How Precious Was That While

HOW PRECIOUS

WAS THAT

WHILE

An Autobiography

Piers Anthony

TOR®

A TOM DOHERTY ASSOCIATES BOOK
NEW YORK

HOW PRECIOUS WAS THAT WHILE: AN AUTOBIOGRAPHY

Edited by Beth Meacham
Book design by Jennifer Ann Daddio

A Tor Book
Published by Tom Doherty Associates, LLC
175 Fifth Avenue
New York, NY 10010

www.tor.com

Tor® is a registered trademark of Tom Doherty Associates, LLC.

Library of Congress Cataloging-in-Publication Data

Anthony, Piers.
    How precious was that while : an autobiography / Piers Anthony.—1st ed.
    p. cm.
    "A Tom Doherty Associates book."
    ISBN 0-312-87464-2 (acid-free paper)
    1. Anthony, Piers.   2. Authors, American—20th Century—Biography.
3. Science fiction—Authorship.   I. Title.

PS3551.N73 Z476 2001
813'.54—dc21
[B]
                                                        2001027475

First Edition: July 2001

Printed in the United States of America

0   9   8   7   6   5   4   3   2   1

Contents

INTRODUCTION

This is a sequel to my autobiography, *Bio of an Ogre (BiOgre)*. That volume covered my life to age fifty, and I thought I would write a sequel if I lived another fifty years. But so much has happened in the intervening decade that I decided to do the sequel at age sixty. It has actually overrun that by a few years.

Rather than repeat myself, I have chosen different episodes for this volume, and to cover the first fifty years more briefly than before. However, I had to write an autobiographical essay for Gale Research so I am using that as a kind of summary of what *BiOgre* covered, herein titled "Reprise." So those who haven't read the first volume may read that to get a concentrated notion. Others may skip that and proceed to Chapter 1, which is new material though it relates to my earliest memories. In the main text I pretty well skim over anything I covered before. The focus is on the last ten years. So the prior volume is not moot, but it is not necessary to read it in order to understand this one. Some of the episodes here are those I deemed unsuitable for the prior volume, but most simply were squeezed out before, in the interest of brevity. This is a fairly hard-hitting volume in certain respects, and it is not intended for juvenile readers. There are some duplications between "Reprise" and Chapter 1, particularly of key occurrences in Spain; I wrote them for different purposes, and found it hard to eliminate overlapping without disrupting the spirit of the narration. There are also scattered duplications elsewhere in the book, as I come at subjects from different perspectives. So readers who read both are welcome to skim when they encounter something familiar.

It should be evident that I have objections to life as we know it, and that if I ran the world, much would change. Some of my notions about the history and future of the world are shown in my serious historical fiction Geodyssey series, which I hope will be the real conclusion of my career. But I don't run the world, or even influence it very much. So this volume is merely a clarification of my experiences and attitudes, and the connections between them, with the hope that others will benefit in some fashion, or at least be entertained. I don't feel that my thoughts are more worthy of publication than the thoughts of others, just that there may be some interest in them because a vagary of fate has given me a certain amount of notoriety. It's as good a basis as the next.

The title derives from an essay on writing that I wrote for *The Writer* magazine, titled "Think of the Reader," which makes the point that the writer must relate to the reader, and care about him/her, sharing feeling. It concludes "We were true friends, for a while. How precious was that while!" I do care about my readers, as will be evident in this volume, and have had many meaningful encounters with them. There will be some samples of what they have written. But in the larger sense, my life is slowly drawing nigh the final harbor, and perspective suggests that my existence is just a blip on the variegated screen of humanity, a brief but intense while. How precious that while is, for every person.

REPRISE

My American grandfather was known as The Mushroom King; he had started growing edible mushrooms in his cellar and built it into a business that made him a millionaire. He didn't have much formal education, but was a savvy businessman; two weeks before the great stock market crash of 1929 he sold the business. I believe that about half of the mushrooms produced in the United States still come from the region around West Chester, Pennsylvania, where he started it, though now it is split between a number of companies. He married, and his wife died of cancer; he remarried, and she also died. He married a third time, Caroline, and she survived him, living to the age of ninety-nine.

My father, Alfred, was the opposite of rich; he was intellectual. I was told that his mother, my grandfather's first wife, was in the hospital, and he visited her there. She asked him to go out and read the words at the entry to her ward, and he did. They were in Latin, and he didn't understand them, but he described them to her as well as he could. She thanked him. Next day she was dead. She seemed to have given up the struggle to live. He always felt guilty, because the words he had conveyed to her identified the ward: it was for incurables. He had given his mother the news that destroyed her hope. He went to England, to continue his education where they took it more seriously than they did in America. He was to graduate from Oxford University, but that isn't my immediate concern. He met a British girl, Joyce, and really liked her. But when summer passed, and a new semester started, she wasn't there. She had caught a fever, maybe typhoid fever, maybe from polluted water when she went camping, and died. He was never to get over that. Again he had been cursed by death. Indeed, I know of only one person who ponders death as much as I do: my father. Later he met another British girl, Norma, who graduated from Oxford with top honors, and she was the one he married. He sent my grandfather a newspaper clipping reporting the marriage: that was the extent of his announcement. Later they both went on to earn Ph.D.s. The relationship didn't work out, but in the course of their marriage my sister and I were born. I arrived in AwGhost 1934, and Teresa in OctOgre 1935. Bear with me on the oddly spelled months; I was later to make my fortune in funny fantasy, and I renamed the months accordingly. There are oddities about me that I will try to explain here; I'm not normal, and I relate well to other abnormals. For now it is enough to know that everyone in my immediate family was academically gifted except me. I was the dunce who made up for it all, pulling the average down.

I think we children were something of an afterthought, because our parents did not seem to be unduly interested in us. Instead they went to Spain to do relief work with the British Friends Service Committee, feeding starving children. They were members of the Religious Society of Friends, more popularly known as Quakers, and the Quakers are known for silent meetings for worship, good business practice, integrity, and good works. This was among the latter. In 1936 the Spanish Civil War started, a kind of prelude to World War II, wherein Spain's own military fought to take over the country from the civilians. In three years it was successful, but it was hell on the children. So my parents were helping to keep those devastated children alive, by importing food and milk and feeding them on a regular basis. It was worthy work, and I don't fault it, but there was a personal cost.

It was not safe for my sister and me during the Spanish war, so we remained in England, cared for by our British grandparents and a nanny. I loved that nanny, whom I thought of as my mother. I remember when she took us to the park in London, and there was a bird hopping on the ground. We feared it was injured, so told the keeper. He picked up the bird and stretched out its wings, to ascertain whether they were broken. He concluded that the bird was all right, and set it down again. I was amazed; it seemed that there was no bird there, just folded wings. I wondered whether it would be possible to make another bird by folding paper cleverly enough. Would it come alive?

I also remember going to the hospital at age four. For years I said I went there to be born, until my mother corrected me: I had been born earlier. She was in a position to know, though she did not acquaint me with the details. So this visit was actually for a tonsillectomy, an operation thought necessary at the time for all children.

In 1939 we joined our parents in Spain, for the war there was then over. This was my first real crisis of identity, because my parents seemed like acquaintances rather than close kin. The nanny was the one I really knew, but she wasn't going. I think of it in retrospect as root pruning: it may be necessary to transplant the young tree, and the tree looks complete, but it isn't. It is hurting where it doesn't show. I had abruptly lost what I valued most, and it was the beginning of a downward spiral that was to leave me depressive even decades later. I never saw the nanny again. I understand she was a Scottish girl, perhaps one of two similar sisters, very good with children. Surely so, for I remember no evil of her; I remember only happiness of a kind I was never to achieve again.

Spain was interesting in new ways. My sister had a nice little Spanish dress. I remember waking alone in my bedroom in Barcelona and seeing moving patterns on the wall. It was the morning sunlight outlining a neighboring palm tree, casting shadows through my window. To me it was like a show; as the wind blew the fronds, the shadows moved back and forth, sometimes almost all the way off the wall. I loved to watch it. Later I got to see a real movie: a cartoon of the three little pigs and the big bad wolf. Absolutely fascinating! Also my first experience with an elevator. Here was this little room we went into, and suddenly it moved, and when the door opened again, everything outside had changed. It was like magic, and for years thereafter I imagined magical rooms that could take me anywhere I wanted to go. And my first ice-cream cone. The funny thing was, the ice cream was square, not round. I think that supplies must have been limited, so that they lacked the tubs and scoops, and had to use packaged ice cream. The man crammed it into a cone, and I ate it and loved it. By the time I reached the bottom of the cone, the ice cream there was melting. But it was a great experience. And we got a pair of sandals made from string; the soles were this mass of coiled string, actually hemp. I don't think they lasted long, because the string tended to unravel, but they were nice. There was also the old man who told me stories and played a trick on me: he gave me a candy, and ate one himself, then took back the wrappers and balled them and wrapped them in another wrapper so cunningly that it looked just like a real candy. Then my sister arrived, and he gave it to her. I could hardly contain myself, waiting to see her dismay as it turned out to be empty. But she unwrapped one, two, three wrappers—and there was a candy inside. The joke had been on me. At one point we went to a hotel in a nearby town, Tossa, about forty miles up the Mediterranean coast from Barcelona, on top of a steep hill; we thought no car could get up that hill, but a man in a motorcycle zoomed right up it, amazing us. I remember swimming in the warm Mediterranean Sea. Actually I couldn't swim; I was floating on an inflated raft. It banged into another, and I fell off, sinking under the salty water. I was quickly rescued—it was only about two feet deep—but it was a memorable experience. I remember the big cigar-shaped balloons that moved silently over the beach: military blimps, I think. Another time I was walking with my family when I realized that I had somehow gotten lost; I was with strangers. I didn't know what to do, so I just kept going. They seemed to accept me; the woman even gave me roasted peanuts. Later my mother came to recover me. It must have been a baby-sitting device; my mother had slipped away unseen so that I wouldn't make a fuss. But that had left me without moorings, uncertain of my fate. I had discovered that my mother could disappear without warning. I never did that to my own children. Another time my father was playing with us, showing us magic blocks. He was really better at games and stories than my mother was. He put a coin on one, and covered it with a block-shaped shell, then removed the shell—and the coin was gone. Where could it be? We looked all over. It occurred to me that it might be hidden under the block, so I picked it up—and another shell came off, with the coin under it. My father departed in a huff; I had spoiled the trick. I really hadn't meant to. And I remember Easter: I was given a huge wooden egg. It opened, and inside was a model of a sailing ship and a number of chocolates. Thereafter I loved Easter, though I think none since has been as great. But I also remember my sister and me standing in the garden with tape stuck across our mouths, evidently our punishment for talking out of turn. I don't approve of that sort of punishment, and don't know whether our parents knew of it. Another time we were with a woman doing laundry in the cellar, which was a converted jail cell, and a young man came and locked the gate, shutting us in. The woman screeched at him so violently that he had to return to let us out. He was Jorge, pronounced "Hor-Hee," and was always fun.

It was in Spain that my sister Teresa and I suffered a shock that was to mark us in separate ways for life. I will tell it first as I saw it. I was in a room, alone, when I heard my sister protesting something. So I followed the sound, going to see what was the matter. I saw her on a counter of some sort, with a group of adults clustered around her. She was trying to get away, but couldn't. Then her screams became piercing; they were torturing her. I saw her little feet pounding the counter as she tried to run away, but could not. They were doing something to her face; I think I saw a splash of water. Then, when they had hurt her enough, they let her go, and turned to see me standing there. "He saw!" one said. At that point my terrible memory fades out. It was to remain for fifty years as a disconnected scene I couldn't explain, until at last it clicked into place, like a piece of a puzzle: that was when my sister had her tonsillectomy. The full story I had learned before, but never connected to my horrible vision. When it was time for her operation, my mother inquired of the local medical facilities, and was told they had no safe anesthetic. The war had devastated Spain, and many supplies were low or gone. So they would have to do it without any painkiller. "Not on *my* child!" my mother said. So they agreed: they would find something. She brought the child in to the clinic, telling me to stay in the waiting room, and took Teresa on in. Whereupon the nurses snatched the child away from her, took her to the counter, propped her mouth open, and cut out her tonsils while she screamed. That was the way it was done in Spain at the time.

I don't think my mother knew that I had seen it happen. I never spoke of it. It was my private horror. I knew then that doctors existed to make children hurt. That was confirmed when I was ill in Spain; a doctor came, checked me over, then asked for a spoon. He turned it over and poked it deep into my mouth until I vomited on the bed. Satisfied, he departed; he had made me hurt enough. Later experiences with horrible needles added to it; I remember one needle being stuck slanting under the skin, and a fluid injected so that the skin swelled up in an excruciating blister while I was held down, screaming. Vaccination, they called it. By whatever name, its point was obvious; no doctor could let a child go without hurting it. My parents, strangely, never protested.

Our departure from Spain was another ugly matter. My father liked

Spain, and wanted to remain there. I have mixed feelings about that; I liked Spain too, but I am not at all sure I would have had a worthwhile life there. But fate took the decision out of our hands. As I understand it, Adolf Hitler of Nazi Germany was trying to get Generalissimo Franco of Spain to join the Axis, and a meeting between them was scheduled. Security was tight. And there was my father, with a lot of money, near the border. He was there to buy food to feed a trainful of Jews being deported from Germany. So they "disappeared" him: they arrested him and dumped him in prison, uncharged. For three days my mother desperately tried to find out what had happened to him. The Spanish authorities denied knowing anything about it. Meanwhile he was confined with other men in a dungeon cell, whose sanitary facility was a trench. There were female prisoners too, in another cell, only theirs had no trench; periodically they were herded to the male cell to do their business, while the men stood around and watched, seeing whatever they could see. One prisoner was allowed a visitor, who brought a hot drink to him in a thermos; Alfred got them to put a postcard of his into the empty thermos, to be taken out and mailed. My mother received the card, and so learned of what had happened. Armed with that, and with the forceful assistance of a wealthy Quaker of influence who could have cost Spain a lot of needed monetary assistance, she was able to get them to admit that they did after all have a prisoner of that name. But dictatorships don't admit mistakes, so they agreed to let him go only on condition that he depart the country. The relief mission of that area was shut down, and thereafter the children had to survive as well as they could without that food. I like to think that some people are alive today because of what my parents did in Spain. I was later to write a novel, *Volk*, relating to Spain and Germany and World War II, but have not as yet found a book publisher for it, because it is controversial. Instead it is on sale on the Internet, at http://www.xlibris.com.

So it was that we left Spain. I remember traveling from Barcelona to Madrid, the capital city, where we toured the big earthworks around the city: its former defenses. Then we went on to Lisbon, Portugal, to catch the ship to America. I remember stopping high in a mountain pass to go touch the spongy bark of a cork tree, and driving way up on a high hill where there was a kind of amusement park. There were many small stands with toy trains. My mother put in a coin, and the little train buzzed around and around its little mountain on its little tracks. Finally, it disappeared into a tunnel and didn't come out: the show was over. In Lisbon we took a taxi, and the cabby unfolded a child seat from the floor or somewhere, a novelty. We also got to ride in paddleboats; foot pedals made the paddles go around, and the boats moved forward. So it was fun. But not without its cautions. I remember seeing my mother naked for the first and only time, there, and being amazed to see that she had hair on her crotch. It had never occurred to me that adults were different from children. But what appalled my mother was the fact that the hotel room was overrun with roaches.

Even our voyage on the ship to America was unusual. I did not know it at the time, but the former King Edward VIII of England was on that ship with us. He had gotten interested in an American divorcée, and had a difficult choice: the crown or the woman. Romance had won, and he gave up his throne and married her. They happened to be in Portugal at this time. The Nazis thought he was sympathetic to their cause, and hoped to abduct him and talk him into supporting them politically. But they fouled up, and didn't get him, and he boarded the ship, going as far as Bermuda. That was the *Excalibur*, the same ship and the same voyage we were on, the last trip out before the war shut off such travel. No, I don't believe I ever saw the erstwhile king, but I do remember seeing his car unloaded in Bermuda: it dangled from a crane line dropped into the hold, and was swung out onto the dock. I had my sixth birthday on the ship, where I had a cake made of sawdust because they lacked provisions for a real one; they brought it to us with the candles burning, and then we couldn't eat it. Later my own children were to be jealous: *they* never got a cake made of sawdust. I was given a harmonica, and I loved it, and played it endlessly as I walked around the deck. I still wonder whether the former king of England was gritting his teeth somewhere, wishing that kid would cut out the noise. And I had my first bout with seasickness; I remember my father holding me up so I could vomit over the rail, seeing it fall down into the distant water. There was also a swimming pool set up on the deck; the canvas had a leak in one corner, and I got to play in that jet of water. I think my elder daughter inherited that delight; she was hyperactive, but could play endlessly in flowing water.

The trip took ten days, and we made it safely to New York. I think I remember seeing the Statue of Liberty, without understanding its significance. I was an immigrant, a subject of the Queen; that statue welcomed folk like me. We docked, and my American grandparents—yes, The Mushroom King, and his third wife, Caroline—met us and drove us to Philadelphia, Pennsylvania, the Quaker City. My mother was uncertain of her reception by my father's folks, for she was not even American, and might be considered an intruder, but Caroline, similarly new to the family, welcomed her, and that started a friendship that was to last fifty years, until they died just a month apart.

My memories of that time are scattered, but some do stand out. My grandfather Edward's house was at the end of a street in West Chester, Pencil Vania (well, I warned you about my funny fantasy), with a fishpond behind and a rolling meadow leading down to the highway and a golf course beyond it. It was like a slice of Heaven. The house was large, and even had a maid's quarters with a separate little winding stairway for her. Fascinating! Grandfather was hard of hearing, so at meals had a hearing aid that looked like a toaster; my father joked about putting bread in it. His wife was known as Aunt Caroline, carried across from the way she was known in her own family. Later I liked to refer to her as my wife's stepgrandmother-in-law. She was a great person, competent and diplomatic and very much a Quaker, speaking with "thee" in the manner of the elder generation. So, as I became acquainted with my American relatives, I liked them.

We spent a while at Grandfather's cabin in Seaside Park, New Jersey (no parody for that state; I already have a mental picture of a freshly purchased garment). That was on the Atlantic beach, and was sheer delight. There was a boardwalk that extended endlessly north and south. There was the white sand and the constant washing sea. There was a telescope on the front porch that seemed magical. Once I saw a tiny dot on the horizon, but when the telescope focused on it, it became a yacht with girls running around its decks and jumping into the water. I never had a city apartment, but can appreciate the lure of a high-rise telescope; who knows what sights one might see. There was an amusement park, with little machines that you looked into, and turned a crank on the side, and they flipped the pages of picture books, making them become animated cartoons. I loved that. Today's more sophisticated animation is far superior, yet I loved those magic moving pictures.

Another time I was ill, and had to be quarantined. Was it German measles? I don't know. I was at a house somewhere else, and only my mother was there with me. I spent the long hours drawing things on a sketch pad. I remember the bread she brought: huge slices that were incredibly delicious with butter. So this illness was a pleasant experience.

We moved to a place called Pendle Hill. It was a kind of Quaker school for adult studies. We had a little apartment squeezed in the rear of one of the buildings. I was given a scooter, and I loved it; I scooted constantly. Years later I learned the penalty: my right leg became an inch longer than the left leg, because I had always pushed with it. That wasn't discovered until a chiropractor looked at me; at a glance he saw my uneven stance, and put me on two scales, one foot to each. I weighed one hundred pounds, divided sixty-forty. I had to wear a corrective shoe to force my stance to change, enabling my legs to grow back to the same length.

It wasn't all fun. A neighbor boy invited me over, but he wasn't necessarily as friendly as he seemed. He had a big dog, which he would encourage a stranger to pet; after a moment the dog would leap up, growling, scaring the child, and the boy would laugh. Another time some of his other friends were there, so he told me to go home. Realizing that I was being dissed, I balked. When he threatened to push me, I threatened to kick him. He stepped in and punched me in the face. Completely defeated, in tears, I fled. I didn't tell, but I remembered. Today when someone tries to push me around, I am apt to find a way to make him regret it. I don't like bullies. When my second daughter was treated exactly the same way, I went immediately to the scene and got it straightened out. Another time, when three boys beat up my two girls, I went and virtually challenged the eldest boy's father; had he not departed quickly, I might have tried to do to him what his boy had done to my girls, and take him down and grind his face in the dirt. As it was, I merely called the police and sent them to the errant household. At any rate, I did make my point; his boy never touched my girls again. When my elder daughter's college treated her contemptuously, I wrote a sharp letter to the college president, to similar effect; their unfair action was instantly reversed. I am not small anymore, and I saw to it that my children did not suffer as I had. I don't claim to be always nice, but there's always justice in my cases, and I have taken down many bullies, in my fashion, though the arena is no longer physical. Few have cared to tangle with me a second time.

I started school. Somehow what I did was never satisfactory to the teacher. She showed me another student's paper, which was much neater than mine, but I couldn't do it the way the teacher wanted. In fact it took me three years and five schools to make it through first grade, because I couldn't learn to read and write. My sister, in contrast, had no trouble at all. She had the good fortune to catch tuberculosis and spent six months in bed, so our mother taught her to read. She entered first grade with a sixth grade reading skill. People would come up to me and say "Aren't you thrilled to have a smart sister like her?" Somehow I didn't see it that way; maybe I was too dull to appreciate such a blessing. In my day things like learning disability or dyslexia didn't exist, just stupid or careless children. It wasn't until I saw the trouble my daughter had in school that I realized what must have been my problem. Actually it was more complicated than that, and I may still not understand the whole of it, slow learner that I am. Theoretically, intelligence doesn't change through life, but tests showed me to be subnormal early, and normal later, and superior later yet, and my success in school and life varied accordingly. So the kid who couldn't read later became an English teacher, and a highly successful writer. How could I have been so dull before, and so smart after, if IQ is fixed?

Well, it's possible. First, I may indeed have had a problem in seeing and learning writing. Eyes do not mature immediately, and some studies have shown that many children suffer measurable ocular damage from the close work demanded in school. That's one reason that so many adults, myself included, need glasses for reading. We protected our dys-lexic daughter by having her wear special glasses in first grade, so that her eyes would not be damaged, and as an adult she didn't need glasses. But most children are not that fortunate. I may also have had something like dyslexia, and it took me time to learn to compensate. It was as if I had an analog mind in a digital world. When I did learn to handle it, I started forging ahead, and in adult life few have ever thought me stupid, and some of those who have, have been surprised when they learned more of me. In fact I think it may be that only those who are not as smart as I am ever think me to be dull. I have an analogy I like: suppose a sports car races with a locomotive. At the starting line, the car races ahead. If the finish line is a hundred yards away, there's no contest. But if the finish line is three thousand miles away, the locomotive will win, because once it gets up steam it proceeds at a very high rate of speed without pausing. So I was a loser as a child, but not as an adult; my locomotive had finally gotten up speed, and it left most others behind.

There is one more thing: I was always slow. I was slow to learn to walk, and to speak. I am still slow to catch on to new things. I was slow to grow, and slow to reach maturity. I am still slow to eat, and still read slowly. That is not a euphemism for stupid; I just take my time, but I get there in the end. Like the locomotive. Give me a timed test and I will not be a high scorer, but I can compete on an open-ended basis. School is timed, but life is an open-ended experience.

So school was difficult for me. It didn't help having to learn a new school, with its different grounds, teachers, students, and rules, every time I started to catch on to the way of one. One teacher, instead of encouraging me, chastised me for mispronouncing my A's: "There's an A in that word! Grass, not grawss." She was trying to correct my English accent. No wonder I had a problem. The students weren't any better. In winter I had a fast little sled, a Flexible Flyer, and that was fun. But at one of the schools the old students threw all the sleds of the new students into the river. They were there in plain view in the water, but the teachers ignored it. Teachers just didn't seem to have much awareness of justice. Or of education. That was over fifty years ago, but I'm not sure it has changed much.

One of the schools was in New York state, with beautiful grounds. It was a boarding school. I was later to see some of the bright caring reports it sent back to my family. They were fantasy; the reality was something else. My main early entertainment was playing in the adjacent garbage dump, because the good facilities were off-limits to us. As a first grader, I was the lowest of the low. Older students took me into a room and told me to take off my clothes. I did so, but gradually became suspicious; to be slow is not to be entirely out of it. So I dressed again and managed to break away, escaping to my own dorm. That night we were watching a movie, and suddenly someone was wading into me, hitting me, pummeling me, beating me up. The teachers paid no attention. I fled out of the building, into the surrounding forest, escaping the beating. I hid behind a tree, wary of pursuit. Indeed it seemed incipient, because as I watched the building, I heard frequent yelling and pounding, as of a gang about to break down the door and charge out. I was terrified. It continued for a long time, and finally I realized that they weren't actually coming out. So I sneaked around to the other side, and up the stairs, and into bed, and they never spied me. Why should they? I hadn't even been missed. Later I realized that what

I had seen was the outside of the indoor basketball court; the pounding had been the ball and people hitting the wall as they played. If only I had realized that earlier, I would have been spared an evening of terror. So what of the boy who was beating on me? It took me years to put that together: I think he was the one who had been guarding the door during my "initiation"; I had pushed by him and escaped, and that made him mad. Bullies don't like to let anyone escape. So next time he saw me he waded into me. A first grader couldn't stand up to a second or third grader. I lived in fear of him, until finally other students decided that enough was enough. They brought us together and had us shake hands, declaring peace. "But what if he goes after me again?" I asked. "Then *we'll* beat *him* up," they said. That did indeed take care of it; they weren't bluffing. Justice had come, no thanks to the teachers or school administration.

Yet such things seldom happen of their own accord, and I suspect there was more to it. An older boy befriended me. His name was Craig Work, and he was the child of a black father and white mother, and his IQ had been tested at 180. I realize, in considerable retrospect, that he must have had thorough experience in the rough-and-tumble of life among children. I didn't know of racism then, and didn't care that his skin was brown, but surely there were others who did. He was a great friend, and once he started associating with me, things started turning better. I think he had something to do with it. His mother later reported something he had said to her: "Mom, I'm a peaceful kind of guy, and I don't like to fight. But they *make* you fight." Yes indeed. Craig helped teach me how to fight, and that in itself made a difference. I was no longer such an easy target. In fact it got so that I never lost unless my opponent was substantially larger than I. I wasn't weak, just small. So later, when others tried me out, and found me tougher than expected, they became friends instead of enemies. But at the beginning, at boarding school, I'm sure the considerable shadow of Craig protected me more than somewhat. And of course there were always boys who *were* substantially larger, so I wasn't yet out of the wilderness.

My experience with Craig was to affect my social attitude. No one ever had to tell me that racism wasn't nice; I knew it from the time I first learned of it. My best friend really *had* been black. When I see racism, I have a kind of mental picture of filth and grubs exposed under a rock. I have trouble understanding how such folk can stand their own company. I don't believe in Hell, but if by some mischance it exists, I think it must be stocked with racists.

But school was only one of the growing problems of my life. I had been toilet trained in England and Spain, but in America I started wetting the bed at night. This continued for several years. I was checked into a hospital, and that was another awful experience: periodically a group of adults would enter my room, and that was always mischief. Sometimes they wanted to poke a finger into my various orifices, including the rectum—the entire medical establishment seemed to be fascinated with that orifice, so that they even had pretty nurses take my temperature that way. Sometimes they brought deadly needles, inflicting pain on me in the manner that doctors always did to children. Once I woke to hear a cluster of nurses just outside my door, whispering avidly. "Just take it and *shove it in!*" one was saying. I was terrified; what were they going to do to me? Was it my turn to be tortured the way my sister had been in Spain? Surely it must be a knife they would use. But nobody said a word to me. I realized that they were planning to do it by surprise; without warning would come that sudden thrust, while I screamed helplessly. All in all, I was never able to truly relax, even in sleep. Since I wet my bed only when soundly asleep, I didn't do it in that hospital. In the end they reported to my parents that there was nothing organically wrong with me; no physical cause for my bedwetting. They were right, in their fashion, but what they didn't know could fill a volume. I learned later that it was supposed to have been a briefer visit, for observation only, but that there had been a delay in the insurance payment, so they had held me as it were at ransom for several extra days, until they got their payment. I had suffered all that extra time because of a bureaucratic snarl. So what was it with the nurses? I think now that they had merely been exchanging stories in the hall, and it was sheer coincidence that my room was the closest one, so that I could overhear. No surgery had been scheduled for me; that fear had been groundless. If only I had known!

So what was the matter with me? My bedwetting did not abate. Then I began to suffer twitches. Every few seconds I would fling my head around, or give a hard shake to both my hands. Why did I do it? It was like a cough: you can hold it back only so long before it has to come out. Naturally these actions brought further ridicule down on my head. It was evident that I was a pretty fouled-up child. Oh, I would have loved to be normal, but I wasn't. Yet that, too, was not the major thing.

It started innocently enough, while I was still in that long first grade. This was in New Hampshire, I think. We went to an amusement park that was all inside a big building, another novelty to me. All kinds of things were going on there. There was a huge hollow man-statue with an entrance at the base and exit at the top; I think there was a spiral stairway inside. People were constantly going through it. Every so often the statue would go HO HO HO and wiggle just a little, and the folk inside it would scream. I think that from inside it seemed that the whole thing was falling. My father went on it while we watched, and reported on what he experienced. At one point, beyond the statue, was a room with a table full of nice watches, and a sign saying TAKE ONE. But when he tried to, he found that it was fastened to the table, and electrified; he got a shock. One has to be wary, in a fun house. Later fun houses had jets of air that blew up girls' dresses so that their underwear showed; somehow the girls didn't find that as amusing as the boys did. Then my father took me on a ride through the horror house. This was weird and exciting. Ghostly creatures appeared and lurched at the cart, scaring me. Then suddenly a stone wall appeared before us, and we were headed right for it, about to crash—and the cart dropped an inch or so to a lower track, feeling just like a crash. We swung on around the wall, safe after all, and in due course emerged from the darkness. It had been a phenomenal thrill.

But that night I had a terrible dream. It consisted of just four pictures, or brief scenes. In the first, my sister and I were walking along a city street with our mother. That was all; nothing remarkable. In the second, she stopped at a standing structure, like a telephone booth. She entered it, but then the door wouldn't open, and she was caught inside. The third picture was a forest glade, with an altar, and a woman was lying on it. I knew it was my mother. At the edge of the glade stood a man, and beside him was a lion. The fourth scene was just the man, lifting the lion up in his arms, as if hefting it for weight. That was all— but it so terrified me that I woke screaming. My mother was soon there to comfort me, but it was not possible to expunge the awfulness. I don't normally believe in dream interpretation; I think that most of it is fantasy, and that even the experts know almost nothing of the real nature of dreams. Right: I alone know their true nature, and I'll cover that in a moment. But this particular dream, simple as it seems, had formidable meaning, and is the very essence of terror. Here is the interpretation: the first picture is just the introduction, and it was taken from experience. The setting was Spain, and my sister and I did walk along the street with our mother. The second picture refers to the time she made a phone call from a booth, and the door stuck; she did get out, but for a moment I was worried. This connected to something that was preying on my mind, even then: she had said that she might have to have an operation. Little was explained to the children, leaving much to the imagination. Just as when she spoke of seeing a book that had been made into a movie, and I thought that meant that they projected the pages of the book onto the screen for everyone to read. I thought that the operation meant that they would stretch her out on a table and cut into her body with knives. It was horrible to contemplate. The memory of the phone booth was twined with the thought of that operation, as if first they had to catch her so they could do it to her. So, later, when that memory returned in the dream scene, the horror was building, for this time she was indeed caught. The third scene was crafted in part from an experience I had had when walking in the country: I had come across an animal skull. It was the vast, bleached, hollow-eyed bone of a cow, and I understood that death had come to this creature, and this was all that was left of it. That setting, between forest and field, was in my dream, and so it was a place of death. My mother was laid out there for the knife. Her absence from the fourth scene was significant: she must have been eaten by the lion, and now the man, who might have been the anonymous surgeon or perhaps was really my father, was weighing the lion to see how much it had gained. My mother was horribly dead.

So this dream was crafted from several assorted memories, assembled into a horrible whole. But why did it occur? The immediate trigger was the emotion of the horror house ride; it had shaken loose deeper fears. But those fears had been building before then, and they were related to my bedwetting and compulsive twitches. This is the root of the larger story. For our family was coming apart. My parents were in the process of separating, though they themselves may not have realized it at that point. The marriage had not been ideal from the start; they were two intelligent, liberal, socially conscious Quakers, but their more subtle differences doomed their union. As I see it, he was a creature of the country, while she was a creature of the city. He liked the self-sufficiency of the farm and forest; she preferred the civilization of the city. He could work quietly logging or gardening alone; she longed for the thickly clustered conveniences of the populated metropolis. He liked being largely free of the works of mankind; she couldn't stand a house without hot water or internal sanitary facilities. Note how the dream sequences with the woman are in the city, and with the man are in the country. Their ideal lifestyles were poles apart. There was, of course, more to it than that, but that was enough; he was headed for the farm and she for the city, and ultimately their marriage sundered, leaving them free to find their ideal habitats. There were quarrels, there were reconciliations, there were negotiations, there were compromises, but the end was inevitable. Later this divergence was to be expressed in my fiction: there was the planet Proton, with cities and pollution, and the magic land of Phaze, with forests and unicorns. Yet they were merely aspects of one realm, the city and the country merging. I liked both, and wanted the two to be joined, but they kept separating.

Meanwhile, it was hell on the children, as divorces usually are. I liken it to standing on a mountain, but then the mountain quakes and collapses, and becomes an island in a heaving sea. I was standing there, and my footing was eroding. It became an iceberg, floating in that treacherous sea, and then the ice split so that one of my feet was on each section. The sections separated, leaving me no way to escape the fate of the icy water. So while I was not physically mistreated, emotionally I was suffering. I spoke of root pruning when I lost the nanny in England; now I was pruned again, having lost the second country—Spain—and the remaining foundation of the unified family. No wonder the stress manifested in various ways, such as bedwetting and twitching; I had no legitimate way to handle it. They say that stupid folk don't have as many emotional problems as smart folk, being too dull to realize how bad things are. The way I was reacting, I must have been far smarter than I seemed.

So how did I survive? There came a point when I realized that my problems were really not of my own making, but stemmed from the stress between my parents. I declared, in effect, emotional independence. I weaned myself away from the family, emotionally, and began building my own framework. It was a long and difficult job, like a climb from a deep and treacherous pit, but in time I got there. My parents were shocked when I stated that they were people I knew and liked, but did not love, yet it was the truth. That was the state I had needed to achieve for emotional survival. It wasn't ideal, it wasn't pretty, but it was the only way. I don't regret the decision; I regret the necessity for it. How would it have been if Joyce, my father's early love, had lived, and they had married, and I had been their child? I suspect I would have been far happier as a child—and never become a writer. So I can't really fault the circumstances that brought me into this realm and made me what I am, however uncomfortable they may have been.

Now on this matter of dreams: I have an insatiable curiosity about the nature of the universe and mankind's place in it, and my profession of writing allows me to explore it all, seeking answers. I have fathomed a number of things to my satisfaction before they were clarified by the scientists, and this is one of them. This discussion will get somewhat intellectual, but I'll try to make it intelligible. It has been said that we waste a third of our lives in sleep. Baloney; nature doesn't work that way. It has been said that we use only ten percent of our brains. Baloney, again. While we are up and about we are constantly receiving impressions. Now consider what happens to them: are they just dumped into a virtual vat in the brain and stored for future use? It may seem that way at first blush, but a little thought shows that this is impractical. If you buy groceries for the next week's meals, do you just dump them pell-mell into the freezer? Chances are you sort them and put them carefully in a number of spots reserved for them, so that you won't find week-old milk squished under the canned beans, or fresh lettuce coated with cocoa powder. So that when you need butter in a hurry, you won't have to unload the whole freezer to find it, and then have to thaw it on the stove. (That reminds me of the story my mother told of the day the refrigeration was too cold: "The ice cream's been in the oven for twenty minutes, and still isn't soft enough to cut." It also reminds me of the time I took a pat of butter and dropped it on my plate, and it clinked.) It takes time to sort things properly, but you learn to do it, because it's better than the alternative. The same is true for anything else; you separate it and sort it and store it for future convenience. So is it any different with memories? Obviously they are well organized, because all our past experience can quickly be brought to bear on a present event. If we spy a small red roughly spherical object before us, we know almost immediately whether it's the dog's rubber ball or a giant cherry bomb, and treat it accordingly. But when did we do the massive sorting and filing of memories that allowed us to classify it so rapidly? For such work does take time. I was for some years a file clerk, and I learned that there is no paper so lost as one that has been misfiled or mislabeled. If you're in an unfamiliar program, with a deadline for an obnoxious assignment, how do you find an article on cooking squash, if your file isn't organized? Under C for Cooking, or S for Squash, or F for Food, or U for Ugh—who wants it? In fact you have not only to file accurately, you have to cross-reference, so that under COOKING is a note saying SEE SQUASH, along with other notes saying SEE POTATOES, SEE BROCCOLI, SEE BALONEY, and so on. Also under FOOD, and under UGH. So that you can quickly find anything, when you don't know how the ditsy file clerk classified it. Well, your brain has to do that job too, only it's a lot more complicated than just a list of recipes. Your entire ongoing life experience has to be sorted and classified and filed in memory for instant retrieval. It doesn't just happen; it has to be organized. When do you do it—in your sleep? Yes, actually. Part of that 90 percent of the brain that ignorant experts think is unused is actually used for that considerable cross-referencing-and-filing chore. And since you are way too busy in the daytime to do it, the chore must wait for the brain's downtime: at night. Think of a computer that has some really hot features you'd like to play with, but someone else is using it now; what do you do? You schedule a session during its downtime, when no one else is using it. That's what your brain does. When you sleep, precious little is coming in from outside. So it calls up the fresh memories of the day, that have been held in temporary storage, and processes them. It takes one memory, such as that of the personable person of the opposite gender who smiled at you during lunch, and compares it rapidly to your prior lifetime's experience, in the manner of a computer checking for a word beginning with WOW. Whenever there's some sort of match, it looks farther, and when there's a significant match, it considers the matter and strengthens the neural pathways that actually make memory. But this aspect takes intelligence, because most of the day's impressions are not very important in terms of the rest of your life, and you don't want to clutter your memory with them. For example, if that person was your sibling, you can dump that memory right there. But if there are matches to a similar smile yesterday by a person you well might want to get lost with in a stranded elevator, this bears further consideration. How would it be, if the two of you are going to the sixth floor, and the power fails, and one of you is a bit scared and the other is a bit protective, and you mesh rather nicely, and then a kiss sort of happens, and then the alarm goes off and it's morning, and all you remember is a rather pleasant dream about an elevator. And so you process everything, and the occasional images that take more serious form as you explore their bypaths are what you call dreams. It's not wasted time at all; it's vital to your well-being. Your whole future may be guided in your dreams. But you can't afford to remember most of them, because they are the sorting process, and any dream you remember has to be treated as a memory and run through that classification mill itself. You would rapidly encounter the phenomenon of diminishing returns.

Now you know what dreams are for. Don't bother to tell your science teacher; he's not ready for this yet. Just be smugly satisfied in your secret understanding of what modern science does not yet know. With luck, you'll dream about that elevator again tonight, and the alarm won't go off so soon.

And so I survived the horror of my devastating dream, though it haunted me every night for three years thereafter. When I closed my eyes I saw that corpse and knew its identity. I tried to make it go away, and in my imagination it would move off-screen, but another would appear, and another, until they were cruising by like the cars of a long train. It may sound funny, but it was killing my sanity. If I seem a bit crazy here, well, now you have half a notion how I got that way. I had an active imagination, and it didn't stop with corpses. By day I saw monsters. They followed me as I walked home from school through the forest alone, and hid behind the trees when I turned to look. They lurked under my bed, ready to grab my ankles if I was careless enough to put them in reach. They were everywhere. I had to have a night-light, for light was the only thing that kept them at bay. Today I put those monsters into my fiction, and I love them. But fantasy monsters don't chase adults, only children. So the dominant emotion of my later childhood was fear. Fear of bigger kids at school, of a monster in the forest, and fear of the corpse. Fear, really, of life. I hated being alone, but others neither understood nor cared, so I was alone a lot. That is, often physically, and almost always emotionally. Today when I get a letter from a reader who feels almost utterly alone, I understand, because I remember.

That wasn't all. One doctor had a simplistic remedy for my bedwetting: I was to have no liquid after 4 P.M. So to my accumulated discomforts was added that of thirst. The bedwetting continued unabated, but I longed for a drink of water. Later in life I had a kidney stone, and I wonder whether it could have started long before, during my years of dehydration.

Meanwhile, I endured, having no alternative. Each morning I would wake soaking in urine, because the rubber sheet that protected the mattress caused the brine to pool around me. I would get up—I remember dancing on the floor in winter, because it was so cold on my feet—go downstairs to the bathroom, which had no toilet but did have a basin of cold water. Once I had to break the ice on the water before I could use it to wash. I would soak the washcloth, grit my teeth, and start washing my chest. After a few strokes my body would warm the cloth, and it would be easier. I would wash my midsection, getting the urine off, then run back shivering upstairs to my room to dress. Sometimes I couldn't resist putting the wet cloth to my mouth and sucking a little of the water out, to abate my thirst, feeling guilty because I wasn't allowed anything to drink until breakfast. Ironically, I now must drink more water than I like, to keep my urine diluted so that I won't have another kidney stone. I developed a real hatred of being cold, having experienced so much of it so unpleasantly; that's one big reason I now live in Florida. Later in the day I would wash out the sheet, a tedious chore with cold water. My parents didn't call it punishment, but it was my penalty for my persistence in wetting the bed: I had to clean up my own mess. I got the message in this and other ways: I was a burden to the family.

My fondest imagination was that one day I would wake up and discover that it had all been a horrible dream, and I was really back in England with the nanny. But it never happened. I pondered my life, and concluded that if I could be given a choice either to live it over exactly as it had been, or never to exist at all, I would prefer the latter. The net balance was negative; though I had never been verbally, physically, or sexually abused, by conventional definition, my existence simply wasn't worth it. My past was unpleasant, and my prospects for the future bleak.

But it wasn't all bad. My parents did care, though they did not understand how the world seemed from my perspective. They encouraged me to paste up gold stars on a chart for every night I remained dry, motivating me to change my behavior. Unfortunately they did not address its true cause, which lay closer to their own behavior than they would have cared to admit, so such things weren't very effective. But there was one thing that did impress me. My father offered two remedies:

he could arrange for a sympathetic group to pray for me, or he could take me on a trip to the city to talk with a knowledgeable woman. I never did have much faith in the supernatural, so I chose the trip. It was always a pleasure to get away from the wilderness and into civilization. I think my love of trains, especially the old steam engines, stems from that: a train was the big, powerful, fascinating machine that carried folk to interesting places. That doesn't mean that I hated the country; today I am an environmentalist, and live on my own tree farm. But I also have central heating, TV, radio, telephone, computer, car, and the other benefits of civilization. I forget whether the trip was to New York or Philadelphia, but the woman was Mrs. West. She explained to me how you could not see electricity, or hear it, or smell it, but nevertheless it existed, and you knew that when you turned on a light or some appliance. Similarly, she said, you couldn't see or hear God, but he nevertheless existed. Now that's a rationale I can accept, and it may be the reason I became an agnostic rather than an atheist. I remember being told about Santa Claus: a jolly fat man who squeezed down the chimney and brought presents to all the children in the world, in a single night. I didn't buy it. Then I was told about God: a big old white man with a long white beard sitting on a cloud, looking down at mortal folk. I don't buy that either. I make my living from fantasy, but I always knew the difference between fantasy and reality. I am a realist. But I understood the difference between lack of evidence, and proof. If you're driving on a mountainous road, and you want to pass the slow car ahead, and you don't see any oncoming traffic, you don't just assume that none exists. You don't pass on a turn. You wait until you can see ahead on a straight stretch. To do otherwise is dangerous. So while I have never seen persuasive evidence of the supernatural, and really don't believe in ghosts or flying saucers, and like the great playwright George Bernard Shaw I am wary of a man whose god is in the sky, I don't feel free to declare that there *is* no God. So I am agnostic, not presuming to define the nature of God. And if you define God as Truth, Justice, Compassion, Beauty, Honor, Decency, and the like, then I do believe. But the bigotry I have seen in so many religions prevents me from joining any of them; I don't think that any great religious leaders, including Jesus Christ, ever intended their followers to practice anything like the Inquisition or Crusades or Jihads, converting others by sword and torture. In fact I think that if Jesus returned to the world today, his tears would flow to see what has been wrought in his name. He was a man of tolerance and peace, and he welcomed even a prostitute to wash his feet. I think that he and I could have a compatible chat, and he would not object to my philosophy any more than I object to his. And I think that the bigots would crucify him again, in the name of religion. So I am agnostic, and satisfied to be so. When I grew up, I married a minister's daughter, and we don't have any quarrels about religion. My background was Quaker, hers Unitarian Universalist, both "liberal" religions, and I like to think that when good work is quietly being done, there is apt to be either a Quaker or a U-U person involved.

So I appreciated Mrs. West's rationale, without being persuaded of the existence of God. After that she took me to a bookstore and bought me a book. No, not a religious one; it was a storybook with games. On one page a little dog had gotten its leash hopelessly tangled in the furniture: could I untangle it? That was an example of a type of fiendishly challenging puzzle I have encountered also in other settings. To solve it, you have to fashion a loop elsewhere, pass it through a couple of holes, and around the dog; then it can be freed. I, being slow on the uptake, must have struggled with it for months. So it was that wonderful book that was my prize from that trip. Perhaps it contributed to my love of books—I, who had had such trouble even learning to read. Today I earn my living by writing books, and many of them incorporate challenges and puzzles.

But the thing that impressed me most about that trip was the proof it represented that my father really did care. He had taken a lot of trouble to make that trip with me, and I enjoyed all of it. When I had children of my own, I made it a point to take them on similar trips, giving them the experience of airplane flights (today's equivalent of the train), hotels, restaurants, and far places. We also read to them, just as my father had read to my sister and me every night. I think that nightly reading, and the daytime storytelling when we worked together outside, was the most important influence on my eventual choice of career. I knew that books contained fascinating adventures, and those stories took me away from my dreary real life. Today I spend even more of my time away from real life; my very name, Piers Anthony, is a pen name relating to the things I imagine. I have entered the realm of stories, and hope never to leave it. So that trip was fundamentally reassuring in a vital way, and I think it helped lay the foundation for my emotional recovery.

And the truth is that though I would not have cared to live my early life over, today the balance has changed, and I would be satisfied to live my whole life over, rather than never to exist. Because my physical life improved too, and though progress has never been easy, taken as a whole my life is a good one. Two major things contribute to that well-being: my wife and my career. Those who seek advice for happiness can have mine: find the right spouse and the right career. Unfortunately today's world makes the achievement of such things difficult.

It would be tedious to detail the rest of my schooling, so I'll skip it, and just say that of the ten schools I attended through college, the third best was Westtown School in Pencil Vania, where I boarded four years and graduated with an indifferent record; the second best was The School in Rose Valley, also in Pencil Vania, where I completed grades five through seven in two years; and the best was Goddard College, in Vermont, where I got my degree in creative writing. In fact Goddard was like entering paradise. It was at the time perhaps the most liberal college in America, with fewer than seventy-five students, no tests or grades, informal clothing, and a pervasive egalitarianism. That is, there was no hierarchy of students, no initiations or discrimination, everyone was friendly and helpful, and teachers were called by their first names. That doesn't mean that everything was perfect, and I did have some severe problems there. At one point I was suspended for a week for opposing a regressive faculty policy, and as with other conflicts I have had, I think it is now generally conceded that I had the right of the case. But overall, Goddard set me on course for my future, with my practice in writing, and my wife, and I now support it generously financially, being one of its richest graduates.

Ah, yes, romance. When I was eleven I loved a girl who was twelve. I'm not one to sneer at puppy love or crushes; it was the most intense love I am aware of experiencing, and it lasted for three years despite a complete lack of encouragement on her part; indeed she was at different schools after the first year. She was slender, had long brown hair, wore glasses, and was a smart and nice person. She taught me to play chess, and today I still work the daily chess puzzles in the newspaper. So in certain respects she defined my interest in the opposite gender. Let's pause, here, for a statement about terms: technically, gender means the grammatical identification of certain classes of words, while sex refers to whether a person or animal is male or female. But because sex also means the activity of procreation, this gets confusing and sometimes embarrassing. There is the story of the woman who filled out a job application form, writing in the box marked SEX "Occasionally." There is the suspicion that the Equal Opportunity Amendment to the Constitution, that would have protected women from discrimination, failed to pass because some people thought it meant sex as in copulation. So I prefer to use the word gender, where there is no confusion, and to hell with the purist grammarians. I never liked the subject of grammar much anyway. At any rate, when I later encountered a smart brown-haired girl with glasses in college, I married her. Now you know why. (My wife says that's an oversimplification. I can't think why. It's been forty years and she still has glasses and brown hair, and handles the family finances and goes on-line with her computer, something I'm not smart enough to do.) She was a tall girl, standing five feet nine inches in bare feet, while I had been the shortest person, male or female, in my high school classes. But in five years, from ninth grade to the second year of college, I grew almost a foot, so was a full inch and a half taller than she. I tease her about that: I had to do it, to be ready for her. Men judge women by their figures; women judge men by their height.

After college, life was rough. My wife and I spent most of a year trying to make a living in northern Vermont, and I had trouble getting work because I insisted that I needed $50 a week to support my family, and most jobs didn't pay that much. I finally landed a dollar an hour, fifty-hour-a-week job with American News, delivering magazines and paperback books to stores. Then, at the end of summer, the boss approached me as I was punching out my time card on Friday. "Don't come in Monday." That was it. It seemed it was a summer job, not the permanent one I had been told. No advance notice, no severance pay, just gone. After that the only job I could get was selling health insurance—and you know, it's rough if you represent the policies honestly and are in an economically depressed region. When driving, I took my eye off the road to verify the address, and at that moment hit a reverse-banked turn and started to go out of control. I hit the brakes—and they locked, and the car sailed off a six-foot bank at forty miles an hour. I remember wondering whether I would recover consciousness after landing. It rolled over, and I found my head in the backseat. The roof had caved in six inches—which was exactly the head clearance our VW Bug had. I was lucky; I came out of it with only a bruised shoulder. That was in the stone age, before seat belts; you bet I've always used one since.

My grandmother Caroline sent money to enable us to get the car repaired, and my mother sent what money she could spare to enable us to live. Meanwhile my wife was pregnant, but having trouble. I took her to the hospital, where she lost the baby. Suddenly we had no prospective child, and I was eligible for the draft. Since I wasn't making it economically anyway, I volunteered to go in immediately. At least it would guarantee a paycheck for two years.

I was lucky, again: I was in the army 1957–59, between Korea and Vietnam. My wife joined me at Fort Sill, Oklahoma, where I was an instructor in basic math and survey. It was an artillery base, and it takes calculation to survey in the big guns, so that they can fire exactly on target. You have to know where you are, before you know where you're going. Later they tried to make us all "volunteer" to sign up for savings bonds, at two and a half percent interest, but we needed the money for groceries and rent, so I didn't sign. So they harassed my whole unit, trying to make it put pressure on me to sign, but the others supported me instead, because nobody likes getting pushed around. Remember, once I got free of childhood, I got ornery about being bullied. I even went to the battalion commander with a charge of extortion against the first sergeant. The lieutenant colonel heard me out courteously for an hour and a half, but did not feel the evidence was conclusive. So I didn't get the sergeant canned, but I made him sweat, and I suspect he got a private reprimand. It was one more notch in the minor Legend I became in the Army. Strangers would come up to shake my hand. But the authorities were not amused. They booted me as instructor and sent me to another unit of the battalion, as well as depriving me of any promotions. It's the Army way. They didn't care as much about quality instruction—I was so effective a teacher that they wouldn't give me leave time to visit home, and in the end they had to pay me extra for over a month of unused leave—as they did about 100 percent bond participation. So, taken as a whole, the Army was a waste of time for me, but it did pay my way, and covered my wife's month-long hospitalization and second miscarriage, a medical expense that could have bankrupted us otherwise.

After the Army, we moved to Florida. I like to say that I traveled from Vermont to Florida the hard way: via two years in the Army. That's how we came in out of the cold. I worked in industry as a technical writer for three years, and later I was an English teacher in high school.

But what I really wanted to do was write, and finally we took the plunge: my wife, having suffered her third miscarriage, went to work, and I stayed home and tried to be a writer. The agreement was that if I didn't make it in a year, I would give up my foolish dream and focus on earning a living in Mundania. I had a fifth cousin who did just that after failing at writing, he became an executive at Sears Roebuck and did well. But I made it; I sold two stories, and in that year earned a total of $160 from writing. Now I'm slow, but finally it penetrated: that wasn't enough income to sustain a family. That's when I actually became a teacher. But I kept writing stories on the side, selling one every six months or so. Finally, in 1966, I retired from teaching, which job I liked no better than the others, and returned again to writing. This time I focused on novels instead of stories, and the larger amounts of money earned from novels allowed me to make a living, barely, though my wife continued to work. So it was lean, but it was writing, and that's what I wanted.

Thereafter, with the help of modern medicine, we were finally able to have two children we could keep. I think of this blessing as being like the monkey's paw. That famous story was about an old couple who had a severed monkey's paw that would grant three wishes, but it granted each wish in such a way that the result was worse than before. So they wished for money—and got it when their son was killed and his insurance came to them. Horrified, they wished for him to return—so the corpse was roused and heading for their door as one of the walking dead, before they wished him gone again and were done with it. I would never have been able to take the risk of staying home and writing, if my wife had not been free to earn the family income instead—and she was free only because all three of our babies had died. Had we had a choice, we would never have let them go. But now I was a successful writer, and we got our two daughters too. Thus we had everything we had wanted: success in writing and a regular family.

But I was never a regular person, as this autobio surely makes clear. My life as a writer was just as problematical as my life elsewhere. I'm a square peg, and life offers mostly round holes. I think I didn't have the most trouble of any writer in the science fiction / fantasy genre, as that dubious honor belongs to Harlan Ellison, but I think I can fairly claim second place. Harlan himself was somewhat baffled by me, and our relations have been mixed. There was a problem with one publisher, so I demanded an accurate statement of account. Instead, I got blacklisted:

publishers refused to buy from me. Even a writer's organization, which supposedly existed to help writers against errant publishers, tacitly sided with the publisher, though in a position to know that I had the right of the case. Writing is not necessarily a nice business, and justice is not always served. I dumped the writer's organization, called SFWA, and have been hostile to it ever since, for good reason. The blacklist was rough; I accumulated eight unsold novels. But one publisher didn't honor the blacklist, so I survived. Also, I got a literary agent, the same one who handled Robert Heinlein, then the genre's leading writer. That messed up the blacklisters, because they knew that if they annoyed that agent, they'd never see work by Heinlein. Meanwhile, a new administration came in at the errant publisher. The new administration hired editors who were friendly to me; they checked the company books and realized what had happened, and invited me to return. I was wary, but tried it, as I really wanted to work with their editor, Lester del Rey. He was in charge of fantasy, so I wrote a fantasy book. That was *A Spell for Chameleon*, the first Xanth novel.

None of us knew it at the time, but fantasy was about to take off for the stratosphere, and the Xanth series rode that rocket right on up. This was, as I see it, for two main reasons: Lester del Rey was an apt editor who knew a commercial novel when he saw one; he developed Stephen Donaldson, Terry Brooks, David Eddings, and others, in addition to me, and became arguably the most successful book editor the genre has seen. The other was his wife, Judy-Lynn del Rey, who named Del Rey Books. I call her a giant, and I wrote her into Xanth as the lovely but deadly Gorgon, and she even sent in puns for it, like Gorgonzola cheese and was duly credited in the Author's Note, like any other young fan. "I *am* a young fan!" she said. But the humor went beyond that, for physically Judy-Lynn was a dwarf, standing something like three and a half feet tall. But she was smart and tough, and she could really promote her books. She was the publisher who first put *Star Wars* into print. So Lester's editing and Judy-Lynn's promotion made a publishing phenomenon like few seen in our time, and Del Rey Books soon dominated the genre. The fifth Xanth novel, *Ogre, Ogre*, became the first original fantasy paperback (that is, one that never had a hardcover edition) to make the big national best-seller lists. My income moved from that initial $160 to more than a million dollars a year, and all our financial problems were behind us. The blacklist was gone, destroyed at its source; all the editors who had blacklisted me were out of power and not eager to advertise what they had done. I wasn't actually responsible for getting them canned, not directly, but I believe that none of them cared to mess with me again. It's that bully syndrome; when the tables turn, the bullies flee.

With success came fan mail, and I do my best to answer it, though about one-third of my working time is now taken up by it. Sometimes it seems that half my readers want to become writers themselves; unfortunately, only about one in a hundred will ever sell anything, because the competition is great. A number of the letters are serious, such as those from suicidally depressed teens. I understand depression, because despite my phenomenal commercial success (not critical success; critics claim that I don't write anything worthwhile) I remain mildly depressive. It seems that most writers and artists are depressive; I guess I'm lucky that it's not worse for me. So though I am old and most of them are young, we relate well. A number have credited me with saving their lives, just by responding and understanding. I drew on what they told me to make the character Colene in the Mode series: age fourteen, smart, pretty, and secretly slicing her wrists. Many have told me how well they relate to her; they wonder how I could know their inner truths so well. I don't know, really, but I listen well. I also have a novel, *Firefly*, that is apt to freak out school officials, because it deals graphically with sexual abuse, but I have had many letters from women who thank me for bringing this ugly matter out into the open. So readers should beware; not all my work is frivolous fantasy. Some of it is savage.

But no glory lasts forever. Judy-Lynn had a stroke, and died. Problems caused me to leave Del Rey Books though I really didn't want to, and in time my career crested and diminished. Publishers made promises and then reneged, to my cost. It remains a perilous business, and as in life, writing skill is not always rewarded, and justice is not necessarily served. There seems to be a small anonymous cadre of critics whose purpose in life is to spread false stories about me. I tackle these head-on when I encounter them, but it's like dealing with pickpockets: they are hard to catch in the act. I have been called a Satanist, maybe because Satan is a character in a couple of my novels, and a possible child molester, and some even hint that I must be into bestiality because there are mythical half-human creatures in my fiction, like centaurs and mermaids. Some accuse me of unethical behavior, though they can't document it. It started with that Ogre business, and hasn't stopped. I presume that other successful folk have similar problems; those who are not successful want to drag down those who are, and are not choosy about their methods. But the great majority of those who write to me are supportive. Still, it's more fun climbing up the mountain of Parnassus—that's what the literary establishment is called—than tumbling down it! Today other fantasy writers are surging ahead, and I wish them well, though I am sorry to be left behind. I still write funny fantasy, and I have answered an average of 150 fan letters a month for a number of years, but my real interest now is in historical fiction. I regard *Tatham Mound*, about the American Indians who encountered the Spanish explorer Hernando do Soto, as the major novel of my career, and the historical GEODYSSEY series as the major work of my career. I am now in my sixties and know I won't live forever, so I'm doing what I always really wanted to do, and that is to explore the whole human condition and help others to understand it. I like to think that those young readers who like funny Xanth will in time graduate to my historical fiction, and find it as satisfying in a different way. I love writing, and when I die I expect to be halfway through a great novel.

EPISODES

My first sexual experience occurred, as I remember, at age four. I was in bed alone when an attractive young adult woman entered the room, uncovered me, removed my pajamas, and addressed my bottom. She was very pleasant and soft spoken, and her touch was gentle. She required me to lie on my right side, facing away from her, and she ran her soft hands across my buttocks and into the cleavage between them until she found my anus. She spread some salve on it, then firmly pushed something in. I jumped, surprised, as this was new to my experience, but she told me to relax, that it was all right, so I eased my clench and let her continue. She reassured me as she worked it well inside me, and I was not really discomfited despite the strange penetration. In fact there was a special quality to the sensation, arousing my interest. It turned out to be the nozzle of a hose, sliding on and on in once the sphincter had been breached. When it was firmly set, quite deep, she lifted the other end of the hose high and used a pitcher to pour water into a funnel. I turned my head so I could see as she smilingly did it. The cool water coursed down the hose and into my rectum, filling me up. There was a transparent place in the hose, where I could see bubbles pass, so I knew the fluid was going into my body. This was a second type of penetration, with its own odd pleasure. But she didn't have enough water; the pitcher ran out, and she had to pause to refill it, with a friendly exclamation of surprise, as if we were accomplishing something unusual. I was evidently taking in more water than expected, but there was no problem; she would keep it going until enough was in. That's about all I remember, over half a century subsequent.

Years later I learned what this procedure was. It was an enema, done to clean out my bowel in preparation for a tonsillectomy. I'm sure I had to sit on the potty thereafter and blow all that water out again—I have a very obscure impression of that—and later I must have been given ether or something to render me unconscious, and later yet I must have had a sore throat. I vaguely remember being told I could eat anything I wanted, like ice cream, but for some reason I wasn't very hungry. So it was done, and nobody thought anything of it. But I remembered that pleasant experience with the young woman who had touched me so intimately and shown me what could be done with that part of my body. My horizon had been broadened in a way I was never to forget, as this narration shows.

Another night, at home, I dreamed. I was with my sister and the nanny, and we stopped at a gas station. I thought the nozzle of the gas pump would be put in the car, to fill its tank, but suddenly I was lying on my stomach on the ground, my bottom was bare, and they were putting it into my anus. I was caught by surprise, just as I had been at the hospital, and exclaimed with protest, but to no avail. The fluid came, filling me, pumping me up, making my body expand, but the feeling was in its way pleasant, with a special extra quality. And so I remembered that dream.

When I was perhaps eight, I dreamed again, of being held in the arms of a lovely young woman who somehow had access to my bottom and was running something deep into my rectum. "Only ten minutes more," she murmured reassuringly. I didn't mind; the whole experience was pleasant in a way I wanted to continue. I did not understand either dream at the time I had it, but, looking back from the vantage of adult sexual and anatomical experience, I believe I do now.

I am thoroughly heterosexual; I love the look and feel of women. I like every part, and really appreciate long hair, but the sight of breasts or inner thighs truly electrifies me. Even a cartoon picture of a woman with her skirt rising attracts my attention. The idea of anal sex with a man repels me. But I think back on the lingering effects of that early anal contact with the hospital nurse, and I wonder whether something like this couldn't make the difference, if a man were of borderline sexuality. If he oriented on the rectum rather than on the woman. Homosexuality surely has a strong genetic component, but there are cases of identical twins, one of whom is homosexual, the other heterosexual. Did someone, in the name of medicine, exploit the private parts of one, and lead him to an orientation that solidified in adulthood? The association of the enema hose, with its copiously jetting fluid, is obvious. I am, as I mentioned in *BiOgre,* suspicious of the medical establishment's seeming fascination with the anus, even using it to take temperatures. Is there a consequence no doctor would like to acknowledge? I have seen comments about men who do "like it in the ass" in the course of heterosexual sex play. I have no real evidence, but at times I do wonder.

There are other things. One of the most traumatic events of my childhood was not something that happened to me, but to my sister. I call it rape. I describe it in the "Reprise" chapter, but since it wasn't in *BiOgre* and had a lifelong effect on my awareness, I'm covering it there too. My memory begins with me alone in a strange room, but I knew my mother and sister were near. Then I heard my sister's voice, rising, protesting, saying no, no! So I walked through the short hall and came to a room where my sister was sort of sitting on a bench or table, and several adults were clustering around her. They held her and did something to her, and she screamed, but they did not relent. They held her arms and head, and I think I saw a splash of water. Mainly I remember her little feet thudding against the surface of the table, as she vainly tried to run away. But they were merciless. They made her hurt as much as they could, then let her go, crying. One of them turned around at that point, and saw me standing there in the doorway. "He saw!" she said. And the memory fades out.

It took me more than fifty years to fit that stark memory into the framework of my other memories, to piece the puzzle together. That was my sister's tonsillectomy, a considerable contrast to my own. Mine was like pleasant sex; hers was like violent rape. It was in Spain, in 1939, time for what was routine minor surgery in those days, though today it seems there is no need for it. But in Spain, so soon after the Spanish Civil War, many things were lacking, including safe anesthetics. So, they said, they would do it without anesthesia; it was after all a small, quick operation. "Not on my child!" my mother exclaimed, and they agreed to find an anesthetic. So she brought us in, left me in the waiting room, and took Teresa on into the clinic.

That's where it changed. The personnel snatched my sister away from her mother, put her on the table, held her in place, jammed a fixture in her mouth so she couldn't close it, reached down her throat, and cut out the tonsils, one, two. Done. My mother was horrified—and so was I, understanding nothing of it except the savagery. So sharply was the memory isolated from the rest of my experience that even when my sister told me later how a man had cut into her throat, I didn't realize that it was that she referred to, and years later when my mother told the story, I still didn't make the connection. They say that traumatic memories can be buried for decades, to surface later in adult life, such as in cases of incestuous rape. Well this memory remained with me throughout, unburied, unconnected, until the isolated puzzle piece suddenly snapped into place, and I understood the meaning of the horror. So I am inclined to believe in the reality of buried memories. Had it happened to me, it might have been submerged completely. But no, my sister remembered it, in fair detail. She doesn't call it rape. What horrifies me additionally in retrospect is that this is the way children are often treated by adults, across the world, and some is more brutal than this.

As a general rule, my early experiences with doctors were negative, as detailed in *BiOgre*. They seemed to exist to hurt children. They jammed spoons down throats to make a child vomit, they stuck painful needles into flesh, they poked tender orifices uncomfortably. Once I was taken to a female doctor, in America. She uncovered my uncircumcised penis, saw that the foreskin covered the glans, took hold and forced the skin down so hard that it split. This had to be done every so often, she explained, so that the skin would not close in again. In the following days my penis slowly healed; a scab formed over the end, causing the urine to splatter, but finally that cleared. I had been punished by another doctor, this time for having a natural penis.

Only when I was about sixty did I learn the meaning of that, listening to Dr. Edell on the radio: doctors have this notion that the foreskin will never be able to retract, if not forced to in childhood. But the fact is, he said, that it loosens naturally at puberty, and should not be interfered with before then. Nature does know what she is doing, and should be allowed to take her course. Apparently this isn't more generally known because so many boys in America are circumcised—a ritual, Dr. Edell explained, which they try to justify on the grounds of hygiene, but which has no real effect other than to reduce sexual sensation. And there's the true unspoken agenda: it is intended to prevent boys from masturbating. It doesn't, of course. With the increasing recognition that masturbation is natural to the human condition, the medical urge to cut away the offending skin seems to be slowly fading.

When my wife was pregnant, the subject of circumcision came up, and I said I would not permit it. We were not Jewish or Arabic, so there was no religious reason. The doctor said, in that forced reasonable tone reserved for unreasonable folk, that he would have to have a talk with me. But as it happened, both my children are daughters, so that battle never was fought. There are countries where they do worse to girls, infibulation, cutting out all their external genital anatomy, apparently without warning or anesthesia, just holding them down and carving while they scream, sometimes killing them in the process. Those cultures have no more sympathy for the "unreasonable" ones who protest this barbarism than certain American doctors have for those who protest circumcision. Culture tends to override reason, and ignorance abounds, in medicine as much as anywhere else, ironically.

So how did this all come about? My grandfather's Quaker family left Ireland because of the onerous vaccination law. In those days it wasn't a simple matter of a quick needle; they sliced open the flesh, and deaths sometimes occurred from the process. When my grandfather, Edward H. Jacob, got established in America, he married Edith Dillingham. They had five sons and a daughter, of which my father Alfred was the fourth.

Alfred graduated from an American high school and went to Dartmouth College. His brothers advised him to make a good effort at the start, to impress the professors; thereafter he could coast. He also chose one of the rarer musical instruments to play, the bassoon, to be more certain of a place in the school orchestra. After breaking in at college, he learned that he ranked something like sixth in a class of six hundred. He hadn't even been trying to learn much, just to make an initial impression. He thought about that, and concluded that American education was not for him. So he set his sights on a better educational institution, the University of Oxford in England, widely considered the finest in the world. That decision was to change his life in more than the academic sense.

First he attended Woodbrooke, a Quaker institution which had no examinations and no pressure; students were there to learn what they wished, in the way they wished. He was interested in biographies, and was studying about Ghandi, the great Indian pacifist. He was happy there. And there he met Joyce Maybery, a quiet girl. Her family had experienced its own tragedy, when her father had gone on the maiden voyage of the *Titanic*, and been lost with the ship, in 1912. Thus Joyce's youngest sister had been born during the absence of her father, whom she was never to know. The relationship of Alfred and Joyce was tentative, subtle rather than overt; they did not even go as far as holding hands. The high point was when they rode to the end of the train line, got off, and walked up a hill there, and talked for the afternoon, just coming to know each other better. But for him, his future had become apparent. He wrote up the experience in detail in his journal of the time. Joyce was the one.

The summer break came, and he didn't see her. He lived for the fall term, when they would be together again. But when it came, she wasn't there. He inquired, for surely she could not have changed her mind about school.

That was when he learned that she had caught a fever, and died. It may have been typhoid fever; she might have drunk tainted water when camping. It may have been misdiagnosed, or she may have been given the wrong medicine. There isn't much way to be sure. Thus suddenly, she was gone.

More than sixty years later it remained difficult for him to talk about Joyce, and I never knew of her till that time had passed. We cannot know how things would have been. Perhaps their acquaintance would have ripened, and they would have married and been happy. I wish it could have been—yet with a certain selfish reservation, because then I would not have existed, and all those who came to know of my novels and the magical land of Xanth would not have encountered them. It is tempting to think that there was some higher purpose in the loss of Joyce, and that it was necessary for the greater good that the well-adjusted child she might have had—not come to exist. So that the gnarled, depressive, imaginative creature later to be known as Piers Anthony could come to be. But I am more cynical than that. I see no higher purpose in the devious and sometimes savage twists of the threads of fate, and I wish my father had not had to suffer that loss.

It is also possible that had Joyce lived, her association with Alfred would have passed. Romances come and go, and there can be many trial associations before the more binding commitments are made. Sometimes relationships don't work out. There was just one small hint, in a comment made by Joyce's mother, "Perhaps that was best," that Joyce's feeling for Alfred did not at that stage match his feeling for her. Yet the relationship was nascent; much could have changed in the next term, had she lived. Women tend to be more cautious about love than men are, but they do achieve it in their own time. And if they were not fated to love and to marry, surely it would have been better to play that out in life, instead of bringing such grief to both Alfred and Joyce's family. They could have gone their separate ways in friendship, without interfering with whatever larger order was destined.

Coincidentally, at that time, Alfred met another young woman, Genevieve. They were acquaintances and friends, but Genevieve was not Joyce, and in due course they moved apart. But there was a good deal more to come, between them, in due course, despite the lack of bells and whistles at the time.

Another time he was to go on a triple date with two friends, but the other two men were unable to make it, so Alfred found himself with all three girls. One of them was Norma Sherlock. As time passed, and he was with one and then another, a friend inquired "Why are you bothering with those others? They aren't close to Norma's quality." He realized it was true, and became serious about Norma.

Norma was the daughter of a doctor, and granddaughter of a Church of England bishop. Her father, Dr. Sherlock, had been devising tests for intelligence, and used his little girl as a model. He assumed she was ordinary. That's why she was named Norma—for normal. Unfortunately for the validity of his norms, she was not; she was an extremely bright child, somewhere in the top percentile of intelligence. She grew up to graduate from Oxford University, taking two Firsts in languages, French and Spanish, an unusual feat. There were four levels, which Americans might see as grades A, B, C, and D. So she had made, in our crude analogy, a double A.

I have a picture of her as she was as a cute child of perhaps three, and another as a young woman of perhaps twenty-three, with typically English floating hairstyle. As a child she had grown her hair so long she could sit on it, but at age twelve decided to cut it. There is said to be a picture of her with her mother, with her shorn hair all on the floor and her mother in tears. I'm with Grandmother; I love long hair on a woman and wince at the notion of such glorious tresses being cut. But my mother was ever a creature of her own will.

Here is an example of her independent mind, quoted from her journal of memories, the entry dated April 21, 1982:

> *Something I heard today on the radio reminded me of another Oxford memory: the entrance examination I took for Somerville in 1928. There was one paper which was designed to test the applicant's ingenuity rather than knowledge, and this contained a question which struck me as so silly that I've remembered it from that day to this. It was: "If you were compelled to fight a war, how would you finance it?" Well, Margaret Thatcher was also at Somerville quite a few years later and I find myself wondering whether she too was asked that question and if so, how she answered it. I didn't; there was a choice and I passed that one up as totally irrelevant to any possible future for a bright girl applying for admission to the world's best women's college.*

How many young women would risk their admission to a highly regarded college in a highly regarded university by declining to answer a question they considered irrelevant?

When she met Alfred, things moved swiftly. "I had forgotten what a handsome man he was," she remarked decades later, when seeing an early picture of them together. Their relationship soon progressed to consideration of marriage. But Alfred was then in therapy, and his therapist disapproved of a patient marrying during therapy. "We'll see about that," Norma said, and went to talk with the man. Thereafter the therapist withdrew his objection. Later, Alfred inquired about their dialogue. "Oh, we didn't talk about it," the therapist said. Then why had he withdrawn his objection? It turned out that the moment Norma walked in, he realized that there would be no compromise with her, so debate was pointless. He yielded to necessity.

Yet that was perhaps a warning signal, because marriage was not the only thing Norma refused to compromise on. She tended to be very sure that she knew what she was doing and that others, when they differed with her, did not. She let Alfred know at the outset that she was the intelligent one in the family, and would brook no argument when she made a decision. This is not the smartest attitude to bring to a marriage, ironically, and indeed, the marriage didn't last. That attitude was to cause trouble with me, too, and unlike my father, I do not gracefully yield when I know I am right. Indeed, there were times I set my mother back by not only asserting myself, but proving that I did have the right of an issue between us. If that bothered her—and it did—at least she knew where I got it from, and perhaps appreciated the kind of a trial she had sometimes been to her own parents and grandparents. But there was a difference between us, because I do my best to make certain that I am right before I make my stand, while she tended to proceed on her own certainty. Substituting certainty for judgment can be disastrous, tempting as it evidently is for many folk.

But at the outset of their association such subtleties were invisible. Love swept away all objections. Well, most of them. Norma had finished at Oxford, but Alfred had not. He was in contention for a First, but was distracted by the romance and did not perform well, so took a Second. That was perhaps part of the basis for Norma's claim that she was smarter—though she was the one responsible for his distraction. In my observation, there are different kinds of intelligence, and those who score high on one kind are apt to have a weakness in another, somewhat in the manner that a hand of cards with strength in spades may be weak in diamonds. Often academics seems to prosper at the expense of social savvy. I think this was the case here.

Actually, I don't regard such unevenness as necessarily bad. Each card is worthy in its own right. Kings have power, but deuces have their role too; most games could not be played without them. I understand that originally aces were the lowest cards, but with the French Revolution, where royalty was slaughtered by the common folk, aces came to be ranked above kings. When deuces are wild, they may be more useful than aces. People are more complicated than cards, and a given person can be a king in one respect and a deuce in another. Each person must be judged in multiple ways, if judged at all. I remember an item in Isaac Asimov's autobiography, wherein he was scheduled to speak at a "Black Tie" event. So he put on a black tie. When he concluded his speech, he noticed that every person there was dressed far more formally than he was. He had never before caught on to the meaning of "black tie"; he had taken it literally. I would have made the same mistake. Asimov was without question a very intelligent and knowledgeable man, but some of his spades were at the expense of diamonds. And his first marriage, too, didn't last, suggesting imperfect social savvy.

And this, also, is not necessarily a fault. One recent study suggests that the human kind is geared to a four-year romance: time enough to generate a child and see it through weaning, which is when the mother is in greatest need of support. Thereafter another romance can commence. So many marriages founder in emotion if not always in appearance at that time. Those that endure longer may have become another kind of association. I suspect that the half of all marriages that end in divorce are merely the more extreme cases; the remaining ones have varying degrees of separation. "Until death do us part" is an unrealistic commitment for the majority. Sometimes it is better simply to recognize that a given marriage is not working, and to dissolve it. That was the case with my parents, who had an amicable divorce after nineteen years. But that action had its price. More on that anon.

Today only a minority of couples seem to wait for marriage before indulging in sex. It was different for my parents, sixty years ago. In fact Alfred, still a student at Oxford, had a curfew; he could not stay out all night. One time Norma was visiting him, and had to go home alone, because the curfew prevented him from going with her. That was all right; she had a bicycle. But let her tell it in her own words, from her journal entry of March 13, 1980:

> We certainly did manage, in that time and place, to enjoy being young, and Oxford was the place to do it. Another of my memories is of the evening when I was visiting Alfred at his lodgings in Headington and missed the last bus home. It was too late for him to drive me back, since as an undergraduate he had to be in by midnight. So he mounted me on his bicycle, which was difficult because I was wearing a tight skirt, and gave me a push at the top of Headington Hill, and down the hill I went and all through the center of Oxford, unable to stop for any red lights because once I got off I'd never be able to get on again. Luckily in the middle of the night there was very little traffic and no police, and I finally managed to fall off outside my own door.

But Norma's sexual education consisted of a quiet briefing by her mother on the eve of her marriage, of the "just close your eyes and think of England" variety calculated to render a young woman frigid. It did.

And so they married in 1933, and though they were in love and meant well, that was probably the beginning of the end of their relationship. Norma was simply unable to enjoy sex, and had to struggle to participate at all. Nevertheless I was born the following year in the

Oxford hospital. They found a thatch house nearby to live in, and my sister was born in that house. I have a painting of the house that my sister commissioned on my study wall, constantly before me as I work. I don't remember it, but appreciate the significance of it in my life, as does my sister even more strongly. But quaint as it was—it remains one of the last such houses in England—my mother hated it. It was primitive, and I think lacked such amenities as running hot water. She was caught there when the labor pains for my sister's birth started, and couldn't get to the hospital. She said Alfred had to carry her upstairs to the bedroom, and she bit him on the arm. Teresa arrived in just twenty minutes, in contrast to the seven hours it had taken me to enter this world. Our subsequent lives followed those examples. My sister was swift, while I was slow. Though she was a year younger, at one point she was five inches taller than I was, and she entered first grade with a sixth grade reading ability, while I took three years to get through first grade because of my inability to learn to read.

Then Alfred and Norma went to Spain to do relief work during the Spanish Civil War. Their effort is detailed by my mother's narrative in an appendix to *Bio of an Ogre*. A Scottish nanny took care of the children. She is actually the first "parent" I remember, and I think my separation from her was the beginning of what turned out, in its various forms, to be a lifelong depression. Apparently there were two of them, sisters, and one may have been named Bunty Stewart. That's all I know. When I think of the happiness of childhood in England, it may actually be the limited time when that competent, gentle young woman was always there. I don't even know whether that was at Oxford, or London, where my mother's parents lived. Probably London, because I remember seeing a double-decker bus, and going to the park, and the vine-covered dead end of the street. And the way my sister and I imitated our grandmother Sherlock, as she held the serving utensils vertically in her hands, ready to serve the food. I'm not sure I remember Oxford at all, unless that was where I had my tonsils out.

Then we went to Spain. I remember seemingly endless train rides, where periodically men would come through and check through all the suitcases, customs inspection. At one point there was revealed something wrapped in light paper or cloth, and my mother indicated what it was by waving her hand. It was a hand fan, the kind that opens out. We don't see many of those today.

Most of my memories of Spain were covered in *BiOgre*, so what remains is scant. I believe it was there that I had my first ice-cream cone. The thing about it is that it was square rather than round: that is, the man put a block of ice cream into the cone. I was surprised, when later in America I found that the ice cream put into cones was round. I conjecture that in Spain they lacked the bulk ice cream and scoops, so the man used a packaged cube instead.

Another memory is trivial, yet it assumes significance now that any memories of the time are precious. Norma had a nice little set of cooking pots with matching lids, perhaps a wedding gift brought from England. One day I saw the cook using one of those little pans on the stove, with a huge foreign lid on it. I was disgusted, that such a sweet little pot should be so abused. In a way, now, it symbolizes the situation of my mother, a bright yet innocent British woman thrown into the appalling situation of war.

When we went to Portugal to catch the ship to America, we had to drive through a high mountain range. There we stopped so we could go out and touch a cork tree. All that cork, just growing as bark! Perhaps that gave me a notion that was later to manifest as the magical trees in the Land of Xanth, that could grow just about anything. We also drove to the very top of one mountain—I remember the road winding around and around, finding its way up the steep slope—until at the top we found some kind of amusement park. There were many entertaining devices. My mother put a coin in a model train set, and we watched the train run along the tracks, as winding as the road had been. In fact, I thought it was a model of the mountain we had just come up. Then the train went into a tunnel, and didn't come out the other side. The game was over.

In Lisbon, Portugal, we stayed at a hotel. At one point my mother walked across the room naked, and I was surprised; I had never seen her that way before (and never since), and marveled that she had some hair low on her belly as well as on her head.

We were leaving Spain because the newly victorious Franco regime had arrested my father, perhaps by mistake, and couldn't admit any error. He had smuggled a note out of prison, and my mother used that, and the leverage of an influential Quaker friend who was in a position to cut off substantial relief funds for Spain, to get him out—on condition that he leave the country. I think dictatorial regimes do not understand folk who try to help suffering families to survive the ravages of war. Compassion, generosity, or fair-mindedness are alien concepts to them. I did not know the reason for our stay in Spain or our departure from it, at the time, but later as I learned, I came to hate dictatorships, and indeed, all dictatorial entities, whatever names they go by.

Here are Norma's notes on the matter, made January 2, 1982:

> There is a report today of a train accident in Spain, on the line which goes from Barcelona up to Zaragosa. I have good reason to remember that train ride, which I took in July 1940, after Alfred disappeared on one of his field trips during the Franco period. As far as we can tell, he was arrested because he was near the frontier with a large sum of money given him by the British Embassy; this was at the time when Hitler's forces took over most of France and British refugees from the Riviera were supposed to be arriving at the Spanish border on their way to Lisbon (I was in Barcelona meanwhile trying to collect enough non-perishable food for a party of perhaps 400 refugees, men, women and children including young infants, for a journey of several days across Spain in a sealed train in August). After several days of trying in vain to find out where Alfred had gone, Mercedes and I received a grubby picture post-card which had been smuggled out of the prison by a fellow prisoner who was being released. I at once took the train ride and went to the prison, only to find that he had been moved to Madrid. So I took another train, at night this time. My chief memory of that is that it was bitterly cold and my fellow-travelers insisted on having the carriage windows open (it's usually supposed to be the English who insist on this). They were very friendly people and shared all their bread and other provisions for the journey with me.

Mercedes was their secretary in Spain, who took pride in being completely competent though I understand she was only seventeen years old. I remember once being in the office when suddenly one adult woman fled, and Norma ran after her. Only decades later when I read my mother's journal, after her death, did I piece together the elements of that scene and realize that that was the time when Norma had jokingly teased Mercedes about not knowing where something was, and Mercedes fled in tears. Norma had to chase after her to make it up. Though she worked for the Liberal Quakers, I understand that Mercedes was a sympathizer for the revolution, believing that much good would come when General Franco won the civil war. But as time continued, and the realities of that government manifested, her idealism took a beating. I think of Coleridge's comment on the French Revolution, here rendered as prose rather than poetry: "The sensual and the dark rebel in vain, slaves by their own compulsion. In mad game they burst their manacles and wear the name of Freedom—graven on a heavier chain." Perhaps there were revolutions other than the American one that brought lasting benefits to their people, but I think not many.

The ship to America was the *Excalibur*, and I understand it was the last passenger voyage departing Europe before World War II cut off such transport. The former King of England, Edward VIII, was another passenger on it, on his way to govern the Bahamas. I got seasick and had my sixth birthday on that ten-day voyage. The sheer immensity of the ship impressed me, so big they even mounted a canvas swimming pool on the deck. But I don't remember our cabin or meals, apart from a vague impression of some tiny cubicle with a round porthole-window.

In due course we reached New York City. I think I remember passing a big statue rising from the water, which would have been the Statue of Liberty, but can't be quite sure. I believe I also remember being met by Alfred's father, Edward H. Jacob, and his wife Caroline Nicholson Jacob. I'm sure I remember the long drive to West Chester, Pennsylvania, where my grandfather lived. His business was mushrooms, and he had been known as The Mushroom King, before selling the business in 1929. Now he was retired, and lived on a nice estate opposite a golf course. I found it to be a fascinating place.

But as I was beginning to come to terms with the strange land of America, a long nemesis struck: school. I was six years old, and it was time. There was trouble from the start. "What's your name?" "Piers." "No, what's your last name?" I had not heard of any other name. "Piers." "Piers Piers?" I was asked derisively. So when I got home I inquired, and learned that I had two or more names. The papers I did were messy and somehow wrong; I remember being shown one and lectured, I suppose the teacher's effort to shame me into trying harder, but I didn't know what the problem was.

It took me three years and five schools to get out of first grade. Not every school was bad, but taken as a whole, it was a nightmare. I remember sitting beside a boy the teacher didn't like, and seeing how she changed the rules, such as being allowed to use the bathroom, to exclude him. Once she went after him with a ruler, but he avoided the blow. That made her angrier. "Didn't feel that, eh? Well, take this!" She wasn't satisfied until she knew he was really hurting. I had not seen such violence before, and hardly knew what to make of it, but the clarity of my memory over fifty years later shows the impression it made on me. A girl told of the worse school she had come from, where they made kids vomit, and then made them lick it up again. I wasn't sure I believed that, but wasn't sure it was untrue, either. Once my sister Teresa, who was now in the same grade I was, encouraged me to go with her to join a throng of children who were playing in a school field. I was doubtful, having experienced some of the new-student syndrome, but went along with her. But they quickly drove us away with epithets.

So did I ever stand up for myself? Well, sometimes I tried. Once I was visiting a neighbor boy, who had been friendly before, but then he had some other friends, so he told me to go away. I demurred, not liking the change in attitude and not yet understanding the gang syndrome in children. He became threatening. I kicked up with one foot, not really at him, just threatening to. He stepped in and punched me in the face. He was bigger than I was, and completely demolished me. I fled in tears, to some jeering. This was my first lesson in the rationale of the bully. Before I was out of first grade I began to learn to fight, and as time went on I got better at it, though inevitably my opponent was larger than I was. When it got so that I could take just about anyone within ten pounds of me, the bullying mostly stopped. But I did take some lumps from those who were considerably larger. One boy outweighed me by about thirty pounds, in ninth grade, when I weighed just under a hundred pounds. I wrestled him down to the floor, then let him go. He got up and started swinging, and his reach was so much longer than mine that I couldn't get at him at all, and got beaten. After that he pushed me around constantly. Another was my own size, so I knew I could take him—but he palled around with a larger boy, and when anyone stood up to him, he brought in the larger boy and they both went at the one. The bullies ruled the roost. I was not the only one who stayed out of trouble mainly by not resisting, though sometimes this meant allowing the bully to copy my homework. I didn't like it, but it was easier to yield my homework than to get beaten up. The school administration was oblivious, as always. That was a Quaker school, preaching the virtues of nonviolence, but those in charge wouldn't have approved of the price of nonviolence had they taken the trouble to look into it. Reality can differ sharply from idealism.

In adulthood the arena became more intellectual than physical. While many boys finish their physical growth at fourteen, I did not; I gained almost a foot thereafter. All physical bullying stopped. Along the way some tested me, and that was as far as it went. One of the notorious bullies wrestled me in a friendly match; he offered to take on two of us together, but the other boy demurred, so I took him on alone. He was older, larger, and stronger, and he did beat me, in a clean match, but evidently he respected my effort, because he never bullied me. Oh, he could have, had he chosen; he could demolish much larger boys. There was a case when another bully was going after one who wasn't fighting him; he kept snapping and snapping with a wet towel, the kind that can leave scars on bare flesh. No one could stop him, being afraid of him. Then the one I had wrestled came on the scene and told the toweler to get the hell out, and the other had to go. I didn't see it, but another boy told me that the toweler started to turn back, to resume his attack— and the other simply swung his straight arm around and cracked him on the side of the head. That ended that. But he and I always got along. I think it was that he respected my attitude: I had tackled alone what another boy had not dared to as a pair, and I had fought cleanly. So he had tacit respect for one who was no threat to him. And I, with a lifelong hatred of bullies, make an exception for him.

I grew intellectually, too. By the time I got out of high school I had a tested IQ of 131, after testing subnormal earlier. In college I was tested at 132 on a similar test. Sure, it's not supposed to be that way; IQ is supposedly constant. Maybe so; as I said, I was always slow, so in effect in the early years I was competing with classmates who were well ahead of me mentally as well as physically. But in time I not only caught up, I went ahead—and stayed ahead, intellectually, in adulthood. But I had come up through a rough school, in more than one sense. I use the qualification "tested" because I question the validity of the IQ concept; a test is only as good as its mechanism, and it has been said an IQ test tests the ability to take IQ tests, rather than true intelligence. I agree.

So what was my problem? It could have been dyslexia. My daughter has it, and her early problems in school were eerily reminiscent of mine, though she quickly learned to read while I spent three years in first grade trying to learn, and never did become a fast reader. My grandfather Edward Jacob never got good at reading, though he was an excellent businessman. So it seems to be something in the family, which looks from some angles like stupidity but from others like intelligence. The evidence is growing that dyslexia is the inability of the language-processing centers of the brain to coordinate, so the dyslexic must think about what others do naturally, so is at a disadvantage until he learns to compensate. Once he does compensate he may go far, because it's not lack of intelligence so much as lack of integration that is the problem. That seems to describe me. I was called stupid in early school, and was not great in later school, but more than one reader has called me genius for the way I write. Maybe I learned to compensate so well that now I do it better than those who never really had to sweat it. Thus my liability became my strength. I don't know; it's just conjecture.

There were other facets of my life, and these, too, were not necessarily good. The marriage of my parents was dissolving, and though it was to take about a decade for the divorce to become official, the stress of it affected me. I began to wet my bed, for several years, and developed compulsive mannerisms, such as shaking my head or hands every few minutes. No one understood why. I was sent to a number of child psychologists, who I concluded did not know beans about children. Fear became the most constant nemesis of my childhood. I was afraid of being alone, and of the dark, and of strangers, and of my own dreams, the most ravaging of all. Sometimes it seemed that my whole life was a bad dream; I wished I could wake up and find myself back in England with the nanny. But it became apparent that there would be no such reprieve.

There came a time when I declared my independence, in a fashion: I told my mother I would not see any more psychologists. She didn't like it, but I was immovable. I date the onset of my recovery from that point. Slowly I assumed increasing control of my own destiny, at first emotional, later intellectual and physical. In effect I cut the problem of my parents off from me, so that the ongoing struggle of their separation and divorce no longer tore me up. The bedwetting stopped, and the twitching. I began to grow again—I had stopped for several years—and my intellectual effectiveness increased. It was no overnight salvation; my problem had taken years to develop, and it took longer to abate. But my life gradually improved on every front. My mother was appalled when I once remarked that my parents were folk I knew and liked, but did not love; she did not understood why that had to be.

Another aspect of my education was sexual. I was originally naive. I remember once playing behind a shed with my sister and a cousin, and of course we came to the point of showing our private parts. I had seen my sister many times, and knew that girls were different. The other boy, though younger than I, had an erection; his penis stood out at right angles, while mine was small and limp. Years later I came to understand that he had understood better than I the naughtiness of what we were doing. I was capable of erections, and sometimes had them, but had not been sexually excited by that scene. But when I sometimes stayed overnight at another house, and had to share a bed with another boy, he was always feeling for my penis, and asking me to feel his. I didn't understand why. He kept working the skin up and down, up and down, interminably. It seemed pointless to me, but I let him do it to mine. One night I felt a strange sensation growing in that region. Alarmed, I asked him to stop, and he did. Only years later did I understand that that would have been my first orgasm. In my ignorance I had stopped it before it was completed. In retrospect, I wish I had been more knowledgeable. Similarly, once I was playing with a girl, and she wanted to share some genital exposure, and I refused. In retrospect, I wish I hadn't. Once I dreamed I was playing with a girl, and she bared her cleft and invited me to enter it, and I was strongly tempted, but knew it would be wrong, so didn't. Then I woke, and cursed myself for not having done it, as all is forgiven in dreams; it would have been perhaps my first wet dream.

One misunderstanding was humorous. My cousin called an erection a "boner." I remembered the term. Then one day I saw a book whose title was *10,000 Classroom Boners*. I was amazed; I wondered just what kind of a class that was. I was somewhat let down later when I learned that a boner was merely a funny mistake.

Another episode was merely mischief, and I was the perpetrator. One summer at Hilltop Farm we got to know other kids our age, which was then early teen. We got a sixty-pound canister of honey by mail order. Now the problem was to transport it to the neighbors with whom we would share it, and on home, a total route of miles. The other boy was big and fat, and he carried it in a pack on his back without undue trouble. But when my turn came, it was rough, because I weighed a scant hundred pounds. When I tried to lift that pack, 60 percent of my own weight, I fell over under its weight. But I tried again, and did manage to hoist it up and walk my walk. It was balance that was my problem, rather than strength; at that time I was able to carry my sister, who weighed more than I did. We took it to the house of Marshall Smith, where his wife Lois supervised the pouring out of some of it. The hole was small and the honey was thick; it oozed out a blob at a time, the string thinning between blobs. Just when a blob was squeezing out, I made an ooomph! urgent grunting sound, as of someone getting out a load in the outhouse. That set off the other boy, who burst out laughing. The woman gave him a severe stare for that transgression. I had gotten away with one.

Back to sex. When I went to boarding school in ninth grade, my roommate straightened me out in a hurry. "Haven't you ever played with yourself?" he asked incredulously. I didn't know what he meant. So he told me, and showed me, and then it all began to fall into place. I was late maturing, being slow in that respect as in others, and didn't reach puberty until age eighteen. But sexuality didn't wait on puberty. The difference, my roommate explained, was that before you got hair on your balls you couldn't ejaculate, so your orgasm was dry. And it was so. I, like most boys, would have been capable of orgasm at any time in childhood, had I known how to masturbate. Now I learned how. There was a joke going around: "Are you one of the 95 percent or the 5 percent?" That meant, the 95 percent who masturbated, or the 5 percent who lied about it. Indeed, it did seem to be universal. Some did claim they didn't; presumably they were among the 5 percent. It was a nightly occurrence, and some kept at it until they orgasmed a second or third time. Some liked to do it in pairs or with several; some preferred alone. One boy would get into bed with anyone who let him, and massage the other's penis, expecting a simultaneous return of the favor. One once demonstrated how far he could spurt; he went into the closet to work himself up, desiring privacy for that, then emerged to jet into the air and onto the floor. But my impression was that as they became interested in girls, masturbation diminished. I doubt that they were having sex with the girls, because the rules were strict and there was almost no opportunity, but they had a new orientation.

Girls. I was the shortest person in my ninth grade class, male or female, and this militated against much of a social life. I have been on only one formal date in my life, and that was an arranged one, required attendance, with a classmate, Nancy Horsefield. We sat together at a program, and I had to take a brief leave to go onstage for a bit part, then return. That was it; there was no mutual interest. I never had further interaction with her, other than seeing her in classes. She was a fully developed girl, and I was far from the equivalent in boys; physiologically she was about five years ahead of me.

However, I was encouraged to attend some evening dances, and did dance with several girls. I was beginning to get into the feel of it. Then a couple of older boys told me that I should cut in on a couple they pointed out to me. In my naïveté I did. It was a practical joke, and they got out of there in a hurry. I had cut in on a senior boy and his steady girlfriend. He was nice about it, cutting back in after a minute, and never seemed to hold it against me. But it was a grievous lapse of etiquette, and when I realized the nature of my transgression, I was totally embarrassed. In four years at that school, I never attended another dance. My social life ended at that point, and did not resume until I was in college.

One of my unkind chronic awarenesses is of death. My two closest calls were a car accident I mention in Chapter 3, and the measles. Normally measles is just another childhood illness, but the later it comes the worse it may be. In my senior year at Westtown one of my friends came back to school with it, and sure enough, two weeks later I got it. I was, I believe, the second worst case among the boys; the worst was my classmate Han Broekman. As I recall, his temperature peaked at 105 3/4, while mine was 105 1/2. For three days I had no appetite, and ate nothing, and so nothing passed through my system. The nurse, whose book of instructions said that there had to be a BM every day regardless, gave me enemas each of those days, looking for what wasn't there. Actually on the third day there was something, though where it came from I don't know. But what bothered me more was the weakness. When I was moved to another infirmary room the poor nurses had to carry me, a difficult job for them, and the disruption made me vomit. I was allowed to take myself to the bathroom, but lacked the strength to get out of bed. I had a cough, and it came to the point where I no longer had the strength to cough, so had to lie there with that nagging tickle in my throat. Then, indeed, did I feel the deepening shadow of the valley of death. They gave me a sleeping pill, but I stayed awake all night until at last they gave me something to counter the pill, and then I slept; apparently the pill had the opposite effect on my metabolism. One night

I developed a terrible thirst; every hour I woke and asked for water. It got so that the nurse was by my bed with a glass of water the moment I stirred. I felt sorry for her; she could get no rest herself, with patients like me. But slowly the crisis passed, and my appetite and strength returned—slowly. I remember when one of the other boys got up to go to the bathroom, ran out of strength, so lay down amicably in the hall for a few minutes to rest, before recovering enough to complete his trip. That was the way of it for us all. As I improved, I was moved back to the main infirmary, where I woke to find a wonderful basket of fruit by my bedside, sent by my Uncle Ed and Aunt Dorothy, the parents of my cousin Teddy Jacob, whose early death colored the rest of my life. It was like emerging into bright daylight after being lost in a dark burial cave. Thereafter it was as if my life had passed a significant marker; Teddy had died, but I was not destined to die just yet.

PEOPLE

No one exists in a vacuum, and certainly I did not. I was shaped by my experiences with other people as much as by my genes.

My outlook was so negative in much of my childhood that I reasoned it out, and concluded that if I could be given the choice to live my life over, exactly as it had been, or never to exist at all, I would prefer the latter. I was not suicidal; I just would have preferred to have been spared the travails of existence. This may suggest that I was strongly depressive, but I think it was rational. Nonexistence is better than negative existence. But probably I was mildly depressive, because I seem to have been that way all my life. That doesn't mean I'm unhappy all the time, just that my thermostat is set lower than the norm, and my joy of existence, taken as a whole, is less. This seems to be the case with many creative types; in fact there is a question whether creative genius is bound together with madness, loosely defined, the most creative being the maddest. I doubt that there is any universal truth in this, but if there is, it is my fortune to be far enough short of the extremes that I am able to function in the real world while taking advantage of my creativity to earn my living. In fact, I may be close to the line of viability, gleaning as strong a trade-off between genius and competence as is feasible. Thus I have not become alcoholic or otherwise nonfunctional, while achieving considerable success as a commercial writer whose interests are not limited to personal well-being. Not many achieve that fortunate a compromise. This was more luck than design, but the underlying balance had to be there.

So why *wasn't* I too fouled-up to achieve anything? I have pondered

that over the years, and concluded that I had enough good support at a
critical time in my life to enable me to become well enough adjusted to
recover from the bad times. I think the first support came early in life,
most of it before I remember: in England, with my parents, and then
with the nanny. The nanny, I suspect, had but one object while on duty,
and that was to take good care of the children in her care. She surely
did that, and that gave me my secure original base. Though I lost my
contact with her, and my well-being eroded, that foundation remained.
Maybe she was only doing her job, but I feel that I owe her much of
my sanity. I always had the memory of happy England to sustain me in
adversity. Perhaps it was a fantasy realm, as I did not know her name
or that there were actually two of her, and I have no memory of her
hair (could she have had long hair? That would explain a lot!), eyes,
form, or face. She's just a presence, always there, always nice.

After that, according to my obviously imperfect memory, there were
my parents. I came to know them, actually, in Spain. They really did
mean well, but they were not naturally endowed for the job of parenting.
Perhaps this is unkind, but I wonder whether the way they so eagerly
volunteered for the challenging job of handling relief work in war-torn
Spain was an indication of their incapacity as parents. They could not
risk the children while the war continued, so we remained in England.
When they were home, according to my mother, she tried to stay away,
so as not to let us become attached, because then we would miss them
when they returned to Spain. Thus it was that the attachment I developed was to the nanny—and my separation from her was just as bad as
it would have been from my mother. Except that, in the case of the
nanny, I was never to see her again. Thus my exile had no end.

Nevertheless, I did come to know them. I don't recall my mother
ever playing with us, but my father did. Once he had a magic trick, in
which he put a coin on the top of a block, covered the block with a
block-shaped shell, lifted the shell—and the coin was gone. Where could
it be? He had a toy rabbit or something, perhaps one of our dolls, and
animated it, looking all over for that lost coin. It was hilarious. Finally
I tried to help. I thought it might be under the block, so I picked up
the block. Instead of coming up whole, a block-shaped shell came up,
and there under it was the original block, with the coin. Disgusted by
my interference, which had ruined the trick, my father picked up block
and shells and departed. We never saw that trick again. So it didn't finish

well, but it was fun while it lasted, and I have been interested in similar tricks since. It did show the way of it: my father was able to play with children, and did so many times; that was the only time I remember it turning out negatively.

In later years he was to tell us stories while we shared in some kind of work, such as digging in the garden, and they were always fascinating. Sometimes he would read the story just before we went out, then retell it, spinning it out. I remember a reference to a prince being given an army with a hundred men; later I checked that story in the book, and it was something like ten thousand men. My father had tailored it to our scale, and indeed, those hundred men made sense to us. He would read to us at night, and we loved those sessions. It was a favor I was to pass along to my own children, later. There is a special togetherness in reading together.

Again, I don't remember my mother reading to us, but surely she did on occasion. She was there for the other things, especially illness, dressing, meals, shopping, and so on. The family fell into different aspects, as is the case with many families. Mother was there for comfort and routine and responsibility; father was there for discipline and fun. It was a workable system. We children had no hint of the ravages the people of Spain suffered; we were insulated from it.

My memories of other people in Spain are mostly slight and passing. There was the young man, Jorge, who sometimes played with us; I understand he spoke no English, so that was when we began to learn Spanish. There was a nursemaid who cared for us for a while; she taught us to brush our teeth and rinse our mouths by letting the discolored water go back in the glass. When we were finished, we each had a glassful of rinse water. Then, on her instruction, we drank the water. I don't know whether this was to save water when perhaps it was precious, or mischief on the part of the maid. Later, with our mother, we started to drink the rinse water and she immediately said of course not. So I think she didn't know. Perhaps it is my imagination, as I re-create the scene, but I think I remember the maid smiling with perhaps too-good humor, so it may have been mischief.

There were too many passing people to remark on when we came to America, so I'll confine it to a few who had more of an impact. We were at Pendle Hill, a Quaker study center, for a while in 1940, and everyone there seemed nice. I remember a story my mother told later, of something I wasn't party to: there was a party, and a fancy meal, but dessert had a problem. The hostess came to announce that they had had the ice cream in the oven for twenty minutes, but it still wasn't soft enough to serve. I also remember being alone one evening while the others were out, and there was a phenomenal thunderstorm, with the lightning flashing and the thunder crashing. I loved it. I lay on the bed and gazed out the night window, watching it all. To me, light and noise were interesting, signifying action and excitement, like a war movie, though I had never seen such a movie. It was quiet that was lonely and frightening. Later the others came home. My mother was concerned that I would be terrified. How little she understood.

We left Pendle Hill, but later were there again for a while. We got a house in nearby Wallingford, and were often on the Pendle Hill campus. I went to The School in Rose Valley—that was its official name—covering grades five, six, and seven in two years, catching up to my grade level. It was the best school I attended, of nine, in my first nine years of schooling. One of the other students there was Herta Payson, who had long brown hair and glasses. She was twelve, and I was eleven, and I had a crush on her that I can't to this day distinguish from love; it was as deep and enduring as any such emotion I have felt, though un-returned. She was on the Pendle Hill campus about as much as I was, so we interacted often. Once when she was bored she taught me to play chess. I was glad to learn anything she had to teach me, and I have been intrigued by chess ever since, though the pressure of workaholism was later to squeeze it out of my life except for the daily newspaper chess problems.

I had thought my attraction to long hair dated from my association with Herta, because she had fairly long straight hair, but now I suspect that I had it backwards; she appealed to me because of the hair, rather than the hair appealing because of her. There doesn't seem to be much way to know, for sure. She also wore glasses, and the woman I later married wore glasses; was there any connection? I doubt it; my mother wore glasses too. I can see beauty in a woman with or without glasses, but a short-haired or blond woman leaves me romantically cold. My sister had long blond hair, and apparently that squelched all possible romantic interest for me in blondes. In other respects, blond hair gives me no problem; I thought my blond cousin Dotsy was a sweet girl, and my daughter Penny has wonderful long blond hair. But for romance, for me, a woman's hair had to be long *and* dark, not one or the other. This preference still affects me, and it remains overwhelmingly strong. But after many years of long hair, my wife finally cut hers short; I felt I did not have the right to demand that she never wear it the length she preferred. I now choose to wear a beard; she doesn't fault me on that, either. Romance is not identical to reality.

One day several of us were playing with homemade slingshots, fashioned from coat hangers and rubber bands, firing small stones at each other. We agreed to aim below the waist, so no one would get hurt. But Herta was struck on the glasses, and a lens cracked. It is not possible to be certain, and there were at least two of us on each side, but it could have been one of my stones that did it. Yes, I was aiming below the waist, but that meant a trajectory that went higher, or the stones would never have gotten far enough. She was nice about it, but of course the game broke up at that point, and I don't think we ever did it again. I remain chagrined, because it just seems too likely that it was my stone that did it, and she was the very last person I wanted to harm in any way.

In due course Herta went to another school, and we seldom saw each other thereafter. There had never been anything between us, other than in my fancy. But my love for her burned brightly for three years before fading, and never faded entirely. Once, years later, a young woman introduced herself to me: "I don't know if you remember, but we knew each other. I'm Herta Payson." Not remember her? *Not remember?* At age sixty I saw a picture of one of my correspondents, a woman in her thirties and something about it fascinated me. Then I realized: there was a faint resemblance to that twelve-year-old girl I had loved, fifteen years before my correspondent was born.

Once I saw a newspaper article about a grisly murder. A woman returned to the apartment she shared with another woman, to find blood all over and the woman dead. I don't know the outcome of that case—I think a boyfriend had done it—but I remember it because the surviving woman was Herta. There too, others thought I might not remember her, and I did not enlighten them. But it would be like not remembering the sun and the moon. I don't know what happened to her thereafter; I presume she followed a normal life course, married, and so on. But I wonder whether any man ever loved her as I did. I have never sneered at "puppy love," because I have felt its power. Adults have more experience than children, and can make better decisions, and have more control over their destinies, so their romances can endure longer. But I'm not sure they are more intense.

After the first time at Pendle Hill we moved to Hilltop Farm in Vermont. Teresa and I had no notion why; only decades later did I come to understand the rationale. Here is my mother's comment, from her journal entry of 1-15-1991, not long before her death:

> When we arrived in America and spent a year in that haunt of peace-lovers, Pendle Hill, we got ourselves involved in a scheme to defeat the war people by living out the disaster on a hilltop in Vermont and then coming down to rebuild society; it didn't take me very long to realize that something was very wrong with our high-flown argument.

Indeed it did not work out as envisioned. I mentioned an indication of that in *BiOgre*: an artist, Cliff Bennet, painted a nice picture of the house as a mural on the kitchen wall, and below it wrote "Let not the seeds of war be found on these our premises." Later those words were erased, I think because it was discovered that the seeds of war—that is, disharmony—were indeed to be found there. I remember telling him that he had painted the roof of the house wrong; the lines of the roofing went at right angles to what he showed. He didn't comment. Later I rechecked the roof: work had been done on it since I had looked, and I was the one who was wrong. I thought about his silence, and realized that I had made a fool of myself. Since then I have always tried to verify my information before challenging anything, and it has spared me many a potential subsequent embarrassment. A number of other people, however, have not learned that lesson, and have challenged me on details without checking, and so have been embarrassed by my refutations. Harlan Ellison was perhaps the most notable of these. Memory is treacherous stuff, and should always be verified before an issue is made. It's like a finder telescope, useful to get you to the ballpark vicinity, but not to be trusted for detail.

My mother hated living, as she put it, like troglodytes, there where there was no electricity, no running water, and no vehicular access in winter. Subsistence farming was definitely not her style. She much preferred the conveniences of the civilized city. But her objection was primarily intellectual:

In the brief excursions I made out into the war-torn world, it became clear to me that it was the people who were living in it and coping as best they could who were in the morally superior position. Whatever their ideology, they simply were better people than we. When I broke away from that and became a fund raiser for the peace movement I still was tormented by ambiguity (I always remember, when I was interviewed for the job by Kitty Arnett. Lee, whom I then didn't know at all, coming through the room and saying "You'll make the bomb-cases but you won't make the bombs—is that it?")

My conclusion is similar. I don't believe that the problems of the world can be significantly alleviated by retreat from them. They need to be actively addressed in some fashion. The conquerors and despoilers don't desist when ignored by their neighbors; they take over their neighbors and often destroy their cultures. So Norma was right to get back into the world, philosophically.

But she left the children behind. Again. It was no fun life. It wasn't abusive in the standard sense, it was just rough in certain ways, physically and emotionally. We had to walk alone through the forest to school, two and a half miles each way (later it was said to be three: they hadn't wanted to make us wary of the distance), sometimes on snowshoes in winter. The snow could reach four feet deep at times, the temperature 30°F below zero. Sometimes the water I washed in was frozen, so I had to break the ice in the basin. But the emotional isolation was worse. I had already started wetting my bed at night; now I developed halfway involuntary twitching of the head or hands. That is, when you have a cough, each cough is voluntary—but you do have to do it soon. Again and again. Though you'd rather be rid of it. Ridicule or punishment won't make it go away. This was that way. And just as a cough is the apparent evidence of a hidden disease in the body, my compulsive twitching and bedwetting was the evidence of the deep emotional distress I was suffering. Picture a child being punished for coughing or having a runny nose. I got punished in certain ways for those reactions. Until finally I figured out for myself what others did not, and began to repair myself, by weaning myself away from emotional dependence on a unified family. But that was a long and difficult process.

A mother's love is traditionally unconditional. But my mother didn't really know how to love. And in this time she was overwhelmed by her own problem. My father had a greater commitment to the family, and though he made mistakes, he was the one who was usually there for me. Unfortunately there was a kind of dichotomy, with male understanding male and female understanding female, so I got along better with our father and my sister got along better with our mother. I remember with some bitterness that in the many altercations I had with my sister, only once did our mother take my side, though I believe that an objective party would have seen the justice of my case at least half the time. Thus I was alienated for cause, and grew up to resent unfairness wherever I encountered it. Our father usually took my side, and so alienated my sister—and when our mother left, she was left in the care of our father. So she has her horror stories too, many also of the subtle kind that don't have significance for those who don't actually experience them. Later we both lived with our mother, and I was the odd one out again.

I remember examples, and to be fair will give one of each: the two of us were playing by a low wall in a garden, when my mother was advised that there was poison ivy there. She immediately hauled us both out of there, and thoroughly washed my sister. I was relieved at the time to escape that. But years later, pondering it, I inquired: why was she the only one? Both mother and sister chastised me for paranoia. So I didn't bring it up again. My observations later in life suggest to me that it is often the one who makes the charge of paranoia who is the one causing the mischief, protecting himself by aggression. Folk hate to have biases exposed, so pretend they don't exist. This also relates to the blame-the-victim syndrome: if the victim is culpable, then other folk, who presume themselves to be superior, will not be similarly hurt.

Now the other example: when we were with our father, Teresa once made a meal, doing what she could at an age when adult skills had not yet arrived. Our father criticized it endlessly: the salad wasn't clean, the vegetables weren't cooked well, the whole thing was slipshod. She finally fled the table in tears. He didn't understand why. Later he asked me, and I explained about the stresses on her—a boy who hadn't been interested, a friend in trouble, and lack of appreciation for the effort she had made. Sympathy for Teresa's situation didn't come naturally to him, just as sympathy for mine did not come naturally to our mother. Though in adulthood we all tried to paper over such schisms, they do remain below. Our parents just weren't perfect at parenting, however well-meaning they were. They tended to think of us as small adults, and were impatient with our childishness, even when we were indeed children. Once, I put the question pointedly to my mother: "If you can't be young when you're young, when can you be?"

Were there times when I had differences with my father, and Teresa with her mother? Oh, yes, some serious ones. But in general—well, let me go to another analogy. Once in adult life I played badminton with an associate from work. His shots were fast and straight and true, while mine just didn't have much force, if they got there at all. He tore me up. Then we changed courts, and the wind was at *my* back, and I tore him up. It had been so slight as to be almost unnoticeable, yet it made all the difference. Well, when we were with my father, the wind was at my back; when with our mother, it was at my sister's back. On major issues the wind did not count, but in the myriad little ones that make up daily life, its effect was constant. My sister and I did not get along well, but I think she would agree with me on this.

At any rate, Hilltop Farm was our lot for about four years, and it had its positive aspects. I developed an abiding love for nature, and today, with the resources to live anywhere in the world I please, I live in a forest with our nearest human neighbor about a mile away by road. No animals are hunted, and we have seen deer, a wildcat, rare birds, and many other creatures close by our house. But we do have electricity, and all that goes with it.

As the group of people who set up Hilltop Farm with such ambition fragmented, replacements were needed. I don't know how it was arranged, but a young—age nineteen, I think—college man came, and brought his girlfriend, later wife. They were Norman and Winifred Williams. They took to the primitive life and made something of it. In fact they were later to buy their own neighboring property and built their own house there. But meanwhile she got a job as a local schoolteacher, and the deserted school in Pikes Falls was reopened, and for two years we went there—all two and a half miles distant. Winnie was, for my taste, a lovely woman and wonderful person, almost too pretty to be seen in a backwoods region like this, and too intelligent to get along well with the sometimes bigoted neighbors. But she made the best of it, and I think it was largely her presence that made those years bearable for me.

Norm Williams was a fine man. My father later told of an experience he had: once a week he opened the back of the privy house, took out the loaded can of refuse, hauled it to the garden, and added it to the compost pile. Compost piles are one of the mainstays of natural farming; all garbage goes there, including the bodies of dead animals, and in the course of a year it all processes into rich soil for the garden. But the details of handling organic refuse aren't really pleasant. One day Norm joined him, observing every detail, and Alfred was glad to explain the whole process and philosophy. Next week Alfred went out as usual— and Norm was already doing the job. Thereafter Norm did it regularly. Alfred hadn't asked him to; Norm had simply found a place where he could be of help, contributing to the farm, and did it. At other times they worked in the woods, cutting and hauling firewood for the winter, and Norm was always a compatible and hardworking companion.

When Winnie started teaching school, the only way we knew to get there through the forest was along an old road about a mile west, then a right-angle turn south for a mile, at which point the forest road inter-sected the Pikes Falls valley road that cars could drive. It was an inter-esting route, but a long one. It seemed too bad that we couldn't simply cut across the square, or the diagonal instead of around the edge. There was a trail that started that way, but it soon petered out, going nowhere. The end of it was even marked by a pretzel-bent tree. In my fantasy, that would be sure sign of the passage an ogre, but in the mundane realm it meant that the Indians had bent a small tree that way, so that it grew up to signal the path. Only there was no path. Well, Norm wondered about that, so he explored more thoroughly—and found the continuation of the trail. It crawled out of the gully and continued in exactly the direction we needed. So on the second day of school, as we two children were walking there with Winnie Williams, she brought us to that dead-end trail—and around the slope to the "new" trail Norm had found. It was a wonderful fresh exploration, as the trail wended its way through the forest. About halfway along, in the center of the "square," was a clearing where blueberries grew. I think it was the rem-nant of an old farmstead; I believe there was a cellar hole there. That region of Vermont had been much better populated in the prior century; there were several cellar holes scattered around our premises. I have often wondered who was there, and what their lives were like, and where they went. We lived, as it were, in the ebb of a once-thriving culture, and it made me ponder. That, too, was later reflected in my fiction. But on this day, we were simply glad to have half a mile cut from our route to school. Just as well, because for the next two years we walked that distance every school day. It was okay when both of us went, but often the teacher had different hours, and sometimes my sister was ill, so I walked it alone, and then a monster always followed me, just out of sight, sneaking ever closer.

Later, the Williamses bought the land around that clearing in the center of the square, named it Welkincroft, and built their stone house there. I came once to baby-sit their daughter when they had a day-long blueberry picking excursion, and that child insisted on exploring the forest road all the way down to the bottom, about half a mile, then declared she was too tired to return, and I had to carry her back. But it did keep her entertained. Later my own daughter Penny would lead me around similarly; I just found it hard to say no. I stayed with the Williamses at Welkincroft the end of the summer between high school and college. I don't think I was as much help as I should have been; I was in the process of reorienting my own life, turning my back on the distress of the past and focusing on the future, and I think not paying enough attention to the present. Such things bother me in retrospect. Today I try to be aware of what I want to accomplish, of whatever nature, and do it at the appropriate time, so as to have no regrets later. But I learned that by assessing my errors of the past. At the end of that summer my grandmother Caroline Jacob came and took me barefoot from the mountain, and I was on my way back to civilization.

One of the people who stayed a while at Hilltop was a conscientious objector (CO) to the draft. Today bad examples of the misplaced priorities of law abound, as nonviolent people are imprisoned for using marijuana while murderers are released early and rapists let go after token sentences, if they serve time at all. Those days had their own bad examples, as fine young men were imprisoned for their opposition to war. They did not try to sneak out of it, they notified the draft boards that they declined to register, and for this they could be severely punished— while criminals might not be, as usual. The CO had spent five years in prison for refusing to carry a draft card. He was finally released—no time off for good behavior—and later was picked up again for the same offense, and spent five more years in prison. Thus American justice in the 1940s. He was with us in the interim between imprisonments, and is the subject of a difficulty of conscience of my own.

As a child I was not conversant with the background. In the summer

I had time on my hands—television did not exist then, but we also lacked radio and close neighbors—so we spent much time outside. The CO found an isolated field and built himself a sod hut. He carefully cut oblongs of sod from the ground and laid them like huge bricks, fashioning walls, and even the roof, over a wooden framework. This process fascinated me, and naturally I went there to watch. But the CO wasn't seeking the company of a seven-year-old boy; he preferred to be alone. So my folks told me to stay away from there. But the fascination was such that I couldn't stay away. "Are you supposed to be here?" "Well . . ." So I guess I was a pest. Then one day I ran afoul of some bees, and got stung on the lip. I raced away, and after that I stayed clear of there, since I knew I wasn't wanted anyway. This satisfied the adults; the problem had been solved.

Well, in due course the CO departed, and his sod hut remained, gradually suffering the depredations of time. The twig of a tree was growing in the slanting roof sod as years passed, it assumed larger stature, and bore down the roof under it, collapsing the house. Eventually, I think, what had been the sod hut was just a tangle of ground around the tree. But the CO existed elsewhere, in prison. Someone mentioned that to me, and I remembered him and inquired whether there was anything I could do. "You could write to him; prisoners don't get much mail." I thought about that, but never did write. Because though I by then appreciated his situation, I couldn't forget that he had not had much sympathy with my own isolation, and I wasn't sure he'd appreciate hearing from that bothersome kid. Now, with a correspondence averaging above 150 letters a month, a significant portion of it to depressed teens or to prisoners, I wonder whether I was right. I think I should have written to him. But of course it's too late.

There were other neighbors, there in the Green Mountains of Vermont. Perhaps most notable was Scott Nearing, a famous radical who had once been tried for treason. He had defended himself and won his case. He was a small man, physically, who shared my birthday, AwGhost 6. And a formidable one intellectually. His politics were leftist, and he was very sure of himself; he brooked little argument. For a time we went every week to listen to his global commentaries. Personally he was generous, having no use for wealth, living well enough directly from the land. My father said that when we were struggling one winter, not having known to cut wood in advance for our stove, so that all we had was green wood, Scott appeared one day with a truckful of seasoned wood for us, a wonderful gift. Scott lived to be a hundred, then starved himself to death, preferring to exit life in his own fashion. His wife Helen carried on; she and I exchanged some books, and she liked my novel *On a Pale Horse*. She lived to 91, and died in a car accident, just after publishing her collection of quotations *Light on Aging and Dying*. I wonder whether she, too, chose the manner of her conclusion, ensuring that no one try to extend her life artificially.

Another neighbor was Marshall Smith, who came as a young man from England, liked the look of what we were trying to do, and bought a farmstead near Welkincroft. He married Lois, a comely young woman, after getting her pregnant in what was arguably a rape. He would come to talk with Alfred late into the night; his marriage was not smooth. She always seemed to be criticizing him. He also seemed to be plagued by bad luck. I remember the way he described getting a horse-drawn mower for hay or wheat; he had it operating just perfectly. Then a bee stung the horse, the horse bolted, hauling the mower along, and it got dented and spoiled for easy mowing. That was heartbreaking for Marshall. It's the kind of disaster that city folk might not understand, but farmers would wince. In the 1990s I heard from two of their daughters, Derika and Sybil, now women in their forties. Sybil had written a novelized account of her mother Lois's early life that was illuminating and beautifully done. I helped her get an agent so she could effectively market it. Through that manuscript I came, belatedly, to know and understand Lois far better than I had when she was our neighbor. I wish I could have known of her situation at the outset; I would have had far more sympathy for her situation.

There were also Harold and Natalie Field. He was knowledgeable about mechanics and electricity, and she was a vivacious small woman, rather pretty as I recall. We visited their farm a number of times, but I never got to know them well. Now I wonder whether I wasn't missing as much as I was with Marshall and Lois Smith. There is evidence that I was. People are so interesting, if only we have opportunity to discover and appreciate how.

I entered my ninth school in ninth grade. The best of the early ones was The School in Rose Valley, where I covered fifth, sixth, and seventh grades in two years and gained confidence and scholastic ability. It had an egalitarian philosophy, and let students democratically choose what they liked to learn, within reasonable limits. Once we voted to play baseball all afternoon, and this was allowed. Finally, we all came back in, having had enough of it, and didn't do it again. We chose our own parts in plays, and put out a school magazine. I don't think The School in Rose Valley was perfect, but overall it came close. I have a chapter on it in *BiOgre*, so won't go into it here, other than my contacts with two other students. Yes, my ideal woman Herta Payson was there, my first year, but then she was gone. There was another girl other students tried to match me with; they would arrange, in the course of other activities, to have the two of us wait alone together in a room. But such ploys were useless; I had no interest in any but Herta. But there were two girls I remember for other reasons.

One was Tanis Fletcher. One morning, in the weekly school assembly, I saw the name TANIS on the back of the chair in front of me. She was one of the Tens, that is, ten-year-olds, a year younger than me. Later when I went to Westtown School, Tanis was there too, though we had no association. Later still she came to the same college, Goddard. When she first came, a year after me, I offered to show her around the campus, but another boy blocked her way at a door, engaging her in conversation. I didn't know how to deal with such rudeness, but since she didn't seem to mind, I realized that she no longer wanted me to show her around, and I left it to the other boy. That perhaps typifies our relationship: we had no binding interaction. But she was the only person, apart from my sister, with whom I shared three schools, or about eight overlapping years. Years later, commenting on a novel by the fine fantasy writer Tanith Lee, I reminisced on my memory of Tanis and speculated whether maybe Tanith lisped. I don't know whether Tanith appreciated the humor.

The other girl was my age, a niece of my stepgrandmother Caroline Nicholson Jacob, so we were nominally related. She was generally quiet, but was one tough girl. Once when I annoyed her, she punched me. Another time she and a friend tried to tie me to a chair, for what purpose I don't know, because I managed to escape. She was horse crazy. Once when *she* annoyed *me*, I drew a picture of a sneering horse, but I lacked the courage to show it to her, for fear it would be too effective. She was athletic, competing on even terms with the boys. I knew her two years at Rose Valley and four years at Westtown, with no close association—I'm not sure we ever even spoke to each other at Westtown—and she took the award as the best female athlete there. Thereafter we saw each other seldom. In one of the ironies of life, her promise faded, while in due course mine flowered. I was nothing at Westtown, but today am widely known for my writing. She was outstanding, but later got involved with a radical war protest group that raided an FBI office and stole papers. She spent a year in prison for that, and disappeared from view thereafter. I met her at our twenty-fifth class reunion, and she said something about wanting to talk to me about writing something, but never followed up. I'm sure she has a considerable story to tell. I saw her as a coiled rattlesnake in the guise of a woman. That's not an insult; it's guarded respect. I get along with rattlesnakes. Maybe we'll meet again.

Another I knew at Westtown was Ronald Bodkin. He was what later came to be called a nerd: academically brilliant, socially unsure. He was a grade behind me, but we associated for three years, and were roommates for one. We got to know each other when we wrestled, routinely when we were supposed to be doing something else. He was constantly ragged by others, while I always had sympathy for the square pegs, being one myself. As I recall, we wrestled cleanly, and I won, as I always did against those my own size, and thereafter we associated increasingly. I stood up for him when I could, and this sometimes had effect. He helped me too, clarifying things like Latin for me, as I was a linguistic dunce. We played a lot of Ping-Pong, and he passed me in skill, to my discomfort—since then I try much harder to be a good sport—and was always way ahead academically. We lost contact after Westtown, until when I was in the U.S. Army my sister, his classmate, on whom he once had a crush, encountered him, and sent me his address, and I wrote. That was 1958, and we have remained in contact since, nigh forty years. He and his family visited us in Florida, and his younger daughter Amy looked so much like my daughter Penny from behind that I could not tell them apart. That was weird. Penny visited them in Canada one Christmas, and loved it, and his elder daughter Christie Lynn visited us in Florida. She had trouble getting along, and later in life committed suicide. So of all the folk I encountered in school, Ron Bodkin has been the most enduring acquaintance. He seemed to grow into life, gaining social stature, and now has better memories of Westtown than I do, though his time there was harder than mine, because of the shunning by so many students. Perhaps he is simply more forgiving than I am. He is now a professor of economics at a university.

One more student had a profound effect on my life. This was my cousin Teddy Jacob. We had known each other before, of course, as we were the closest in age of Grandfather Edward's grandchildren. He was a year younger than I, and in my sister's class at Westtown. I discussed him in *BiOgre*, so won't go into detail here, except to say that he seemed to be the happy one with everything to live for, while I was the unhappy one with nothing to live for. Then, suddenly, he was dead. Why had he been taken, while I was spared? The shock of the fact of his death, so difficult to accept, and that question of *why* haunted me. Like a virus, it had no seeming initial effect, but in time it wrought a profound change in my outlook. I became a vegetarian, because I didn't want to contribute to death, and later I wrote about Death in my novels. I tried to make something of my life, and Teddy's death is one of the prime factors in that effort. An irony is that if he had lived, he probably would have had little effect on me; it was the seeming unfairness of his death that shook my forming equilibrium. That was a significant part of what I was wrestling with, as I made ready to go on to college. I don't think I ever have managed to come completely to terms with the fact of death, but that was when I had to make my best effort.

There were others who were incidental to my life, but who did have some effect. There were, of course, the teachers at the various schools; teachers seldom get full credit for the good work they do. At Goddard there was Robert Mattuck, my first counselor and the drama coach; from him I learned how to address an audience so as to be heard, though I did not become comfortable on a stage until I became a teacher. There was John Pierce, a dynamic teacher who did not talk down to his students and made me realize how wonderful the geology of the world is, the way the rivers carve the valleys, and who hosted folk-singing sessions I liked. I remember the first of these I attended, early in my time at Goddard, and suddenly I felt at home. "For each one who got rich by mining, perceiving that hundreds grew poor, I made up my mind to try farming, the only pursuit that was sure," he sang with a good, strong voice. He was always at home to students, and I remember him with perhaps the greatest nostalgia. He liked science fiction and the outdoors. He was great to be with and great to learn from. In the end his association with students became too close, leading to serious problems in his life, but I remember him as an extraordinary man who died too soon. I learned that he was aware of my later career as a novelist, and was pleased by my success. That's gratifying.

And, of course, there was Will Hamlin, my writing teacher, whom I later wrote into *Tarot*. He went over my first novel, *The Unstilled World*, whose title he suggested, and encouraged me to keep working at my writing. He did not find my writing to be of high level, and I don't fault him for that; he was correct. It wasn't until six years after I left Goddard that I started selling my fiction, having finally worked up to publishable level. But my time with Hamlin was a necessary step in the growing process. He also stood by me when I had serious trouble with the college administration, resulting in my suspension, and he was a character witness who helped me get my American citizenship. Later, when I started supporting Goddard generously with money, I made it clear that it was Will Hamlin's continued presence there that influenced me. Thus I stood by him in somewhat the manner he had stood by me.

Students, too, had impact on my outlook. Some I mention in Chapter 3. Most were passing acquaintances, but they could leave vivid spot memories, as of the girl who sat in class with her legs spread wide open. She was wearing jeans, but still it seemed suggestive. Another wore tight jeans that were frayed to the point of having holes in the rear, so that her panties showed; evidently she didn't care. Both girls were comely, and my subsequent reflection satisfies me that their appearance did reflect their attitudes toward sex; they were experienced. Thus my slightly prudish innocence was rapidly abated at Goddard, never to return. There was one with whom my association was tangential, yet he taught me some things without meaning to. He was another student, whose height, build, Ping-Pong-playing ability, and IQ were all closely parallel to mine, and he could do fine art when he chose to, but we were not friends. He was older, a veteran, and he was the campus radical, accounting for the one Communist Party vote in the town of Plainfield at elections. I saw him at a night beer party on a hill off campus, and it looked as if he were kissing another man. No, it turned out to be his mannishly thin girlfriend. But once he did a sculpture of two women making love, and they were beautiful women, so obviously he knew what was what in that respect. I inquired why two women, instead of a man and a woman, and am not sure I got an answer from him, but another person said that the most beautiful thing in the world was two women making love. I was curious about the reality of the Communist philosophy, so I made his acquaintance, just to observe. I signed up for the kitchen chore of washing the pots and pans, because he was the other on that crew. I hardly ever saw him there, so wound up doing most of them alone. He said just to do my share and leave the others for him, but it was hard to judge what was fair. When there was a Red Cross drive handled by another student, the student ran it on the honor system: he put out a box for contributions "for needy persons," and the contributor could then take one of the little crosses. But all the money and crosses disappeared. It turned out that this person had come by, said "Well, I'm a needy person," and taken the works. When I worked with the Goddard Co-op, we set up a candy machine. He vehemently opposed it, so I talked to him, trying to ascertain his reasoning. What it came down to, as near as I could tell, was that he personally did not like vending machines, so he opposed it for the community. Once he gave me a haircut and wouldn't take anything for it; later when he needed soap I gave him a bar. He offered to pay, but I said "for the haircut," and he agreed; it was fair barter. But in other cases he simply took what he wanted without asking. So by capitalistic definitions, he was a thief. And when the milk at my dining room table ran out, I went to the next table to ask for some; the pitchers were put on every table, but some had more people than others, so it was shared. Others at the table were amenable, but this one was there, and angrily dissented. "Go get a CARE package," he told me snidely. So I went to another table, but I was upset. So where was the doctrine of "From each according to his ability, to each according to his need"? It was said of him that his philosophy was "What's yours is mine, what's mine is mine." So it seemed. So, in the end, I deemed him a hypocrite, and I judged Communism by his example, and never had any use for it. It's one thing to be individualistic, which he was, and to have strong political opinions, which he did, but a philosophy that is consistent only in terms of selfishness is not one I respect. This was how this radical influenced me: by an example which, taken as a whole, was neither consistent nor well thought-out. He was no Scott Nearing. I have tended to be wary of radicals since; they may be radical only for the sake of being different, and that's a substitute for real thinking. I don't think it was that simple a case with him, but neither was it worthwhile by my definition.

Three

MARRIAGE

I had not expected to go to college, or to get married. So much for expectations. My life is fraught with the unexpected, and many times courses I would not have chosen nevertheless turned out best. It was a Westtown tradition for all students to go on to college, so school officials encouraged me, but I was then coming into the attitudes that were to typify my adult life, and was ready to say no. I was tired of the key decisions of my life being made by others, especially when they were bad decisions. I'd rather make my own decisions, and suffer the consequences of them, for good or ill. But I was not in a position to assert myself absolutely, so I set difficult strictures: I would attend only a college that did not require foreign languages for admission, and one in the state of Vermont. Of course there could be no such place; I think college requirements then were even more irrelevant to life and success than they are today.

Then one day I received a notice from Goddard College: I had qualified for an eight-hundred-dollar tuition reduction, based on the financial need of my family. This amazed me; no academic standards? No interview? I got interested, and ascertained that those other criteria existed; it was just that if I qualified otherwise, I would not be denied because of lack of money. I perceived that as an act of faith and generosity, and it impressed me. I remember such things; today I have contributed several hundred times as much to that college as it contributed monetarily to me. The perspective of time shows that it was a good investment for them. And lo—Goddard was in Vermont, and required no languages, and had no grades. It was at that time one of the most liberal colleges in the nation, though by today's standards it would be ordinary. And so I went four years to Goddard—and it was there I met my future wife. So the effort made by my mother and concerned folk at Westtown did affect my life significantly.

I have covered my experience at Goddard in *BiOgre*, and in my novel *Tarot*, so will gloss over the details. Overall, it was the best experience of my-life-to-that-date, and I wouldn't trade it. Yet even paradise had its problems, and in time I had a serious problem there. The working rules of the campus were set by the community meeting, with students and faculty voting as individuals. But one year the faculty decided to preempt the rules governing dormitory lounges, and close them to members of the opposite gender at 10:00 P.M. until morning. They did not go through the community meeting, they just declared the new rules to be in force. By the conventions of the community government, this was akin to illegal assumption of power by a tyrant. Naturally the students protested, and to this day I feel that the right of the case was with the students. But Tim Pitkin, the college president, declared that he would close the college if the students did not honor this rule. If this seems to resemble a madman putting a gun to the head of a hostage and declaring he'll shoot if not given ransom money—yes, I think a case can be made. But what do others do, in such a situation? It varies, but usually they will yield to the madman—until the hostages are freed, or dead. That doesn't signify agreement, merely expedience. And so it was with us, and I was one of those suspended for a week, because I had been one of three males conversing with three females at 10:40 P.M. and refused to apologize or confess wrongdoing. I still say openly that the college administration was wrong. Decades later, when invited to become a member of the college's governing board, I declined, giving the suspension as the reason. I contributed substantially only when all those associated with my suspension were gone from there, and again I told them why. Not a peep in response, perhaps not oddly. Setting ethical judgments of right and wrong aside, this does not necessarily signal a change of heart on the part of the perpetrators, but rather the shift of power. In those days I needed the college more than it needed me; now it needs me more than I need it. But I suspect that those in charge now can more readily see my case, regardless.

So our serious difference has passed, and what remains is my gratitude to the college that gave me so much in every other respect. I still recommend Goddard College to those in search of a good, personal, liberal education at a small institution.

I began to get into boy-girl relations at Goddard, with the encouragement of my roommate, Joel Fedder. For a while I was with Bunny Leder, Goddard's smallest and one of the most attractive girls in terms of face and figure. But she was playing the field, and I was soon enough part of her past. My closest friend was Barbara Baller, a minister's daughter and highly expressive girl five months my senior. But she had dyed her hair blond, so I took her for a blonde, and that ruled out any romantic attachment on my part. She was a great girl, and we had many common interests, such as science fiction, and I think she helped me become more social. We called it our "plutonic" friendship, as in platonic and Pluto, the farthest planet and god of the nether realm. We shared many confidences, including sexual ones, and I saw from what she told me how men can really mess up the emotional states of women. I had, of course, thought before that it was all the other way. Barbara believed in many supernatural things, while I was an absolute skeptic, and we argued without harming our friendship. It was her ambition to marry a nuclear physicist, and later she did that, though I don't think it lasted. At any rate, we kept close company for two years, and she helped me see my sister to the University of Vermont. Barbara couldn't go anywhere without discovering somebody she knew, and sure enough, there at the end of the registration line was a girl she knew, and so she introduced her to Teresa, making that event easier. Later I began to be intrigued by a thin girl about a year my junior, and finally approached her and made my interest known. But she told me politely that she wasn't interested. She was almost apologetic, and there was really no rebuff, and no affront; she was a nice girl who simply had other interests. I appreciated her candor and left her alone. Later I learned what her other interest was: she was seeing a married professor and eventually married him. No wonder I hadn't known; they would hardly have bruited that about the campus. Goddard wasn't *that* liberal. That was, however, not the only student/faculty affair going on at the time. I suspect that every institution has similar secrets.

There was one minor incident associated with Barbara that I remember with a certain irrelevant fondness. I never had much money, and oil paints were expensive, so I tried not to waste them. We were expected to put dabs of paint on the palette, drawing from each as needed for the painting, mixing them to obtain intermediate shades. Sometimes I used up a dab and had to put out more; more often I had some left over. So at the end of the session I would squeeze the appropriate tube in such a way as to make it suck in instead of push out, and take up most of the surplus paint that would otherwise have been wasted. It made sense to me, extending the life of a tube of paint perhaps 50 percent. But the female art teacher was appalled. "Never marry a man who does that," she told Barbara. I suppose she felt that the natural mission of a phallically shaped tube of paint was to emit thick liquid substance, not to take it in. Barbara herself was intrigued when she learned that electrical connections have male and female plugs. "Shall we?" she asked, holding one of each, as if merging them was a sexual act. She once painted a picture, deliberately incorporating every sexual symbol she could think of, including clocks, female symbols because of periods. A visiting psychologist saw that picture on display and almost freaked out, not realizing that it was a joke.

My third year at Goddard, after a summer of logging with Robert Pancoast and Malcolm Stewart, we all found girlfriends. Mine was Carol Ann Marble, nicknamed Cam after her initials, the daughter of a Unitarian Universalist minister, about three years younger than I, two years behind me in college. I had not been much aware of her at first, and she had a different boyfriend before me, but as time passed her other relationship broke up and I became aware of her signals. Barbara helped, telling me that Cam was the smartest of the new students. Oh, there were others with reputed astronomical IQ's, but these were never really documented or evident in behavior. I value intelligence, and I wanted smart children. So we associated—and suddenly I was in love. I can't say it was easy or smooth throughout, and I did come to know the awful pangs of separation and "breaking up," but in the end we couldn't stay apart, and we agreed to marry.

It was not a decision I ever regretted. Our marriage, like our lives, was fraught with many problems, but we handled them together, and endured. I don't think I could have found a better wife. As I review my life, seeking the most significant turning points, I conclude that one was coming to America, another was going to Goddard College, and a third was marrying Cam. Later there was my decision to become a professional writer, and to give a publisher that had blacklisted me a second chance. Yet there is always the idle speculation about what might have been, and there was for me. Suppose that thin girl had not alienated me for a year by an unkind remark, so that I might have approached her before she developed her interest in the married professor? How many lives might have been changed, in what ways? Or was it too late from the outset? There was a girl I knew mainly in art classes, Rosemarie Sonnenwald, nicknamed Sonny, a fine painter. She was pretty enough, and I'm not entirely clear why she didn't have a boyfriend. I was told once that she was interested in a man who was engaged to another woman, so it was hopeless, and she simply remained uninvolved. In the time when Cam and I were broken up, Sonny once expressed an interest in me. She was talking with several other people, and I happened to be standing nearby, and she looked at me and encouraged me to join them. I hesitated, and she invited me again, smiling. There could be no doubting the opening she was making to me, and in any other circumstance I would have taken her up on it, and quite possibly our lives would have changed. She was certainly an acceptable partner, and that one invitation tugged strongly at me. But I ignored it and departed. Why? Because I had just made up with Cam, something known at that time only to the two of us, and was on my way to meet her. Sonny was quite in order to approach me; her timing was just about one day off, through no fault of hers. And ever since I have regretted turning her down in that way, and wondered what might have been. Even though I remain convinced that the association I made with Cam was the best for both of us. It is human nature to dream of the might-have-beens, even those common sense indicates were not meant to be. And I still feel guilt for not dealing as forthrightly with Sonny as the other had with me. I wonder at times whether the thin girl learned of my later career and pondered whether she had made a mistake, but I also wonder what happened to Sonny. The realm of might-be is infinitely larger and more interesting than reality; it has the fascination of speculation. One tends to see the warts in real life, and the halos in fantasy life, so those far pastures are indeed greenest. Yet my reality was far to surpass any dreams I had in those days, and that reality was with Cam. If I could return to those days and change reality, I wouldn't trade it for a gamble on an alternate.

These were not the only ones. There were three other girls with whom I associated on occasion. Everybody knew everybody at Goddard, of course, and there were girls who could have interested me had they shown the slightest return interest, and ones who would have been encouraged had I shown the slightest return interest. The college years, in my day, were prime matching opportunities, as boys and girls sought passing or lasting unions. Several marriages occurred among the people I knew, and several heartbreaks too. The major guilt I feel in this connection was when I was discussing girls with Dick Weissman, at one time my roommate and then the Vermont state Ping-Pong champion. We had both been interested in Bunny Leder—who stayed with neither of us—and I had mentioned another girl I might consider. But it was a passing thought, and further consideration satisfied me that that was not the direction I wanted to go. But I think word reached her, and it soon became evident that she liked me in much the way I had liked Herta Payson. Herta never made any pretense of interest in me, but she was never unkind to me in any way. I tried to be the same with this one; I was never impolite, just neutral. But I hated leading her on, though it was my very presence that did it. When we danced, I knew the closeness meant everything to her, though it meant nothing other than that guilt to me. I should never have mentioned her name, even in confidence, thus perhaps giving her a false hope. There were others, but I did not have the same guilt about them; I had not ever named them, as it were. So it was clear that I served others as others served me, and if there were those who saw me as not worthwhile, I was doing the same to others. I wish I could have avoided both receiving and giving heartbreak; it is no kind thing. But it was perhaps a necessary education, for all of us.

Today, as a successful writer, I attract the attention and often interest of many more women, but I tread a very careful path. I am married, intend to remain so, and am looking for no affairs on the side. I try always to have a wife or daughter present when I meet with any female reader of mine, so that there can be no misunderstanding. It is not that I find other women uninteresting—my interest in the entire female gender is intense—or that my wife doesn't trust me—she is not a jealous woman. It is that I want neither the appearance of illicit liaison, nor any temptation for the reality, however discreetly accomplished. Especially since I have come to have some quite intimate contacts by mail. So I am polite, and sometimes candid, when a woman makes known her interest in having an affair with me: what might be tempting indeed, were I single, is not a present prospect. There is more on this in Chapter 12, "Readers."

And so, when I graduated, Cam and I jammed into our Volkswagen

sedan with Charles Gasset, who served as my best man, and my sister
Teresa, the maid of honor, for a wild ride to Florida. That little car had
its own special history: when my parents were in England, money was
tight. Their musical friend Anthony Baines (yes, I think that was the
inspiration for my Anthony name) borrowed Alfred's bassoon, which he
had brought with him from America, and showed it to the first bas-
soonist of the London Philharmonic Orchestra, who tried it and liked it
so well that he just had to have it. He offered a generous price for it.
Alfred did not want to give it up, but the man was insistent, and finally
the instrument did change hands. My father put the money in a fund
to be saved for my education. But when it came due, as it were, my
parents were divorced, and I was already most of the way through college
and preparing to get married. So it was used to buy our first car instead,
and that was to make life and work possible for us, so it was well spent.
But I'm sorry that Alfred had to give up his treasured bassoon for my
car. At least I have been able to repay the monetary aspect, later in life,
by helping support my father, as described in Chapter 16.

My mother came down for the wedding. These, apart from Cam's
mother, Elizabeth Marble, and little sister Jane Marble, then ten years
old, were just about all the people there I knew. Cam's father, the Rev-
erend Ernest Marble, married us in his little church on Mirror Lake in
St. Petersburg. Cam was just nineteen, and naturally she was a lovely
bride. The ideal age for a woman, ever since, to my mind, has been
nineteen. With long dark hair.

We took a slightly more leisurely trip back north, seeing Rainbow
Springs and the Luray Caverns, in lieu of a honeymoon, dropping Char-
lie off in Philadelphia. We rented an apartment in Plainfield, Vermont,
near the college, so Cam could continue her studies, and I set out to
find work. College had been more or less idyllic; now we were up against
mundane reality. It was rough going, and we lived exceedingly close to
the wire, sustained mainly by the checks I received from the Jacob Trust
Fund: $125.00 every three months, and several $25 checks my mother
sent, when she could manage it. We never argued about money; not
then, when we didn't have it, or later, when we had a great deal; we
discussed things and spent wisely. Our one luxury expense in that time
was a caged parakeet we bought for ten dollars; we named it Lucky,
short for Luxury. We wished we could go to Florida, but we lacked the
money. Then I had a rollover that could have killed me but gave me

only a bruised shoulder and a bashed car; Cam got pregnant and had a miscarriage; and in March 1953 I was drafted into the U.S. Army, having volunteered for an early draft call. I hated the separation from Cam, during basic training, but at least it gave us two years of relative (if lean) financial security, with my private's pay and an allotment for my wife. Two years later, released from the Army, we settled in Florida; I like to say that we traveled to Florida the hard way, via the U.S. Army.

With all the major things happening in our lives, one of the most poignant memories I have is of something trivial. I was in the bedroom, putting on my jacket, I think, and turned on the little radio there. A song came on, and it fascinated me. It was "Remember Me," or "The Girl in the Wood," about a boy who saw a lovely woman with eyes like green grassy pools and hair like an autumn tree, who told him that he would never see a girl as lovely as she was. And when he grew up, he never did, so remained a bachelor. The vision of that lovely girl in the wood had spoiled him for marriage. I heard that song only once, but it had a phenomenal impact on my imagination. It became the basis for the plot of my first published novel, *Chthon*, and I searched for it for decades. Until at last two readers wrote to identify it for me, and I got both versions, and listened until I had memorized it. The song just took me right back to that bleak first year of marriage, when love was new, but the winter was cold, and money was scarce. More on that in Chapter 13, "Incidentals."

The Army took me first to Fort Dix in New Jersey for basic training. They tried to make it hell on earth, and succeeded to a reasonable extent. It was rougher for me than some, because the meals weren't geared to a vegetarian diet, but I gulped a lot of milk and stuffed rolls in my pockets, and got through. I caught a bug that was going around, but managed to finesse a weekend pass. I went to my mother in Philadelphia, and she put me to bed and brought the doctor in. He said I seemed to have a cross between pneumonia and strep throat. He urged me to report on sick call when I returned to the base. So I did, and was put on KP for the rest of the day. But the rest and treatment I had gotten over the weekend sufficed, and I recovered, and made it through training with my cycle. The single event that scared me most was when we did a mock encroachment on an enemy position, crawling under barbed wire, while other trainees fired live ammunition just above us—about waist height. I was afraid someone would aim just a bit too low, and I'd get a bullet up my ass, literally. Cam came to see me—and managed to slam the taxi door on her left thumb; I was notified that my wife had had an accident. I rushed there, and soon we were at the base hospital, where an officer bandaged her thumb—all medical personnel seemed to be officers—and I took her around in a wheelchair. I suppose it was a lot of fuss over not much, but she had cracked the bone, and pretty young women weren't common on Army bases. Another time, Teresa visited; one of the other trainees saw this striking blonde, and ever after his endorsement of me was "You got a nice sister!"

The second part of basic training was at Fort Sill, Oklahoma. I got leave between the sessions and went home to Cam. What a wonderful reprieve! But all too soon it was over, and I had to prepare for the three-day bus trip. We checked schedules and found that the train would get me there in only two days. It was more expensive, but we decided that we'd rather have the extra day together, and paid for the train. I don't regret it. We had our pictures taken then, and still have those portraits. We look so young! I'm handsome at twenty-two, with my military crew cut growing out, and she's lovely at nineteen, with her lustrous long brown hair. I had much more than her appearance in mind when I asked her to marry me, but oh, my, she's beautiful.

I did better in the intellectual portion of training than I had in the physical portion, and was one of two top cycle graduates to be chosen to become survey instructors. I was eager to do it, because it meant I would remain in the States, instead of being shipped on to Germany. Cam shut down things in Vermont, drove to Philadelphia to help my father move belongings, and to North Carolina to meet her folks. She drove to Florida with them, and then to Oklahoma to join me. It was a wonderful reunion. I believe she became pregnant again, the day we met. I remember two of the songs on the radio during that time of separation, their poignancy enhanced by my longing for Cam. One was "Tammy," and the other was "Dark Moon." The first was on the radio for decades thereafter, a standby, while the second faded from the scene. I was bemused by the way their histories differed, when they had seemed similarly beautiful to me. Today I have both in my collection of popular songs.

But more troubles came. My career in the Army effectively ended when I made the mistake of standing up for my rights and declining to sign for a coercive savings bond deal. Few soldiers wanted to sign up, but only two of us actually held out long. The saying was "They can't make you do it, but they can make you wish you had." Exactly—even when their demands are illicit. The others in my unit were hassled too, in the hope that they would pressure me to capitulate, but they were glad to see *someone* holding out, and tacitly supported me. Meanwhile, Cam had difficulties with her pregnancy, and spent a cumulative month in the hospital with threatening miscarriage, and finally did lose the baby. Once when I wanted to visit her in the hospital, I had guard duty, and had to wait for my time off before leaving the post. I arrived just after visiting hours closed, and they wouldn't let me see her. Cam, in her room, could hear my voice, but there was no visit. I went back to the post and resumed guard duty. It seems to me that the hospital staff, knowing the circumstances, could have relented a trifle, but of course they didn't care. It's too bad that hospitals tend to be known for their supreme indifference to human sensitivities and suffering, but it's an earned reputation. Even today they may not give effective pain medication to terminal patients, for fear they become addicted to it, as if addiction matters to a dead man. So not only must folk die, they must die in avoidable agony. That's de facto sadism. A sergeant I knew had a worse experience: his wife had a heart attack, but their house was just beyond the military ambulance's territorial limit, so it didn't fetch her, and she died. But, he said, they did give her a nice funeral, later. At least the financial burden was not bad; I paid $25, and the military insurance paid all the rest. That saved us from a financial wipeout. But we had lost our second baby.

I had seriously considered making the Army a career, oddly, because it really wasn't as bad as anticipated and did offer financial security, albeit of a low level. But the trouble I had satisfied me that it was not the place for me; I do need an environment where there is some individual freedom and justice. So when my term was up we departed Oklahoma and drove to Florida. A trip from there fetched our things from Vermont and Pennsylvania. We were in Sunny Florida to stay, at last.

But even in that relative paradise, things were not easy. I looked for a job—and found none. Our savings diminished, and finally I put in for unemployment compensation—only to learn that there was a thirty-day waiting period after qualifying. I should have applied *before* I needed to, to get that waiting out of the way. What to do? Well, Cam's folks, the Marbles, helped; they had us in for supper every day, greatly easing our food budget. My grandmother Caroline helped, letting us use her house, rent-free. Family is great in emergencies, and I really appreciated it. In my later novel *With a Tangled Skein* I showed that: a beautiful young woman was required to marry a younger man, really a stripling, in part because he was of good family. That was a poor consolation for her—but later, when she was widowed with a baby, and had the opportunity to step into a phenomenal position, the man's family took her son and raised him well and lovingly. That made it possible, and then she understood about good families. That sequence was a reflection of what I had found, when our families were there for us.

There was an electronics company in St. Petersburg, so I gave it a try, expecting the usual demurral. I walked in and inquired whether they could use a writer. "We do have an opening," I was told, and I was sent to be interviewed by Harold Snider. I had my B.A. in writing, but no knowledge of technical writing—but as it turned out, they were willing to train someone. So suddenly I had not only a job, but a good job, paying twice what I had made in the Army including all allotments. I worked with Sam Day, a man in his fifties. He knew his job and I was an apt learner, so it was fine. Subsequently it soured, in part because Sam and others there were strong conservatives, supporting Richard Nixon, while I was liberal and openly supported John Kennedy. Kennedy won in 1960, and later Nixon showed his nature more openly in Watergate, but the signs were there throughout his career. I had trouble seeing how anyone could support such a dishonest, unscrupulous man— and that made me a petunia in an onion patch. Other factors come in, and eventually I lost my job, for reasons other than competence; it was one of the significant disillusions of my life, and it damaged my health.

Cam got a job too; she took a training course in accounting and typing, and that led to a position with Pittsburgh Plate Glass. As a temporary employee she was not eligible for compensation during illness, but when she was sick for a week they paid her anyway. My sympathy for big companies is minimal, but that act of generosity on the part of that company impressed me, and if I ever have a chance to do a favor for Pittsburgh Plate Glass, I'll give it serious consideration.

Then she went to work for St. Petersburg Junior College (SPJC), in an office. Her boss was Dr. Jack Mauny, Registrar, second only to the college president, and a nice guy. He happened to be our neighbor, living directly across the street from us. He supervised the office of Admissions and Records. She worked there for two years, compatibly, before another difficult pregnancy required her to depart. Her sister Jane, then fifteen, was interested in gaining experience and earning some money, so Cam brought her into the office and paid her a small amount herself. Later Jane studied dental hygiene at SPJC, which impressed me; she wasn't just a typical teen. Part of the training required students to bring in people to practice on. Thus Cam went in, and I did, among others. But what floored the hygiene director was when Jane brought in some of the ranking officials of the college, including Dr. Mauny himself, whom she had gotten to know during her office assistant days. Needless to say, Jane passed the course, and indeed spent many years as a hygienist. Her specialty enabled her to find work wherever her husband, Cary McConnell, a geologist she had met as another SPJC student, was transferred.

I believe it was May 3, 1962, when the bad currents struck together. That day I lost my job, and Cam lost our third baby, and the internist I went to about my mysterious chronic fatigue informed me that it was all in my head. He even suggested that when my wife had her baby normally, my fatigue would disappear. "She's in the hospital losing it right now," I said sourly. The truth was that it wasn't my illness that was all in my head, but his diagnosis that was all in *his* head. Thereafter my insurance ridered me for *all* mental disease. Oh, the doctor had tried, but found nothing physically wrong with me, so set out to confirm the suspected psychological aspect. He had had me strip to the waist and sit on a table alone in a room, without explanation, for half an hour, I presume to work up my nervousness. Then I was called to the door, which opened suddenly with a noise to reveal a man-sized spook. It was the doctor in fancy laboratory costume, somewhat like a diving outfit complete with mask. I just looked at him, hardly in the mood for Halloween pranks. But despite my failure to faint or leap for the ceiling, and the nonimaginary nature of my job and baby concerns, he concluded that I was neurasthenic—a word the insurance company translated as crazy. Is it any wonder I am cynical about the medical profession? Its ignorance was my grief.

But when you are at the nadir, there isn't much place to go but up. I had checked prospects, and had taken a placement test, and had a likely new job as a state social worker. Its reduced pay and benefits made it about half as remunerative as my prior position, but at least it had a positive thrust. Instead of working indirectly for the defense industry I would be working to help needy people. Unfortunately, this didn't work out. The people were nice enough, and the clients were needy enough, but the rules were such that I seemed to spend most of my time explaining to folk in genuine need why the state of Florida would not help them. Later the Supreme Court would throw out some of the abusive requirements, but I couldn't tolerate them in the interim. So I left within a few months.

Cam came to my rescue: suppose she went back to work, and I stayed home and tried to make it as a writer? That had been my dream, but seven years of part-time efforts had garnered only rejections. Yet I had come close in 1958, when editor Damon Knight had accepted a story for *IF* magazine—only to have the magazine fold before publication. So it just might be that a full-time effort would finally enable me to crack through to professional sales. I agonized over the decision, torn between the need to secure a family income and the desire to be a writer. Cam's willingness to go to work again made the difference. I know many young wives support their husbands through training, and that many husbands subsequently turn around and dump those wives after success is achieved. I regard such men as turds. My wife enabled me to try seriously for my dream, and my gratitude for that will never abate.

So we tried it—and in three months I made my first story sale, and in another seven months, my second. But my total earnings from writing of $160 were not sufficient to support a family, so I reluctantly returned to gainful employment. Cam had meanwhile had difficulty finding a job, getting turned down for being overqualified, so she had to pay an employment agency to get a worse job, ironically. But later she got a job with the *St. Petersburg Times*, working at their dummy desk. No, this didn't mean she was a dummy, but that she dummied the pages, fitting in the articles and ads so that no space was blank. So she had a regular job, and I was able to prepare for mine by going back to school to get a teaching certificate. Thus my wife supported us a second year.

I went to the University of South Florida (USF), through the barrage of "education" courses that in retrospect strike me as featherbedding for professors. It was not that there was no value in the classes, but that they were, taken as a whole, largely irrelevant to teaching, and I think that if they were all boiled down to just one class, the actual ability of new teachers to teach would not suffer. I saw favoritism, and a negative agenda, and incompetence, mixed in with some dedicated and even brilliant teaching. A mixed bag, and I suspect the university administration did not know or really care which was which. It was during this period that President Kennedy was assassinated; I learned of his death in an education class. So I can't claim that I learned nothing significant. I did have the pleasure of a class with Wesley Ford Davis, a published novelist, whom I came to like as novelist, teacher, and person. My appreciation of modern fiction and poetry was enhanced by his guidance.

I got my teaching certificate, but was ill prepared to teach, so had to take further classes at SPJC on my own to gain competence in subject matter. There I found a similar mix of competence. But early judgments are treacherous. One teacher, Mrs. Major, seemed at first to be the epitome of the pointlessly fussy bureaucrat. For example, she insisted that essays be written with a black pen only. But as I observed her behavior in class, I saw how smart and alert she was; she could cut through ignorant bluster in a hurry. When I asked about the pen color, she explained: her vision was good, but she could see black penmanship most clearly, and so could grade the papers faster and more accurately. It made sense. When I got a regular job teaching, I asked her for guidance, and in about three hours she gave me more relevant and good advice about the practicalities of teaching than I had received in the entire battery of education courses. I didn't follow all of it—and looking back, I wish I had, because she was right on. I wish I could thank her now, but she was then of middle age and is surely dead now. But I try to be as considerate and accurate myself, now, when asked for advice on writing, passing on the kind of favor I appreciated.

Substitute teaching was hellish, but then I got a position at Admiral Farragut Academy, filling out the last two months of the school year in 1965 left vacant by the departure of another teacher. Some of the students seemed to be there because they had been disciplinary problems elsewhere, and I had a problem keeping the discipline. But some were good cadets. So this experience was rather like that of the U.S. Army: it paid my way long enough for other prospects to fall into place. It had come at a very fortunate time: I had been about to return to USF, reluctantly, to go for a higher degree, so as to have a better chance to get a regular teaching job. We would have had to buy another car, as my wife needed one for her job. But Farragut was adjacent to our property, and so I could walk to work. So it saved us the price of a car, and saved me from what I suspect would have been a vain quest for a decent teaching position. As it was, the experience at Farragut satisfied me that teaching was not for me: I could handle the subject material, but trying to keep discipline with students who had no interest in learning, with a school administration that seemed to have little notion of reality, was nightmarish. I never want to teach again, but I have thought that if I did, the first thing I would do would be to speak to the principal in this manner: "If I send a troublemaker to the office for discipline, and he comes back smiling, you will have to hire a new teacher the next day." I suspect that most teachers will understand.

So in the summer of 1966 I retired to writing a second time. I had continued writing stories, and now had about nine story sales and was marketing a novel. So my prospects were better than they had been before; I was developing a track record. Cam was still working, and our finances were better than before. This time I didn't simply want to make a sale, I wanted to earn my living as a writer. I would prefer to make a meager living as a writer than a good one in some other employment. If it didn't work out, again, then I would see what mundane job I could get. But I really hoped I could make it, this time.

Meanwhile, we had better prospects on the family scene. During the third miscarriage it had turned out that the reason was a septum in Cam's uterus, that divided it and prevented the fetus from utilizing the whole of it. This had triggered early expulsions. The doctor tried something new: to break down that wall of tissue manually, right after the birth. "I put my fist in there," he said descriptively. But he didn't think it had worked, so Cam went in for X-rays preparatory to surgery. The pictures were astonishing: there was no septum. The doctor *had* succeeded in eliminating it. I'm not sure, but I think this was the first time this manual procedure had been effective, anywhere. So we were spared the discomfort and expense of surgery, and the prospects for natural childbirth seemed good. We had understood that one miscarriage happened, that two happened, but that if a woman had three, her chances for ever carrying a baby to term were remote. We had pondered adoption, but suspected that a fussy agency would not give a baby to a vegetarian science fiction writer. Now we had reason to believe the jinx was off. And so it turned out to be; we waited five years, but the biological clock was ticking, so it was time. In 1967, at the age of twenty-nine, Cam was pregnant again, and at the age of thirty she gave birth to a full-term healthy baby: Penelope Carolyn. That, Cam and I agree, was to change our daily lives more than our marriage itself had. In 1970 our second daughter, Cheryl Pierra, arrived. After her, we broke the mold; Cam had a hysterectomy. She had originally wanted to have three children, but we were aware of the growing crisis overpopulation represents, and decided that two sufficed. So now we were a family of four, and our dreams of publication and children had both been realized. We were to enter different realms from those we had known before.

Indeed, in certain respects our lives had just begun. The survival of our fourth and fifth babies, after loss of the first three, ushered in what was to be a twenty-one-year span of family life that was exactly the kind we had dreamed of, raising our own children, with all its joys and travails.

And what a welter of memories there are of that period! Penny associated more with me, and Cheryl more with Cam, so most of my images are of Penny, but we definitely had two daughters. Penny was our vanilla hair, and Cheryl our chocolate hair. Penny's hair was never cut; from childhood on she always had tresses down beyond her waist. I explained to others that this must be the source of her hyperactivity; like the biblical Samson, she derived her energy from her hair. Cheryl's hair was periodically cut short by her mother, so she was a quieter child, but in adulthood she let it grow until her tresses actually became longer than Penny's, more than a yard in length. I can select only a few episodes as examples of this period, for the sake of economy.

There was the time when the grandparents on the distaff side visited, Ernest and Elizabeth Marble. Or maybe we were visiting them. Cam and I were elsewhere in the house, while Penny, still crawling, was in the living room with the grandparents. Then we heard her crying, and came to investigate. She had tried to find one of us, being shy, and knew the way, but her grandfather had balked her by having his legs in the way. Evidently his chair was near the exit. He recounted with evident pleasure how she had tried to crawl over his legs, but he had raised them, so she had tried to crawl under, but he had lowered them, so that she could not get through. That was when she started crying. He thought it was hilarious, but I thought it was cruel. I didn't say anything, but I was thereafter wary of leaving Penny alone with them.

There was a much worse incident where I was at fault, when Penny was about eighteen months old. Our porch was cluttered, and there were things out there that could hurt an unsupervised child. So when Penny went out there while I was brushing my teeth, I told her no. Next thing

I knew, she was out there anyway. My mouth was full of toothpaste or whatever, so I couldn't speak, so I left the brush in my mouth, picked her up by the elbows, carried her to the kitchen where her mother was, and set her firmly on her feet. I turned away to close the door to the porch and rinse my mouth. Suddenly Penny was screaming and Cam was trying to comfort her. She seemed really hurt. What had happened? We couldn't figure it out. But years later—maybe decades later—I pieced together what could have happened. Penny had had for a while a "cute" trick of refusing to be set down; when we tried to set her on her feet, she would stick her feet out in front of her, so she couldn't land on them. Of course we wouldn't just drop her. What I realized, so very much later, was that that trick had abruptly stopped—and just about that time. When I set her firmly on her feet and turned away, distracted, maybe she had put her feet out, and thus I had without realizing dropped her on her bottom on the floor. That would have hurt, accounting for the screaming, and for the end of that trick. I would never have done it, had I realized, and am appalled in retrospect.

One day in a store we found a little doll mounted in a frame, titled "Portrait of Penny." It looked much like Penny as she was then, about two. I suppose all children have a certain similarity, so it was really coincidence, but I liked it, and bought it, and put on the wall. But as Penny got older she got hold of it, took out the doll, washed its hair, stripped off its clothing, and ruined it so that we had to throw it away. She was just playing as a child does, but I wish I could have kept that one doll away from her, because it was a precious reminder of the cuteness of Penny at an early age. I hope that someday I'll see a catalog of past dolls, and will find another copy of "Portrait of Penny."

As Penny grew older, she wanted to become adult faster than nature indicated, and was impatient with our cautions. "When will I stop being a child?" she demanded of me once. "When you are no longer afraid of the dark," I replied. She looked thoughtful, and never asked that question again. Sometimes we come across the right answers—the ones that are self-defining. This was similar in its way to one I had in *A Spell for Chameleon*: a creature wanted to know if he had a soul, and the Good Magician replied "Only those who have souls are concerned about them." Later Xanth history indicates that that's not entirely true, but it certainly reassured the monster.

There was another mistake I appreciated only in long retrospect.

Cheryl was invited to a party of her classmates. Penny asked whether she could go too. Cautiously, I said she could if the hosts invited her. But when we delivered Cheryl, the hosts said nothing, so Penny stayed with me. Nothing more was said, and we went on home. But thereafter Penny's jealously of her sister increased, leading to friction in the family. I realized too late that I should have found something else to do at that time with Penny—go to a park, or buy an ice-cream cone, anything that served in lieu of the party she missed. It just hadn't entered my mind, and I had other work to do. But had I that afternoon to do over again, I would find something nice for Penny.

Apart from such errors, I always got along well with my daughters; indeed I don't see why the average family is so eager for sons, as if they are more valuable. We shared many tastes, and I think had a similar sense of humor. Once when we were walking along a forest trail we passed a section in which large acorns lay on the ground, but the nearest tree was a small pine. "Aren't those big acorns for such a small pine tree?" I inquired. "Yes, Daddy," they agreed, smiling.

Years later, perhaps learning from experience, we managed to play a potentially mischievous situation right. It was when computers were coming into the schools, and Cheryl was fascinated, and wanted one at home, so she could play the games on it. We shopped around, and got an Atari, that could be used for games or word processing. Penny resented the fact that we were catering to her sister, and expressed objection to the computer. But when it arrived, and we set it up, Penny surprised us by immediately sitting down to try it. Perhaps she expected us to say "No, that's for your sister," but Cam and I kept our mouths shut. Penny was into computers from that time on, and there was never any trouble. Later we got good systems for each of them, and today every member of the family has one or more computer systems. Now that the daughters are grown and on their own, members of my family exchange e-mail messages and go on-line. I, being of another generation, was the last to get connected, having no idea how to do any of that stuff. But I'm learning.

When Penny went to Eckerd College, we had good hopes. But it turned out to be not as good as anticipated, and there were some aggravating problems. One was the food service. It cost about a thousand dollars a semester, and Penny reported that there was meat mixed into everything. She was a vegetarian, like her sister, and while we did not require this of our children, we support them in their choice. So Penny went through channels, formally requesting to be relieved of the requirement that she eat on campus, as she couldn't get enough food that way. We helped her make out the forms, and I wrote my own letter of explanation. There was a board of three professors to make the decision. As it happened, Penny knew one of them, and he told her that he never saw her form. It was summarily denied. Well, now. "I'm going to show you how the real world works," I told Penny. I collected the material and sent it to the college president with a brief cover letter, concluding "I shall consider this to be an involuntary contribution to the college. You may be sure I will not make a voluntary one." That occurred at the time that we were making a total of $75,000 in donations to support the University of Florida's excavation of Tatham Mound and excavation of a de Soto campsite in the Tallahassee area. I suspect that college presidents have ways of knowing who makes what-sized donations to educational institutions. My letter crossed with an Eckerd College solicitation for donations. And just like that, the food service decision was reversed. So Penny remained at Eckerd, and we did make voluntary contributions to the college, but on the order of $500 a time, while donations of five and six figures went to other institutions. I don't respect those who do what is right only under the gun.

But there are memories of Cheryl too. Her first day at Sunday school she did beautifully. Then when she saw me coming to pick her up, she burst into tears. As I make it, she behaved with poise, but was really worried about the absence of her parents. When she saw me she knew she could relax, and her feelings abruptly overwhelmed her. I picked her up and took her to Cam. She had no further trouble with Sunday school, knowing that she was not being deserted. I had resolved never to do that sort of thing to my own children, remembering what it felt like in my own childhood, especially once in Spain, but I hadn't set this one up, and I think Cam didn't realize how Cheryl would miss her.

On our bicycle rides through town we discovered a little park with swings, slide, and a whirl-a-round. It was overgrown with prickly sandspurs, known in Xanth as curse burrs, so I called it Sandspur Park, and we went there often. When the girls got big enough to have their own bicycles, we would stand them at the edge, several feet off the street. One day a car backed out of an adjacent driveway, across both lanes of the street, and knocked down our bicycles. Then it moved forward without ever stopping. We picked up the bikes, staring after the car; it was singularly bad and arrogant driving. Fortunately the bikes weren't damaged. A few days later a woman came from the house to speak with us: she was sorry about the accident, but the bikes really shouldn't have been in the way. I didn't answer. It had been the car that was at fault, backing onto the park, and she had not been the one driving. The clumsy male never had the grace to come out, and the woman was actually trying to blame *us* for his breach of the rules of driving. I comment elsewhere, notably in Chapter 12, on the blame-the-victim syndrome.

Penny was dyslexic and hyperactive, so had trouble in school, with grades like mine: mediocre. Cheryl had no such problems, so excelled in school from day-school on. But once there was a problem of a different nature. At one point her academic record deteriorated, so we investigated. We never drove our children to excellence, but Cheryl drove herself; something was wrong. We found that sometimes she was not given the grades she earned. Other parents of the brightest children found similar discrimination. I put it bluntly to the school officials: "When my child earns an A but is given a C no matter how hard she tries, next time she *earns* a C. She's not stupid." A phenomenal understatement. In middle school the teacher scheduled key tests for the days Cheryl would be away at her enhanced learning classes. That was subtle harassment that generated mischief, and we protested, and finally got it changed. But one standardized test she never did catch up on, because it was a one-time one administered by others, so that blank in her academic record remained. Once those problems were straightened out, she resumed her straight A grades.

When Cheryl graduated from high school, she was probably the most competent student in her class. Others had higher grade averages, but they had not carried her workload; it's easier to score well if you stick to the "safe" classes. At the graduation ceremonies Cheryl got a total of eighteen awards, scholarships, and recognitions, and her SAT score was the highest in the history of the school at that time. She had gone as an undergraduate to summer school at Harvard University, and made an A there. I joked that I had had to struggle to get rich enough to send my children to college—and then Cheryl went on scholarship.

It had taken time to get our new house on the tree farm built, and by the time we were able to move in, on Cam's birthday in Mayhem 1988, Penny was off at college and Cheryl would be with us only that summer before departing herself. But we set each up with good rooms, so that they could always return. I was just sorry that we had had to be so crowded before, but of course this was typical of families of middle income. Despite Cheryl's relatively brief stay there, when she left, I suffered awful pangs of loss. The house seemed huge and empty, like the ruins of the palace of Knossos on Crete, about which I had just been doing research. I had had the book *Lost World of the Aegean* for a dozen years, and used it before, but this time the picture on the cover, of two young women playing with a pet monkey by the stately columns, entranced me. I loved their multitiered skirts and bare breasts, but the root of my sudden fascination was deeper: we had lost our two young women to the greater world, and were alone in our large house. Our twenty-one years of "family" had ended. Of course we kept in touch with both daughters, and they visited regularly, but it wasn't the same. In time that sweet sorrow faded, but I think I will always feel nostalgia for the Minoan civilization of Crete, because of that personal association.

Cheryl went on to New College, perhaps the finest public college in the nation, on a par with Harvard, and in Florida, so she could still visit home on occasion. I had advised her that one workaholic—me—was enough for the family, and this time it seemed she listened. Maybe she shouldn't have. The freedom of a gradeless college set her somewhat adrift, and she took an off-campus job before finishing school. In fact it was eight years before she graduated. Then she got a conventional job in the area, and disappeared into routine adulthood.

So Cam and I made our marriage, and carried it through our daughters' childhood, education, and entry into adult life. At one time it had seemed that we would be unable to have children, but we had after all gotten our family, and it was great.

IRONIES

One of the problems in my first trial year of writing was writing. That is, keeping at it. I liken it to running: can you run? Of course you can. But can you run a mile? You might think you could, but if you tried it, you would discover your distance is more like one- or two-tenths of a mile, at speed, before laboring breath, a side stitch, or leg cramps took you out. You need conditioning. If you run every three days, you will build up, until you can run a mile or more. But it takes time and persistence. It turned out that writing is similar. Interest is great at first, but there are mental muscles that need to be developed before the pace can be sustained. Thus almost all writers suffer the dread Writer's Block at some stage. They want to write, they have time to write, but they somehow lack inspiration. This is independent of talent. Theodore Sturgeon was one of the finest genre writers of the day, but he had an awful time sitting down to actually write. Damon Knight was a fine writer, but once mentioned having a siege of Writer's Block that lasted three years. And many, many hopeful writers don't actually like to write; they crave the supposed fame and wealth of success, but just aren't much for actually trotting the turf, alone in a room with a pencil, typewriter, or computer. Actually completing a story takes endurance, and a novel is like a marathon. A writer isn't physically hurting, but Writer's Block is the equivalent. He needs to build up to the point where he can maintain his pace indefinitely.

So that was part of what I learned in my first trial year of writing: how to keep going, to avoid Writer's Block. Block was something I simply couldn't afford. So I eliminated it, and have not suffered from it since. Any other writer could use my system to eliminate it also. But just as an alcoholic may arrange to "forget" to take the medication that keeps him straight, and relapses, some writers aren't much interested in learning how to sustain writing. Thus I feel that for many, the root of their Writer's Block is a lack of interest in actually writing. For them there is not much hope. It's an irony, for some do have talent.

This statement of mine, that Writer's Block may be mainly an excuse not to do what they don't want to do, has aroused wrath in some. There are women who get similarly angry at me for suggesting that the various reasons they have for avoiding sex derive from a profound lack of interest, or even distaste, for sex. It's a fair parallel. Of course there are many writers who really do want to write, but are prevented by circumstance, and there are many women who would like idealized sex, etc. But there are also many who don't, and don't want to admit it. So let me go into my system for abating Block, and those who find it boring are probably not serious about writing. Those who are not hopeful writers should find this chapter increasingly uninteresting, so should skip on to the next, which is about suicidal teens.

My system consists of a series of plays, devices, and tactics, any of which may work in a particular case, and some will work in any case. One is variety: if you are bogging down in a heavy project, try switching to a light one, or at least a different one. I discovered this when I was writing *Omnivore* and proceeding an inch an hour. Then my wife had to work late, and would be coming home around midnight, and I just didn't like the notion of her walking alone a couple of blocks to her car in the parking lot at that hour. So I went with her, and took along a notion for a separate project, *Sos the Rope*. This was to be an adaptation of a chapter from my first, unsold novel *The Unstilled World*, and I hadn't actually done any writing on it, so could take just pencil and paper along and play with it. I don't like to take substantial projects out of the house, lest they be lost. So I sat in an empty office for several hours, and gave it a try—and to my surprise it moved phenomenally. It moved so well that next day, at home, I just kept working on it. Why mess with a winning game? And in about ten days I had written about forty thousand words, which was just about all of the first draft of the novel. Later I typed it and retyped it, and it expanded to sixty-two thousand words, so I think it took about a month in all. I entered it in a contest, and it won, and suddenly I had $5,000 and a published novel.

Then I returned to *Omnivore*, and still it crawled. So it wasn't me, it was the material; action-adventure *Sos the Rope* moved much more readily than intellectual *Omnivore*. So I remembered, and thereafter tried to keep more than one project in the hopper, so as to be able to switch between them, and work on whatever was moving at the time. This abated much of my problem. Summary: if A doesn't move, try B, or C, or D.

Another is what I call my bracket system, which started when I was writing or typing first draft text, BC (Before Computers). When I came to a hangup, I'd simply use brackets (this worked with pencil, too) to give me privacy and wrestle with the problem therein: [Now I need a good example here; what offers? I've used the-falling-in-a-hole how-to-get-out problem before, and I've used the man-embracing-girl-and-not-knowing-what-to-say-next problem too. I need something new. What haven't I used, that's interesting? Little green men from space? So what's the problem, and how is it solved? Maybe they are here to solve the problem of Block? They have a ton of AntiBlock they need to jettison? Okay.] So then I emerged from the brackets and got on with my text, having a better notion where it was going. When I typed my second draft, I deleted the brackets and their contents; they had done their job. When I computerized I made a macro to delete the brackets when editing, and when I got a multiple-file program I dispensed with the brackets and had a whole separate parallel Notes file instead for the purpose. I still use it. Typically, my writing day begins with notes, and shifts increasingly to text as the day progresses. Then I print out both notes and text and save them, and assemble my text into the ongoing novel. Sometimes I'll forget a notion I was playing with, and check back through the notes for prior days to find it: maybe there *is* a place for little green men from space. Regardless, I keep writing, if not on the text itself, then on why the text isn't moving, until I solve the problem. So I'm always working, one way or another. Most notes are brief, but sometimes they last for days and thousands of words, as I break down the problem [Just what *is* the nature of ultimate reality?] and get a handle on it. [Self does not exist.] This works for me, and I have heard from others who have tried it, and it works for them too. It doesn't guarantee quality writing, or publication, but it does abolish Writer's Block. For those who aren't just using Block as an excuse not to write.

Another device was to keep a record of each day's accomplishments. I started that Work Record the day I began my Second Attempt to be a full-time writer, in JeJune 1966, and maintained it for twenty-one years without a break. Then a computer hard disk crash wiped out three months of it, and I quit, shifting to a more personal diary of daily thoughts. But four years later I resumed it, and now I have both diary and record. With multiple computer files it's convenient, and both serve their purpose. The record of thoughts helps clear my creatively seething brain of distractions so I can settle down to paying writing, so represents another AntiBlock device. The Work Record goads me to continuing performance, because if I goof off, it makes that clear.

So with that system, I kept writing. In fact I became a writaholic. On a typical day I write about 5,000 words: 1,000 in the Personal file, 1,000 in the Novel Notes file, and 3,000 in the Novel Text. But it varies widely with the difficulty of the novel and the number of other distractions I have, such as phone calls or family crises. This text, for example, was delayed by the need to sign twenty copies of contracts that arrived today, then interrupted by the phone at this point: a reader had driven from California to Inverness just to meet me. So my writing day ended right here, at 1,750 words text.

The following day was spent exchanging haircuts with my wife—we stopped going to barbers when their prices passed one dollar—exercising, and answering letters, which included two faxes from alarmed collaborators about the proposed scheduling of their novels. One arrived near midnight, waking me, and I lost a couple hours sleep because of it. So the next day, typing this text, I was logy and inefficient. The weather complicated it by putting our area into a major storm warning from the system that had flooded California a week before; there could be ferocious thunderstorms and even tornadoes. Indeed, it rained several inches, and there's always the threat of power failures, which aren't fun when you're trying to use a computer. It didn't help that I received a letter from a friend of forty-five years, Ronald Bodkin (mentioned in Chapter 2), that his elder daughter Christie Lynn, who once visited us for a week in Florida, had committed suicide. Meanwhile my word processor had decided to right-justify my text, so I had to delve in and reset it to normal. This too is part of the business of writing. The outside world seems to be constantly striving to prevent a writer from writing in peace, interspersing major or minor distractions. A writer has to learn to write regularly despite whatever the world does to interfere. My first year of writing wasn't phenomenally efficient, but by its end I had pretty well learned to write on a sustained basis. I had developed my intellectual writing muscles, learned to handle interruptions, and made progress in becoming independent of mood. A writer who waits for inspiration may wait forever. A real writer writes when he has time, his inspiration on tap when he needs it.

I have an analogy for that, too. Ping-Pong was my one good sport, because I was small and automatically frozen out of things like basketball, and I played in some tournaments while in college and the Army. I wasn't of champion caliber, just one of those good but not great players a rung or three down from the championship level. As I worked my way up in high school, I had great games and awful games. Gradually I improved by raising my lows, so that I could play consistently near my best. I made it a point to warm up by playing lightly for fifteen minutes or more early in the day. That warm-up zeroed me in so that I could make my shots instead of missing them, and it normally lasted for the day. I won many games from equivalent players, because they didn't realize that they weren't playing well at the start. Okay—my writing progressed similarly. I had on days and off days. But as a professional I couldn't afford off days, so I learned to write as well as I could whenever I could. I eliminated the lows. Inspiration? It pretty much ceased to be a factor.

Now this concept can freak out some hopeful writers. They think a piece of fiction should spring fully formed from the head of Zeus, as it were, and isn't valid otherwise. That a writer should write only from overwhelming inspiration. Nonsense. A real writer should generate his inspiration as a tool, ready whenever he needs it. I have another analogy. I'm great for analogies; they are part of what make me a writer.

Think of a highway. As you drive blithely along it at ten miles an hour over the speed limit, cursing the idiots who are trying to slow you down by five miles an hour, and wishing the authorities had had the sense to make the road more direct and with fewer potholes, do you ever ponder just how much work has gone into the preparation of that long strip of asphalt? Suppose you were the contractor in charge of building such a highway? Would you wait for inspiration? Would you hold your breath and strain until suddenly the fully formed road burst out of your left ear and spread itself in a ribbon across the landscape, instantly perfect? Only in your dreams!

No, in real life you would start at the beginning, reviewing maps of increasingly fine detail to ascertain the best route, considering the mountains, chasms, deserts, rivers, cities, and other natural hazards obstructing the way. You would study charts of likely traffic flow, so as to determine where the highway should be six-laned and where two lanes would do. You would figure out the most practical course, all things considered. Then you would set about gaining the right of way. It would turn out that your best route between cities crosses a nature park protected from development by federal law; you must go around. Your best site for a major intersection is owned by a reclusive billionaire who will sue you and tie you up in court for two and a half centuries if you even think of paving over his duck pond; you'll never make your deadline there. Your best place, geographically, to bridge across the river is surrounded by Hell's Bells Bog, so deep it would take fifteen umptillion tons of special fill to stabilize it, putting you over your budget. The second-best place for the bridge is an earthquake zone: do you gamble that you can complete your project and get well away before the ground shakes? So you route it down past the quiet marina subdivision, where there's already a bridge you can upgrade for heavier traffic, and the neighbors set up a deafening clamor: Not In My Backyard! So by the time you have settled on your (distinctly awkward) route, and gained the necessary (ruinously costly) permissions, the project has lost much of its luster—and you haven't yet moved the first spadeful of dirt.

Thereafter you must get the physical job done. Every foot of it has its own character and challenge, and most of the surprises are unpleasant. Some of the vital materials arrive late, and others are flawed, and some of your crews go out on a wildcat sympathy strike because of an incident not connected to you. But by dint of superhuman effort you manage to get it done, one hour before the deadline and one dollar within the budget. It opens for traffic—and the local newspapers condemn it for not being more conveniently and scenically routed. All this money and time wasted on this poor effort? Obviously, they say, an imbecile was in charge.

Now, about writing a novel with a set wordage and a set deadline for a schlock publisher, and receiving the usual courtesies of critics . . .

The fact is, the average full-time freelance fiction writer is not far from the poverty line. My first piece of advice for any seriously hopeful writer is "Have a working spouse." Because then maybe you'll have a secure income. Don't write for riches, because your chances for achieving them this way are remote. Oh, sure, I made it—but I liken it to winning a lottery. It's great for the winner, but you're far more likely to be a loser. I don't think there are any accurate statistics, but my understanding is that only one of every hundred seriously hopeful writers will ever get anything published by a paying market, and only one in a hundred of published fiction writers will make a significant livelihood by it. Of course there are other kinds of writers, such as journalists or technical writers, and these have better chances. It's freelance fiction that's the Lorelei.

And so it was for me. My spouse did go to work, and we did just barely struggle along. But there were real signs of progress. Two weeks after commencing my Second Attempt at full-time writing, I sold a novel. I had written *Chthon* over the course of seven years, bit by bit as time permitted, a big section written during leave time in the Army, and much done at the end of the first trial year of writing. I had been marketing it for a year, and three hardcover publishers had rejected it. In fact, hardcover publishers never did give me the time of day; the way I finally broke into hardcover print was when Del Rey developed its own hardcover line and took its paperback writers along. So I had finally submitted *Chthon* to a paperback house, Ballantine. After five months passed without any word, I queried—and received news from Betty Ballantine that they had wrestled with it for some time and finally decided to publish it. So I had my first novel sale, for $1,500, with 4 percent royalties. It was a great breakthrough. Because I couldn't make a living by selling one story in four, for one or two cents a word, as my first trial year had shown. But if I could sell a couple of novels a year, survival was possible.

You're still game? You say if you had the same kind of setup I did, knowing what I learned by trial and error, you'd be just as successful as I ever was? All you need is the chance to prove it, and you'd dive in tomorrow, so as to have time today to buy a handful of red peppers to soak in hot sauce and shove up your boss's left nostril (or somewhere) as you inform him politely that you are leaving this rathole at Mach 3 and won't return no matter how pitifully he begs you.

Very well. Let's say you do what I did, and take a trial year writing while your obliging spouse works, so you have time to write without starving. Let's say you have no family or friends to distract you, so you can work all day without interruption. Let's further say that you have read this book and know how to avoid Writer's Block. And that you have had the impossibly good fortune to have a contract: you wrote to a publisher saying "I have this great notion for a novel about how this ordinary Joe gets shanghaied into space by aliens and forced into stud service for a harem of 365 luscious creatures, each of whom would make the sexiest human starlet look dull, because they are sick of parthenogenic reproduction and need to get some male offspring to make things interesting." And the publisher was so impressed it sent a contract by return mail, specifying payment of $10,000 on delivery of the 80,000-word manuscript, with a deadline of six months. (WARNING: don't try this at home. I could get a contract this way, but you couldn't, because you are unknown. In fact you probably wouldn't even get a reply to your letter. This is merely a thought experiment.)

Six months? Hell, you'll do it in three! Why wait any longer than you have to, for your money and fame? So you start in, and write like mad, and it goes great, and in only three days you have the whole thing done. And it's 8,000 words long, half of which consists of bedroom scenes that, well, when you show it to your spouse, she looks at you a bit oddly and says "I thought you threw out that bachelor porn as you promised to when we got married." You realize that it's a female editor you have to deal with, and the fine print of your contract says "nothing libelous or obscene." It doesn't help when your spouse inquires when you are going to get into the story. "But that *is* the story!" you protest. "No it isn't," she retorts. "It's a masturbation fantasy." Then, as an afterthought, "You know, Ditchdiggers Amalgamated is hiring unskilled workers now. Maybe if you hurry—"

So you realize that more is required. If Spouse doesn't go for it, Editor probably won't either. All those women are on the same dull wavelength. Your great idea doesn't seem quite as great anymore. "What kind of a story were you expecting?" you inquire cunningly. "One where Joe realizes that it's impossible and not very interesting to have a different woman in bed every night, and falls in love with the only creature who has split ends and a slight weight problem, and tries to escape with her," she replies, inhaling a bit self-consciously.

So you start over, this time beginning with your map, or rather, outline. You lay out ten chapters, each of which should be the length of your whole original story; that will guarantee you an 80,000-word novel. You use the Bracket System to figure out plot complications: Joe doesn't know why the aliens are after him, so Chapter 1 is all about his desperate attempt to escape capture, concluding with an 80-mph car chase that ends with his vehicle mired in the Hell's Bells Bog and slowly sinking as the alien saucer descends with grapplers extended. Chapter 2 has his seeming rescue as eight lovely young women appear and haul him out just as the car sucks out of sight under the mud. But instead of letting him go, they carry him to the saucer, and he realizes that these are the aliens. His feelings are mixed, because though they are phenomenally pretty, he's afraid that they may be taking him to something utterly awful. One of them, with a really rather slight weight problem, and who's looking at her hair anyway? is assigned to watch him while the others see to the operation of the alien craft. He tries to leap out the porthole, but she tackles him and they struggle, and her alien smock/dress comes undone and she's even more luscious than he had thought, and—and it's going too fast, and you have to back off and restructure. Again. This highway, uh, novel, just can't go exactly the way you thought it would, in your naïveté before you actually tried writing it. It's ironic: here you are, the god of this fictive realm, and yet you can't write it quite the way you want. Because 80,000 words turns out to be a whole lot more fiction than you figured. Funny; it never seemed that long when you were driving other folks' highways—er, reading their novels. You realize that the infrastructure of a novel is actually quite intricate and carefully planned.

So it continues, as you discover that what you need to write in Chapter 6 conflicts with what you've already written in Chapter 3; one or the other has to go. Ouch! You have expended all this sweat getting those words down, and now you have to throw them away. Why don't you cut your finger and let it bleed into the toilet a while, while you're at it? Each chapter is its own challenge, and sometimes they seem to compete against each other. One diversion, intended only to fill out a too-short chapter, takes hold and fills two and a half chapters. In fact you realize that she's probably a better match for Joe than the original woman of Chapter 2. But if you change it, you'll have to change half a slew of cross-references along the way, not to mention the hurt feelings of Spouse.

You also have to work on characterization, because most of the alien women, being parthenogenic clones, are so similar you can't tell them apart, and description, because without it that alien saucer is just an unconvincing shell. You also discover that you have an inadequate climax, no pun: at the end Joe escapes with the right woman, returns home, and resumes garden-variety life. If that doesn't satisfy you, it surely won't satisfy the editor, and maybe not the reader either. But what else is there? He has destroyed the alien saucer, so the adventure is over, but no one will believe him, so he has to shut up about it. It's romantic, sure, and Spouse likes it—especially the way Joe concludes that the no-longer-alien woman's weight problem is all in her mind, she's fine just as she is, and he gives her money for a new hair styling—but the finale has become ordinary. That's no good for a rousing climax. And it's still somewhat short; who would have thought it would be so hard to stretch it up to full length? You are halfway sick of the thing, but you can't quit, because now the deadline looms within a month—how did the time pass so swiftly?—and you've got to finish. Your dream has become something of an albatross. At night you dream that it's suddenly a month beyond the deadline, which you somehow forgot about, and you didn't get it done in time, and all your work was for nothing.

So you rip out your last chapter and rework the finale: Joe has the alien saucer in the sights of his laser blaster, but finds that he just can't bring himself to destroy those 364 luscious creatures who had labored so diligently to please him. Sure, they abducted him, sure they have some maybe malign alien purpose. But lusciousness just shouldn't be destroyed. So he lets them go, knowing that they'll probably be back. For a sequel, maybe. Spouse isn't quite sanguine about that; she thinks that one such adventure is more than enough. But it leaves the novel with a chance for something wild in the future, and that's better, despite Spouse's misgivings. Compromise is the name of the game, after all.

Then there's the editing. You start at the beginning and try to review it objectively, and discover fouled-up sentences and misspelled words. But actually it reads better than you feared. The most surprising thing is that the scene that you struggled three days to write and thought you'd have to edit down to manageable length is actually only one page long and passes without notice. All that work, disappearing into the fill for one incidental puddle! You also realize that you have used too many exclamation points!!! You have your computer count them in one chapter, and there are 179. And 38 ellipses. And each one struggles to avoid being eliminated, when you try to edit them out without messing up the flow of your narrative.

So one day before the dread deadline you have it done: 80,000 words exactly, if you round it off upward. You have made it! (Oops, delete that exclamation point!) You ship it off. And learn, in due course, that the editor has changed, and the new one is automatically rejecting all the novels commissioned by his predecessor. But he can't do that, can he? Unfortunately he can: the small print (which masquerades as regular-size print—it's better hidden that way) says that the novel must be acceptable—in the sole judgment of the publisher. It says nothing about any change of editors. So the manuscript is back on your hands, and naturally every other publisher, having apparently been alerted by instantaneous telepathy, rejects it also. You are a has-been who never was.

So what's my point, you inquire in a justifiably aggrieved tone. It's that in writing, as in other things, there are no free lunches, no guarantees, and even a solid contract does not necessarily protect you from arbitrary rejection. The average publisher does not give a swell foop whether you live or die, let alone whether you have a dream. This one risked nothing, and was able to change its mind on any whim it cared to. And you were an open-season target. Had you had a literary agent, he would have required the publisher to pay half the money on signature of the contract, nonreturnable unless you sold the novel elsewhere. He would have inserted an arbitration clause in the contract, the cost to be borne by the publisher if bad faith were demonstrated. He would have protected you to the degree he was able. But you didn't have an agent, because the truth is that your writing ability is only a third as good as you think it is, and your novel is unsalable, and agents won't touch you. Sure, that FAMOUS MAKE BRAND-NAME AUTHORS' COURSE, that charged by the page for critiques, said you had real potential. That's how it makes its money: by preying on the dreams of unexceptional hopefuls. You fool.

Oh, sure, not every hopeful writer has this experience. Most never even get a contract. Even if your manuscript is publishable, that's no sign that it actually will be published. Many publishers won't even look at it unless it comes through an agent, and most agents won't take on any writers who haven't already sold material. It's a Catch-22 situation loaded against the hopeful writer. So it requires considerable determination, persistence, and luck as well as talent to find the crevices in the protective armor of Parnassus, and if you want to avoid heartache, it's best to pin your dreams on some other donkey.

However, I had, by dint of the above qualities, managed to become a selling novelist. But even so, I soon ran into trouble. This is covered in detail in *BiOgre* so is capsulized here: I had had a problem with Ballantine Books, so I demanded a correct accounting. Instead I seem to have gotten blacklisted. What really riled me was the way the Science Fiction Writers of America (SFWA, now SFFWA to include Fantasy), an organization supposedly instituted to help writers against bad publishers, in effect sided with Ballantine. Talk of blaming the victim! Lies were spread about me and my markets dried up. There never has been an explanation or apology for that misconduct. So I did three things:

1. I dumped SFWA, and have remained hostile to it since. There is evidence that some of its members are *still* spreading falsehoods about me. Well, if push ever comes to shove, I will put it out of business. Because today I have the resources to sue, as I did not before, and I always did have the right of the case, then and now. All I need is the pretext. My hostility is not to individual members, who for the most part were blithely ignorant of what the officers were doing in their name, but to the officers who either promoted this wrong, or who knowingly allowed it to happen without protest. And to those who learned of it—and slandered me, as described in Chapter 10.

2. I got a New York lawyer. The publisher instantly sent me just enough of the money owing to make what remained too little to be worth a lawyer's while, so there was no lawsuit. It wanted me to shut up. I refused. At least I had demonstrated the justice of my case. The blacklist continued, but wasn't tight; one publisher, Avon, continued to buy from me. That meant that my finances were lean but not prohibitive; I could survive.

3. I got a literary agent. This was Lurton Blassingame, an old-timer who also represented the leading genre writer of the day, Robert Heinlein. This effectively ended the blacklist. I doubt that it was ever stated in so many words, but what publisher would care to aggravate the agent of Robert Heinlein? Oh, a few editors continued it, but I think not only are those editors now mostly out of business, so are their publishers.

But of course the problem remained at Ballantine Books. Until Ian and Betty Ballantine abruptly left their own company. I never saw an explanation for this in print—the fan press can be pusillanimous about the truth, as well as covering up for those it favors, however undeserving of such favor. Judy-Lynn del Rey was now in charge of their SF/fantasy genre division, and her husband Lester del Rey was their fantasy editor. I had worked with them when they were at *Galaxy* and *IF* magazines. They queried me, saying they understood; indeed they were quite candid about what had been going on under the prior administration. Lester said he himself had been similarly treated, being credited with less than half his actual book sales for his royalties. And so I wrote a fantasy novel, because I had always wanted to work with Lester del Rey, and my science fiction was committed elsewhere. That novel was *A Spell for Chameleon*— the first Xanth. None of us realized it at the time, but that was the beginning of the phenomenal success that I was to achieve in fantasy. *Spell* was to become my best-selling novel, with a million paperback copies sold—without ever making a significant best-seller list.

Judy-Lynn del Rey herself was a remarkable person. I call her a giant. This was because she was the driving force behind the massive surge that the subgenre of fantasy made. Lester located the good novels, and Judy-Lynn promoted them effectively, and suddenly sales were rising. She brooked little opposition; she always found a way to accomplish her purpose. She published the first *Star Wars* material. She made Del Rey a hardcover publisher. She abolished the remaining tacit blacklist the Science Fiction Book Club had against me. She lifted the Del Rey lead titles to parallel status with the Ballantine lead titles. She was a wonder. Nothing seemed to stand against her. It became evident that it was not wise to cross her; others learned. Yet according to my memory and judgment, Judy-Lynn stood about three and a half feet tall. She was a dwarf, literally. In fantasy, dwarfs tend to be magically powerful. So was Judy-Lynn. I think everyone who really knew her respected her, and even her detractors, who I think mainly resented her success, did not question her ability. When she died she was voted an award—which Lester declined, because of its hypocrisy. Of what value was an award from folk who had hardly given her any deserved credit while she lived? I agree completely.

Cam and I met her and Lester when they were in Florida. Our daughters met them in Dallas, at the American Booksellers Association (ABA) Convention in 1983. I hate Dallas, because of its complicity in the murder of President Kennedy, and bungling of the subsequent actions. (Steven King had a pointed commentary, I think in *The Tommyknockers*, about the incompetence of the Dallas police. They went to other places where they continued to bungle, in his fiction. But he missed one, as I see it: that was a Dallas police inspector who moved on to NASA, where he became the inspector of O-rings just before *Challenger* blew up—because of faulty O-rings.) But that several-day visit with the del Reys was great. Penny, then sixteen, liked Lester's science fiction novels, and she got to sit beside him, with the publisher paying for the meal. Both daughters liked Judy-Lynn. Lester and I, apart from generally agreeing on the proper nature of fantasy and the inanities of critics, also shared an idiosyncrasy of typing: we were the only two people in the world we knew of to have put the quote marks on the unshift position on our typewriters. In fiction, quotes are used far more often than most other symbols, so it made sense, but the rest of the world was too dull to see that. I liked Lester, and I think he liked me. I still think he was 90 percent right on everything, and wish I hadn't run afoul of the 10 percent.

But Judy-Lynn died tragically. One day she was talking with someone in the Del Rey office, when she stopped making sense. Then she stopped talking entirely. She had had a stroke, and was in a coma for some time. She died without recovering consciousness. Lester was arguably the most successful editor of all time, having edited more national best-selling writers who made it under his auspices than any other I know of, but his personal life was fraught with tragedies, this being the third wife suddenly dead. But the empire of fantasy they had made continued. And my career was part of it. They changed my life, because my fantasy success brought money and made me financially independent, so that we could live where we wished, in what style we wished, and give our daughters what we felt was best without being limited by money. They put me on the map. Without them, I believe, I would be just another writer, unknown outside the circle of science fiction devotees. Instead I had a decade or so with twenty-one *New York Times* paperback best-sellers, during which time I earned ten million dollars—before taxes. But it isn't just the money, because my desire to write is independent of that. It's that I had the chance to do what I most wanted to do, to realize my dream of being a really successful writer, and make my mark on the genre I love. Few folk get to live their dream. I succeeded mostly because of the del Reys.

Yet I left them, and the roots of that were before Judy-Lynn died.

That is part of a complicated story that made the decade of my fifties (1984–94) as turbulent as my prior ones. There was heartache in that, and I wish it had not had to be. But if I had the chance to live it over, I would do the same. Life and business just do not necessarily follow ideal courses, and there can be great irony in events.

I think the root of the problem was that Lester del Rey got old. One of his great strengths as an editor was his experience as a writer; he knew what it felt like to have one's material editorially cut up. So he was cautious about doing it to others. He knew a lot about writing in general, and fantasy in particular, so his critiques were on target. He recommended a number of changes in *Spell*, and I saw their justice, and made them, and the novel stood improved. For example I had a more violent beginning that was not in keeping with the remainder of the novel; at his direction I edited that down. I had too many *underlinings* (manuscript code for *italics*); he pointed out that this can have a bad effect, and I saw it was so, and have watched it ever since. Not everything he did was perfectly on target, by my definition; he deleted some italics that were necessary to the shade of meaning I intended, and when Bink was transformed into a dog so he could sniff out Chameleon, the part where he smelled the intriguing scent of urine was deleted. Dogs do find the scent of urine intriguing, and I don't think it is wrong to recognize that, even in fantasy. But overall, what he did was good, and the novel benefited.

But as time passed, I zeroed in more accurately on fantasy, while Lester became more arbitrary and less on target. I had gone along with his early changes not because he was the editor, but because they made sense. I began to balk at the later ones because they didn't make sense. For example, he thought a line quoted in *On a Pale Horse* was from a Beatles' song, and under copyright, so he deleted it. But the scene didn't make sense without that line, so he deleted the whole scene. Naturally I protested; you don't cut off an arm because of a sore finger. He yielded enough to allow the scene back in, provided I changed the quote, though I had shown that the line was from a folk song that predated the Beatles. So I did, and the novel suffered because of the inferior line I had to use, but not as much as it would have had it lost the entire scene of Luna's bereavement after the death of her father. Other cuts I let stand, though I questioned their validity. One reviewer objected to the novel because she said it didn't have enough humor, not knowing that the humor had been editorially excised. I could use that as an indication the editor was wrong, except that the reviewer showed no understanding of the novel as a whole, so her judgment was not to be respected. Probably Lester was right in that case.

It got worse. Lester alienated best-selling fantasy writer Stephen Donaldson by insisting that irrelevant text be added to one of his novels so that a particular illustration could be used, and the publisher almost lost Donaldson at that time. But he was given a different editor, and so that altercation did not have a consequence, other than Lester's refusal to put the Del Rey fantasy emblem on his novels thereafter. I understand two other major writers were similarly alienated.

Then Lester cut the entire first chapter of Xanth #8, *Crewel Lye*, because he said it had too many puns. Now he had a point; I had used many reader-suggested notions there, and it was probably the weakest chapter in the book. But he was mistaken in more than one way. First, the relevance of the chapter to the rest of the novel was arguable; I pace my novels carefully, and the deletion of that material made the opening jumpy, confusing some readers. I also was using it to set up forthcoming elements of future Xanth novels that Lester did not yet know about, such as Tangleman, the tangle tree turned into a man, and that too was messed up. In any event, the fact that a chapter is weak does not necessarily mean it should be cut off. My left hand is weaker than my right, but I want no one to do me the supposed favor of lopping it off. Second, Lester had lost sight of the fact that the author writes the novel and gets the praise or blame for what's in it; he was requiring me to damage my novel and take the consequence, when he was the one damaging it. He was out of line. He was treating me like an employee who had no choice. That was a fundamental mistake, because not only was I not an employee, I was one of the more assertive freelance professionals. He was asking for a good deal more trouble than the chapter was worth. He even held back part of the advance, a matter of about seven thousand dollars, as a further inducement for my compliance. This added insult to injury; if I was not then a millionaire from my writing, I was close to it, and the advance was ludicrously small compared to the royalties my novels were earning. The very notion that he could threaten me with such a puny stick showed a contempt for reality. I seethed, but Del Rey had made me a major best-seller, and I didn't want to break with it, so I compromised: I yielded the chapter, but resolved not to allow that to happen again. I carefully wrote the following novel, *Golem in the Gears*, to be short enough that it would not be possible to cut anything from it. That's not the best way to write, and I do feel that novel suffered because of that, but I was trying to preserve my text without a quarrel. I was seeking an alternative between capitulation and the A-bomb.

Then Lester tried to cut the entire Author's Note from the fourth Incarnations novel, *Wielding a Red Sword*. He said it was too long, and anyway, they were in the business of publishing fiction, not nonfiction. This was the Note in which I described my computerization—I had until then written my novels in pencil and then typed them with a manual machine, so it was a significant step for me—and introduced Ligeia, the suicidally depressive fourteen-year-old girl who was to have such an effect on my career. I had already been angered by the editing of the Incarnations series, such as when my correct spelling "gantlet" (running through a battering) was changed to "gauntlet" (an armored glove) and my correction overruled so that it was published wrong, making me look ignorant. But this was the limit. I believe I have received only three objections to the Author's Notes, and two of those were by reviewers, who are almost by definition wrong, and the third reader clarified when questioned that she didn't really object, she just thought it was a lot of work for me. The Notes have been perhaps my most universally praised aspect, receiving much attention from readers, who love them. Many tell me that they read the Notes before the novels, and some don't even read the novels, just the Notes. But Lester demanded that this one be cut.

I have tried to figure out why, since he had approved the Notes before. It was a good and significant Note, and it should have been easy for him to let it be. Why had he changed, and why was he so determined, even to the extent of violating my contract, which gave me the final decision? There are fights that need to be fought, regardless of the consequences, but this hardly seemed to be one of them, for him. I believe I have figured it out. And the issue is so stupidly minor that it amplifies the question of his judgment.

My fan mail was increasing enormously with my success. My fantasy generates the most, my serious work the least, generally. Perhaps this is because younger readers are attracted to the fantasy, and they tend to write more. They have dreams, and more time, and less cynicism. Most publishers save up the mail for a month or so and forward it as small packages, unopened. Del Rey opened and read the letters, then sent them on to me in flat packages, open, their envelopes stapled to them. Sometimes Judy-Lynn would scribble a note on one, as she did when a reader remarked on how I shouldn't let the publisher's gorgonlike stare dissuade me from answering my mail. It didn't start that way, but Lester had become the gnarled, grumpy, always correct Good Magician Humfrey, and Judy-Lynn had become the Gorgon, a nice person with a potentially deadly gaze. So she marked "Ha!" on the letter's note about the Gorgon. All good fun. Judy-Lynn also sent in suggestions for the Gorgon, as noted in the Reprise. But one day I received a package of eighty-seven fan letters. I stopped writing my then-current novel, *Red Sword*, and worked for several days, answering those letters. I mentioned that in the Author's Note, with some comments on the letters. Then I addressed the matter of why I should bother answering my fan mail, when many other writers didn't answer theirs. That led into Ligeia, who will be amplified in Chapter 5. I still feel it was a good, fair, and significant discussion, and my fan mail in the ensuing decade endorses that. But my agent relayed a remark Lester had made, to the effect that I shouldn't be taking my time on fan mail. I asked the agent what business it was of the editor's. But that was the hint: not only was the Author's Note too long, by the editor's standard, and not only did it address computers, which he, being then uncomputerized, felt were not of great interest; it discussed the way I handled fan mail. A perceptive reader would realize that the publisher had been holding my mail too long, so that it piled up and messed up my schedule, as well as opening and reading it. That reflected adversely on the publisher. Now you might think the proper response would have been to clean up its act and forward fan mail more rapidly, sealed. But that's not the way such things work. The response was actually to try to cover up the embarrassment. By eliminating the Note that publicized the situation. Just as Lester had tried to cut an entire scene for the sake of one (to him) questionable quote, he tried to cut the whole Author's Note for the sake of one embarrassing reference. And of course he could not come out and say that directly.

How much mischief misplaced pride makes! Lester didn't know that I had resolved to allow no further wholesale cutting of my material, and apparently did not remember how unyielding I could be when crossed. I was the one who had survived blacklisting by that same publisher, and essentially won my case. Judy-Lynn, as tough as any in adversity, was caught in the middle. Certain hints she gave indicated that she agreed with my case, but she would not contravene her husband. So she tried to negotiate, and might have succeeded, for she was skilled; she and I discussed the matter on the phone at some length. But then she died, and there was then no mediator with the power to make her will felt by both parties. Things fell apart; the center could no longer hold.

My agent, Kirby McCauley, did what he could. I also wrote to Lester, explaining my position. He did not respond. I didn't want to leave Del Rey, but I was not going to allow this worsening editing to continue. Finally, I suggested that they give me another editor at Del Rey, as they had for Donaldson. But Lester said No Way; he had sworn he would not be had that way again. (The similarity in our attitudes toward things becomes painful; what had unified us was now driving us apart.) That was the critical point. I decided to leave Del Rey.

We queried my other main publisher, Avon: would it be interested in Incarnations #4–#7? The one whose Note Lester was trying to delete, and the one following it, plus two more to be written. Yes, Avon was eager, and for a good deal more advance money than Del Rey had paid. There were several ways in which Del Rey was foolish, and maintaining low advances was one, because that made its writers easy prey for other publishers. At one point I had said to Judy-Lynn that I knew I was not her million-dollar writer (Arthur Clarke was that) or her hundred-thousand-dollar writer (Larry Niven was that), but that my fiction was likely to do as well as theirs. Actually it fell between those two, in earnings per novel, but taken as a whole, in terms of actual sales and profit margins and quantity, my fiction was probably more important to the publisher's welfare than that of either other writer. Del Rey did not take the hint, until it was too late; then it offered more, but I was already gone.

So we came to an agreement with Avon, for $75,000 per novel and no imperative editing. We sought to refund the portions of the $25,000 or $27,500 advances paid on Incarnations #4 and #5—and Del Rey balked. It wouldn't give up those novels. This was another mistake. Apparently the publisher, now without Judy-Lynn's sure hand, thought it had overwhelming power. It had made a mistake in alienating me for cause by arrogant editing, and was proceeding on a similar course. Publishers just don't think in terms of author's rights. As with the Roman general who lost a battle to Sparticus's rebellious slave army, when asked how he could have been so careless, explained "But they were only

slaves!" I was only a writer. So I pulled out the next stop: I brought
Xanth out of the temporary retirement I had put it into when the editing
got too bad, and inquired how Avon would like three unwritten Xanths
in lieu of the two written. Incarnations. Avon nearly expired with delight.
And so it was that Xanth changed publishers. It was done.

Not quite. Lester phoned me, on the eve of my signature of the Avon
contracts. Apparently I hadn't gotten a letter he had written, he said.
No I hadn't. So I phoned the agent and we held up, and soon the letter
came, agreeing to run the Note with a cosmetic compromise in format.
But it was too late, and I was by this time a bit cynical: Lester never
said he had *sent* that letter before, just that he had written it. He had
not wanted to yield anything until there was no alternative. But it was
too little, too late. Del Rey kept two Incarnations novels, but I was gone
from there, with Xanth.

Lester also accepted the fourth Adept novel, but had taken so long
to do it—about six months—that I had quit on that too, and turned
down his offer when it came and sold it instead to Putnam/Berkley at
the $75,000 rate. It wasn't the money; I just was tired of the oppressive
editing and writer-be-damned attitude. Resolving not to let all my fantasy
eggs be in one basket again, I split it between two publishers. Thus Del
Rey lost all three fantasy series I had been doing for it—because stage
by stage, it would not yield to common sense. Had Lester yielded at the
outset on the Note, all my fantasy would have remained there. Had he
allowed me to have another editor, it would have remained. Had he let
the two Incarnations novels in question go, only the Incarnations and
Adept series would have been lost. Xanth would have waited quiescently
for an eventual change of heart about the editing, because I still didn't
want to take it from Del Rey. But the hard line led to the hard response.
I was sorry to do it, but satisfied that it was the necessary course.

And so I left the publisher that had put me on the big map, and the
editor who had lifted the blacklist and made me a millionaire. Ironies
abounded. I had not wanted to go, and Del Rey had not wanted to lose
me, but Lester's intransigence had made it happen. Looking back on
those trying events, I don't see any alternative to what I did. I feel my
course was reasonable in the circumstances. I protected my novels from
increasingly damaging editing. But I wish I had not had to.

Five

THE EARLY PART
OF DYING

As my books became best-sellers, my fan mail increased enormously. I felt that a sincere letter deserved a sincere answer, so I answered. But what happens when there get to be too many letters to answer? That's why assorted celebrities don't answer their fan mail, or they have a secretary send printed forms in response. Someone who receives a thousand letters a week simply can't keep up with them all. Fortunately my fan mail did not reach that level. But I did type almost nineteen hundred letters in 1994, and more in 1995, taking two or more days each week on my mail. Where is the reasonable limit? My correspondence has squeezed out my reading time and my free time; I am in harness, as it were, all day, every day, seven days a week. I'm a workaholic, so it doesn't hurt me, but I would like to ease off a bit. The computer has enabled me to keep up, but it remains a constant effort.

So why not do what others do, and simply ignore fan mail? That's not an option for me either, and this chapter will show the main reason why. I think most readers will agree that certain correspondence has to be maintained.

The title of this chapter derives from a song. I listen to songs on the radio constantly while I work; I need to be alone, but not totally alone, and the radio represents about the right level of company. I like the type of songs that were popular in the late 1940s and early 1950s. I have zeroed my radio in on those stations that provide such music, and that's it. One song caught my attention: the words I heard were "It's hard to lose a lover in the early part of dying." In due course it turned out that I had misheard; it was actually "the early part of autumn," with the last two words pronounced so that I heard a D sound. But by the time I figured this out, I was enamored of the words I had thought I heard, because my correspondence had brought me nearer to death. I'm slightly depressive anyway; maybe it wasn't coincidence that I chose to hear the word "dying." So I have kept those words.

It started with an ordinary fan letter from a girl of thirteen: how she liked my fantasy novels. I answered routinely. Then, abruptly, her letters became serious: she was suicidally depressed, and wanted to die. Her envelopes were decorated with cute little girl decals, but inside was raw pain. She sliced her wrists often. Her favorite subjects were love, sex, and death, and she wanted to talk to me about all of them. I responded carefully, but "careful" was hardly in her lexicon. Soon she was telephoning me, and she could talk indefinitely. She declared that she loved me, and she wanted me to say I returned that love. I declined. It wasn't that I disliked her; she was intelligent and creative. It was that her love, apart from being unrealistic in any practical sense, had strong currents of sexuality, and I felt any such discussion between us was inappropriate. I was fifty, she thirteen; I was married, she was underage; I was stable, she was wildly unstable; I had other things to occupy my interest, such as earning my living; she evidently had time to spare. She was locked on to love, death, and sex, and she would have liked me to engage in what amounted to phone sex with her. What she desired simply could not be, and not just because she was three months younger that my younger daughter. It wasn't just a generation gap, it was a sanity gap. But she did not care to hear my protestations. My daughters began to resent the time this girl took, and I couldn't blame them. Yet she *was* hurting, and I did not want to cast her out.

So I compromised in various ways. I limited her phoning to one hour a month, cumulatively; she could talk for an hour straight, or for five minutes at a time, but I was prepared to cut her off when the hour was complete. I demurred on certain topics, staying within the bounds of what I felt was fitting. I put her in touch with another correspondent, a woman who knew something about the stresses on women, having been a victim of rape. I encouraged her to get in touch with counselors at school. After she turned fourteen, I wrote a fourteen-line poem, each line fourteen words, "The Ugly Unicorn," and sent it to her one "chapter" at a time. I wrote about her in the Author's Note in the fourth Incarnations of Immortality novel, *Wielding a Red Sword*, assigning her the name of a character in that novel, Ligeia, as a pseudonym. I also used a notion of hers in the novel: a cemetery where there were thoughts instead of people, though for some reason I don't understand I confused it into a church. I can't blame her for being annoyed.

But her severe depression did not ease. She continued to slice her wrists, once sending me a letter signed in her blood, another time exclaiming in pain as she cut at her wrists while on the phone with me. It was evident that her depression was no simple thing; it verged on insanity. When I said that her long long-distance phone calls were a financial burden on her family, she said "I don't care." In fact she didn't care about anything much except herself. One time she played with candles, perhaps a mortuary ritual, and it got out of hand and set fire to the house. The house burned down, rendering her family homeless until they could make other arrangements. But next week she was back on the phone as usual, seemingly unaffected.

It was clear that something had to be done, and in due course her family did it. They sent her to a special hospital in another state, supposedly temporarily. She was going to send me her new address the following week. But I never heard from her again. It was evident that she had been institutionalized, and that she was allowed no private contact with the outside world. I once worked at a mental hospital; I knew how it was. It might seem cruel, but I think her family had no better choice. Ligeia was dangerous. I did not try to write to her again, knowing that it was pointless; I had no correct address, and I could not ethically contact her family about her. But for years I had this concern that one day the phone would ring, and I would hear this soft voice: "I'm back." I dreaded the prospect of its starting over.

After the novel was published, I heard from another fourteen-year-old, suicidally depressive girl, who had read about the first one. I call her Ligeia 2, though she hated being categorized as if she had no individuality. Indeed she was an individual, highly artistic; she decorated her envelopes with her drawings, and I remember one with a human eye, a single tear falling from it. Her family wanted her to train to be a doctor, rather than wasting her time on art. Her family didn't know it was in danger of losing her entirely. But because of complications in which I had some guilt, mentioned in the Author's Note for *Virtual Mode*, she overdosed (OD'd) on pills, was caught in time, and phoned me collect from the hospital. But that finally brought home to her family what was going on, and they gave her more freedom, and she improved and stopped writing to me. I heard from her once four years later, in response to *Virtual Mode*, so knew that she survived, though her life was not perfect. It does seem that severe depression may be only one symptom of a broader malady, though that symptom does need to be treated.

Thereafter there were many Ligeias, and I stopped numbering them. They are all simply Ligeia, though I know them individually as correspondents and they are all different. Some merely need some understanding, and though my mild depressiveness isn't much of a base, it does enable me to sympathize. Some have said they love me, and I, remembering Herta, have sympathy for that too. But understanding and sympathy is as far as it can go. I have never been aware of meeting any of them personally. (After I wrote the first draft of this, I did meet two. Both seemed perfectly normal in person, but their inner agonies continued.) It is possible that some have been among the fans I meet at conventions, but I did not know it. Indeed, I think now that one did mention our correspondence, when we met, and I did not remember; when I got home I looked up the name and there it was. I wrote her a note of apology. My memory for events is good, but for names, bad. That's just as well, perhaps, because my gut emotions with respect to these particular correspondents are compounded of sympathy, obligation, fascination, and fear.

I put a number of them together for the main character in the Mode series, calling her Colene, and seem to have defined the type accurately enough, according to the girls themselves and those who know them: typically bright, sensitive, artistic, young, depressed, sorely in need of love, and willing to do just about anything to get it. Would she use sex appeal? Oh yes; it's a prime weapon. Do I feel the same emotions with respect to Colene? Yes. If she existed in the mundane realm, and fixed on a person, that pretty, smart, driven, underage creature might destroy any man.

This chapter has many feeling poems written by the Ligeias, for I think no one can tell their feelings quite the way they can. But let me start with the one I wrote for Ligeia 1. My taste in poetry is old-fashioned; I like rhyme, meter, alliteration, assonance, and untwisted sentence structure. Blank verse, to me, is like blindness or kissing your sister, and free verse is like prose. But I have learned appreciation for those other forms, and do utilize them myself. Ultimately it's the meaning and force that count. So here it is, with no rhyme, meter, or anything except its word patterning, imagery, and message:

THE UGLY UNICORN

Once upon a time, there was a little unicorn. She lived in a shell.
There was a funny thing about this shell. No one else could see it.
But to her, it was very heavy, as if an elephant were on it.
Sometimes that shell just seemed to crush all the happiness right out
*   of her.*
Of course, she wasn't really a unicorn, because little unicorns don't live
*   in shells.*
She was really an alicorn, which is a flying unicorn. Her mane was
*   brown.*
Alicorns live in shells, because they like privacy. When anyone comes near,
*   they close.*
Of course that means that hardly anyone ever sees an alicorn, which is
*   unfortunate.*
Because alicorns are really very special creatures, when they come out of
*   their shells.*
But the little unicorn didn't know she was an alicorn. She wanted to die.
This is because a magical creature who stifles her magic is in deep trouble.
No one else understood about this, because no one else could see the shell.
Except for maybe one old centaur—but he was too far away to help.
He hoped the little unicorn would learn to fly, before she learned to die.

Unfortunately she did not learn to fly, and if she remains alive today, her wings have surely been clipped. But many other Ligeias do seem to have made it through the treacherous shoals of the teens and achieved ordinary lives, and some are even happily married now. A number of them credit me with saving their lives. I suspect they give me too much credit, but if I have helped even one, it helps to justify my own once-tormented existence. So what Ligeia 1, in her fashion, started, has benefited others.

Not all of them were female. Boys get depressed too. But I heard mostly from girls. My theory is that this reflects the statistics: most of the attempted suicides are by girls, but most of the successes are by boys. The ratio is something like four to one, in each case. I suspect this is because a girl will try the more gentle, inefficient ways, like wrist cutting or pills, while a boy will try the more violent, efficient ways, like crashing a car or pulling the trigger of a gun. But I don't know.

The poems vary in quality, judged by professional standards. But that is not the point; all of these folk are amateurs with respect to writing, and most are young. Nevertheless, the feeling comes through. Many of these are also anonymous, by the authors' requests; I am assigning the pen name Colene to some and Oenone to others. Colene is depressive; Oenone is sexually abused. They come from the main characters in *Virtual Mode* and *Firefly*. The categories can overlap, so my categorization is approximate. The Colene poems can be painful in their desolation; the Oenone poems can be horrifying in their implication.

As it turned out, there were problems about running these poems. I was careful to ask permission for each one, and this was never denied. But some were under the legal age of consent, and they were not about to ask their parents for permission. In several cases, their abusive parents were what they were writing about. I hoped to protect them by using the house pseudonyms, but the publisher's legal department wasn't satisfied. By the time this volume was to be published, several years had passed, bringing the younger authors up to the age of consent—but by then I had lost touch with most of the contributors. Those I could reach quickly granted adult permission; the others I had either to delete or excerpt from in accordance with the "Fair Use" doctrine. So there are fewer poems here than I intended, and some who expected to be represented here are not, because of the irony of circumstance. I regret this, and if any "lost" ones discover this and contact me via my Web site, www.hipiers.com, I will run their poems there if they wish. If any who are anonymous here wish to be revealed there, I will name them. In all cases the literary rights are with the authors, and should there be requests to reprint any, I will contact the authors and put them in touch if this is possible.

Here, in no special order, are the poems.

STILL
Colene

I am still
Dead silence surrounds

No one is near
Nobody found
Black as the night, thick as twilight
Where absence of sound
Meets a perilous plight
No more confusion
End disillusion
Standing on the precipice
Overlooking the abyss
Last thought I have
Bears no turning back
Here comes the peace
Turn to pitch black.

Note the themes of stillness and peace; Ligeias typically look forward to death as relief.

SILENCE
Colene

She is silent. Not
In the sense of a
Chilled night with great
Diamond-studded heavens.
But in the sense of a
Rape victim's
Muffled shriek.
The quiet she feels
Is a fathomless void,
One that fights night and day
To make her shrink into her
Fighting soul.
She is being steadily possessed
By a paper-thin shell.
A monster that slaps on different faces
Like young children with masks
On the night before Halloween,
Her intensity is struggling;

Emptiness, thick and dark and heavy,
Like maple syrup,
Gushes through the peepholes.
She reaches for help, but . . .
No one is there.

Again, silence, and hopelessness, the emptiness behind the mask of the face so great that it seems as thick as syrup. This one does seek help, but finds none. She was twelve when she wrote it. Fortunately, her life has improved since.

Some of my correspondences are extended, because I have some empathy for depressives. One of the Ligeias, in her twenties, I can identify here, because I collaborated with her on a novel, *Dream a Little Dream*, now in print. She is lovely, artistic, perceptive, and caring, but seemingly cursed with bad breaks, and I fear for her continued life even as I write this. Here is one of her poems, showing that she does belong in this group:

THE UNDEAD
Julie Brady

The raven sometimes sings for me
And shakes her darker wings
She wraps her black around me
She tells me I am wrong
And she cursed me with her song.
The terror rolls in like a thunderhead
It booms in my life's sky;
The raven takes wing singing
Into my death she will fly
Never mourning and never a tear will fall.
For me there is no misery
Quite like living through it all.
Undead I am
Death upon my soul
Yet my feet still turn the road
My shoulders still burden the load.
Undead I am

Wishing to be free
Free to die
Free to fly
Free not to see
What I don't want to see.

I have also heard from a number of prisoners. Some men slice their wrists too. Here is the view of one:

I ONLY FELT THE THORN
Marvin W. Scofield

I've always wanted to see a rose.
But I only felt the thorn.
It's a beautiful thing, so I've been told.
But I only felt the thorn.
"A soft and gentle scent,"
But I only felt the thorn.

A splendid sight, for one to see.
But I only felt the thorn.
As soft as silk, so I've been told.
But I only felt the thorn.
"Life is as beautiful as a rose"
But I only felt the thorn.

Now my finger bleeds, and
My heart continues to weep,
'Cause I only felt the thorn.

But not all male depressives are in prison. Here's one who even draws the poison boxes popularized by the Colene of the novel:

STARS
Colene

Tiny points of brilliance float
Within a vast dark void.

They call out to me, begging for me to come:
What is it that they promise?
I look up to the stars, searching for an answer:
Why am I so alone?
A drop of blood falls into the void.
Splash. It sits for a moment, and then it is gone.
Forever cast into oblivion, eternally nothing.
Flat drop of my life is gone.
And yet something calls me, something
Stays my hand—something keeps the blade from my throat.
What is it? Again I look at the stars,
And they continue to shine, as before,
Tiny points of brilliance within a black void of despair.
Brief flashes, hints of joy in an endless existence of pain.

Some are depressed for reasons others can understand. Actually, there's always a reason, but often it's invisible to others. A person can have all the material comforts of life, and strong emotional support, yet want to die. Or a person can have a life of tragedy, yet be of good spirit. Chronic depression is independent of external circumstances. But this one has the debilitating malady of juvenile rheumatoid arthritis, which twists the limbs to the point where the hip joints may have to be replaced, and greatly restricts mobility and independent motion. This is one I had to summarize and excerpt, presenting the mere shadow of the original. She is well taken care of, yet—

THE YOUNG PRISONER
Colene

The girl sits in cell,
Saddened by distant hopes.

She wants to understand, yet desperately wishes to be freed from her prison:

The iron bars of a disease.
A punishment for a sin in the eyes of God.

For if she cannot be free, her trapped passions will destroy her, and

She shall be no more.

I think the oldest poem is this one, written by a young man of sixteen, in 1981:

THE BEAST
Michael Rosenberg

A spirit's breath
On my cheek,
A cold winter's
Night, down by dead creek,
Whispers of shadows
Playing in the dark,
Searching for freedom
And the man with the mark.
Crying is not just for children
You see,
I saw the beast
Cry for me.

The themes of love and death come in often, and not necessarily as opposites. The correspondent addresses this from several converging angles.

BLACK CLOAKED MAN
Ariane Racer

I see him standing over me.
I look up at his black cloaked body.
Then up to his piercing red eyes.
His beady red eyes are set into a bleached, white skull.
They burn holes into me,
Ready to take my life away.
He reaches for me,
I won't take his skeletal hand.

I tremble with fear.
I was obsessed with Death.
Now I fear him.
I wanted him to take my life.
Now, I push him back.
Away.
Leave me alone.
Though, I'm not scared to die,
I fear Death

TRAIL OF TEARS
Ariane Racer

Not one day has gone by,
Where I don't have a nightmare,
Where I don't cry.
He's always there,
Always behind,
Following my trail of tears.
He knows I'm frightened,
By the slightest movement,
By the slightest noise.
He knew that I was weak,
And that is when he struck.
In my puddle of tears,
My puddle of blood,
My puddle of fears.
He leaves me in a heap,
All hurt and dying,
Not caring or looking back,
At the life he has fucked.

THE ONE I LOVE
Ariane Racer

As I stand here,
Trapped behind the door of depression,
The door of love,

The door of loneliness,
A door of solid feelings.
I lost all sense of life,
Something went with him when he left me,
Now as I wait for something to take the pain away,
My outreaching arms yearning to hug a live,
Loving, caring, happy, warm body.
Someone to love and love me back.
To put back the shield of protection,
To put back the love.
To switch my lifeless,
Shattered heart with a warm, beating one.
But do I dare?
Do I dare try once again?
Should I spare another heart to once again be shattered?
Should I take the chance?
Shall I once again live the darkening,
Chewing pain I feel now?
Do I give up on life completely?
Just because I lost the one I love?
Still love,
Always will for eternity?
Is suicide really the answer?
Why do I cut my wrist up
And watch the blood run?
In my dreams, only, he loves me still.

No Where to Run
Ariane Racer

There's no where to run,
There's no where to hide.
Every where I go,
He follows me,
Deep inside.
Night is here. Sleep has overpowered the fear,
But still,
Nightmares come,

They turn to reality,
Scaring me.
I don't feel safe,
Not even in my own home,
Not even in my own bed.
He haunts me every night,
Every day.
What can I do?
Where can I go?
I just want to forget,
Never remembering.
No more nightmares,
No more fears.
Peace and quiet.
Home.

But there is male perspective on that, too. Men are not necessarily trying to haunt women; they may be trying merely to find their own way.

DREAMING
Stephen Fitch

Where is my sunshine
The light of my life
Where is my dream
Mine infinite longing
Where is my salvation
The last bastion of hope.
How will I know her
When I have seen naught but darkness
How can I care for her
When I have felt naught but pain
How can she love me
When I do not love myself

When her sister committed suicide, one girl was thrown into deep doubt. She wanted to protect her family, yet how was she to handle this? "Now the anniversary is coming up, and though I have come to terms with it intellectually, my heart has different ideas. I can't let go! I don't want to. I'm scared that if I do, all I believe in will be gone. I am starting to have doubts about whether or not anything I do even matters. I can't stand it. I feel as if I am standing on an island in the Void, and in front of me are answers, to my right happiness, my left paradise, behind me is Hell, and the island is a sort of limbo where I will stay the same. I am uncertain about everything and nothing. I am going to insert a short poem here—never read, published, etc., trying to describe this . . .

"I must warn you, my poems go where they will; I only hold the pen."

UNTITLED
Elena Bush

In the black pit of night
Where the demons dwell,
Desolation takes a hold
And rules my mind.

What am I to do?
—But stay where I am.
Lest my struggles rip out
A vital part of my being?

A cry for help
Brings nothing but echoes,
For my special Demon
Has its own instinct of self-preservation.

A decision must come quickly, though,
Because every breath I take
Draws the end swiftly closer,
And Evil is putrefying my soul . . .
What can I do?

This one, by the author's request, has no commentary. (The word "sidhe" is pronounced "shee" and refers to the things of the fairies. Thus bean sidhe is banshee.)

The Sacrifice

Robyn Johnson

O beautiful in cloudy skies,
Where skies flash salmon gray
When the bean sidhe storm blows in the roost
When the falcon turns away
Turn the seasons all around,
Let the winds come blowing down
Offer up the sacrifice
Dance the music
Pay the price.

Arise, the sun is shining still,
Eagle's wings the sky will fill
Sprays of foam come shining down
In flecks of salmon gray.
Let the sun come blowing down,
Let the warmth flow all around you
Dance the music
Pay the price
This is another sacrifice.

O earthbound trees
With earthbound roots.
O falcon high
With pinion shoots.
A creaking cry
Mid screaming sighs.
Upon the winds so high.
Shaded leaves fall all around you
Color bold in dying tribute
Dance the music
Pay the price
The winds demand the sacrifice.

Sparrows sing and breezes blow
Freedoms come with its new blow

Working, crying, with the strain
Play again of life's own game.
Let the green grow all around you
Let the breeze blow all around you.
Dance the music
Pay the price
In rebirth comes a sacrifice.

Oh beautiful for starkissed skies
Sun's brightness in dawn filled eyes
When the sidhe winds blow so high.
Once again a falcon's cry
And night to dawn fill twilight eyes.
As salmon-hued wings fill the sky
Offer up a sacrifice
Dance the music
Pay the price.

Turn the seasons all around you
Let wind's touch blow all around you
Dance the music
Pay the price
In innocence is sacrifice
And dying is life's final price.

Sometimes the author is aware of the danger she may represent to others. One is tempted to picture a sad, nice, gentle victim, who lacks only a supportive contact. But just as an abused animal can turn ugly, so can an abused person. This one is summarized and excerpted.

INSIDE MY HEART
Angel Lynn

Terror stalks and attacks its prey.

But do not set me free,
For there is hell inside my heart.

She feels the pain of a thousand years and of a moment, but it can't touch the hell in her heart. There are nightmares and beauty.

So here, hold my hand, my mind, my soul,

But beware that hell in her heart.

There are many causes for distress, and I don't know which is most difficult to handle, but I suspect that it is death out of turn, especially of a close family member. Here is one by a girl whose father died when she was ten. Sometimes it is the seemingly incidental detail that strikes through to the spirit. Perhaps it is that the horror of death cannot be approached head-on, so it is blanked out to a degree, in much the manner one blocks out the direct disk of the sun in order to look at its corona. In this case it was the smell of her father's shoe polish, and for years I called her "my shoe polish girl." Now, checking the poem, I find no such smell. It was the shine of his shoes, and the smell of his sweaters. She herself is a grown woman now, active in adult pursuits, and a published novelist, but still I think of her with the aura of shoe polish. She visited me, with friends, all the way from England, and I regret that circumstances prevented us from just sitting down and talking about anything or nothing. I might have been some comfort to her, if only because I was someone's father and she was someone's daughter. But we couldn't talk, so whatever there was went unsaid. When she got home she wrote this:

MUTE
Justina Robson

I think I had something to say.
It was about my father, or maybe
it was to him.
Yes.
It was about the shine of his shoes,
his early morning whistle
and the smell of his sweaters;
the long steps of the University Hall
that always smelled of chemicals and wood.

I saw his friends and students
Turn their hands to easy work.

Now they have lost their champion
as have I.
We walk alone, each watching
every white-haired man in the street;
running ahead,
tripping over the flagstones,
our mouths bursting with something that
we'll never say.

We know who it isn't.
His friends come eagerly to see us.
They look at me
as if his words which they so need
will come out of
my mouth.

Mother only has no message.
She said goodbye
although she did not want to.

But I have to tell someone
who has some idea about something.

Sometimes there is no abuse, no seeming cause for distress, yet there is the feeling of confusion and loss. This one is by one of identical twin girls, after they went to separate colleges. It was sent to me by her twin, Abby:

APART FROM YOU
Mandy Wray

There were two children, and not many could tell one from the other.

For we are twins, born minutes apart:
For we are twins, heart to heart

Yet at last they had to separate:

As the years went by we began to see
That you had to be you and I had to be me.

And each thought the other was stronger, better able to handle that separation.

I just hope I can find me
Apart from you.

As it happened, they visited me with their parents. I could not tell those two pretty girls apart, but that ache of their separation from each other still haunts me.

Some are older, and they may have perspectives the younger ones lack, but they are hurting too. Here is one written at age seventy:

70 AND STILL DREAMING
Marte Johnson

Today I am moved to send
A message to the future
As I stand on this high ridge
Of a long and convoluted life.

There are not many years left to me,
At least many less than I have had already.
Seventy so far, and to hope for thirty more
Is like asking for a miracle.

I did so want to leave my mark
For everyone to see: the Great Deed,
The Best Seller, the Last Stand in some
Beleaguered castle. I didn't do it.

I must now call myself content, resting
On these Laurels—a lasting marriage,

Beautiful children and grandchildren, even
Some small comforting of wayfarers.

It has to be enough. I don't have time now
To defend that Bridge against all odds.
The blaze of glory is somehow not for me.
But oh! I did want it, more than you know.

I guess this is the message: I dreamed
Great dreams—but they didn't happen.
I had great plans that died unborn.
Still, life is good—worth living.

Lord, I'd like to believe that the Great Deed
May be still ahead of me. How lovely if it is!
But if not, then Your will, and not mine.
Until You call my name and time is ended.

Here is one by a writer who is twenty-four years of age:

SPECTRUM
Josh Robbins

We are all colors
in the spectrum of life—
equal, yet different.
Each being has its role to play;
no hue takes precedence.
There are many moments
in the circular rainbow
that is time.

And one by a woman of thirty-four who understands loneliness. The form of this one is different, yet it, too, is a poem, and has its feeling and its beauty.

The Loneliest Heart
Jody Oakes

The heart continues to beat, yet the life has been drained from it mercilessly. Leaving an emptiness, a void, a gap: tragic enough to equal that of a shore never touched by the sea, or maybe a hollow earth frail enough to shatter at the next gentle rain.

It's the heart that screams in pain when no one is listening, yet clothes itself in festive garb when strangers' eyes are present. And although the clothing is transparent, those peering in are assumed to be blind, as none see the tombstone erected on the very spot it died.

But even in its death the heart continues to cry. It cries out to be noticed, to be needed, to be touched. It cries in mourning over that it knew of, but never really knew.

And when it cries out for help, nobody hears, for its voice has become weak. When the cry is somehow heard, the heart retreats. Sometimes in fear, but more often because the true hope of being revived has vanished.

And when the day comes the heart can no longer produce even the faintest whisper, that is when the final beat of the heart will be heard. One endless beat . . .
    heard over . . .
      . . . and over . . .

    echoing on relentlessly

          . . . still in search of that it knew of . . .
          but never really knew.

Here is one that has an appealing rhyme pattern, as well as a key question:

WHEN RAINBOWS FADE
Erin Kane

When rainbows fade
And the mist is gone
All that is left is the rain
When youth fades
And childhood is gone
We've nothing left to gain
When true love fades
And that spark is gone
All that is left is pain
When memories fade
And pain is gone
How do we stay sane?

When the colors fade
And the leaves are gone
All that is left is snow
When the moonlight fades
And the snow is gone
We know that we must grow
When the pain fades
And the rain is gone
To be touched by the sun's bright glow
But when the sunlight fades
And the flowers are gone
Where are we to go?

I had closed out this volume, but an unexpected delay prevented me from sending it off to my literary agent. In that time I heard from one more, with a poem so raw and specific that I had to add it to this collection, concluding the suicidal statements:

A LETTER TO NO ONE
Shawna Toupin

My death didn't make the front page
Many like me die each day

only to be remembered as a statistic
         Your cruel tongues taunted me
Your malicious action shunned me

My death, self-inflicted,   was not a surprise

I didn't kill myself
         All of you murdered me

my hands   these toys of death
Were merely puppets upon your stage

Each one of you held the strings

                         Twisting and pulling

You tuned out your ears to my screams of pain
(turned silent) muted

You programmed me to self-destruct

         my soul was torn and maimed

and then my soul fled

         So I remained empty until the blessed end

Here is the first portion of a longer poem, drawing a nice analogy:

GARDENING AND CHILDREN
Phyllis Alexia Eileen Barker

Of gardening and children my sons and daughter—and husband too—
     think I'm wrong
You water and you plant, you trim and fertilize
You watch with loving care—each petal grow
Now children I have found—you fertilize with care

You feed with information from Encyclopedia, TV, or information oh so
  rare—or not so rare
Be careful of the pruning—a tree cut back too soon or too much will not
  bear
A child like a tree you see—needs careful pruning too
For it can cut too deep—it can cut a limb off where growth should
  shoot
If you prune back hard my dears with harsh words and filth
Where there should be love and understanding
It will stunt the growth
Now little boys and girls I know
Need hair cut and nails trimmed
The edges on the lawns you see so very badly trimmed
If you will look at gardens friend
Be careful of the bud—a little petal might be
forming like a little girl should
Petal is a loving name for a little girl I once knew
To understand a rose's growth, honeysuckle and birch too
An apple blossom like the tree is a Chinese painting I once knew
The front garden had one too—if you could but see
The honey-suckle—don't you see
The bees they say—if you will but tell it your secrets they will grant
Like a mother's understanding of a special want
A need just quietly mentioned—in a wistful voice perhaps
Oh flowers and trees have genes just as we do
Names and meanings too if you have time to study
Strappings and slappings you see—a walnut tree I'm told
Will bear better and more nuts—if at the right time this is administered—
  and no mother should have to hear "Slut"
Or like the temper if controlled properly
Better still—a father who will understand both sides
And correct before it is too late

Of watering my dears
A garden needs just enough you see
In the hot summer sun—like swimming or a cup of coffee
Like showers or the bath too—like attention to the loo

Like tears gently shed or rushing like a torrent
Too much will rot the roots—enough set the bud
If one is stinting with the water
On the honey-suckle, bean or bud—old bean
The hot tomato or potato—referred to by some boys
Needs careful building up, pruning, budding and packaging
And this means money too
For she one day you will see bear sons and daughters just like you and me

Teach of caring and love and understanding too
Teach of sex and drugs and drinking too
Teach of books and TV but of the heart too
Teach of imagination and of striving too
Teach of wood-work or cooking—and give each its due
Teach of cleanliness in thought and word and love of God too
The weeds in the garden my children
Tackled so zealously with rake or hoe or lovingly with hand care
Like weeds in our minds—bad thoughts filth and despair
Remember God's words my dears—to honor, love and respect
To take care of a partner as one's own body
The marriage ceremony says—read it and read it true—
Remember that the body will bear
The fruit like the flowers and the bees
When two bodies are made one body.

Now we come to some by Oenone. She did not get good gardening. In *Firefly* she had sex with a grown man at the age of five. Many stores refused to put the novel on their shelves, keeping it under the counter, so that only those who asked for it got it; this tacit censorship greatly reduced sales. But the response from readers was overwhelmingly positive. Most was from women, and the essence was "It's about time someone brought this out into the open." They told me their stories, and I realized that I had understated the case. There's a lot more incestuous sex going on, mostly forced by grown men or adolescent boys on female children, than our society cares to admit. In fact, there seems to be an inverse ratio: the more society suppresses information about sex, especially for children, the more of it there is—especially for children. In the name of religion, of decency, of morals, in the name of protecting the innocence of the young, a far different reality is visited on too many children. It is a dark secret that can destroy lives. Knowledgeable, consenting sex between adults can be one of life's beautiful things, but forced sex can have malign effect well beyond the physical. As these poems show.

First the more subdued one:

DADDY SAYS SO SO IT'S SO
Oenone

Mother isn't home so Daddy's cooking
eggs he always cooks eggs & gives
us cereal he can't cook but he
wants us to have something hot
so he cooks eggs & makes cereal
& we eat in the den & drink coke
from a straw as a treat

The game is over for the night
& now he's cooking eggs
I hate the smell of eggs
bland meaty rot of jungle reek
I never eat them unless he makes me
& then I puke & have to clean it up
Daddy says I did it so it's my job
& I'm lucky he doesn't
make me eat it but
he wouldn't do that he's
my daddy & he loves me very much
he says so when we play our game
and Daddy says so so it's so.

Almost time to eat so
I take off my clothes & put
my pj's on the yellow ones with
blue flowers & floppy feet
my clothes are damp
with the slick sticky sheen of
(spunk jizzum jungle juice cum)

sweat my father sweats
when we play his game

I stuff my clothes into a pillowcase
(my Snoopy pillowcase that says
"Happiness is a warm puppy")
& go to my brother's room
he lies in a tangle of curled
legs & arms & head burrowed
into the pillow I cannot see
his face but I hear low cries
& breathy sobs & moans
a quiet knotted agony
& all alone
because I have my job to do
(it's the first time Daddy ever
played his game with you
I'm sorry, I guess, but now you know
that Daddy loves you too)

I do what Daddy told me to
I pick up Timmy's pair of shorts
lying crumpled by the door
they are white with red wet
stains & I take them to the bathroom sink
and use cold water like my mother
taught me to wash the blood away
it's my job Daddy says five is
plenty old enough to be
responsible Timmy's older
but I'm the girl it's my job
& someday I'll be a good wife
Daddy says
and if Daddy says it's so it's so

I take the pillowcase to Daddy
& he kisses me says thank you
Timmy's sick, I think. I say

& Daddy says no he's sulking just
sulking, can't get his way, don't worry
we'll eat alone tonight, angel,
you and me, okay? & I say sure, Daddy
& I hope he doesn't
make me eat the eggs

Even so, it wasn't always safe. When she was seven or eight he tried to kill her. He had her down under the table, choking her. Her brother threw a ketchup bottle, hitting their father and getting ketchup all over him. "I will remember that stipple of ketchup in my father's black bushy left eyebrow all my life." It distracted him long enough for her to scramble out from under the table, and gave him time to gain control of himself. "I don't think my dad ever meant for it to go that far—he just loses it sometimes. My brother probably saved my life that day, & at great risk to himself." Indeed, her brother, two years older, supported her throughout a childhood that involved sex and drugs; he held her hand throughout an eighteen-hour ordeal of a bad LSD trip. "He is my big brother. And I love him."

She was in and out of mental institutions as she grew older, and required speech therapy to ease her stuttering. She read my books, and appreciated *Wielding a Red Sword* because of its stuttering protagonist. Then, half a year later, she sent this, written at age twenty-two, in an institution. The subtlety is gone; the gloves are off. I regard this as the most telling statement of its type I have encountered, and a fine, if horrible, poem. It's all there: the instruction, the rationalization, the sex, the ignorant mother, the threats, the secrecy, the pain, the flair of artistic revelation. This is terrible beauty:

I KNEW TO BE A WOMAN
Oenone

I knew to be a woman
I learned at seven
How to read a clock
I learned at seven
How to suck a cock
I knew to be a woman

He said to me he said
Your mother she doesn't
She doesn't understand
She doesn't satisfy me, doesn't
Make me happy, not
The way you do, show me, show me.
Won't you show me how,
Show me how much you love me?

I knew to be a woman
Eight times seven
Is fifty six
Eight years old
And turning tricks
My father, my lover
In the whispering night
He enters my room
He enters me
Comes when he will
Takes what he wants
Leaving me
With the moon in my window
Our sweat on the pillow
And the bed slick against my skin

I knew to be a woman
Mother screams
Why don't you smile?
What's wrong with you?
*   I say nothing*
Why won't you eat?
Why won't you sleep?
What's wrong with you?
*   I say nothing*

('Cause if you tell
I'll take you away

To a far-away place
A place in the city
A place I know
And you'll probably die
And you'll never come home.
You'll never come home
'Cause if you tell
I won't love you anymore
Mommy won't love you anymore
We'll send you off
To a far-off place
And you'll never come home,
You'll never come home
'Cause if you tell
I won't love you anymore
I'll know you don't love me
And I won't love you anymore)

I knew to be a woman
Don't you understand
I'm doing this for you
So you'll be, oh so you'll be
You'll be a good wife
See don't you see don't you
See I love you
So won't you show me
Won't you show me how
Show me how much you love me?

My father, my lover
Taught me to tie my shoes
To ride a bike
And to be a woman
To love to hate to shame
To hurt and to be silent

I knew to be a woman.

And so some go from child to woman without passing through adolescence. Therein, it seems, they lose something vital. I do not know how such lives can be repaired.

Let's conclude with one that at this point should need no discussion:

WATCHES
Kaaiohelo Jensen

Sometimes
On the lonely
Hours of the evening
I sit & watch the sun go down
And cry.

⬩ ———————————————————— ⬩

S i x

BETRAYALS

I made a comment once in a weekly letter to Jenny that bears repeating here: it was a formula I invented for explaining the ways of publishers. TPB = SOD. What does it mean? Typical Publisher Behavior is Shitting On Dreams. I think it's a shame that something as creative and vital to the nature of the human species as storytelling is largely controlled by the soulless cretins known as publishers. Perhaps every person has his dream, and many of those dreams are expressed in writing, but they will never be promulgated because the means of doing so are in the cynical hands of those whose only dreams are money and power. In this chapter I'll give examples of my ongoing battle with those whose avarice seemed exceeded only by their incompetence. In other words, typical publishers.

I worried that I would not be able to write fantasy well without Lester del Rey's editing. But instead it was like a burden lifting from my shoulders. Suddenly I was free of the incubus of oppressive editing. No longer would Xanth be pruned of both its puns and its realistic references. The first novel I wrote for Avon, *Vale of the Vole*, proceeded at a record pace, and was complete in six and a half weeks. Characters it introduced, such as the Demoness Metria and Chex the winged centaur filly, have endured to be strong regulars in following Xanth novels. I was free to experiment, and to have realistic references, such as the way Chex was completely free of concern about natural functions, as outdoor animals are. I could have any puns I wanted. I believe that the novels following my separation from Del Rey are stronger than those preceding it. Lester may have thought I would self-destruct, but if he read any of those novels, I think he would have seen that their standard had not suffered. He had claimed that my writing had deteriorated after I computerized. My writing *had* declined, but not for that reason. It had suffered because of Lester's editing, and the preventive measures I had had to take to prevent him from doing even more damage. All that had changed. I was now dealing with editors who didn't understand my fantasy, so left it alone. And it did well, continuing to make the national best-seller lists despite underprintings that required publishers to return immediately to press to fill reorders.

In fact, that was an annoyance from the start. Avon printed 370,000 copies of *Vole* instead of the 400,000 or more Del Rey had before. I figured Avon would learn, and correct its error next time, but it never did; the fifth Xanth novel it had, *Question Quest*, had an initial printing of 365,000, and so had to be reprinted immediately. So what difference did it make, if they were ready to reprint so readily? It's hard to tell, but in my judgment, every sale gained from a quick reorder represents two sales lost because of the buyers who hadn't had a chance to buy at the outset. When stocks at stores run out, they reorder, but there is delay; if they have more copies two weeks later, many readers have gone on to other novels that have arrived in the interim. Some readers are dedicated and seek out what they want, and I have many such dedicated ones. But more are impulse buyers who will grab a book when they see it new, but won't look for it two weeks later. It's vital that the initial exposure be there, especially since many stores will put new books up front, then move them back as other new books come in. And of course for every store that reorders, there may be another that doesn't. One of the things the big chain stores did was computerize, so they could keep constant track of all titles, and they made sure to have enough of what was moving well. But the old-fashioned stores didn't necessarily have that philosophy; they marketed what was there, and didn't go to any trouble to seek what ran out. Some seemed not to know how well a book would do, so if they started with ten copies, they sold ten and forgot about it, though they might have sold thirty copies if they had had them. It's too late, after the first flush has passed, just as it's too late to catch the plane after it has taken off.

So why did publishers do it? I have taken years—decades!—trying to get a line on the obscure thought processes of publishers, and have some tentative answers. I refer to publishers, but actually they are composed of individual people. They would not express it this way, of course, but essentially each little person in that big organization is intent on covering his own ass. If too many copies are printed, there will be too many returns, and that's lost money. So it's safer to print too few copies, and go back to press when reorders come. Sure, there are less total sales, but no provable losses are incurred. In fact, suppose a brash editor doubled the print order, and sold 50 percent more copies? That novel has done much better than it would have—but what of all those extra unsold copies? That looks bad. He should have printed only 50 percent more, the reasoning goes, and taken no losses. Meanwhile, other editors who underprint have the "success" of selling even better than anticipated. So some, in rare moments of candor, will say it openly: they would rather print conservatively and have fewer returns, than print more and sell more. I was told that Stephen King, then a promising writer on his way up, ran up against a publisher that absolutely refused to print more than 75,000 hardcover copies. But he could sell twice that many, the agent protested. It made no matter; the publisher had a policy, and the limit was the limit. So, as with me in a different respect, King finally had to leave that publisher. And the new publisher printed and sold 175,000 copies. Sometimes changing publishers is the only way. Where would King have been, if he had stayed with that limited editor? Not where he is now, for sure!

Berkley was worse. Its first Adept novel, *Out of Phaze*, was reported by *Publishers Weekly* to have an initial paperback printing of 450,000. That novel spent three consecutive weeks as #7 on the *New York Times* best-seller list, a very strong showing. So what did they do for the following novel? They cut the print order! They printed 350,000 copies. And of course that novel's sales were lower. It made the *NYT* best-seller list, but around #14. What had they expected? Indeed, they continued to underprint, and finally succeeded in taking that series off the national best-seller lists. Sure, they had fewer returns—at the expense of my career.

Did I regret leaving Del Rey? I watched David Eddings fantasy series at Del Rey rise up and pass mine in sales, his income advancing accordingly, and yes, I was sorry to be gone. But I wouldn't pay the price Eddings may have paid, sacrificing the integrity of my text. I surely would have had better sales at Del Rey, but my fiction would not have had the same quality. That's why I would do the same again: I care more about quality than money. Yes, even with such seemingly frivolous fantasy as Xanth. There are elements there the critics know nothing of.

It was to get worse. Whatever Berkley did, Avon did also; the two publishers became in my mind like gasoline companies, whose prices rise and fall in perfect tandem. Avon finally did make an effort with the hardcover edition of the final Incarnations novel, *And Eternity*, printing 47,500 copies, of which all but 500 went out to the stores—and it made the *Publishers Weekly* hardcover best-seller list, the first of my novels to do so. I was a best-seller in paperback, but not in hardcover. That novel was obviously ready to take off in paperback. So what did Avon do? Right; it cut the print order, and sales dropped from those of the prior novel in that series. In fact that series, whose first six novels had all been paperback national best-sellers, didn't make the list with the seventh. No, it wasn't because the novel was inferior; the consensus of my fan mail was that it was second best after *On a Pale Horse*, the first novel in that series. It simply had a publisher that wouldn't address its market.

It gets still worse. At times my mind boggled at what was happening. It was as if these publishers had a death wish, and wanted each novel to sell fewer copies than the prior one. Indeed, this is built into the philosophies of many publishers, to the amazement and chagrin of their writers. The explanation for this becomes complicated, so is separated into its own chapter, "Dynamics." For now we'll continue with my own more limited view.

At one point, with what may be the genre record for paperback best-sellers—it totaled twenty-one novels before the string broke—I looked ahead to a likely breakthrough into hardcover bestsellerdom too. I had resolved before I ever became a best-seller that I would not be one of those who were lifted and lowered like chips floating on the tide, and would act intelligently to preserve my fortune. I tried to do that, with good writing, good agenting, and a general comprehension of contracts and markets. There are writers who write well enough, but who seem to have little financial sense; I can handle numbers as well as notions, and make it a point to understand royalty statements. But I had reckoned without the duplicity and sometimes idiocy of publishers.

A good sample case history is *Total Recall*, my novelization of an Arnold Schwarzenegger movie. One day I received a call from Avon: would I be interested in novelizing a movie based on a Philip K. Dick story? I have admired Dick's work; it has a special, peculiar, halfway-crazy quality that appeals to many of us who aren't as crazy as he was. So I asked to see the script, so that I could judge whether this was for me. Tri-Star promptly sent me a copy of their revised script. I read it and liked it, though there were some hilarious science errors. But I could fix those. So I agreed to do it. I took only a token advance, $1,000, but asked for half the royalties. That is, 5 percent, with the movie folk getting the other 5 percent. Actually they probably had a different financial arrangement; they owned the movie, and the publisher had to pay them for the right to novelize it. But ordinarily writers receive only 2 percent royalties for such projects, so it was a good enough deal for me. I thought.

Working from the script, as if it were a collaboration, I completed the novel in a month. Writing is much faster when you don't have to stop to figure out where you're going or how to end it. I fixed the problems, such as Arnold dispatching thirteen of the twelve uglies who attacked him, and the science, such as talking by phone between Earth and Mars with no time delay. Well, in a fashion; I had to spot invent an instantaneous transmitter, so that the poky speed of light wouldn't make for ten minute or more travel times. I've never taken a chemistry course, but I knew it wouldn't be possible to make breathable air on Planet Mars simply by evaporating a glacier. So I made up some chemistry to make it possible. And I filled in the aliens who had built the nuclear power plant, eons ago. I didn't touch the settings or dialogue, because they were in the original material, but I did fill in around them so as to provide more clarity and impact. I regretted having to use the four-letter expletives, which I normally don't use in my fiction, but didn't feel free to change them. It was my first novelization, but I believe I did the job. Indeed, later fan mail informed me that the book was better than the movie.

The book was published first in hardcover, well before the movie. The publisher had obtained the novelization rights in part with the promise of doing a good job of promotion. But not much promotion was apparent, and the print order was a medium 15,000 copies. The movie folk, disturbed by this, sent a man to New York to remonstrate with the publisher, and I understand even paid money to facilitate promotion and a larger printing. Okay, the print order was doubled, to 30,000, which is respectable but not big. Only when the time came, only 15,000 copies were printed. It seemed that the doubled figure was only if enough orders came in, and they didn't. Why should they, with no extra promotion? I understand the movie folk were disgusted, and so was I; it smelled like reneging.

As they made the movie, there kept being changes. So the editor said they would hire someone to splice those changes into the text of the novel, so that the paperback edition would match the movie. They did so, and showed me the revisions, which consisted mainly of deleting certain scenes and paragraphs of mine and substituting larger passages matching the movie scenes. I checked them and approved them. But when the paperback was published, some idiot had left the original paragraphs in, so that in four places things happened twice. This perplexed readers, who wondered whether I didn't proofread my material. It's the writer who gets the blame for the editor's mistakes. Then the movie itself had further changes. Thus there were three versions: the hardcover, the paperback, and the movie. I did learn from the experience though. For one thing, I found that it isn't just good books the scriptwriters maul, it's their own original scripts. There was a lovely scene in the original that wasn't in the paperback or movie: Arnold, at work as a construction worker, takes a lunch break. Several men are watching a lovely nude dancing girl, there in the middle of the construction site. He walks right through her. Oh—she's a girlie holograph! He knew it; we didn't, until then. The men have a lot of fun with that kind of entertainment, even changing her size so she's forty feet tall, so they can stand directly below and look up. Men will be men. But all that was gone from the finished movie. So did they correct the erring science while they were at it? No; it was apparent that they paid no attention to my corrections. Too bad; I think it would have been a better movie if they had.

The movie *Total Recall* was one of the blockbusters of 1990. How about the novel? Novelizations are sneered at by critics, but of course it seems that *everything* that's interesting is panned by critics. Books based on best-selling movies commonly do make the best-seller lists. How many copies of the tie-in paperback would Avon print? Oh, a million, for this one, the editor said. That was great; my largest prior paperback printing had been 450,000. Morrow had printed only half the indicated number of hardcover copies, but the paperback was where the big promise was, for this one. But as the time grew near, the editor backed off somewhat. Only 600,000 would be printed. Well, that was a comedown, but still a good size, easily enough to make a good showing on the best-seller lists. But it didn't make those lists. What had happened? We checked—and learned that they had printed only 300,000 copies. They had to rush back to press as the book sold out in the stores, but of course it was too late; by the time the replacement orders reached the stores, the tide had ebbed. An almost sure best-seller had been denied in the only way possible: by printing too few copies to allow it to happen.

Why had they done it? If they were going to print 300,00, why did they tell us 600,000? Well, as I encountered this phenomenon repeatedly, always to my cost, I slowly realized that there is in place an unwritten policy in Parnassus: they inflate their figures to double what they actually intend to print. It's routine; they don't consider it lying. Why? Because they want to appear to be bigger players than they are. In hardcover, you aren't considered to be a contender for a best-seller unless your printing is at least 100,000. So they announce that, then print 50,000. Everyone knows it—except, it seems, folk like me, who deal in straight figures. So when I asked the size of a coming print order, and was given a figure, I believed it. And then was confounded when it turned out to be only half that. The trouble was, I knew how many copies had to be out there to make the best-seller lists, and sometimes I sold novels based on publishers' promises—which then turned out to be double what they actually intended to do. They don't consider it lying, but I do, and I don't like doing business with liars.

But that was just one book, and not exactly great literature. What about more serious material? Well, Morrow/Avon was eager for my future novels, and in a conference call with me and my agent they said: however many hardcover copies of the final Incarnations novel *And Eternity* they sold, they would double it with my provocative singleton mainstream sex-abuse novel *Firefly*, and double it again with the major novel of my career, the historical *Tatham Mound*. No hard figures there, but relative ones—so the fudge factor shouldn't apply. So did they do it?

Well, they printed 47,500 hardcover copies of *And Eternity*, and it sold well, even making the *Publishers Weekly* hardcover best-seller list. It just kept selling, so it seemed that returns would be negligible. In the end there were some; it sold about 36,000. So that meant 72,000 for *Firefly*. They actually printed 52,000. But they insisted on marketing the novel as horror, which meant that the genre horror readers would be disappointed because it had nothing to do with vampires or werewolves or ghosts and not much to do with really mean people, and its real market would not know it existed. Sure enough, tacit censorship caused many stores not to put it on their shelves or to tell readers they had it. Those who found it and read it were mostly very positive; a typical female comment was "It's about time this was brought out into the open!" But the return rate was 50 percent, which was a disaster for a hardcover edition. Because it had been marketed as a genre novel, in a genre that doesn't get into the realities of sexual abuse the way *Firefly* does.

The next was *Tatham Mound*, a 200,000-word story of the American Indians who encountered the Spanish explorer Hernando de Soto. It was based on the bones found in a burial mound discovered about ten miles from where we live. I had contributed $75,000 to the University of Florida and a related project to enable them to excavate it, and I believe that project helped define our knowledge of the people who lived here at the time the Europeans discovered America. So this was THE novel, for me, finally getting seriously into the type of writing I had wanted to do for a quarter century. By the publisher's original promise, made at the time of purchase, the hardcover printing should have been 144,000—enough to make it a significant best-seller. Now of course it isn't enough just to print copies; there has to be promotion and distribution geared to it, so that the stores and the public know what's coming. When they spoke of a printing, I thought they were actually promising that whole major effort. So how many did they actually print? They were cagey about figures, but they did not promote it as one of their 50,000+ efforts, despite telling me that they did plan to print that many. Not 144,000? Why weren't they promoting as they had promised? Well, the word came back, Anthony wasn't a big enough name to justify their doing any real promotion. They only promoted the names who didn't need it? Something was weird here.

I swung into action. I had been working with others to set up Hi Piers, a marketing operation for my books. We arranged for me to attend the 1991 ABA convention being held in New York City, so I could promote the novel there. Morrow protested that a book-signing couldn't be arranged. Yes it could; we had cleared it with the ABA personnel, and they were waiting for Morrow's call. So finally, reluctantly, they made the call and it was scheduled. What about books to send out for review? Morrow's effort was so inadequate that I bought 600 copies of the bound galleys at $5 each, and we sent them out for review, and garnered a number of favorable reviews. I paid my own way and rented my own booth at ABA. The signing was a success; many bookstore personnel were interested. We made up and handed out *Tatham Mound* T-shirts. We did the whole bit. It's hard to be precise on figures, not knowing what should be counted for what, but my wife estimates that the promotional effort cost us about $50,000. All because the publisher wouldn't do it. But the worst was still to come. Morrow had dragged its heels throughout, and finally trumped our best efforts: apparently they actually printed about 20,000 copies. That made it impossible to do well, no matter how many readers wanted it. They had to go immediately back to press, so it nudged up to about 25,000—or half the amount they had told me when I queried, and perhaps a sixth what they had originally promised. When I tried to reach the editor he was always out of the office. He did forward me what he said was a favorable blurb comment on it—but the envelope was empty except for his letter. Later Morrow sent me *only the indifferent* reviews of it, really rubbing it in.

Why did they do it? Why did they so determinedly renege, doing just about everything possible to torpedo their own book? I finally figured that out. After they had so badly blown *Firefly*, they decided that my next novel would never sell. Never mind that it was a completely different type of book, in a different genre; if they promoted it well and it sold well, it would prove them wrong. I suspect at this point they wanted to demonstrate that Anthony was not a good-selling writer. And some editors would rather torpedo their writers and publishers than admit significant error. Covering his own wretched ass. Crazy? You bet. But it happened. If there was some other reason, I'd like to know it. One evidence of their inadequacy is the returns. There are always some returns, as some stores change their minds or fail to put books on the shelves, as happened massively with *Firefly*. But when Hi Piers then sought to buy leftover hardcovers to fill its requests, it could not: there were none. There were no copies of the hardcover edition of *Tatham Mound* remaining. So further orders for the novel could not be filled. Morrow had made absolutely sure the novel would fail, despite its market.

Yet I understand that Avon was astounded to learn that I was leaving that publisher, and taking Xanth elsewhere. Carolyn Reidy, president of Avon, who had not been at fault in this instance, because Avon is the paperback arm, called me, and I explained how I felt about reneging on a promise made to obtain an important novel. "That just isn't done, with me; it just isn't done," I concluded. She listened and did not comment. Then she resigned her position at Avon. So how was this received by the publisher? Did the errant hardcover editor pay any penalty for what he had done? No; they promoted him. Later he left Morrow and was involved in the notorious four-and-a-half-million-dollar Newt Gingrich deal. The odor was par for the course.

In due course it became apparent that Morrow/Avon was in trouble, and it was put up for sale. But even as offers came in, it was losing writers—guess why!—and its value was declining. Finally, a sale to Putnam fell through, so it continued on its own, not the publisher it had been. I wonder if the matter of integrity ever came up in its board meetings, or the likely consequence of stiffing its writers. Avon had for years been my best publisher, and I had not expected to leave it, but with Morrow's considerable help it demonstrated that it had the ability to alienate me. I say this with regret; I had not wished to be alienated, but I think this capsule history shows that there was little point in remaining there.

So where was I to go with Xanth? This was a matter of deep concern. I considered each of the other publishers with whom I had done business carefully, because I prefer to stay with the known than risk the unknown. These were Berkley, Del Rey, Baen, and TOR. There were others, but these were more significant or current, so warranted first consideration.

My history with Berkley was mixed. My first sale there was *Hasan*, in 1969—but then the editor changed, and the new one wrote it off unpublished. Par for the course, but not the best beginning. My next sale there was *Prostho Plus*, after a hassle which included the report of the manuscript being lost; only when I got a copy of the galley proofs from the about-to-be-published British edition, so it was clear that I was ready to remarket it elsewhere, did Berkley manage to find its own copy and make an offer. It seems that manuscripts can be lost and found at publishers' convenience. I accepted, and in another two years it was published. My next sale there was *Kiai!*, a collaborative martial arts novel with Roberto Fuentes. Berkley had rejected it before, but when *Kung Fu* was a hit on TV, the editor asked for it back, because of the sudden martial arts craze, and bought it, and published it in only seven months. It continued with four sequels. Then *Chthon*, which I had taken from Ballantine during the blacklisting there, together with its sequel *Phthor*.

Their first edition was okay, but their later reissue was missing ten pages. I didn't know of this, because they didn't send me an author's copy; I learned of it only when a reader wrote from Australia to ask a number of stupid questions—which turned out to be not stupid at all. He had in fact been paying attention, and discovered the missing pages by comparing editions. "Dump Berkley!" I told my agent, furious. But he was wiser than I, and put me in touch with their hardcover arm, Putnam, which was to do quite well for a time with my revived Adept series.

Except for that underprinting syndrome. Berkley paid good money, had a good contract, and good (i.e., minimal) editing, but that business of printing fewer copies each time drove me crazy. However, that was the tail end of a series inherited from another publisher; maybe Berkley would do better with its own series. So I generated Mode, featuring cute, smart, suicidally depressive Colene, her ideal man Darius, her telepathic horse Seqiro, and a grand multiuniverse adventure. This would put me on the hardcover best-seller list, the catalog said. Since it generally takes at least 50,000 copies printed to do that, I was really interested. So what happened? The readers loved it, but they printed only about 25,000 hardcover copies, and had to go back to press twice in a hurry, but of course had ruined its potential. We checked with a store: how was it selling? "You mean *Virtual Mode* has been published?" the bookseller asked, amazed. "I've been waiting for it!" The salesman had never come, so the store had not known of it, and so not ordered any copies. No wonder the initial orders were small! So how about the big chain stores, which know what they want and get it at reduced prices, and keep computer track of sales? One woman reported checking eighteen Waldenbooks stores before she found a copy on sale. Obviously they felt no urgency about keeping that title in stock. They must have sent out something like two copies per store, sold out immediately, and not noticed. That says something more about the type of promotion and follow-up the publisher had done, not to mention the chain store. Suddenly I knew what had happened—too late. They applied the lower printing rule to the sequels, of course, and didn't do anything special with the paperback editions, which tend to be pegged on the hardcover performances. So there was nothing to do but shut down the series, which was going nowhere despite the avid response from those readers who had found it on sale. Berkley had many big ideas about marketing, but somehow never carried them through very well. For example, they sent me on a promotional tour to California—where I had a phone interview which could have been done at my home in Florida, autographed at two stores, and was interviewed personally for a radio broadcast by Richard Lupoff, himself one of the more talented and lesser-known genre writers. He mentioned that he had a project at Berkley with no report for a year and a half. So when I got home I mentioned the matter to Susan Allison of Berkley, with this innocent surely-this-can't-be-true? attitude, and she got on it and contacted Lupoff. I think he never knew who had jogged her into action at last, but I was glad to help. He thought I was one of his un-friends, having been cautioned by Robert Silverberg, whose malign influences on my relations were described in part in *BiOgre.* I had been scheduled to stop in Los Angeles, but I said I didn't want to be interviewed by Harlan Ellison, so they simply cut LA out of the tour, leaving the local Dalton in the lurch. Another reader told me how the Dalton store still had signs up for the autographing, not knowing that the publisher had pulled the rug out from under. Apparently they were afraid to tell Ellison no, though I was ready to do so. More on that in Chapter 10. Taken as a whole, the tour was a waste of time; the publisher simply had nothing worth the effort. But it was typical of its inability to carry through an idea effectively. Had the editors told me how little they had, I would have declined the trip, but naturally they concealed the relevant information.

There was one more thing. That publisher was the distributor for Richard and Wendy Pini's graphic adaptation of Xanth #13, *Isle of View.* The ElfQuest folk did a nice job on the first half, finding an artist whose drawings were a delight. The first half of the novel was rendered into pictures as *Return to Centaur.* They planned to print 30,000 copies, but early reports were so good that Berkley required them to double it to 60,000. That last-minute change caused a delay while they got the extra printing done. The copies went out—and suddenly, it seemed like a week later but must have been longer, things slammed into reverse, and two-thirds of the copies were back on their hands. I have not been able to find out exactly what happened, but my impression is some character came along and said, "This stuff won't sell" and swept it off the shelves before the readers had much of a chance to see it. Thus it was a self-fulfilling prophecy. Parnassus is great on that sort of thing. And of course Berkley said it would take only one-third as many of the sequel, applying that sell-through ratio. The ratio that had occurred because *they* doubled the print order, then wouldn't let the copies be sold. I call it holding and hitting. Of course the Pinis took a financial beating, when they would have had a nice success, had they been allowed to market it their own way. They knew the nature of their market, as the big publisher did not. The big publishers are like bullies in the schoolyard, pushing around anyone they can, imposing their sometimes stupid rules, heedless of their own ignorance, and thus making commercial disasters of potential winners.

That was pretty much the clincher. If Berkley treated a Xanth adaptation that way, I sure as hell wasn't going to give it Xanth itself. Berkley had taken Adept off the best-seller list, and failed to make a reasonable effort on Mode, and torpedoed an aspect of Xanth. The handwriting on that wall was plain enough. Berkley was out.

Del Rey had lost my business because of the editing, but half a dozen years had passed and now could offer me what would have kept me there before: an editor other than Lester Del Rey. Owen Lock had visited me at my house in Florida and was a fascinating and erudite man, quite candid about aspects of publishing. I had a meal with him and editor Veronica Chapman, a dark-haired sweet-looking young woman who surely would not say "Boo" to me about anything I might write. Del Rey had put Xanth on the best-seller map, and would love to have it back. It was tempting, very tempting, because I had never wanted to leave Del Rey, and would have felt at home there. It could do what it had before, putting real muscle into marketing—the kind of treatment Avon and Berkley had so singularly (doubly?) failed to do.

But there were two problems. One was licensing: a clause in the contract that limited the publisher's right to sell copies of the novels to a given period, perhaps twelve years, after which the novels reverted to the author. For a series that never goes out of print, like Xanth, this is important, because it returns control to the author, who can then sell it again elsewhere, or leave it where it is, as he chooses. It really helps keep a publisher honest. That's why publishers don't like to do it. In Europe licensing is common, but in America it isn't, for books; a writer has to fight for it. I had done so, because I had learned what's-what on contracts. I had licensing on virtually all my other material, but my seventeen novels at Del Rey lacked it. A condition of my returning was that these be put on license. And the publisher had a policy against licensing. Owen hemmed and hawed, and didn't say no, but never could quite commit to that matter. But I insisted on it, so knew that this publisher was chancy. Publishers have ways of avoiding, "forgetting," nullifying, or reneging on commitments they don't like; I've had ample experience, to my cost. This wasn't worthwhile.

The other problem was the Xanth calendar. I had paid $30,000 for the art and assembly of a beautiful all-new calendar, and signed it over to Del Rey on a special deal: if it sold more than about 30,000 copies, I would get repaid for my original costs. There were several stages, but that was the essence. I knew it could do far better than that. The prior Xanth calendar, consisting mainly of recycled cover art, had sold that many, and this was an improved job. I was considering whether to return to that publisher, but after twice leaving it for cause, I was cautious. I wanted to see how they did with a relatively small project before I trusted them with the big one. So what happened? Del Rey printed about 33,000, which means that it would be almost impossible to crack over into paying territory for me. Owen had said that Del Rey was concerned that they could not do well enough with it to satisfy me, but I had figured that Del Rey would at least try to address its market, and would be pleasantly surprised. But once it was published, and we wanted to know how it was doing, Owen was chronically "out of the office" for the entire sales period. Instead came a report from the sales department: why did they have to handle this stuff, instead of the real Xanth? So evidently they resented it and didn't try very hard to market it. I had reports from stores: one had sold out the morning the calendar was put on sale, and latecomers couldn't get it because the publisher would not go back to press on it. Another store had never heard of it; a third had sold out. The sampling told the story. So it was a combination of bad marketing, inadequate printing, and determination not to admit obvious error. I received queries about the calendar from interested readers who couldn't find it on sale, and even one great suggestion from a reader: why didn't I do a Xanth calendar? He had no idea that it already existed. That showed the lack of promotion; how many readers who would have bought it never learned of its existence? When we set up Hi Piers, to market my books for those who couldn't find them, we had requests for the calendar, though it was now well out of date. So we queried Owen: we would buy the returned copies, at the regular wholesale rate, because *we* could sell them even if Del Rey couldn't. "Oh, we destroyed those," he replied. Right: thereby making it absolutely impossible to sell enough to pass the threshold for repayment. If there really had been any significant returns. But why should they have tried? They made a good profit, at my expense, by *not* selling more copies: by this device the publisher neatly hit me with a $30,000 loss and, of course, made that much more itself. I remarked on that to an agent, later. "I trusted them," I said ruefully. He just looked at me with that "You fool" expression. Of course I had been a fool. That was what really stuck in my craw, as I pondered whether to return to Del Rey. Judy-Lynn del Rey was dead; straight playing was dead; the bean counters were in charge there now. They had stuck me for a five-figure loss. That bit of cleverness bordering on bad faith may have cost them a seven-figure profit that they could have made on the return of Xanth, had they not alienated me on the rapprochement project. Which is why bean-counter companies tend to lose out in the long run to those with a larger view. Short-term profit can indeed mean long-term loss, as the American car companies discovered the hard way. So Del Rey was out—and when I finally made that decision, a weight lifted from me. An incubus was gone.

I had not done much business with Baen, but what there was was interesting. Jim Baen offered a copublishing deal, splitting the profits with me. So I tried it on two novels: the paperback edition of my collaboration with Robert Kornwise, *Through the Ice*, and an arranged collaboration with Mercedes Lackey, *If I Pay Thee Not in Gold*. They told me I would get a blizzard of paper from day one—all the documents relating to the process of printing, promoting, and so on. But there was none. Baen never tried to honor that. The actual money, when it came, late, was good, but I saw that this was another promise-them-anything, give-them-nothing-much publisher. That abrogation of the verbal understanding, and the actual violation of contracts by late payments, satisfied me that this was not the place to put my major series. Later I did agree to place a series of collaborations there, because there wasn't much market for them the moment Xanth came off the best-seller lists; we agreed on terms and expected the contracts. Baen did not deliver them. After more than six months with no explanation, and five ignored queries from my agent, I had had enough; I dumped the deal. *Then* came the explanation: Baen had wanted to take foreign rights, for which I have my own foreign agent. Apparently the publisher had figured that if it waited long enough, we'd grow so desperate that we'd agree to anything. For that I have a maxim publishers should heed: they may push around poor writers, but they can't do it to rich writers. And some of the poor writers later get rich, and they do remember. I'm one. Baen was out.

TOR had published a number of my less-commercial novels, and done well with them. I liked TOR's boss, Tom Doherty, personally; he was my age and a genial man. His competence had advanced TOR from a fledging publisher to arguably the major one in the genre, in the course of a decade or so. Was it time to give it my major commercial work? Well, TOR wasn't perfect. It wouldn't pay the size advances other publishers offered, and it had very few actual best-sellers. All my TOR advances had readily earned out, but I actually made more money elsewhere. When I had sold it a group of novels, the contract specified publication within eighteen months; TOR had actually taken several years. One book, *But What of Earth*, TOR had seemed to want to write off; only when it became apparent that I would give it no new novels until that one was scheduled did *Earth* finally see print. At one point its accounts had been so disastrously wrong that I sent a stiff letter detailing the errors. "Thank you, thank you, thank you!" chief editor Beth Meacham wrote—and got the errors fixed. Now that was interesting. I make it a point to read and understand contracts and statements of account, after getting shafted by Ballantine in the early days, and always challenged incorrect reports. Ballantine had blacklisted me rather than correct the errors; Del Rey I regarded as a different publisher, and its accounts were squeaky-clean; the only error I caught, about the royalty rate of an early novel, turned out to be my misunderstanding. (The matter of the Xanth Calendar wasn't incorrect accounting, but incorrect marketing.) Avon took its time but did fix theirs; Berkley had some spectacular errors, but fixed them, and when I audited them, they were clean. But TOR had actually thanked me. I was pleasantly surprised.

TOR had done well with the novels, probably better than would have been the case with on-time publication, so I hadn't made an issue. The fact that I don't challenge a given violation doesn't necessarily mean that I don't notice it; I choose my ground carefully. Some fights aren't worth it. Indeed, few publishers seem to have understood my underlying reasons for doing or not doing business with them. Money counts, and editing, and promotion, and so on, but so do the hidden things. I'm paying attention in ways that they are not, judging where my best interests lie. I confess that sometimes I get the impression that I am dealing with relative idiots, but that's their problem, had they the wit to realize it, not mine. I have not been phenomenally stupid since childhood.

In short, TOR's assets were okay, and debits were mild. I was mindful of the statement Tom Doherty had made to me, that Avon's printing of 375,000 paperback copies was exactly half what it should have been for the big best-seller lists. I'd love to have a printing of 750,000 copies! But TOR wasn't much for big advances, which indicated a publisher's real commitment, and because of the importance of Xanth to my career, there had to be a competitive advance. However, in this case TOR was ready to play with the big boys. But other publishers with whom I had not done much, if any, business were interested, and they did have considerable clout on the marketplace, so my agent let them put in their bids. All the offers were for $250,000 per novel, but only one publisher came through with the subtle but vitally important term: licensing. That made the decision easy: TOR. And so Xanth came at last to TOR. Who made a fine effort on the hardcover, multiplying its sales tenfold, but printed only 400,000 paperback copies, 40,000 of which were used for the "Companions of Xanth" computer game, and took Xanth off the national best-seller lists. Sigh. That 360,000 net printing was, you guessed it, less than half the figure Tom Doherty had implied his publisher would print. The editor, Beth Meacham, asked amazed how I had ever gotten the notion that more would be printed. She really didn't know? That was hard to believe. Well, I had been taken. Again. That meant the next time that publisher pulled a fast one, I responded with greater force, as will be seen in Chapter 8. I learn slowly, but well.

S e v e n

DYNAMICS

So are publishers really as rapacious and idiotic as they seem? Yes and no. Just as the intelligence and conscience of a lynch mob may be less than that of any individual person within it, so may the net savvy of a publisher be below that of any of its components. But the publisher also has its own perspective, which differs from that of human beings in much the manner of predator from prey. It's like politics: what makes sense to a liberal may be nonsense to a conservative. Much depends on the viewpoint. Mine is that of the writer, so this will not be a friendly analysis, but it should clarify some matters. Those who aren't interested in technical matters should skip this chapter. Here's how it works:

First, it must be recognized that power will tell. There is a thought experiment that is instructive. Take a ten-dollar bill and offer it to a person, on condition that he/she find one other person with whom to share it. Of course Person A will make the deal, and will soon find a Person B to cooperate with. So they each get $5. Or do they? Soon A will realize that there is nothing in the deal that specifies the shares; he can change the terms. So he offers B $4, and B will take it, because that's still better than nothing. Or $3, or $2. Whatever the market will bear. If B turns it down, he loses easy money, and A will make the deal with someone else. So chances are that A will wind up with most of the benefit, because he has a superior bargaining position: he controls the money. Okay—now translate this to publishing. The publisher is Person A, and the writer is Person B. Guess who gets the better deal. It's not discrimination, it's not cheating, it's the nature of the game. So the publisher makes most of the rules, and the writer agrees to them or gets left out of the game. Thus the dynamics are those of the publisher rather than those of the writer. Perhaps if writers ran the show, they would be making similarly sharp deals and foolish errors. But they aren't.

The bean counters have a formula for printings. Indeed, Parnassus is formula driven. Formulas are the salvation of those who lack real intelligence or judgment. They look at the sell-through for the first year—that is, how many copies of a book are actually reported back from booksellers as sold—and limit the print order for the author's next book to that. This might seem reasonable, except for the actual way of sales. There are always returns, because some stores don't put all their books on the shelves, and may even return whole boxes of books unopened. I once worked for a distributor, and saw the way of it: the store manager gets one look at the cover, and says "No, we don't carry that kind here." So it goes back unseen by anyone else. Maybe some readers would be interested, but they don't even know that the book exists. Because the store manager objected to the partially clad young woman on the cover, or thought the book would be dull, or had space only for the existing best-seller list, or had some other private agenda. Sure, other stores may carry it, but if it is a one-bookstore town, many who might have bought it will not have the chance. So that book is returned. It's a self-fulfilling prophecy: what the manager doesn't think will sell (or doesn't want to sell) doesn't sell, because it isn't given the chance. The publisher doesn't want to pay the shipping charges for returned books, so they make it easy: just tear the cover off and return that instead. What happens to the rest of the book? It's against the law to sell it, but many do get sold; I've had fan letters from readers who liked the books, but wondered why they weren't sold with covers on. It's a dandy way for an unscrupulous person to make more money: why accept only part of the cover price, when he can tear the cover off, sell the book for half price, and keep all of that? So the cover is returned, and the author's next print order is reduced accordingly, even though his actual sales (including coverless copies) were good. Other books are honestly put out for sale, but don't sell all at once; some folk visit a bookstore every week, or every month, or less often. They may buy a lot when they do visit, stocking up for the interval—but by that time many books have been removed from the shelves and returned. The booksellers just can't keep all the books on sale forever; their space is limited, so they focus on the fastest sellers and send the slower ones back. You guessed it: after the first week or so, a fantasy novel is apt to become a slow seller.

So in a general way, the more copies are printed and distributed, the more sales there are—but also more returns. Obviously a publisher doesn't want too many returns, because they represent losses for the costs of printing and shipping. Suppose 100,000 paperbacks are shipped, and 50,000 are returned: that's a 50 percent sell-through. Is that a disaster? No, it's about average for paperbacks. If it costs, say, a dollar a copy to print, and the sale price is five dollars, you might think a 50 percent sell-through would still make a profit. That is, $250,000 in sales, minus the $100,000 printing costs. But of course it's not that simple, because the publisher doesn't get all that money, it gets only maybe 30 percent of it, and it has editing and overhead and such to pay for. So the dynamics can get complicated. For now, let's assume that a 50 percent sell-through is the break-even point. The author gets royalties on 50,000 copies. So if the publisher doubles the print order to 200,000, and more sales are made, that's good for the author, but if the sell-through drops to 40 percent it may be bad for the publisher. That is, 80,000 copies are sold, so the author gets royalties on an additional 30,000 copies, but the publisher has losses on 70,000 more returns. While if it lowers the print order to 50,000, and the sell-through rises to 75 percent, that's bad for the author but may be good for the publisher. The author gets royalties on 37,500 copies, and the publisher has only 12,500 returns. So the publisher tends to underprint. And that tends to drive the author crazy, as my own reactions of the prior chapter demonstrate. And yes, when Berkley cut the print order in my best-selling series, the sell-through was in the neighborhood of 73 percent.

But it isn't necessarily feasible for a publisher to cut down too far, because there are certain initial costs, such as the advance paid to the author, the wage paid the editor, the rental on the building, the art for the cover, and so on. Let's say that the publisher's initial costs for a paperback original, including everything, are $100,000. If it sells 50,000 copies, at $5 per, and receives 40 percent of the money, it will make $100,000. Right: it breaks even. If it made those sales by a 50 percent sell-through of a 100,000 printing, what happens if it cuts the printing on the next? Its sell-through may rise to 75 percent, and so its losses on the printing are cut. But the other expenses, such as the $25,000 advance paid the author, don't shrink. The author may have a good contract with

8 percent royalties, so he earns 40¢ a copy, or $20,000. That advance has not earned out, so the publisher is $5,000 in the hole. If the printing is cut, the publisher will be further in the hole. But if the publisher doubles the print order, and the sell-through drops to 40 percent, it sells 80,000 copies, receives $160,000, and is ahead despite grudgingly paying the author another $7,000 when his advance earns out and royalties are owing. And the editorial, art, rental, promotion, and similar fixed costs don't rise at all. So it may be better for the publisher to absorb the cost of the extra returns, for the sake of the larger picture. Up to a point. Too high a return ratio could wipe out everything despite increased sales.

So the real issue is between sell-through and total copies sold. A printing of 100,000 with a sell-through of 40 percent might lose because it wouldn't earn back the initial costs, while a printing of 25,000 with a sell-through of 100 percent would lose also. There's another dynamic with respect to the author: royalties are more or less fixed, but advances are negotiable. My early novels all earned out their advances and paid royalties, some of them ten or twenty or even fifty times over. *A Spell for Chameleon* had an advance of $5,000, but earned more than $300,000. I may have had the genre record for the number of novels remaining in print and paying royalties at the same time: about seventy-five. I thought that was great. But I lost ground to others whose sales were less but whose advances were larger. What happened?

One of the things about the publisher mind-set is the way the advance keys into promotion. It is said that folk value only what they pay for. So if the water you drink costs cents per gallon, and the air you breathe is free, you hardly think about them, though they are two of the things your body needs most. While a little diamond ring that makes no physical difference to your welfare you may pay a fortune for, and value accordingly. If a publisher pays a million dollars for a novel, you bet that novel is going to receive a lot more care and attention than the one it got for five thousand dollars. Or the calendar it got for nothing. Even if the cheap one is actually a better piece of writing than the expensive one. So while I was satisfied to be earning royalties on my titles, there were other writers who didn't earn extra royalties, yet whom the publishers evidently valued more. Because of the advances. The publishers worked harder to promote those writers, not because they cared about them as people—does Satan care for the marks he corrupts?—but because they needed to sell enough copies to get back their investment.

So why did they pay those larger advances to others and not to me? Because I wasn't demanding them; only rarely did I make an issue of that, and I won my case when I did. While other writers were pushing for the largest advances they could get. When I saw how I was losing ground, I finally had my agent go for the larger advances, and the price of some of my novels went from four figures to six figures. I didn't do it for the money, but to encourage the publishers to promote my novels more effectively. Thus *Macroscope* had an advance of $5,000, while the similarly sized and researched *Tatham Mound* went for $350,000 to the same publisher. The former paid back over a dozen times its advance, while the latter may never come close to earning out, but you bet I made a lot more money on it.

But why would publishers pay big advances in the first place? Even the small advances seldom earn out, and the big ones generally fall farther short, I believe. So publishers are taking large losses on their big novels, with respect to the advances. Is this more idiocy? Not entirely. This is where the dynamics come in again. If a publisher breaks even with 50,000 paperback copies sold, it doesn't do twice as well with 100,000 sold, assuming that the sell-through remains reasonably constant. It does much better. Because most of its costs have been covered at the lower level. The higher the sales go, the better the ratio of profit to sales.

I don't have figures for most publishers—they tend to treat them as secrets—but I do have some. The indications are that for every dollar a publisher has to pay in royalties, above the earned-out advance, it is making two or three dollars itself. Let's say a book sells a lot of copies, and makes a 32 percent profit. That is, 32¢ of each dollar of the cover price. The author may do handsomely, getting 8¢ of that dollar, but the publisher is getting 24¢ for itself. I suspect that's the way it is with *A Spell for Chameleon*. Three-quarters of a million dollars profit on one novel? Yes, it may be, though I suspect the publisher will never tell. And sixteen other novels with that publisher, building similarly. So suppose Del Rey had known it would be like that, at the outset: how big an advance would it have been prepared to pay? Suppose it had paid half a million dollars, and only half of that ever earned out? It still would have made half a million dollars for itself. Thus its nominal quarter-million-dollar loss would be an actual profit of twice that amount. Thus it's really a question of how the pie is to be shared. Would you take half of a million dollars—or insist on three-quarters of it, and watch the author take his novel to a different publisher who was willing to go fifty-fifty? Publishers are realists in this respect; most will give up some of the pie for the sake of the remaining riches it offers. Good agents know the figures, and bargain shrewdly for the writers they represent. Which means that the agents, who make ten or fifteen percent of what their writers get, wind up with maybe $50,000 on a single sale—and are worth it to the writers.

But I have remarked, without smiling, that publishers tend to be idiots. So they make mistakes—sometimes horrendous ones. Every little part of the big organization is busy covering its own ass, of course, and so sales can conflict with editing, and accounting with promotion. Publishers who get it all together can do better than those that don't. But even when they get together, they can follow a flawed philosophy and really mess up. They tend to go for the mega-best-seller, forgetting that the best money is usually made in the quiet steady sales of the backlist, and so they tend to ignore the "midlist" offerings. This can lead to mischief in several ways. They tend to orient on last year's megahit, which may prove to be passé this year, so their pale imitations are always a step behind the times. They also may have to compete for their prospective winner with other publishers, who are just as rich and stupid; so the price can escalate beyond reason. And when they get it, they can bobble their play and throw away their victory. They can also encounter plain bad luck, as sports figures crash their images or politicians are exposed, rendering their expensive ghost-written titles valueless. So every year there are big hopes—and big disappointments. While little-suspected, largely ignored titles rise to the heights, surprising everyone. Waller's *The Bridges of Madison County* is an example. I understand that this maiden effort by an unknown professor attracted so little notice that it was sold to a publisher by an agent's secretary—then spent years on the hardcover best-seller lists.

So will publishers get halfway smart and focus again on plain, solid, plotted, lucidly styled fiction in many genres? Don't bet on it. They think they know better.

Another frustration for me was another bean-counter formula: they would print ten times as many paperback copies as they had hardcover copies. Normally that is the ratio of sales. But I was never strong in hardcover, and my ratio of paperback sales to hardcover sales was more like twenty to one. Thus the formula stifled my paperback sales. I tried to get through to editors about this, but editors are like doctors in this respect: they don't listen to the one most concerned. One editor denied that they used such a formula, though I had the figures showing that they were indeed following it. So instead of putting me on the hardcover best-seller lists, they were taking me off the paperback best-seller lists. The one-year sell-through formula was also bad for me, because my novels keep on selling. At least that can be corrected by going back to press as new orders come. But sometimes they balk, refusing to go back to press regardless, because that would be like admitting their mistake. It's maddening.

However, the story hardly ends with the publishers. It isn't just a matter of paying bills and printing copies. One of the vital aspects of the business of writing is distribution. A publisher doesn't just print up 100,000 copies of *Awful Space Crap* or *Sickly Sweet Romance* and set them on the doorstep for passersby to buy. It has to get them out to the stores across the nation. And there are outfits that do just that. They are called distributors.

The distributor takes the printed copies from the publishers and parcels them out to the myriad little bookstores, newsstands, grocery stores, or holes in the wall that sell books. It does its own accounts, essentially buying the books in large quantities from the publishers and selling them in small quantities to the stores. It has its own regular delivery routes. I worked for one, once, and spent a lot of time making up parcels of books and magazines for individual stores according to the list the manager made out, and driving the route around part of the states of Vermont and New Hampshire. That's why I have a notion of the reaction of store managers to books, and how many titles get returned without ever going on the shelves. The publisher has to reimburse the distributor for the returns. And for this service, the distributor may receive 20 percent of the cover price, or more than twice the amount the author is likely to see on it. Yes, it pays better to move a book than to write it, in that sense. But let's (with an effort) be fair: the distributor has to handle every book physically, while the author doesn't touch it after he turns in the manuscript. He still gets his 8 percent of every copy sold. The guy driving the delivery truck would be glad to change places with him. I know; I have played both roles.

But distributors suffer similar effects of scale as do the publishers. It's not just a mom-and-pop business delivering books in the manner of a newspaper route. They are linked from the local to the national level, and are multimillion-dollar businesses. Know what that means? Right: they start thinking of themselves as the masters rather than the servants. They don't just distribute the books the publishers offer, they decide what books they'll take, and even what publishers they will handle. There are a few big publishers and many small ones, and the small ones are apt to be frozen out. No (another heroic effort to be fair), it isn't necessarily invidious discrimination. Small publishers can be uneconomic to handle. They have maybe one title in six months, and there's no promotion, and nobody much cares about it, and it'll probably be returned. Why bother, when the big publishers have hundreds of thousands of selling copies? Small publishers are likely to have weak finances, so someone may get stuck for the price of the books. And there are so many of them! Why deal with the grains of sand on the beach, when it's a hell of a lot more efficient to toss a few boulders on the truck? So small publishers get the smelly end of the stick because that's the end of the economy of scale that they are on; it's inherent.

But this necessity to choose can readily become abusive. There are stories of extra payoffs to get certain books distributed, regardless of their merit. If the publisher doesn't pay, its books don't get out to the market. So to stay in business, it pays, in addition to the official rates for the service. I don't have details on that; naturally no one gets very specific. But the smell is in the air.

Also, they can get arbitrary about titles. Small publishers especially can get hung on whims: they may have good titles, but are doomed because distributors won't take them, no reasons given. Thus we have faceless functionaries deciding what the public may see. Just because they can.

Then there are the stores themselves. They choose from among the titles the publishers publish and the distributors distribute. They don't necessarily choose wisely. Some want only the best-sellers, which makes their offerings derivative. Do you ever wonder why the latest Stephen King novel is in every store? (Which is not to disparage King; he has good material, and his daughter Naomi was a leading fan of mine.) You bought it in the first store, and hoped to find something else elsewhere, but the racks mirror each other. That's why. To them, books are just a product, and King sells better than Brand X. Your desire as a customer hardly matters; you're not economic.

So are there ways around this, to get other titles into the stores so they have a chance? Yes, but they aren't necessarily nice ways. The reading public is treated like a vast ignorant clod, and unfortunately that assessment is often borne out by the numbers. The public buys what is laid out in front of it, and doesn't miss what isn't. Oh, some stores do care, and do make an effort, but too few to make much of a difference. Thus a book on a prominent shelf in the front of the store sells copies, and one in the back nook doesn't. So how does a given title get a place in the sun? Right. It does it the old-fashioned way: it buys it. Books are not prominently displayed because the management believes they are the best books that readers will most appreciate, they are there because of something similar to what in radio is called payola. If a publisher wants a book up front, it buys the shelf for that week. It's that simple, in a business that in other ways isn't necessarily simple. It comes under the heading of "promotion." Does it work? You bet. When Morrow paid for shelf space for *And Eternity*, that week it made the *Publisher's Weekly* hardcover national best-seller list—the only one of my hardcover titles ever to make such a list. As far as I know, the only one ever to have such shelf space bought for it. The other titles didn't have a chance.

So much for the little stores. What about the big ones—the chains? There the impact is multiplied. When you buy a front shelf, they double their order, and your book goes on display in every one of their stores.

And if the big chains, who have their own distribution, decide not to take your book, the publisher may cancel its publication, because about half its market is eliminated right there. Thus the faceless folk in the chains are deciding to an increasing extent what may or may not be published. They can be just as arbitrary as anyone else. When *BiOgre* was published in hardcover, Waldenbooks took it and B Dalton did not, so it lost a major market share. Even so, the publisher had to go back to press. How well would it have done, had B Dalton carried it? We'll never know. Would they have lost money on it? Surely not. But the big boys have the power to be arbitrary, and they exercise it. Of course B Dalton, once the leading bookseller nationwide, made too many such bad decisions, and became #2—until Waldenbooks lost its compass, and its sales and market position eroded in turn. Mismanagement does lead to consequences, in time, and idiocy is hardly limited to publishers.

So how do I feel about those big boys? Mixed. Their arbitrariness has cost me and my readers more than once. But they were the ones

who helped make me a national best-seller in paperback. They are driven
by money, and larger sales mean more money, and if they think a given
title will sell, they'll give it a push and see if they can help it really sell.
They are computerized, and keep close track of exactly what is and is
not moving, and they reorder rapidly when something does move. In
short, they specialize in the real world of sales, rather than some untested
notion, such as "fantasy won't sell." They figured that Anthony fantasy
could make it, so they tried. And while the smaller old-fashioned stores
were ignoring me, the big chains sold most of my copies, and put me
on the map. No, I know the big chains didn't give half a crap about me
personally, or the quality of my writing; they just evened the playing
field and went with what worked. And lo, when more readers had an
even chance to try my fiction, they liked it. So for all that philosophically
I distrust the big chains, and know that they don't have the welfare of
literature at heart, privately I do appreciate them. And for all the concern
about their supposed bad effect on literature, and the way they drive
conventional bookstores out of business, I think they are only half-guilty.
Because they didn't take over the market so much as they added to it;
they put their stores in malls and made books readily available to the
public. They did the marketing job the old stores should have done, but
weren't doing. And each individual store in the chain does have its own
people, who in my experience care just as much or little about literature
as those of regular bookstores do. I do not accept the notion that only
things published a century or more ago are literature, or that only things
written in obscure language are worthwhile. The material that the average
person likes to read is literature too, and it's better that he be reading
it, than that he be letting his mind sink into a slough of inertia. If the
chains make reading easier, they are doing more good for the world than
the elitists who seek to channel everyone into the limited elitist mode.

So if the publisher does effective promotion, and gets wide distribution, and buys decent placement on the shelves, it can make a world
of difference in the sales of a given book. But there are constraints here,
too. There are thousands of books published every year; they can't all fit
in any one store, let alone all take the prominent shelf. There has to be
a pretty severe selection process. This is mainly the province of the publishers. They publish many things, but they promote only a few. Most
they pigeonhole conveniently in the ghettos of the genres, where a certain
level of sales are pretty much guaranteed. They are unlikely to take losses

on those titles—but also unlikely to have best-sellers there either. Rare is the writer who manages to break out of that dread prison. Most are doomed to be locked in for their entire careers. Because they are categorized by their first books, and publishers and distributors seem constitutionally unable to recognize that a given writer is capable of writing in more than one genre. On occasion they manage to jump from one ship to another, as John Jakes did, going from fantasy to historical fiction in a package deal. Sometimes they escape by writing the same material, but getting the genre label removed; Dean Koontz's sales took off when he finally prevailed on his publisher to do that. Sometimes they achieve the recognition of the genre-ignorant critics by pretending that they don't write what they write, as Kurt Vonnegut did. Sometimes they remain within the genre, but attract enough readers beyond it to achieve larger success, as Larry Niven did in science fiction and I did in fantasy. I seem to have many readers who read no fantasy except for mine. But most writers will not be seen beyond the genre enclosures. Because the publishers do not care to take the risk of marketing them more widely, and aren't about to put any money into promotion so that outside readers might learn of their existence. The single greatest source for new readers appears to be word of mouth. But if the publishers don't realize that, they don't get the copies out. Too many of my readers are looking for my books and not finding them, even if they learn that they have been published. I suspect other writers have the same problem.

I was lucky enough to get some effective promotion and distribution, back when Judy-Lynn was running Del Rey, and so I had the pleasure of making the big best-seller lists for a decade. That was nice, but it became apparent that those lists are imperfect. Some best-selling books aren't listed, like the Bible. One writer sued because a too-low position on the *New York Times* list damaged his situation. The *Times* defense was not that its list was accurate, but that a person couldn't claim defamation for *not* being listed, even if he *should* have been. Too bad, because some contracts specify bonuses when a book makes such lists, and failure to list a book that should have been listed does indeed hurt that writer. The *Times* list uses a ballot of suggested titles that key booksellers fill out; if a book isn't there, it may not make the list despite its sales, because the *Times* didn't see it coming. Similarly, an anticipated title may make the list, though it shouldn't have. I believe I have had both happen with my titles. In addition, sometimes the lists are stacked;

shills are sent to the key stores to buy copies, to jack up the apparent sales. It's not supposed to happen, but it does. But even when accurate, such lists can be inaccurate, odd as that may sound. Because what they actually measure is velocity rather than total sales. If a title sells rapidly for a few weeks, it gets listed; if it then drops dead, the listing is still there in the record. Slower, steady sellers may sell more copies, cumulatively, without making the lists. Thus my leading paperback seller, *A Spell for Chameleon*, with about a million sold, never made a significant best-seller list. I'm sure my experience is not unique. Readers should take such lists with a grain of salt; they are an indication, but not the final word.

When a publisher tells me that it just filled the orders it received for my books, I know that it was acting like a salesman who stays home and waits for clients to come to him. He will not have the success of one who hustles. And I know that the publisher chose to put forth its best efforts for some other writer, not for me. And I look for another publisher. Because otherwise I will soon enough be back in the pack, unknown outside the genre stockade. I saw it happen to other writers, some who had scaled the heights, and resolved that if I ever reached those heights, not to go gently into that good night. Because I saw that if success is likened to a surfer's ride on a big wave, he had better not tumble off that wave until it has run its course. It has been some ride, as publishers have tried to denature my text, or underprint, or just plain renege on commitments. Sometimes I feel like a beautiful woman: every man seeks her favor, and she suspects it's not her mind they are interested in, but when she mentions lasting commitment, bbrrrtt! and they're gone. She knows she won't be beautiful forever, so she has some concern to achieve her potential before her appeal fades. Like the petunia in the onion patch, she doesn't necessarily find it easy.

Let's conclude with a direct analysis of one novel for which I have comprehensive figures. This is *Through the Ice*, my collaboration with Robert Kornwise. I finished it in July 1988, and it was published a year later in hardcover by the small press Underwood-Miller. It paid an advance of $2,000 in two installments: at the time of the contract signature, and at publication. I sent the first payment to the Robert Kornwise Memorial Fund, kept the second, and then tithed the paperback royalties. In the course of five years Underwood sold 3,091 copies at assorted prices, paying me a total $5,634.43. Small press is not big business, because it doesn't get much distribution or publicity.

Meanwhile Baen Books paid a one-dollar advance for the paperback rights and published its edition April 1992. This was a copublishing deal, wherein the author shared the profits evenly. It did promotion, including the distribution of advertising T-shirts, and in the course of two years shipped 188, 458 copies out to booksellers. Returns for that period were 79,729. Had the royalties been 8 percent, I would have received $51,410.13 at that point, plus $9,342.24 Canadian income, bringing the total to a generous $60,000. I actually received $94,778.94, which the publisher informed me was the equivalent of a 19.5 percent royalty rate less half the costs incurred. So on the American sales, in crudely rounded-off terms, I made about $85,000 instead of about $50,000, or an effective royalty rate of about 13 percent. So it was a good deal for me, commercially. But more important, it gave me the figures so I could fathom what the publisher actually made on such a novel. A normal 8 percent deal would have paid the author about $50,000, and the publisher would have had $120,000. This wasn't a best-seller; it was just a novel buried in the throng. The publisher could have paid an advance of $100,000, and marked the author as being in the hole by $50,000, while actually having a profit of $70,000 the author didn't know about. That's why publishers are close-fisted about their real figures. All these writers who think that their publishers are losing money on them, because their advances haven't earned out, and maybe feeling guilty because of it, or maybe getting their royalties on other novels docked to make up the "loss," are living in a fool's hell. The publishers just don't want to share any more of the pie than they have to, and they keep the writers in the dark as much as possible. It's much easier to deal with an ignorant writer. That's why any writer who is going anywhere needs a good agent. The writer may still be a fool about money, but the agent helps get him a bigger slice of pie. Sometimes the agent makes such a shrewd deal that the writer winds up better off than the publisher. That's a fool's paradise, because he won't get any more such deals. I've had those, too.

E i g h t

COLLABORATIONS

B y the time I had done a hundred and ten books (that is, through 1994), twenty-five of them were collaborations. Not quite one in four. That's a substantial number. What led me to this proportion, when I have no trouble writing and placing my solo efforts?

Back when I first started selling, in 1962, I also joined a fan organization, the National Fantasy Fan Federation or NFFF or N3F. I never was much of a fan in the usual sense; conventions and fanzines (amateur magazines) didn't turn me on so much as the prospect of finding other seriously hopeful writers. NFFF turned out to be so sloppily organized and run that I dropped it after a year, as someone else put it "for the usual reasons." But I did get a few contacts. An occasional pro and active fan named Alma Hill contacted me and several others who had joined about the same time, and organized us into what she called the Pro/2 group. Among the others were Robert E. "Rem" Margroff, H. James Hotaling, and soon one brought in by Margroff, Frances T. Hall. We exchanged our pieces for comment, and I feel that all of us profited from this, because we all took it seriously. This was exactly what I had been looking for. Before long I had gotten collaborative stories published with each of those three. Then I had a bright historical notion, was uncertain whether I could handle it myself, so more or less dragged Frances Hall into it with me. In due course we had completed *The Pretender*, set in ancient Babylon. The original notion was mine, of a religion that tried to prevent people from joining it. We discussed outline and scenes, and I think I wrote some and she wrote some, and then we went over each other's, integrating them into the whole. When a decade went by without success in getting it published, I revised it into a science fiction novel and we placed it with the small press Borgo for hardcover, and later with TOR for paperback. Frances was a good collaborator, and I stand by the quality of the novel. Later we had a blowout and became estranged, but I don't regret working with her in Pro/2 or our collaborative story "The Message," or the novel. So that was the first collaborative novel I wrote, though not the first to be published. We split the money evenly, not trying to determine who contributed how much of what, and that has been the rule on most of my collaborations.

My second collaborative novel was with Robert Margroff, Rem. Again, I had the idea, of a system of justice that enforced law abidance by criminals via a ring on finger or toe that generated prohibitive pain when they erred. It was inspired by a fairy tale about a prince who wore just such a ring. Rem wrote the first draft, and I revised it. *The Ring* sold quickly and was published as an Ace Special in 1968.

That was the first of seven collaborations I eventually did with Rem. The second derived from our Pro/2 activity: Rem attended a world science convention and gave us a full report. I remarked that the light spirit he showed there could be turned to fiction, and challenged him to try a funny fantasy piece. He did, and it worked; it became a hilariously naughty novel, *The Rumpleskin Brat*. But he had trouble selling it, and finally I undertook to rework it to see if I could get it sold, because I didn't like seeing his effort be wasted on a project I had encouraged. I have a fanatic loyalty to any piece of writing I associate with, and can't rest until it has found its natural repose in print. He was trying an agent, who placed the collaboration, but did it in such a way—lying to the publisher about the rights we had agreed to sell, then blaming me when I held to the original agreement—that I refused to have anything further to do with him. The publisher retitled it *The E.S.P. Worm*, which was okay though not as good as Rem's original title.

Later yet Rem approached me about a fantasy novel, *Dragon's Gold*, that he felt should have found a publisher but hadn't. I thought so too, so tackled it as a collaboration, making some wholesale changes. I converted a brother into a sister, and added a romantic theme. He had one character, a half brother, who got killed at the end. I felt he was too nice a person to die, so I banished him to an alternate reality instead. Rem was not completely pleased with all my changes, but went along with them. We showed it to editor Beth Meacham of TOR, who liked the novel and said it was obviously the first of a series, because of the alternate reality setup. It was? We hastily agreed, and thus came to be the five-novel series that did well with TOR. Rem, impressed, told me to ignore any future objections he might have to what I did, but I knew as well as any how sheerly lucky we had been, and paid careful attention to all his points, which were always good ones. He was a solid writer, who just happened to lack the stylistic flair that scores on editors. Rem did the hard work of writing the original novels, while I revised and retyped them into my computer. So was it fair to split the money evenly? I feel it was, because though he was working harder than I was on them, I provided better marketing because my name now brought higher prices and better sales. In fact I could earn more money working alone, because publishers paid more for my individual work, and I didn't have to split the money. So my contribution was only partly in the revising. That doesn't mean that I don't value the novels; I feel Rem did good work, and I am glad to have participated. It's just that the vagaries of success, that brought me fame as much by chance as by talent, changed the dynamics of collaboration. Early in our association I had thought that Rem was more likely to have such success than I was, but it turned out that I was the one who, to adapt a saying of my high school days, got dinked by the dangling dork of destiny.

Another collaborator came by fickle chance. The realm of amateur magazines, called fanzines, ranges from polite to internecinely combative. Some fan editors—faneds—are great human beings, and some are turds. I never suffered fools or knaves—or turds—gladly, so I am proud of the roster of enemies I made in fandom by calling the shots accurately. There were those who came at me with guns blazing, who soon retreated again into their festering holes. Few, if any, ever cared to challenge me twice to my face, mainly because I did my homework before shooting off my mouth and could support anything I said—and I could say it well. But some turds did not play fair; they would change the letters of contributors to make them look foolish. You can't beat a cheater in his own fanzine. Once such, out to get me, printed a derogatory comment by one Roberto Fuentes. I remembered my year in Spain, so I wrote directly to Fuentes to inquire whether he was Spanish. He replied no, he was Cuban—and that his remarks about me had been distorted. He had a most interesting background, and was a remarkably intelligent and knowledgeable person. Because English was not his first language, he could not write for American publication, but he had endless notions. One thing led to another, and soon we were involved in a Latin America/ time travel collaboration, *Dead Morn*. It didn't sell. Meanwhile Roberto and his wife and son visited us, and my daughter Penny and I went with them to see a judo class in Tampa. Roberto had once been the judo champion of Cuba, before the Castro revolution that drove him out. While watching the class, I found my mind turning to fiction, and I worked out a story, "Kiai!" for which Roberto supplied the authentic martial arts detail. It didn't sell. We did another, and a third, and finally put them all together as chapters in a novel, *Kiai!*, which was bounced by several publishers. Then the TV series *Kung Fu* started, and suddenly there was interest in martial arts, and two publishers asked to see our novel again. Thus came to be the five-novel martial arts series. It was cut off prematurely by an editor with a grudge against me, and Roberto went to Miami, where he became a top insurance salesman before having problems. And finally, the better part of two decades after it was written, *Dead Morn* was sold, for more money than all the martial arts novels combined. All because a turd faned had printed only the critical part of a letter about me.

Other collaborations developed in similarly diverse ways. Martin Greenberg approached me about doing a collaborative anthology of stories. As it happened, there are some stories that are not well-known that I feel should be better known. For example, "The Night of Hoggy Darn" by R. M. McKenna, a writer held in high esteem for other works. Actually, I understand there is a question whether this story is really by him, or by a person of the same name. I heard that a publisher approached his estate for permission to reprint "Hoggy Darn," and was told that McKenna had written no such story. Interesting. Regardless who wrote it, I remember it as an outstanding adventure. There was another in the *Magazine of Fantasy & Science Fiction* whose title and author I don't remember (but I think was "Myrrha" by Gary Jennings) only the editor's succinct introduction "This is a horrible story." Yes it is, brilliantly so. So I agreed to do the anthology.

So what happened? None of my favorite genre stories were included. How did this happen? Because others did the initial research in the magazines, digging up stories for me to approve or disapprove, and their tastes weren't the same as mine. There were good stories, just not my favorites. So I chose the best, in this way appreciating the problem I think most awards have: the judges aren't given the chance to choose what they deem to be the best material published, only the best of a preselected roster. In addition, one of the other editors had a favorite piece, so I agreed to include it, though it didn't rate as well with me. Then he rearranged the order of the stories without my knowledge so that his choice was first in the volume. That messed up my introduction, which had been written with a different leading story in mind. It also caused the volume to start with a story that would not really grab the average reader. Without putting too fine a point on this at this time, I will say that I have a fair notion of what the average genre reader likes— and the average critic lacks that notion, if he even cares. Naturally *Uncollected Stars* did not do well on the market. I decided not to do that sort of project again.

Later I was approached for another such project. But this was an original anthology, not a reprint anthology, and there was only one other editor, who seemed likely to be more responsive to my judgments. Also, it related to a subject I felt needed promotion: the situation of the American Indians. Thus I agreed to collaborate with Richard Gilliam on *Tales from the Great Turtle*, an anthology of stories by or about American Indians. Richard did most of the work, while I reviewed the stories he presented and wrote an introduction and a story, "Tortoise Shell," for it. Because the money was tight, I put money for advances in to supplement the publisher's advance, and took no payment for my own story. If the volume earns more money, I'll get paid. Richard hardly got the value of his time back, either. But it does have some good pieces by or about American Indians, and I think is worth doing. Once.

Bill Fawcett approached me about projects he and his wife were interested in, such as a series of gamebooks based on the genre realms of established writers. His wife was Jody Lynn Nye, a woman who disproved the theory about ability being inversely proportional to appearance: she was quite attractive, and showed a wicked way with puns. She wrote two Xanth gamebooks, wherein the reader is given choices every so often, and can pursue the results of his choice, in the manner of a computer game in book form. Then she and I collaborated on a compendium of Xanth characters, creatures, places, and things, the *Visual Guide To Xanth*. That goes further out of date with each passing year, because of the new material in later Xanth novels, but is a nice volume for those who need a reference to all the early things of Xanth. Jody wrote the first draft, and I reviewed it and added in pieces of my own. Some errors did sneak in, as sharp-eyed readers gleefully inform me, but that's par for the course.

Perhaps my favorite collaboration is also the most tragic. I received a letter from the friends of Robert Kornwise, who had been killed by a reckless driver. He had been working on a novel: would I complete it collaboratively? I was sympathetic, but advised them that it wasn't that simple; that partial novel was part of his estate, and only his family could give permission for it to be so used. Robert's father promptly gave that permission, assigning the rights to me. All he asked, essentially, was that Robert's name be included in the credits, and that mention be made of the fund set up in Robert's memory. Thus came to be *Through the Ice*, published in hardcover by Underwood-Miller, and later in paperback by Baen Books. It won a small award, but more important to me was the fact that Robert's family felt that the finished novel was true to the nature of Robert's writing. I had tried to stay within the boundaries he set, fleshing out and extending the story. I believe I succeeded in that, and made the kind of novel Robert would have made, had he lived to pursue it. That is why it is my favorite: because it helps make known the essence of Robert in a way that was otherwise not possible.

My most illustrious collaborator is Philip José Farmer. This one has a quarter century history. Farmer came to my attention when his short novel *The Lovers* was run in *Startling Stories* in 1952. The "better" genre magazines had turned it down, evidently because of its provocative sexual theme, which shows part of what has generally been wrong with their standards. *The Lovers* made Farmer's fame, and he continued with a fine career, in due course achieving hardcover bestsellerdom with his Riverworld series. In college I collaborated with a friend, Barbara Baller, on an oil painting inspired by that novel: huge insect merged with lovely nude woman. I painted the bug, she painted the woman. When, a decade later, my first published story shared a magazine issue with a Farmer novelette, Barbara was impressed.

But the tide of genre writing lifts some boats while it lowers others, independent of merit. I scored with funny fantasy and became a bestseller myself, while Farmer's sales receded. Publishers who were treating me with sudden respect were treating him with disrespect. Such things anger me. So when a former editor of mine, Charles Platt, suggested that I get together with Farmer, I was pleased to do it. The hell with what publishers may think; to me he is one of the great figures of the field.

It came about in an unlikely manner. Hank Stine, a former editor and adverse critic of my writing, had a dream: to put ten significant genre writers together for a galaxy-ranging adventure novel, each doing one chapter. He assembled an impressive list of names, and got a contract with Charles Platt's publisher for it. He asked me to write the first chapter. I was caught by surprise; I had expected to come somewhere in the middle. So I pondered, and concluded that it would be best to start off in a thoroughly mundane manner, to hook mundane readers, then get into the wild depths of space and carry them along. And I had a piece I could adapt to fit that bill: my story "Tappuah." I had written it in 1962, about a blind, maimed, depressed thirteen-year-old girl named Tappuah (Tappy for short), who was to be transported through New England by a young hopeful artist in need of a job. His sympathy for the ill-treated girl got out of hand, and they made love one time. Then he pondered the penalty of statutory rape, and realized he needed to get out of there—but he couldn't leave Tappy, who was coming to love him. That story had been rejected by numerous magazines, and remained unsold after twenty-five years. So I adapted it to be that first chapter of the novel. The editor was pleased with it, and the project went on to the next writer, Philip José Farmer, who took the couple to a far and strange planet. But following writers had problems, and Charles Platt finally rejected the book. Then, years later, Platt suggested that Farmer and I rescue an aspect of the project by doing the full book ourselves, alternating chapters. I agreed, and Farmer agreed. But the rights were encumbered, and the original contract was sloppy as hell. In the end, I simply bought the project, paying off publisher and both editors. So I had been paid $167 for my chapter, but it cost me $7,000 to buy it back. I returned the rights to the other chapters to their authors, and Farmer and I were on our way. Neither of us knew where it would end, but it was an interesting journey. Thus came to be *The Caterpillar's Question*, my most unusual collaboration. My agent sold it for $150,000, so it was worth it monetarily as well as for the rescue of Tappy from oblivion and the chance to work with Farmer. I regard it as an irony that my name came first in the credits; it will never be first in my mind.

I had placed the paperback edition of *Through the Ice* with Baen. Now Jim Baen proposed that I do a collaborative novel for him. So I dusted off a notion for a major fantasy novel I had developed a decade before, summarized it in detail, and sent it to him. He arranged for Mercedes Lackey, a highly successful novelist in her own right, to collaborate on it. She sent me a letter with some sample text wherein she emulated my style, and I saw that there was a problem. She seemed to feel that *italics* made *effective* writing, and that since I kept such usage to a minimum, my writing was less feeling than hers. This was an arrogant kind of mistake on her part. I wrote her a long letter, explaining as well as I could, and rewriting her sample to be more like my actual style of writing. My interest was in making it easy for her to write in my general style. But apparently she took offense at my assumption that I understood Piers-Anthony-style fantasy writing better than she did, because when the manuscript draft arrived, she had done everything opposite to my advice, and it had *italics* and exclamation! points! galore! This in-your-face response to my well-meaning helpfulness angered me. Jim Baen told me that he regarded her version as publishable, with a few small adjustments; I replied that it didn't meet my standards, and thereafter I distrusted his judgment. I had to struggle to restyle the whole thing, and shore up the lapses of logic and taste and drama so as to make the novel presentable. My wife and daughter went over it too, helping eliminate the myriad flaws. When the copyedited manuscript arrived, it looked as if the copy editor from hell had had at it, with marks on every page and a remark about my weird sentence structure. I checked, and found that all the cited cases were Lackey's sentences, which had escaped my correction in the sheer welter of errors. Thus came to be *If I Pay Thee Not in Gold*, intended as the first novel in a series which will never be pursued. I refused to try to deal with that attitude again. I'm sorry I ever let a good fantasy project be handled that way.

Then science writer Clifford Pickover approached me: here was his novel—would I revise it collaboratively? I read it and saw that it had good promise but did need work. It was essentially a horror novel, and I was unwilling to do straight horror with no redeeming social value, so I incorporated an ecological theme. I also shored up the romantic element. Thus came to be *Spider Legs*, wherein a monster from the sea attacks boats around Newfoundland.

Then Alfred Tella approached me similarly. He had had a good fantasy novel published by a small publisher, but was interested in more. So I read his manuscript, and it had beautiful aspects and style, but also needed work on unification and character identification. So I agreed to collaborate, and thus came to be *The Willing Spirit*, set in medieval India, a fantasy of a young man's quest for meaning—but instead he finds love.

I sent the two novels to my agent, who marketed them. Publishers had been phenomenally interested, but the moment the novels were actually ready, that interest evaporated. Why publishers annoy me: let me count the ways. Collectively they can seem like little children, getting really enthusiastic one minute, and not even remembering it the next minute. It wasn't a question of quality; they didn't even want to *look* at the novels. What had happened? I finally figured out part of it: when we originally broached the notion of a collaborative series, I was a regular on the national best-seller lists. But when TOR took Xanth off those lists, interest in my work plummeted. So it had never been a question of quality; they had just wanted anything by a best-seller—and nothing by a non-best-seller. The quality or originality of writing had never been a consideration. Then finally Baen Books made an offer for the two. But there were strings: heavy editing would be required on *Spider Legs*. Oh—after I had reworked it? I didn't trust this. As a general rule, editing is like government: the less of it, the better. After my novel *But What of Earth?* was destroyed by editing, my nose for this sort of mischief sharpened. So I asked to see exactly what kind of editing was required. In due course sample copyedited pages were sent. Sure enough, it was mostly make-work, just an expression of the editor's power to mess in. If such an editor saw a document beginning "When in the course of human events, it becomes necessary to" he would change it to "It becomes necessary in the course of human events to." But let's get specific: on page 25 of the manuscript the original sentence read "Before he fell asleep he thought about the sea." This was changed to "Before he fell asleep thinking about the sea." Apart from being pointless, that's not a complete sentence, and the cadence has been damaged. On page 29, the original was "Although an iceberg could be as big as an entire village, any sailor would have rather been shipwrecked on land than on such ice." The revision made it "Any sailor would rather have been shipwrecked on the worst lee shore than on an iceberg, even one as big as an entire village." Okay, granted that the original sentence is awkward, and that the "have rather" needed fixing (my theory is that such errors grow on the manuscript after the final proofreading is done), why was the rest changed? It's not that the revision is bad, just that it's unnecessary, in the manner of the change I mentioned in the Declaration of Independence. On page 32 a dream is described, and in the dream he feeds a fish: "Occasionally, he supplemented the diet"; this was changed to "Occasionally, just as he had in reality, his dream-self supplemented the diet" etc. This, to my mind, interrupts the flow of what was to become a frightening dream; I didn't want reminders that it was a dream, I wanted it to seem increasingly real until the end. So the change was deleterious. However, taken as a whole, the editing was annoying rather than ruinous, so I went along with it.

I received that sample editing October 15, 1993. After I reluctantly accepted it, my agent proceeded with the negotiation for the sale for the two novels. The contracts should have arrived in a month or so, and payment of the first part of the advance by the end of the year. The advance arrived, but, oddly, not the contracts. The agent queried the publisher, and got no answer. When June 1994, passed, and there were still no contracts after eight months and five increasingly urgent queries, I had had enough. We returned the advances and dumped the deal. *Then* came word from the publisher: he had been holding out to get foreign rights. I do not normally give those to American publishers, as I have my own foreign agent who can get me better deals overseas. But the curiosity remained: if Baen wanted those rights, why hadn't it said so? Why the eight-month silence? I am wary of dealing with seeming insanity.

So we remarketed the two collaborations. Meanwhile I had been working on others. There was *The Secret of Spring* with JoAnne Taeusch, a nice science fantasy featuring man/plant crossbreeds. There was *The Gutbucket Quest* with Ron Leming, about a blues player in an alternate reality where blues magic was real. And there was *Dream a Little Dream* with Julie Brady, a fantasy featuring unicorns and a suicidal girl. Baen had bounced one and not reported on the others, so wasn't turning out to be the ideal publisher regardless. In fact, it was apparent that Baen really wasn't into the spirit of copublishing; it was acting just like a regular, teasingly arbitrary, distributor, giving me no powers of decision. So there were now five to remarket.

I had become aware of something. The publishers who had been so interested in the collaborations had stopped being interested not only when I came off the best-seller lists, but also when it was evident that we weren't offering more than those particular novels. That is, that the

Xanth series was not part of the deal. And the publisher who got Xanth, TOR, had lost the interest it used to have in my collaborations when it got what it wanted: Xanth. I have an analogy I use for such a situation, as described in Chapter 7, and will amplify now: I feel like a beautiful woman. That is, a lovely woman is pursued by many men—but when she mentions commitment, most of them vanish. Some vanish when they find they can't get her into bed on the first date. Others vanish after they *do* get her into bed. So she becomes cynical; it is evident that most of those ardent suitors are insincere; all they want is her body for a night, rather than an enduring relationship, unless she happens to be rich. All the publishers really wanted from me was my best-selling series, Xanth—and both those who lost it and those who got it tended to vanish as far as my other novels went. Especially the collaborations.

I pondered, and my agent pondered, and it was my wife, who evidently understands the situation of beautiful women, who came up with an effective notion: link the one to the other. Make a package deal of Xanth and the collaborations. So when the time for a new multinovel Xanth contract came up, we put it to TOR: double or nothing. If this man wanted to get this woman in bed again, there would have to be marriage—though TOR's chief editor Beth Meacham is female, and I'm male. Publishing, like politics, makes strange bedfellows and stranger inversions. But the point is the dynamics: TOR knew that if it rejected this offer, we would make it to another publisher, and chances were that we would find one who would make the deal. So TOR agreed. But with a caveat: space the collaborations out, one a year. This dropped a stink bomb into the soup, because some of my collaborators were in desperate situations, and none wanted to wait another five years, after the year's delay already suffered. But gradually we worked it out, and the deal was made.

But there was one more collaboration in the offing, not part of this deal. This was a novel by James Richey Goolsby. He had tried every market himself with no success, and wanted advice on what to do next. So I suggested that he send a sample to me, so I could see what its level was. At times it seems that half my readers are hopeful writers, but that doesn't mean they are all good writers. He sent about fifty pages, and it seemed to me that the text was essentially good enough. Maybe all it needed was agenting. So I recommended it to my agent, based on those fifty pages. My agent liked the novel and marketed it—with no success.

Now I don't like building up a writer's hopes for nothing. So when it was apparent that the novel wouldn't sell on its own, I suggested that I try revising it as a collaboration.

Richey sent *Quest for the Fallen Star*—and suddenly I had a problem. No, it was a good novel, that ought to do well with readers. Yes, now that I was reading the whole thing, critically, I found work that needed to be done. The problem was that it was 240,000 words long. As a massive high fantasy adventure novel, this is okay; readers like big efforts, if they are readable. But I had budgeted about two weeks to revise it. This would take me ten weeks. That would disrupt my schedule in my third GEODYSSEY novel. What to do? I discussed it with my researcher, Alan Riggs, and he had a notion: suppose he tried doing the initial revision, which consisted of some simplification of story line and merging of characters to make the main theme clearer, as well as a number of stylistic adjustments. Richey tended to have doors open to "emit" people, and such wrinkles needed to be ironed out. Then I could go over the novel much more rapidly, saving about six weeks of time. That notion appealed, because Alan had a good notion of my tastes in writing and knows something about writing himself. His first story was published in *Turtle*, after all. No, I hadn't put it there; I recused myself from judging it, and the other editor made the decision, and the story has been well received by others. So I wrote to Richey: would he be amenable to making this a three-way collaboration, Anthony/Goolsby/Riggs? Richey agreed, so Alan took the huge manuscript and began working on it.

But we hadn't reckoned on two things: first, Alan had not had the thirty years experience I had had in writing. I do what I do swiftly. Think of typing on a keyboard: a beginner picks out the keys slowly. An experienced typist knows where they are and goes much faster. Both may type the same piece with similar literary competence, but what takes the touch typist one minute takes the novice ten minutes. Thus with Alan. What he did was good, but he lacked the touch-typing reflexes, as it were. So the revision did indeed take him several times as long as it would have taken me. Second, he was destined to have an unparalleled run of distractions. Four friends or family members died, requiring his attention and clouding his mind; his mother had to have breast surgery for cancer; he made plans to get married; and he got ill himself. No, no necessary connection between them, other than the way they slowed his work. So the job stretched out six, seven, eight months. It ran out of

1994 and into 1995, technically beyond the scope of this discussion, but had its influence within that year.

That meant that I was deprived of my researcher for that time. I use a researcher because I am a slow reader, and the GEODYSSEY series requires a lot of research. I could do it myself, but then I would be the one taking several times as long to do the same quality job. Since my work alternates between high research historical fiction and nonresearch fantasy fiction, it did not make sense for me to do the research at this time; by the time I finished, Alan would be off the collaboration and back on-line, as it were—just in time for me to be on a Xanth novel, with nothing for him to do. That did not compute. So I filled in with other things, such as a Xanth novel ahead of schedule, learning a new word processor, and portions of this sequel autobiography. I also did some research, because there are books I do need to digest myself; I just don't read as many when I have Alan to read them for me. As I like to put it: when I was young I read a lot, but lacked the money to buy all the books I wanted. When I got successful as a writer, I could afford to buy what I wanted, but lacked the time even to keep up with the books publishers sent me free. Finally, I reached the point where I bought the books I really wanted to read—and paid Alan to read them for me. There are certain ironies to success. At any rate, my schedule wound up being disrupted more than it would have been had I simply done the collaboration myself. But just about everything is worthwhile in its own fashion, and this was clearly the time for me to tackle the new word processor, which was an ogre: extremely powerful and often extremely stupid, wasting my time in big sweaty globs.

Thus twenty-six collaborative books, total, and I stand by every one of them, but I doubt I'll be doing many more.

But as it happened, the story wasn't over. I wrote it up in fictionalized form for the Hi Piers Newsletter, and here is that item, which should be clear enough:

Mountain Climbing

Pedro had done 24 collaborative novels, as well as two collaborative anthologies and some collaborative stories. In general he could do better on his own, because he didn't have to coordinate with others, and could have every scene all his own way. Also, Pedro made more money on his individual novels, in two ways: he didn't have to split with anyone else, and publishers actually paid more for a straight Pedro novel than they did for a collaboration. In fact it had become increasingly evident that publishers would rather not have Pedro collaborations at all, regardless of their quality. And thereby hung a tale.

From 1993 to 1995 Pedro did six collaborations. Call them, for simplicity, *Spider, Spirit, Spring, Gut, Dream,* and *Quest,* with, respectively, Cliff, Al, JoAnne, Ron, Julie, and Richey. Each was of the type that has proved to be simplest for him: the other writer had a complete manuscript that hadn't found a publisher, so Pedro took it over and revised it as necessary to make it publishable. His rule was to do as little as he could to it, for two reasons. First, no one liked getting his prose messed with; editors who insisted on interfering with the text of the writers they published became unpopular. Robert Heinlein may have said it best: after the editor pisses on the manuscript, he likes the taste better. But the authors didn't. Pedro never liked tasting piss, and had been known to change publishers to avoid it. So, applying the Golden Rule, he tried not to do it to other writers, and to do it only where it was clearly necessary. So he focused on finding the one word change that would make the book publishable, or the hundred words, or whatever. He tried not to make it over in his own image, but preferred to enhance the original flavor, so that it remained the other author's story, done better. Second, his time was precious, so he tried not to waste it, and making unnecessary changes was a waste. Even so, in some cases there were substantial revisions, and Pedro's writing schedule had been severely disrupted.

They were all good novels, and Pedro thought some should have been able to get published in their original versions, were editors more competent than they were. But the novels became his also, and that included not only revision, but marketing. Writing a publishable novel got an author about halfway there; selling it was the other half. They placed the first two with PEA PUBLICATIONS, but then PEA stalled for eight months on the contracts, ignoring increasingly urgent queries, until at last the authors dumped the deal. Pedro just didn't like getting peed on. So his agent remarketed them together with the next three, and made a deal with CRAG: four individual Zamph novels for one million bux, five collaborations at 25G each in a package deal. That reflected not the quality of the novels, but their respective marketability in a market that had its idiosyncrasies. CRAG protested that it couldn't possibly publish them faster than one a year, which would take the deal up to the year 2000. Publishers had this notion that if a book by a given author was published, it sold X many copies; if two books were published in a year, they divided that market, and if more were published they divided it further. It was nonsensical, but one of the entrenched editorial beliefs. Genius was not a job requirement for editing. It was one reason why some writers used multiple pseudonyms: to get around lunacy. So, reluctantly, Pedro and the agent agreed. The publisher said they would have to take no advance on the first one, which would be a paperback original. Again they agreed, refusing to be driven away from the deal. CRAG rushed through the Zamph contracts. Mindful of past experience, Pedro held them for six weeks until receiving confirmation that all five collaborations had been accepted. CRAG had half a fit; how could he delay on a million bux contract like that? Because Pedro hadn't made the deal for the money, he had made it for the collaborations. This was the kind of leverage required to make a publisher publish good novels despite its reluctance. Once Pedro had specific confirmation, he signed the Zamph contracts, in Jamboree 1995.

Time passed, but the collaborative contracts did not appear. A parallel to PEA was appearing. His agent, of the RESTORATION agency, pressed CRAG more closely. And the CRAG editor said she had lost one collaboration and never received another. What? More likely, it seemed, they "lost" both, because they were the two to be scheduled earliest. So Pedro ran off new copies of each and sent them in. And, in AwGhost, eight months after CRAG had confirmed the collaborations, he finally got the contracts. Pedro filled them out and signed them and passed them on to the collaborators, who signed them and relayed them to the agent, who sent them to the publisher. It should have been quick and routine from that point on: copies of the countersigned contracts returned for the agent and writers, a share of the advances paid, and the novels scheduled for publication.

Time passed. The agent queried the editor, and got no response.

He queried Cragerty of CRAG, with no response. He phoned the editor, who said she had another call and would get right back to him—then never called back. When four months had passed with no word on the contracts, Pedro and the agent knew there was mischief. Had the publisher cynically processed only the Zamph contracts, while stalling in various ways on the collaborations? The endless delays, the lost manuscripts, the stonewall silence, began to shape into a pattern they had already seen elsewhere. More than a year after the deal had been made, they had no completions on those collaborations, while the first of the Zamph novels in the deal was already scheduled for publication. Pedro consulted with a writer's union, but they felt that a mere query by them would not be effective in as egregious a case as this. None of them had ever before seen this blatant a reneging by a reputable publisher. It seemed that CRAG, having gotten what it wanted, was daring author and agent to do anything about the rest. The deal had been arranged mainly verbally, as most deals were; the confirmation was in the contracts— and only the Zamphs had been implemented.

But just in case there could be some misunderstanding, they gave it one more try: the agent sent a careful query to CRAG, with a copy to the editor, rehearsing the situation and suggesting that it would be a shame to get into legal action over a misunderstanding. Such a missive, however politely worded, could no more be ignored than a tax lien or an eviction notice. Yet the month passed—with no response at all.

Now Pedro never much liked the bully in the schoolyard. The bully gets away with it because anyone who tries to stand up for his rights gets smashed. But it had been some time since Pedro was the smallest boy in class. Those who tried to bully him today generally regretted it, thought the arena was not physical. So Pedro acted. He engaged a top Parnassus law firm, Mott & Bailey, who studied the situation, then sent a hand-carried missive stating, in part:

> Indeed, as noted above, in view of CRAG's actions over the last year, there is good reason to believe that CRAG never intended to fulfill its agreement to publish the five collaborations and that its reassurances to Pedro were knowing misrepresentations to obtain his signature on the

Zamph agreements . . . Absent some further agreement, all of the agreements in question are hereby terminated.

So if CRAG failed to respond *this* time, it would lose everything by default. That was the cherry bomb in the privy. It did get CRAG's attention. Cragerty phoned RESTORATION, and he phoned Pedro: it was all a mistake, they weren't trying to renege, this was really the first he had heard about it, and anyway, they had never received the completed contracts. Oh? Those contracts had made it from CRAG to RESTORATION, thence to Pedro, thence to the collaborators, thence back to the agent, who had shipped them in two special DOWNS packages to the publisher. So it seemed that CRAG had stepped up the scale of its "losses," and never bothered to query the agent about the supposed absence of the contracts, or to respond to RESTORATION's repeated queries to CRAG. They had never noticed that they were in violation of the deal that had been hammered out? Thus Pedro's blunt response to Cragerty: "I don't believe you." The pattern of stalling had become too obvious for further excuses. CRAG's lawyer sent a response that didn't help, denying that there was a deal, saying "You must be joking." Oh?

But there was doubt, because they couldn't actually prove it hadn't been an amazing series of foul-ups. The fact that the publisher had stalled more than a year, had lost manuscripts and contracts, and the agent could get no response to queries until Pedro made a legal issue was indicative of the way the wind was blowing, but not legal proof. So when CRAG agreed to publish the collaborations at eight month intervals, they agreed. Pedro had to go through the nuisance of signing them all again, in quintuplicate, and this time he initialed the pages too, just to be sure; it took 350 initials in all. Thus the issue was settled, for the nonce.

And for reasons no one else might understand, Pedro thought it doubtful that he would be doing any more collaborations. He wasn't looking for more mountains to climb.

N i n e

COMPUTERS

I got into computers just two months before the end of *Bio of an Ogre*, when I turned fifty, so I did not have a lot to say about them there. In the ensuing decade all my writing was done on the computer, and it was vital to my profession. But the course was not always easy. The computer can be the most frustrating thing, but like the opposite gender, it also offers rare delights.

I was actually one of the later writers to computerize. This wasn't because of any inherent conservatism—I am seldom accused of that— but because I type on a nonstandard keyboard, and that was an option slow to come. Oh, sure, it was supposed to be readily available, but that wasn't necessarily so. For example we inquired at Wang, and were told that they had offered Dvorak for years. But it seemed that they didn't have it on their nice new computer; it was on a prior version, really a minicomputer, requiring a more complicated setup that proved to be impractical for my study in the pasture. And they charged an extra $1,000 per unit to put Dvorak on.

Part of the complication was that I learned Dvorak before the computer industry did, so I typed on the original Dvorak keyboard. For reasons that have never been clarified, the computer industry later established a standard that scrambled the punctuation. So when I typed a comma, I got something else, like a colon. That gets old in a hurry. No, I wasn't willing to retrain myself; I felt that the computer should give me the keys where I wanted them. So I didn't computerize; I was waiting until the computer industry wanted my business enough to give me what I wanted.

But when I had used my nice Olympia office manual typewriter a decade, the company stopped making them. That meant that if my machine ever broke down, I would be in trouble. So I decided to computerize before that crisis came. Some bridges are indeed best crossed ahead of time. So we started actively searching. Some computers were tempting, but we learned of liabilities, such as a get-lost attitude when repairs were needed. We queried Atari, because it had a nice computer for games that could do word processing. But it was slow, and had no Dvorak keyboard; I had to dictate letters to my wife for typing on the regular QWERTY keyboard, which was awkward for us both. I wrote to Atari urging that it provide an option for Dvorak, but the company seemed to feel that wasn't worth responding to. Scratch Atari, and in due course the company crashed; it had evidently been indifferent to too many potential purchasers. Arrogance really does often precede a fall. Apple was no good; for personal reasons I refused to do business with it. Also, at that time its notion of a typewriter keyboard was ALL CAPITALS, and its idea of cut and paste was to print out the material, then take scissors and glue to it. How Apple ever got away with claiming to be a leader in computing I don't know, and I wonder about the qualifications of "experts" who detail this company's history of leadership. Maybe they weren't shopping when I was, in the early 1980s. But the man at Digital (DEC) was very good. He wasn't a high-pressure salesman; it was that everything he told us was true. He said DEC had an excellent dedicated word processor, but when he asked whether it would give out the specs on the keyboard so that Dvorak could be put in it, that section of the company balked. That superproprietary attitude soon cost it the business of regular users, and the machine foundered. But there was also the Rainbow, another section of the company. He did some research and found a software program called SmartKey was just then coming out with a program to enable the user to redefine every key on the DEC Rainbow keyboard any way he wanted. Ideal!

So I became a user of the DEC Rainbow. It was a nice system, with the industry's best-designed keyboard, and it didn't require air-conditioning, so I could use it in my study. It had a ten-megabyte hard disk, and would run either CP/M or MS-DOS, the two main operating systems of the day. I commented in an Author's Note how Captain M, a retired seaman, had a boardinghouse fifteen stories high, and his tenants each had one floor and were called Users. Ms. Dos didn't like such accommodations, so instead had a garden with paths leading to directories. I started with CP/M, and it was okay, but had some aggravations. For example, the first time I tried to copy a file using its obscure PIP mechanism, I naturally first defined the file I wanted to copy, then defined where I wanted to send it. ZZapp! CP/M destroyed my file. It seemed it had to be done backwards: first tell where it's going, then tell what's going there. If you did it wrong it didn't flash an error message, it trashed your file. Thus I became acquainted with the concept User Unfriendly, a quality computer programmers seem avidly to strive for. But CP/M did have one very nice feature: MAINT, for file maintenance, where you could list the files you had, and delete outdated ones. Because MS-DOS lacked that feature, I stayed with CP/M.

DEC's authorized word processor was Select 86. It was awful. It was clunky, and though it would do a lot if you had the patience to figure out its nuances, it was so slow that reformatting a paragraph because of a one-word change took as long as thirty seconds. You could not save a file without exiting it, and then calling it back up was a cumbersome process. It was not WYSIWYG—What You See Is What You Get—and responded quirkily to formatting commands. Once I tried to use a smaller type, but it didn't work. Later, when I printed that file for another purpose—it came out in that smaller type it hadn't done before. How could that be, when I had made no change in the interim? It is claimed that programs have no self-will, and do only what you tell them to, always the same way. HA! Anyone who uses a computer knows better. The first book I did on it was my restoration of *But What of Earth?*, a novel that had been just about destroyed by the publisher's idiotic copy editors. It had over 150 footnotes, and every footnote took thirty seconds to copy, and thirty more to paste, so that it took me three days to collect them all in the back of the book. I had had enough.

I learned of a text processor, which seemed to be a simplified word processor. This was PTP-100, and it was beautiful. It was simple and fast and versatile, and it allowed me to make macros—that is, I could assign a series of keystrokes to a single key, simplifying a complicated chore—that made it even more of a pleasure to use. I loved it. As a general rule, it had the simplest form of a function on one key, and that key plus SHIFT would extend that function, and that key plus CONTROL would extend it more. So DELETE would take out one character, and

SHIFT DELETE would take out a line, and CONTROL DELETE would take out everything to the end of the file. Something like that; I no longer remember precisely. It also showed underlining on-screen, something not every program did. Simplicity and power: PTP had it.

But PTP had one limitation that drove me increasingly crazy. It addressed only 128K of memory. I had 250K, and could use only half of it. Any file that went over 6,000 words had to be broken into two. As a novelist, I often had longer files, and it was a pain when printing to do half a chapter, then have some blank space on the page before the second half of the chapter began on the next page. The proprietors kept promising to increase its capacity, but never did. Not in CP/M. Also, its later revision tended to trample on special symbols I used, without showing that on the screen, so that what I printed was missing certain key elements. PTP was great, but it was devolving.

I discovered that dishonesty was rampant in computing, as it is elsewhere. For sure, much software is pirated, though I now see quiet steps Microsoft is taking to deal with it; one day a number of pirates will hang. Every file made by Word has hidden text detailing the system and the original purchaser and other information. If it is on the wrong system, beware; if they ever check—and they may do so, on the Internet or via transferred files—they will catch you. But hardware companies rip off their customers too, making false claims for performance and compatibility, and so do software outfits. I saw an ad for a promising word processor, and it was on a special sale: $100 instead of $150. So I decided to try it. My wife does the ordering and writes the checks in our family—as I have said, we're a typical family, in that I earn it and she spends it—but she picked up the wrong ad, and paid full price of $150. So what did they do? They held up the order for two weeks, until the day the sale ran out, then sent it with a bill for postage. So they knew they were cheating me. And it was incompatible with my system. I wrote a letter, and enclosed the payment for postage; I am not governed by the standards of others, and one cheater does not justify another. So did they refund the $50? Or the whole thing, since I couldn't use it? No, they simply kept the money. Since then my sympathy for software outfits has diminished, though I do pay for all mine. I even paid for two copies of my current word processor, though I am the only one using them, because I have two systems: my main one and my backup. Others who heard about this were disgusted, and so am I—but that's the way the license reads. So while I neither practice nor approve software piracy, I can appreciate the attitude of some of those who do.

Then after a year I saw an ad for Edward, that promised to address all my memory. So I sent for it. It did indeed double my capacity overnight. Not only that, it had multiple files: I could call up to fifteen files simultaneously. From it I gained the concept of buffers: each file was actually a buffer, or region of a larger file in memory, and I could page rapidly between buffers, incorporate one into another, copy/paste from one to another, and so on. So I had come to Edward for its larger capacity, but I loved it for its multiple files. Now I could have a text file to write on, and a table of contents file to keep ongoing track of my chapters, and a notes file for my thoughts on how to work out the story. I had been using my "bracket" system, wherein I worked out my plotting problems [in brackets]; now I could have a whole separate file there instead. Edward also had many more macros, so that I was able to tailor it nicely to my needs. Unfortunately, its printing was no good for me; it was necessary to go back to insert an extra symbol at the end of each paragraph, or the paragraphs would all be run together when printed. So I used PTP to print it. PTP didn't like that, and pulled some dirty tricks, but overall it worked.

But CP/M was not being supported, and I was coming up against its limits. With DOS I could address a larger hard disk, and that was becoming important. So I kept Edward, but moved across to its DOS version. That was a struggle, because SmartKey, that I used to get my modified Dvorak keyboard, was not compatible in DOS. I had to hit every key twice, to have its effect: AA to get A, BB to get B, and so on. But we changed to another version of the keyboard, the Finnish, and that solved the problem. I hired the proprietor to craft a better version of Edward for me, with special features. It cost about $1,500 all told, but gave me the ideal word processor. That was great, except for one thing: about once a day, Edward would softly and silently fade away. I would be left with the DOS prompt in the middle of my screen, surrounded by my ongoing novel text—which I could neither address nor save. Wipeout. That, too, gets old very quickly.

Then I met the other Dvorak typist in my area, Lois Wickstrom. She put me on to the program she used: Final Word. It did everything Edward did, and more. For example, it had twenty-four files, and yet more macros. The literature assured me that it was compatible with all other programs, such as SmartKey. So I bought it—and it was not compatible with SmartKey. The Final Word folk said the problem must be with SmartKey. Yeah, sure; it's always the other party who is incompatible. But Final Word allowed the redefinition of every key, including the regular typing keys, so I used that feature to redefine it, key by key, to my Dvorak. That worked fine—except that it didn't work for commands. So I had to hunt and peck for the QWERTY keys for commands, a real nuisance. It seemed that every program just had to have its torpedo. The Big Book of Computer Rules decreed that nothing could ever be completely right; there had to be a stink bomb somewhere. Final Word also was not WYSIWYG, and though it claimed there were no invisible commands, there were. Every so often my text, fine on the screen, would print out with all the words going down the left side of the page. I finally learned that the key was a triple space: one space between words was fine, or two spaces, but three spaces was interpreted as a command to set the right margin right there. This was mentioned somewhere in the manual, like maybe page 365 footnote B, where no one would ever find it. So an innocent typo, three spaces instead of two between sentences, could destroy the printout, with the effect not showing on-screen, so there was no warning. Lois once sent Final Word a disk with that error on it, demanding to know how come, but received no answer. Things like underlining did not show on-screen; there had to be embedded commands, like @U<underline>. Nevertheless, it was a powerful program, and I used it for two years.

Then Final Word was bought out by Borland, and its upgrade was Sprint. Sprint was supposed to run on anything that Final Word did. Wrong! It would not run on DEC. Well, parts of it did, but not the whole. For example, I could get on-screen underlining with Sprint. So how come that had been impossible for Edward and Final Word? Sprint did everything Final Word did, and was WYSIWYG: my ideal word processor. What to do? I pondered, and made a fateful decision: for the sake of the $100 Sprint program, I would invest about $13,000 in IBM clone computer systems.

So, after four years on Digital computers, I made the shift to IBM-compatible 286 systems. Our procedure was simple: we looked in the phone book for local dealers, and phoned one. The phone book was out-of-date, and he had moved, but our message got through. It turned out that he didn't have an office, but he would come to our house. Okay.

This might seem to be a formula for disaster, but it turned out quite well. He recommended a brand we had never heard of: Acer. We were willing to give it a try, so we bought two Acer systems. They worked well, and Sprint ran on them. Sprint was everything I had hoped for, and so was the hardware. With Digital we had had three hard disk crashes, causing untold mischief; with Acer we never crashed at all. The main annoyance was when we had to have a $500 repair for a $20 printer part, a counter, that had been installed defective, but didn't show up until just after the one-year warranty ran out. Apart from that, the solid Acer laser printer gave excellent service.

We made three experiments, when we went to the new equipment: a color monitor, a 3.5-inch disk drive, and a mouse. I loved the monitor, and have used color ever since. I loved the 3.5-inch disks, and have used them ever since. But I didn't like the mouse. However, that can't be considered a failure, because later I had to use the mouse regardless of my preferences. I solved half the problem by getting a trackball instead: no pad needed, and cursor control was better. So on the whole, computing was better than it had been.

But Sprint had some liabilities, and these became more annoying with time. The speller was well set up, but had an absolute genius for getting the wrong word. It would challenge a word like "revved" and offer as a replacement "revved." That's right: the same spelling. It would be unable to guess at obvious errors, and would challenge some words repeatedly despite being given the okay. It would miss some misspelled words. This sort of thing drove me crazy. Nevertheless, I stuck with Sprint, as it was malleable, allowing me to have all my functions where I wanted them, and I could even modify them to perform in the manner I desired. So I stayed with Sprint for six years. But by then it was getting dated. It had never had an update, and Borland seemed to have no intention of doing anything more with it. Other word processors were moving ahead with new features. When we upgraded to 486s, skipping the 366, we had to get a special patch to enable Sprint to run. Chances were that there would be more trouble with further hardware upgrades.

So at last we looked at what else there was. There seemed to be only two really solid word processors surviving the winnowing process: WordPerfect and Microsoft Word. I had been watching WordPerfect, and knew that it had not incorporated an Oops feature until its fifth major revision—so much for its attention to the needs of its users!—

and would call up only two files at a time, with limits on those. With Sprint I had up to twenty-four files, and six windows, and could look simultaneously at several places in one file if I wanted to. That was helpful when I wanted to compare similar sections, and do some editing on them. I had nine working files I called up every day; I couldn't do that with Word Perfect. So I looked at MS Word, and found that the DOS version would call up nine files in nine windows. Okay, that was the one.

But it soon became apparent that it was the Windows version of MS Word that was getting most of Microsoft's attention. It looked as if I would have to shift to it sooner or later. So I made it sooner, upgrading to it. Of the six word processors I had used, it was the most difficult to learn, and the most user unfriendly. Nice Sprint features, such as the ability to park my set up—nine files, cursor places kept—and turn off for the night, and restore it complete the next day—did not exist in Word. There was no ongoing "saved" indication. The text cursor was an almost invisible "I" bar that could disappear entirely in dialogue boxes, and there was no way to turn it into a square or other visible shape. In Sprint I had defined the number-pad ENTER key as SAVE, distinct from the main keyboard ENTER; it was absolutely impossible to do that in Windows, because it refused to recognize the keys as separate. Odd that in six years, Word had been unable to catch up to Sprint in such respects. Its manual was a marvel of seeming clarity that was often useless, because some key step was omitted; apparently they had never had newcomers to the program try it and give their comments. Same for its on-screen help system. And slow: you haven't seen slow until you have worked in Windows. DOS is like lightning in comparison. So it is necessary to buy ever faster equipment, with ever larger memory and storage, just to function at a reasonable speed.

On the other hand, Word was more powerful. In fact it was like an eighteen-wheeler truck, compared to the passenger cars of prior word processors. It had True Type, wherein the fonts were defined by the program itself, so could be printed exactly as they looked on the screen, any size, any style. It had variable sizes on-screen, so I could squeeze the print into tininess, or magnify it to double, making it easier to read, without affecting the actual printing size. It had AutoCorrect, wherein my chronically uncapitalized *i*'s were automatically corrected as I typed. My reflexes dated from my thirty years on manual typewriters, so my finger came off the cap key just before striking the "I" key, so as to avoid flying caps; the faster responses of the computer keyboard meant that I left many letters uncapped, a nuisance. It had files and windows limited only by the size of the system's memory. I called up forty-three files and windows at one point, testing it. More than I would ever need. I never tested it on my later Pentium system; obviously the limit was way beyond my need. And it had a good speller—later upgraded to an almost perfect speller in Word 7. Its Revision Mode and Spike—a function enabling copying of multiple items at one time—greatly facilitated my process of revising text, once I figured out how to get around the torpedo: you couldn't spike text without deleting it from the original document. What genius idiot devised that nonsense? But frequent use of the CONTROL Z undo key restores the text.

Windows has aggravating propensities for imposing its will on the user, and for cutting in with the message THIS APPLICATION HAS PERFORMED AN ILLEGAL ACT, AND WILL BE SHUT DOWN, and then doing it, wiping out your recent text. When you have done nothing "illegal"; it is just its own malfunction, for which it punishes you without giving you a chance to save your material. It happened three times while I was editing this book, so that I had to do parts of chapters over. The program trips over its own feet, and seems to be blaming the user, who really can't do anything illegal in that sense. Yet at other times it can be quite helpful. So though aspects are absolutely maddening, taken as a whole, it is the best operating system and word processor I have encountered, and it seems likely to be with me the rest of my career. Of course I still print out and back up my material every day, being sensibly paranoid about the intentions of the system.

So I went from Word for DOS to Word for Windows, and the two were not the same. Then, after a year, came Win95, the operating system upgrade. I did not like Windows; it was a struggle to get through, and was best avoided whenever possible. But Win95 was a substantial improvement. It was actually possible to get around in it from the start, and it did do useful things like background printing that the prior windows had claimed to do, but tended to mess up. Win95 eliminated the cute little analog clock, but we copied it back in, and now I have that in the corner as well as the digital readout. The clock also puts the date in the taskbar, so I have that too; since I work seven days a week I tend to lose track, and that helps.

I don't use many third party programs, but did try INFOPEDIA, one of the dictionary/encyclopedia/atlas CD disks, and that does help me with spelling and definitions when the regular speller is stumped. Since this, and any other program, can be kept on standby, once invoked, it is convenient in a way that such programs were not, prior to Windows. I have a collection of physical dictionaries, discussed in Chapter 15, which I treasure, but INFOPEDIA is preempting them, because with it I can generally get what I want faster.

I also found some nice wallpaper, which is the background when there is no program overlaying Windows. I have several nice pictures I can put there, as my mood dictates, and when I take a break for lunch or whatever I minimize all windows and show the picture: Penny on her farm, or a state capitol building, or colorful Wonder Woman, or whatever. This is not the same as a screen saver; for that I have the words coursing by, WHAT ARE YOU LOOKING AT THIS FOR? before it clicks into current-saving sleep mode after five minutes.

Sometimes I listen to a CD on the system stereo speakers. There are also different sounds that can apply to miskeying or the invocation of particular functions: musical notes, buzzes, or groans. Fun.

There was also the Microsoft Natural Keyboard, which was ergonomic. It looks like a Salvador Dali painting, as if the keyboard has been melted and bent and pulled partly apart in the center. But it enables the hands to fall naturally on the keys, with less strain to the wrists, and by damn, it has eased the carpal tunnel syndrome I suffered when I computerized. Later we saw an ad for the Cirque Wave Keyboard, which has a similar layout, but with a built-in trackpad that's so nice that it even converted my wife to that design. It's a little panel, a generous two inches by one and a half, and you stroke it with your finger to make the cursor move, and tap it to click. Two taps are a double click, and to drag it's one tap and slide. It does have two buttons to use if the tapping seems uncertain. Because it's sealed in, it won't get clogged with grime as the trackballs do, and it needs no extra space. So I think this has solved most of the rest of our problem with the mouse.

So though I hate being corralled into doing business with the big boys, who hardly care about the needs of ordinary users, I must say that computing has never been better. This material is written on a Pentium system with a 1 Gigabyte hard disk and 16 M memory; that's what it takes to make Win95 and Word 7 function at reasonable velocity. But function it does. I continue to explore its recesses, adapting new functions to my convenience. For example, when writing this book I had to check constantly to see whether I had or had not already covered any one of myriad subjects. The FIND TEXT feature does an instant search for whatever words I want, listing the chapters in which they appear, and then I can readily call up those files and do a spot search for the exact place. In bygone days I had to have a separate program to do a multiple-files search. Now it's easy. Also, I made a forty-two-keystroke macro to split the screen into two panes, with four different "zoom" sizes of print available. I have 10 percent in the upper pane so that I can see my pages forming as I type, and know how far along I am on a given page, and 140 percent in the lower pane for supremely easy reading. I have a brown background screen with green Courier New font for my novel text, and yellow Times New Roman font for my associated notes. Thus I always know exactly what I'm doing; I'm color coded. I love it.

Lester del Rey muttered that when I computerized, my writing deteriorated. I don't think so. It was his ham-handed editing toward the end that hurt my writing; when I got away from that, things improved. The computer enables me to make any spot change right when I think of it. I can pause in what I'm doing, call in a chapter from a different novel, make the change, put it away, and resume work on my current project, which remains conveniently there. I don't have to sweat whether to make a change, knowing it will require me to retype the page; I can do it on the screen with no loss of time. The speller catches most typos. I can do a search to verify whether I have said something before, thus eliminating repetition unless it's intentional. There are so many little ways the computer facilitates not only the writing, but the editing process, that I'm sure the net effect is an improvement in the finished text. And the speed—I used to do three drafts, but now I type it only once, and edit on the screen, so that I save about 40 percent of my working time, with less frustration. I expect this efficiency to continue as I move on into the Linux operating system.

Let's face it: I was dragged, figuratively, kicking and screaming into the computer age. But now I love the computer, and would dread going back to the old way.

PROFESSIONALS

Originally, when I read, I paid little attention to the title of a book, and none to the author. Only gradually did this change. When I went to college, my friend Barbara Baller asked me what I thought of the works of Ray Bradbury, and I drew a blank: who was Ray Bradbury? So she showed me *The Martian Chronicles* and *The Illustrated Man*, and then I knew who Bradbury was. Actually his stories did not strike me as particularly apt or forceful; it was as though he were writing for children, with simple language and concepts and not much point. In later years I have come to have more respect for that writer, who is actually one of the best known the genre has produced. But this marks the point at which I began to be aware of authors: lo, there were *people* writing the stories and books I liked.

I saw many comments about one Isaac Asimov. So I read one of his short stories. It wasn't much. It was about a man who went back in time to get valuable documents, which he then brought to the present to sell for the inflated price such rare items would be worth today. But he couldn't sell them, because they were deemed to be fakes. He demanded to know why, since he knew (without telling them how he had gotten them) that the items were genuine. They admitted that they could find nothing wrong with them, but were still sure they were fakes— because they were *new*. How could a new document be over a hundred years old?

As with Bradbury, I came to appreciate Asimov more, with time. The fact that this seemed to me to be a minor story didn't mean that it was a bad story, or that Asimov was a bad writer. In fact today I resent being judged similarly by youths as ignorant as I was then, who have little understanding of the craft of writing but are very free with pronouncements on what is good and bad. It is mostly their own pulse they are taking, not that of my fiction. Some have written to me, saying that years later they had reread material of mine they had dismissed, and this time discovered more of its depth. Precisely. Fortunately I did not quit with one Asimov story; I went on to read *The Second Foundation*, and there by damn was a great novel. Later I got the complete Foundation trilogy—since then it has expanded into any number of additional volumes, but then it was a trilogy—and found the first Foundation stories to be okay but not special, while *Foundation and Empire* was a great improvement, but my favorite remained *The Second Foundation*.

This, of course, was par for the reader's course: no later books can match the sense of wonder of the first one he reads, even if he reads them out of order. That is what is in operation with readers (and reviewers, a pox on all their houses) who claim that the only decent Xanth novel was the first. Those who start with a later novel, then go back to read the first novel, don't say that. In fact one reader read, as I recall, the first nine novels in reverse order, finishing with *Spell*, and reported with regret that *Spell* just wasn't up to the quality of the others. I cherish that comment, because of the way it demonstrates my point. There are crudities in *Spell* that I eliminated in later novels, so I agree: it's not up to the later standard. But it is a good novel.

But I was talking about Isaac Asimov. I went on to read his Robot series and others, and generally enjoyed his work, though he was stronger on imagination than style. His nonfiction was always interesting and lucid. As he said of himself, he discovered that he was a born explainer. I read his massive two-volume autobiography, *In Memory Yet Green 1920–1954* and *In Joy Still Felt 1954–1978*, and found it altogether too detailed, but nevertheless interesting. Asimov was at least straightforward. I was guided in part by that when I wrote my own autobiography; I tried for clarity, honesty, and brevity, rather than for style. Though there was little actual sex in his fiction, and romance was not his strongest suit, Asimov was no literary prude; he could write about sex in considerable detail, fictively and nonfictively, when he chose. He had the courage to suggest that one solution to the population crisis could be alternative sexual expression: homosexuality, oral sex, masturbation, and so on. Sex without procreation. He knew that the only practical way to control human population was by reducing the birth rate. There were a couple of ways in which I identified closely with Asimov—in fact as I read his autobiography, I found many strong correlations, but of course those who read my own autobiography report similar identification with me, so I think it's mostly one human being relating to another. Isaac was a foreign-born, naturalized American; so was I. He was a writaholic, living to write above all else; so am I. I wrote more fiction than he did, but he was by far the more prolific writer overall, because of his nonfiction. Both of us took our work with us, always returning to writing when a spare moment offered. I gather that other writers find this odd; they live to go to conventions or to find other excuses not to be at the keyboard. But I think I understand Asimov in this respect about as well as anyone does.

I did have some small interactions with the man. Once I wrote in response to one of his *Magazine of Fantasy & Science Fiction* columns about the problem of matter forming out of nothing. He had a problem figuring out how it could appear one atom at a time. I suggested that energy, instead of matter, could be forming, then being shaped into atoms. He responded with a brief card, saying it would still have to form one quantum at a time, so the problem remained. I don't think I agree with that; he was thinking digital, while I was thinking analog: not in chunks, but in a spectrum. But there's still a problem about anything appearing from nothing that bothers most rational folk.

That was it; I didn't write him again. This showed that he did answer his mail, another thing I do. He also used autograph labels, to avoid shipping books through the mail, as I do. Great minds run in similar channels. (That's mild humor. This announcement is to forestall critics who will otherwise take off on me for daring to consider myself great.) Later he referred to me in a fanzine, saying that he lacked the time to participate that Piers Anthony evidently had. I replied to the effect that it only looked that way, because I made my words count so that they seemed to be more lengthy than they were. As I said: minor interactions. I was sorry when Asimov died; he was a remarkable presence in the genre and in writing.

Which is not to say that he was perfect. He loved women a bit too well, and could not keep his hands off them, literally. He compulsively grabbed for breasts and bottoms, in public. I warned my daughters: if they ever encountered Asimov, keep out of reach of his hands. I believe one writer, no delicate flower, grabbed Asimov *back*, on the bottom, making a real scene. But his compulsion could not be controlled. Fortunately for him, his aura as a celebrity enabled him to get away with it. One fan remarked with awe how Asimov shook hands with him, and shook the breast of his girlfriend. And no, this is not one of my affinities with Asimov; I love women too, but I do not grab, I just look. I suspect that just as a genius is apt to be short a few cards in some other respect, Asimov's short suit was in personal control; he lacked the formidable social cautions that most of us possess. When he abruptly lost his will to write, I knew that death was hard upon him, because writing was his greatest passion, as it is mine. When a flying bird loses the power of flight, it is near the end.

For decades the genre had its "Big Three"; Isaac Asimov, Robert Heinlein, and Arthur Clarke. My interactions with the other two were as slight as with Asimov, but in the case of Heinlein may have more significance than has been recognized. I was introduced to Heinlein's fiction via a collection of stories titled, as I dimly recall, *The Man Who Sold the Moon*. I was surprised by their quality; this was one sharp writer. I went on to his novels. My opinion concurred with that of the majority: of the Big Three, Heinlein was the best actual writer, though in his later career certain flaws did grow. It is an irony that writing was not his ambition; he was a Navy man, but illness forced him out, so he turned to writing instead. His military background shows; he tended to have a hard right slant to his fiction. But he was so intelligent, consistent, and imaginative that even liberals like me had to accede to his greatness. Late in his career his novels became too long and rambling, until he sharpened up and got back on track. So probably Early Heinlein was the best Heinlein.

But about my limited interactions with the man: there were three, and perhaps the least significant was this: I was told that when I was blacklisted (more on that in a moment), and the writer's organization SWFA tacitly sided with the errant publisher—you can read all about it in *Bio of an Ogre*, or in more limited detail here, as I seem to be the only one talking about that, unsurprisingly—Heinlein considered that matter, made no comment, but then let his membership in SFWA lapse. That was comment enough.

Heinlein was represented by the literary agent Lurton Blassingame. When I had that trouble with a publisher and got blacklisted for my temerity in demanding a correct statement of accounts, I took one significant step to stop the blacklist: I took Lurton Blassingame as my agent. Editors knew that if they irritated Blassingame by blacklisting one of his clients, they might never see the work of another of his clients, Robert Heinlein. That pretty much knocked the wind out of it, and my unplaced novels started getting placed, and later, given a level playing field, I was able to make my own mark on the genre. So Heinlein's long shadow helped me, and I remember it as a favor though it was nothing he did, or perhaps even knew about, directly. Without Heinlein, Piers Anthony might never have achieved fame.

But there was more: when Blassingame retired, two younger agents took over his agency: Elinor Wood and Kirby McCauley. I was assigned to Wood, and Heinlein to McCauley. That's when the feces hit the fan. Wood sent me a contract that was simply not acceptable, so I bounced both the contract and the agent. Yes, I got my way, with a much-improved contract and with a change of agents. Meanwhile, Heinlein did not like McCauley, or the story I heard was that his wife didn't. Later I heard that Heinlein was jealous of the huge advances another McCauley client, the upstart Stephen King, was making, so refused to share an agent with him. That aspect didn't bother me; I figured the agent might do something similar for me, in due course, and in due course he did. No, he didn't get me contracts of the eight-figure magnitude King got, but he did get me three separate seven-figure deals. So the two writers, or agents, were switched, and Heinlein got Wood while I got McCauley. You might not think that would be a fair exchange, but it turned out to be, because Heinlein was fading while I was rising, and I think McCauley actually made more in commissions from my business than he would have with Heinlein's business. So it was a neat fix, benefiting us both, because Wood turned out to be competent for Heinlein, and McCauley was a genius as an agent who helped put me on the commercial map. He became perhaps the leading genre agent, for a while. But that's a separate story. This story is about Heinlein, and the subtle but considerable debt I owe to his presence. We never met, we never spoke, we never exchanged letters, our philosophies differed, but I believe I owe him, and I cherish his memory.

I encountered the works of Arthur Clarke, too, in college. I was taking a class in the nature of mankind, and another student had bought a paperback book titled *Childhood's End* that he gave to me as a possible reference for that. It turned out to be not a treatise on how children mature, but a science fiction novel by Arthur Clarke. I read it, and it was a great story. Actually it *was* about the end of childhood—the childhood of mankind as a species. It presented our species as the larval stage of a greater species, about to emerge in the manner of a butterfly from a cocoon. After that I knew who Clarke was. When I was writing *A Piece of Cake*, published as *Triple Détente* (I hate the way publishers mess with titles), I was concerned that a portion of it was too similar to a portion of *Childhood's End*. They were quite different novels, but I did not want to seem to be copying any other writer in style or substance. So I compared the two sequences in detail, and concluded that no, they were not at all that similar, fortunately. To my surprise, I also saw that mine was better written. My maturing as a writer brought me a closer awareness of style, so what had thrilled me in college I later could see was not as great as I had once taken it to be. Indeed, Clarke's style was, I think, the clumsiest of the Big Three, and his plotting wasn't necessarily apt, and his handling of romance was weak. On occasion he even had an error in physics. He made it on ideas, and they were grand ideas. One of his outstanding pieces was a short story, "The Star," in which it turned out that a supernova that destroyed a great civilized species was the one that had been seen on Earth at the time of the birth of Jesus Christ. It concluded, approximately (I'm going from memory): "What was the need to give these people to the fire, that the light of their passing might shine above Bethlehem?" What a notion! I advised my British mother of his work, and she became a devotee, not of science fiction, but of Clarke's novels.

There was a comment in one Clarke interview that Piers Anthony was one of a number of up-and-coming writers, so I knew Clarke knew of me. And once I received a cryptic letter from Ceylon—Sri Lanka—where he lived, commenting on *Macroscope*. I couldn't make head or tail of it, and neither could any of my acquaintances, so I responded simply, expressing my confusion, and remarking that the only novel I had done relating to Ceylon was *Hasan*. I never heard again. The name on the letter was an obvious put-on, so I have wondered ever since whether that was actually Arthur Clarke. I suppose only a thorough exploration of his papers would tell. I see no reason for him to play such a joke, so maybe it was someone else. A subsequent letter indicated that was the case.

Back when I was getting started, I learned of an established writer who lived near me. He was Keith Laumer, a writer of fairly superficial but compelling adventure science fiction, and noted mainly for his Retief series of adventures. So I contacted him, and arranged to visit him. In the summer of 1966 my wife and I drove up to his place near Brooksville, taking along sandwiches for our lunch on the way back. We arrived in midmorning at his lovely house in the wetlands, trees all around. Laumer was gracious, and though we were alert for a suitable time to go, it never came, and we wound up staying all day, having supper there, and driving home after dark, our sandwiches never eaten. He told us how Retief was actually based on things he had noted during his years in the civil service. In person he was more intelligent and broader than his fiction. He had good commentary on all aspects of writing. He asked how I liked the writing of Jack Vance, and I said I liked it, except for Vance's wooden dialogue. "Not wooden, carved," Laumer said. That made me pause; he was right, and I appreciated Vance more after that, and indeed, now consider him to be the genre's finest fantasy writer. I remarked on my problem with *Astounding Science Fiction*, later called *Analog*: the editor, John W. Campbell, seemed increasingly bigoted, giving no credit to blacks for anything. Yet overall he was the fairest editor and best market. Should I sell to him, or not? Laumer cautioned me about making the wrong associations. He agreed that the editor was bigoted, but it was only his job as editor that should concern me; I couldn't let irrelevant considerations guide my marketing. It was a fine distinction, and I think a correct one; what an editor thinks of racial considerations is really not my business, while how he treats my manuscripts *is* my business. So Laumer's balanced advice helped me. He told how the German physicist Willy Ley had done a collaboration with a lesser-known female writer. Ley had sent voluminous scientific material, that she had to somehow digest as the basis for a novel. She struggled through, and later brought the manuscript to Ley's house. At one point he exclaimed that she was just trying to use his name to make personal gains. Outraged by this unfair charge, she picked up the manuscript and threw it into the blazing fire. Ley had to scramble to save it. She had made her point. He told how H. L. Gold, the editor of *Galaxy* magazine, was agoraphobic; he couldn't stand to leave his apartment, lest something bad happen. Friends finally prevailed on him to take a drive with them—and on that trip the car was twice involved in accidents. So much for that effort. That told me something about Gold that was reassuring: this arrogant editor, who liked to step on faces, was mentally unbalanced. Laumer was full of such fascinating bits, and his wife and family seemed nice. So he made a very good impression on us.

Later that year I met him again at the Milford Conference in Pennsylvania, and he was affable and congratulated me on my intervening sale of my first novel, *Chthon*. When that novel was published, Laumer sent me a card saying it was great, and that he had instantly nominated it for the Nebula Award. At the conference itself he seemed more interested in the social aspect than in the critiquing of manuscripts, its nominal purpose. I don't remember his specific story now, but do remember my comment, which was that it was salable as it stood, though not ambitious, and he should send it off and get it published. It soon became apparent how right I was: after everyone had made comments, intended to help him improve the piece, he simply said that he had already sold it to a magazine. So all our comments, it was evident, were pointless; the story was already history. Apparently Laumer didn't see anything wrong with this; he had tossed in whatever was handy so as to officially participate, but he wasn't interested in the actual comments. I suppose a person can attend such a function for whatever reason he chooses. Certainly my own motives were mixed; I wanted comment on my story, "Tappuah," and got it, but I also wanted to get to know some of the figures in the genre, and as it turned out, this was the single best event for that in all my career. I did not, however, feel the need to repeat; I had learned what I needed to in that one week. I believe Laumer was a regular attendee of the Milford events, and as far as I know, he was popular there. So why not? It evidently served a need for him other than commentary.

It may seem strange, then, to say that I may never know how much evil came of that association, or how much mischief Laumer caused me. Later I reviewed things, looking for hints that might have given me the clue, but they were few and scattered, and I don't think I was unduly naive to have taken Laumer at face value. Others have been similarly impressed by him. I had visited his house; I invited him for a return visit to mine. But though he had research to do in St. Petersburg, where I lived, he said he was too busy to stop by. When I agreed to visit Joe Green, across the state at Cape Kennedy, Laumer was also invited. He asked who else was going, and when told I was, he decided not to go. So I began to wonder whether my wife and I had been mousetrapped, when we visited Laumer. Had he enjoyed himself showing off his knowledge, keeping us there, even phoning his agent in our presence despite having no pressing business to conduct, so as to make an impression—then condemned us for wasting his time after we left? He was close to Damon Knight, organizer of the Milford Conference; Knight had been interested in buying a story of mine for an anthology, but after I attended Milford, he made continual excuses to avoid buying anything from me, and it became apparent that that market was now closed to me. Maybe my fiction just wasn't to Knight's taste, though it did see successful publication elsewhere, or maybe Knight didn't like me personally. I have always been forthright in my statements, and perhaps it is not surprising how often those who are not forthright take offense, without being able to refute me. But just maybe it was Laumer.

Much of this I learned after his death. Laumer was two-faced. He could be very nice to people, to their faces, but could also torpedo them behind their backs: Thinking back, I remembered how sour he had been about Larry Niven, as well as Willy Ley, and others. Perhaps his attitude is clarified by his marriage. He seemed to have a compulsion to sleep with any pretty woman he could get. His wife finally had enough and dumped him, and apparently to the day he died, he never understood why she did that. He didn't understand? Only a person without much conscience could suffer such confusion. Then he suffered a stroke. Friends who tried to help him, to take him to the hospital, were reviled; he claimed they were trying to kill him. He survived, but now the mask came off. He could still be charming, but seldom saw reason to be. Instead of cursing folk behind their backs, he now was more likely to do it to their faces. Gordon Dickson took the trouble to visit him, and when Dickson left, Laumer bad-mouthed him. Laumer went to a bookstore and said he was a writer. Oh, they asked, interested. Which one? "Guess!" he snarled, waving his cane at the entire genre section. He went to conventions, where it was reported he acted like an ogre. He had become one mean man.

And there is where it impacted me. Because others got it confused, and accused *me* of being the convention ogre. I had this direct from a fan who met me. "You don't seem like an ogre," he remarked. I inquired, and he explained about the stories circulating about me at conventions. "I have never been to a convention," I said. He looked at me, surprised. It was true; from the time I attended the Milford Conference, which was a private gathering of writers, to my first science fiction convention, was seventeen years. Even then, I was always well behaved at conventions, as I was elsewhere; compared to some other writers, I am a model of decorum, as anyone who has actually met me knows. I don't get drunk, or use foul language, or grab for women; instead I try to meet and talk with all those who wish to meet me, trying to relate to their interests. People had confused one genre writer for another. Yet that story was to dog my entire career. I made something of it by becoming the ogre: I titled a Xanth novel *Ogre, Ogre*, and it become my first national bestseller. So now there was ample evidence that the Piers Anthony ogre was not the kind that disrupted conventions. Yet it seemed that many folk out there clung to the false stories, not much interested in the truth. Even in 1992, at the World Science Fiction Convention in Orlando, Florida, when I met Jerry Pournelle, he accused me of something Laumer had evidently done: writing him a letter when he was SFWA president, castigating him as a Nazi. I never did anything like that, to anyone. Pournelle would not accept my denial, and would not apologize when it became evident that what he said was false. (I had SFWA look up the correspondence records, showing that there was no such letter to be found.) This is one root for my gradual and increasing contempt for fandom, and for some pro writers too. I am not much interested in those who have agendas other than fairness. It all started with Keith Laumer, but maybe it was carried on by others, who didn't have the excuse of suffering strokes.

Laumer's life after the stroke was not good. His family avoided him. As far as I know, he wrote very little after that, but he wanted to consider himself the genre's finest writer. He suffered outbursts of scatological swearing in the middle of ordinary conversations. He wanted female companionship, but he was too grabby and abusive, and women were wary of him. I had vivid descriptions from two of my correspondents who had interacted with him. A simple trip to a gas station with him could become a scene that no woman would care to repeat. He could control himself when he chose to, but seldom chose to unless there was something he very much wanted from a person, and he could be insidiously cruel. It was as though the stroke had severed his conscience. One woman called him "an evil man." I lived about forty miles from him, but never sought to renew our acquaintance, because I knew that he would deeply resent me for replacing him as the best-known genre writer of the area. Yet that isn't what he said. I was told that he cursed me for offering him advice on landscaping. Huh? I don't know what he was thinking of, unless he confused me with someone else. So finally he died, and his long travail was done. Yet the meetings and correspondence I had with him were positive, and I think is only fair to put the good on record with the bad. Perhaps the best way to give those who never knew him an image is to mention the movie *Scent of a Woman*, wherein Al Pacino played a blind man who was embittered and cutting toward others. I was not the only one who thought of Laumer when I saw that characterization. But in the course of the movie, the man's better characteristics gradually emerged, until at the end he came across with stunning brilliance, redeeming himself and the young man he sought to help. Laumer might have been that way, had it been his sight instead of his conscience destroyed by the stroke. In his heyday, Keith Laumer was an exciting writer and a winning personality, and perhaps his faults were no worse than those of others. It's just that the stroke made his faults become glaringly obvious, and destroyed a career that might have become what mine did become. He was well started on such a career, at the time we met. What might have happened, had he turned his narrative talent to fantasy? It was a tragedy, and surely what I suffered from his deeds was only a shadow of what he suffered himself. May he rest in peace.

I mentioned Gordon Dickson, one of Laumer's friends. Back when I did my first year's effort of writing, I read widely and studied the work of successful writers. I also worked on an index of reviews, and listed the authors of stories in the several genre magazines. Damon Knight had remarked that Poul Anderson was probably the genre writer with the most stories in print. My survey confirmed that, and indicated that Dickson was #3. I forget who was #2. I met Poul Anderson and his wife Karen in New York, and we rode the bus together to Milford, where I met many others, including Dickson. Dickson was like Bacchus, the god of wine, and I don't mean that in an unkind sense. He was convivial, the center of the party, and yes, he drank, but he was a great person to know. He was smart, too, perceptive and considerate. We had had some slight correspondence before; he had enclosed a note with one of his SFWA-distributed novels saying that writers needed more feedback, so he was inviting comment on his book. I sent in comment, and then did the same with my first published novel, *Chthon*. At the conference he read my entry, and took extra time to consider his response, so as to make the nature of his comment amicably clear; he was a thoughtful person. Dickson was later to become president of SFWA, and his motives and courage were good. But he tended to delay on things. When my novel *Macroscope* was excluded from the ballot for Nebula, because members had been waiting for free distribution from the publisher, which was late so that it missed the nomination deadline, I wrote to Dickson, asking him to allow write-in ballots. He declined. He read the novel, and said he did consider it good enough to nominate, but he did not feel that the existing policy should be changed. I disagreed with this, and it resulted in a major contender—*Macroscope* came in #3 on the Hugo Award ballot for that year, and at the time the Nebula and Hugo normally went to the same novels—being unfairly denied consideration. But Dickson was forthright, and that I can respect. When I had my problem with the publisher, Dickson suggested that SFWA mediate the issue. I agreed. But then he took so long to get around to it that the matter died unfulfilled, and I had to get a lawyer instead. So again, Dickson's neglect cost me heavily, because I got blacklisted when I should have been vindicated. But he was not a bad man. I liken it to the cop on the beat who is looking the other way when a mugging occurs; he should be more alert, because if he's not there to stop crimes, what's the point? Dickson was a prolific writer, but also a good one; I loved his *Dorsai!* series. In 1976 his fantasy novel *The Dragon and the George* was published by Ballantine (Del Rey), wherein the dragons were the heroes oppressed by charging human knights. I read it and liked it, though I could see where he had used a loop—that is, an inserted episode that didn't relate to the rest of the novel—to lengthen it to exactly 100,000 words, to make Lester del Rey's minimum for the fantasy line. It won the British Fantasy Award for that year. The following year my *A Spell for Chameleon* won the same award, and the year after that Stephen Donaldson's massive Unbeliever series with the same publisher won it. Donaldson and I moved right ahead with our fantasy, doing sequels, becoming best-sellers, but Dickson waited fourteen years to do the sequel to his fantasy. The course he might have followed can be seen by mine, riding fantasy to the top. But as time went on, he faded, and when I met him again years later at a convention, I saw why: his glass of whiskey was constantly with him, and he sipped continuously. I sat beside him on a panel, and he kept right on drinking. Now he is gone, his work unfinished, and I regret that.

Jack Williamson was an old-time writer of special significance to me. When I first discovered science fiction as a genre, in the form of a copy of *Astounding Science Fiction* magazine left in my mother's office in 1947, it was a Jack Williamson story titled "The Equalizer" that led off the issue and captivated me. A space mission returned to find the moon base deserted, and Earth rendered back to a nontechnological culture. What had happened? I never reread the story, and no longer have the magazine—it was the March 1947 issue—so the details fog, but the magic of it remains with me forever. So it was really Jack Williamson who hauled me into the genre, and I never really left it. My own world of the time was not very interesting or joyful, and the stories in the magazine gave me endless new worlds in which to dwell. I think science fiction was a significant buttress for my sanity.

I was eager to find the next magazine, which was April 1948, a year later. No, I hadn't waited a year; I had been in my mother's office around the Christmas season, so it was an old magazine, and in the three months it took to discover that these things were sold at newsstands and such, that became the current issue. There was part two of a serialized novel by Jack Williamson, *And Searching Mind*. It was absolutely compelling. Later it was published in book form as *The Humanoids*—a worse title, I think, as the original had been a novelette followed by the novel, the set titled "With Folded Hands . . . And Searching Mind." But editors change titles all the time, usually for the worse, I think; it's their way of showing their power. This novel introduced me to the wonders of Psi power, wherein a man could move mountains by the force of his thoughts alone. Glorious! There was a nine-year-old girl in it, and when my daughter was nine I read that novel to her. That was in 1976, and as I have mentioned, my taste in fiction had matured since 1946, and I found it less compelling than I remembered. But it remained a good novel, and I was glad to share the experience with my daughter. Along the way I had the chance to meet Jack Williamson himself; in fact Joe Green brought him to my house for an evening in 1969, when he attended the Milford Conference that had moved to the local Florida beaches, and I was able to show him my collection of magazines, and the original *Astoundings* with his material, and tell him how important it was to me. He said he would have to have his head shrunk after all that praise. He met my daughter Penny, who was then only two years old. It is one of the gratifications of my life that I was able to have

Williamson over and entertain him for that evening; it would be hard to think of a writer I would rather have had there. Later yet, in 1987, when I was Guest of Honor at the World Fantasy Convention in Nashville, Tennessee, Williamson was another guest, and I was able to tell him again of his importance to me, in public with an audience of a couple of hundred, gaining him applause. "Thanks for bringing me into this world of wonder," I said. So it's not that I think that Williamson is the greatest writer ever, but he is a good one, and he was the one who captured the thirteen-year-old who was to become Piers Anthony. Without him it might never have happened.

Theodore Sturgeon was I think generally conceded to be the finest stylist in the genre. Certainly I considered him so. His life, I learned in due course, had been unkind. When his stern stepfather discovered his collection of science fiction magazines, he cut them into pieces. There could hardly be a worse, or less deserved, punishment for a child. Yet that same stepfather, as I understand it, also drilled him in proper English usage, so may be part of the source of Sturgeon's marvelous ability to express himself. But only part, for Sturgeon's imagination and sensitivity were phenomenal. Unfortunately, he didn't like to write. So if someone were to ask me what a hack like me ever had that Sturgeon didn't, I could give two answers, either of which would have sufficed: discipline, and a love of writing. When I decide to do something, I do it—but I don't need that discipline when it comes to writing, because I love the process of writing. It was said that Sturgeon lost his status as a writer when he became a good convention man. I think that's reversed; he attended conventions because he couldn't stand to apply himself to the lonely writing exercise. I wanted to say to him, "Ted, you write so well; why don't you go home and do it?" But I didn't, knowing it was pointless. I did, later, write him a letter, and send him a novel notion that a fan had sent me, because I believed he could do a better job of it than I could. But he didn't like to write letters either, and didn't reply. So Sturgeon, who could have been phenomenally successful as a writer, was instead a writer's writer, admired by other writers, but not well-known beyond the genre. What a waste.

When I was invited to attend the 1982 SFRA (that's Science Fiction Research Association, different from SFWA) meeting, and I saw that Sturgeon would be there, I decided to go. Actually I wanted to meet the proprietor, James Gunn, too, for he had written one of my all-time favorite stories, that had transfixed me in 1953: "Breaking Point." So I went, and took my younger daughter Cheryl, who was then just twelve years old. I did meet Sturgeon, and talk with him, and got him to autograph my copy of *More Than Human*, which I had read in the magazines as "Baby is Three," and that was nice. We sat beside each other on a panel, and there was a surprise: Cheryl was in the audience, and Sturgeon focused on her the entire session, somewhat to her discomfort. In due course I figured it out: some called Sturgeon the Apostle of Love, because he often wrote sensitively about love. Cheryl was just then coming into womanhood, and was the very image of a nascent maiden. That's what Sturgeon saw, and he was right. Later I met *his* daughter, and no, I didn't stare at her; at one point she and I might have collaborated on a project, but I turned that down for different reasons. I was sorry when Sturgeon died, but glad I had taken the chance to meet him when I could.

Harlan Ellison, as others know, is a case unto himself. I met him, also, at the 1966 Milford Conference. He was small in physical stature but large in presence. I had felt that his fiction tended too much to the grotesque, wherein men found themselves mired in garbage. But I was interested in him, partly because he was about my age, being three months older. I like to think that those of my generation, which means for this purpose within a year or so of me, are making their mark on the world. Ellison was making his mark. He was a showman, and he evidently felt a compulsion to make himself known in any group in which he found himself, even if it was simply a matter of telling one dirty joke after another. He took his work with him, and he had his typewriter set up in one of the rooms, with his story in progress there for anyone to see. At other times he would write a story while in a store window. He had a chip on his shoulder about the way the establishment had treated him, and I think it was justified. I learned that James Blish, a respected writer and fine critic (I know that sounds like an oxymoron, but a literary critic in the pure sense can have genuine perception, and he was on occasion that type), had in a prior year told Ellison that he would never sell a thing. How wrong (and wrongheaded) he was on that score! So Ellison repeated that, then said, "Well, here I am." He proved his point; in the course of his career he won many awards for his fiction. I liked his attitude in that respect, though I had my differences with him. I noticed how he would courteously wait his turn as each manuscript traveled around the circle for comment, then make his own comment, which was generally thoughtful, then depart. He wasn't interested in whatever anyone following him might say. That seemed somewhat self-centered to me. Yet he was always generous to James Blish, oddly, treating him with deference, and arranging for extra money to be paid to his widow when Blish died. So Ellison was a man of contrasts.

We interacted brightly at Milford. I described some of his work as being like vomit flying through the air toward the reader's face, and I didn't think much of his story "Pretty Maggie Moneyeyes" either; it was, as I think another writer commented, dollar writing for a dime theme. Then when I was commenting on another writer's story, Ellison made a show of ridicule for my comment, finally fetching a fly swatter as if to deal with me. He was mistaken, as were others who agreed with him; they thought I was confused about a character in the story that I thought was female when it was actually male. It was Joanna Russ who told me it was a male character. No, it turned out that the author had done two versions of the story, and in one she had changed the gender of that character. The version I read had the woman comparing the size of her breasts to that of another woman's: something hard to confuse, gender-wise. This messed up Chip Delany too, who then said that his entire commentary should be discarded. Delany certainly was aware of the distinction, as he is gay. So, for that matter, is Russ, if others interpreted her subsequent statement on the matter correctly. I have wondered since then just how apt a story is, if a female character can be changed to a male one, without otherwise affecting the story. The distinction between male and female is far more significant than that, to me. But it seemed that few others thought of it that way. This was one of two cases where I differed from most or all of the other writers, and where I feel I was right and they were wrong. Ellison was not only extremely discourteous, he gave me no credit for correctly reading the version of the story I had seen.

But when he submitted a second story for consideration by the group, "I Have No Mouth, And I Must Scream," I said that I knew this was going to make trouble, but I had to speak my mind: I liked that story. Then I ticked off why I liked it. This was exactly the kind of stick and carrot commentary that Ellison has done to others; I do at times use folk's own techniques against them, which may account for some of my unpopularity in some quarters. Ellison made a show of sinking in his chair, as if reprieved from execution. My judgment was vindicated by the public; that story went on to win an award. I made it a point to join his table when we had a banquet-style meal. That's when he learned that I was a vegetarian. I believe it was Norman Spinrad who asked me about things like shoes, and I showed my cloth shoes. Ellison later commented in print on being impressed at the way I handled the matter. So our association, after a mixed start, was amicable.

Ellison was then in the process of putting together a massive anthology titled *Dangerous Visions*. I was interested in markets, and mentioned it when talking with Damon Knight, as I recall. Ellison was near, so Knight asked him then: what about it? Ellison said it was already 50 percent oversubscribed, so he didn't need any more. Okay, no market there. But later I saw him make a deal with Chip Delany for a story. So I got the real message: the volume wasn't open for *me*. Actually, the Delany story won an award, though I have never been able to find anything special in it. I took this snub as a challenge. When *Dangerous Visions* was published, I reviewed it in detail in a fanzine, and stated with humorous threat that if there ever was a sequel volume, I intended to be in it, because I could more than match the prevailing level of vision therein. And this must be said about Ellison: he can take it as well as dish it out. When a sequel, *Again Dangerous Visions*, was announced, I submitted a story, and he not only accepted it, he asked for revision that would strengthen it. Thus "In the Barn" appeared therein, a provocative story that I think made my case: I had more than matched the prevailing level. It was about an alternate world where all bovine mammals had died out, yet there was a thriving milk industry. Just what was *in* the barn, if not cows? It turned out to be enormously breasted human women. It was not a sweet story; the women were systematically deprived of their intelligence so they would make good cows, and bred to a prize human bull. The surplus males were killed. The story received mixed reviews. Ted White claimed I was covering myself in shit. The *Science Fiction Encyclopedia* dismissed it as vegetarian fiction. Guess who never read the story! But over the years I received letters from readers who had found it truly memorable. So I give Ellison credit for meaning it when he said he wanted provocative stories that would have trouble finding publication elsewhere. The advance from it was nice, and later there were royalties that brought the story's earnings up to over $500. More was promised, as another major sale of the volume had been made—but the statements and payments abruptly stopped. I suspect that Ellison got behind on the accounts and never returned to them. I was in any event better off than the contributors to the third volume, *The Last Dangerous Visions*, which at this writing twenty years later still has not been published.

Which leads me to the manner of my breaking with Ellison. We were nominally friends, with a great deal in common. As I said, I tested him on things, and he came out combative but true to his word. I understand that sort of thing as well as I understand myself. He remarked at Milford on how some folk thought him to be quarrelsome. "But look at how you come at me!" He had a point; anyone would react if attacked the way Ellison has been. It doesn't all start with him. I have been similarly condemned, when what I have done was paste back those who came at me with slurs or lies. Of course a liar doesn't admit his error; he merely learns to repeat his stories where they can't be immediately refuted. Ellison rails at things that are well worth railing at. I haven't seen his nongenre newspaper column, but I understand it's more of the same, and that's good. I suspect that if you compared our politics, there would be 95 percent agreement; we're both prime liberal and proud of it. I believe Ellison hates the way Parnassus is run; so do I. A person can disagree with him and still be respected by him. There's a great deal there to be respected. Once there was a hint of motion picture interest in one of my works; Ellison phoned me to recommend competent representation for it. Unfortunately the publisher controlled the movie rights, and it went nowhere. But I did appreciate Ellison's kindness.

So why would I break with him? Because I came to the conclusion that he was a loose cannon. The problem with such a cannon is that it is more dangerous to its friends than to its enemies. I had suffered such looseness before, when he berated me in the Introduction to *Dangerous Visions* on a matter where he, rather than I, was in error, as he could have ascertained had he inquired. He tended to shoot off his mouth first and ask questions later, often to the considerable embarrassment of himself and others. The point of decision came when he wrote to me to say that I shouldn't be alienating people in my Author's Notes. It was obvious that he had never understood those Notes, which are not at all the hurtful missives he seemed to think. I responded carefully, and I think gently enough, hinting that he should get a better notion of my Notes before commenting. To do his homework. I also had to say that should he repeat in print some of the accusations he made in private, I would have to take legal action. I said this not to aggravate him, but to warn him off, because I would indeed sue if libeled, and I didn't want to have to do it to a friend. If I had to give advice to anyone who didn't know me about dealing with Piers Anthony, it would be "Don't cross him; he'll destroy you." I would give the same advice about Harlan Ellison, with the qualification that unlike me, he does not do his homework before launching his missiles, so he makes mistakes I don't. Apart from that, my long letter was positive. He responded that he had seldom received such a dismaying letter, and told me of three thoughtful things I might have said but had not said. Oh? I responded briefly, quoting those very same three things from the first page of my prior letter. Apparently he hadn't even assimilated that before sounding off! That, to my mind, made the case hopeless; the cannon would not be anchored. I concluded "Farewell, Harlan."

That was the kiss-off; I never contacted him again. I seldom if ever even mention him elsewhere. I understand via the grapevine that he never understood my withdrawal. Sure, the way Keith Laumer never understood why his wife left him. I left him so we could remain nominal friends; I truly did not want to fight him. There are so many turds out there that need to be shelled, it would be a shame for either of us to waste our ammunition on each other. Yes, he has a problem of overreacting without checking, and firing off explosive verbal shells before verifying their targets. He can be supremely arrogant. He can go ballistic over trivial nuisances. So the pattern of alienation he thought he saw in my Author's Notes was more likely a reading of his own pulse. But he's not a bad person, and he has formidable recommendations. So I must be his friend from afar. I will regret it if he dies without understanding that.

Roger Zelazny broke into genre print shortly before I did, in the same magazines. He was smart and nice and extremely talented, and his progress was like a blazing meteor as he swept up awards. He was a few years younger than I, but because he come onto the scene when I did, I regard him as a kind of contemporary. Actually he was two weeks older than my wife, who he said had a nice voice. He had struggled to break into print as I had, with thirteen years of college publications and rejection slips compared to my eight years; he had started younger. Of course the rest of the world hardly saw us as occupying the same universe. He was deemed a great writer, while I was unnoticed. But he himself seemed untouched by the adulation heaped upon him. He was in touch with me, and he treated me like an equal. It was clear that he did notice my work, and he complimented it, personally and in print. Once he phoned me to invite me to attend a convention he would be at. We met at Milford, and he was nice to me though everyone was seeking his attention. When I remarked on how an editor, Lawrence Ashmead of Doubleday, had solicited, then rejected my Arabian Nights fantasy novel *Hasan* as not sufficiently interesting, another writer said that probably the editor was right. But Zelazny said that the same editor had similarly rejected a novel of his, *And Call Me Conrad*, later republished as *This Immortal*—then chided him for not showing the same novel first to that editor, after it won an award when published elsewhere. Zelazny looked from one hand to the other, as if comparing the two letters from that editor: what was he to make of that? That pretty well scotched any further siding with that editor about my novel—and indeed, *Hasan* was to do well in later print. It also showed that Zelazny, too, had early problems with "How's that again?" editing, just like the rest of us. It was a warm implied endorsement of my position, which I appreciated. He was a devotee of Persian fantasy, just as I was of Arabian fantasy. So it was from him that I learned what I call the Zelazny lesson: it's hard to resent a person's great success when he's constantly complimenting you. Everybody liked him, with reason.

Years passed, and things changed. I discovered commercial gold with funny fantasy, while his career stalled. For a time we both had the same literary agent, and the same publisher, and it was clear that I, rather than he, was now the prize prospect. But I remembered, and it was my turn to compliment him, if I had the chance. But it bothered me. He had had such brilliance in writing, but later novels I read were downright pedestrian, with no sign of the prior flair. What had happened? He remained the darling of the critics, and with my success I became the anathema of the critics, but the reality was that my novels now had more imagination and style than his. (I speak of the couple of novels I read; it is possible that others I didn't read were better.) How could such a marvelous writer fall so low? He continued to win awards for his short pieces, and perhaps they were worthy, but obviously something was wrong. When I met him in a later year he seemed almost blank, without real focus. Maybe he was preoccupied with something else. I did compliment him as we shared lunch with some mutual fans, telling him of "the Zelazny lesson." But it was not reassuring. My best guess is that he fell afoul of some malady, and the medication had a dire effect on his ability to write, so that his full skill returned only briefly for some stories, and could not be maintained for longer works. He was not one to complain, and indeed, his death in 1995 at the age of fifty-eight caught the genre by surprise, for he had not let it be widely known that he was terminally ill with cancer. In fact it was reported that toward the end he would prepare for a public appearance by having a blood transfusion, so that he would appear healthier than he was. Maybe that cancer explains his decline. One real regret I have is that when I was asked to blurb—that is, to read and give favorable comment on—one of his later books (a signal of how far our respective fortunes had changed), I had to decline, because I knew my readers would not understand that book. It was a collection of literary stories, with Zelazny's elliptical luster, rather than straightforward narrative, suitable for critics but not for garden variety readers. So though I really wanted to do Zelazny a return favor, considering his early kindness to me, I couldn't. Now he is dead and I will never have another chance.

John Brunner was born in Oxfordshire, England, seven weeks after I was born in Oxford, England, so we were about as close in age and origin as any two genre writers are. His childhood was marked by isolation and illness, and he had problems at school. That remains reasonably close to my own less than happy childhood, though he remained in England while I came to America. He dropped out of school at age seventeen planning to become a writer; I had thought I would not go to college, which would have ended my education at the same age, but circumstances changed my course for the better, and I did go on to college, got married, and embarked on life. But I didn't get serious about writing until I was twenty, and took another eight years to make my first sale. Brunner, in contrast, started selling at age seventeen, and by the time we met at the Milford Conference, he had sold forty novels to my one. I didn't realize until his death that a story I had liked in *Astounding Science Fiction*, "Thou Good and Faithful," was written by him; it was published under a pseudonym. More than forty years later, it's hard for me to re-create it in my mind, but my memory says that it was about a robot that did very long service (centuries, I think) for little reward, just the words from its master "Well done, thou good and faithful servant." Later he published *Quicksand* and *Stand on Zanzibar*, both outstanding novels, one of which won awards. He was an ardent liberal, more so than I, because he actually participated in marches and sit-ins, and social comment colored his serious work. Maybe that's why I liked his more ambitious novels so much. He earned his living with conventional adventure fiction, but his heart was in the provocative mindexpanding work, as came to be the case for me too. In person he was a sharp, almost dapper man, extremely quick-witted and with knowledge of many things; his discussion of the nature of space-time awed the writers at Milford. My interaction then with him was slight. Alexei Panshin had made a deal with me to share a motel room, splitting the costs, but then he roomed with Brunner instead, latching onto the betterknown writer, leaving me stuck to pay my whole cost. On the last day I shared the room with Brunner, though I was asleep before he retired, and he was asleep when I departed. I left him a note: "Thanks." At one point a cape turned up, and folk delighted in draping it over whoever was handy and requiring that person to do or say something significant. I couldn't think of anything when my turn came, so I repeated a joke instead: "TB or not TB—that is the congestion." Brunner made a clever, punish remark that I don't recall. Mainly, that experience taught me to be careful never to get put onstage unprepared, a caution I have maintained since.

One thing that annoyed me was when I brought up a question I had seen in print, I think by Algis Budrys: was it smart for a male writer to do a first person singular story or novel from the female viewpoint, or vice versa, when it was obvious that it couldn't be true? Brunner took some time to lecture me on my perversion for raising the question, and the whole group broke out in applause. Well, obviously I was out of step with the rest of the writers there, but it is my contention that I was right and they were all wrong. I was not expressing opposition—after all, I have done a good deal of "female" writing myself, and have been complimented on it by female readers, so I evidently have a feel for its nature—but raising a valid question in a discussion group. To which I got no valid answer, merely a personal attack. Since when is it right to attack a person's sexuality instead of addressing the question he raises? I find it significant that no writer there was sharp enough to see the point. This was the second example of error at Milford, and it seems to me that both Harlan Ellison and John Brunner should have been ashamed of their performances in that respect. Both played to the crowd instead of taking the trouble to see accurately. This is something I have noted elsewhere; writers are in general no better than others in operating on prejudice or fuzzy thinking instead of fathoming the precise issue. But they should be. Brunner, in being eloquent, could also be wrong-headed.

Nevertheless, I supported Brunner when he had trouble with an American publisher (and explained to him why I felt he was wrong on the gender issue), and received his terse note of thanks. We had some correspondence, comparing notes. Despite his success, he was barely making a living at writing, and I was not even doing that; my wife was working to support us. But as time passed, I got one phenomenal break, getting into fantasy at the time it was taking off, and my career took off, while his faded. I actually had more novels published than he did, by the 1990s, and had made considerably more money, despite his formidable head start. He is another one I think could have done similar fantasy; why didn't he? Others have commented on some disastrous career decisions he made; perhaps that was one of them. In the end he died in 1995 at age sixty, of a stroke at the World Science Fiction convention in Glasgow, disillusioned and unhappy. For all that our limited association was mixed, and I had the impression that he didn't think much of my intelligence, we had close affinities of origin and social awareness, and his demise brought me pain. He was a genuinely talented and versatile writer, with an enviable liberal passion. The system had ground him up and spat him out, as it does so many writers. I hate the system.

There were too many writers and too many interactions at Milford to cover here. I wrote up a complete personal report at the time and sent it to Damon Knight, who replied that it was more grist for the papers. Perhaps that report, which used alternate names for the participants, remains in the files of some university collection. Knight himself was a pleasant host who I think kept most of his thoughts to himself. He had been a reviewer whose acid wit I had really appreciated, and though he did not write a lot, he could write well. At one point I remarked on my experience with hard-boiled eggs: I would crack them against my skull, and if I did not strike hard enough, the shell would not crack and would bruise my head. But when I struck hard enough, the egg cracked open and my head was okay. Knight said he found that a nice analogy of my attitude in other respects. He may have been correct; I have always taken pains to express myself plainly and with suffi-cient force. But though Knight has good skills as writer and critic, I don't regard him as a true professional writer, because he admitted to suffering Writer's Block that lasted for years. As I comment elsewhere in this volume, such blocking is not to be tolerated by a true professional, and must be rooted in a lack of discipline and lack of true desire to write.

I think I annoyed Knight, too, in my approach to James Blish: Blish submitted a truly awful piece for examination, saying that he had finally discovered the nature of commercial writing. Others were diffident, avoiding straight comment, until my turn came. I put it on the line: it was poorly written, poorly characterized, poorly plotted, and without thematic value. In short, junk. Blish turned red in the face. He could dish it out, but it was now apparent that he couldn't take it. I was not out to get him; I was simply telling the truth about his manuscript. After I had broken that ice, other writers agreed, and even Damon Knight had to agree that the piece wasn't much. Apparently Blish had thought that commercial fiction made a point of having no writing values. He was 180 degrees wrong. Good commercial fiction is the epitome of good writing, having values that the "literary" purists evidently don't under-stand. Mainly, it's readable and interesting and moving, and often has a point. So it wasn't Ellison who took Blish down, it was me. I believe Blish never forgave me for the sin of uttering truth to his discredit, and it may be that Knight did not forgive me either. If so, both were wrong, for I was only doing what the conference was nominally about: straight, honest, accurate comment on the manuscript.

Later the comment was on my piece, "Tappuah," which finally ap-peared in print a quarter century later as the first chapter of my collab-oration with Philip José Farmer, *The Caterpillar's Question*. The story was generally praised, but Knight was negative. Again, time fogs the details, but I remember him poking fun at my mention of the "budding bulges" in the thirteen-year-old girl's shirt, showing that she was starting to develop. Okay, I changed that, though no one else had objected. He also pointed out that her leg brace was mentioned as showing one time on the foot, and another time on the leg: "Which is it?" he demanded, as if such a brace, which covers the length of the leg from knee to foot, had to be one or the other. I was distinctly unimpressed by that com-mentary, and not just because it was negative. Knight was simply trying to take me down, perhaps getting even for what I had done to Blish. But that is not the way critiquing is supposed to be. Not a series of writers trying to torpedo other writers, but trying genuinely to understand and analyze the pieces in question, and to separate the wheat from the chaff without fudging the issue. I could certainly play the game of torpedo, but even in the case of Ellison I wasn't trying to do so. Attacking a writer because he speaks a truth you don't necessarily like is not the way it is supposed to be, and my judgment of Knight declined. I can't say I think much of the way Blish praised his own work, critiquing it under a pseudonym, either. I regard it as intellectual dishonesty. Yet for all that, Blish was a fine writer, and so was Knight, on occasion. Perhaps they would have been more successful if they had had a better comprehension of the parameters of integrity, which go well beyond the Thou Shalt Nots.

These were by no means the only writers with whom I interacted; in the course of my career I brushed with most of the figures of the field, and some who are on the fringes, like Stephen King, whose daughter was a fan of mine, and Dean Koontz, with whom I used to battle in the fanzines, before we both got too successful to have time for that sort of thing. This is just a selection of those who came to mind. I should say also that my focus on Milford is on the daytime manuscript commentary sessions. There were also evening sessions of general discussion, where much excellent thought was brought out. But they ran late, and I tended to get sleepy, and I also don't like to break in on others, and could hardly get a word in edgewise. So what was probably the best part of Milford largely passed me by. There was also a Milford meeting with Sol Cohen, publisher of *Amazing Stories* and *Fantastic*, who was reprinting stories without payment. SFWA blacklisted the magazines for that, and Cohen wanted to get the blacklist lifted, so he came to make his case. The result was inconclusive, but it was an honorable encounter. So, taken as a whole, Milford was a great experience. But I never felt the need to attend again. I stopped by to say hello when it moved to Florida, and that was all. The later flourishing of my career owed little or nothing to it. Yet the acquaintances I made there, and the insights I gained on the hidden social currents of the genre, such as the formidable impact Milford had on the Nebula awards, were well worthwhile.

Let me conclude with one lighter note. I was asked by a small publisher to blurb a novel by a new writer, J. F. Rivken. I read her novel,

Silverglass, and enjoyed it. It was published by Ace in 1986—apparently the small publisher, W. S. Mercador, had been bought out—and my blurb was run—expurgated. What I had said was "It's fun to see a tall, handsome, hard fighting, hard drinking, womanizing barbarian hero—who is female." They cut the word "womanizing," though it was true, at least in the edition I read. Too bad; I think readers would have been intrigued.

Eleven

FANS

I actually entered prodom and fandom simultaneously. I had been an avid reader of the genre since my discovery of it in 1947. Fifteen years later, when I tried my first full-time writing year, I submitted stories to the magazines and joined the National Fantasy Fan Federation, NFFF or N3F, as mentioned in Chapter 8, "Collaborations." But I was never much of a fan in the regular fannish sense. Essentially I went from avid reader to professional, with limited fan activity on the side. Most of my participation in fandom has been as a professional. Oh, yes, fandom includes professionals; it's the arena where fans and pros interact. It has two broad categories: fanzines and conventions, and now a third is developing on the Internet. Fanzines are amateur magazines published by fans or pros for the interest and benefit of fans and pros, while conventions are gatherings put on by fan clubs with pro writers as guests, and publishers may also participate. The fans must pay to attend, while the pros attend free, and guests of honor have their travel expenses and accommodations paid. Over the years I have participated in both, and had some interesting experiences, but they have always been peripheral activities.

My fanzine experience has been so varied and detailed that it is pointless to try to cover it solidly here. I'll try to cover the essence, however, and some more detailed examples. The N3F, which had been started by Damon Knight and then turned loose, had a lot of services for new members—"neofans"—and that was helpful, and it did introduce me to several other hopeful writers, with whom I did collaborations that were published. But it was so sloppily run that I dropped it after a year as a

waste of time. There was a Los Angeles area science fiction society—
LASFS—that published a fanzine to which I wrote. But soon my practice
year of writing ended and I had to orient again on paying work. I had
at that point sold two stories, and I continued to sell stories at the rate
of two or three a year, so that I was building a gradual professional base.
But my time for fanzine participation and correspondence was squeezed
out by classes and homework.

When I returned to full-time writing in 1966 I had more time available, but I was focusing on writing novels, so really didn't get into it for
a while. One of the contacts I had made during my first year of writing,
in 1962–63, was Ed Meskys, who helped me work on my Review Index.
Later he left the Lawrence Radiation Lab and moved to New York, where
he published a fanzine, *Niekas,* which is Lithuanian for "nothing." I
wrote an article about the *Arabian Nights* for him, based on my re-
searches for *Hasan,* which was well received. In fact, *Niekas* won the
Hugo Award for that year. When I attended the 1966 Milford Conference in Pennsylvania, I rode the bus to New York City, where Meskys
met me and took me to his home for the night. He took me to a party
where Poul and Karen Anderson were, and I enjoyed talking with them
and riding the bus with them to Milford, Pennsylvania, the next day.
Meskys inquired whether I'd like to do another article for *Niekas,* and I
mentioned my interest in dinosaurs. But he didn't think that subject
would do, so nothing came of it. But I did continue to write letters for
the fanzine. At one point it suffered a ten-year hiatus, then picked up
exactly where it had left off, including one of my ten-year-old letters.
But eventually it ran my address, a no-no I have made plain throughout
my career, because I don't want to be further deluged with letters from
strangers, so I dropped it. It really wasn't Meskys's fault; he had gone
blind, so others had to do much of the work; one of them "accidentally"
did it. But my policy in that respect is inflexible—any fanzine that runs
my address loses me. Those who test me, verify it the hard way. I apply
the same rule to publications such as *Who's Who;* when one violated my
stipulation, I cut it from my list, and it has been sadly out-of-date on
me ever since. I don't even answer its queries, because that would give
it my current address, and it has shown that it doesn't respect my wishes.
I am not being entirely arbitrary here; I have a correspondence averaging
over 150 letters a month, that cuts deeply into my working time, and I
want to cut it down without hurting feelings. Publication of my address

would greatly enlarge the inflow of mail. There is also the matter of the danger of strangers having free access to "celebrity" addresses: every so often there is the one who wants to come and kill the celebrity and maybe take his place. Maybe if that happened to an editor of *Who's Who*, those thoughtless folk would begin to understand. But mostly it's fans who simply want to come and take an afternoon of my time, without being concerned about whatever else I might have wanted to do with that time, such as completing a piece on a deadline. But Ed Meskys remains a good guy, and *Niekas* remains a good fanzine.

In 1968 or '69 I encountered a fanzine called *Psychotic*, edited by an erotic genre writer called Richard Geis. He earned his living doing sex novels, but his heart was evidently in his fannish activity, and *Psychotic* was a sparkling magazine, featuring the likes of Poul Anderson and Harlan Ellison. A number of professionals wrote to it, and some had columns in it. Geis on occasion would publish dialogues with his alter ego, who was a cleverly opinionated character I rather liked. I started writing to it, and soon Geis, impressed by the level of my comment, offered me a column. So for a time I commented on a number of things, stirring up interest and arguments. The fact is, any successful professional writer who chooses to turn his hand to the less formal amateur writing can do a good job of it, because he knows how to write well and has a base of information drawn from his professional activity. But I was more provocative than most, because when someone hurled something smelly at me, I hurled it right back. In time the name of that fanzine changed to *SF Review*, and in more time Geis lost interest and folded it, and I took my column to Bill Bowers's *Outworlds*. The question came up whether I should resume submitting material to *Amazing* and *Fantastic*, now edited by Ted White, with whom I had had some encounters in the fanzines, but he had also published my novel *Hasan*. They remained marginal markets, yet they were the magazines where I had gotten my first start as a published writer, and that is always something precious. So I wrote "Rationale of an Indecision," and asked the readers to vote on the matter. The vote was to submit to the magazine, so I sent it *Dead Morn*, my collaboration with Roberto Fuentes. There was never a decision on that, but it was a worthwhile experiment. I also wrote a review of *Again, Dangerous Visions*, which as I remember started a series of reactions and counterreactions that lasted two years. When we moved to the backwoods of north Florida in 1977 I lost the issues of *Outworlds* so didn't comment, and I guess I was cut off; I thought it had folded, but years later heard from the editor, with it still going. But it had been quite a time. Later Geis's *SF Review* revived, and I wrote to it again, but then in a fit of pique he published my address, and I was through with him. Years thereafter he asked me to contribute to a new magazine with which he was associated; I did not answer. As I said, some folk have to learn the hard way. He had at one point called me naive for answering my fan mail; he seemed proud of not answering similar mail himself. So maybe this time he discovered what that felt like at the other end. But in his heyday, Geis was about the best fanzine publisher ever, at least in my limited experience.

Another fanzine was Frank Lunney's *Beabohema.* He offered me a column, I agreed, and the resulting controversy elevated his fanzine to Hugo-nominee status. When another faned (= fan editor) asked me to contribute to his fanzine, and I politely declined, being already over-committed, he then published an attack on me by several other writers, including Wilson Tucker, and didn't send me a copy. Several pros responded in my defense, including Harry Harrison and Harlan Ellison. When I finally got a copy via other channels, I responded in *Beabohema*, so that the errant faned wouldn't get the benefit, and refuted all the charges, which were pretty much made from whole cloth. So that, too, was quite a ride. Eventually *Beabohema* flagged, and my fanzine activity faded out. I was, after all, then rising onto the national best-seller lists, and had plenty else to keep me busy.

Later, in 1986 I think, I was sent a copy of *Fosfax*, a club fanzine, and for a year or so acknowledged with postcards, which were duly printed. Then I started doing full letters, and for another year it became like the old days, with considerable interaction. The proprietors were conservative, while I am liberal, but we both took free expression seriously. Actually I think they considered themselves libertarians, whose philosophy is so far to the right that it closes the circle and comes back on the left, as it were. Lawrence Watt Evans wrote regularly to the fanzine, and Poul Anderson also wrote. Once Dean Koontz wrote, commenting on something I had said. He and I had fought savagely in fanzines in bygone days, but had no wish to do so now. I introduced my collaborator Robert Margroff to it, and he wrote regular and good letters, which is what a faned really appreciates; the heart of most fanzines is in their letter column. I mentioned it to others, but they did not necessarily follow up. Then I showed a couple of copies to a correspondent, John Brewer, who was a prisoner on death row for murdering his girlfriend. There will be more about him in Chapter 12, "Readers"; this is only as he relates to *Fosfax*. He liked the fanzine, being conservative and interested in the supernatural, and wrote in and subscribed. They ran a couple of his letters, then abruptly cut him off because they didn't like him. I think what they actually didn't like was this evidence of a conservative who espoused their values, but was a killer; it hit too close to home. But this bothered me, because it was a violation of their supposed policy of free expression; apparently what they actually meant was free expression only for those they liked or agreed with, or wished to have represented for notoriety. That, by my definition, was hypocrisy. So I wrote them one more letter, expressing my objection, and sent them one article, on my experience meeting Jenny Elf at a convention—more about that too, in "Readers"—and when they did not relent, I dropped them. Thereafter they bad-mouthed me for years, even apparently trying to blame *me* for dropping John Brewer. Hypocrisy indeed.

A couple of other examples: one person in Fosfax claimed that I had misused the word "logarithmic" in my novel *But What of Earth* and berated my supposed ignorance. He said that logarithms were actually very small numbers. Now it happens I was an instructor of basic math in the U.S. Army, and one of the things I taught there was logarithms. Small numbers? Hardly! A logarithm is an exponent in decimal form, and can magnify a given number by any amount. My actual sentence in the novel was "Inflation was becoming logarithmic rather than linear." That is correct usage; a logarithmic scale is more potent than a linear one. But no one in Fosfax corrected him, which gives an indication of the math level of that readership. Then later, when I was Guest of Honor at Necronomicon in 1991 my daughter and I encountered a man in an elevator. He said that he and I had "crossed swords." I drew a blank, as I didn't know him, and shrugged it off. But then I saw him bad-mouthing me in Fosfax, and made the connection, I think: when I had sent two issues of the magazine to John Brewer, I told him to ignore my pencil check marks in the margin, as they were just indicating references to me. When he returned the magazines, he informed me that I had missed one. So I had: someone had challenged my statement that I was an agnostic and called me an atheist. He didn't explain his authority for changing my religious status, or say what would be wrong with being an atheist, but evidently he thought he had scored a point. I had never responded, since I had overlooked that remark. That must have been his "crossing swords." My neglecting to answer him in kind had evidently not pacified him, because now he was remarking on his elevator encounter with me, saying that I was an also-attendee—he named another writer as *the* Guest of Honor—and that he saw me as curiously empty. I had, because I didn't recognize him, treated him with complete pacifism, but that seemed to have incited him to further attack, which continued intermittently for years, at times bordering on libel. Again, it seemed that no one at *Fosfax* knew the actual guests of honor at that convention, or cared to check the truth about any other statements. When last heard from, he was accusing me of dropping John Brewer, having used him only to demean *Fosfax*. But I never have been clear on why this person hates me, given the entirely one-sided nature of our interaction. *Fosfax,* of course, is glad to pretend that it wasn't the entity at fault. Robert Margroff finally got fed up with the misrepresentations and sent in a hard-hitting letter correcting them. And they refused to run his letter, claiming that it violated their standards of civility. He and I found it interesting that false statements about me were not considered uncivil, only the corrections. They did summarize his letter, though—in a misleading way. So it is apparent that it is not editorial confusion operating here; it is indeed a malign agenda.

Thereafter I stayed clear of fanzines. There had been a number of others over the years, and my contributions would probably fill a book in themselves. I recommend them to those who want to be in touch with like-minded folk of the genre. They range from great-hearts to turds, and the category they occupy is not always immediately apparent, as my experience shows. They come and go; one will shine brightly for a time, then fade, and others will brighten. Some become major centers of interaction; others have standards similar to those described, with ignorant opinionated editors who will never admit being wrong. Most are mixed bags. I took one, the *Knarley Knews,* apart in my column in the Hi Piers Newsletter, giving the editor space to respond. He had openly questioned my integrity in print, and never had the grace to apologize when fully refuted. That's unfortunately typical. Anyone with a ditto machine, or now a computer printer, can became a fanzine publisher; all he needs is postage and a mailing list. If you publish, they will come. Normally fanzines are free for the contribution of a letter of comment, called a LoC, but they can also be had by subscription. I am not aware of any general listing of them all, so can't say how to get in touch with the first one. A standing joke is the Secret Master of Fandom: obviously fandom is ungoverned and ungovernable, and how could it be controlled in secret anyway? Sometimes this is amplified to the League of the Secret Masters. I once told Geis that I was going to report him to the Secret Masters, a threat that surely scared him for all of an eighth of a second. Today I understand there are similar associations on the computer nets, with fanzines being replaced by bulletin boards, chat rooms, pages, and so on. Indeed, some magazines have gone into cyberspace, no longer being published as physical entities. The beauty of cyberspace is that it's inherently uncensorable; it, too, has no secret master, though certain governments are making the attempt to assume that role. So it may represent the spirit of fanzine fandom in its heyday.

Out of this welter have come a few semiprofessional or fully professional magazines, such as the "newszines" *LOCUS* and *SF Chronicle*. Of those two, Locus is larger, with more news, reviews, and ads, but also with a more evident agenda, at least in my case: its rule seems to be that if it can't pan my books, it won't review them at all. When it reviewed *Bio of an Ogre* it used so many derogatory terms as to make the review seem a joke, and even put the term "(sic)" by a supposed error that wasn't in the published book. I received word from readers that they had protested the unfair review, but *LOCUS* never acknowledged that. I tried to fathom why *LOCUS* turned hostile, as I was a subscriber from its origin as a one-staple news-sheet and had been courteous to it. I think I finally ran it down, though the incident is so small as to be almost beyond belief as a motive. As I remember, it ran a note that Piers Anthony had sold a story to a magazine. I commented that since thousands of stories are sold to magazines in a year, this hardly seemed worthy of note; why not save the space for significant events? After that, the magazine turned hostile. When my first Xanth novel, *A Spell for Chameleon*, won the British Fantasy Award, that was the one year that *LOCUS* skipped listing that award. When a chain store counted the genre authors with the most novels on its "favorites" list, and Anthony led with twelve to Robert Heinlein's eleven, *LOCUS* didn't mention it. It even missed my first—and apparently the genre's first—original paperback national best-seller, *Ogre, Ogre*, though it didn't seem to have trouble picking up on the successes of other writers. It has been an ongoing pattern. And the turning point, as far as I can tell, was that one innocuous comment of mine, made in a private letter to the editor. I still subscribe to *LOCUS*, because it is one of the only games in town, but I don't respect it, because if it distorts my record, how many other records is it similarly distorting? SF *Chronicle* seems to lack such an agenda, though I was not pleased when its editor accepted my subscription to a prior magazine he published, then shut it down with my subscription incomplete, no refund, while sending a grand final issue free to a number of folk but apparently not to subscribers, because I never received it. This sort of thing seems endemic in fandom, and isn't its prettiest aspect. Nevertheless, I recommend both of these magazines to those who want to know most of what's going on in the genre. You won't find much about me there, but coverage in other respects is fair to good.

Another aspect of fandom is the network of conventions. All over the world there are periodic gatherings of fans, readers, and professionals, though I think most of them are in the United States. Just about every major city in the U.S. has a fan convention at some time, and a number have regular annual ones. They try to fit the word "con" in, for convention, often humorously. Thus we have Chattacon in Chattanooga, Tennessee; Rockon in Little Rock, Arkansas; Wiscon in Wisconsin; NorWescon in Seattle, Washington; DeepSouthCon in the deep south; Hurricon on the Florida beaches; Aggiecon at Texas A&M; Confusion, Con-Dor, Con-Cave, Contact, Conduit, Confluence, Leprecon, Contradiction, and so on. There is a World Science Fiction Convention that travels to a different city each year, and a World Fantasy Con that moves similarly; local fan clubs bid for the privilege of hosting them.

So what is the use of conventions? They serve as physical meeting places, where fans can find enormous arrays of genre books, magazines, and artifacts on display and sale. They bring in professionals, so that readers can finally get to meet their favorite authors. They put on assorted panels and shows of interest to readers. But mainly, they establish for a few days a community of common interest. Genre devotees can join the group and not feel strange, because everyone else there has a similar devotion to the genre. Wild-eyed fans can feel at home there. Indeed, there seem to be convention addicts, who go to all the conventions they can manage. They don't necessarily read the genre, they don't attend the functions, they just go to hang out in the compatible atmosphere. Some of them are called BNFs, or Big Name Fans. Some are called BOFs, or Boring Old Farts.

After I attended the Milford Writer's Conference in 1966, which was not a convention but a gathering purely of writers, I did not rush to go to the other kind of gathering. But when I was invited to attend the Science Fiction Research Association annual meeting in 1982, I pondered. I don't like to travel, but Theodore Sturgeon would be there, a writer I have much admired, along with Harry Harrison, James Gunn, and others. We had a policy of giving our daughters experience when we can, and Penny had visited Canada, so this time I took Cheryl along. Oh, it's not one-way; if I must travel, I'd much rather have company. So I had her read at least one novel by each of the writers we would be meeting, so she would know them, and that's when she discovered Harry Harrison's Stainless Steel Rat series, and loved it. We went to Kansas, and I did meet the folk I wanted to. It was dull for Cheryl, until she got together with the Miller family, and learned to play Ping-Pong, after which for a couple of years we played that game at home and she became good at it. I remember when I was washing up in the bathroom of our hotel room, and she called "Daddy, you'd better come see this!" She was watching cable TV, and on it was a splendidly bare-breasted woman, twirling thongs from her nipples. We don't see that sort of thing on broadcast TV. I remember also attending a writing seminar, and the proprietor inquired how many had actually submitted material for publication, and everyone laughed when I was one of those raising a hand. One unfortunate thing was a confusion about the time we were heading home; James Gunn's son was a fan of mine, but he had understood my departure was one day later, and his schedule caused him to miss me. I hate it when that sort of thing happens, but I did autograph his collection of my novels in his absence. I was bemused by the fact that it was a story of James Gunn that became perhaps my all-time favorite, "Breaking Point." I read it in the March 1953 *Space Science Fiction*, my favorite magazine of the time, edited by Lester del Rey. I was working at a warehouse and living in a cooperative boardinghouse called the Brudercoop, and both work and residence were okay, but I felt somewhat alone. Science fiction was my continuing salvation, and it transported me to another dimension. I was tired when I read that story, alone in the evening, and when I finished it I looked up, and the whole room seemed to be turning inside out. Then it began to shake, and the shaking got worse, until I grew alarmed and moved, and the effect dissipated. So there were a number of elements, but one of them was that phenomenal story, wherein a spaceship landed on a foreign planet and was subjected to a mind siege that severely tested every member of the crew. Psychological science fiction, a great piece of writing. I found it awesome to think that the son of this great writer was a fan of mine. Perhaps also that Theodore Sturgeon's daughter read my fiction. Sturgeon's story "The Girl Had Guts" is another classic, in my mind, along with Walter M. Miller's "Vengeance for Nikolai," both of them appearing in *Venture* in 1957. So I had an experience at that function that partook of my own fandom, with the odd juxtaposition of others seeing me as the author of pieces that moved them. Was I fan or writer? Emotionally that has never quite clarified for me. That SFRA meeting took on some convention-like attributes, and had an autographing session, and that was where I learned how such things are done. So this was not a fan convention, but it enabled me to handle fan conventions thereafter, so I think deserves a place here. I am glad that I attended it.

Next year we received a surprise invitation from Judy-Lynn del Rey: how about having the whole family come to Dallas to attend the American Booksellers Convention there that year, and autograph copies for the publisher? Now Dallas was the last place I wanted to visit, because that's where the first president I got to vote for, John F. Kennedy, was shot, when some kook took the campaign against him in that region seriously and thought he was doing the world a favor. But Dallas was where the ABA was, and I had either to accept or decline. I thought of the great experience it would be for my daughters, then ages fifteen and thirteen, and agreed to go. The ABA is an annual convention that moves around, and it resembled a genre convention on a larger scale. A typical one might have twenty thousand attendees, and their myriad autographing sessions are always well attended, because the books are provided free. Many other promotional things are given out free, so my daughters had a ball. We got to eat several meals with Lester and Judy-Lynn del Rey, and the girls enjoyed themselves. At one point we were supposed to eat with my agent, Kirby McCauley, but he didn't show up, so the del Reys took us in hand. But the addition of the four of us made theirs a party of eight rather than the four they had planned, so they had a problem at the restaurant. Judy-Lynn was afraid it wouldn't work out, but Lester said it would. And in a few minutes there was a cancellation of a party of eight, which made room for us. Lester in effect told his wife "I told you so!" Thus we shared a meal with Charles Brown, editor of LOCUS, back before his magazine's increasingly negative slant on me was apparent. At another meal the girls were stuffed full, but the proprietors were required to show us their complete cart full of fancy desserts; this must have been like heaven offering, but they had to turn it all down, tragically. Overall, we had a good experience at the Dallas ABA, but I still don't like the city.

Necronomicon in Tampa invited me to be their Guest of Honor. I pondered, and concluded that I had to break the ice sometime, with respect to regular fandom, and it was close by (I don't much like to travel), and my daughters should like the experience. So I accepted, and in 1983 we went for our first actual small genre convention. It was an instant hit with Penny and Cheryl, and thereafter they became convention freaks, and today they have attended many more conventions than I have. The fan Guest of Honor was Bill Ritch, and he was to have a considerable effect on our lives. He visited us, and showed us how his VCR worked. We had heard of these devices, but never actually seen one in operation. It was just like a movie, on our own TV! Cheryl was an instant convert, and soon we got one of our own. He also educated us on computers, and in due course we got computerized.

Two years later I went to Fall-Con (Falcon) in Gainesville, Florida, as Guest of Honor. The daughters joined me, though my wife stayed home to take care of the pets. By this time I was used to conventions and knew it to be typical. It was there I met the genre writer Meredith Ann Pierce, whose distinction in my eyes was that she had black hair that reached to the floor. Maybe she thought I was teasing her when I commented on it, but I just love long hair on a woman.

Now understand, I'm a long-married man, and I'm not about to do anything to mess that up. But she became a mental image of my dream girl, because of the hair, foolish as it is to orient on one thing. When I read her fantasy novels, I liked them too; she strikes me as a good writer and a nice person. But I would hardly have noticed her, were it not for the hair. The rest of the convention was routine; I enjoyed it, and I believe that the attendees enjoyed meeting me. It is my policy to protect my privacy most of the time, but to make myself fully available to readers when I make public appearances. So while some guest writers disappear most of the time, I don't; I'm amidst my readers. It's not that I love attention; I really don't crave that much, which is why I limit my public appearances. But whatever I do, I try to do as it should be done.

In 1987 I changed publishers, and that led to a busy year. I did a tour and attended three conventions. Avon Books, to whom I had taken the Xanth series, took me to the ABA convention in Washington, DC. That was my first and only experience with a first-class ticket in an airplane. Thanks, but no thanks, thereafter; why should I pay three times as much for a little more room? But it was nice, once. Avon did not have a book of mine coming out at that time, so I wound up with an autographing session for Berkley. I wore a participant's badge, and the guard at the entrance was letting only regular members in. Thus the line was forming for the books I was to sign, but I couldn't get in to sign them. Idiocy! The publisher had to sneak me in the back way so I could meet my commitment. I did address a dinner event Avon set up, where caviar was served; as a vegetarian I skipped it, and wished they had been a bit more sensitive. Folk can eat what they want, but I dislike being the supposed reason for meat being served. I also was cautious with the two types of wine served, with the two glasses kept constantly filled; I'm not much of a drinker, and in public I prefer not to drink at all, so as to keep my mental facilities. One attendee was obviously drunk, not making the kind of impression she supposed she was making. But the Washington ABA was a nice enough event, all things considered.

The tour was arranged by Berkley to promote my Adept series, and took my wife and me to San Francisco, as discussed in Chapter 6. In that chapter I discussed some of the professional aspects of that trip; here I'll cover some of the fan aspects. I remember watching the movie *Little Shop of Horrors* without sound on the huge airplane going there, because we didn't care to pay four dollars for earphones. Later, at home, we watched it with the sound, and it wasn't as interesting. I remember how one of my fans flew from Los Angeles to San Francisco so as to come to my book signing, and the store personnel told her I wanted her to leave. It was a lie, devastating her, causing much mischief, and that is what governs my emotional connection to that city: it had liars. Apparently they felt she was a disruption, because she was black. I remember also the woman who came to the bookstore in Berkeley, across the bay, who felt compelled to give me a number of little gifts, including a nice model bird. I set it on the empty chair next to me and continued my autographing, because there was a crowd—the best single day in the history of that store, I was told later—and someone else came and sat on the model. I took it home and it seemed all right, but I always feel guilty when I look at it, as if it was the woman herself who got sat on. I remember seeing the edge of the Pacific Ocean, and the south end of the Golden Gate Bridge. And being alarmed in Oakland, because the lady who drove us there said she was concerned about her brakes, which were whining, and the streets went straight up and down the steep hills. A brake failure could have been fatal. We stopped at the *LOCUS* headquarters, where I signed the huge collection of my novels that the proprietor got free for reviewing—as if *LOCUS* would ever voluntarily do any of my books the favor of a good review. Their chief reviewer remained cloistered in her room the whole time, refusing to come out and speak with me. If I did as bad a job on anyone's books as she did on mine, I'd hide too. But competence and objectivity are not requirements for reviewing. Things were sociable enough on the surface, but I'm sure the folk there were no more comfortable with me than I was with them. On the way back to Florida we were jammed in the back of the plane, next to an engine, because that was the section for smokers, and my wife smokes. That gave me the feel of segregation; the smokers were definitely being made to feel unwelcome.

Then I was pro guest of honor at the 1987 Necronomicon again, in Tampa. They normally have two guests of honor, but the other, Fred Pohl, had to cancel because his wife had a heart attack. I had arranged to interview him there, and of course that couldn't be done, so I came back for one day the following year and we did it. Pohl is one of the premier writers of the genre and a great person, for all that I never liked him in his editing days. I teased him about that, reading an "anonymous" criticism of him, holding up the book so the audience could see that it was one of mine. Pohl grabbed for it a couple of times, as if trying to find out who the critic was. It was a fun interview, of a writer I really do respect. I asked him whether, the year before, he had told his wife he was going to be interviewed by an ogre, and she had a heart attack. I met his wife, briefly, and was surprised when, years later, she was reported as finding me to be shy. Perhaps she had confused me with someone else, or maybe she meant shy for an ogre.

The 1987 finale was the World Fantasy Convention in Nashville, Tennessee. I agreed to be their Guest of Honor only because I felt I owed a debt to fantasy, because it had put me on the best-seller list. I learned that this traveling convention, more than any other, was a gathering for professionals. It turned out to be well run, and was attended by many publishers, too. Indeed, all my main meals were with publishers, and each made a banquet of it. I would have preferred less attention, and I did not attend another World Fantasy Con. But there were good aspects. I think my favorite memory is of having three breakfasts with Andre Norton, who at this point is one of the few genre writers who has had more novels published than I have. She was of my mother's generation, and had been publishing novels since 1951. One floor of the hotel was reserved for professionals, and a buffet-style breakfast was laid out for their use. I'm an early riser, and it turned out that Andre Norton was too, while our companions were not, so I asked if I could join her, and we had a compatible meal together. We had first met at Necronomicon, and my daughter Penny and I had taken her and her friend to dinner, so we knew each other. We compared notes on agents and such, and her input was one reason I did not take a certain agent when I had the opportunity. But there were other things at that convention. I met with Stephen Donaldson, who had forged into fantasy best-selling status with Del Rey the same time I did, and who encountered similar trouble with the editing. My wife and I had a meal with the prominent genre artist Kelly Freas. I had admired his work from way back, on covers and in *Mad* magazine. I asked him whether he would like to handle my upcoming Xanth Calendar, but he had just taken a job as genre art director for the Scientologists and wasn't available. But he pondered, and contacted the convention Art Guest of Honor, Ron Lindahn, with whom I was later to have a considerable association. And I met someone there I hardly noticed, but she was to become a collaborator on a novel: Jo Anne Taeusch. She and her husband came through my autograph line, and he seemed huge while she looked like a child in comparison. Then she showed up at my reading, never saying a word. But later I received humorous love letters from her, and after a few years I finally made the connection. So a lot happened at that convention, thanks mainly to the strong presence of other professionals and publishers. I noticed that the readings, including my own, were not well attended; six to a dozen folk might show up, and Donaldson said this was typical. But the awards banquet, in contrast, was jammed. I pondered this, and concluded that most of the attendees simply were not interested in the genre, but liked the big social gathering. So these were not actually my kind of people, as I love the genre but am not much for parties.

So I never really developed a taste for conventions, and preferred to avoid them. I told Andre Norton that I regard the two of us as being in a contest to see who could attend the fewest conventions, and she laughed. Indeed, neither of us goes often, and it was unusual for us both to be at the same one, though it had happened at Necronomicon. But in 1989 something special came up. I was invited to be GoH at Sci-Con in Virginia, and declined. Then I discovered that Jenny, my paralyzed correspondent, lived in that area. So I arranged to go, so that I could meet her. More on that in the next chapter. Kelly Freas was there—it turned out that he had long been associated with that convention—and Ron and Val Lindahn, and the GoH was the artist who had done the *Visual Guide to Xanth*, Todd Cameron Hamilton. And it was this almost coincidental convention that I regard as my most compatible one. They had it well organized, the convention hotel was well laid out, and the usual and often infuriating foul-ups did not occur. The staff was thoughtful, and this facilitated the presence of Jenny. So this convention was, in contrast to some, a pleasure.

In 1990 I was GoH at Phoenixcon in Atlanta, arranged by Bill Ritch, who had introduced us to video and computers. It was a nice little convention, where I understand they tried very hard to make things go well. Because I don't like being in the position where every program I attend I'm onstage, I went to the first program of the morning reading of another writer—and the only attendees were Bill Ritch and I. It was a good piece and a good reading. I said it was too bad he didn't have a better audience, and he said he had a good audience, just not a big one. But this continues to bother me: if the attendees of conventions aren't interested in writers sharing their material, isn't it a sad situation? Are conventions just big parties after all? But I did do some business there: I met with Ron Lindahn's business partner, Ed Maul, and we discussed setting up what was to become Hi Piers. That will be covered in a separate chapter.

Later in 1990 I attended SeaCon in Orlando, a regional American Booksellers Association convention, to promote Hi Piers. I wasn't a guest, just an attendee, or rather, an exhibitor, with a Hi Piers booth. And later still, the World Fantasy Convention in Chicago, again not as a guest but in connection with Hi Piers. There I received a note: would I pose for a photographer? It seemed that all the professionals were being done, at fifteen-minute intervals during the convention. So I showed up for my slot at the appointed time. The photographer turned out to be an attractive young woman. I remarked, as I usually do, on the anomaly of pretty girls taking pictures of ugly old men: a reversal of the natural order. Then I told bystanders how we used to play "Picture" when I was a boy. Just as the camera was about to click, I turned my head, put my spread fingers to my ears, and stuck out my tongue. Flash! She got the picture. Of course she took many others, so surely had some good ones, but I suspect that was her favorite.

In 1991 I went to the ABA convention in New York, again for Hi Piers. All this traveling was not anything I did for the joy of it. Again I had my own booth, and also promoted the major novel of my career, *Tatham Mound*, as described in Chapter 6. It was a good convention, well laid out, so that there were no logjams at key places.

Then I went to DragonCon in Atlanta, again because of Hi Piers, which the convention helped promote, though for this one I was a Guest of Honor. It was a big convention, well organized, with many professionals attending; I'm sure most folk enjoy it. But I ran afoul of a special situation: after a full day, I was developing a headache and wanted to go to my room to sleep. But all the elevators were full, and they never got empty. It turned out that fans were staging an "Elevator Party," wherein they never got off the elevators, preventing them from being used legitimately. I was unable to get to my room. I had to go to the hotel manager, who put me on a private hotel elevator. That sort of thing turns me off conventions. If attendees have nothing better to do than interfere with other folk, and the convention authorities don't care enough to prevent such mischief, they can do without me. I never went to another DragonCon.

And later that year I was GoH at Necronomicon again, in Tampa. I paid my own way completely, so I was no expense to them; this enabled them to use the money they had budgeted for me to have a third Guest of Honor. I donated one of my bound galleys of *Tatham Mound* to their book auction, and it went for $150. I met all their fans and signed autographs, as usual. My daughters attended also. The convention worked me hard, so that I was perpetually hurrying from one program to another. Normally the Guest of Honor gets a free convention T-shirt, but they ran out of them and hadn't set any aside for me. The working time I lost by attending was worth approximately $10,000. I think it would have been nice if they had at least said "thank you." But the only report I saw on that convention criticized me for always hurrying, and named me as an also-ran, not a Guest of Honor. So much for accuracy. When they invited me to be Guest of Honor for 1996, my reply was brief: "Thanks, no." I suspect they didn't understand why.

In 1992 we went to the World Science Fiction Convention in Orlando, Florida. I had never been to a World SF Con before, and I did it right: I made no advance commitments, and attended pretty much as a walk-in fan, paying my own way. That left me free to go to the programs that interested me, instead of being prechanneled. The convention center in Orlando, like that in New York, was well laid out, so there were no frustrating delays at elevators. As we walked in, we spied Tom Doherty of TOR, and he invited us to dinner. We hadn't anticipated that, but agreed, and had a nice one with him and his new wife from Russia. She was learning English, so did not speak much, but I made her laugh when I described how the scriptwriters for the movie I novelized, *Total Recall*, thought that all that was necessary to make breathable air on the planet Mars was to vaporize a huge glacier. She was a chemist; she knew better. Vaporize a typical glacier and you have water vapor, not air. After that meal we adjourned to the lobby, where we met Jerry Pournelle—who proceeded to accuse me of writing a letter vilifying him, as described in Chapter 10. That turned a good day into a bad one. I was so upset that I stayed awake all night. Oh, I know, one should not let the false words of those who ought to know better get to one, but my hide is not that thick; this lie caught me entirely unprepared. Then I had to sleep during the day, missing some of the programs I had wanted to attend. But I did meet a number of acquaintances; conventions are good places to do that, and some folk are met only at conventions. I attended the "Coffee Klatch" for Hal Clement, an old-time genre writer whose work I respected; *Mission of Gravity* was a classic. This was a gathering at a table where readers could have a more extended dialogue with given writers, and I was glad to meet another of the giants of my genre-formative years. After it, we talked, and I told him how I had worried that I was copying him when I used alien symbiosis to convert my collaborative novel *The Pretender* to science fiction, similar to what he had in *Needle*. He wasn't concerned. Andre Norton had her klatch elsewhere in the large room; I hadn't signed for hers because it was already oversubscribed, but my wife and I stopped by afterwards to say hello. I also met with Richard Gilliam, and we set up for a collaborative anthology, *Tales from the Great Turtle*. So the convention, taken as a whole, was worthwhile for me. We picked up literature for the next one, to be held in Glasgow, Scotland, and planned to go, so I could see the old country after more than fifty years, but things got complicated and we didn't go.

Early in 1994 I was GoH at Hurricon, in the Florida panhandle. It was a typical convention, which meant that for most of my party there was a lack of convention badges and hotel reservations, though we had all set up well in advance, and were all paying our own way. Anything that required preparation hadn't been done, so at one point I found myself in front of an expectant audience and had to tell them that the planned program had foundered. Fortunately they were willing to settle for just my candid talk. But I was fed up with the persistent amateurishness of amateur-run conventions, and though I had up until then been trying to limit my conventions to one a year, thereafter my object was to limit them to none a year. Oh, the readers are great, and there's a lot going on at any convention that's worthwhile; it's just that I do learn from experience, albeit slowly, and concluded that conventions, like fanzines, weren't worth it.

Conventions figure in my life in another way, even when I don't attend them. They are centers for the exchange of information, true and false. Once my collaborator Robert E. Margroff attended a convention, and talked with an editor, and learned that that editor was desperate for material. Margroff told me, so I sent my then-unsold novel *Hasan* to the editor, and he liked it and bought it for an advance of $1,500. We were then tight financially, and that money gave us leeway that eased our condition, even though later another editor come in and, of course, dumped the novel. That's what new editors do, killing the offspring of their predecessors. So it was never published there, but we got to keep the money. But there are negatives too; I left the genre writer's organization SFWA because of its bad actions, and since then various SFWA members have maligned me at conventions. For example, I understand that at the 1990 DeepSouthCon, a SFWA Southeastern representative writer named Robin Bailey was publicly bad-mouthing me for my supposed free ride in the SFWA audit of Berkley Books. My daughter was there, and she approached Bailey to challenge him, but he refused to listen to her. The fact is that I supported the audit of Berkley before SFWA did, and when SFWA took it over I held my nose and not only paid my own way, but that of another writer, a SFWA member, who couldn't afford it himself. The SFWA officer with whom I interacted on that occasion was Greg Bear, who had tried to level a similar charge at me and been thoroughly refuted, as I believe he will agree. (Those who brush with me directly seldom seek return engagements.) Later another writer was saying at another convention that I had told him that I would rather write a poor novel for more money than a good one for less money. This must be a confusion. I don't recall talking with him, but if I did, I think my comment would have been that I would rather write thoughtful material, but if the market is open only to frivolous fantasy, I will write that, because I'd rather be writing any kind of fiction than lose my career as a writer through poverty. This is true for virtually all professional writers, even if some don't admit it. I have never tried to write a poor novel, though some turn out better than others, and even my frivolous fantasy is the best of that kind I can do, always. If I have a choice between a serious novel and light fantasy, which also has its merits, and have time to do only one or the other, and the publisher will pay in six figures for the fantasy and in four figures for the serious one, then I will write the fantasy. That's not the same thing as preferring to write poorly for money, as any writer ought to know.

So while I don't say I'll never attend another convention, my appearances are likely to be few, and unpredictable. Recently I have received reports that people have met me at conventions and found me to be an arrogant, pompous ass. If that report dates from within six years, it's an obvious lie, as I haven't attended any SF conventions in that time, and in any event I have never acted that way at any convention, ever. Those who really have met me know that. Before I attended my first convention, I was accused of being an ogre at conventions, as mentioned before, hence my ogre theme; it seems that charge is still going around, with no better basis. It doesn't endear conventions to me. But I wonder: is someone impersonating me? Sometimes that happens to writers, and I think no writer is pleased by such antics.

When Robert A. Heinlein died, his wife did two things I know of that I deem commendable. First, she worked to get the original uncut versions of his novels into print, such as *The Puppet Masters* and *Stranger in a Strange Land*. I reread both, and feel that they should have been published in that form at the outset. The idea of a great writer like Heinlein having to take months to shorten such novels at the behest of an ignorant editor is infuriating. Second, she assembled *Grumbles from the Grave*, a book of Heinlein's letters and incidental pieces. He had planned to do a book of that title himself, really putting his concerns on the line, and certainly he had things to say. But he never got around to it. So she used the title and drew on his papers to enable him to do at least a bit of grumbling from the grave. When I read it, I was struck by how well I related to it. He had run afoul of so many of the things I did, with seemingly idiotic and greedy publishers, demanding fans, and malicious gossip. He remarked on the prospect of getting formal coaching in writing from Thomas Uzzell, a well-known "story doctor," and declined. I relate to that because I actually took Uzzell's course, and concluded that it was hardly worth my time. Uzzell meant well, but he didn't know the genre, and was floored by ordinary science fiction, thinking I must be joking, as shown in the appendix to *BiOgre*. The Uzzells were long on principles and short on relevance. For sure, there was little there for Heinlein. He referred to writing—that is, the modern form of Tale Telling—as the second oldest profession. He wanted to do serious writing for adults, instead of being typecast as a writer of juveniles. Yes. He also had to move to have room for his papers and books, which evidently accumulated with his success. Right; no matter how far ahead I plan, my books and papers soon threaten to overwhelm the territory. That's one reason I donate them to university archives. He struggled with the inanities and duplicities of builders, a route we learned too. But mainly it was the fans.

One of the chapter titles is "Fan Mail and Other Time Wasters." So many letters came in that he didn't have time to write. I detail my own experience of that type in Chapter 12. He said that there were endless requests for him to go here, speak there, donate mss, advise a beginning writer, and so on. He tried using a secretary, but it just cost him money and didn't save time. Uh-huh. Form letters didn't serve because there was too much variety in the incoming mail. Each fan felt that *he* was different, expecting Heinlein to stop whatever he was doing and make a full answer. Finally, his wife took over the correspondence, as a way to answer without encouraging more. I have not followed him in that, in part because my wife is not comfortable writing letters, but at least the computer increases my efficiency in answering. Invitations to speak used up yet more time, so he learned to avoid them. Yes. I'm sure he felt the same way about fan conventions and stopped attending them, as I have.

But mainly I like his response to a fan who wrote to ask why he was unsympathetic to the aims of a fan group. He replied that he had very little contact with organized fandom, and objected to malicious allegations from faceless strangers, with "experts" on him who really didn't know him. Yep. Then he said that he wrote for three reasons: to support himself, to entertain readers, and if possible, to make his readers think. He said that if a writer did not entertain his readers, all he was producing was paper dirty on one side. Or, simplified, he wrote for money. He felt that any other short answer was dishonest. Here I differ with him; I write for the love of writing. But I do also write for money, and find no shame in it. Fans and reviewers and critics who endlessly take off on me because I am a successful commercial writer would do well to read *Grumbles*.

And of course I should make my own comment on reviewers and critics, which for my purpose are more serious reviewers. A reviewer may briefly describe a book and say it's great or it stinks; a critic goes more deeply into it, identifying its themes and strengths and fallacies and educating the reader on fundamentals that might otherwise be missed. I feel that these are good and necessary endeavors, because there is such a mass of fiction coming out that ordinary readers can't keep up with it. If they can read the comment of a competent reviewer, they can discover what novels will be to their taste, and avoid those that aren't.

Unfortunately, that often doesn't happen. Folk in other professions must undergo serious training and prove their qualifications before being allowed to practice. Writers must labor to learn their craft, and only about one in a hundred succeeds in this competitive endeavor. But there are no standards for reviewers or critics; anyone can, as it were, set up his shingle and think himself an expert. Few are. Thus ignorant or thoughtless opinions are given the same weight as serious and informed ones. Some have agendas: they may be unsuccessful writers who wish to condemn those who succeed as writers. They may wish to prove that they, the reviewers, could have written it better, by tearing up what they see. They may like one type of fiction and hate another, so they praise the one and condemn the other regardless of actual merit. They may wish to do personal favors or indulge in grudges. Anonymous reviews are great for that, and magazines that publish them evidently don't care much about fairness. In a general way, many reviewers have a bias against success, so they try to bring down the most successful fiction while promoting the least successful. Thus the novels that are most widely praised by reviewers can be unreadable by regular readers. Some readers have learned to tune in specific reviewers, and go for the novels that are panned while avoiding those that are praised. But most, disgusted, seem to avoid reviews entirely. In the circumstance, that seems sensible.

When challenged on evident bias and inaccuracy, a reviewer may say "It's just my opinion," as if that justifies it. It is not a question of free speech, but of competence. This is a forum where an ignorant opinion is not good enough. The reviewer is there to perform a service for the readers of that publication, and therefore he must do his best to make it an informed opinion. This is a different creature from an uninformed one. Any idiot can watch a football game on TV and berate the coach for a stupid decision; his opinion has no force. But the coach himself has a responsibility to his team to make the best decisions he can, and if those aren't good enough, he will in due course lose his position. Similarly any idiot can condemn a book without even opening it, but a reviewer is abrogating his responsibility if he does that. Any idiot can stick a pin in a newspaper and pick a horse or stock to recommend, but a professional with significant money on the outcome takes pains to inform himself as thoroughly as he can. Similarly, a reviewer should learn his trade, so as to make his opinion informed and worthwhile. Otherwise, he is wasting everyone's time. He is not there to toss off ignorant quips or to impose his personal foibles on the material; when he does that he is toying with the trust of the reader, the livelihood of the writer, and the reputation of the publication in which the reviewer appears. In literary terms, he is a criminal. He needs to be removed so that a more responsible or competent reviewer can have the forum.

There are writers who think that the only good review is a favorable one, and they curse any negative review. They are mistaken. There is considerable subjectivity; nevertheless, some novels are by most standards excellent; others are not. The deciding criterion is the taste of the book's intended readership, and the reviewer needs to ascertain this and relate to it. A good review is one that successfully separates the wheat from the chaff, and identifies the best, worst, and indifferent works for their intended readership. A bad review is one that fails to do this. Thus there can be a negative review that is good: it has correctly called a bad novel what it is. There can be a bad positive review, that praises a novel that readers won't much like. The proprietors of publications that print reviews should fire any reviewer who is evidently unable or unwilling to make those distinctions. The fact that they seldom do eliminate bad reviewers suggests that such publishers neither know nor care about quality reviewing. They are just filling space. So they, too, are defaulting on their obligation to their readers, and deserve the eventual loss of circulation they will achieve.

In short, the reviewing industry needs to clean up its act. At present it is held in generally, and deservedly, low regard.

Twelve

READERS

t first fan mail was a rarity. But when I got into the Xanth fantasy series, the letters multiplied. I felt that a fair letter deserved a fair answer, and a number of correspondences developed. It gradually rose to the level of 150 a month, and that is where I have tried to hold the line, because it takes me about ten days of each month to keep up with it, and that's one-third of my working time. Every so often I will receive a sarcastic or condemnatory missive from a reader who resents my statements that I'd rather have less mail; my standard response is to the effect of "Do *you* spend a third of your working time answering letters for no pay?" and that generally shuts them up. I have no statistics on this, but I suspect that there are very few novelists who answer more mail, more responsively, than I do. I don't guarantee to answer more than the first letter, but if the reader is serious, I usually do answer others. So I judge that about half my mail is from first timers, and half from repeaters. Originally my impression was that it ran about 60–40 male-female, but a more recent survey indicated that the ratio had reversed, and I now correspond with more women/girls than men/boys. Concerned that I might be selecting the girls for answers—I'm a man, and highly aware of the opposite gender—I limited my count to new letters—and it still ran predominantly female. So I conclude that my fantasy and novels like *Virtual Mode* and *Firefly* cause more women to react than men.

Every person is an individual, and so is every letter. That's why I don't use forms to respond, though I do have a number of "canned paragraphs" so that I don't have to type the same information about an upcoming novel over and over. But over the months and years they tend to merge into broad fuzzy groups. My memory for names is poor, so few stand out in my memory. But there are some, and I'll discuss some of those here.

One early one was difficult. I learn well from experience, but experience can be a hard teacher, and new things are not always easy to play correctly. I heard from a woman who was a devoted fan of my works, intelligent, expressive, and interesting. Her letters always drew me out, getting me into extended discussions. They also contained hints that she found me romantically interesting, and would be amenable to something along that line. Later, other correspondents came on to me similarly, and they ranged in age from thirteen to over sixty and from moderately to extremely attractive. But I was alert to the signs, and responded courteously but with no suggestion that I was looking for what they offered. If I lost my wife, in due course I would want to remarry, because I can't face the thought of living alone. But it will be death that parts us, and whatever I can do to preserve her life and health I will do, within reason. I can't make her stop smoking or get into a sustained exercise program, so I fear she will die before me. But I have to let her live her life in the way she chooses, and support her in that, just as she lets me live mine and supports me. It is a good marriage, and we differ on very few things, and compatibly on those. We have what I call a conventional marriage: I earn the money, she spends it. In fact she keeps the accounts and does the taxes, which are complicated. I decide on the big things, like the significance of world events, and she decides the small things, like everything else. We trust each other, and communicate constantly. I'm glad I married her, and believe that I would not be where I am today without her. But if I should find myself alone, I would then consider more carefully what else offers, with strong cautions from my life experience. Meanwhile I have a small category of correspondents I treat politely: those who profess or imply love for me. Some I would never marry, regardless, but I don't want to bring them the grief of direct rejection. They are, as a rule, good women, and I never like the notion of breaking hearts or treading on dreams. Very generally, my proscriptions relate to age—I'm wary of women younger than my daughters, and doubly wary of teens, and think that reasonable boundaries would be within twenty years of my own age, older or younger. And to healthy lifestyle—any excesses of smoking, drinking, gambling, drugs, spending, temper, weight, politics, religion, or the like would be suspect, and I could not love one who was not a vegetarian. I also have a strong bias toward intelligence, creativity, and honor. So I guess I would be pretty damn choosy. But I think I could find such a woman, because what I would offer in return would be a compatible nature that meets the same requirements, and absolute financial security. Were I to enter a singles ad, it would be something like "Old vegetarian ogre ISO (in search of) the usual." Those who don't know ogres as I define them would be scared away, simplifying the search. So do I ponder in my fancy any particular women now, though I am not on the market? Yes, in much the way most men reflect what it would be like to spend a night with particular women, despite knowing there is no chance of it happening. No, I will not name my most likely choice. Yes, my wife knows who it is. Is she jealous? I doubt it. Does the woman herself know? I think not. My wife also knows that I have no desire to lose her, and no intention of crossing any lines. I think of the way I know roughly where my wife is, when we are separated in a group: I hear her ready laugh. That says so much. If there comes a time when I no longer hear it, that will be bleak.

Most correspondences consist of one fan letter and my response. A number go several letters, when there is a series of points to cover. I try to discourage letters just for the sake of letters, and most readers realize that my time is not infinite. But on occasion they refuse to take the hints of spaced-out responses or increasingly brief ones. Sometimes I stop answering, but they continue writing, demanding responses. Sometimes I simply have to say that I am terminating the correspondence. One reader was so upset by this, when I terminated him at the twenty-letter point, that he rented a car and drove by my house, then wrote a letter condemning me, my property, and my work. Another had his psychologist write to me to urge me to resume correspondence. I answered the psychologist, approximately: "Do you work for free? I have already taken $2,000 worth of my time on this, and it's enough." It was true, and it shut him up. Some few write to berate me on something, and will continue as long as I respond; when it is apparent that they have an agenda that is other than reasonable, I stop responding. One reader condemned my supposedly harsh treatment of the copy editors who destroyed *But What of Earth?* demanding answers when I sought to demur. So I let him have it, but didn't persuade him. I showed the correspondence to another person, to ascertain whether I was dealing fairly with the issues, and was told I was. So I let him go; there was no further point. I don't drop someone just because he disagrees with me; I'm not looking for yes-men. Sometimes there is ground for reasonable debate. Sometimes there is formidable reversal. A reader named Roberto Fuentes criticized me—and later became a friend and collaborator for six published novels. A pro reader objected to my interpretation of Neandertal man, who I believe was not ancestral to modern man; we differ, but he knows a lot, and I respect it. One woman called my novel *Firefly* "trash," but I maintained a correspondence with her because I saw that she was a good person, sacrificing herself for the sake of her ailing husband. Agreement with me is no sure ticket to correspondence, nor does disagreeing with me bar it; my perspective is wider than that.

One category of correspondent I have discussed in Chapter 5: the suicidally depressive, whom I call Ligeia. They can be either gender, but the great majority are female. Normally they write to me when they are unhappy, and cease when their outlook improves. Some cross over into the romantic category, perhaps in the manner of the transference psychologists or psychiatrists encounter. This can be difficult, as it was with the first Ligeia, but I respond to them with sympathy, not love.

Some write to me for advice on myriad subjects. I'm not an expert in anything much other than writing fantasy, but I try to answer reasonably. One young man was with his girlfriend when an attractive mutual acquaintance said that she was curious about sex and would like to try it with him, no other obligation. His girlfriend said it was okay with her, but he wasn't sure, so asked me. My answer, in essence, was: if you decide to have sex with anyone, have it with your regular girlfriend, or you will lose her, regardless what she tells you now. One girl told me that she loved her pony, but could see it only once a week. Should she sell it, which would be good for the pony but would break the girl's heart? I suggested that she sell it to a neighbor with a stipulation that she be granted regular visiting rights. She reported later than she did that, and it solved the problem; the pony was well cared for and happy, and she did visit it as often as she wished.

Some are routine correspondences, that suddenly emerge as memorable. That was the case when a girl sent me a newspaper clipping of the volunteer work she did nursing injured wild raptors—birds of prey— back to health. That lifted her right out of the ordinary; how many people do such work on a volunteer basis? I dubbed her The Bird

Maiden, after a character in my novel *Hasan* who married a woman who could don a bird suit and fly, and mentioned her when that novel was reissued. I still hear from her annually; she is married, lived in Germany for several years, and now lives in the United States.

Some are remarkable from the start. One reader was not a correspondent, but met me personally in New York. She had been spelunking in a phenomenally extensive newly discovered cave system out west, and had broken her leg and had to be hauled out. The horror of the situation and degree of challenge made national headlines. She was in a wheelchair, with a cast on her leg, when she came to meet me. I told her I was thrilled to have a reader who was famous. Another was a survivor of Waco, when the government stormed the stronghold of the David Koresh cult. My reader hid under a bed with her children, having no way to escape the situation. Her husband was shot to death, her four children were taken from her, and she was convicted of "resisting arrest" and sent to prison, where I heard from her: my novels helped bring her solace in a most difficult time. Another was Janet Hines, who had been stricken as a teenager with a debilitating disease that gradually deprived her of her sight and motion, leaving her by age thirty completely blind and paralyzed. But she enjoyed hearing my books read to her, or on tape. She was learning to use an eye-controlled computer, because though she was blind, she could still move her eyes. She was in my area, and in due course I visited her, and held her hand, talked with her, and kissed her on the cheek. She could respond only with a kind of laugh, but she certainly knew who I was. Later she died, and I wrote her into Xanth, her faculties restored, and in that manner gave her a nice life and marriage. Another correspondent bred new types of iris flowers, and I put him in touch with Janet's family, and he named a new iris after Janet. He also named one after Jenny Elf.

Some have had special experiences. Once a woman who had been violently raped asked to be put in touch with others who had suffered similarly. In such cases I am even more careful than usual; I must get permission from both parties before giving out any addresses. In due course I introduced her to three others, and I believe those turned out to be lasting correspondences. Rape is not something I am in much position to understand, and perhaps only a victim is in such a position. But I pay attention to what my correspondents tell me, and so have been able to write about it with more authority than would otherwise have been possible. Individual cases can be tragic. A little girl saw her father unhappy, and tried to cheer him—and he raped her. No, that's not the one in Chapter 5, "I knew to be a Woman." Another girl, sixteen, went on a date with a high school sports hero, who took her into a barn, took a hammer to her, and raped her. She thought he was trying to kill her, but apparently he was only making sure she wouldn't resist by hammering her into submission first. She never told her family, pretending she had taken a fall and bruised herself. Some fall! She asked me whether I would want to know it, if someone did that to one of my daughters. That was no easy question, and I'm not sure how I answered it, but did say that I'd probably want to kill the perpetrator. So I understood her silence, though I was appalled that the rapist thus got away with it. Another girl went on a date at age thirteen, and didn't understand why her date took her to his house for a party, but soon discovered that *she* was the entertainment. There were four of them, and she could go along with it, or be subjected to it more violently. So she didn't scream or cry, but she nevertheless felt the shock of rape, and thought that she must have been at fault somehow, and didn't tell, though it fouled up her life thereafter. Another woman accepted a ride home from a passing acquaintance, who instead drove her to his apartment where he and a friend threatened her with a gun, stripped her, raped her, and subjected her to humiliations, such as poking the muzzle of the pistol in her rectum and daring her to protest. When she tried to tell, she wasn't believed, even by those closest to her. Feminists like to claim that sex isn't the object, that it's just that men want to humiliate women. I regard that as nonsense; why not just rub feces in her hair or spit on her? Humiliation is not the object; it's a tool to break down her resistance. The object is sex. But humiliation does in some cases become a significant part of it, when men have been taught that sex is dirty. So they try to make the women dirty, to degrade them, so that they become fit objects for sex. So that they will be too ashamed to tell. And often it works, and the women do blame themselves, and feel worthless, and so are silent. Blame that on a warped society, which pretends that sex is shameful or unnatural. Rape is bad enough, without the enormous social burden, the tacit condemnation, that is put on the victims. Another young woman happened to be nearby when two "friends" grabbed her, stripped her, and replayed a scene they had seen in a movie, taking toothless bites of her flesh all over her body and running a tongue into her vagina. When they let her

go, she went to an isolated spot and contemplated suicide, blaming herself. When she told me about it, she was apologetic, because she said she
hadn't really been raped. As if she didn't have anything to fuss about. I
gave her the odd comfort of correcting her on that: penetration by any
organ constitutes technical rape.

The number of women who suffered incestuous sex as children seems
beyond counting, and it is not just stepfathers; blood fathers do it too,
and brothers. One brother "sold" his little sister to the neighbor man,
who had repeated sex with her, and she didn't feel free to tell. It may
be easy for those not involved to say that a girl should report such abuse,
but it's not easy for the girls themselves, who may have been threatened
or beaten, who may not be believed, and who may be blamed for bringing it on themselves. Yeah, sure: they brought it on themselves by being
female and innocent and within range; by the time they discover what
it's all about, they feel so worthless that there seems to be no point in
protesting. They may be told that this is perfectly normal, that everyone
does it, that it's what they owe their fathers who take care of them. One
girl was visiting with a friend her own age, who persuaded her to strip
for the friend's father, for oral sex. The father offered a gift, a special
doll. The friend even demonstrated how simple it was, spreading her
own legs for the man's mouth. It was easy, it was fun—see? Reluctantly
persuaded, and truly desiring the doll, the girl acceded, focusing determinedly on the doll instead of what was happening between her legs.
She felt deeply disgusted ever after, but she loved the doll, and no one
else ever understood exactly what she had paid for it. "I never actually
said no," they tell me. "It didn't really hurt, so it can't have been rape."
"It's my own fault, for being so foolish." "I thought he was my friend."
One girl, supposedly on a date, didn't understand why they stopped in
a forest, until she got raped by one of two men. The other man then
began to attack her, threatening to mutilate her, and the rapist had to
protect her from that. How could she turn him in, when he had protected her from worse? One girl, put into foster care to protect her from
further sexual molestation, was surprised when the official who was driving her there pulled over to the side of the road and raped her. "They'll
never believe you," he told her, and she knew he was right. Who would
believe a girl who made a habit of accusing every man with whom she
came in contact? She didn't tell, then; she told me—thirty years later.
One girl, fourteen when she wrote to me, told me of how she had had

to go into prostitution when she was twelve to get money to live on. She cried all the way through her indoctrination by the pimp, who was the first to try his wares, but it was indeed a way to get money. The moment she was able to get out of that situation, she did so, and the sex stopped, and she turned happy—and no longer wrote to me.

It must be asked: why would anyone write to a distant stranger about such a violation, when she didn't tell those close to her or report it to the police? The answer, as I see it, is that I am not really a stranger to them; I have written novels and Author's Notes to which they relate, so they know me even if I don't know them. They feel the need to tell someone, someone who will understand and not condemn, and who is not personally known or likely to be encountered, so that there is a shield, as it were. I am indeed sympathetic, but I don't violate their confidence by reporting it, though I may tell them that they should report it themselves. These episodes are all from memory, no names attached, mixed in together so as to be anonymous, the peripheral details fudged. My reaction is savagely mixed; I condemn the brutality and abuse, and I condemn the way these girls are blamed for being victims, suffering twice. Yet as a man I understand the sexual appeal of the female form, and can see how those without sufficient conscience would seek sex with what they can get. Women of any age are interesting, and as a general rule, the younger a woman is, the more interesting she is, because natural selection dictates that the man who controls the greatest part of a woman's fertile years will have the most children. A girl of twelve may have breasts and be a young woman in appearance; she is sexually desirable, regardless of law or custom. A girl of eleven may lack the breasts but be of similar general appearance, and her clothing masks her lack of maturity. So it is evident that some men aren't concerned about the distinction, and go for the vagina regardless. Indeed, with the separation of sex from reproduction, some men may prefer the girl who can't yet get pregnant; she is "safe." Obviously it happens, and I hear from a distressing number of the victims. It makes me feel guilty for being a man. When I wrote *Firefly* I expected some readers to be repelled; what surprised and dismayed me was the much greater number of responses I received from women who warmly endorsed it, because for the first time what they had experienced was being brought out into the open. I don't have a direct count, but my impression is that there are more than twenty very positive responses for every negative one. Probably most of the negatives don't bother to write to me, skewing the statistics. I also learned that I had underestimated the case; these horrors are not the rarities I had supposed. In fact some surveys indicate that one of every four, or perhaps even three, girls is sexually molested before reaching legal maturity. One man told me how he had been seduced at age seven by a girl a year younger, who had learned the art from her brother. It was a game to her. I understand that the sexual researcher Kinsey faked some of his statistics, but it seems that a lot does go on. I read my mail, and I learn what I never knew when I was young.

I hear from a number of prisoners, mostly male. I don't approve of whatever they did to get imprisoned, but I respond to them as I do to anyone else, because they need contacts too. One was an American Indian grandfather who sent me nice handcrafted art, and indeed, others have been artists too. Some of what they tell me is amazing. One described his encounters with four girls age ten and under, who came on to him, wanting to play with his penis, to hold contests to see who could make it spurt the farthest, wanting to see if it could be fitted into a small vagina, even when they were in a public swimming pool with many other people nearby, oblivious, and who blackmailed him with the threat of exposure when he tried to demur. He did like girls of any age, and was vulnerable to their aggressive interest, so his demurrals were not strong enough. No doubt he was guilty of statutory rape, but if it was as he described it, what of the girls who used him, then turned him in? What of the man elsewhere who had turned them on to sex at that age, who was not turned in? Justice is not necessarily a simple thing.

One prisoner was on death row for murder. That was John Brewer. At first he wrote as a reader, having discovered my books in prison. Then he told why he was there: for killing his girlfriend. He thought that would so revolt me that I would cut him off immediately. No, I respond to meaningful letters, without regard to my approval or disapproval of their originators. But when I don't cut off a correspondence, it may continue indefinitely, as happens with the Ligeias. Still, I couldn't see cutting off someone on death row, so it continued. I would try to space out my letters, but he always wrote back promptly. He asked favors, such as my writing to gain him some privilege, and I declined. I sent him a copy of *Bio of an Ogre*, and his reaction was odd: he thought I had made it up to parody his life. Why I should go to so much trouble he didn't say. As I see it, there was not much parallel between our lives. In due course, perhaps having encountered other prisoners who had read the book, he realized that it was legitimate. He was a hard-line conservative, law & order type, and said that murderers should be executed—and that held especially true for himself. He had done it, and he intended to be executed. But bleeding heart lawyers kept putting in appeals that he didn't want, stretching things out. He also believed in supernatural things, like flying saucers—UFOs—so I had a bright idea and put him in touch with a fanzine featuring conservatives like him and some who believed in UFOs; I thought he would feel at home there. He loved the issues of *Fosfax* I lent him, and promptly subscribed and began writing letters. Then the editors abruptly cut him off, and I quit the magazine in disgust; I don't support magazines whose doctrine of free expression extends only to expression they personally like. One of their editors, who had opposed the cutoff, corresponded with him, and so did I. But when the total number of letters reached approximately forty—my computer count showed more, but there may have been a couple of letters to a different person with the same last name—I had to ease off. I preferred to answer first-time letters, rather than to continue indefinitely with a correspondent who had already had a great number. So I explained this to Brewer. But I put him in touch with my daughter Penny, the age of Brewer's former girlfriend, and she wrote to him until his death. When something important came up, Brewer would write to me and I would answer; it wasn't a complete cutoff, just an abatement because of the volume of my mail. When a new lawyer wrote to me, trying to get my cooperation in arranging for another appeal I knew Brewer opposed, I refused to cooperate, and sent the letter on to Brewer, who appreciated my information. Then Penny and I filled out affidavits attesting to Brewer's soundness of mind, so that his death sentence couldn't be over-turned on the basis of insanity. It may seem strange, actively helping a man to die, but this was Brewer's decision and we supported it. And so he was duly executed. Later I heard from his attorney, a woman it seemed he had trusted, thanking me for my participation, and explaining that Brewer had written a novel. I sent $40 to cover duplication and shipping, and read the manuscript with an eye to possible collaboration, something the lawyer said Brewer had hoped for. But though it could have been done, the novel was not really special, and it was only partial, despite being a hundred thousand words long; it was the first portion of a longer story. With Brewer not available to do his continuation, true sequels would not be possible, and I did not think publishers would want an incomplete story. So I declined, with mixed feelings. I described the novel in my newsletter Hi Piers. Thus ended my association with John Brewer.

One nagging thought remains: the nature of his crime. My sympathy was with the girl, who by all accounts was decent and loyal, and hardly deserved to die like this. Brewer would allow no ill to be spoken of her. His mother had tried to condemn her, and that alienated him from his mother, with whom he would not speak. I wanted to understand: why had he suddenly killed the young woman who loved him? He explained it to me once, evidently feeling that the matter was shameful and asking me to forget it, but I couldn't. So from memory, because I don't care to get into the painful correspondence again, here is my impression. It had been a brutal murder, in which he struggled with her for, I think he once said, an hour, until he managed to get his hands around her neck and throttle her to death. Her last words were "I love you!" When she was dead he stripped her and raped the body. Then he turned himself in to the police, demanding to be executed. Why? I asked him that: if he didn't want to be with her, why not just let her go? Why kill her? They had been traveling together, and she was pregnant with his child; she supported him throughout. Then, suddenly, this. Why? There had to be a rationale, however twisted. She was trying to help him, and he was a dependent person; he could not go anywhere alone. He asked her to help him. She finally persuaded him that he needed to learn at least how to take a ten-minute walk alone. He agreed, and went to the motel door. Then he turned, and attacked her, and killed her. Why? It happened in that moment that he looked out the door, realizing that he was on the verge of being able to do it: to leave her there and walk alone, and return. A trial run, proving it was possible. He suffered a revelationon that freaked him out. What was it? He said only that when he realized what this meant, his decision came, and death was the answer. So I must piece it together myself. John Brewer realized that if he proved he could walk alone, he would no longer be absolutely dependent on her. He would be capable of existing alone. She would not have to stay with him; her constant support would no longer be essential. It would become possible for them to break up. And that was anathema. Just as too many men will kill the women they love rather than let them go, Brewer could not face even the possibility of losing his fiancée. He had bound her to him by his absolute dependency; now that was threatened. So, suddenly, he acted to prevent it from ever happening.

My major correspondence started suddenly. I received a letter from a woman whose daughter had been struck by a drunk driver, almost killed, and put into a coma then coming up on three months. This did not mean complete unconsciousness, but rather a retreat into mostly oblivion. When they showed her pictures of her favorite cats, she would sigh and disappear again. She was a fan of mine; Xanth was all around their house. Maybe if I wrote a letter to her, she would be roused by it. So I wrote the letter. My expectation was not great, but certainly it was worth trying. And thus began my series of letters to Jenny, the first year of which was published as *Letters To Jenny*. Because my first letter did bring her out of it, but it turned out that she was almost totally paralyzed. She could wiggle one toe, and move her right hand a little, and blink her eyes. She couldn't talk. This put me into a crisis of conscience: had I been wrong to write the letter? Should I have let well enough alone? Would it have been kinder simply to let Jenny fade out in her own time? But I had written the letter, and hauled her into the awfulness that was now her real life; I could not undo that. So I did the next best thing: I tried to make her life bearable, to the extent I could. By writing to cheer her. Every week. I thought at first that it would be temporary, until she recovered enough to get back on her feet and active, but her recovery has been glacially slow, and it now seems unlikely that she will ever be other than mostly paralyzed. It has been twelve years now, and I still write her weekly, a full-page letter designed to make her think, make her react, make her laugh. I suspect that a small but significant part of her education has been through my letters, because I cover just about everything in them. Originally the letters were read to her by her mother, father, or a friend; now I think she reads them herself, propped up in her bed, perhaps with her special glasses that turn her vision at right angles so she doesn't have to strain to see the pages of a letter. Every so often her mother phones and updates us on Jenny's progress. She is twenty-four now, and I no longer hide adult subjects under the cover of the Adult Conspiracy. She doesn't answer my letters, because typing is for her an enormous task, but I know she appreciates my words. As described in *Letters*, I met her at Psi-Con in 1989, and she has attended those conventions since. My purpose was to get her into the open, to see that she needn't hide, and now she does go in public. I receive many letters in response to the book, and queries about a continuation; the material exists, eleven more years of letters, but the publisher has expressed no interest. So it will continue, and I must admit it's fun writing to Jenny; it's like a weekly summary of my activities, phrased to be interesting.

I have covered the positive or significant correspondence. There are a good many types of letters I could readily live without, but I don't know whether it's worthwhile describing them all here. Perhaps a sampling will do: possibly the main nuisance is celebrity auctions. Folk have the idea that they can raise money by getting incidental things from actors or politicians or writers. But if I gave away things to each requester, I'd soon enough be down to my shorts. When I got three such solicitations in a single day, I got fed up, and now I normally don't answer them. But some schools get their children to do it for them. The child will write a fan letter, gee I love your books (not necessarily naming any), and by the way will you please contribute to our auction? So do I write and explain why not—a letter that will not be appreciated? Or do I ignore it as a solicitation. Sometimes I compromise, politely explaining. Once I received an angry letter from a school official, castigating me for doing that and hurting the kid's feelings. So I wrote to that school's principal, spelling out more bluntly my objection to making children beg favors from strangers, and didn't hear from that source again. I guess it's easier just not to answer, when the opposition gets pointed.

I also don't much like proselytizing, where some fifteen-year-old boy seeks to acquaint me with Jesus Christ. As it happens I already know Jesus, having made him a character in my major philosophical novel *Tarot*, and think he's a fine person—so fine that the bigots couldn't stand him, and crucified him—and if he came again to Earth, those same bigots would crucify him again, in the name of Christianity. In any event I don't care to be lectured on morality or religion by those who hardly understand the message of tolerance that Jesus preached. Then there are the fans who send copies—sometimes whole boxes full— of my books for autographing. They should ask first; then I would tell them that it's far easier, cheaper, and safer to use bookplates instead. I don't tell them another truth: that handling those books takes more in the value of my lost time than the book is worth, literally. So it's a netloss game; they get their autograph, I lose my working time. There are those who want to lecture me for saying I'd rather have fewer letters, informing me that I am dependent on my readers, and without them I'd be nothing. Well, I do need readers, but if the only readers I had were those with whom I corresponded, I'd be out of business before I started. I don't even demand that readers buy my books; I encourage them to use the libraries. The readers who support me are the vast majority who never write to me. There are those who want to collaborate with me. One person wrote saying, approximately, "Share the wealth! I'll write the novels, you put your name on them, and we'll split the money." As if no one would know the difference. Some folks' idea of collaboration is for them to suggest an idea, for me to make it into a novel, and share the money. As if I didn't have ideas of my own. The truth is that it takes a hell of a lot more than an idea to make a decent novel. Suppose I said to an architect "I have this idea: design a house that is hexagonal, and send me half your fees." Would he consider it to be a fair deal? So as a general rule, I'm not interested in collaborations. One reader wrote to a different writer, but the publisher accidentally forwarded the letter to me instead—publishers can be careless with mail, because they don't make money from it—so I forwarded it, but also gave him my own answer, which was that he would probably do better trying to establish his own reputation as a writer, assuming he was good enough, rather than trying to get together with a busy pro. "You don't understand," he responded hotly. "I don't have *time* for that. I have bills to pay *now*." He added disparagement about those of us who, he thought, were salable only because we had names. How did he think we *got* those names? We did it by taking the time and effort to learn our craft, as he was evidently not interested in doing. It's a thankless task, trying to educate a determined amateur, which is surely why most pros simply ignore such queries. Much as I hate to admit it, this does show me the reason for *Galaxy* editor H. L. Gold's attitude; he must have been deluged with amateurs wanting easy money. So he had an automatic lecture he delivered, which I received when I finally had to use a registered letter just to get a response from him after months of silence on my submissions. He remarked on folk trying to get rich by the flick of a typewriter, and recommended that I aim only a bit higher than I could shoot and not try to compete with the big boys. I felt this was unfair, considering that all I had done was try to get a response for my pieces, and later had the pleasure of remarking in print how my career as a writer had gone well beyond what his ever had. Of course he was known as an editor rather than a writer, but he was a writer first, and sometimes published his own fiction in his magazine. So I never liked this arrogant man, and there have been many other writers who felt as I did about him, from Robert Heinlein and Theodore Sturgeon on down. But he did have a point about unrealistic amateurs. In any event, there's not much easy money to be had by writing, with only about one in a hundred hopefuls ever selling anything, and that for mostly pittances. I have done a number of collaborations, as Chapter 8 details, but almost always with those who have an excellent notion of what is entailed. The exception was *Through the Ice*, whose author was dead before the collaboration started.

Then there are the kids with school papers to do, so they decide to write about me, and send me pages of questions that take inordinate time to answer, and maybe their letters arrive after the deadline for their papers anyway. They want me to write their papers for them. Once I took an afternoon off to answer such a letter, but his deadline was so short I could make it only by faxing my letter to him—and for three days I tried, but he had given me a wrong number. This kid's carelessness wasted my afternoon. I do try to answer such requests, but do so increasingly with canned paragraphs and advice to read *Bio of an Ogre*, where most of their questions are answered. Some are thoughtful, and it's no chore to answer them. A number of students told me later that my help enabled them to get A's on their papers. Good for them. But I'm trying to standardize my answers, to save time.

Another category of letter is the "How come you're an atheist?" query, sometimes phrased as "How come you're a Satanist?" I'm not; I'm agnostic, which means I don't presume to define the nature of God. There seems to be no tangible evidence on the subject, just assorted faiths who readily kill those of other faiths. I see no evidence of divine order in the universe, but neither is there any absolute refutation. So I don't believe in Heaven, Hell, or any Afterlife, or in any kindly white man with a beard in the sky, or in any burning red man with a pitchfork underground, but there does seem to be a certain order in the universe for which the explanation is obscure, and perhaps that would be evidence of a divine presence. Our universe seems to have started fifteen or twenty billion years ago in a great explosion that brought matter, energy, and time into existence; what made that explosion, and what came before it? Did it all form out of nothing? Maybe so; I can appreciate how the sum of all the things of the universe might be zero, like an equation $3+4+5 = 6+6$. Simplify it and you have 0, yet the equation itself exists. Does every electron have a positron, the hole left in vacuum when the electron was cut out? Does all the terrene matter have equivalent contra-terrene matter, its exact opposite? If so, and if the universe were simplified by putting together each bit of matter and antimatter, it would all cancel out and there would be nothing. Then only the fact that the universe is too chaotic for all the bits to get together accounts for its continued existence. So maybe it could have come from nothing. But why did it happen? Wouldn't it have been easier just to stay nothing? Maybe that "why" could be called God. Are there intangible things, like Honor, Compassion, and Realism (my personal triad), and if so, who created them? I don't know. So I'm agnostic. I think my mind is more open and inquiring than are the minds of most religionists or atheists, so I believe I am more likely to ascertain the truth, if there is any such thing to be ascertained. And I really don't favor being lectured by those whose minds are evidently closed.

Another category is the pleas for me to clean up my novels, stop writing trash; after all, many young folk are exposed to my fiction. The root of this objection is generally sex, and I suspect that if I could get the folk to express themselves candidly, they would say that they believe that sex itself is evil and should be abolished. Now I feel that sex is a natural part of human life, and should be treated in fiction as other aspects of life are. This does not mean that grown men should be forcing sex on little girls; that's mischief, as I have shown in Chapter 5 and in this chapter. But adult, consenting, mutually pleasurable sexuality is one of the major spices of life, and I'm for it, and that is reflected in the strong sexual current in my fiction. I think that those who consider anything containing sex is trash, have attitudes that are trash. So, no, I won't clean it up, though I do believe in labeling, so that those who seek fictive sex can readily find it, and those who dislike it can as readily avoid it. In general, my Xanth fantasies are sexual show without substance; full-bodied nymphs run around nude, and the sight of panties freaks out male observers, but the dread Ellipsis always obscures the details of how the stork is summoned. Even that is too much for some adults, though the young folk can handle it well enough. My adult mainstream fiction, such as *Firefly*, can get deeply into those details, so I recommend caution for those who are freakable out by natural processes. And my erotic fantasy *Pornucopia* is a truly dirty entertainment, whose sale is restricted to those who will sign a statement that they are eighteen or over. So anyone who doesn't like sex in my fiction is welcome to avoid it—but not to censor it. There are others who do enjoy it.

The same goes for those who don't like puns: so skip Xanth, but don't deny it to those who do like puns. Then there are the gosh-wow readers of limited experience: "I'm your biggest fan! I've read every book you've ever written! All nine Zanths!" "Gee Mr. Anthony, why don't you make a movie from Xanth?" Because I'm not the one who makes that decision; the boys with the big money do, and they are not known for either their intelligence or their taste. Maybe someday it will happen; I hope so. And there is a category of letters I find awkward, though not objectionable: the ones that solicit my congratulations for a Boy Scout's achievement of Eagle Scout status, or Bar Mitzvah, or similar. I was never a Boy Scout, so am not conversant with its processes, and I was never a Jew, so am similarly ignorant there. I don't know the people concerned. So what am I to say? I try, but I worry that my responses may be inadequate to the occasion. Generally I say congratulations, and if you were in Xanth, you would be going for Roc Scout. I hope that's not in poor taste; it's well intended. And last and least, are the letters that are demanding answers, when they have little point other than to prove that somebody really did get an answer from me. Letters with make-work questions. How are you? (As ever, thanks.) How are your horses? (Sky Blue died several years ago.) Say hi to your daughters. (Both have grown up and flown the coop.) "Gee, this is my 8th letter to you; how come you didn't answer the last one?" Gee, I don't know; I must have been crazy.

But, taken as a whole, my fan mail represents tremendous support for my work and life, and I appreciate it. Every person is an individual, and I respect that. I suspect I have a closer relationship with my readers than most writers do, and I do care about them, despite occasional annoyances. There are among them many men I wouldn't mind having as friends, and many women I wouldn't mind marrying, circumstances permitting. Of course what I see in a fan letter is only a tiny portion of the whole person, so my comfortable mental images are mostly illusion. But a pleasant one, the reflection of the largely illusory figure my readers see in me.

Thirteen

HI PIERS

It all started with the Xanth calendar. When my novel *Ogre, Ogre* made the best-seller lists in October 1982, ushering in my decade of best-sellerdom, I renamed the month OctOgre. Then, bit by bit, I pondered similar names for the other months of the year. November was a problem, but I finally came up with NoRemember. February was another problem; I couldn't find a suitable equivalent. Then my daughter Penny suggested FeBlueberry. I laughed, not taking it seriously—but the more I thought about it, the better it sounded, and finally it became one of my favorites. And so at last I had the full year: Jamboree, when the ogres celebrate with iceball fights. FeBlueberry, when the redberries are blue with cold. Marsh, when the snows melt, turning the ground into mud: mudball fights are almost as much fun. Apull, when they have a big tug-of-war contest, a Pull which lasts all month, having forgotten to schedule a month for a Push. Mayhem, which is entirely too pleasant for ogres, driving them crazy, so they do wild things. Nobody messes with an ogre then—or any other time. JeJune, which is so pleasant they can't stand it, so they sleep through it, making the month pleasant for all other creatures. Jewel-Lye, parodying the novel title *Crewel Lye*, when the ogres bash fist-sized jewels into fragments that scatter widely for others to find. AwGhost, when an ogre imbibed too deeply from a beerbarrel tree, so that it gave up the ghost, causing the ogre to say "Aw, Ghost." Sap-Timber, when the ogres bash trees into splinters with their hamfists, making sap fly and trees fall, thus ushering in the fall season. OctOgre which the ogres reckoned to be the eighth month of the year, showing that ogres can't count well beyond the toes of one foot; but it was still their very own month. NoRemember, because it was hard for a stupid ogre to remember anything that late in the year. And Dismember, with really bad weather, which the ogres love, causing them to celebrate rather violently.

I broached the matter to Judy-Lynn del Rey: how about a Xanth calendar? She loved the notion, and so it came to be, fashioned mostly from existing covers of the novels recycled for this purpose. Thus the 1987 Xanth Ogre calendar. It sold 50,000 copies, which is good. But then, slowly, returns came in, until it had sold only 30,000. This demonstrates the rationale behind publishers' reluctance to overprint; returns vitiate the profits. They had already paid me royalties on the larger figure, but I didn't think that was right, so later refunded about $7,000 to the publisher.

Later I decided to do a Xanth calendar with all original art. So I met with the leading genre artist Kelly Freas at the World Fantasy Convention in 1987 and asked him whether he would be interested in handling it. But he had just taken another position. But he introduced me to Ron Lindahn, and we talked, and moved ahead with it. Thus came to be the 1990 Xanth calendar, a beautiful production. Del Rey books agreed to handle it, but limited the print order even after the increased market for the calendar was apparent, as described in Chapter 6, turning a likely best-seller into an also-ran, at my expense. They never even gave us a report on the following calendar, but held it indefinitely without either accepting or rejecting it.

So we expanded the calendar operation and formed Hi Piers to market it ourselves. Ron Lindahn introduced us to his business partner Ed Maul. Would it work, without a regular publisher? We just had to try it and see. But the calendar did not seem enough to sustain such an operation, so we added in my book titles. Ron and Ed set up a phone center with an 800 number in Georgia, and that was the origin of the name. We tried to get a number spelling out ANTHONY, but none was available, so we oriented on my first name instead, which may have been just as well. (There are other Anthony writers, but very few Piers writers. Piers Paul Reid is the only one that comes to mind.) The number was 44-74377, with the last 5 digits spelling out PIERS. My wife came up with the rest of it: 44 = HI. A perfect fit.

But calls don't just come in; the number has to be publicized. So we set up for ads on cable television. That meant making the ads. And so

I found myself before the camera at Channel 5 in Orlando, Florida, which would rent out to people for such work on off days. It was interesting, because not only did we get to see their studios, we saw them in operation. For example, those little promo spots that advise the viewer of some hot item of news coming up at 6 P.M. are done perhaps at noon, and the announcers come in, sit at the counter, and speak their pieces. It's all done in a couple of minutes and they're gone. It may look comfortable and homey when you see it on TV, but that's the only part of the studio that is so; the rest consists of concrete floor with complicated wires winding like tangled serpents across it. There are assorted backdrops to put behind the speakers. Just about none of it is real, except the people, who are acting. It may be cold, too, because the lights are hot and they need to compensate.

We worked out the ads, and I discovered the use of the TV prompter. You may think that the people on the screen are speaking from memory or extemporaneously, but they seldom are; their lines are on a screen beside the camera lens, and when they look directly at the camera, they are reading. The lines move as the people speak, keeping up, so that they never run out. Usually. Once the prompter cut off, and I stalled, not knowing what to say; others thought it was stage fright, but it was lack of material.

Which is another thing: I am long accustomed to speaking before audiences of any size, thanks to my experience in drama and as a teacher. Originally I suffered from stage fright, but day in and day out addressing classes wears that out, and I am comfortable before people. In fact I prefer to speak from limited notes, or from none, so that I can maintain eye contact with the audience. I do it also when I am reading from a novel, but then I have to read a sentence and speak it while I look around, then return to the text to get new words before the old ones run out. I do it, but straight speaking is easier. But here was something new: no audience, just a camera lens, with even its operator invisible to me. And I had to read my lines not from a page before me, but from that screen some distance in front of me. I wasn't used to that, and it gave me, if not actual stage fright, at least a certain awkwardness. The fact is, there are different kinds of stage fright, and to be inured to one is not necessarily to be free from others. When I was tested for my green belt in judo class I suffered physical stage fright; I knew the throws, but my body tended to balk at performing them, much as an actor may forget a line of a play that he never had trouble with during rehearsal. So I found it distinctly awkward because it didn't fit my accustomed mode. I read lines clumsily that I should have read smoothly.

I also found that it wasn't easy to play the part—even though the part was Piers Anthony. When I talk naturally, there are foibles of speech and manner that are mine. When I read lines, it becomes artificial. My reading manner differs from my speaking manner, as is the case with most folk. But this was reading from an odd screen, and trying to make it seem as if I'm speaking naturally. Experienced TV actors seem to have no trouble, but this was new to me. It wasn't just the fact of the camera, because when Ron Lindahn interviewed me for the Ogre Interview, I felt comfortable, answering his questions without notes, and it worked well. It was reading from that prompting screen. I just couldn't get the hang of it. So I realized ruefully that I was making a mess of acting myself, weird as that may seem. It was a new experience.

But we made the commercials, and they were run on several cable TV channels. I was annoyed when one was censored. It was a humorous one: "Hello, this is Piers Anthony. This is to-to-oh, just buy the bleeping book!" followed immediately by Ed's loud "Perfect!" at which point I looked toward him, disgusted. CNN claimed it had a bad word. When challenged about what was the matter with "bleeping," they made other excuses, each time a different one, and finally just said the commercial was too silly. Oh? How about some of the stuff on broadcast TV? You can't get much sillier than that. But they were adamant. There is no free speech on CNN. It's something I remember when solicited to sign up for cable TV as an alternative to the regular commercial networks. So far we haven't signed, though the day may come for satellite TV.

When the commercials ran, giving the 800 number, the calls came in with a rush. It took a crew of phone operators to handle them. That was fine, but it required a number of phoners for a short period, while at other times there wasn't much business. That was inefficient, as the phone center had to be maintained throughout. Also, most of the calls were queries or requests for a free sample issue of the Hi Piers Newsletter. In due course I calculated how much each name that actually ordered anything cost to acquire, and it was a hundred dollars. Since an order might consist of one calendar or a few paperback books, this was a money-losing enterprise.

In fact for a time Hi Piers was costing me $20,000 a month to operate: about half of it for TV ads, the rest for office rental, wages, and overhead expenses. It wasn't bringing in nearly that much. This rate of loss would run me broke.

We looked for alternatives. I tried putting the Hi Piers notices at the end of my novels, which was essentially free advertising to the most likely clientele: my readers. But of course those readers would already have the most likely book they wanted: the one wherein they saw the message. In addition, any book they bought by mail was more expensive than the same book in the store, because of the postage; that was a built-in discouragement. Nevertheless, it improved things in two ways: it cut the costs, and it made for a more steady response, so that we could have a smaller staff handling the calls throughout the day. We gave up on the TV ads, nice as some of them were. The experience of Image Marketing indicated that the steady stream of calls from the book ads would continue for years.

But it remained a losing operation. The 1991 calendar alone lost $50,000. That is, it cost $60,000 to make and publish, and it sold $10,000 worth. And that was only part of it. I had invested in the stock of books needed to supply Hi Piers. We bought them at wholesale rates from the publishers, a box or two of each of my titles. That meant the better part of a hundred titles; some were out of print and unavailable. I spent about $150,000 on that aspect. We also bought up the remaindered stock of the hardcover edition of *Bio of an Ogre*. There was a considerable accumulation of boxes of those books and calendars, a storage problem. In all, the whole Hi Piers operation—books, calendar, advertising, office, personnel, 800 line fees and so on—put me in the hole about half a million dollars. It was becoming apparent that I would never get it back. In fact losses continued at about $50,000 a year. This thing was a money pit. I hadn't gotten into it for money, but rather to support the Xanth calendar and to provide a service for my readers, but a continuing loss of this magnitude was not sustainable.

That wasn't even counting the value of my time. Planning it, setting it up, meetings to iron out the details, phone calls, and writing the material for the newsletters added up, and my time was worth a fair amount. There is no sure way to figure the worth of a writer's time when he's working on books that won't be published for months or years and whose ultimate value is determined by royalties, licenses, and publicity, so I use a simplified guide: take my average annual income and divide it by the time I work. Since I was then earning an average of one million dollars a year (gross, not net), this came to about $20,000 a week (figuring 50 working weeks in a year) or $500 an hour (figuring a 40-hour working week). Actually I worked more like 60-hour weeks, but the extra was taken by the voluminous mail, which wasn't earning any money. So if I took an eight-hour day to prepare material for the newsletter, that was $4,000 in my time. When I took several days off to go to a convention to help promote Hi Piers, that might be $20,000 in my time. Because it always comes out of paying time; the letters pile up in my absence and have to be handled, and so it is my novel-writing time that suffers. I haven't added up all the value of the time expended for Hi Piers, but it is considerable.

That wasn't all. It became apparent that there were problems in the Georgia operation. It was taking them six months to publish an issue of the newsletter, so that its material was dated by the time it saw print. What was the matter? They said it was at the printer, but the printer didn't get it done. We weren't told more. But in time we figured it out: the printer wouldn't print the next newsletter until it got paid for the last one. That wasn't the only bill that wasn't getting paid. There was bad feeling being generated for me, because some of our suppliers weren't getting paid, and they thought I was the one who was stiffing them. I was subsidizing the operation at the rate of $25,000 a year, but apparently that wasn't enough.

There was more. Ed Maul's Image Marketing liked to get a percentage of the action, on the theory that not all of its efforts could be tangibly measured. It was difficult to figure what their effort on Hi Piers's behalf was worth, but it was hoped that it would help my career, and thus lead to greater income for me. So I agreed to try it. Since I was already making a very good living, with or without their efforts, we set up a formula by which a certain portion of my earning above that would be shared with them. The details were more complicated, but one year I did send them about $18,000 on the formula. Unfortunately, it was becoming apparent that their efforts were not improving my image; in fact my image was being savaged in some respects, and the indication was that my career had crested and was commencing a decline. So I honored the deal we made, but do not believe it was worth it for me.

Finally, we took action. My wife took over the operation and moved it to Tampa, where we would have complete control. She hired an office manager and an assistant, and did the accounts herself. My researcher Alan drove to Georgia and brought a truckload of books and calendars down. We trained our own people, whose loyalty was directly to us. Thereafter the newsletter came out five times a year and all bills were paid, including about $20,000 worth that were owing from before our in-house takeover, that we hadn't known about until we got the accounts.

It turned out that the losses were worse even than that. The folk in Georgia had been selling the books I had bought from the publishers but had not been restocking them. In effect, they had been selling free books. So the apparent losses were only half the real losses.

So how did we do in Tampa? It took a while to get it straight, because there were no proper accounts from Georgia. We had trusted others to know their business, and our trust had been misplaced. But in due course we did get a notion: Hi Piers was still losing $50,000 a year. This was an improvement, because these accounts were straight, with due allowance made for restocking the books actually sold. But it was apparent that Hi Piers could not continue indefinitely.

My daughter Penny's husband took an interest in the third Xanth calendar, which we had made up but not yet marketed, and worked to get it published. He had me write a full story for it, about Jenny Elf's quest to leave Xanth and return to the World of Two Moons, and he lined up a printer and queried stores and distributors. Most of the big distributors turned it down. This is the big problem for small publishers: you can't sell your wares if you can't get good distribution, because most folk choose from what they see in the stores and don't inquire about what isn't on display there. It was a nice calendar, that many folk would like and buy—if they knew it existed. But the powers that be in the realm of distribution don't care about that; they don't care to deal with small outfits, and that's that. We sent information to the individual stores, but they tend to buy from their regular distributors, not direct from small publishers. So commercial failure for this one was virtually guaranteed, through no fault of the calendar itself. But at least we got it published, and advertised it in the newsletter, so that my most ardent readers could get it by mail.

That wrapped up the Xanth calendars. I lost about $100,000 on them collectively. I think they could all have been best-sellers and more than paid their way, but we were up against a system rigged against this sort of enterprise. I don't mind having given it a try, but I do learn from experience, and in time I tend to lose my taste for losing large amounts of money.

Meanwhile Hi Piers has served as a useful liaison. It is the surest and fastest way for my readers to reach me, or to locate my books that can't be found in the stores. Publishers forward letters, but it takes them anywhere from two weeks to a year to do so, with the normal delay being one or two months. Hi Piers forwards letters weekly. Gradually the majority of incoming fan mail has shifted from the publisher to Hi Piers. Of course I would prefer to have less mail, rather than more, but if there has to be mail, I prefer that it reach me reasonably promptly. And, as described in Chapter 12, reader correspondence can be interesting. Sometimes a business connection calls. This hasn't actually happened, but I like to think that if a movie studio suddenly decided to make a phenomenal best-selling picture from one of my obscure novels, it could get in touch quickly. Of course Hi Piers would simply refer it to my Hollywood agent for negotiation, but at least the contact would have been made.

So what is the future of Hi Piers? We had to close it, although readers did appreciate it. Its long-term outlook was bleak. Chalk it up to experience: so now we know whether a prolific, popular writer can market his own books by mail and make a profit while making his readers happy. The answer is no. So Hi Piers had to be shut down, but one aspect of it remains: www.hipiers.com on the Internet. That actually was to grow in importance until it reached many more readers than the original physical Hi Piers did.

Fourteen

ANIMALS

When my family moved to Hilltop Farm, in the Green Mountains of Vermont, in 1940, we soon had animals. At first their names began with J, matching our own surname: Jacob. So there was our first goat, Junie, and our dog, Juliet. Later there were to be many more animals, including a herd of goats and some sheep, and a woolly angora goat that looked much like a sheep. Also hens, including one called Halfchick, who had hatched from an egg laid by one variety of chicken, and incubated by a hen of another breed, so seemed to be half and half. Also angora rabbits, whose tempers were not sweet. My memories of the first animals are faded, except for two unpleasantly striking ones relating to the dog.

Juliet was undisciplined, and she thought that the goats were her natural prey. She was a small dog, who had no chance against them, but the goats didn't want trouble, so tried to ignore her. One day a goat walked from the barn to the house, a distance of several hundred feet, and Juliet kept growling and leaping at her neck. The goat paid no attention, not striking back at all, just waiting for the annoyance to pass, but the dog simply would not give up. Finally, my father Alfred snapped; as they passed him, he kicked the dog so hard she sailed into the air with a pained yipe. That ended that; the dog left the goats alone thereafter. At the time my sympathy was with the dog, but today it is with the goat. Sometimes obnoxiousness needs to be curbed unequivocally. But it was also an early lesson for me in the futility of pacifism. The pacifism of the goat seemed to encourage more of the bad behavior on the part of the dog. My father was a pacifist, except when it came to the crunch. I remembered that. To me, a philosophy that endures only so long as it is convenient is inconsistent. I have seen similar inconsistency in many other people, notably in would-be censors: "This isn't censorship; we just don't like this view, so must suppress it." Uh-huh.

One time when we were traveling in our battered old converted telephone truck, we had the animals in back: two goats and the dog. They didn't get along well, but the goats were tied, so all the dog had to do was stay clear of them. We drove a stretch of perhaps twenty miles, then stopped to check in back—and Juliet was gone. We drove back over the whole stretch, looking at the road and along the sides, but there was no sign of her. She must have jumped out and run away. We never saw her again. I hope she found a good home.

The first kids—that is, baby goats—born, were when we were away from Hilltop, in New Hampshire, I think. They were male and female, and we named them Peter and Penny. The odd thing about that was that years later my sister Teresa's first child was named Peter, and our own first surviving child was Penny. I think that was coincidence, but it's an odd one. Sometimes I tease our Penny, saying she's just a kid.

Cam and I lived for eleven years as a childless couple before we got two children we could keep. When children came, so did pets. But we did have one set of pets before then. It started coincidentally rather than intentionally.

Back in the 1960s Cam's sister Jane got a parakeet. It was cinnamon-winged green, so she named it Cinnamon. When she moved, she gave the bird to us. It didn't seem right to have a bird without company of its own kind, so we arranged to get another from an acquaintance: a blue parakeet. To keep the style of naming, we called that one Nutmeg. Then we got Clove, who was gray. We built a larger birdcage from fencing wire, three feet long, so they could fly, with perches at each end, because it didn't seem right for a bird not to fly, and we didn't have them trained well enough to be loose in the house. They did seem to like it. We bought one from Meares, a big plant nursery in St. Petersburg; Mr. Meares also had a bird hobby. We named that one Ginger. Then we were given two more: a hyperactive yellow one we called Saffron, and a blue one we called Angelica, another kind of spice. We weren't quite certain of the gender of any of them; theoretically a brown bar above the beak means female, and blue means male, but Clove's beak changed from one to the other, and the others were mostly nondescript brown. But we thought of Ginger and Saffron as male. They got along okay, and seemed happy. We had had a parakeet called Lucky in our first year of marriage, in Vermont; now we had six. They all had personalities. Cinnamon was taciturn, while Saffron was endlessly perky; he could dance up to another bird and dare it to respond. Once he came up to another, and the other went chiiirp! negatively, the language plain: Don't bother me! Angelica had an illness, and her beak was warped; we learned later that mites can infect the bills. We could have had her treated, had we known in time; we thought she just had a rough beak. Her wings had been clipped so that she couldn't fly; they were slowly growing out, and we hoped that she would recover her power of flight in due course. The other birds tended to shun her. Then Ginger grew ill, and sat on a low perch. Angelica came to nudge up against him, and he was too ill to move or drive her off; she took it as a welcome. Again, we see similar in people, misunderstanding each other's motives. Next day Ginger was sitting on the floor of the cage, where the birds never stayed voluntarily. We watched helplessly. Then he died. We took the body to Mr. Meares, wondering whether there could be an autopsy or something, but he said these things just happened. We were much saddened by the loss; it seemed that little birds should not die like that. We think it was a heart problem. We learned that birds died of the same ailments that human beings do, when in captivity. In the wild, of course, it's another matter; predators keep lives short. Later, there was news of an exotic malady spreading among birds; to stop it, whole populations of exotic birds had to be killed, and Meares's phenomenal collection, which ranged far, far beyond parakeets, was wiped out. I think it destroyed the man's interest in life. It seemed like a cruel sequel: we had bought one bird from him, and lost it; he had lost them all. Our other birds went one by one, of different causes, until only Cinnamon and Saffron were left. The mites infected Saffron's feet, but now we knew of them, and got them eradicated; he died of complications of age, and I think was the last to go. I remember when Nutmeg was ailing, and died; I was afraid Cam would cry when I told her, but I was wrong; I was the one who cried. It reminded me of the terrible shock when President Kennedy was assassinated. That was a national calamity, affecting every citizen of the United States, and to a diminishing degree, the world. The death of the bird was a minor thing, but very close to us, and just as a penny may hide a mountain, if held close to the eye, the close death of the bird hit me almost as hard as the distant death of a president. When the last bird died, we decided to have no more; it was too painful for us. Later I wrote them into a story, "Beak By Beak," published in *Analog*. I think the length of our time with the parakeets was six or seven years. After that we had children, and they required other types of pets, which was how we got into dogs and cats.

I described our first dog, Canute, in *Bio of an Ogre*, and our cat Pandora II. After him we got Conny, a hyperfriendly crossbreed, part Basenji, part fox terrier. We thought she would outgrow her puppylike friendliness, but she never did. When our local veterinarian, Dr. Richard Shinn, saved the life of a full Basenji that had been brought to him, and couldn't find the owner, he gave him to us. We named him Cenji Basenji. He was a housebroken dog with one complication: he hated all other animals and would attack them on sight. Except Conny, who he evidently realized had prior tenure at our house. He learned to climb our high wire fence, so as to escape and attack other dogs; we had to put L braces all around, so that it bent at right angles inward at the top, to stop him. We got a brace chain, so we could take them walking together, and Cenji's full Basenji lines brought out the Basenji lines of Conny, improving her looks. And so for eleven years we had them both, until Cenji quietly faded. He just stopped eating, until he died. That upset Conny; she missed him, and perhaps feared that she would be next. I buried him in the garden, saddened by the sight of one of his ears sticking up out of the cardboard box-coffin as I shoveled dirt on it; it seemed wrong that such a pretty ear should meet such a fate. I hadn't really liked Cenji; we had a truce, whose nature was he didn't bite me, and I didn't bash his head into a tree. But his death hurt me anyway. As did Conny's, a year or two later. Little things can get to you, in such events; I had a good night's sleep, came downstairs, and saw a blank space: no dog dish there anymore. That was like an arrow through the heart, suddenly catching me. I think we block out the big things, but then are prey to the myriad little things that escape the block.

Meanwhile we had adopted an outside dog, Lucky; the neighbors had taken in a stray, who had puppies, and Lucky was the smallest and prettiest, always yipping as he got the worst of a pileup. He took to sleeping under our car, away from the others, to get some peace, and so gradually he became ours. With proper feeding and care he thrived, and became the largest and strongest of the litter. Once he encountered one of the other dogs, and she thought to push him around, as in the old days; ROAR! and a show of teeth forever abolished that notion. I can see it. But when he was a puppy he had tried to be friendly with Cenji, when the indoor dog was out, and been roughly disabused, and thereafter stayed clear. Then one day, when I was in the hospital with a kidney stone, Cenji got loose outside and took off after Lucky. Lucky tried to flee, but could not, in the fenced yard, so finally he turned around and fought. He clamped his jaws on Cenji so hard that it took a couple of neighbor men to pry them off. After that Lucky took no guff from Cenji, either. Lucky was now a much bigger dog, and stronger, and knew it. Cenji had brought it on himself, really. Lucky, on the other hand, welcomed company. When we adopted a puppy from a following neighborly litter, and took a second to keep the first warm, Lucky welcomed them, and the three dogs got along well for the rest of their lives. Thus Lucky didn't attack those who hadn't attacked him first. That, too, I find compatible. But then it turned out he had a genetic skin ailment that treatment couldn't cure. He would lie on his back, rubbing at the itch until the fur wore off, leaving a bare patch. We hated to see it, but there wasn't much we could do about it. As an adult he turned vicious to strangers, but was always good with family members. We didn't train him to be that way; it may have been that he had some pit-bull ancestry, and there was also the matter of his experiences when young, when he had to learn to fight. Again, I understand, seeing a parallel to my own experience. It's not easy to learn how to fight to survive, but it's no easier to unlearn it. He would fight to protect the two females, long after they were grown.

We had two because though Cheryl adopted one, Tipsy—because she had white on her body, but none on the tipsy of her tailsy, in defiance of the rule about dog coloration (one wonders whether "experts" ever actually look at the creatures to whom they apply rules), Cam had boarded a second puppy, Bubbles, because she was afraid one puppy could not survive the cold outside weather alone. Bubbles was for the neighbor boy, and he could take her anytime he wished; meanwhile we fed her and cared for her. There was a bit more to it than that: there were too many puppies to keep, so they planned to take them to a pet store. But we feared that was just what they told the children, and that the puppies were actually headed for the pound—and that Bubbles would be taken too. So we intervened, tacitly, to prevent that. One day he took her into their house, and she pooped on their floor, and that effectively ended that, and she just stayed with us. We offered to buy her, but they told us just to keep her. So Cam adopted Bubbles, who was named by the neighbor boy, perhaps after an older canine cousin Bubba. Of the two females, Bubbles grew larger and more solidly fleshed. At first she seemed bolder, but Lucky informed her in no uncertain manner that she was the boss of no dog yard, and she became shy. Tipsy was lean and fast, as an unfortunate rabbit discovered just before it died. When a raccoon (we think) broke into our chicken coop and stole a hen, we let the dogs out into the main yard at night, and thereafter nothing invaded it. Once in a while the two bitches (that is after all the name for female dogs) had an argument and would fight, and we would have to break it up. Lucky was never involved in that. Cheryl was traumatized by it once; she tried to separate the dogs, and was almost bitten, and at the time they were not much smaller than she was.

When we moved, we made a huge forest dog yard with a big doghouse. We would have preferred to let them run free, but couldn't; we wanted neither destruction of forest creatures nor destruction of our pets when they encountered rattlesnakes. Their mother had died when she tackled a big rattlesnake. Then Tipsy ailed. There was another fight with Bubbles, and I went out and let Tipsy into the house yard, to separate them. I conjecture that Bubbles came, and said "Hey, let's play!" and Tipsy snapped at her. Tipsy walked through the yard, and to the screened door of the pool enclosure, which had stuck open, and settled down beside the pool. I hadn't intended this, but realized that it might be for the best. So we got her a cushion to lie on, and a blanket to cover her, and she stayed there. We put baffles up so that she wouldn't wander into the pool, though she seemed to be savvy about that. But she was fading. She would get up to go out for natural functions, but barely had strength to walk. Finally, we bundled her up and took her to the vet, who concluded that she had a bad fever. He boarded her and fought to get the fever down. After several days he phoned: the fever was down, and in another day or so we could pick her up. But next day he phoned again, regretfully: Tipsy had cancer. It had been concealed by the other illness, but now was apparent. She was terminal. There was nothing to do but put her down. Cheryl seemed to be jinxed; every pet she had died early, through no fault of hers. So Tipsy was gone, and we were down to two. I worried how Bubbles would be, when Lucky died. The dogs knew the horses, but would that be company enough? Then in February 1991 Lucky faded. He wasn't moving, but lifted his head when I checked on him; it was a cold night, and soon he was dead. I put him on the wheelbarrow and took him to the forest and dug a grave and buried him.

Bubbles seemed not to understand. Now she was alone. We let her into the backyard, closer to the house. Then, experimenting, we let her into the house for the day—and though she had never been a house dog, she behaved perfectly. We put her out for the nights, and she slept close by. After a few days we gambled again, and left her in for the night—and she remained housebroken. Thus the outdoor dog became an indoor dog, and she turned out to be the best indoor dog we had had. It wasn't just that she was house trained, it was that she was so well behaved generally. She messed on nothing, she chewed on nothing, she made no clamor. This dog, adopted more or less incidentally, and always an also-ran in our awareness, though Cam did like her and considered her her own, at the age of about twelve won our hearts anew. All she wanted was to be reasonably close to us, and she treated us equally, without jealousy. When we separated in the house, she would settle down halfway between. It took her time to learn to navigate the stairs, because they were new to her experience and daunting. Once she was with me in the study, and I was going downstairs in the evening, and it was growing dark. She hesitated at the top, so I called to her to come on down. She started down, lost her footing, and tumbled several stairs to the landing. She wasn't hurt, but I was chagrined; now I realized that her caution had been because she couldn't see well enough to be sure of her footing in the dusk. Thereafter I always turned on the light, and never pressed her; she knew her limits. She was not used to much attention; it took her time to get used to my patting her or rubbing her ears in passing. Cam gradually taught her to play. In her old age, she was finally learning the joys of being a family dog. She would sleep on the floor in our bedroom at night, and I would take her out first thing in the morning, when I fed the horses. I found she didn't need a leash; she stayed with me, and behaved around the horses. She enjoyed licking up the feed they spilled. So it was compatible.

But after almost a year she was evidently failing; she started to be incontinent. One morning I woke to find Cam gone, and she was sleeping on the couch downstairs, because Bubbles hadn't been able to make it upstairs. We took the dog to the vet, who X-rayed her: she had a big tumor, which they could remove surgically, but they felt it was probably not worth the pain and distress for the dog being ill in a strange place. It had been bad enough for Tipsy, whom we would have spared the last week's pain had we known there was to be no recovery. So we made the decision to put her down. Cam stayed in the waiting room while I went in with vet and dog, and stroked her head while the vet gave her the fatal shot. There was no pain, no alarm; she just laid her head down and was gone. We were glad that at least we had been able to give her that one scant year of comfort; she was with us at the end, and we were with her. We had never punished her for anything in her life; she was just a nice dog, never offending.

I would have been satisfied to be without pets at that point, and so we were, for a year and a half. Then Penny saw a box of puppies at the entrance to a store, free to good homes. In the afternoon when she passed again there was only one left. They said they would take her to the pound. Penny couldn't stand the thought, so she took the puppy and named her Obsidian, because her back was glossy black. But Penny already had one or two dogs—it depends on how one counts a long-term boarder—and couldn't keep another. She did it right from the outset, keeping Obsidian in a dog crate for the nights; dogs really don't mind, and just sleep, and there is no chewing of furniture or messing of rugs. She hoped the hearing ear folk would take her for training, but they found the dog too active. Indeed, Obsidian was hyperactive, super-friendly but impossible to turn off. Just as Penny herself had been, as a child. Cam pondered it for months, and finally in September 1993 drove down and took Obsidian off Penny's hands. Thus she became our seventh dog, following Canute, Conny, Cenji, Lucky, Tipsy, and Bubbles, and the largest, peaking at 96½ pounds. She was thought to be part Labrador and part Rottweiler, but though her color was Rottweiler, she wasn't solid enough. She nevertheless filled out into one supremely robust, healthy dog, in our care. She loved people, but had never learned to play people style; she played dog style, chasing, playing keep-away with toys, and pretend-fighting. So I learned to chase her, and growl at her, and pretend to attack her. I would grab her paw, not hard, and she would set her teeth on my hand, not hard, in fake attack and counter. I tried to teach her how to be petted, but she never quite caught on to that. She also had trouble learning not to jam her nose into people's crotches, a regular embarrassment with visitors. Whoever was newest was most interesting. But she truly liked those she knew of old, such as Penny, John, Alan, and Peg, and when one of them visited, she would get so excited she leaked urine on the rug. For all her pushiness, she was sensitive, and couldn't stand to be among strangers. When we boarded her for a few days she was so upset that she wasn't eating or drinking, and wouldn't come out of the cage; Cam had to go back and get her directly. It wasn't that she had been mistreated; she just longed to be home. So when we considered attending the 1995 World Science Fiction convention in Glasgow, Scotland, we thought about Obsidian spending two weeks in the kennel, and weren't sure she would survive it. She couldn't board with Penny or Alan, because they were going to Scotland too. So in the end we stayed home, and I used the time to read Terry Goodkind's huge *Stone of Tears*, which took one week, and learned to use Windows 95 and Word 7 on my new Pentium computer system instead. So the novel got a blurb, and I was secure in my new system. I would have liked to see the old country, England, after fifty-five years, but it wasn't to be. As time passed, Obsidian oriented increasingly on Cam, and it got to the point where she growled at me whenever I approached my wife. Since we do have a lot of business together, even after forty years of marriage, that has been a source of stress for the dog. It disturbs her when I even walk by the chair Cam is sitting in. I had thought our mistake with our first dog, Canute, was bringing him into a changing family situation; Cheryl's arrival as a baby made the dog think he was being displaced. But here was Obsidian in a steady situation, yet she developed her own notions and stresses. So maybe Canute's stress and kidney stones that took him out young would have happened anyway.

A sidelight on the animals: our vet in Gulfport, Florida, was just the closest one we could find that we liked. He was a character. His name was Dr. Shinn, and he truly had the welfare of the animals at heart. We got lectured about caring for them, and if we didn't heed his words, we could just find another vet. Everyone got lectured similarly. His words made sense to us, and we did heed them, and got along well. When our dog Canute developed kidney stones, it took more than one session of surgery to get them out. Times were lean for us then, and Dr. Shinn knew it, and did not charge us for the surgery. When we brought a stray cat in to get spayed, so that an animal shelter would take her, he didn't charge us. He was an opinionated conservative politically, while we were liberal, but it didn't matter; we all cared about the animals. When Panda Cat got hit by a car, and his back was broken, we brought him in to that office; he couldn't be saved, and had to be put down, but the assistant vet mentioned a Basenji dog they had patched up, hurt similarly on the road. We took him, and that was Cenji Basenji, free from the vet, despite what would have been a horrendous medical bill for the original owner. I wrote a newspaper article on the vet, with his permission and cooperation, that many readers liked and the veterinary association did not. Shinn was a maverick, with his own methods, not universally approved of. But they worked. Later my career advanced, as I caught hold of the skyrocket that was fantasy, and my financial troubles were over. But we had moved, and Dr. Shinn was no longer our vet. When I had occasion to get in touch with him again, when Cenji died eleven years later, I wrote to inform Dr. Shinn of the extent to which he had extended that dog's life. Then, later, when I spoke at a writing seminar, Dr. Shinn sent me a message through the proprietor, and a copy of his book, *Shinnanigans*, about his experiences as a vet, some of which I remembered. And I thought, how can I repay this good man for his prior kindnesses to us and our animals? I was sure he would not accept belated payment for the free surgeries, and in any event intervening inflation had made the amounts meaningless. Then I got it. I wrote to him, saying that my fortunes had changed, and I would now like to make a donation to any charitable cause he espoused, in his name, of the approximate value of the charges he had forgiven us. I judged these to be about $1,000 in contemporary dollars. He could not decline that. So it was that we donated that amount to his alma mater, Auburn University, their veterinary department, in his name. In that way we gave him open credit for the good he had done us in a way he surely appreciated. He deserved it.

We also had horses. Penny was a girl, and girls love horses, but we couldn't keep a horse in the city. But when we moved to the forest in 1977, Penny said "Well?" So in 1978 we got Sky Blue, a twenty-year-old pedigreed hackney mare, a former harness racer. She was a small horse, fourteen hands, but well trained and well behaved. She was black, with white "socks"; they were low around her hind hooves, and I said that in her age her socks were sagging. Penny was ten at the time, half Blue's age. Penny said that the happiest day of her life was when she got

Blue. We got a second horse, Misty, because once again we didn't like the idea of an animal alone. Horses crave company of their own kind. Misty was white (that is, light gray) and said to be so gentle a child could ride her. Half-true; a child could sit on her, but couldn't make her mind; she just ignored the child. Blue was perfectly trained, but her beautiful trot felt like riding a washboard. For a time we did ride; I started on Misty, the larger horse, and Cam rode Blue, but Cam didn't like that trot; and we switched horses in mid-ride, and from then on, I always rode Blue. Penny rode too, of course, but she had school activities, and then went away to college, so we were really the ones who stayed with the horses. When we bought horse feed, the local supplier had two types: regular and "sweet," for extra energy. One was Carnation Roundup, the other Carnation Saddle-up; I forget which was which. Blue could choke on sweet, so we used it sparingly. I was always tempted to walk in to the store and ask for Tarnation Roundworm and Saddlesore, but never quite had the nerve; the proprietor might not have appreciated the humor. Once we had the horses grazing near where the school bus stopped, so I put up a big sign we had: WHOA! The children loved it, but the lady bus driver was Not Amused. Though Misty was younger, thirteen when we got her, she developed laminitis, an inflammation of the lining of the hoofs, and it was progressive, resisting all that the vet could do. It got to the point where she couldn't stand in comfort, so she lay, getting up only to eat and drink. Then it got worse, and I brought water and food to her. We had to fence Blue off, because now Blue was eager to prove she had become the dominant horse and would attack Misty. It was ironic; Blue longed for company, but mistreated it when she got it. Once more we could see the problems that human beings have illustrated more openly in animals. Misty lasted for some time on the ground, but a horse is built to stand, and her left lung collapsed. Finally, reluctantly, we had her put down; we don't like to see an animal suffer, with no hope of reprieve. We hired a man with a bulldozer to dig a hole to bury her. It was a sad event. I hate death, and it always is painful. I came daily to her grave in the pasture. On the third day I felt the grief let go a bit, but still for a month or so I came, just to stand by the grave a moment. As time passed grass started growing over it, and longleaf pine seedlings started of their own accord; most did not survive, but when we left that property, one endured, and I like to think that a new tree marked Misty's grave.

Meanwhile the vet brought us a young horse who had been a ten-thousand-dollar animal, but had suffered bad illness in youth and could not be raced or ridden. We were no longer interested in riding; Blue was too old. We just wanted company for her, and had good pasture. This was a filly called Fantasy, named elsewhere but quite fitting for us. She was brown with a large white blaze on her forehead. I remarked that Blue was black, and faded into the shadows, while Fantasy was brown, and faded into the woodwork. She had been raised among people, because of her illness, and was completely friendly. I had learned early that I couldn't use a shovel to clean out the stall when Blue was near; she must have had experience with sticks. With Fantasy there was no trouble at all; she had never been mistreated. She was a delight; you could pet her, for she would come to you. After a bad couple of nights she and Blue came to terms, and became friendly; I saw them grooming each other once, which is something Blue and Misty didn't do. So Blue had company again, and it was great; together they ranged the farthest pastures, as had not been possible with Misty for the prior year. We considered Fantasy to be Cheryl's horse, because Misty had been hers. But then Fantasy developed a swelling around the chest. We thought perhaps she had gotten a thorn embedded, but it was more than that. The vet was grim. He took her back, and brought a white pony to replace her, again with no charge; we just wanted company for Blue, and he wanted a suitable home for certain animals. We learned that Fantasy died, and the autopsy showed that it was her heart: it had indeed been damaged by that illness, and had taken time to take her out. She had seemed so healthy! We had her only four months, but she was a lovely horse, and we are glad to have known her for that time.

Meanwhile the white pony had no name we knew of. She had been boarded with the vet, but the family had never claimed her; a big bill was left unpaid. So now she was boarding with us; we didn't own her, any more than we had owned Fantasy. So we named her Snowflake, because of the color and because I had had a horse named that in the Adept series; Penny reminded me. She turned out to be just as good for our purpose as Fantasy had been; she and Blue got along well from the outset, perhaps because there was no debate as to who bossed the pasture. When we moved in 1988, we built a little barn just like the one at our prior property, so that the horses had something familiar. The new property wasn't as good for pasture, but was larger, and they had the range of about fifty acres of pine and oak trees. I cut a path through the brush—I was always good at paths—to where there was a semblance of grazing, but we didn't depend on it; we fed them well. They used the path, and seemed to like to range among the pine trees of the tree farm. There was a pole barn out there, but they didn't use it much. There was also an old bathtub with a pump, and we kept it filled so they could drink, but mostly they used the tub we had at the regular barn. Still, sometimes we saw them up by Ogre Corner, half a mile from the barn, looking out at our driveway. They seemed satisfied with the premises.

But Blue was old, past thirty, and her digestion was frail; her manure emerged in a liquid stream like urine. She seemed otherwise healthy, but her head was turning white. Finally she sickened at the turn of the year, 1991–92. On New Year's Day she seemed healthy, but on the second she was ill and off her feed, and on the third morning I phoned the vet: "I fear for her life." He had morning chores to do, so it was about four hours before he arrived. Blue was lying by the barnyard gate. I saw her take a breath as we entered—but she was dead as the vet knelt beside her. We think it was rampaging infection from a tear in her intestinal system; that liquid manure had gotten into her blood and destroyed her system. So, again, we hired a dozer to dig a hole; we got same-day service because the owner's son was a fan of my novels. So Blue was gone, and this was the worst one yet; she was just shy of thirty-four years old, and we had had her almost fourteen years. Penny came to pay her respects; she had been away to college, and Blue no longer knew her, but Blue was Penny's horse, and I knew her loss was awful. I used to say that Blue's business was raising girls; her prior mistress, Joanne Monck, had been ten when she got Blue, and was fifteen when she sold Blue to Penny, who was then ten. Joanne got married when she was twenty, so we knew that Blue had taught her the necessary aspects, and later Penny got married too. We gave Snowflake back to the vet, who had another horse who needed company. My main regret was that the vet's van had broken, so we had to wait for other transportation, which meant that for two weeks Snowflake was alone. She could not see well or walk well, but she searched the whole tree farm, looking for Blue, unable to realize that Blue was forever gone. It was so sad. And so we were out of the horse business, as it were. For a week after Snowflake left I still went to the barn every morning, as if to feed the horses, Just Because. It was hard to let go of them. But we knew better than to start in on any new horses. It was a segment of our lives that was done.

In due course Penny set up her own establishment near Tampa, where she kept goats and geese as well as dogs and cats. Later she moved to Oregon, taking the animals along and adding new ones. I had told her the stories of my early life on a goat farm, and she had read *Bio of an Ogre*, and something must have made an impression. The goats had kids, so she had the pleasure of getting to know them too, as I had. I would report in my monthly family letter with my usual whimsy that Penny had two more kids. So the tradition of animals continued.

F i f t e e n

INCIDENTALS

I have tried to cover major aspects of my continuing life with some subject grouping for clarity, but there remains a huge collection of fragmentary episodes that don't readily fit into the existing structure. This is the nature of human life. This chapter consists of selections from that collection.

Over the years certain songs have become associated with particular novels of mine. This usually happens when a popular song is playing on the radio—I always have it on when I'm working, as background company—at the time I'm doing creative work on a particular scene. Those incidental associations remain indefinitely, and later when I hear those songs, I think of the relevant novel. One example is "My Heart Belongs to Me," which must have been playing in 1977 when I was working on the second Xanth novel, *The Source of Magic*. The nymph Jewel happened to be in the vicinity when Bink inadvertently drank from a love spring, and she was the first woman he saw thereafter. He was married to Chameleon, but love elixir takes no note of marital status; he loved her as well as his wife, and constantly sought to get closer to her, to her discomfort. But gradually he won her over, and she came to love him too. Then the Time of No Magic wiped out the spell on him, and he lost his love for Jewel. But Jewel's love for Bink was natural, not magical, and did not fade. That was her tragedy, which she bore gracefully. And there is the association with the song, actually in reverse: Jewel's heart has been lost, though Bink is no longer chasing her. So I am always sad when I hear the song, remembering Jewel and the unfairness of it. Fortunately, another man took a liking to her, and came after her with a love spell, so in the end she was happy and married. In fact she was the mother of Tandy, who was patterned after my daughter Cheryl, and later grew up to marry Smash Ogre.

Two songs associate with the third Mode novel, *Chaos Mode*. I was long familiar with both, but they are still occasionally played on the radio, and when I had a relevant scene for Colene, the feisty depressive fourteen-year-old heroine, those songs joined in. Colene, then thirteen, was trying to get close to her ninth grade science teacher, on whom she had a crush. She hummed the songs "To Know Him Is to Love Him," and "Why Was I Born Too Late?" Finally, she found a pretext to kiss him, and was thrilled when she realized that he had had time to dodge away, but had allowed her to score. No, he was a good man, and never took advantage of her, and was quite helpful in saving Burgess, her ailing alien friend.

Another song, "Eternal Flame," associates with Colene in the first novel of that series, *Virtual Mode*, when she lands a man she can keep. I tried to get permission to quote thirteen words of it in the Author's Note, but they demanded payment of thirty dollars per word, so I dumped that. But I still think of Colene taking his hand and holding it to her bosom, longing for his love.

I had reference to a folk song in the first Incarnations of Immortality novel, *On a Pale Horse*, in a scene where lovely Luna is suffering the recent death of her father: "Come Let Me Hold Your Hand." The lines were "It's a long time, girl, may never see you, come let me hold your hand." But the editor mistook the song for the Beatles' "I Wanna Hold Your Hand," and took it out. Since it was well integrated with its scene, as my elements normally are, he took out the whole scene. I protested, and he allowed the scene back in if I substituted other words. He couldn't admit his error, and that attitude was soon enough to destroy our relationship. I was one of several of that publisher's best-selling writers to depart, because I am not the only one who can't stand to have good text destroyed by bad editing. The song signaled the coming mischief.

In the third volume in that series, the song was "Believe in Me," wherein a young man is wishing that the woman he loves would truly believe in him. That associates with Cedric, who as a youth of sixteen was married to Niobe, a woman of twenty-one, the most beautiful of her generation. He stands in complete awe of her, while she regards him as like a gangling puppy and wonders whether he will grow into his huge hands and feet. Yet he is far more man than she dreams, as events prove. But at the time of the marriage she doesn't truly believe in him. And this story, interestingly, derives from another song, "The Bonnie Boy," which dates from a prior generation. I heard it on a record by Mary O'Hara, an Irish singer. For years I searched for her music, and finally on a visit to New York around 1960 we found a store which carried her records. Later that song, with a fifteen-year-old man marrying a twenty-two-year-old woman, and soon dying, inspired the situation of my novel. I believe Joan Baez recorded it too, but I worked from the earlier version. It is ironic that I came to associate my scene with a different song, but these things don't necessarily have much logic. In fact, there is a different song quoted in the scene, which Cedric sings to Niobe, trying belatedly to court her: "Come Live with Me and Be My Love," which dates centuries back. Here is how it happened:

> And we will sit upon the rocks.
> Seeing the shepherds feed their flocks.

As he sang, he reached forth to take her hand.

> By shallow rivers, to whose falls
> Melodious birds sing madrigals.

At his touch, something happened. Suddenly there was music, as of a mighty orchestra, filling the forest with the power of its sound. His voice seemed to become amplified, magnificent, evocative, compelling, beautiful. She sat stunned, mesmerized by his amazing presence, by the phenomenal music, and she only came out of it when the song ended.

> If these delights thy mind may move.
> Then live with me, and be my love.

As he stopped singing, the grand music also died away.

For that was his magic: to be accompanied by the unseen orchestra when he sang, making his untrained voice become wonderful. It was the beginning of love for Niobe. I still like the scene, though today I wince at one line, which should be "and she came out of it only when the song ended." The placement of the word "only" is one of those nuances I picked up on too late for this novel.

The fifth novel in my Incarnations series, *Being a Green Mother*, associates with a hymn. I needed one as the theme for Orb's wedding to Satan, and couldn't find anything suitable. I was about to buy an album of something like a hundred hymns and listen to them all, searching for the right one. But then my wife and I returned late to our house, I think from a local speaking engagement I had had in Inverness, and turned on the TV, and caught the last two minutes of *Cheers*, a favorite program. It seemed an acquaintance had died, and nobody much had liked him, so they would not do him honor in a memorial service. Then the woman, Diane, stood alone and began singing "Amazing Grace," and the men, shamed, came back in and joined her in a kindly memorial. I was long familiar with that song, but I had never heard it quite that way before. "Amazing Grace, how sweet the sound, that saves a wretch like me"—"That's it!" I thought, and so it entered my novel.

Then there was "Islands in the Stream," sung I believe by Dolly Parton, that I came to associate with the second Space Tyrant novel, *Mercenary*, wherein the protagonist Hope Hubris marries a fiery and beautiful pirate lass named Roulette for political reason, and soon loves her, and in time she loves him too. But circumstances force them apart, and he has a vision of the two of them being on separate islands, which are inexorably separating. A second song associates with her, "Rue," which I remembered from my collection of folk songs. Key lines are "And when your thyme is past and gone, he'll care no more for you, you; And every day that your garden is waste, will spread all over with rue, rue." It uses garden analogies with a social point, warning women of the fickle ways of men.

When I started that series, I wrote the first novel, *Refugee*, in pencil in the winter, because my typewriter was in the study, too cold to use. Then I set it aside and wrote the first Incarnation novel, *On a Pale Horse* similarly in pencil. When spring came I typed them both, and both were similarly strong fiction, with similarly broad themes that the critics wouldn't admit existed, though it was the latter that made the best-seller lists. Next winter I wrote the second novel in each series, and the odd thing was that when I finished *Mercenary* I suffered awful pangs of separation from it. Since the first novel in the series was the more savage of the two, I'm not sure why, but I hated to leave this one. I don't always understand my own feelings.

Then there was the song "Remember Me," also called "The Girl in the Wood," which is both the earliest and the latest, and associates with two of my novels. In 1956, the year I was married, I heard it once, and it inspired a sequence in my first published novel *Chthon*, as described in Chapter 3. Then about thirty-five years later, readers identified it for me, and I wrote another such sequence into the eighteenth Xanth novel, *Geis of the Gargoyle*, which was not far short of my hundredth published novel. Ah, that lovely girl in the wood! The song described a boy who went into the wood and saw there a beautiful woman, who told him that he would never see a girl as lovely as she was. Her eyes were as green as grassy pools, looking right at him, and her hair was red as autumn leaves, and she completely enchanted him. And me. He never married, because no woman measured up to that image; fortunately I was already married when I heard it. It wasn't until I recovered the song, in the 1990s, that I realized that the girl in the wood was a dryad, a spirit of a tree. No wonder she had so fascinated me! I remember being a bit disappointed on the first hearing, when the girl moved her tiny hands and made a little turn, because she was obviously showing off, diminishing my impression of her as serious. But I did remember her, for all that time, and memorized the song when I recovered it. I always liked trees, and lovely women, and magic, and stories, and songs, and there they all were in one.

Songs aren't the only things with associations for me. There was a movie about an American nuclear bomber gone awry, and it destroyed a Russian city. The Russians were naturally upset, and World War III threatened, but it was diffused when the Americans agreed to bomb an equivalent city. How would the Russians know when that had been done? By having a phone connection to that city; when the bomb detonated, the phone would be vaporized, and there would be a shrill whine. Now when our phone changes over to receive a fax, it makes a sound just like that, and I always think of the phone vaporizing. It's a bit unnerving.

Often I need to go to a dictionary to check a word. I try to use words precisely, and if I am in doubt about a nuance, I look it up. I have four major dictionaries: the *Oxford English Dictionary*, in the condensed form, with the update supplement that makes it current to 1987;

I have to use a magnifying glass to make out the tiny print. The 1913 *Funk & Wagnalls* I got for my tenth birthday in 1944. The 1945 *Webster's New International* I inherited from my wife's father. And the 1987 Random House. All are unabridged, ranging from 2,500 pages to 5,000—or 20,000, if you count each compacted page of the *OED*. I love them all. I also have a big fake 1973 Webster that I don't respect. I made up a list of test words that defeat some dictionaries, thus rating them in my own fashion. The updated *OED* is the only one that has all eleven test worlds: *neoteny, bindlestiff, phthore, tesseract, parsec, googolplex, fart, ouroborus, eidetic, geis,* and *menarche.* Random comes second with eight, missing *phthore, ouroborus,* and *geis.* Webster is third with six; it gets *tesseract,* but misses *googolplex* and *fart,* but those are forgivable because the one is too recent, and the other is dirty. Funk gets only four, which is a shame, because it's always been my dictionary, but it suffers because of the number of words that simply didn't exist in its day. And the fake Webster is last with only two: *bindlestiff* and *parsec.* So I generally use Random, and go to *OED* if I have to, because it's less convenient. But here is where the association comes in: in the U.S. Army Artillery training we had to judge how far away a particular target was. One was deceptive; it looked reasonably close, but wasn't, so our figurative rounds kept falling short. The lesson: always bracket your target. Put one shot beyond it, one before it, then close in. I use that when I look for a word in my dictionaries, because otherwise I can turn pages wastefully. So when I look up a word like *kris,* a Malay dagger, I bracket it, going back and forth: *I, M, K, L, KA, LA,* and finally *KR.* Only Funk and OED have it. And I think of that Army lesson, ranging with the artillery shells. Every time. And wonder whether there's a better way to zero in. Actually, a late development produced one: Infopedia, mentioned in Chapter 9, jumps to your likely word as you type it in. It scores 8 on the word list, missing on the archaic terms. That's not bad.

Incidentally, I have an objection to the definition of *googolplex.* A googol is ten to the hundredth power, or a 1 with a hundred zeros following it. It seems to me that a googolplex should be a googol to the googol power, but according to the dictionaries it is a relatively puny ten to the googol power. Maybe we need a new term for my concept: goOogol. That's one big number!

There was one more song association, minor yet enduring. I was hitchhiking north to Vermont in 1953, and a song played on the radio of a car that gave me a ride. I remember the words of the refrain, which experience has taught me not to quote directly: he was glad he had kissed other lips first, so that he knew how different it was this time. Years, maybe decades later I saw Eddie Fisher sing that song on TV, so I realized it was his. It wasn't that it was an especially great song, just that it associated with that time in my life, coincidentally between the first lips I kissed as man/woman at Goddard in 1952, and the second, in 1954, and there was a difference, and I married the second. So I sought that song, and couldn't find it. Finally I prevailed on my wife to buy me a $100 book for my sixtieth birthday, Lissaur's *Encyclopedia of Popular Music in America*, 1688–1989, and there at last I found it: "Many Times," Eddie Fisher, 1953 hit song. But when I finally heard it—it wasn't the song, so it's still missing.

Which reminds me of another book Cam gave me: *Woods Unabridged Rhyming Dictionary*. Sometimes—rarely—I try to versify, and it's frustrating to get stuck on a missing rhyme. I can go through the alphabet in my head, searching: *ale, bale, dale, fail, gale, hale, jail, kale, mail, nail*, and so on, but I'm apt to miss *ail, Braille, flail, frail, regale, hail*, and similar. So she got me the book, and it remains precious to me, including her dedication in front: "To Piers—This dictionary,/ As you can see,/ Is meant for rhymes/ Like me, be, thee.// But 'cause the book/ Is just for you,/ I will not look/ To make this work. Your Cam, Christmas 1960."

My collection of dictionaries, of various types, is just part of my interest in books. I have about twenty atlases, the first major one being the *National Geographic Atlas of the World*, which Cam gave me for Christmas in 1970. And of course now I have a whole small library of research books, mostly on history and the nature of mankind, shelved and indexed according to the system used by the Library of Congress. Affluence has allowed me to acquire any good book I want, and there are more and more good books. Now I have three thousand reference books. But those early gifts are the treasures.

But about songs: I always loved them, and used to sing them to myself, though I learned to do it only when alone, because of ridicule by family and other children. I collected my favorite songs, memorizing them and writing them out. Once at Goddard I came across a book of songs in a lounge, and exclaimed with delight as I recognized old favorites, such as "Lady of Spain." "Lady of Spain," a girl echoed derisively.

It was as if she resented my delight in finding a song. Some folk are like that. They remind me of reviewers.

There is another bemused memory of a song associated with Goddard College. There were two girls, close friends, who I think were unrelated but they looked almost like twins. One was dark brunette, the other pale blond, both with long straight tresses, if my errant memory doesn't deceive me. They went everywhere together, these slender, pretty creatures. Then something changed, and the brunette discovered sex. She indulged in it wildly, seeming to want to seduce as many of the boys as she could, just for the challenge of it, and succeeding often. One boy was said to have had sex with her six times in one night. I know she had a way about her, because once she was standing near me as I sat in a chair, and she sort of nudged close, silently hinting at what she had, and she did have it; I felt the gravitic pull of it as I saw the clothed outline of her breast near my face. But I had my own girlfriend and wasn't looking for anything on the side, so I ignored her, and she moved on, leaving me with a memory of that revelation: that girl was a woman, physically. She took no precautions at all against VD or pregnancy, and the other girls in her dormitory became so alarmed that they scheduled a session on the use of contraception, so that the one among them who needed the information most, without knowing that she did, could be educated without being pointed out. The faculty adviser adamantly opposed that, so they weren't able to do it, which shows the folly of such "adult" attitudes. If the girl had gotten pregnant by an unknown man, much of the blame could have been laid to the faculty member. But the girl was lucky, and escaped mischief, as far as I know. Meanwhile her friend the blonde was left out in the cold, as it were. They remained close, but the blonde did not go the sexual route. Instead she became obsessed by a song, which she was always singing to herself, whose words were "I wish I were a fascinating bitch," with verses going on to all the things she would do, such as taking a holiday once a month and driving her customers wild. It finished "I wish I were a fascinating bitch—instead of a motherless child."

The girls at Goddard could have a mischievous humor about songs; I remember my first semester, when at an open house they were singing with gusto a song with at least ten verses, each suggestive: "Oh this is number one, it's going to be fun, roll me over, lay me down, and do it again; roll me over, in the clover, roll me over, lay me down, and do it again." It finished, I think, "Oh this is number ten, HE'S DOING IT AGAIN!" But the Motherless Child song was straight from the heart, in this case.

Sometimes my associations don't work out. Back in the 1970s Edmund Scientific Company, whose catalog of minor scientific marvels was always intriguing, had a contest to name their new telescope. It looked like a basketball with a projecting tube. I wrote to suggest "Macroscope," which was by no coincidence the name of the truly powerful orbiting telescope I had invented for my novel of that name. They ignored me and named it Astroscan. Okay, it was their choice. I conjecture that when they realized that toilets would be needed in space, they named their potty-shaped device Astro's-can.

Any life is filled mostly with incidentals, far too numerous to describe. When I read Isaac Asimov's massive two-volume autobiography I found it interesting, but concluded that the minutia of daily existence are seldom worth recording for posterity. So I tried to be more selective in *Bio of an Ogre*, and though I am going into things here that I did not there, so as to make a complementary rather than a duplicative volume, there are still many more notes than I can accommodate without becoming tedious. So I'll will give samples, selected as much for general interest as for biographical validity.

My experience in the U.S. Army was not fun. It paid my way for two years and enabled my wife and me to survive until we could get to Florida. I went into detail on the problems in *Bio of an Ogre*, so won't repeat them here. But there were some lighter episodes.

There was a joke I learned, using a quarter. In the old days quarters were silver, and had a flying eagle on one side. The joke was to hold the eagle upside down and cover its small head with the thumb, so that only the downward pointing wings showed. In that position they resembled the chaps of a cowboy's legs. "What direction is the cowboy walking?" The other person would say "that way," pointing the obvious direction. Then you pulled your thumb off, showing the upside-down eagle head, which resembled a penis. "Damn right!" When I was a survey instructor in the U.S. Army, and the material wasn't urgent, I would bring out my quarter and show the joke to the first student in the class, who would in turn show it to the next, and so on as the class progressed, until I got my quarter back from the last student. There would be chuckles as the coin slowly made its way. That joke is no longer current because with the erosion of the value of the dollar the government issued nonsilver coins, and speculators collected all the real silver coins. For years I saved my "Pecker Quarter," but lost it somewhere along the way. Too bad.

When I worked on the staff of *The Observer*, the battalion newspaper, I noticed a heading the chief editor, Bob Ransom, had written. I did a double take, then realized that it was relevant, so didn't challenge it. It was about the mail clerk for the battalion, who had been highly successful in sports. The editor was not aware that there was anything odd about it. Later the post newspaper, *The Cannoneer*, picked up on it, remarking on the humor. Thus came post notoriety for that headline: BATTALION MAIL CLERK HOLDS SIX LETTERS.

I identify with most living things, and try to avoid hurting them if I can. There are obvious limits, such as the impossibility of surviving without eating, and though I don't eat animals, I do eat plants. So constant compromise is the price of life. But I also identify with many inanimate things. When a good machine has served me well, I don't like to junk it. We have had a number of bicycles, including two tandems, which we used to take our daughters to school when they were small, and I was really sorry when one got trodden on by a horse and couldn't be repaired. The other we finally gave to Penny when she was on her own, because we no longer had a use for it and I preferred that it be used. Something that isn't used is dead. But there's one special guilt I have about another type of thing: curtains. In the 1960s when I was writing, I sat by the window and worked, but then I got the allergic sneezes. Cam thought it was the curtains, so she took them out and bought new ones. It turned out to be the northeast wind; from that direction it set me off, and that was the window on that side. So the curtains were innocent, and it still bothers me that they were falsely blamed. I wish we could recover them and put them up again, but of course three decades have passed and they are long since gone.

That allergy started bothering me after we moved to Florida. My nose got chronically stuffed, inhibiting my breathing, and sometimes I would have daylong sieges of runny nose, so that I had to wad tissue into it to stop it from dripping onto my keyboard as I typed. I asked a doctor about it, but he said that I must be allergic to some common substance, and it would take two years of testing to run it down, and then they wouldn't be able to do anything about it anyway. So I suffered through it, though at times I couldn't eat well, because I could not both chew and breathe, and my mouth would get completely dry at night, so that I couldn't get my tongue unstuck from the floor of my mouth. Until finally it was diagnosed as a deviated septum in the nose. I had surgery for that, and it improved my nose breathing somewhat—and, incidentally, abolished most of my allergy to the northeast wind. I was always more allergic to weather than my wife was, but now the situation has reversed.

When I went to Goddard College in 1952 I was still growing. In two years I outgrew my collection of plaid shirts, and girls asked me for them. No, I had no relationship with any of them; apparently they simply liked the shirts. It would be tempting to imply that these were payments for favors rendered, but it wasn't so. So for a time a number of girls were wearing my old plaid shirts. I think those shirts looked better on them than they had on me.

When credit cards became popular, we avoided them for some time. We always managed our money well, back when we didn't have much, and also later when we had plenty. One of the gratifications of my marriage is that my wife is even less likely to waste money than I am. I tease her about her spending money, but teasing is all it is. Once I was shopping for Christmas gifts with my daughters, and I kept seeing nice things to buy; Cheryl kept demurring along cost/value lines, while Penny said "that's why I like to shop with Daddy." But eventually we concluded that a credit card could be useful, because though I don't much like to travel, on occasion family or business concerns require it, and a credit card can be invaluable then. So we applied for what we deemed to be the best one: the Sears Discover card. And they turned me down, because I hadn't been in debt enough. I was a millionaire with no bad debts, ever, and they didn't like that? Later that card ran into financial problems of its own. No wonder! When you turn down the best credit risks, you are left with the other kind. Maybe a publishing executive got in their works, counting his beans in the usual fashion. Meanwhile we applied next to MasterCard, whose solicitations we had been throwing away for years. They carried no grudge, and accepted me without any fuss at all. Later yet we diversified, deliberately, so that if a card was lost or stolen we would not be caught short in Timbuktu or wherever, so now in addition to our joint MasterCard Cam has an AT&T card and I have a Wilderness Society VISA card. My main disappointment there was that the ad for it showed a lovely wilderness scene on the card, while the one they actually issued me is dull brown. I was tempted to protest the false representation, but it hardly seemed worth my energy.

At one point one of my readers came to visit me. I generally discourage this, so as not to have all my time taken up, but we had corresponded for a number of years and he had offered to do some professional work for me on a project that never quite jelled. His second visit occurred when my father-in-law was extremely ill, with a fifty percent chance of death, and my mother-in-law needed support, so Cam was away with her mother. Penny, Cheryl, and I were running the household. The visitor brought his girlfriend, and we talked about this and that. He thought I was great, but his friend thought I was terrible. Why? Because, she said, I did not meet her gaze. Now this intrigued me. When I pondered the matter, I concluded that she was right: I had hardly made eye contact with her. But why not? I have met thousands of people, and never had trouble with eye contact; I relate closely with my readers, and can handle other relationships well enough. So what was the matter here? And I realized that it hadn't been me, it had been her. When the man and I talked, I had more than once looked over to the woman and invited her to participate, but she had demurred, saying that she was good at listening. So I hadn't met her gaze because I hadn't been talking to her— by her preference. And I learned why: he had come this time to ask my advice on whether they should marry and keep the baby that the woman was carrying. This was not something I felt it was my province to decide on for anyone else, but I did give my opinion: yes, I don't like abortion, because it destroys a life that deserves its fair chance. So he decided to do that. But the woman had assumed that I would argue the opposite case, and she resented my seeming power over her reproduction, understandably. So she had viewed me with hostility from the outset. And herein were several lessons for me. One, of course, was not to prejudge; the woman had done that to me, and then blamed me for her own cutoff of communication. Another was not to be too ready to assume I was at fault when I didn't get along with someone; sometimes the other person comes with a preformed grudge and a determination not to get along. I have seen that notably in fanzines; one fan editor followed me for twenty years from one fanzine to another, having no seeming purpose other than to cut me down. I wasn't even aware of him until near the end of that time, and don't know what bothered him about me, other than my success as a writer. Another lesson was that I may have no notion what is going on in a dialogue; sometimes I come up against a hostile agenda that bears no relation to reason. So I remember that reader visit for reasons other than the usual. So what happened between that reader and his girlfriend? Later they had an argument, and she went next day and got an abortion, and they broke up. So my advice counted for just about nothing.

Abortion is one of those difficult issues that keeps me firmly on the fence. I don't like it—but then, I don't think anyone *does* like it. I am a vegetarian because I don't like the unnecessary taking of life, and a baby is a life. But some others who oppose abortion seem to stand for nothing much else I approve. They don't really support life, because they tend to approve the death penalty, they bomb clinics, and they murder doctors and others associated with abortion clinics. I also have a problem, because I believe that the overpopulation of the world with people is perhaps the major threat to the continuation of civilization as we know it, and if every baby is saved, that will only get worse. I would much prefer to see effective contraception, so that an unwanted baby would never be conceived. There seems little point in requiring an unwanted baby to be brought into a hostile situation. So I hesitate to second-guess the women who seek abortions. But I hate the thought of the most truly innocent of creatures, unborn babies, suffering the death penalty.

The death penalty is another difficult issue for me. I don't like it in general, and I see its racist application, but there are specific cases where it does seem justified. Some people seem to exist only to harm others, and I just don't see why they should be allowed either to be free to rob, rape, abuse, or kill others, or to be supported at society's expense in prison. So this is another case where I figuratively hold my nose and let it be.

At Goddard, in one of the classes we tried growing plants, to see how they were affected by different conditions. But at the end of the semester I had my trays of seedlings left. I couldn't take them with me, and I couldn't do anything with them; it was winter and they would have died outside. I didn't want to simply kill them. So I put them in the attic. At the next term, after the two-month winter hiatus that Goddard had to save heating costs, I returned to college and checked on the plants. They were dead, of course, but what got me was that they had stretched way out and to the side, seeking the dim light of a distant window. They had tried so hard to survive, but had no chance. I had in effect murdered them. I don't know what else I could have done, but still I feel the guilt. I don't like to see plants suffer either.

But there was a more pleasant sequel. One of the things I learned from that plant project was that soil made a difference. I stayed with my mother that work term, and she had an African violet that was languishing, with only a few leaves. So I applied my new knowledge: I bought good potting soil and transplanted the poor rootbound thing into better conditions. Many months later when I returned to visit my mother, there was the plant, with about five centers and flowers all over, absolutely thriving. All because of what I had done for it. Now I try never to plant seeds that I am not prepared to care for. Plants are living things too, and deserve fair treatment.

Some stray items relate to names. I was never good at names, and still am not; they slip through my consciousness like slippery fish. One name I do remember nevertheless balks me. When we came to America, I remember how my grandfather liked to listen to the news in the early evening. He had a favorite commentator whose name, as I remember it, was Bawkage—I don't know the spelling. He had a very authoritative tone. Ever since I have tried to verify that, and have not been able to. Who cast the news in Pennsylvania in 1940? No one seems to know.

In high school I was at a party of some sort where placards bearing the names of celebrities were attached to our backs, where we wouldn't see them. Then we had to talk with others, asking questions, trying to guess whose name we carried. I knew I wouldn't be able to guess mine, and I was right. It turned out to be Fred Astaire. I had never heard of him. But thereafter I remembered the name, and learned that he was a dancer in the movies, quite well-known.

When Cam and I got married in Florida, we had very little money. Our honeymoon was the drive back north, with our best man Charles Gasset traveling with us. We stopped at the Luray Caverns in Virginia—I always liked caves—and they were impressive. But the thing I remember most was the way the guide informed us at one point that we were standing at the lowest point in the explored caverns. But not far from there was a fenced-off section, with stairs going down.

The last conventional employment I had, before retiring permanently to writing, was as a teacher. Two linked aspects stand out in my memory. I discussed my limited teaching career in Chapter 3, but one aspect didn't properly fit there. Part of the preparation for teaching was practice teaching, supervised by a regular teacher. Mine was with John Humphreys, who taught twelfth grade English at Northeast High School in St. Petersburg, Florida. He was a good teacher and I liked him, but he had in my estimation an Achilles' heel. He was a tough grader, sometimes brutally tough, but that wasn't it. It was that he stood up for his rights. I respect that, but it carries a price, and he ran afoul of that price, in what I saw as painful pseudo-justice.

My first day in his classroom, I saw a girl in the front row, crying. John asked her contemptuously if she had some complaint, but she didn't answer. Later he told me that she was one of the brightest students, but she had made one mistake: when working out test answers on scratch paper, she had gotten her lines crossed, and copied the answer for B to the line for A, and C to B, D to C and so on down. Humphreys had seen that, and saw that all her answers were correct, just misplaced. In such a case, I would have given her one error, and given credit for the rest, as the test was supposed to be of her knowledge of the subject. But Humphreys had given her no credit on that section, so she had an indifferent or even failing exam instead of a top score. All her work studying and preparing had gone for nothing; one misalignment had done her in, and she was crying at the loss. High school grades are important for admission to college; I have no way of knowing how much damage this did to her. I have suffered similar penalties myself, so have sympathy. I felt that Humphreys had been needlessly cruel, and that the grade he gave her did not reflect her competence as a student. But I was only an observer. Perhaps he was teaching a hard lesson that would profit the girl later in life.

Later came what was called the Florida teachers' strike for better conditions. Legally they couldn't strike, so they resigned instead. Humphreys supported it, and resigned with the others. The conclusion was mixed; I don't think the teachers got much of what they wanted, and Florida education continued its decline. I was not part of the scene, having been unable to get a job in the public school system; I taught at a private school. But I would have had to join the strike, had I not been on the sidelines. So the strike ended, but with a difference: the state school boards were vengeance-minded, and they accepted back only those teachers they wanted. They excluded the troublemakers, who were as a general class the most caring and effective teachers, in favor of the duller ones, who would make no peep of protest about bad school conditions.

So they excluded John Humphreys, and he lost his livelihood. He was, as far as I know, never to teach in the public school system in Florida again; he was blacklisted. Later, when my little girl and his little girl were friends, and I went to his house to pick mine up from a visit, his wife told me how hard it had been financially. He had paid a terrible price. Why? Because he had given the authorities the chance to get him, and they had struck ruthlessly the moment they could. They didn't care that he was an effective teacher; they didn't really care about education. Only about who went along with a stupid system and who made trouble. They had taught him a harsh lesson. The same one he had taught that girl.

So was it poetic justice? I doubt it. The parallel exists only in my own perception. But I wish that Humphreys had been kinder to that girl, and that the school system had been kinder to him. Neither victim deserved that magnitude of punishment for relatively small errors in judgment. Nature does indeed teach such harsh lessons, and lives are lost simply because a creature forgot to check the whereabouts of a predator, or happened to be too young or slow to avoid it, or was simply unlucky. But we as human beings have the capacity to rise above brutality. But of course I'm an idealist. I also watch my back, so as not to be caught as either of them were. When that fails, as it does when there is bad faith, I fight. Thus I have fought a lot, in my life and career. It's not a perfect world.

I have always appreciated humor, and see it as one of the defining characteristics of our species. It is universal, and permeates every aspect of our society, so that perhaps much of it passes unnoticed. I made my fortune with humorous fantasy replete with puns. As my roommate at Westtown asked me once: "If the pun is the lowest form of humor, is the bun the lowest form of bread?" As has been said elsewhere, the only thing worse than a pun is two puns. Another monstrous category is dirty humor. Theoretically children aren't supposed to know it, but they are just as much into it as the adult realm is. So one of the things I remember from Westtown is the illicit and pun-ish humor. At the time we were learning the formulae of physics relating to measurements such as the square-cube law for calculating volume or the vectors and angles and thrust of motion, a mock formula circulated. I never heard the whole of it, so have had to reconstruct it. It was, approximately, the formula for the Measure of the Pleasure: The Square of the Hair over the Mass of the Ass, times the Thrust of the Bust over the Angle of the Dangle. Over forty years later I still find it intriguing. There was another episode I found hilarious: someone rigged a joke car bomb to the vehicle of one of the teachers. When he turned the ignition, there was a high whistle, as of something sailing through the air, then a loud bang, and black smoke poured out from under the hood.

But I have elected not to support Westtown financially, though the school continues to solicit me, and all graduates. My reasons are both simple and subtle. I feel that a person should contribute to those causes he values, and I do, approximately tithing my income. By the same token, he should not be obliged to contribute to those he doesn't value, merely because they keep asking. Since I decided to let Westtown be part of my past, I didn't contribute—and the more persistently it solicited me, the more negative I found myself becoming. With each solicitation I explored my decision, and discovered to my surprise that it was not apathy that kept me apart, it was hostility. Yet Westtown was one of the best schools I attended—#3 of ten in my private ranking, and I do contribute to #1 Goddard College and #2 The School in Rose Valley, and to others that aren't on my list, for different reasons.

So what was the matter? I covered some of this in *BiOgre*, so will add examples not given there: in bygone days, wealthy Quakers had donated formidable sums to the school to be used to pay part of the tuition of Quaker students. I counted as Quaker, because my family was Quaker, so got the benefit of that. Then the headmaster decided that the school could use that money better elsewhere, and took it, so that no student got its benefit anymore. Now the justice of contributing money for some students' tuition and not for others may be debatable, but this was a private Quaker school, so it seemed in order. In any event, the money had been accepted with that proviso, so when it was then taken for other purposes, that might be questioned. The same applied to students' personal money: we were required to keep most of it in personal envelopes in the office, for safekeeping. But when I came the weekend after a year of school ended, to recover my money, I could not; they had taken it to apply to expenses they charged to me. So I lost my personal money. That smelled like stealing, but there was nothing I could do about it, then. When my cousin Teddy Jacob died, his family invited me to join them in Florida during the Christmas holiday. I got along well with their daughter Dotsy, and served somewhat in lieu of a brother for her. This invitation was a great prospect for me, and I loved the idea of visiting wonderful warm Florida for two weeks. But there was a problem: their schedule meant that if I were to ride down with them, I would have to miss one day of school at Westtown. So we went to ask the principal for permission to miss that day. He was polite, but said that he could not grant such an exception for one student without doing it for others. So he turned us down. The result was that I had to take the train, and the inefficiency of scheduling and other factors resulted in a Florida stay of just one day. It destroyed the vacation; most of my time was spent traveling. But the school policy had been upheld. It wasn't a waste, actually, but neither was it what it could have been. The message I got was that a school rule was more important than human experience, and that the school did not care how much its consistency cost others. I can't fault that on technical grounds, but it left me with a keen awareness of the possible costs of foolish consistency. So when in later years the school wanted something from me, I concluded that I should be true to my policy of contributing only to those causes I wished to, and not make an exception merely because I could readily spare the money. If the school doesn't perceive the logic, well, it is being served as it served me. I learn some lessons well.

Some incidents are of a lighter nature. Once my sister Teresa was talking about an interaction with someone, and said she wasn't trying to curry favor. "Favor is the name of a horse," I quipped, and we all laughed. Back in those days I wasn't known for humor, but perhaps there were signals.

When I was in the Army, it was said "There's the right way, the wrong way, and the Army way." This applied to clothing too. The U.S. Army regulation issue undershorts were not well designed. The civilian variant advertised that there was no chafing center seam. Sure enough there wasn't; instead there were two chafing side seams. Their fly was designed so that if a man wanted to use a urinal, it would be most comfortable if that urinal were set in the ceiling. Also in the Army: we normally wore fatigues at work, but weren't allowed to wear the regulation fatigue cap; instead use of a civilian cap with a raised, flat top was universal. Once another soldier asked me "What's that thing in your hat?" "My head," I responded, and he was silent. Later I looked at my hat and saw that someone had put a bit of wire through two of its holes. I had been set up for a joke, but had inadvertently diffused it by jumping to the punch line. Jokes were not necessarily kind. I had several flat tires, then one day saw a nail propped against my rear tire in such as way that when I backed out of the parking lot, it would be driven in, giving me a flat in due course. That explained much. Thereafter I circled my car each time before using it, making sure there was no trap. The actual humor of such vandalism escapes me. I had a notion of who was responsible, and why: he had been friendly until it turned out that I was the superior Ping-Pong player. I made no issue, because I lacked proof, but I chalked it up as another little lesson of life.

When I was in the second half of basic training in the Army, learning the survey that I was later to teach in that same unit, I worked hard to maintain my average, for only the top two in my class would be kept as instructors. The problem was that the Army itself didn't seem to care much; it routinely took students from classes for KP, guard duty, and whatever else. When I missed a day of classes because of some such assignment, I found a way to learn the material anyway. One soldier was slow to grasp the material, but he wanted to do well, so I would go over it with him. He would tell me what they had covered, and show me his homework, and I would figure it out and explain it to him. Thus he was able to keep up, and I was able to learn the material despite not being in class. There was one time that I had studying to do, and I was terrified that my time for it would be taken away. This was when they told us that there was post baseball, of semipro quality, and any of us who wished to could attend the game free. No one was interested. Jokes started flying. Someone farted. Another trainee whirled, imitating an officer: "Who fired that shot?" That annoyed the cadre, so they started assigning "volunteers" in the usual Army manner, sending the jokers and others taken at random to the waiting truck to be taken to the game. I was afraid I too would be hauled off, and stood with perfectly still face, hoping to escape. I was in luck; I wasn't taken. Thus I got my study time and maintained my average. It would have been ironic if I had lost my average, and thus my chance to remain as an instructor, and to bring my wife to join me so that the Army could become bearable, for the sake of a baseball game. I had very little interest in baseball anyway.

Another time there was to be a big battalion inspection. Inspections were the bane of military life; the barracks had to be scrubbed throughout, everything polished, and our clothing laid out perfectly. After several inspections, unused uniforms had to be dry-cleaned again, because of the wear entailed in the inspections. We even had to have packs of cigarettes laid out, including the nonsmokers, and they all had to be the same brand, Lucky Strike. It seemed like a lot of sound and fury, signifying nothing. But there was hell to pay if anyone messed up. One day we were preparing for inspection, but the cadre came by and said that our barracks had been postponed for several hours, so we were to do a GI party (scrubbing the floor) instead. It didn't matter whether the floor had just been scrubbed; I suspect that cleanliness wasn't the point anyway. We started in—and then suddenly the inspection party arrived, catching us in disarray. We had to run to our bunks and stand at attention as we were—in fatigues, with shirts out, hands soiled, buckets sitting there, mops leaning against bunks. One soldier had one boot on and one boot off, and had to remain that way. But the inspection team must have realized that there was a problem, and the officers went through the normal routine as if everything were completely in order, not commenting on the disarray. Maybe they had changed the route deliberately, in order to catch a barracks off guard, so as to verify actual preparedness. Since we were obviously working, and not goofing off, we were okay.

When I hitchhiked home from college, the day got late and rides were scarce. As dusk fell, a car passed me, then stopped. I ran up, and it was a single woman. She said she wasn't going to pick me up, but then she thought of how far I would have to walk otherwise, knowing that no one else would stop, so she had stopped. She was so relieved to find that I was a harmless college student that she drove three miles out of her way to help me on mine. I really appreciated that. I still had a long walk in the dark, and at one point cows were chasing me, and I feared I would walk into a porcupine, but it was about six miles shorter than it would otherwise have been. Today I wish I could thank that woman personally for that favor, but I don't even know her name. So I'll just say that if any woman reads this who gave a ride at dusk to a college kid in Vermont the summer of 1953 or '54, THANK YOU, Fair Lady!

For a time I collected stamps. Once a man sent me a huge batch of stamps on paper torn from envelopes. The deal was that if I soaked them and got them safely off the paper, I could have any I wanted, plus some special ones. I expressed interest in triangular stamps, and I believe he did find me some. The job itself was interesting, and I sent him a batch of cleanly separated stamps. About half of them were common British ones. Later I encountered big fancy stamps from Tannu Tuva, and so I looked up that little Asiatic country. I discovered that the *Encyclopedia Americana* had an entry: TANNU TUVA—SEE TUVA. And under TUVA it said SEE TANNU TUVA. So much for that edition!

When we lived on the farm in Vermont, back when I was about seven years old, at one point we visited elsewhere. The folk were very friendly, and brought out a big box with many interesting items. My sister and I were encouraged to take something from it as a gift. There was a harmonica in it, and I wanted that, but the woman guided my hand and had me pick something else. This bothered me; she hadn't understood what I really wanted. So later, when the others left the room, I took the harmonica and put it in my pocket. But I knew it wasn't right. On the way home my mother, checking in my pocket for a handkerchief, found the harmonica. "You can't keep this!" she said. "I know," I said. That was all. She sent it back to the owners, and I was ashamed. It was one of the defining lessons of my early life, and by the time I had wrestled it through I concluded that stealing was wrong. There's always a rationale, that a person needs something, or that somebody else cheated him so deserves to be cheated back, but it's still wrong. When I was in the Army, there was a box of blue/red colored pencils for general use; I took one, and I think it was never missed, but later I pondered and concluded that that too was stealing. The Army cheated me in an enormously greater manner, but that didn't make it right to cheat it back. Thus I continued to refine my philosophy, closing gradually on my ideal: total honesty. It's not an easy course, and I know of no one who is more concerned with it than I am, and I can't claim to be perfect in this. It's an ideal whose difficulty seems to vary inversely with proximity. What of social "white lies"? Do you tell a hurtful truth in the name of honesty? I think not. What is the distinction between privacy and truth? I conclude that there are things that are properly no one else's business. So if there is an embarrassment in someone's life, he or she does not have to advertise it to others. There is also the problem of keeping confidences. When a depressive teen writes to me of contemplating suicide, I feel bound not to report that to authorities; it is privileged information. But it means that something I know, that might save a life if I told, I will not tell. That's a difficult kind of integrity. So in the end there are no clear answers, and I must settle for fudgy guideline answers that may later turn out to be in error. I must have tolerance for standards I may deplore.

There was an isolated odd incident in the Army. When I was in basic training at Fort Dix, New Jersey, it quickly became known that I was a vegetarian. They nicknamed me "No meat." It was good-humored, and I suffered no discrimination or unkindness because of my diet. Once another trainee questioned me about it, and I answered him, but got the impression that there was a sarcastic edge, and was privately annoyed. Later I was told that when he went home on leave, his girlfriend dumped him, and he committed suicide. No connection between that and our dialogue, except in my mind: maybe his girlfriend didn't like muted sarcasm either.

Sometimes I'm stupid. This is annoying when I'm taking an IQ test. I remember being unable to figure out what was wrong with a particular picture of a man standing outdoors, so when the test was done, I inquired, and was told: his shadow was pointing into the sun instead of away from it. Ouch! So obvious, yet I had missed it. Years later, taking another such test, I saw another picture of a man in the sun, and remarked on the idiotic way I had missed. But this one was not in error that way; the man's shadow was not falling toward the sun. So I missed it. Afterward, I inquired, and learned that there was no shadow at all. Double ouch!

My politics are generally liberal, and I am not shy about them, though I value integrity more than philosophy. For example, those "liberal" students who shout down conservative speakers are not making a political statement, as I see it, but rather are demonstrating their lack of appreciation for freedom of expression. They need an education in courtesy and the First Amendment before they can claim to be true liberals. If they object to what conservatives say, they should skip the program, or, better, listen carefully, then make reasoned statements of refutation. But I must say that most of the illiberalism I see is on the conservative side, and their agendas often disgust me. I tried subscribing to the *Wall Street Journal* in the late 1960s or early 1970s, to be fair-minded, but dropped it when I saw how narrow its intellectual base was. For example, this was the time when Richard Nixon was president, and it was evident from the start that he was a man of no scruples—his congressional campaign against Helen Gahagan Douglas showed that—but the *Journal* could see no evil in him. Then one day they had an editorial criticizing him. Well, now; what was this? So I read it with interest. So what was its criticism? It said that he wasn't being hard enough on his critics. What a sham! In the 1980s I tried *American Spectator,* and quickly saw that its idea of savvy commentary on Democrat candidates for president was that they were "weird." That was it? In the 1990s I tried the *National Review,* opened it at random, and read that all the charges against Speaker of the House Newt Gingrich were either trumped up or irrelevant. Apparently they hadn't heard of the way he had cheated on his wife, dumped her when she had cancer, stiffed her on child support, then campaigned for "family values." Or the way he drove another congressman out because of a smelly book deal, only to make his own smelly book deals. Trumped up? Irrelevant? Maybe there exists a conservative publication that is fair-minded and opposes hypocrisy in conservatives as well as in liberals; I just haven't encountered it yet. I, as a liberal, do oppose bad behavior regardless of ideology, as mentioned above, and don't support a given politician merely because he spoon-feeds me compatible views. Without integrity, those views are valueless.

Sometimes qualities emerge that show unsuspected facets of people. At Westtown School there was a Vespers program every Sunday evening that students were required to attend. In one of them a woman told little stories and sang songs of her own composition to accompany them. It really was nice, but as the program progressed she seemed to become increasingly nervous, and finally she looked at the audience as if about to break down entirely. Then someone caught on, and began to applaud. Normally there was no applause at Vespers; evidently the headmaster had forgotten to tell her, and she thought that she was failing entirely in her presentation, without being able to fathom why. It must have seemed like the audience from hell, offering no clue about its nonresponse. The one who caught on, and who started the applause, which was then given for her following songs, was a student in my class named Marvin Flicker. He was a large, aggressive, militant Jew who took no crap from anyone about his religion, and sometimes got into fights because of it. But he normally defused it by another device: he would lead any anti-Jew songs. He knew them all. At times he seemed somewhat insensitive about the feelings of others. But this was the time when he was the first to catch on to a problem, and to deal with it appropriately.

And sometimes something unexpected happens that generates awkwardness. When we moved to Citrus County, Florida, our closest neighbors had several children, and their two girls were about the age of our girls, so they were around somewhat. I got the impression that at times the other girls might have preferred our family to their own. Once when I was working in the crawl space under my study, moving something in the dirt there, one of their girls came under with me. She just seemed to like my company. I was a bit wary, without saying anything; as a general rule, men don't crawl under buildings with the neighbor's girls. Another time we went walking in the forest, and spied a nest on a low branch, so I lifted my girls up so they could look in the nest, which I think had eggs. My girls were then aged seven and ten, and big for their ages, so were solid enough for me to have to exert a fair amount of power for the hoist. I stood behind them and put my hands under their arms, heaving each up in turn so that their heads were higher than mine, so they could see into the nest. Naturally the neighbor's girls wanted to see too, so I heaved up the younger one, then the older one. I became aware somewhere in mid-hoist that the last one had a different feel; she wasn't lighter, but she was softer. It did not take much reflection to realize that when I put my hands under their arms, my fingers pressed into their chests—or breasts. The older girl may have been eleven or twelve, and must have been starting to develop. I had inadvertently fondled her. She wanted to be lifted up again, but I demurred, not giving a reason. What could I have said? What bothered me in retrospect was that she might have realized what my fingers were pressing. It is my hope that that was not the case, and that she soon forgot the contact I did not forget. I did no more such lifting thereafter.

Let me conclude this chapter on nominally less serious notes: one is rubber bands. When we were away, and our daughter Cheryl came to baby-sit the house and dog, she discovered the box of rubber bands I had saved. I don't throw away useful things like paper clips and rubber bands, so they accumulate. So Cheryl made them into two rubber band balls, one big, one small. I had never thought of that, and was intrigued. So I added new bands to the balls, and then made my own ball from scratch, and kept adding to it until it was the largest of the three. I learned that they are true rubber balls; you can play toss and catch with them, and they bounce. Imagine a poor child who can't afford what he most wants: a ball. Save stray rubber bands, and in time he can have one. But it became more than that, for me. I wanted to form my ball perfectly, so I tried to put each new band around it on a course not done before. But somehow it always crossed a major nexus, or followed almost the same course of a prior band. Since the ball is made entirely of bands, it's impossible to add a band without overlaying what has been done before. Nevertheless it remains a challenge for me, to find as new a course as possible, and I can turn the ball around and over for some time before putting on a band. And it seems to me that this is another analogy of life: no matter how original you try to be, someone else has always been there before, and a critic will point this out to you. The critic can't see that you are forming a fine ball from unlikely material; all he sees is the negative aspect of unoriginality. That's part of what's wrong with critics.

Another incidental note is our pool. When we built our final house, it had everything, including a pool. That's when we discovered how much work a pool is to maintain. It wasn't heated, and we learned that 80°F water isn't hot to get in, it's cold; we needed it up around 85° for comfortable swimming. So we swam only about once a year, on the hottest day. But that pool had to be maintained every day. Organic material filtered down through the mesh of the pool enclosure, and algae was determined to grow. We used chlorine and whatever other chemicals we were supposed to, but they were never fully effective. So we had to scrape it off the sides. That job wore Cam out, so I took it over, and it took time every few days. Finally, we changed the formula, and that helped. But it was a lot of expense and effort for a pool we really weren't using. We also had to keep adding water. Then the pump broke—and we decided to let it be. So we let the pool go natural. It wasn't a pretty process. The algae flourished, and formed mats that floated to the top, and sank, and floated. The water turned dark. Plants sprang up around it, including copious resurrection ferns and a number of rare coonties. An outdoor tree extended a branch down, poking a hole in the mesh of the roof. Dragonflies hatched out of it, and we had to catch them in butterfly nets and take them outside lest they starve. One day I took thirty-two of them out. Frogs moved in, and we had hundreds of tadpoles, and then dozens of little frogs, which grew into larger frogs. On rainy days we would open the door and shoo batches of them out, so they could forage in the forestland where the insects were. Snakes came in: black racers, a water snake, a large yellow rat snake, and once a pretty coral snake. We caught them and took them out, but one racer came back in, so we let it be; it evidently wasn't lost. We also discovered that the pool no longer lost water; in fact rainfall kept overfilling it, so we had to siphon off the surplus. The pump must have leaked. And so our artificial pool became a forest pond, and perhaps that's no bad thing. Nature has recovered some of its own, and given us the company of pretty dragonflies and cute frogs. But we'll see about repairing that break in the roof. Maybe we can convert the pool into a greenhouse/pond.

✧ —————————————————————————— ✧

Sixteen

Conclusions

Much happened in the interim between the cutoff date for *BioOgre* and the writing of *Precious*, as this volume clarifies. As time proceeds, we all age and finally die, and the old order passes. I am intrigued by the past and by the future, as my various writings show, but at the same time I dread both in various respects. There are so many things I regret about my past, and things I regret to see in the future. It is as if the present is the high point of a landscape, with the future ahead and the past behind, each with its mountains and pits and hidden recesses. Each with its hopes and fears, its joys and regrets. Much of each can be fully appreciated only with the perspective of distance. So it is with nostalgia and mixed pleasure and misgiving that I consider that portion of the whole I am able to compass at this stage.

My wife's mother, Elizabeth Marble, died in 1982, before *BiOgre* was done. My wife's father, Ernest Marble, had fallen ill with a rare disease, Wegener's Syndrome, that nearly killed him. But the doctors tried one thing after another, and finally a stopgap measure they didn't really think would work, did work, and he recovered. But it was hell on Elizabeth, and she needed support. Their three children, Carol, Curtis, and Jane, took turns staying with her, a week or more at a time. Jane was first, then Cam, then Curt, and Cam was there again, because she lived closest. It was a fine family effort that gave Elizabeth great comfort when she needed it most, tiding her through the seven weeks of the crisis. I was pleased, incidentally, that when Ernest had to be put on temporary kidney dialysis, I was able to reassure Elizabeth about its nature, having learned about it when working on the book *Death or Dialysis*, though that was never published. At least that research did someone some good.

Ernest returned home, and improved daily, though he had lost a lot of weight and strength. But Elizabeth wasn't feeling well, and she checked with the doctor—and it turned out that she had cancer of the pancreas. Surely it was worsened by the stress of her husband's illness. She was scheduled for treatment, and we made plans for a family reunion in the summer, to be a pleasant surprise for her, but we did not know how fast and deadly this particular type of cancer is. Friends came to visit them, and she sat up on the couch where she was lying to greet them—and fell back, dead. At least it was quick and painless. That was early in 1982.

We see aspects of people when there is severe stress that we may not ordinarily be aware of. My mother-in-law had always struck me as a sensible, secure woman who knew her way around. The siege of her husband's illness stripped much of that away, and she became dependent. We were prepared to take her in if Ernest died; we would have built a small house for her on our property, as our house was barely sufficient for the four of us. So there would have been supportive contact. She couldn't bear the thought of being alone. Her husband was everything; without him, she had no real bearings. I understand that; while there was a time when I didn't expect to marry, all that changed forever when I encountered the right girl, and I soon knew that I could not endure unmarried. But it was apparent that my understanding of my mother-in-law's situation was not matched by her comprehension of me. There were ways in which she truly did not fathom me. At times she seemed to have objected to things about me, of which I was not guilty, and she seemed to regard me as intemperate. Now it is true that when I have a quarrel, I finish it, but I do not seek quarrels, and do my best to make sure my case is sound before I get into any. That is why I seldom lose. It may be that she assigned to me certain qualities that she objected to in her husband or others, and when she saw that she was wrong, was unable to say so. It would not be kind to go into specifics here, but it's a common enough phenomenon. So I think she did not want to join us, not because of any problem with Cam, but because of the way she saw me. I think she would almost rather have died than to be in any way dependent on me. She did not know that Ernest was destined to survive. So her will to live was not strong, and she died sooner than she might have. But probably contemporary medicine was unable to save her, regardless.

Ernest was much better equipped, emotionally, to endure alone. His health was not strong, and as time passed the damage Wegener's Syndrome had done to his system required him to get regular kidney dialysis, but he handled it. He did not enter a retirement home; he drove his car, he shopped, and he did well enough. He and I had never gotten along well, under the surface, because from the outset he was critical of me in chronic minor ways. He had done a fine job on our wedding, at which he officiated, and he and his wife were always supportive in practical ways, but there was a personal pique that others may not have seen. Two examples suffice: when I was writing the Cluster series, which related to interstellar empires, I made it a point to study the stars. I got a huge book of star maps, and I did my best to ascertain how far distant the stars of constellations like Orion's Belt were. I discovered that very little was known of actual distances, so I had to guess, which I didn't like. I spent time outside at night, contemplating the stars, which I find inherently fascinating. When Penny was little, I showed her Orion's Belt and its associated stars, Rigel, Betelgeuse ("Beetle Juice"), and the nearby Pleiades. When we moved from the city to the country, I was pleased to see something that the city illumination had made impossible: the Milky Way. So I remarked on that in passing, once, when we were visiting—and Ernest said "Then you haven't been looking at the stars." He had simply assumed that I must be wrong, though he was the one who hadn't been looking. He always assumed I was wrong. Another time we and the Marbles were visiting with my grandmother, Caroline Nicholson Jacob, with our toddler Penny. Penny started to get into trouble, and I was caught with a dish of food and glass of liquid in my hands, unable to act at the moment. But Ernest immediately blamed me, and only me. Because I was by definition wrong. I think any man who married his daughter was destined to be the object of his hostility. I didn't like it at all, but held my peace throughout, because I did not want to put my wife in a difficult position. But it was like being Archie Bunker's son-in-law. Then when Elizabeth died, and Ernest was not in good health, I received a call from an organization whose purpose was to ascertain whether he was capable of living alone. I said he was, because it was true, and gave some supporting detail. Then, later, to my surprise, Ernest said to me "Thank you for giving me a good reference." He was not being sarcastic, though he was perhaps a bit rueful. It seemed that my affirmation had made the difference, so that they had allowed him his freedom, and they had told him that, and he appreciated it. At that point I was glad that I had held my peace, and had been fair to him when it counted. I had done what was right because it was right, as I always try to do (sometimes I don't know what's right), but perhaps as he saw it, I had done him good when in a position to do him harm.

As time passed, and our affluence expanded, we bought a tree farm as an investment property, and liked it so well that later we built on it and moved there. Ernest visited, and helped us assemble a cabinet for my sound system in the study. I had to be constantly here and there, getting us moved in, and Cam was similarly busy, so most of the work on the cabinet was done by Ernest and Cheryl, his granddaughter. I was glad to see them getting along well. They got it done, and that cabinet has served me well ever since. He stayed the night, and drove himself back to Tampa next day. I believe he visited another time, compatibly. For the first time in our marriage since the arrival of our children, we had a house with room for such visitors without crowding. I admit that I was privately gratified to have this tangible evidence that I was providing well for my wife.

With fall came unusual rains. We had eight inches in four days, and areas near us flooded, though we had no trouble. We have always been careful about the lay of the local land, sometimes shopping for houses during inclement weather, to be sure there would be no problem. It rained heavily in Tampa too, and communications became spotty. Cam couldn't reach her father by phone, to check on him. Thus it was via a family friend that we were reached: did we know that Ernest was in the hospital? He had not been feeling well, and his doctor apparently hadn't taken his condition seriously, so he had driven himself to the hospital and checked in. He was ill, all right. We conjecture that it was an infection from dialysis, that spread to his heart, clogging it. Now that heart was throwing off clots, and they were reaching other parts of his body and destroying him. His right arm was paralyzed, and he had a stroke. We visited him, and he knew us, but was unable to move. His main concern was that some due bills be paid. Cam took the information, and then we left, saying good-bye. "Good-bye," he said faintly. Then, with a second effort, louder: "Good-bye." From there it was downhill. They scheduled heart surgery. The doctor asked Cam whether heroic measures should be taken to preserve his life, and she said no; he would not want to survive dependent, as he would be without the use of his arm. And so he wound down, and faded out before it came to the heart surgery late in 1988. I don't like second-guessing those on the scene, but it seemed to me that if his doctor had listened when he complained about not feeling well, they might have caught his developing condition in time and been able to treat the sepsis. Doctors don't listen well—and they should. Of course we all have to go sometime, but it shouldn't be because of neglect.

The memorial service was at the church on Mirror Lake, in St. Petersburg, where Ernest Marble had been the minister for fourteen years. He had married us there in 1956, and his three children had grown up in that vicinity. Now they were all there, with their families. The service was for both Ernest and Elizabeth, nicely done by the current Unitarian Universalist minister. The families attended, and then we had a big dinner together, with the first cousins that were the grandchildren getting reacquainted. There was no difficulty about the disposition of the family properties; the estate was in good order, with Cam the administrator, and incidental items were shared amicably. That's the way it should be, and I think it was a fitting legacy: all three of the children of Ernest and Elizabeth Marble were in enduring marriages with unified families. Something had been done right.

My own family, in contrast, was much less unified. My parents were divorced in 1952 after nineteen years whose last decade had been essentially null, and my father remarried. My stepmother, Genevieve, was a truly nice person who died in 1987. My mother, Norma Jacob, lived in a Quaker retirement community in Pennsylvania (I like to refer to it as Pencil Vania when writing my monthly family letters); my father Alfred lived in a different retirement development in another city. Of the two, Norma seemed to be doing better. She visited us at our new house in the tree farm twice, in 1988 and 1990. I was especially pleased by the second visit, because I knew she never would have returned if she hadn't liked the first one. This was because she didn't like the wilderness. But though we were isolated, with no close neighbors, our long drive was paved, and we had all the amenities of the modern world. We rented *Crocodile Dundee* on video and watched it with her. I liked the scene where a mugger is threatening the party with a knife, and Crocodile seems bemused. "That's not a knife. *This* is a knife." And he draws his huge blade, and drives off the mugger. Norma didn't seem to appreciate that scene, though, and I think it was because the mugger was black: she was so politically correct that she couldn't appreciate any black person being in the wrong. I don't care what the color is, a mugger is a mugger, and I'm glad to see one foiled. That movie was careful to be racially balanced, so the limo driver Crocodile encountered, another black man, won his respect. He wasn't racist, the movie wasn't racist, and it wasn't racist to enjoy the good scenes, regardless of the colors of their participants. So I differed with my mother on that, though nothing was said.

In fact I differed with her on a lot. When I declared my emotional independence from the tangled situation of my parentage, I maintained it adamantly. But I did want to help my mother where I could, when my means grew to be well beyond hers. She would not accept much, so I had to be cautious. When her TV broke down, we arranged with my sister and her family to get Norma a nice new one: we sent the money, and they took her to the store and bought it, complete with a remote control that made it easier for her to use. When she visited her native England, I arranged for my literary agent there, Pamela Buckmaster, to give Norma some more money for shopping, from my British funds. When she revised the book written by another Quaker, digesting it down to publishable length, and needed to find a way to finance its publication, I sent the thousand dollars, which was in due course repaid from proceeds. Thus I facilitated her effort without any actual monetary cost to me, so it wasn't a gift. So I did what I could, though it wasn't as much as I wished. She had arranged things so as not to be a burden on her children, and that was it. Had she ever needed money to remain in the retirement center, I was ready to provide it, but it never came to that.

In 1991 she was checked, and the blood vessels around her heart were found to be 80 percent clogged. So they scheduled quadruple bypass surgery, the cost entirely covered by insurance. A number of her friends had had it, so she felt it was safe. She got through the surgery successfully, but it seems that her digestive system closed down, not operating at all, and she did not feel well. Still, as the days passed, I felt that the crisis was over. We sent her a little floating balloon display in lieu of flowers, as the hospital did not encourage the latter. I received a card of acknowledgment, amidst a pile of something like seventeen fan letters, so hardly paid attention. Then that evening came a call from my sister

Teresa: Norma didn't make it. Teresa was with her when she suddenly said, "Oh, I'm going!" and died, in May 1991.

My emotions were severely mixed. Norma had always been too sure of herself, and this was true right up until the end. When researching for my novel *Volk* I had encountered evidence that America, as well as Nazi Germany, had kept death camps. Only these were for disarmed German soldiers. The Allies systematically killed more than a million of them, in order to cripple any likely military future for Germany. The reference was *Other Losses* by James Bacque. I read it carefully, then had my researcher Alan read it. What I wanted to know was whether this was true. Alan went over it, checked out the math, and concluded that yes, it seemed to be true. So I used it in my novel. And mentioned it in my monthly family letter. Norma said it couldn't possibly be true, but just to be sure, she checked with a Quaker friend who had been in Germany during the war. He agreed that it couldn't be true. Therefore Norma, with no further research, informed me that I was credulous, like my father. She didn't need to read the book; she already knew. Then the *New York Times Book Review* ran a "killer" review of the book, which said it was nonsense. Alan went over the review, and concluded that the book was right and the review was wrong. Norma sent me a copy of that review, to prove her point. Then came the responses to that review—from people who had actually been there, including a prisoner whose camp had been transferred to the British, who had shut it down and freed the prisoners, and a guard who had reported being required to machine-gun down prisoners who had made a break to get to the nearby river so they could drink. Supplies had been sent for the prisoners—and rejected by the authorities. There was no question that the atrocity had been committed, and not by any oversight. Naturally I commented on that in my family letter, but Norma died before receiving her copy. This was of course not the only factor, but I suspect that she would rather have died than be proven so drastically wrong—and had done so. It was like a religious person's loss of faith, when God despite all pleas allows ill to happen to the favored. I regret it, if I had that part in it, yet she *was* wrong, both in the fact and in her attitude, and she should have known from long experience not to challenge me on such a matter. Certainty in lieu of judgment is dangerous folly. Yet I took no joy at all in my mother's death. Right after that I read in a health newsletter that heart bypass surgery is not the best option; that there are drugs to treat the condition in a much safer and less costly manner. So I deem her death at that time unnecessary. Had I known in time of the drug option, I would have urged it on her. But I believe that she would have dismissed me as credulous and had the surgery anyway. So she died of her faith in contemporary medicine. It was a shame.

I attended the memorial service with Penny and Cheryl. We met their cousin Patrick at the Philadelphia airport, and we rented a car and drove in. It was a family gathering, of a sort. Teresa attended, of course, with her daughters Erin and Caroline, and Alfred did too. There were many others; Norma seemed to have cut quite a swath in the retirement community, always standing up actively for what she believed in, and her agenda, by my definition, was a good one. So there were many there to thank her for her support, this last time. But there was also a hint that I was not the only one to have run afoul of her rigidity, though of course no one would speak it aloud on such an occasion. I spoke, and likened her travel to the next realm to a ride on a train bound for Eternity. "And though I am so sad to see her go," I concluded, "I hope she rides that train forever." The complete comment is at the end of the Author's Note in the novel I was then writing, *The Color of Her Panties*. I don't believe in any Afterlife, but it is a pleasant fiction.

It is said that imperfect relationships can be more difficult to let go than good ones. That may be so, for mine with my mother was far from ideal. She had hurt me by her misguided certainties when I was young, and I hurt her by my refutations when I was adult. It was an awful shock to me when she died, and it colored my awareness for years. I remembered the little things she had done for us, including the gift of a nice little rug I still have to cushion my feet as I type this. When she gave us a poster of one of Vincent van Gogh's paintings, we put it up on a wall, and I got interested in the artist, and there were references to him in more than one of my later novels. I now have a big volume containing all van Gogh's art. But I don't think my mother knew of all this. I read a portion of a poem she had chosen for her memorial, "The Soldier," by Rupert Brooke; when I got home I looked it up, memorized the whole poem, and repeated it to myself every day for six months as I rode out each morning to fetch in the newspapers, and every Sunday thereafter for four years before I made myself stop. Yet I know from her journal, which I read after her death, and have quoted from in this volume, that this was only an incidental thing. She had not expected to die, and she didn't think much of the sentiment in the poem; it was just something she was required to provide, just in case. Yet this was what became her memorial, so it became precious to me. My mother may have been misguided in some respects, and wrongheaded in some, but she had virtues too, and she has always been there. Her abrupt absence left a painful hole in my awareness. The woman who had brought me into this world was gone.

How much worse, then, it was for my sister Teresa. She was much closer to Norma than I was, in geography and spirit. I believe that Norma was her main support in her own travails, which included a bad marriage, difficult relations with her children, and chronic financial stress. I was not close to my sister; we had been usually at odds as children and not all that compatible as adults, and I was satisfied to live a thousand miles away from her as well as from my parents. But she is my closest kin, and I was the one who shared her loss of a mother. I felt that when our mother died, the effective responsibility for the support of the family devolved on me. This was not a moralistic thing, but mainly one of stability and means. Teresa handled Norma's estate, for which I am grateful, and I pondered ways to do my part. In the end it was my daughter Penny who made the key suggestion: guarantee that Teresa could retire to the community she most wanted to join. That was Kendal at Longwood, where Norma had found happiness. I had resolved long since to see that Norma never had to leave it, should any financial problem come up. It had been like paradise for her, and while I think it would be less than that for Teresa, it is nevertheless the place for her to be. If she is capable of happiness, that is where she is most likely to find it. So I arranged for a small trust, to which I contributed annually, of an amount sufficient to ensure that Teresa would qualify financially to go there. I think Norma would approve.

As I write this, my father Alfred survives, but is winding down at age ninety-plus. He was in good shape while Genevieve lived, but was cast adrift when she died. At that point I began calling him every month on the sixteenth, at 6 P.M., just to talk. The calls gradually expanded to two hours, where they are cut off by supper here. My daughter Penny also calls him every week. We have some formidable differences, mainly in that area of credulity, but can converse compatibly on a wide range of subjects. He believes in many things that I do not, from the afterlife to socialism, and I can appreciate how my parents differed so drastically on things, each being, by my definition, at an erroneous fringe. But at least my father's mind is open, as my mother's was not in certain areas.

When it became apparent that Alfred was declining physically, I stepped in, again prompted by Penny. She had a friend who knew of a service for elders; I had the money. So we arranged for ElderCare in Pennsylvania to assist Alfred in what ways were feasible. He has several major needs, not all of which he acknowledges, and ElderCare helps provide them. He needs compatible company, and that is not easy to find for a person whose set of beliefs differs substantially from the norm. He needs help making arrangements, for he is not well adapted to the modern world. For example, he has difficulty using the telephone. He can receive calls, but must struggle to make them. I understand this, for I had the same problem. I was jinxed by the phone. Once in high school my roommate decided to show me how ridiculous my fear of phones was. So the two of us jammed into a phone booth and he tried to get the operator, as in those days there was no direct dial. After twenty minutes he gave up in disgust. I had proved my point. But as I became successful in writing, I had to learn to handle the phone, because the mail was too slow and unreliable. So I worked at it. I knew I had graduated when I made a call on my own to a party I didn't know in South Africa. I still don't really *like* the phone, but I can handle it. Here and there among my readers are those who have a similar aversion. So Alfred doesn't make phone calls, but the lady from ElderCare does so on his behalf, and gets his other business in order, such as the annual tax forms. Another area is driving: we were concerned about decreasing ability here, but he saw no problem. Finally, ElderCare arranged to get him tested, and he lost his driving license. He couldn't understand why; the fact that he was unable to read traffic signs until parked directly in front of them seemed irrelevant. But this relieved us of the fear that we would one day get a report of a terrible accident. Now an ElderCare lady drives him wherever he needs to go. When he fell, fracturing his hip, and couldn't get up, it was ElderCare that found him and persuaded him to go to the hospital and have surgery. The cost of this supplementary service would be formidable for an ordinary family, but money is now one of my assets. So in this way I provide increasing support for my father, so that I don't suddenly discover he is gone, as was the case with my mother.

I don't like death, but it is a necessary part of life. Every creature in the animal kingdom seems to be blessed with the instinct of survival, and it is strong enough to override almost all else. But if every creature survived indefinitely, the world would soon stifle. Consider what happens when some cells of the body decide not to self-destruct when their allotted time ends: it is called cancer. It may be that the human species represents a kind of cancer of the world, that will destroy everything because it is running amok. That is a growing concern of mine, explored in my GEODYSSEY series. Death is necessary, as well as inevitable. So I must contemplate the eventual death of my wife, and of myself. Also, of the species, for I fear that as a species we are headed for a lethal crash as we use up the limited resources of the world. But about all I can do is to help cry warning, which I expect to be ignored, and prepare for the assorted terminations I see coming. I fear that I am not writing for posterity, because there won't be much posterity. So, to a degree, I must simply live for the present, doing what good I can along the way and hoping for the best.

Meanwhile the following generation is getting established. My daughter Penny had several serious relationships before she married in 1995; later they bought country property in Oregon and moved there. My daughter Cheryl works for the local newspaper. The nation, like the world, is becoming more difficult for newcomers; there is less virgin territory to move into, and more competition for it. So I don't know how my daughters will fare, and fear they will live to see the dreadful reckoning when the support systems of our species break down. I fear they will not live beyond it. But we will support them in their courses, hoping that things turn out more positively than I foresee.

But let me comment on a happier memory relating to our daughters. The generation gap is ever-present, in every family, with the parents deploring the wild new directions of the children, and the children dismissing the parents as hopelessly dated. I, like any other parent, wanted to demonstrate at least once just how accurate my generation's judgment could be. Penny and Cheryl wanted to see the Disney movie, *The Rescuers*, a fun mouse story. Okay: we agreed to attend "their" movie as a family, provided they attended "our" movie too. The daughters had never heard of ours, but were willing to see the challenge through. They would prove to us how great their movie was, and how dull ours was. Well, ours was *Star Wars*, the one that was to usher in an era. I had heard about it on the excellent radio program *All Things Considered*, and I trusted these folk's judgment. And I believe that even the daughters admit that we won that one.

In the interim, I try to take care of my health and that of my tiny bit of the world. When I suffered chronic fatigue, and the doctors couldn't diagnose it, I was considered neurasthenic and ridered for all mental diseases, as mentioned in Chapter 3. After ten years a test suggested that I was not mentally diseased but mildly diabetic, so for twenty years I was a Type II diabetic, with insurance trouble because the underwriters claimed not to know the difference between the moderate Type II and the deadly Type I. Then another test indicated that I was not diabetic after all. I did not pursue it further, as I didn't want to be considered crazy again. So my fatigue continues, undiagnosed. So does my mild depression; as I like to put it, if what others have is a depression, what I have is a recession. It gives me appreciation for what others suffer, without being much hampered by it myself. I also had spot surgery in 1992: three in one, to remove an ugly wart on the right side of my face, to take a pie-shaped slice from my right ear to eliminate a spot of basal cell carcinoma, and to fix the deviated septum in my nose that had obstructed my breathing for thirty years, as covered in Chapter 15. Therefore I wore a hat outside, to keep the sun off my ears, and I breathed better. I also had a filled root canal in a tooth go bad, and had to have expensive dental surgery to rebuild that tooth. After that I had a siege of shingles, perhaps triggered by the dental surgery, because the same right tri-facial nerve was affected. I learned that this is a complication of chicken pox, in my case fifty years later. The herpes zoster virus remains in the nerves, and strikes when the body's immune system has finally forgotten it. Fortunately it was a light case, not subjecting me to the unbearable pain for which the condition is notorious; my right jaw was merely extremely sensitive to cold, so that I could not even drink room-temperature water without going into orbit. So I heated water to drink, and even to brush my teeth. There were also sores along the nerve line, but the doctor assured me that it could have been much worse. In the course of a month it passed, except for a lingering slight cold sensitivity. Apart from such things, I'm healthy enough for my age.

I started a regular exercise program in 1975 when I was taking judo classes, and continue it. Sandspurs, biting flies, thorns, sugar sand, brush, and weather interfered, so I finally had to quit my three-mile runs and exercise inside, going to a stationary bicycle and "manual" treadmill, catching up on reading while exercising. In 1996 I saw a closeout sale on a compound bow, so bought it, and it turned out to be a brute whose bowstring I couldn't even draw. But I kept working at it, and made progress firing right-handed at 150 feet and left-handed at 100 feet with fair accuracy. Later I gave up the exercycle and treadmill—they kept breaking down, and didn't offer enough exercise—and returned to jogging outside, this time along the drive to fetch in the morning newspapers. It's a 1.5-mile round-trip, only half my former distance, and slower, but I didn't care to do at sixty-two what I had at fifty-two. I also got a recumbent bicycle, an expensive novelty, but a superior design—I'm a sucker for those, as my wave-shaped Dvorak computer keyboard shows—and learned to ride while almost lying on my back. Weird but good. And I got hand weights, to help exercise my arms, along with the rowing machine. Every day, I'm doing something vigorously physical, to keep in shape, and it seems to be paying off: at the age where other writers are fading and dying, my foot remains far from kicking the bucket.

Meanwhile my wife had a scare: when we sought to take out a major life insurance policy, in the course of organizing our estate, the comprehensive physical examination indicated that my wife could have a heart problem. So she had a cardiac catheterization, wherein they ran a tube through her veins and into her heart, and injected dye, so that they could visually trace the blood flow. It turned out that there was no blockage; it was just that her heart squeezes rather than pumps, so that performance is less. She's a heavy smoker, which is a risk factor, but has a healthy diet, so seems to have escaped the lethal consequences. Doctors seem not to want to know just what something like Vitamin C can do to abate the effects of smoking, but we know. I have known for forty years, through my experience with her, that smoking is addictive; she can't just quit. If I thought she could, I'd encourage her to stop; as it is, I let it be. We have a good marriage; we don't hassle each other pointlessly.

Thus as I face the future, I expect to continue with Xanth, which may have taught more children to read than some teachers have, and which has brought comfort to many who could not find it elsewhere. Critics may condemn funny fantasy on principle; critics can be idiots without principles. And I will continue with projects like GEODYSSEY, exploring the nature and history of my species. And I hope to watch my daughters and readers advance in life, again hoping for the best.

Thus my memories are mixed. I have had a fine career as a writer, but I may have alienated more publishers than any other fantastic genre best-seller. I can count the editors who won't speak to me. There was Betty Ballantine, who treated me unfairly, as detailed in *BiOgre*; when I attended the World Fantasy Convention as Guest of Honor I understand that she was there, but I never saw her. For sure, she didn't want to meet me! Later when Lester del Rey wanted to do destructive cutting of my novels, and I balked, he didn't speak to me for a year or so, until I left Del Rey Books. When Morrow promised me a best-seller in *Tatham Mound*, then torpedoed it instead, I knew there was mischief afoot when I couldn't get the editor on the phone. Editors hide when they know they are doing wrong. When I left Morrow/Avon because of that and took Xanth to TOR, Susan Allison, president of Berkeley/Ace, called me: why hadn't I taken Xanth to them? I told her that they had already taken one best-seller series, Adept, off the best-seller list, so I wouldn't let them do it with Xanth. That ended things with her; later when I phoned to tell her about the movie option on *Killobyte*, a novel they published that could profit handsomely, she was out of the office, and has been out ever since, to any communication of mine. In prior times, when my wife and I were in New York and attended a Putnam/Berkley party, Susan Allison took the whole evening to accompany us, though we did not want such attention; later when my daughter introduced herself at the World Science Fiction Convention in Glasgow, Susan Allison broke off abruptly and left the building. Maybe she thought that I was in the vicinity. And when we made a package deal, five collaborations with Xanth, because no publisher would take one without the other, TOR was free to turn down the deal if it couldn't stomach the notion of publishing good collaborative novels. Instead they accepted it, then tried to renege on the collaborations, as described in Chapter 8, and editor Beth Meacham has not spoken to me since, and seems to be similarly freezing my agent. I think she had wanted dessert without the vegetables. So I have been frozen out by a number of publishers or editors, but I stand by my position in every case. I never wanted either the extra attention at the height, or the snub at the depth; I reject both extremes as pointless affectation. All I wanted was for the publishers to do their job competently, and to treat writers with businesslike integrity. As it was, their efforts remind me of a scene from the *M*A*S*H* TV series, wherein instead of doing emergency surgery, the doctor kept showing fancy card tricks to a mortally sick patient, and couldn't understand why the patient didn't get better. Why focus on conventions and parties, instead of getting the books made so their pages won't fall out, and into the stores where the readers can find them? When you think of a publisher, think of a used-car dealer, with the editor as the salesman. Much glitter and flash, but that breed has peculiar definitions of business practice and integrity, and the writer must watch his back. Woe betide the writer who stands up for his rights. When I did so in the early days, I got blacklisted; when I did so in the later days, going to law when I had to, I got the freeze treatment. Most writers don't have the clout to enforce agreements, so most writers die poor. I started poor and finished rich, but my attitude hasn't changed. I expect publishers to honor their given word—at the point of a lawsuit, if that's the only way to make them understand. Too often it is. All their card tricks are as nothing, without competence and integrity.

What of my intellectual horizons? I'm a writer, of course; when I was fifty, I had done fifty novels, and when I was sixty I had published one hundred books, with more in the pipeline. But that's merely the commercial reflection of my career. What of the personal values behind the prolific writer? This volume surely suggests them, but a more compact summary may be in order. When I went to a convention in Virginia to meet Jenny, Ron Lindahn asked me to write a few words and sign his autograph book. I pondered and put down three words that summarize much of my attitude: Honor, Compassion, Realism. Now I'll explore what I mean by this triad.

Honor: I believe in honesty, but it is not necessarily easy to apply, as when folk really don't want the truth. If a woman asks how she looks, she doesn't want to be told she is fat as a pig; she means are her clothing and hairstyle all right, and is she doing well with what she has. So what is true is not always relevant. Honor, as I see it, is integrity with a moral dimension. It is a whole system of righteousness in life, based on understanding and consistency. Honor does not seek to use the truth to hurt others, but to deal fairly with the larger situation. Honor can keep a secret. Thus when I know a young reader of mine is suicidal, I don't write to her parents about it, because I regard it as a privileged communication. I try to do what I think is right, and I try my best to understand what is right. That doesn't mean that I am always right; I do make mistakes. But I constantly try to eliminate the errors in my own thinking, and to home in on the fairest standards. Others have said that I seem very sure of myself, as if that is a disparagement. Actually my certainty is constantly being challenged by my own thinking and observation, and I am adjusting my views in much the way I adjust my course when driving a car, to stay on the proper course. I try to be fair and balanced in my outlook. When I took judo classes I learned that you can't throw a person who is physically balanced. It's also hard to throw a person who is mentally balanced. So when others challenge me, I normally respond, refuting them. They assume that I am in error, and I seldom am, because all my life I have striven to eliminate error. But I don't simply assume that I am right; those who substitute certainty for judgment are very likely wrong. I do my best to understand the opposing position, and sometimes it does prevail. When I interacted with Neil Shulman, an ardent gun advocate, author of *Stopping Power*, and onetime Internet distributor of *Volk*, I found some of his arguments persuasive, and I am in the process of shifting my position on guns, from abolition to free access. Because he satisfied me that the Constitution does guarantee the right to keep and bear arms, and that an armed person is less likely to be a victim than an unarmed one. I am disgusted with those who habitually coddle error, like the racists and bigots, lying to cover what they have to know is falsity. When one of them comes at me, I may let him have it, and I prefer to do it in a public forum, so that others can see where the truth lies. I don't pretend to be sweet or peaceful about it; it is an expressive sword I wield. It isn't a crusade to eliminate dishonor; that's impossible, and I normally live and let live. But when dishonor comes at me, I destroy it if I can. Thus I can say almost categorically that when a story circulates about my supposed hypocrisy or cheating or error, it is a lie promulgated by those who know they can't face me directly and spread by those who ought to know better. In some cases such charges come from folk who seem to resent my efforts to maintain a standard of honor that they lack the gumption to emulate, so they try to pretend that mine is false. I have encountered few who seem to know or care about the nature of honor, but it is an underlying tenet of my fiction and I have heard from young readers who do pick up on it. More power to them. Honor is truly a way of life.

Compassion: human beings are not machines, and should not try to be. I remember a story by another writer—I wish I could remember the title and author—telling of a man in a spaceship who had been injured and was dying. There was a doctor aboard who could have helped the man, but did not. Why? Because the man had not asked for help. But because of his injury, the man was unable to ask for help—and the doctor knew this. So why didn't the doctor act? Because the doctor was a machine that acted only within its set parameters, and these required that help not be given unless specifically requested. A human doctor would have cut through this folly and saved the victim. But the machine would not. Thus the plaque on that ship: A MACHINE DOES NOT CARE. And there it is. The machine may have an inhuman standard of honor, being incapable of violating its directives. But it doesn't have compassion. So this is one of the things that separates living creatures from nonliving ones: living ones care. They are sympathetic, and wish to alleviate suffering. It is true that many animals are indifferent to the fate of others, apart from their immediate relatives or associates, but they do have the capacity to care. It is also true that many people are indifferent or even hostile to the welfare of others. But the ideal person, as I see it, does have compassion. It is one of the liberal virtues, in contrast to the me-first, the-hell-with-you conservative credo. This may be limited by practical concerns, but most folk will try to help neighbors in distress, or others who come to their attention. Most people will not be cruel to animals simply because they have the power to hurt. Thus I answer my mail responsively, though it costs me enormously in lost working time and, indeed, in lost relaxation time, because I care about the feelings of my readers. I hold in a certain contempt those writers who don't care about their readers. Without compassion, how is a person better than a machine?

Realism: I mentioned practical limitations. I wish the whole world could be happy and at peace, with every person achieving his desired destiny. But I know that not only is the world not that way, there is nothing I can do to make it so. I can't even bring about perfect harmony within my own immediate family. I also would like to meet every person worth meeting, but know that there are many more worthwhile people than I could ever meet, even if I spent my whole life going around doing it. I would like to read every good book, but know that there are many more books available that would genuinely please me and profit me than I can ever catch up on. So I school myself in realism: it is not possible to have it all. And this is a necessary condition of life. A certain tolerance is required, for the things a person can't do much about, though he may not like them. How can one act with perfect honor, when faced with choices that are imperfect? How can one help every person or creature or tree that needs help, when that person's resources are woefully inadequate to the challenge? I am constantly deluged with appeals for money or time, and every cause is worthy, and I have lost track of how much I have contributed where, but if I try to oblige them all, I will be broke and worn-out, and still will have made no discernible difference on the global scale. So lines have to be drawn, boundaries made, realizing that only a limited amount can be accomplished. This is why I don't try to change the whole world: realism gets in the way. So I try to target certain aspects and causes, to understand them, and focus most of my attention and effort on those. Otherwise my money and time and effort may be foolishly expended, or even have a negative impact. My wife and I carefully consider each case, and we have given in six figures to three different educational institutions, and in five figures to other worthy causes, and in lesser figures to individuals, trying to use our money wisely as well as generously. We spend more on others than on ourselves. But the need on every front overwhelms our resources. We have heard of do-gooders who don't do their homework, so wind up hurting the cause they seek to help. It is best to consider before acting, and to study any prospects, to ascertain how best to approach them. Sometimes a seemingly token effort can have enormous impact. Sometimes enormous effort will be almost unproductive. A person needs to be rational, to view things with a clear eye, and to understand his own purposes and abilities. Without realism, honor and compassion may be wasted.

Honor, Compassion, Realism: these are by no means the only concepts in my philosophy, and I could ponder similarly on Intelligence, Love, and Decency, or on other triads, but these do serve as a convenient framework on which to build. I'm still building. Having by whatever fortune achieved considerable success, I am trying to be worthy of it. It is my hope to leave the world marginally better than I found it, through my efforts: personal, monetary, and literary.

I'll finish on a related matter. I encountered a simple question, whose answer turned out to be un-simple. "What would it take to make you happy?" I realized quickly that top-of-the-head answers like winning the lottery and becoming a millionaire did not relate; I already have that kind of money. Neither does the pat twofold wish: to be happy, and not to know that this was the result of a wish. If I wanted simply to shut out the world and cater to my own appetites, I could do so. To a degree I am already doing so, as I live in a forest and spend my time doing what I love, writing novels. But I am minded of a story told me by my one-time roommate Ronald Bodkin in high school: a wise man was deploring the hunger and misfortune of the world. A friend said "But you have a good life here; why not ignore the rest and enjoy yourself?" And the wise man replied, "It's not the kind of happiness I care for." Indeed it is not; I could not be happy when others are not. I finally broke my answer down into three parts, with three sections in each part, to keep it manageable. The parts are **Personal, Interpersonal**, and **Global**. The sections of **Personal** are: 1) *Health*, wherein I would be free of my fatigue, depression, bad knees, and any other malady. 2) *Success,* wherein I would be a bestseller again, writing truly meaningful books, with an oxymoronically perfect publisher, and competent and honest reviews. 3) *Knowledge,* wherein I could learn and appreciate all the secrets of the universe. The sections of **Interpersonal** are: 1) *Health,* wherein my wife would have the body she had at age nineteen and lose her cigarette addiction, and all my correspondents and acquaintances would be similarly well off, including especially Jenny, who was paralyzed by a drunk driver but who would now rise, take up her bed, and walk. 2) *Success,* wherein all of them achieve their respective delights of whatever nature. 3) *Attitude,* wherein all of them would know that it was my wish that brought them this good fortune. The sections of **Global:** are: 1) *Society,* wherein the social order and economics of all human cultures would be equitable, with decent folk rewarded and indecent folk put away, and there would be no starvation, torture, bad reviews, or otherwise unkind treatment of anyone. 2) *Knowledge,* wherein the arts and sciences are universally valued and encouraged, so that research continues to make breakthroughs to amaze people, including especially me, and the Perfect Computer Program would be distributed free. 3) *Environment,* wherein the human population of the world is reduced painlessly (maybe by emigration to other planets) to perhaps a tenth of its present level, disease is eliminated, and the habitats and population of all wild species are restored and extended so that all flourish, and the air, earth, and waters of the world are made clean and whole. I realize that all this is a tall order, unlikely to be fulfilled, and that I am therefore doomed not to be happy. It is nevertheless the kind of unhappiness I care for.

The
HIDDEN
CHRIST

Beneath the Surface of the
Old Testament

❧

JAMES L. FERRELL

DESERET
BOOK

SALT LAKE CITY, UTAH

Library of Congress Cataloging-in-Publication Data

Ferrell, James L.
  The hidden Christ : beneath the surface of the Old Testament / James
L. Ferrell.
      p.   cm.
  Includes bibliographical references and index.
  ISBN 978-1-59038-477-0 (hardbound : alk. paper)
  1. Jesus Christ.   2. Bible. O.T.—Criticism, interpretation, etc.   3. Church of Jesus Christ of Latter-day Saints—Doctrines.   4. Mormon Church—Doctrines.   I. Title.
  BX8643.J4F47 2009
  232—dc22   2009012142

Printed in the United States of America
Edwards Brothers Incorporated, Ann Arbor, MI

10   9   8   7   6   5   4   3   2   1

CONTENTS

PART FOUR
CHRIST AND THE WRITINGS

APPENDICES

PREFACE

If you are like me, you are afraid of the Old Testament. At least, that is what I used to be. Today I can honestly say that there is no work I would rather study—no source that rewards inquiry so richly as that large, visually intimidating collection of prophetic stories, history, and writings. If, as latter-day prophets have stated, the Book of Mormon is the keystone standard work of our religion, and the Doctrine and Covenants the capstone, the Old Testament is the foundation stone. All of the other standard works, the New Testament included, are built upon the spiritual history and tradition recorded in the Old Testament. This fact alone merits its study.

But it is always a chore to study something simply because it is merited or scheduled or obligated or assigned. I admit that when I first cracked open the cover of my lightly read Old Testament intent on reading and studying it, I was opening it out of obligation. I had been asked to teach a course on the Old Testament. That meant it was high time to learn what it said and study what it meant!

What I discovered was a veritable wonderland of truth, insight, and mystery. I say "mystery" because many stories in the book don't seem to add up. But when I learned to assume that everything in the book made sense, and then set about to see how *this* odd story or *that* apparently out-of-place passage made sense, I discovered an almost hidden world of insight and meaning.

As this understanding opened to me, I began to see how a particular pattern, woven in and through the Old Testament narrative, gave new and deeper meaning to nearly everything I was reading. I believe the Apostle Paul was referring to this deep pattern when he wrote, "for until this day remaineth the same vail untaken away in the reading of the old testament; which vail is done away in Christ" (2 Corinthians 3:14). Paul seems to be telling us that the key to reading and understanding the Old Testament is discovering the extent to which Christ is hidden within it. When I began to see how fully that is the case—how, for example, the lives of so many of the characters in the Old Testament prefigure *his* life—the lessons in the book began to multiply and penetrate both my mind and my heart. With his light blazing through and illuminating its pages, a myriad of clarifying and testimony-building insights came into view concerning the Lord, ourselves, the plan of happiness, and the Restoration of the gospel in the latter days.

I don't mean to say that I now have anything close to a complete understanding of the Old Testament. Far from it. More than any book I have encountered, each page reminds me how little I yet understand. But with this gentle chastisement, the Old Testament invites the reader into further and deeper conversations.

In my own case, perhaps the love I have discovered for the Old Testament is in an odd way a reflection of the neglect with which I treated it for most of my years. That is, perhaps the insights it offers are exhilarating to me because I hadn't before paid the price to see them, and because I hadn't known the stories enough to assume that I already knew what they meant. If so, I suspect I am not alone in this neglect, and in the opportunity it creates. Surprising rewards lie ready to be discovered by anyone who picks up that frequently avoided book and begins to ask it questions. Looking back, I don't think I began to really understand the gospel until I began to understand its foundational work of scripture.

Having said that, this book, *The Hidden Christ,* does not pretend to be an exhaustive study of the Old Testament. It is rather an account of my own personal journey in its pages and the related pages of the Pearl of Great Price during a period of my life when I was concentrating on them almost exclusively. The next time I venture into the Old Testament with the same kind of sustained focus, I would hope and expect to discover an entirely new slate of insights and fresh perspectives that will lift my soul all over again.

For any who have read my earlier books *The Peacegiver* and *The Holy*

Secret, you will recognize a few chapters in *The Hidden Christ* that seem to cover familiar ideas—in particular chapter 2 on agency, chapter 10 on the purpose of the law, chapter 14 on Abigail, chapter 15 on the houses of the kings and the house of the Lord, chapter 17 on Jonah, and Appendix B on the ordinances of the temple. You will also discover that the first few pages of the introduction echo almost verbatim words that the grandpa character in *The Peacegiver* spoke to his struggling grandson, Ricky. This is no accident, as this book, *The Hidden Christ,* actually came first—both in conception and in actual fact. I wrote the first draft of this book some five years before *The Peacegiver* and *The Holy Secret* were even ideas. Those books happened only because of a host of things that I learned while reading and pondering the Old Testament—ideas that grabbed hold of me and wouldn't let me go.

One final note on the relationship between this book and my earlier ones. Stylistically, they couldn't be more different, as this book, unlike the others, does not unfold as a story. At a deeper level, however, the books share a key similarity: They are each about discovering surprising truths in new, unexpected, and inspiring places, and in each of them, those truths center on Christ. While *The Peacegiver* and *The Holy Secret* are records of a conversation between Old-Testament-steeped elders and younger men, *The Hidden Christ* is the record of my own conversation with the Old Testament. In that sense, I suppose, it is no less a story.

As one who was once afraid, I hope you will join with me in asking questions of and conversing with the Old Testament—a book that I have come to know as a most gentle and generous friend. I have yet to be disappointed with any of its answers, and its insights have nearly always filled me with wonder, gratitude, and surprise.

May the questions and conversations we will engage together in this book be only the beginning. And may you too discover in the original Testament an old and cherished friend.

~~~~~~

THE STORY BENEATH THE SCRIPTURAL STORY

The Things Concerning Himself

"What if I don't like the Old Testament?"

That is the question I used to ask—until I discovered what I had been missing, and absolutely fell head over heels in love with the book. But I had to discover something before I fell in love: I had to discover that the most powerful messages—about the gospel and about life—lie hidden just below the surface of the stories in the book. When I learned to ask questions that penetrated the surface, the Old Testament opened up to reveal a wonderland of inspiring truth and practical insight.

What kinds of questions do that?

One question in particular . . .

Three days after the death of Christ, two believers walked the road to Emmaus, trying to make sense of it all. Jesus, whom they recognized as a great prophet[1] and trusted would be the Redeemer of Israel,[2] was dead, his body gone. They wanted to believe the testimony of the women who said they had "seen a vision of angels, which said that he was alive,"[3] but seemed to struggle at the thought. In their own words, they were "astonished" by the story.

These good men were confused and troubled. What they had "trusted" in did not turn out as they thought it would. "How could the Redeemer of Israel die before Israel was redeemed?" they wondered. Faith shaken, they struggled to find meaning in a tragedy that seemed to snatch all meaning from their lives.[4] Perhaps no road seemed longer than the road they were walking that day.

But, as with every long road we walk, these men did not walk it alone. The Redeemer they had hoped for not only lived, he was walking beside them. "And he said unto them, What manner of communications are these that ye have one to another, as ye walk, and are sad?"[5] After hearing their troubled response, the Lord made this key remark: "O fools, and slow of heart to believe all that the prophets have spoken: Ought not Christ to have suffered these things, and to enter into his glory? *And beginning at Moses and all the prophets, he expounded unto them in all the scriptures the things concerning himself.*"[6]

In other words, had the disciples understood the scriptures, they wouldn't have been surprised by the events that troubled them. All of the scriptures testified of the Savior's life, suffering, and death. These humble disciples just hadn't seen how before.

They were not alone. As the eleven apostles discussed these events, "Jesus himself stood in the midst of them, and saith unto them, Peace be unto you."[7] The apostles "were terrified and affrighted, and supposed that they had seen a spirit."[8] With tender caring, he said, "Why are ye troubled? And why do thoughts arise in your hearts?"[9]

Even those who knew the Savior best in mortality, who had learned at his feet, seemed to have misunderstood the message of redemption. Their understanding of the scriptures did not allow for the terrible death they had witnessed—a death that seemed so premature. Therefore they could not yet believe "for joy," even after handling the Lord's flesh.[10] The Lord's rhetorical "why?" in each of his soothing questions revealed that it didn't have to be that way. The understanding they lacked was available in the scriptures. Everything they witnessed that troubled them had been revealed for generations: "And he said unto them, These are the words which I spake unto you, while I was yet with you, that all things must be fulfilled, which were written in the law of Moses, and in the prophets, and in the psalms, concerning me. *Then he opened their understanding, that they might understand the scriptures,* And said unto them, Thus it is written, and thus it behoved Christ to suffer, and to rise from the dead the third day."[11]

The apostles did not understand the scriptures until they understood how fully the scriptures testified of the Savior. Only after the Lord "opened" the scriptures to them did faith and joy supplant doubt and apprehension.[12] This implies that many of the most important elements of Messianic testimony and prophecy lie below the surface of scriptural narrative—hidden in a way that remained obscure even to those who knew the Savior, and the scriptures, well. "For until this day remaineth the same vail untaken away in the reading of the old testament," Paul wrote to the Corinthians, "which vail is done away in Christ."[13]

So in what ways might critical meaning in the scriptures lie beneath the narrative of the stories? And how might such meaning be "opened" to us? Perhaps Nephi revealed a crucial clue when he wrote: "Behold, my soul delighteth in proving unto my people the truth of the coming of Christ; for, for this end hath the law of Moses been given; *and all things which have been given of God from the beginning of the world, unto man, are the typifying of him.*"[14]

In accordance with that statement, we find that the first thing revealed to Adam after the Fall—the law of sacrifice—was "a similitude of the sacrifice of the Only Begotten of the Father, which is full of grace and truth."[15] The Lord then revealed that this similitude was but the beginning, for "*all things have their likeness,* and all things are created and made to bear record of me, both things which are temporal, and things which are spiritual; things which are in the heavens above, and things which are on the earth, and things which are in the earth, and things which are under the earth, both above and beneath: *all things bear record of me.*"[16]

If everything given of God from the beginning bears record of Christ, then it follows that our understanding on any particular matter is incomplete until we see *how* it bears record of Christ. So of every scriptural element and story, we should ask, "How does this typify or bear record of the Savior?"

When we ask this divine question of every element and story in the Old Testament, the scriptures come alive with redemptive meaning. For example, the Noah story takes on new and deeper significance when we see how Noah's story is also the Savior's story:

- He preached tirelessly to people who largely rejected him[17]
- He was grieved by the sins of the people[18]

- He was just and perfect in his generation[19]
- He was mocked by the people[20]
- He did all that the Lord commanded him[21]
- People sought to kill him[22]
- He constructed the means of saving all mankind[23]
- Those who followed him were saved from death[24]
- Only those who were his family were saved[25]

When we see that the ark is a similitude of the Lord's Atonement, our views of the ark and the Atonement are forever enriched. We understand in a clear way the absolute necessity, for example, of being born again in Christ and taking his name upon us—for only *his* family will be saved. And we see in the flood not only the end of a sinful generation but the predicament of spiritual death that we *all* face unless we accept the invitation to board the ark—leaving behind whatever else might have seemed important or enticing, and submitting to every requirement of passage.

Could Noah's likeness to the Savior be coincidental? Perhaps. But suppose that similitudes accumulate, and likenesses pile on likenesses. Suppose we discover that nearly every major biblical figure and element points inextricably to Him. If "every whit point[s] to [the] great and last sacrifice . . . [of] the Son of God,"[26] then coincidence is out of the question. The world might ignore the evidence, or perhaps even regard it as a hoax perpetrated by biblical authors. But there can be no coincidence where testimony is so deep and pervasive.

In the chapters that follow, we will discover that this is precisely the case. Similitudes accumulate, and likenesses pile on likenesses.[27] Adam's story, for example, is not merely an account of his life but also in a deep sense a chronicle of the Savior's. Likewise, Seth, the perfect son who was the very likeness of his father, points to the perfect Son of God. Noah, Melchizedek, Isaac, Joseph, Moses, and so on, all point in the particulars of their lives to the life of Jesus of Nazareth. As discussed more fully in chapter 18 of this book, even the house of Israel itself is in similitude of him.

Believers in the Old Testament who dispute the divinity of Christ are confronted with the following question: Why would the lives of so many figures in the Old Testament parallel so closely the life of Jesus of

Nazareth? The parallel figures themselves testify of the reason: He was the one prepared as the means of deliverance from certain death, a truth illustrated by the story of the brazen serpent[28]; like Adam, he took upon himself death so that all might live[29]; like Noah, he constructed the means of saving all mankind; like Moses, he will deliver Israel from bondage[30]; and, as we learn though the amazing story of Abigail, all those who hearken to and follow him shall receive peace.[31] Because life itself depends on Christ and Christ alone, "all things," Nephi tells us, "are the typifying of him."[32]

There is no greater testament of Christ and his divinity and mission than the testament hidden below the surface of the Old Testament. Every story is *his* story, preserved at a level that would survive the loss of every plain and precious thing. Everything, from the beginning to the end, is revealed, sometimes directly, but more often indirectly through parallelism and similitude—the light revealing itself through the shadows it casts. No wonder the risen Lord had to "open"[33] the Old Testament to his disciples in order to teach them "the things concerning himself."[34] Only then did they "understand the scriptures."[35] And only then did they know joy.[36]

The chapters that follow explore these and many other types, shadows, and parallelisms that lie preserved and hidden beneath the surface of the scriptural narrative. In revealing the Lord, these literary devices also reveal much of his plan from beginning to end, including the restoration of the gospel in the latter days, and what he would have us be doing, moment to moment and day by day. Each chapter begins with a brief description of the ideas contained in the chapter. This makes it possible to approach the book in different ways. If you read it cover to cover you will acquire a sweeping view of the gospel, as the gospel's grand truths shine radiantly from beneath the pages and stories of the Old Testament. You can also read the book topically, concentrating on chapters with messages that interest you most. (You might scan the chapter descriptions at the beginning of each chapter to locate particular areas of interest.) However you choose to begin this book, I hope that you become captured by the Old Testament, and that your newly discovered passion for *that* book will lead you to explore it in its fulness.

These chapters do not add up to a comprehensive look at the Old Testament; no single work could achieve that feat. Rather, what follows marks the beginning of my own journey in and through and beneath its pages. This book is, I suppose, a travelogue of sorts—a record of faith-building discoveries along a road I had too long avoided. For me, this road, like the road to Emmaus two millennia ago, has been a walk characterized by divine surprise. It is a journey I long to continue.

I hope you will join and journey far beyond me.

PART ONE

CHRIST AND THE FOUNDATION OF THE WORLD

CHAPTER 1

⌒

THE PARALLEL CREATION

All Things Are Created and Made to Bear Record of Me

> *"What does the Creation story have to do with me, today?"*
>
> For most of my life, I thought the Creation story was just about the formation of an earth. I wasn't so sure that it mattered much today.
>
> But then I noticed something amazing: The Creation story was about me.
>
> I'm quite serious. The Creation is not merely the story of a heavenly body. It is also, metaphorically, the story of the creation of heavenly beings—me, you, all of us. So when we study the creative progression of the earth, we're actually also learning about our own mortal and eternal progression. When we see that, the Creation matters. Today.

The ancient scriptures' hidden testimony starts at the very beginning, with the account of the Creation. The Creation story is contained in three books of scripture: the book of Genesis in the Old Testament and the books of Moses and Abraham in the Pearl of Great Price. (These accounts of the Creation are presented in parallel form in Appendix C of this book.) While similar, these accounts of the Creation differ in interesting ways. These differences have been treated elsewhere,[1] so I will not repeat them here. I would like to focus rather on an aspect of the Creation story that has received little, if any notice: the context for the Creation story that we find in the book of Abraham—a context that suggests a deeper reading of the Creation story than we normally give to it.

You are probably familiar with Abraham's vision of the premortal spirits, and his account of the Council in Heaven where he saw many of the "noble and great ones."[2] This vision immediately precedes Abraham's account of the Creation, and we often talk about it in connection with the Creation. However, most of us are not as familiar with another of Abraham's visions—a vision that immediately precedes the vision of the premortal existence—except to note that it is a rather deep-sounding vision about the heavenly bodies, including some star named Kolob, which, we are told, is the nearest star unto God.[3]

We will discover that these two visions—first, the vision of the heavenly bodies, and second, the vision of the spirits—unfold in precisely parallel ways. I'd like to suggest that this parallelism implies a deeper reading and meaning than we normally give to the Creation story that follows the visions, a reading of the story that makes it more than simply an account of the earth's creation—a reading that actually makes it about *us*.

Let's begin by considering the content and structure of Abraham's vision of the heavenly bodies:

1. If two heavenly bodies exist, one whose reckoning of time is longer than another's, there shall be another heavenly body whose reckoning of time is longer still.[4]
2. There are many great ones—stars—that are near unto the throne of God.[5]
3. These are "the governing ones."[6]
4. One among them—the "greatest"—is "nearest unto the throne of God," or, as God says: "nearest unto me." This great one is called "Kolob" *because* it is nearest unto God, and its reckoning is after the reckoning of the Lord's time.[7]
5. Kolob is "set . . . to govern" the earth and other planets of the same order.[8]

Compare this to the vision of the spirits that follows it:

1. If two spirits exist, one being more intelligent than the other, there shall be another more intelligent than they.[9]

2. There were many noble and great ones who dwelt in the midst of God.[10]

3. These will be made "rulers."[11]

4. "And there stood one among them that was like unto God."[12]

5. This one was sent to make an earth to "prove them herewith," and he rules "in the heavens above, and in the earth beneath, in all wisdom and prudence, over all the intelligences [Abraham's] eyes have seen from the beginning."[13]

The parallelism is quite stunning. The stars and the spirits each increase in greatness as they approach God. There are many spirits who "dwell in the midst of God" just as there are many stars that "are near unto the throne of God." These spirits are called the "noble and great ones," and these stars are called "great ones." These noble and great spirits shall be made "rulers," similar to the great stars, which are "the governing ones." The greatest star, Kolob, derives its greatness from its proximity to God—from its being like unto God in its reckoning. Even so, there stood one among the spirits, the Savior, who was "like unto God." And finally, for both stars and spirits, this greatest one—the one nearest unto God—rules the heaven and earth.

Given the strikingly parallel structures of these visions, the vision of the stars gives us a way to visualize the relationship of the spirits with God—that is, *our* relationship with God. Picture a great star at the center, nearest to the throne of God. We might think of this as companion stars at the center of the heavenly expanse—at the center of a great galaxy, for example, or perhaps at the center of a universe. Like Jesus, this star nearest to God is the "first creation"[14] and the closest unto God. We are told in the explanation of Facsimile No. 2 in the book of Abraham that there is another—a third—standing next to Kolob that also holds the "key of power" or right to govern over the other heavenly bodies.[15] So we have three entities at the center that govern all things, perhaps in similitude of the Father, the Son, and the Holy Ghost.

Around these three at the center are arrayed many other great stars that, along with the greatest, Kolob, are set to "govern" all. "Governing" in this sense can be considered as the pull of their gravitational forces. The great stars around Kolob are great precisely because they are orbiting around the greatest of all—that is, because they are *obeying* the gravitational commands of Kolob. These great stars that are orbiting around Kolob then exert their own gravitational forces on the bodies that are still farther away, and these lesser bodies, by obeying the gravitational pull of these governing ones, themselves orbit around the greatest of all. In this way, through obedience to those in authority over them, the heavenly bodies take up their orbits around the heavenly body that is in similitude of the Son of God. Any bit of matter that decides it can do better on its own falls out of this divine orbit and is left to itself.

Applied to ourselves, this vision of things is illuminating, as it tells us that the first order of heaven is to obey and take up orbit around the stars—or leaders—that have been set up by the Lord to govern. The great stars are great only to the degree they have acted in obedience to the commands of the greatest. So it is with the spirits, as the noble and great ones—those who are made "rulers"—have been made leaders in the Lord's kingdom only because they have demonstrated their willingness to follow the Lord's will.

There was one among the spirit children of God who was not content to follow, of course, and he fell out of heaven, along with all those who chose to "orbit" around him.[16] "And the great dragon was cast out, that old serpent, called the Devil, and Satan, which deceiveth the whole world: he was cast out into the earth, and his angels were cast out with him."[17]

THE BIG PICTURE—APPROACHING GOD'S PRESENCE

As instructive as these implications are, so far they seem incomplete, as the end of man is not merely to orbit *around* the Lord but to be *with* him—to be with the Greatest, in his kingdom, in his presence, to obtain eternal life.[18] To this larger point, the parallel visions suggest an additional answer. These visions suggest that spirits relate to God in precisely the same way and according to the same laws as heavenly bodies relate to God. What immediately follows this parallelism is an account of the creation of a heavenly body being made fit for the presence of God. This implies that the story of a heavenly body being prepared for God is also the story of man being prepared for God. The first step in such preparation is to take up orbit around those who have been called to govern on the Lord's behalf. By obeying in this way, we signal our willingness to obey the Lord. Having taken up such an orbit, we are then prepared for the Lord to work on us just as he worked on the earth, preparing us, as the earth, for his presence.

"We will go down," the Lord said, "and we will make an earth whereon these [spirits] may dwell."[19] Why? In order "to see if they will do all things whatsoever the Lord their God shall command them."[20] "They who [do] shall have glory added upon their heads for ever and ever"[21]— "glory in the same kingdom"[22] with God himself.[23]

THE MIRACULOUS TRANSFORMATION OF THE CREATION

To begin with, let's consider the Creation in broad strokes to see how completely the earth was transformed by the creative process, and how that change mirrors the conversion that is offered to man.

In the beginning, before it had taken up orbit around a source of light, the earth was empty, desolate, and dark.[24] This seems a pretty good description of man's state so long as he insists on living for himself, on his own terms, refusing to hearken to the light of Christ. But the Spirit moved upon this darkness,[25] and the earth moved into proximity with the light.[26] Under the influence of the light, a "firmament" or atmosphere of life-sustaining air was formed above and around the earth.[27] In application to ourselves, we might consider this to be a representation of the nourishing influence of the Spirit in our lives. Under the influence of this light and within the protective canopy of this air or spirit, the earth began to come to life.[28] Isn't this exactly what happens to us when we are nourished by the Spirit and bathed by the light? We, too, come to life, as it were, and begin to bring forth good fruit.

Interestingly, it is at this point in the process, after the Lord has sown his seeds and nourished his creation by his own light and spirit, that he then guides that creation into the orbit of those that he has set up to govern—the "lights in the firmament of the heaven," the "greater light to rule the day, and the lesser light to rule the night."[29] This too, I think, is analogous to what happens with us, as the light of Christ and the whisperings of the Spirit both enliven us and direct us to the Lord's representatives on earth. These representatives, who have been called to govern in this sphere, then shed forth the Lord's light on the issues of our day, helping us to discern the light from the darkness. "And God set them in the firmament of the heaven to give light upon the earth, and to rule over the day and over the night, and to divide the light from the darkness."[30]

As we obey the counsel of these governing ones and follow in the light they reveal, our early spiritual growth flowers more fully under their influence, and we, like the earth, bring forth more abundantly. In fact, under the combined influence of the light of Christ, the Spirit, and the direction of those called to govern over the earth, the earth itself becomes a sustaining source of life, nourishing and strengthening everything in its presence—fish, fowls, insects, animals.[31] As the earth grows more abundant and more beautiful, finally, the life that appears on the earth begins to be in the image of God.[32]

Isn't this how we grow as well? As we stay in the orbit, as it were, of the light of Christ, the Spirit, and the Lord's representatives on earth, and as we observe and follow that light, do we not bring forth more abundantly? Do we not sustain and nourish all that is around us? Do we not ultimately receive the image of God in our countenances?

At this point in the Creation story, the parallelism between man and the heavenly body known as the earth becomes one: The earth in its abundant beauty, and man and woman joined together in innocence,[33] are able to stand in the presence of God,[34] this being the purpose of the process of creation, the fate of all linked through time and eternity.[35]

THE CREATOR WHO MAKES IT POSSIBLE

The parallelism implies that the being who was able to create an earth that could come into the presence of God is the same being who can bring *us* into the presence of God. That being, of course, is the Savior. "Behold, I reveal unto you concerning this heaven and this earth," Moses was told. "By mine Only Begotten I created these things."[36]

The Savior's various names testify of his creative role. On the first day, the "light of the world"[37] introduced light.[38] On the second day, "he that giveth breath unto the people"[39] introduced air.[40] On the third, the "living water"[41] and "true vine"[42] introduced water, soil, and vegetation.[43] On the fourth day, "the light which is in all things"[44] caused the sun, the moon, and the stars to shine on the earth according to the appointed rotation of the earth.[45] On the fifth day, the "fisher of men" prepared the earth to bring forth fishes and fowls.[46] On day six, the "Good Shepherd"[47] and Lamb of God"[48] prepared the earth to bring forth the animals and all creeping things, and the "Son of man"[49] formed man and woman "in the image of God."[50]

Just as it was the Savior who transformed the earth, so, too, it is the Savior who transforms man.

> For the natural man is an enemy to God, and has been from the fall of Adam, and will be, forever and ever, unless he yields to the enticings of the Holy Spirit, and putteth off the natural man and becometh a saint *through the atonement of Christ the Lord.*[51]

> There is no other name given whereby salvation cometh; therefore, I would that ye should take upon you the name of Christ, all you that have entered into the covenant with God that ye should be obedient unto the end of your lives. And it shall come to pass that whosoever doeth this shall be found at the right hand of God, for he shall know the name by which he is called; for he shall be called by the name of Christ.[52]

As with the earth, the transformation from dark, desolate solitude to glorious abundance in the presence of God is in and through the power of Christ. He is the creator of heaven and earth.[53]

The Key to Progression from One Stage of Creation to the Next

The Abraham and Moses accounts reveal the key to the Creation process. At the end of day one of the Creation, the Moses account says: "and it was done as I spake."[54] At the end of day two, the Moses account says, "it was so even as I spake,"[55] and the Abraham account echoes: "and it was so, even as [the Gods] ordered."[56] At the end of day three, the Abraham account tells us that "the Gods saw that *they were obeyed*."[57] Day four ends with this interesting detail: "And the Gods watched those things which they had ordered *until they obeyed*."[58] Similarly, at the end of day five, the Abraham account tells us: "And the Gods saw that *they would be obeyed*."[59] And at the end of day six, the Gods said: "We will do everything that we have said, and organize them; and behold, *they shall be very obedient*."[60]

So, for the earth, the key to each stage of progression was obedience. Obedience was so important that the Lord waited until the elements obeyed before proceeding to each successive stage of creation—which is to say that the earth progressed from its desolate state only as its elements strictly obeyed the Lord's commands.

This is as true of man's progression as it was for the earth's, as we are here to be tried to see if we "will do all things whatsoever the Lord [our] God shall command [us]."[61] Like the earth, we progress and are made perfect only through obedience to the Savior. If we seek "to become a law unto [ourselves]," we "cannot be sanctified by law, neither by mercy, justice, nor judgment."[62]

Christ is himself the greatest mortal example of the kind of obedience demonstrated by the elements of the earth in its creation—the kind of obedience that allows ultimate sanctification. At the doorstep of the final stage of the Atonement, when the full import of what he was about to endure was becoming pressingly clear, he said: "O my Father, if it be possible, let this cup pass from me: nevertheless not as I will, but as thou wilt."[63]

From the earth, and its Creator, we learn clearly that *our* will should be to do *His* will. Only then will we be as worthy as the dust of the earth, and with that dust abide in the presence of the Lord.

OUR OWN AND THE EARTH'S SANCTIFICATION

Although Adam and Eve were brought into the presence of the Lord in the Garden of Eden, from latter-day revelation we know that the

Eden-era earth was not yet a fully glorified sphere but rather a sphere of paradisiacal—or terrestrial—glory.[64] The earth will be restored to this state at Christ's Second Coming.[65] Then, after the thousand-year preparation known as the Millennium, the earth will be "sanctified from all unrighteousness, that it may be prepared for the celestial glory; for after it hath filled the measure of its creation, it shall be crowned with glory, even with the presence of God the Father."[66]

Here, too, the earth's progression is linked to man's, for its sanctification unto celestial glory is in order that "bodies who are of the celestial kingdom may possess it forever and ever; for, for this intent was it made and created, and for this intent are they sanctified."[67]

How is this level of sanctification made possible? This is the singular question at the heart of the gospel. The Creation set the stage for the unfolding of God's plan to sanctify his children. Adam and Eve had to progress from a state of immortal *innocence from sin* to a state of eternal holiness that *would never countenance sin*. In order for this purification process to happen, sin itself had to be overcome.

Which leads us from the story of the Creation to the story of the Fall.

CHAPTER 2

THE FALL AND REDEMPTION OF AGENCY

Because They Are Redeemed from the Fall They Have Become Free Forever

> *"If you can show me why the Fall matters—in this moment—then maybe I'll listen. If not, the kids are crying, and I have reality to deal with."*
>
> Here's why the Fall matters today: While it is true that mankind fell from the presence of God with the Fall of Adam and Eve, the fall is repeated anew, many times over, by each of us. And with every personal fall we give away something precious beyond measure—something surprising, even shocking: the very agency we fought to keep in the premortal world. Were it not for the Lord's Atonement, we would be lost not only eternally but in each and every moment, enslaved to the anger, frustration, resentment, and despair that crush us as we fall. So the Fall is as much a modern event as an ancient one, as is the Lord's Atonement, which is the lifting remedy that rescues us from the doom and gloom we may feel stuck within. That's why an understanding of the Fall and the Atonement matters so much today and every day—even, and maybe especially, when the kids are crying.

As we discovered in chapter 1, the earth progressed in glory at each stage of its creation through obedience to the will of God. By the end of the seventh creative period, the earth was a place of such stunning beauty that it was fit for God himself. But after all of that—after perhaps eons of time (according to our current reckoning) spent in the creation process, and after millions of acts of obedience by the elements that ultimately formed the earth—all it took for the entire creation to fall from its station near unto God was a single act of disobedience.

Clearly, if we are to understand the Fall, we must understand what was at stake in Adam and Eve's exercise of agency. However, Adam and Eve were not the first to fall on account of the disobedient exercise of agency. An inquiry into the fall of man must begin with the fall that predated that one—the fall of Lucifer the archangel. For a war was fought in heaven over this issue of agency, and we learn from the scriptures that *that* war—the same war concerning agency—was renewed beneath a tree in Eden.

In the Grand Council in Heaven, the plan for man's progression became a subject of intense debate. Speaking on behalf of the Father, to whom he gave all glory, the premortal Savior announced a plan whereby we would progress toward the Father as we chose to exercise our own will to do His.[1] This plan necessarily meant that some, and perhaps many, would fall short.

To this, Lucifer stepped forward with an alternative. "Behold, here am I," he said to the Father, "I will be thy son, and I will redeem all mankind, *that one soul shall not be lost.*"[2] The Lord described Lucifer's plan and its aftermath as a rebellion wherein he "sought to destroy the agency of man."[3] It is easy to dismiss his alternative out of hand as an obviously wrongheaded play for power. However, the fact that a full third of the hosts of heaven felt so strongly about it that they were willing to lose their exaltation fighting for it[4] suggests that his plan was sophisticated and serious. Enough so to blind his followers to its fundamental contradiction: that one could become as God by fighting against His will.

For this rebellion against God and the plan of agency, Satan and his sympathizers were "cast down" to the earth, where, we are told, they set about "to deceive and to blind men, and to lead them captive at [Satan's] will."[5] Notice: Satan's design on earth is to *lead us captive at his will.* In other words, the war over agency didn't end at Satan's fall. His premortal plan for mankind was to lead us captive at his will in order to save us. After he was cast down, his plan became to lead us captive at his will in order to destroy us. In its essence—the destruction of our agency through the capture of our wills—his plan hasn't changed from the beginning.

In this light, let us consider the events in the Garden of Eden, which appear in the book of Moses immediately after the statement that Satan seeks to lead us captive at his will here on earth. This juxtaposition is no accident, as the events in the garden demonstrate how Satan captures our wills in mortality.

"Of every tree of the garden thou mayest freely eat," God explained to Adam, "But of the tree of the knowledge of good and evil, thou shalt not eat of it, nevertheless, thou mayest choose for thyself, for it is given unto thee; but, remember that I forbid it, for in the day thou eatest thereof thou shalt surely die."[6]

By granting Adam the ability to choose for himself between things that were allowed by the Lord (the good) and things that were forbidden (the evil), the Lord allowed Adam his "agency." As used in the scriptures, "agency" is most helpfully understood to be the capacity we have to choose whom we will follow—the Lord of Light or the lord of darkness. Although limits or constraints—even severe ones—can be put on many other choices in our lives, this deep choice cannot be taken from us. Even a person who is physically restrained in chains retains in his heart the ability to choose whom he will follow and how he will act on that commitment under the circumstances. Indeed, such agency appears to be a condition of existence.[7] However, we learn from the story of Adam and Eve, and from the history of man since, that although the capacity we have to choose whom we will follow cannot be taken from us, we can, through the sinful exercise of this agency, effectively give away our ability to exercise it. "Here is the agency of man," the Lord declares, "and here is the condemnation of man. . . . That wicked one cometh and taketh away light and truth, through disobedience, from the children of men."[8]

We are warned of this from the very beginning. The Lord taught that Adam and Eve's choice to eat of the tree of knowledge of good and evil put their ability to freely exercise their agency at risk. By this transgression, he declared—even this *single* transgression—they became "subject to the will of the devil, because [they] yielded unto temptation."[9] This was the beginning of Satan's plan to compel toward hell all those he had previously proposed to compel toward heaven, to "lead them captive at his will, even as many as would not hearken unto [the Lord's] voice."[10]

Abinadi taught that all mankind have "subject[ed] themselves to the devil" in just this way, becoming "carnal, sensual, [and] devilish" because of their sins.[11] As we choose to follow darkness, our hearts become darkened, which makes it increasingly difficult for us to see the light. Sin, in this way, compromises our ability to withstand further sin. "Whosoever committeth sin," the Savior declared—and that includes everyone—"is the servant of sin,"[12] which is to say that the being who entices us to sin has become our master. Were it not for the Lord's atoning offering, the transgression in the garden and all further sins and transgressions would have destroyed man's ability to follow the Lord. Satan, in the garden, was attempting the usurpation of the agency of man.

How does this usurpation happen? Consider what happened with Adam and Eve immediately after they partook of the fruit:

"And I, the Lord God, called unto Adam, and said unto him: Where goest thou?

"And he said: I heard thy voice in the garden, and I was afraid, because I beheld that I was naked, and I hid myself.

"And I, the Lord God, said unto Adam: Who told thee thou wast naked? Hast thou eaten of the tree whereof I commanded thee that thou shouldst not eat, if so thou shouldst surely die?"[13]

The answer to that question, of course, could have been a simple "Yes." But that wasn't how Adam answered. It is rarely how *we* answer either, when we do something that is less than we know to be right. When my twin girls were very young, for example, and did something they knew I had told them not to do, they first tried to run and hide from me, and then, upon being found, each immediately pointed at the other twin and tried to pass the blame. In fact, they actually said, while pointing at the other, "*That* one." They did this even though they were in a state of innocence, not being morally culpable for their actions.

What is true of innocent children and an innocent Adam and Eve is true as well of not-so-innocent adults. The story of Adam and Eve suggests, and our own lives confirm, that when we act against our understanding of what is right, we typically begin to find ways to justify what we have done. We blame others, our circumstances, genetic tendencies, and so on. The consequence of all this self-justification is that we lose sight of the extent of our own responsibility for our transgressions. Losing sight of our own responsibility for sin, we lose sight of our own need for repentance. And losing sight of our own need to repent, we lose sight of our total and utter need for the Savior. We therefore become less likely to notice, regret, and repent of our sins and transgressions. Thus our ability to exercise our agency to follow the Lord becomes compromised.

Consider how Adam's answer to the Lord's question and Eve's subsequent response illustrate this damning consequence of sin and transgression. After first hiding from their Father (a desire that never could have been planted within them had they not transgressed), they gave the following answers when the Lord asked whether they had partaken of the fruit:

"And [Adam answered]: The woman thou gavest me, and commandest that she should remain with me, she gave me of the fruit of the tree and I did eat.

"And I, the Lord God, said unto the woman: What is this thing which thou hast done? And the woman said: The serpent beguiled me, and I did eat."[14]

In other words, instead of just admitting, "Yes, we ate of the fruit that you commanded us not to eat," Adam and Eve each pointed elsewhere and, like my twins, said, in effect, "*That* one." "*That* one (Satan) tricked me into doing it, or *that* one (Eve) invited me to do it, or *that* one (God) required me to do it." What Adam and Eve said was true, it just wasn't the simplest, meekest truth.

I don't want to be misunderstood on this point. This reaction by Adam and Eve does not make them bad, only fallen. The story simply illustrates what our own lives confirm: Part of the trap of transgression or sin is that we immediately begin seeing the world in ways that justify our transgressions and sins. Because we are created from "intelligence, or the light of truth,"[15] any turning away from the light that burns within apparently creates in us the need to feel justified for our having turned away. Our divine nature being good,[16] we construe the world in a way that preserves a claim of goodness even when we are doing evil. Although we are blind to our predicament when in the throes of wickedness, our excuses nevertheless testify of our sins.

Because of this need to feel justified that comes with sin, we end up feeling less than totally responsible for our own transgressions. This is a serious and damning consequence, for if we do not see the extent of our sins, we will not feel the need to repent as we must. Unless our sin-excusing feelings can be overcome, they will keep us from fully and humbly coming to the Lord, which is our only protection against what the prophet Lehi described as Satan's ability to "captivate" us through "the will of the flesh and the evil which is therein, . . . to bring [us] down to hell."[17] In this way, our ability to choose to follow the Lord—our agency—becomes impaired through sin.

The predicament of sin, then, is much bigger than the fact that we commit individual sinful acts. The larger problem is that with each capitulation to Satan's will we give Satan power over our hearts and begin to become sinful *ourselves*—hard-hearted, stiff-necked, dark. We no longer see clearly but, as Paul warned, "through a glass, darkly,"[18] which is according to Satan's plan to "blind the eyes and harden the hearts of the children of men."[19] The scriptures declare that this is "a snare of the adversary, which he has laid to catch this people, that he might bring [us] into subjection unto him, that he might encircle [us] about with his chains, that he might chain [us] down to everlasting destruction, according to the power of his captivity."[20]

Once we have become sinful in our hearts, acts and thoughts that were formerly reprehensible become desirable. We come to desire to do what we shouldn't (for example, Adam and Eve's post-transgression desire to hide from the Lord[21]) and lose our desire to do what we should. In the words of Paul, we think ourselves "something"—better than, more deserving—when we are in fact "nothing," and are therefore "deceive[d]" about our sinfulness.[22] Losing sight of our sinfulness, we lose sight of our need for the One who has come to heal the sinner. Like Laman and Lemuel in the Book of Mormon, being hard in our hearts, we do not "look unto the Lord as [we] ought."[23]

This, again, is what is meant in the scriptures by the "chains" or "captivity" of sin: Precisely when we are most in need of repentance, we least feel the desire or need to repent. This is the predicament of sin. And this is why the Lord himself declared, "I, the Lord, require the hearts of the children of men,"[24] *and* why the prophets have uniformly declared that what is required is not just a cessation of sinful "acts," but a "mighty change in [our] hearts." It is as the prophet Alma taught: Only this mighty change of heart can loose us from the chains of hell.[25] We need that mighty change of heart because, through sin, our hearts have become captured. We, of ourselves, are no longer free.

Satan must have rejoiced in the moment of the transgression in Eden, believing that by capturing Adam and Eve's will he had put in motion events that would destroy the great plan of God. However, "he knew not the mind of God."[26] All of these events "[were] done in the wisdom of him who knoweth all things."[27] This is what Satan had missed: He was blind to the fact that his attempt to destroy agency was what enabled a full exercise of agency in the first place. For, although God gave man the choice to partake of the fruit of the tree of knowledge of good and evil, there was nothing in Adam and Eve's innocence that would have enticed them to partake of it. In their innocent state, their love of God and their desire to keep his commandments would have kept them from partaking of the fruit, probably forever. In such a state, Adam and Eve would not really have had the agency to choose even though the choice had been granted them because, as Lehi taught his sons, "man could not act for himself save it should be that he was enticed by the one" (the tree of life, toward which Adam and Eve were enticed by the Lord himself) "or the other" (the forbidden fruit, toward which they would not have been enticed unless Satan had come to entice them).[28]

By providing an enticement to disobey in opposition to the enticement God provided to obey, Satan unwittingly created the very condition he was trying to destroy: real, meaningful choice. For "it must needs be," the Lord taught, "that the devil should tempt the children of men, or they could not be agents unto themselves."[29] So while as a result of Satan's temptation the agency of man itself was threatened, there could have been no meaningful agency in the first place without his temptation.

Nevertheless, once sin had been introduced into the world, with the resulting corruption and bondage, all would have been lost unless the blindness that sin introduces could be overcome by a sight-restoring, sin-cleansing act of redemption. Adam and Eve would not have had a meaningful choice had there not been an enticement to do evil in opposition to the enticement they already felt to do good. Similarly, we would not have a meaningful choice out of the darkness that blinds our souls if it were not for the introduction of a piercing light that awakens us to, and invites us out of, our sins. "It must needs be," the scriptures teach, "that there is an opposition in all things. If not so . . . righteousness could not be brought to pass, neither wickedness, neither holiness nor misery, neither good nor bad."[30]

In order for mankind to be redeemed from the Fall, the Atonement would have to redeem man's ability to choose to fully follow the Lord. It would have to break us free from the bondage of our corrupted hearts. This is precisely what we are told was the result of the Atonement: "I will take away the stony heart out of your flesh," the Lord declared. "A new heart . . . will I give you, and a new spirit will I put within you."[31] We are made free only because of the Atonement that makes this change of heart possible. "*Because* [the children of men] are redeemed from the fall they have become free forever," Lehi taught, "knowing good from evil; to act for themselves and not to be acted upon."[32] Had we not been redeemed though the Atonement, we would not have been free at all, but would have become "subject to that angel who fell from before the presence of the Eternal God, and became the devil. . . . And our spirits must have become like unto him, and we become devils, angels to a devil, to be shut out from the presence of our God."[33] We "would have been endlessly lost were it not that God redeemed [us] from [our] lost and fallen state."[34]

So how did the Atonement do this? How has the Lord prepared new hearts for us that are free from the bondage of corruption? How did he restore choice that would have been lost had there been nothing to remedy the effects of the Fall?

According to the Lord, agency was preserved in precisely the way it was threatened. "*As* thou hast fallen," the Lord told Adam, "thou mayest be redeemed,"[35] the word *as* suggesting that the atoning act that would restore man's agency would parallel the act that precipitated its fall. So it is no accident that the Atonement would begin, as did the Fall, in a garden. And it is no accident as well that the individuals in those gardens were each sinless, or that the events in those gardens centered on their exercise of agency—for Adam, whether he would partake of the bitter fruit, and for the Savior, whether he would partake of the bitter cup. The Savior and Adam faced a similar choice: If they did not partake, they would become lone men in paradise. Both partook that man might be. And by partaking of that bitterness, Adam came to know good and evil, and the Savior came to know all of the good and evil that had and would transpire in the hearts of men through all generations of time.

If it is true that the atoning act that restores man's agency parallels the act that precipitated its loss, then the Savior had to endure what Adam did after his fall, and then redeem man from the effects of it. In order to re-deem mankind from the predicament of our captivity to sin, the Savior had to take upon himself that captivity—in its fulness—and then find a way to break free from it. Because of the power that Satan obtained through the fall over the will of the flesh,[36] man's agency could be re-deemed only if all the powers of captivity that had been hardwired into the flesh by every sin of mankind could be overcome by an opposing power—by someone who could take our captivity upon himself and yet escape from it, thereby providing a way of escape for us. That is what the Savior did. In order to free us from the captivity of sinfulness, he took upon himself all the sins of mankind, the "iniquities of us all."[37] In order to redeem us from the chains of sin, the Savior took upon himself all of the chains that bind us to sin—in the words of Paul, to be "in all points tempted like as we are."[38] He had to shoulder "the burden of the combined weight of the sins of the world"[39]—our sinful desires, our predispositions and addictions toward sin, our darkened hearts. It was as Paul said: He "who knew no sin" was "made . . . to be sin for us."[40]

Luke describes the Savior's struggle in the garden using the Greek word *agon* (translated in Luke as "an agony"[41]), which means, literally, "a contest, struggle, or fight, facing an opponent."[42] Latter-day prophets have referred to it as "indescribable anguish" and "overpowering torture,"[43] a "supreme contest with the powers of evil," an "hour of anguish when Christ had to meet and overcome all the horrors that Satan could inflict."[44] With all of our sinfulness heaped upon him, he had to withstand the unimaginable onslaught of the entire power and fury of the forces of hell, and do so, as Paul described further, "yet [remaining] without sin."[45] For Satan knew that if he could wield the power of his captivity—the chains of our sinfulness that lay ready to bind the Savior—and entice the Savior to sin, he would bring the Savior into his captivity as well. Then the destruction of agency would be complete, and mankind would be left without a way for their hearts to be purified and cleansed. There would therefore be no way for any of us to return to the Father, where only the clean and pure can dwell.

Is it any wonder, as Enoch witnessed, that Satan "looked up and laughed" when he held the entire earth in his chains?[46] Throughout the Savior's life, and as he struggled under the weight of our transgressions in Gethsemane, Satan was only one sin away from holding all creation in his hand.

But the Savior withstood in the aggregate what no man has been able to withstand individually. He refused to submit to Satan's will even though he was fully subject to it. Even with all of the mortal effects of our sins heaped upon and pulling at him, and with Satan and his hosts attempting to drag him down by that power to sin, the Savior was able to withstand and resist. By opposing perfectly what for mankind had been an overpowering enticement, the Savior redeemed agency by opening up a way of escape from the captivity of sin. He is himself that way—the "enmity" that was placed between Satan and mankind,[47] who would release mankind, "even as many as will,"[48] from the grasp of sin. The promise of the Atonement is that, on condition of repentance and faith in Christ, the Lord will replace our sinful hearts with his own—with a heart that is free from the captivity of the devil.

Although the Savior's Atonement preserved man's ability to choose and follow the Lord, it did not destroy Satan's ability to captivate us individually and subject us to his will. After the Fall, Satan came among the posterity of Adam and Eve, tempting them, and those who yielded to his temptations relinquished their agency to Satan as surely as Adam and Eve did, for they "began from that time forth to be carnal, sensual, and devilish."[49] Abinadi taught that "he that persists in his own carnal nature, and goes on in the ways of sin and rebellion against God, remaineth in his fallen state and the devil hath all power over him. Therefore he is as though there was no redemption made."[50]

So "awake!" Lehi exhorted his sons, "awake from a deep sleep, yea, even from the sleep of hell, and shake off the awful chains by which ye are bound, which are the chains which bind the children of men, that they are carried away captive down to the eternal gulf of misery and woe."[51] "*Because* . . . [the children of men] are redeemed from the fall," Lehi continued, "they are free to choose liberty and eternal life, through the great Mediator of all men, or to choose captivity and death, according to the captivity and power of the devil."[52]

Eternal life or death rests on our choice of wills—a choice that is available to us only by virtue of the Atonement. We can "look to the great Mediator, and hearken unto his great commandments; and be faithful unto his words, and choose eternal life, *according to the will of his Holy Spirit,*" or we can "choose eternal death, *according to the will of the flesh* and the evil which is therein, which giveth the spirit of the devil power to captivate, to bring [us] down to hell."[53]

By the Fall, mankind came to know good and evil. But it is only because of the infinite Atonement that mankind is able to choose between them. "Men are, that they *might* have joy,"[54] Lehi exclaimed, emphasizing again the necessity of agency. Whether we *will* have joy depends on whose "will" we choose—our own will that has been corrupted by sin, or the Lord's will that conquered sin. The exercise of agency is the choice of whose agent we will be.

CHAPTER 3

GOD AND MAN AFTER THE FALL

In Similitude of the Only Begotten

> *"What can we do when we are struggling with children who persist in doing what they shouldn't be doing? For example, when kids have separated themselves—physically, emotionally, or spiritually—what can we do?"*
>
> This is the same question the Lord faced from the beginning—the question for which the gospel itself was designed to be the answer. In this case, however, *we* are the struggling, separated children.

The fall of Adam introduced both physical and spiritual death—physical death because man had become mortal and would "surely die,"[1] and spiritual death because man was now separated from God. This separation was more than a mere physical separation. It was rather the reality that man, now sinful, was unable to be with God.

So what could be done? How can we be reconciled back to God so that we can reenter his presence? That is the question. Let's explore God's answer.

THE PROBLEM OF ENDURING GOD'S PRESENCE

The scriptures teach that our inability to be with God is just that—an inability, and not simply a whimsical punishment imposed by God on his disobedient children. "He who is not able to abide the law of a celestial kingdom *cannot* abide a celestial glory,"[2] the Lord tells us, for "no unclean thing *can* dwell there, or dwell in his presence."[3] This state of being cut off was for man's own protection. For, as the Prophet Joseph taught, "God

Almighty Himself dwells in eternal fire; flesh and blood cannot go there, for all corruption is devoured by the fire. Our God is consuming fire."[4] The Lord was referring to this inability of fallen man to abide his presence when he told Moses, "no sinful man hath at any time, neither shall there be any sinful man at any time, that shall see my face *and live*."[5] "For my presence shall not go up in their midst, lest I destroy them."[6]

"Thus we see," Alma taught his son, "that all mankind were fallen, and they were in the grasp of justice; yea, the justice of God, which consigneth them forever to be cut off from his presence."[7] This, then, is the predicament of man: Having become sinful, we *cannot* abide the glory of sinlessness. "All have sinned," Paul wrote. We therefore "come short of the glory of God."[8]

This, of course, is not the end of the story, as we know that through the Atonement we can become sanctified, through the Lord's grace, and once again dwell in the presence of God. Notice, however, that this plan of redemption required the condescension of God into the mortal realm. In so noticing, consider the genius and beauty of the plan: Separated from us by the Fall and our resulting sinfulness, which has rendered us unable to endure his presence, God the Father sent a mediator to reconcile man with God—a mortal mediator whose presence mankind *could* endure.[9] Not just any mediator, either, but a mediator who was the Son of God, identical to his Father even in his physical appearance,[10] a mediator whose very will was the will of the Father.[11] The oneness of the Father and the Son is so complete that Jesus said, "he that hath seen me hath seen the Father."[12] This oneness enabled mankind to be taught, as it were, by the Father, in the personage of his very physical and spiritual likeness, the Son. "God was in Christ manifesting himself to the world," we are taught, "a gracious and condescending thing for the Eternal Father to do."[13] In this way, the Father from whom we cut ourselves off devised a way that we could come to know him—through his Son. And then the mortal Son, by offering himself in atonement, opened the way by which we can once again enter into the presence of the Father.

The events recorded in Moses, chapter 1, show us that the healing power of the infinite Atonement, operating forward and backward into eternity, opened a way for us to be redeemed from the effects of sin and to be able to endure again the Lord's presence even in *this* life. These events demonstrate the conditions upon which this redemption back into the Lord's presence—whether in this life or the next—rests. The story also answers many fundamental questions regarding the nature of man's relationship to God after the Fall.

BECOMING BORN AGAIN, AS CHILDREN OF CHRIST

Moses 1 begins with a meeting between God and Moses on "an exceedingly high mountain."[14] President Joseph Fielding Smith taught that this meeting was with God the Son, not God the Father. "All revelation since the fall has come through Jesus Christ," he taught, "who is the Jehovah of the Old Testament. In all of the scriptures, where God is mentioned and where he has appeared, it was Jehovah who talked with Abraham, with Noah, Enoch, Moses and all the prophets. He is the God of Israel, the Holy One of Israel; the one who led that nation out of Egyptian bondage, and who gave and fulfilled the Law of Moses. The Father has never dealt with man directly and personally since the fall, and he has never appeared except to introduce and bear record of the Son."[15]

After this sacred experience, the premortal Savior withdrew his presence, and Moses was left to himself.[16] The experience drained Moses of strength for many hours,[17] after which time Satan appeared to him, tempting him.[18] After Moses had rebuked Satan, Jehovah again appeared and then proceeded to show to Moses the creation of the earth,[19] the habitation of the earth by Adam and Eve and their family,[20] and the proceedings of mankind down through the time of Noah and the great flood.[21] It is through Moses that we have knowledge of these events, which are recorded in the books of Genesis and Moses.[22]

This story raises an important question: If we, in our fallen condition, are unable to endure the presence of God, how is it that Moses was able to endure the divine presence? An interesting feature in Moses 1 offers a first clue.

You might have noticed while reading Moses 1 that Jehovah and Satan refer differently to Moses. Satan calls Moses a "son of man,"[23] while

Jehovah always addresses him as "my son" (this happens four times—in verses 4, 6, 7 and 40).[24] Why the difference? Might it be significant?

On the surface, the difference might simply appear to be an example of Satan tearing Moses down while God is building him up. But this seems too simple a reading, as Jehovah himself throughout the chapter refers to humankind as "children of men."[25] So again, what significance, if any, might there be to the different way that God specifically refers to *Moses*? To begin with, let's consider why God might refer generally to mankind as "children of men."

Although one of the tenets of our faith is that we are spirit children of God the Father, when we are born into mortality we also become children of mortal parents. With respect to mortal life, then, we are sons and daughters of men, extending back to Adam. The title "son (or daughter) of man" refers to our membership, by virtue of physical birth, in the family of Adam—the family of mortal man. In and of itself, "son of man" is not a pejorative term. It is simply a statement regarding our mortal status. Moses, like the rest of us, is a "son of man."

But if Moses is a son of man, why did God—again, God the Son in this case—specifically call him something different whenever He addressed him? What significance might there be in being called "my son"? Is this only in reference to Moses' identity as a spiritual child of God, or might there be some other, and greater, meaning?

In order to ponder this question, let's consider the following scriptures:

> Behold, I am he who was prepared from the foundation of the world to redeem my people. Behold, I am Jesus Christ. I am the Father and the Son. In me shall all mankind have life, and that eternally, even they who shall believe on my name; and they shall become my sons and my daughters.[26]

> And now, because of the covenant which ye have made ye shall be called the children of Christ, his sons, and his daughters; for behold, this day he hath spiritually begotten you; for ye say that your hearts are changed through faith on his name;

therefore, ye are born of him and have become his sons and his daughters.[27]

These and many other scriptures declare that we can inherit eternal life only by becoming sons and daughters of Christ. But what does that mean, exactly? And how does it happen?

This new birth is the "mighty change of heart" referred to in the scriptures. It is the change desired by the father of King Lamoni when he pined, "What shall I do that I may be born of God, having this wicked spirit rooted out of my breast, and receive his Spirit?"[28] Speaking of those who had become born again, Alma said: "[The Lord] changed their hearts"[29]— a miraculous change made possible by the Atonement offering discussed in chapter 2. And then Alma asked those of the Church, "Have ye spiritually been born of God? Have ye received his image in your countenances? Have ye experienced this mighty change in your hearts?"[30]

The labor of this new birth was performed in Gethsemane and on the cross at Calvary. As discussed in chapter 2, through the blood shed in Gethsemane for the remission of our sins, the Lord prepared for each of us this new heart—his Spirit, which yearns to enter into and enliven man. And because of his offering on Calvary, and his subsequent resurrection, the Lord has also prepared new bodies for us. Because the Lord has prepared for us both a new spirit and a new body, he is literally the father of the new birth, the creator of eternal life.

"Whose sons and whose daughters do we become when we are born again?" Elder Bruce R. McConkie asked rhetorically, "Who is our new Father? The answer is, Christ is our Father; . . . he makes us members of his family."[31] Expanding on this point, he added: "Few doctrines are better known by members of the true church than the doctrine of preexistence. We are well aware that all men are the children of God, the offspring of the Father, his sons and daughters. . . . What is not so well known," he continued, "is that nearly all passages of scripture, both ancient and modern, which speak of God as our Father and of men on earth being sons of God, *have no reference to our birth in preexistence as the children of Elohim, but teach rather that Jehovah [Christ] is our Father and we are his children.*"[32]

The First Presidency of the Church made the same point when they declared, "If it be proper to speak of those who accept and abide in the Gospel as Christ's sons and daughters—and upon this matter the scriptures are explicit and cannot be gainsaid or denied—it is consistently proper to speak of Jesus Christ as the Father of the righteous, they having become His children and He having been made their Father through the second birth—the baptismal regeneration."[33]

This new birth is marked symbolically by the first ordinance of the gospel—baptism by immersion for the remission of sins—then by the gift of the Holy Ghost (i.e., the new Spirit), which is received by the laying on of hands.[34] Baptism into and out of the water is itself in similitude of Christ's burial and resurrection, signifying that when we receive our new body in the Resurrection, if we have been born again in Christ, having already received his Spirit, we will then have received both a new body and a new spirit through him, becoming children of Christ in the eternities.

But is it just that easy? Do we simply need to be baptized and receive the Holy Ghost? Is that, alone, all that is required for the new birth?

No, for remember, the first two principles of the gospel must be lived as well,[35] both before and after these first two ordinances. We must live with faith in the Lord Jesus Christ, and we must always be repenting of our sins. This is why, to those who had already been baptized and had received the gift of the Holy Ghost, Alma said, "if ye have experienced [this mighty] change of heart . . . I would ask, can ye feel so now? Have ye walked, keeping yourselves blameless before God?"[36] Which is to say that this change of heart or rebirth must be *retained,* by living faithfully in Christ, and by continually repenting of sins. "If ye do this," King Benjamin taught, "ye shall always rejoice, and be filled with the love of God, and always retain a remission of your sins."[37] Abinadi explained, "All those who have hearkened unto [the words of the prophets], and believed that the Lord would redeem his people, and have looked forward to that day for a remission of their sins," and "have kept the commandments of God, these are his seed."[38]

Significantly, when we are baptized, just as we do when we are born into mortality, we take upon us the name of our father. "There is no other name given whereby salvation cometh," King Benjamin taught, "therefore,

I would that ye should take upon you the name of Christ, . . . [and] whosoever doeth this shall be found at the right hand of God, for he shall know the name by which he is called; for he shall be called by the name of Christ."[39]

With all of this in mind, consider the potential significance of the premortal Savior referring to Moses as "my son"—that is, the son of the premortal Savior. The implication is that the Savior called Moses "my son" because Moses had by then been born again in Christ.

The Rebirth and Enduring God's Presence

The second verse of Moses 1 tells us that Moses "saw God face to face," and that "the glory of God was upon Moses." Which means, the verse continues, "[that] Moses could endure his presence." The question is, how? How is it that Moses was able to endure God's presence? The use of the word *wherefore* in verse 4 suggests that it was precisely because Moses had become a child of Christ that he was granted the vision of the Lord: "And, behold, thou art my son; *wherefore* look, and I will show thee the workmanship of mine hands."[40] "But not all," he continued, teaching Moses that even more is required in order to abide the *fulness* of the glory of God. "No man can behold all my works, except he behold all my glory; and no man can behold all my glory, and afterwards remain in the flesh on the earth."[41]

The fact that Moses was able to enjoy the Lord's glory in any degree means that the power of the spiritual deliverance of Christ was operative from the foundation of the world—even before Christ actually came in the flesh to work out the Atonement. "The atonement was retroactive; it was for all men of all ages; its effect was past, present, future."[42] So after the Fall, for those who became sons and daughters of Christ through faith in his future Atonement, it was as if spiritual death had already been overcome, and they could be transfigured and caught up as was Moses into the presence of God, able to endure at least a portion of his glory.[43] As the premortal Christ explained to the brother of Jared: "[Because of your faith in the Savior who is to come,] ye are redeemed from the fall; therefore ye are brought back into my presence; therefore I show myself unto you."[44]

Of course, our ultimate goal is to be able to abide not just a portion but a *fulness* of God's glory and to receive eternal life. When Jesus was born into this mortal realm, his premortal glory was cloaked, as it were, by the veil of his flesh[45] to the level of a telestial glory so that all mankind could be with him in the flesh. When he comes again a second time, he will appear at a terrestrial level of glory. This means that only those who have abided a terrestrial or celestial law here on earth will be able to survive his coming,[46] the rest being burned as stubble.[47] It will then take the thousand years of the Millennium to prepare mankind for the coming of celestial glory—the fulness of the glory of the Father.

For a discussion of the way prepared for us to become sanctified to abide not just a portion but the *fulness* of the glory of the Father, see Appendix B.

TEACHING CHRIST AND THE REBIRTH FROM THE BEGINNING

Able to abide the presence of at least a partially glorified Savior because of his status as a son of Christ, Moses was shown a vision of the early history of the world. Through Moses' accounts of these visions, we learn that Christ's Atonement, and the new birth required to make it efficacious unto eternal life, was preached from the very beginning to Adam and Eve.

After Adam and Eve were cast out of the garden, the Lord by his voice "gave unto them commandments, that they should worship the Lord their God, and should offer the firstlings of their flocks, for an offering unto the Lord."[48]

After Adam sustained this obedience for "many days," an angel appeared and taught him the significance of the sacrificial ordinance: "This thing is a similitude of the sacrifice of the Only Begotten of the Father, which is full of grace and truth. Wherefore, thou shalt do all that thou doest in the name of the Son, and thou shalt repent and call upon God in the name of the Son forevermore."[49]

The Lord then called upon Adam, saying: "If thou wilt [1] turn unto me, and [2] hearken unto my voice, and [3] believe, and [4] repent of all thy transgressions, and [5] be baptized, even in water, in the name of mine Only Begotten Son, who is full of grace and truth, which is Jesus Christ, the only name which shall be given under heaven, whereby salvation shall come unto the children of men, [then] [6] ye shall receive the gift of the Holy Ghost, asking all things in his name, and whatsoever ye shall ask, it shall be given you."[50]

After being taught the necessity of the new birth, Adam then became the first to be born again: "And [Adam] was caught away by the Spirit of the Lord, and was carried down into the water, and was laid under the water, and was brought forth out of the water. And thus he was baptized, and the Spirit of God descended upon him, and thus he was born of the Spirit, and became quickened in the inner man. And he heard a voice out of heaven, saying . . . *Behold, thou art one in me, a son of God; and thus may all become my sons.*"[51]

So in the very beginning, the Savior's atoning role was made central, foundational, all-encompassing. The sacrificial ordinance—in similitude of his infinite and eternal sacrifice—was instituted to keep mankind turned to him. Likewise, the ordinance of baptism—in similitude of his death and saving return to life—was instituted to keep him in remembrance unto repentance. This was "the plan of salvation unto all men," the Lord told Adam, "through the blood of mine Only Begotten, who shall come in the meridian of time."[52]

Living in Similitude of Christ

Those who become Christ's sons and daughters grow to be like him, for they live by the Spirit, which shows them "all things what [they] should do."[53] So, of born-again Moses, the Lord said, "thou art in the similitude of mine Only Begotten; and mine Only Begotten is and shall be the Savior, for he is full of grace and truth."[54]

One could ponder a lifetime over what it means to be "in similitude of mine Only Begotten." Of the many similitudes one could mention, one seems foundational: Our son-ship or daughter-ship in Christ must be in similitude of Christ's son-ship in the Father. *His* son-ship must be the model for ours.

The foundational feature of the relationship between God the Father and God the Son is their complete unity or oneness: "I am in the Father, and the Father in me, and the Father and I are one."[55] Is such unity required of us? The Savior himself answered that question in his great intercessory prayer: "That they all may be one," he prayed, "as thou, Father, art in me, and I in thee, that they also may be one in us."[56]

The Lord emphasized this same requirement of oneness to Joseph Smith: "I am Jesus Christ, the Son of God, who was crucified for the sins of the world, even as many as will believe on my name, that they may become the sons of God, *even one in me as I am one in the Father, as the Father is one in me, that we may be one.*"[57]

"Ye do the deeds of your father," the Savior taught.[58] To be a son or daughter of Christ therefore implies a certain kind of work. Moses, whose mission it was to "deliver [the Lord's] people from bondage, even Israel [the Lord's] chosen,"[59] was united with the Lord in His work. We must be too, if we, like Moses, are to become children in the Lord's eternal family, able to endure his glory in this world and in the world to come.

PART TWO

CHRIST AND
THE PATRIARCHS

CHAPTER 4

~~~⌐

EXPLORING THE ABRAHAMIC COVENANT

After the Order of the Son of God

> *"Frankly, I don't really understand why the Abrahamic covenant is so important."*
>
> In the last chapter we discovered how we must become children of Christ in order to become sons and daughters in the eternal family of God. Birth into mortality is in similitude of our birth into eternity.
>
> Here's where Abraham comes in: Parenthood too has a similitude in eternity, and this miracle—the miracle of eternal parenthood—is made possible through the Abrahamic covenant. Which is to say that we, like Abraham, can become the "father (or mother) of many nations." But we can become this only because of Christ—who, as we shall see, is at the center of this and every other covenant.

The first verse of Abraham 1 begins with one of the great understatements of all time: After his father and others had conspired to offer Abraham up as a human sacrifice to heathen gods,[1] Abraham says: "In the land of the Chaldeans, at the residence of my fathers, I, Abraham, saw that it was needful for me to obtain another place of residence."

Abraham then continues: "And, finding there was greater happiness and peace and rest for me, I sought for the blessings of the fathers, and the right whereunto I should be ordained to administer the same."[2] Accordingly, he sought for his "appointment unto the Priesthood according to the appointment of God unto the fathers concerning the seed."[3]

One hears in this account of Abraham the unmistakable echo of the

Lord's promise regarding Elijah and his mission: "Behold, I will reveal unto you the Priesthood, by the hand of Elijah the prophet, before the coming of the great and dreadful day of the Lord. . . . *And he shall plant in the hearts of the children the promises made to the fathers, and the hearts of the children shall turn to their fathers.* If it were not so, the whole earth would be utterly wasted at his coming."[4]

Abraham is certainly an example of one whose heart was turned to his fathers regarding the priesthood. The similarity with the description of Elijah's mission suggests that God's covenant with Abraham may be connected to the priesthood keys that were later entrusted to Elijah.[5] This possible connection between Abraham and the keys held by Elijah is made explicit in a vision received by Joseph Smith and Oliver Cowdery in the Kirtland Temple on April 3, 1836.

> After [seeing the Savior], the heavens were again opened unto us; and Moses appeared before us, and committed unto us the keys of the gathering of Israel from the four parts of the earth, and the leading of the ten tribes from the land of the north.
>
> After this, Elias appeared, and *committed the dispensation of the gospel of Abraham,* saying that in us and our seed all generations after us should be blessed.
>
> After this vision had closed, another great and glorious vision burst upon us; for Elijah the prophet . . . stood before us, and said: Behold, the time has fully come, which was spoken of by the mouth of Malachi—testifying that he [Elijah] should be sent, before the great and dreadful day of the Lord come—To turn the hearts of the fathers to the children, and the children to the fathers, lest the whole earth be smitten with a curse— Therefore, *the keys of this dispensation are committed into your hands.*[6]

In this experience, Elias committed to the Prophet Joseph the "dispensation" of the gospel of Abraham, and then Elijah committed into the prophet's hands "the *keys* of this dispensation"—meaning that Elijah effectively committed to Joseph the keys of the dispensation of Abraham. From this we can see that whatever the "dispensation of Abraham" is, and whatever the "Abrahamic covenant" is, they apparently involve the keys committed by Elijah—keys that provide for the sealing of family relationships into the eternities, with the binding together of children and fathers and fathers and children, enabling these relationships to continue eternally in the presence of God.

Although we refer to the collection of promises made by the Lord to Abraham as "the Abrahamic covenant," in most respects these promises were simply bestowals upon Abraham of promises that had been made to each of the patriarchal fathers from the beginning. It was through the realization of the promises of this covenant, for example, that Enoch and his people were able to be received as a people into the glorified presence of God.[7] This "everlasting covenant,"[8] known after the restoration of the gospel in the latter days as the "new and everlasting covenant,"[9] was "instituted for the fulness of [God's] glory"—that is, in order to prepare mankind and their relationships to withstand the fulness of God's glory.[10] It "came down from the fathers, from the beginning of time, yea, even from the beginning, or before the foundation of the earth, down to [Abraham]."[11] As used by Abraham, "the fathers" refers to the great patriarchs from Adam down to Melchizedek (from whom Abraham received his ordination), as those patriarchs were the holders of the keys of the priesthood in their days.

The Prophet Joseph taught that Adam was "the first and father of all, not only by [physical] progeny, but the first to hold the spiritual blessings, to whom was made known the plan of ordinances for the salvation of his posterity unto the end,"[12] ordinances that prepare man to enter into the glory of God.[13] To him "all things were confirmed . . . by an holy ordinance,"[14] including the "grand Key-words of the Holy Priesthood."[15] These promises were then passed down from Adam to Seth, and then respectively to Enos, Cainan, Mahalaleel, Jared, Enoch, Methuselah, Lamech, Noah, and Shem.[16] Abraham was nine generations removed from Shem. Given how long the Bible says these people lived, however, Shem would have been alive at the time of Abraham, and there is an interesting case to be made that the "great high priest"[17] known as Melchizedek was actually

Shem himself.[18] There also is scriptural evidence that Melchizedek and his people were translated just as the city of Enoch had been, leaving Abraham as the head of a new dispensation.[19] Whether or not such was the case, it was from Melchizedek that Abraham received the priesthood, with the attendant ordinances and promises that had been passed down from the fathers.[20]

So Adam was the first to enter into the priesthood covenant that then continued down through the fathers to Abraham. Through Abraham we learn the details of this covenant, and the power by which it is made available to mankind.

GOD'S COVENANT WITH ABRAHAM

Having yearned for "the blessings of the fathers, and the right whereunto [he] should be ordained to administer the same,"[21] ninety-nine-year-old[22] Abram—like Moses, called "my son" by the premortal Savior[23]—was graced with the Lord's presence and received what the Lord called "an everlasting covenant."[24] The Lord gave him a new name—Abraham[25]—and promised him and his posterity the land of Canaan as an "everlasting possession."[26] Concerning the "appointment of God unto the fathers concerning the seed,"[27] which by Abraham's own record was his chief object in inquiring of the Lord, the Lord promised Abraham that he would "multiply [him] exceedingly"—both as the sands on the seashore and as the stars in the heavens.[28] Furthermore, the Lord declared that Abraham and his seed after him would "bear [the Lord's] Priesthood unto all nations,"[29] and that through that priesthood "all the families of the earth [would] be blessed, even with the blessings of the Gospel, which are the blessings of salvation, even of life eternal."[30]

So Abraham received promises concerning land, posterity, and priesthood. As we shall see, the spiritual realization of those promises depended on the impact of a fourth promise: that the Savior of the world would be among Abraham's descendants.

The clearest statement of the Lord's promises to Abraham is in the second chapter of the book of Abraham:

I have purposed to . . . make of thee a minister to bear my name in a strange land which I will give unto thy seed after thee for an everlasting possession, when they hearken to my voice. . . .

My name is Jehovah, and I know the end from the beginning; therefore my hand shall be over thee. And I will make of thee a great nation, and I will bless thee above measure, and make thy name great among all nations, and thou shalt be a blessing unto thy seed after thee, that in their hands they shall bear this ministry and Priesthood unto all nations;

And I will bless them through thy name; for as many as receive this Gospel shall be called after thy name, and shall be accounted thy seed, and shall rise up and bless thee, as their father; And I will bless them that bless thee, and curse them that curse thee; and in thee (that is, in thy Priesthood) and in thy seed (that is, thy Priesthood), for I give unto thee a promise that this right shall continue in thee, and in thy seed after thee (that is to say, the literal seed, or the seed of the body) shall all the families of the earth be blessed, even with the blessings of the Gospel, which are the blessings of salvation, even of life eternal.[31]

Here, Jehovah—the premortal Christ—was speaking to Abraham. Notice how he said that he—Christ—will make Abraham a great nation and that he—Christ—will bless Abraham above measure. This suggests that it will be *because* of Christ that Abraham is made a great nation and will be blessed above measure.

After the Lord told Abraham that he would be "a blessing unto [his] seed after [him],"[32] he defined Abraham's seed in a most interesting way: "As many as receive this Gospel shall be called after thy name," he told Abraham, "and shall be *accounted* thy seed."[33] This implies that those who do not accept the gospel shall *not* be accounted Abraham's seed, including those who are the literal seed of Abraham in the flesh! Abraham's literal or physical seed would be as innumerable as the sands upon the seashore, to be sure, but the greater promises of the covenant pertain to Abraham's spiritual progeny, who, the Lord promised, would be as the stars in the heavens.[34] The Lord's covenant to Abraham pertains to the spiritual or eternal nature of fatherhood, and not merely to its temporal or physical nature.

The enabling foundation of the Abrahamic covenant is contained in Abraham 2:11: "And in thee (that is, in thy Priesthood) and in thy seed (that is, thy Priesthood), for I give unto thee a promise that this right shall continue in thee, and in thy seed after thee (that is to say, the literal seed, or the seed of the body) shall all the families of the earth be blessed, even with the blessings of the Gospel, which are the blessings of salvation, even of life eternal."

So while Abraham was promised that all who accepted the gospel would be accounted his seed in the eternities, in addition, he was promised that his *literal* seed—the actual seed of his body—would bless all the families of the earth, "even with the blessings of the Gospel, which are the blessings of salvation, even of life eternal."[35] The implication is that Abraham's literal, physical seed would somehow make it possible for all mankind to receive the blessings of salvation and eternal life and thereby be accounted part of Abraham's family in the eternities. The Apostle Paul declared that this portion of the covenant that applies to Abraham's actual physical seed refers to a single, physical descendant of Abraham—Christ—and not to Abraham's mortal descendants generally:

> Now to Abraham and his seed were the promises made. He saith not, And to seeds, as of many; but as of one, And to thy seed, which is Christ.
>
> . . . There is one mediator of the new covenant, who is Christ, as it is written in the law concerning the promises made to Abraham and his seed. Now Christ is the mediator of life; for this is the promise which God made unto Abraham. . . .
>
> For ye are all the children of God by faith in Christ Jesus. For as many of you as have been baptized into Christ have put on Christ. There is neither Jew nor Greek, there is neither bond nor free, there is neither male nor female: for ye are all one in Christ Jesus. And if ye be Christ's, then are ye Abraham's seed, and heirs according to the promise.[36]

Here Paul explains that Christ himself was the literal seed of Abraham that would bless "all the families of the earth . . . with the blessings of . . . salvation [and] life eternal."[37] This portion of the Abrahamic covenant pertains to seed "as of one"—i.e., Christ—not "as of many" (i.e., the physical descendants of Abraham as a whole).

This blessing that the Savior would come through the literal seed of Abraham had this effect: All who accept the gospel, thereby becoming Christ's sons and daughters, are therefore accounted as the seed of Abraham because Christ is himself the literal seed of Abraham. This is why "if ye be Christ's, then are ye Abraham's seed, and heirs according to the promise."[38] With this in mind, the Lord's promise in Abraham 2:9—that he himself would make Abraham a great nation—is literally true: Because Christ came through Abraham's line, all who become sons and daughters of Christ as to eternal life are also accounted Abraham's seed (and also the seed of the righteous fathers before Abraham) in the eternities. They become part of and make up his "nation," as it were.

This illustrates the mistake in traditional Jewish belief that the holy priesthood and the blessings thereof were committed to man by virtue of their literal, physical link to Abraham. While that literal connection is true of the lesser or Levitical Priesthood, the greater or Melchizedek Priesthood is not established "by man, nor the will of man; neither by father nor mother," but is "delivered unto men by the calling of [the Lord's] own voice, according to his own will, unto as many as believed on his name."[39]

So the blessings and rights of the holy priesthood come not through lineage, but through belief in Christ. Or, put another way, the lineage that *is* important in receiving the blessings and rights of the holy priesthood is the lineage that one obtains *through* belief in Christ—lineage as *his* children. If we are to be fathers and mothers in the eternities, we must first qualify as sons and daughters in eternity—sons and daughters of Christ, and therefore heirs of the promises to Abraham.

THE COVENANT RENEWED IN US

With the coming of Elijah in the latter days and his restoration of the keys of the dispensation of Abraham,[40] our hearts can turn to our fathers[41] just as Abraham's did. We who have become Abraham's seed through the new birth in Christ can receive, according to the everlasting covenant that has come down from the fathers, the promises of glory and posterity in the eternities.

"Abraham received promises concerning his seed, and of the fruit of his loins . . . which were to continue so long as they were in the world; and as touching Abraham and his seed, *out of the world they should continue;* both in the world and out of the world should they continue as innumerable as the stars; or, if ye were to count the sand upon the seashore ye could not number them. This promise is yours also, because ye are of Abraham [i.e., his children by virtue of having become children of Christ], and the promise was made unto Abraham."[42]

In the temple, through the keys of the "dispensation of Abraham," which were committed to Joseph Smith by Elijah,[43] we, like the patriarchs of old, can have "all things . . . confirmed . . . by an holy ordinance."[44] Husbands and wives can be sealed to each other and to their righteous posterity into the eternities. And all can become sanctified to inherit the eternal promised land in the presence of the fulness of the glory of God. No one who rejects this new and everlasting covenant, the scriptures say, can "be permitted to enter [God's] glory."[45] Neither will their "covenants, contracts, bonds, obligations, oaths, vows, performances, connections, associations, or expectations" entered into in this life survive the Resurrection.[46] These blessings and promises of Abraham—both an eternal promised land in the presence of God and the continuation of the associations of posterity into the eternities—are committed anew to us, for we "are of Abraham."[47] This is the "appointment of God unto the fathers concerning the seed."[48]

Concerning this binding or sealing power and its relation to Christ, the scriptures tell us that we are joined one to another in the eternities by him.[49] In other words, the sealing power that is exercised through the priesthood is made possible only in and through the Savior. It is his power delegated to man. He is *himself* the binding link that stands between mortality and eternity and binds them together, as well as the welding power through which we in mortality can be bound to one another in the eternities. Being both the Father and the Son, he is the embodiment of the power to become both. Accordingly, we learn that the seed of Abraham—

Christ—*is* the priesthood, for Abraham was told that his "seed," identified in Galatians 3 to be a reference to Christ, "*is* [the] Priesthood."[50]

No wonder the priesthood was originally called after his name—"The Holy Priesthood, after the order of the Son of God."[51] And no wonder as well that the fulness of his priesthood is described as having the effect of turning "the heart of the fathers to the children, and the heart of the children to their fathers."[52] Mortality is in similitude of eternity. Christ's oath and covenant with Abraham and with us is that through him we can join the eternal family, both as sons and daughters *and* as fathers and mothers—all of us in the presence of God.

CHAPTER 5

ANOTHER LOOK AT ABRAHAM AND ISAAC

God Will Provide Himself a Lamb

> *"Everyone knows the Abraham and Isaac story,*
> *and that Isaac is in similitude of Christ."*
>
> Yes, but do we know the story of Abraham's other son—the son that is in similitude of *us?* When we read the Isaac story in the context of this other story—*our* story—we'll never see Abraham and Isaac the same way again.

An aging father rose early in the morning to gaze upon his sleeping son. Rousing him, the father enlisted his help with preparations to go offer sacrifice to the Lord. They saddled the ass and loaded wood, a knife, and provisions for the journey—the father with his life almost spent, the son with his life and promise before him.

Three days into that heartbreaking walk, the place of sacrifice rose before them. The son, carrying the wood of the sacrifice on his back, and the father, with flint for fire and the knife in his hand, ascended the desert slope. Righteous Isaac, following in his father's steps, and with humble knowing in his voice, asked: "Behold the fire and the wood: but where is the lamb for a burnt offering?"[1] The father stopped and turned. Gazing into the submissive eyes of his righteous son, his own eyes and heart overflowing, he reached out and slowly lifted his hand to the cheek of the promised heir. How long might they have looked on one another? Oh, to be such a son! Oh, to be such a father! "My son," he replied—mine only son, whom I love[2]—"God will provide himself a lamb."[3] With hearts heavy and full, they turned back up the slope, "and went both of them together."[4]

Many years earlier, in the hot early morning, this same father had arisen, as he was told, to bid good-bye to another. "O that [this boy] might live before thee!" the father had pleaded heavenward.[5] And the Lord heard him, and blessed the boy.[6] This blessed boy, with so much promise—with so many promises—must go. With breaking heart, the father took the boy in his arms and held him. How does one bid good-bye to a son?

As the sun crested the hills, he delivered the boy to his mother. Then he gave them bread and a bottle of water.[7] Perhaps he loaded for them an ass. And perhaps Ishmael asked, "Father, where will we get more water?" And perhaps the father raised his hand to the young lad's cheek, and said, "My son"—whom I love—"God will provide." And he "sent [them] away."[8] The father, now separated from his child, watched after him.

I scarce can take it in. One son is unimaginable. But two? Oh, Abraham, father Abraham, how you knew love, joy, and grief.

The Abraham and Isaac story of sacrifice is well-known. Less well-known, it seems, is the Abraham and Ishmael story. But it too was a story of sacrifice—a story, in fact, where Abraham really *had* to sacrifice his son. One father, two sons, two stories of sacrifice, with nearly parallel structures, in successive chapters of scripture. What are the chances of that?

Appearing as it does in the chapter immediately preceding the Isaac story, the Ishmael story provides a context for the Isaac story—a powerful and beautiful context that makes the Isaac story even more majestic than it would be alone.

ISHMAEL'S SEPARATION FROM HIS FATHER

After years of childlessness, Sarah (at the time still called Sarai) begged Abraham (at that time still called Abram) to take her handmaid, Hagar, to wife, that by chance through her she might supply Abraham with children. Abraham "hearkened to the voice of [his wife]" and received Hagar as a second wife.[9] Hagar conceived and bore Abraham a son. They named him Ishmael, as commanded by the angel of the Lord.[10]

Thirteen years later, the Lord appeared to Abraham and established a covenant with him and his seed forever.[11] The Lord announced as well that Sarah would bear him a son and be a mother of nations.[12] Abraham laughed at the notion, as Sarah was ninety and he himself was ninety and nine.[13] "O that Ishmael might live before thee!" he exclaimed, exhorting the Lord to fulfill the promises through the son he already had and loved.[14] The Lord heard his plea for Ishmael, and promised that he would make him fruitful, the father of twelve princes and of a great nation.[15] But he announced that the covenant he was making with Abraham would be renewed through Sarah's son, whom they were to call Isaac.[16]

This chosen son was born a year later. Some two or three years after that, when Isaac was weaned, Sarah saw Ishmael—by then about sixteen—mocking Isaac. The scriptures do not say what Ishmael said or did, but Sarah took great offense at it and demanded that Abraham cast out Hagar and Ishmael from among them, for, she said, "the son of this bondwoman shall not be heir with my son, even with Isaac."[17]

Then, in a heartbreaking verse, we are told that "the thing was very grievous in Abraham's sight because of his son."[18] Of course it would be! Only a few short years earlier it had been his hope to have the Lord's covenant established through Ishmael. Ishmael had been his only son—in his mind, the only child he would ever have. He must have put everything he had into raising and teaching the boy. Ishmael must have been precious to him beyond measure.

And now Sarah was demanding that Abraham cast him out, that he sever the relationship, that Ishmael, in effect, be no more accounted Abraham's son! In effect, she was asking Abraham to sacrifice the boy.

Evidently downtrodden, he took the matter to the Lord in prayer. Probably to his surprise, the Lord added to his grief. He directed Abraham to do as his wife had said! Abraham was to send the young lad and his mother away.

Would Abraham's feelings with regard to Ishmael have been much different from the grief he felt years later when the Lord demanded that he sacrifice his second son as well? Most people have pondered the story of Abraham and Isaac. But what about the story of Abraham and Ishmael? In both stories Abraham is commanded to sacrifice a son. In both stories he is grieved, but rises up early in the morning to prepare provisions. With

Isaac, he is saved from separation by a last-second intervention by an angel. With Ishmael, there is no intervention. Hagar and his beloved Ishmael trudged over the horizon and out of his sight.

It is well known that Isaac is in similitude of Christ. (A chart that lists the likenesses between them is included in Appendix A.) But if Isaac is a type of someone else, it bears asking whether Ishmael might also be a type. In order to ponder that possibility, consider the following elements of the Ishmael story.

- He committed sin.[19]
- He was cast out of his father's presence as a result of that sin.[20]
- He was not, himself, the heir of his father; heirship was instead through the only begotten son.[21]
- He inhabited the lone and dreary world.[22]
- He was subject to death, with no independent power of life.[23]
- He lived a life of hardship.[24]
- God sent messengers to teach him.[25]
- God rescued him from death.[26]

When we consider these elements, it seems that Ishmael can also be considered a type. Ishmael is in similitude of *us*—of fallen man.

THE ISAAC STORY AS THE WAY FOR ISHMAEL (THAT IS, US) TO BE RESCUED FROM DEATH

It is often said that the Isaac story gives us a window into God the Father's experience in offering up his Only Begotten. In reading about Abraham and Isaac, we get a feel for the pain God the Father must have felt in having to allow the suffering of his Son.

But consider how much more we learn about the Father when we see not only that Isaac is Christ, but that *we* are Ishmael. In that heartbreaking story, we see a new aspect of the Father's love for us, his fallen children. We see the pain the Father must feel at our separation from him: "And the thing [sending Ishmael away] was *very grievous in Abraham's sight because of his son.*"[27] Abraham would be losing a son—a son he had raised and nourished for sixteen years. Oh, how he would miss him! The love of

Abraham for his son—and of God for us—is manifest in the care Abraham took *personally* to supply the son and the boy's mother with the means for physical sustenance: "And Abraham rose up early in the morning, and took bread, and a bottle of water, and gave it unto [them]."[28] This was a difficult morning. He could have had someone else face mother and son. But he went himself. He himself prepared and delivered their food. They had to go, but they would leave in the knowledge of his love.

We also see in the Ishmael story how the difficulties we face in life can be an act of love, as the challenges themselves invite us to cry heavenward and allow us to return again to the Father who longs for our return. Abraham had supplied Hagar and Ishmael with a single bottle of water. When it was spent, Ishmael lifted up his voice to God, and the Lord heard his cry and revealed a well of water that would sustain them.[29] In our own empty bottles[30] lie the seeds of our salvation, for it is in our struggles that we turn to Him who is the source of everlasting water.[31]

I believe it is no accident that the Isaac story—the story of redeeming atonement—appears immediately after the Ishmael story—the story of the fall. Considering the stories metaphorically, the Isaac story, as the story of atonement and redemption, is made necessary *because of* the Ishmael story, a story of fall and separation. Seen metaphorically, when Abraham and Isaac made their trek to Moriah, they did so to redeem their son and brother, Ishmael. The way to the redemption of Ishmael (that is, fallen man) is revealed through the Isaac story.

As I mentioned, Isaac is in similitude of the Savior. But he is in similitude only up to a point: He is in the Lord's likeness until Abraham raises the knife. At that moment, the "angel of the Lord" appeared and delivered Isaac from death. For the Savior, there would be no such deliverance.

Who was the delivering agent in the Isaac story? The text says "the angel of the Lord": "And Abraham stretched forth his hand, and took the knife to slay his son. And *the angel of the Lord* called unto him out of heaven, and said, Abraham, Abraham. . . . Lay not thine hand upon the lad."[32]

In a similar situation, years earlier, when Abraham was about to be offered as a sacrifice to pagan gods, he was delivered from death by "the angel of [the Lord's] presence."[33] It seems likely that "the angel of [the Lord's] presence" who called to and delivered Abraham earlier in his life at an altar would be the same being as "the angel of the Lord" who calls to and delivers him, and Isaac, at the altar at Moriah. In the book of Abraham, Abraham tells us that the "angel of [the Lord's] presence" was Jehovah himself: "[And the angel of the Lord's presence said:] Abraham, Abraham, behold, my name is Jehovah, and I have heard thee, and have come down to deliver thee."[34] That the "angel of the Lord" at Moriah might also have been the Lord is supported by the angel's statement: "for now I know that thou fearest God, seeing thou hast not withheld thy son, thine only son *from me*."[35] The angel who delivered Isaac at Moriah may well have been the Savior himself.

Abraham then "lifted up his eyes, and looked, and behold behind him a ram caught in a thicket by his horns: and Abraham went and took the ram, and offered him up for a burnt offering in the stead of his son."[36] In place of Isaac, it was sufficient that a ram—merely caught by his horns, and by implication therefore unblemished—be sacrificed in his stead. Of whom is the ram a type and shadow? Of course, the Lord Jesus Christ.

So the saving aspects of the Isaac story all point to Christ. He is the delivering agent, our Redeemer, the salvation for Isaac, and the infinite and eternal sacrifice on behalf of Ishmael—or fallen man. "He saved others; himself he cannot save," the people ironically mocked,[37] missing the point that the Lord saved us precisely because he *would not* save himself. Isaac and Ishmael both live because one, who didn't have to, died in their—and our—stead.

To Isaac's question, "Where is the lamb for a burnt offering?" Abraham answered: "God will provide himself a lamb."[38] Notice that he didn't say, "God will provide a lamb." Rather, he said, "God will provide *himself* a lamb." How prophetic this answer turned out to be, as the Lord ultimately offered *himself* in sacrifice. The Lamb of God is our redemption. We who have been sent away, as Ishmael, with some bread and a bottle of water, can turn to him for everlasting nourishment. Our father, who has been watching after us prodigals since our departure, awaits our return:

> And when [Ishmael] came to himself, he said, How many
> hired servants of my father's have bread enough and to spare,

and I perish with hunger! I will arise and go to my father, and will say unto him, Father, I have sinned against heaven, and before thee, and am no more worthy to be called thy son: make me as one of thy hired servants.

And he arose, and came to his father. But when he was yet a great way off, his father saw him, and had compassion, and ran, and fell on his neck, and kissed him. . . .

[Ishmael] was dead, and is alive again; and was lost, and is found.[39]

CHAPTER 6

CHRIST AND THE PATRIARCHAL ORDER

His Younger Brother Shall Be Greater Than He

> *"What's all this business about the oldest sons getting the special blessings? Isn't that a little outdated and unfair?"*
>
> Although the Bible seems to set everything up in favor of eldest sons, it turns out that through the generations of the central patriarchs, most of them were, in fact, the youngest sons in their families. Why might that be? What might the Lord be trying to tell us by that? And what does it have to do with us?

In the Isaac and Ishmael dramas, we see the importance placed by Old Testament peoples on the social convention of birthright. In Hebrew, *birthright* and *firstborn* are the same word, showing the strong patriarchal nature of the culture. Birthright privileges passed from father to eldest son, who received a double portion of inheritance compared with any of the other children, and who then assumed the role of father for the family in the event of the father's death. In addition to the temporal advantages and responsibilities that came with the birthright, as we have also seen through Abraham's story with his two sons, key spiritual blessings and responsibilities also passed with the birthright, at least among the spiritually inclined. In the case of Ishmael and Isaac, the question of birthright was invested with the added significance of the promise of the Savior, for Abraham had been promised that the Savior of the world would proceed from the lineage of his chosen, or birthright, son.

As we have discussed, Hagar and Sarah battled each other on behalf of their sons over this issue of birthright, each of them believing that it was her own son's right. It is a battle still being played out on the world stage, as Jews and Christians look to Isaac as the chosen or "birthright" son, while Muslims believe that Ishmael was the chosen one. The importance of the birthright and the blessings attached to it was underscored when the "losers" in this battle (a version of history that Muslims reject, by the way)—Hagar and Ishmael—were cast out as a result of this disagreement.

In the next generation, the birthright battle was renewed. Esau and Jacob competed, as it were, for the birthright blessing, with Jacob receiving it only after his mother, Rebekah, apparently deceived her husband, Isaac, into giving the blessing to him rather than to Esau.[1] The battle renewed again among the twelve sons of Jacob, with the birthright ultimately going, controversially, to Joseph.[2] And then, among Joseph's children, Ephraim received the birthright even though it would have appeared to have been Manasseh's right.

There is almost a fixation throughout these stories on the patriarchal issue of birthright. Just what was the birthright, and why is it such a central issue in these stories?

To begin with, we should be careful to distinguish the temporal patriarchal order from the spiritual patriarchal order. The spiritual patriarchal order, as discussed in chapter 4, refers to the order of the eternal family— each member bound upward in the family as children of Christ, and bound "downward" as fathers and mothers in eternity through the blessings of the Abrahamic covenant. In the eternities, we will be ordered in the kingdom in this way, as sons and daughters and fathers and mothers in the eternal family made possible by Christ, and the priesthood will be held and exercised in this structure, and not in a structure we might recognize today as the structure of Church government. This family ordering and functioning of the priesthood is known as "the patriarchal order of the priesthood." In our day we get a taste for this ordering of the priesthood in the temple, and in the workings within our own homes and families. At the time of the patriarchs, however, there was no church structure, and the priesthood was organized around the family unit. In fact, the priesthood itself was passed down by right among the families of "the fathers,"[3] and families outside this line did not possess it.[4] Even the promise to Abraham that the priesthood—that is, Christ[5]—would come through his lineage was a promise of priesthood within the family context.

In addition to this spiritual patriarchal order, the people of the Old Testament followed conventions that might be thought of as a kind of *social* patriarchal order. These conventions were followed by all families, regardless of whether the family members themselves held priesthood authority. In this social order, eldest sons occupied a favored place in the social structure. They were invested with more authority, more responsibility, and more of the family's economic wealth. In addition to the traditional "double portion" of property received by the birthright son, special family possessions often passed to this son as well—outward emblems of the birthright that were not the birthright blessing in and of themselves. The story of Esau selling his "birthright" to Jacob for a mess of pottage[6] likely involved just such a physical asset (or assets), as it is clear later in the story that Esau and his father both expected Esau to receive the birthright blessing notwithstanding Esau's earlier "sale" of his "birthright."[7] In fact, Esau himself distinguished between the temporal emblems of the birthright and the spiritual birthright when he complained that "[Jacob] took away my birthright; and, behold, now he hath taken away my blessing."[8] The garment Jacob later gave to his son Joseph, known in the scriptures as the "coat of many colors," may well have been an item of worth or historical value to the family—a physical asset that symbolized the birthright. In fact, it is possible that it was this very garment, perhaps along with other valued family items, that Jacob purchased from Esau.

This is all well and good, but a larger question looms: Why birthrights at all? And why the deep, linguistically linked convention that the birthright—whether temporal, spiritual, or both—goes to the firstborn son? Is this simply social custom, or is there more to it? In particular, is there spiritual significance to this convention?

The discussions in chapters 3 and 4 suggest that the idea of the "firstborn" has at least two spiritually significant applications, each of which points us to Christ. The first is Christ's identity as the firstborn of God the Father. As the firstborn of the Father—both in the spirit and in the flesh—any social convention that elevates the position of the firstborn can reasonably be considered to be in similitude of Christ, the whole system inviting us to continually remember him. The scriptures refer to this similitude: "I am the Firstborn,"[9] the Lord declared. To which Paul added, "he is the image of the invisible God, the firstborn of every creature."[10] The narrative of Christ's birth ties him to the birthright tradition as well: Mary "brought forth her firstborn son: and . . . called his name Jesus."[11]

The second spiritually significant meaning of "firstborn" has to do with the necessity that we be born again in Christ and become his "children." In this respect, as discussed in chapter 3, Adam was the "firstborn" of the Son, showing each of us that we also must be born again in Christ and become members of the "church of the Firstborn."[12] "All those," the Lord declared, "who are begotten through me are partakers of the glory of the same, and are the church of the Firstborn."[13]

For at least these two reasons—Christ's position as the firstborn son of God, and the necessity that we become born again through Christ, as was Adam, who was the "firstborn" of Christ in this new birth—the ancient patriarchal conventions surrounding the "birthright" or "firstborn" point us to Christ. When a firstborn male child received the blessings of his father, it was in similitude of the blessings Christ received from the Father of all. And when the birthright sons of ancient families assumed the role of father at their fathers' deaths, taking upon themselves the obligation to care for their families, we are reminded of how Christ, upon our own spiritual and physical separation from our Father, took upon himself the role of father, and assumed the responsibility of caring for the family of man. In these ways, the patriarchal birthright convention points us fully to Christ.

However, if this is the case, the stories of the central Hebrew patriarchs—Abraham, Isaac, Jacob, Joseph, and Ephraim—might seem confusing, because, as it turns out, none among them was the firstborn in his family. In fact, not only were these recipients of the birthright blessings not the firstborn in their families, at least three and possibly four of the five were actually the *last* born, with the exception of Joseph, who barely escaped the last position by being the eleventh of Jacob's twelve sons (and perhaps Abraham as well, who appears not to have been the firstborn, but who may have been either the second or the third and final son[14]). This exceptional similarity among these recipients of the birthright is the first of an interesting pattern of similarities between them. Consider the following:

ABRAHAM	ISAAC	JACOB	JOSEPH	EPHRAIM
Youngest (or second youngest) son	Youngest son	Youngest son	Eleventh son of twelve	Youngest son
Father tried to kill him	Father prepared to kill him	Brother tried to kill him	Brothers tried to kill him	
Found refuge in foreign land	Found refuge in foreign land	Found refuge in foreign land	Found refuge in foreign land	
Wife barren	Wife barren	Wife barren		
Wife conceives though power of God	Wife conceives through power of God	Wife conceives through power of God		
Wife designates the birthright son	Wife designates the birthright son	Birthright son is the son of the favored wife		

So what are we to make of this multigenerational exception to the "firstborn gets birthright" convention, and to the continued similarities that emerge afterward?

With respect to the birthright, the differences in two of the generations can perhaps be explained upon technical grounds. First, although Isaac was the second born, he was the firstborn of the first wife, suggesting that in ancient polygynous societies the birthright had to do not only with birth order but also with marriage order. The first wife appears to have occupied a favored position in the social structure, her firstborn son having first claim to the birthright, even when he was not, in fact, born first. The operation of the birthright within polygynous societies is developed further in the case of Joseph. Although Joseph was the eleventh born, he was the firstborn of Jacob's second wife, Rachel. The firstborn of Jacob's first wife, Leah, was Reuben, who was also the firstborn of all the sons. As such, Reuben would appear to have been entitled to the birthright under any application of the rules. However, because he "defiled his father's bed"[15] by committing adultery with one of his father's wives (Bilhah),[16] his birthright was taken from him and given to another.[17] This removal of the blessing because of sin shows—and this is important—that the birthright position was a function not only of birth order but also of righteousness. That the birthright passed not to the first wife's (Leah's) second son but to the second wife's (Rachel's) *first* son implies a second application of the birthright rule in polygynous societies: If the birthright is removed from the firstborn of one wife, it moves not to the second son, but to the next "firstborn" son, which in this case was Joseph, the eleventh son overall.

So with respect to Isaac and Joseph, it would appear that the mechanical operation of birthright rules and practices in polygynous contexts might explain why they each received the birthright in their families. However, there is no such mechanical explanation for Abraham, Jacob, or Ephraim. Jacob's and Ephraim's cases are particularly interesting. Jacob received the birthright blessing only because his mother, Rebekah, who had been told by the Lord that her "elder son shall serve the younger,"[18] helped pass Jacob off as Esau, whom Isaac favored.[19] Two generations later, Joseph fully intended for his firstborn son, Manasseh, to receive the birthright. However, Grandfather Jacob, to Joseph's displeasure, said, regarding the eldest, "his younger brother shall be greater than he,"[20] and he extended his right hand to the younger son, Ephraim, and gave him the birthright blessing.[21] In each of these cases, the Lord specifically instructed that the birthright be given to the last of the sons.

So what are we to make of this? If the patriarchal birthright system is in similitude of Christ, then why would the birth orders of these central patriarchs each violate the rule? Consider this possibility: that the exceptions to the rule are just as much in similitude of Christ as the rule itself.

For the reasons discussed earlier, the rule itself can be thought to be in similitude of Christ's *spiritual* role and identity. By contrast, exceptions to the rule can be thought to be in similitude of Christ's *temporal* role and identity. That is, the one who would come as Messiah would not come in the way most would expect. He would not be mighty in appearance or in political or military power. He would be a Savior who to the spiritually undiscerning would appear unable to save even himself—one whom Isaiah described as having "no form nor comeliness; and when we shall see him, there is no beauty that we should desire him . . . despised and rejected of men . . . esteem[ed as] stricken, smitten of God, and afflicted."[22] In short, the Savior of the world would not be great in the eyes of the world. He would come in a form that was unexpected, and his lowly station in life would hide his divine origin and mission from those who were without faith. He was, as it were, in the eyes of the world, the younger son—one without station or claim to position or greatness. He was the second son in another respect as well—what Paul called the "last Adam"[23]—as he came to redeem the world from the effect of the transgression of the "first" son, Adam.

In this second respect, then, the rule of primogeniture is important not because of what the rule itself communicates, but rather because of what the *exception* communicates, which message was made possible only because there was such a rule that could be violated. Said more plainly, one reason the rule may have been created was to emphasize the *exception* to the rule, in order to communicate a central truth about the Lord's identity. The exception also communicates a central truth about our own identity: Exaltation does not come as a matter of right, whether by physical birth or by religious affiliation. Using the birthright convention metaphorically, being an "eldest son"—either because one comes from a certain lineage, for example, or simply belongs to a certain faith—does not entitle one to the blessings of the firstborn. Such blessings come through being born again in Christ, whereby we become members of the "church of the Firstborn,"[24] and therefore become joint-heirs with him.[25]

Failure to understand the relevance of the exceptions to the rule led many at the time of Christ both to miss who he was and to misunderstand who they themselves were. Mere membership in the family of Abraham did not entitle them to his blessings. The blessings of heaven did not come then, nor do they come now, merely by blood or paper membership in any lineage or church. Rather, the blessings of heaven come to those who, to the best of their abilities given the knowledge they possess, come unto Christ. All of us, whatever our lineage or affiliation, are prodigal sons after the manner of the Lord's parable that we discussed in the last chapter.[26] Those who insist upon their "right" as eldest sons are as the eldest son in that parable—left out of the Lord's feast. Only the humbly repentant attend. The parable of the prodigal son ends without us knowing whether the eldest son ended up attending the feast of his father. He would do so only if he realized how he too was prodigal, and repented of his sin of feeling entitled to his father's blessings, the same as his younger brother came to realize his own unworthiness after he had squandered his own "entitlements." The common pattern among the central patriarchs communicates, among other things, that we are entitled to nothing in and of ourselves, and that we need to repent of such feelings of entitlement if we have them.

The patterns that continue among the patriarchs beyond the common fact that they were not actual firstborn sons also point us to Christ. Himself a "youngest son" in the manner of his station and appearance, Christ too, like Abraham, Isaac, Jacob, and Joseph before him, was the focus of violence and intended for death by members of his "family"—in the Savior's case, by those of his same house of Israel. He too found refuge in a foreign land, when Joseph and Mary were commanded to flee into Egypt. Like Isaac, Jacob, and Joseph, he too was the product of a miraculous birth, being born of one who should have been barren—a virgin. She, like Sarah, Rebekah, and Rachel before her, conceived through the power of God. And as was the case with these ancient matriarchs, the birthright son was identified in large part by the calling, place, and miraculous conception by his mother.

It is interesting that while the parallelism between Abraham, Isaac, and Jacob appears to be complete, in Joseph's and Ephraim's cases the parallelism seems incomplete. In Ephraim's case, for example, he appears similar to the others only with respect to the initial commonality: his status as a younger son. Are these exceptions to this pattern among the patriarchs significant in the way that the exception to the standard rule of primogeniture appears to be significant?

I would suggest the answer to this question is yes. To begin with, Abraham, Isaac, and Jacob share something else in common that the others do not: The Savior was promised to come through their lines. The promise of the Lord's seed was split from the rest of the birthright blessing in Joseph's generation. Jacob, whose name had by then been changed to Israel,[27] blessed Joseph's brother, Judah, with the blessing of the Lord's seed.[28] He then conferred the rest of the blessings upon Joseph[29] and upon Joseph's son Ephraim.[30] You will notice that the similarities between Abraham, Isaac, and Jacob that Joseph does not share are similarities that foreshadow the Savior's birth—barren wife who conceives through the power of God, and so on. Since these characteristics foreshadow the birth of the Lord, it is entirely proper that they would cease where the line of the Savior's birth turns elsewhere.

In the next chapter, I will suggest an even more important reason for the apparent break in the patriarchal patterns between Jacob and Joseph. We will explore how the later characteristics that appear to be missing in Joseph and Ephraim—regarding a barren wife, for example, and bringing forth a child through the power of God—actually are not missing at all. They are just fulfilled at a later time—not by Joseph and Ephraim in their own generations, but in the generations of their spiritual posterity, through whom the gospel would be restored to a barren earth in the latter days, in a foreign land of refuge.

PART THREE

CHRIST AND
THE HOUSE OF ISRAEL

CHAPTER 7

TEMPORAL AND SPIRITUAL SALVATION THROUGH JOSEPH

God Did Send Me Before You to Preserve Life

> The story of Joseph in Egypt is one of the most stunning in all of scripture. There is far more to Joseph and his story than meets the eye, however. For example, do you know that the story of his saving Israel from the drought is exactly parallel to the story of how Israel is being saved through the Book of Mormon in the latter days (a parallelism that was revealed by his dreams)? And do you know the extent and depth to which Joseph's story is parallel to the Savior's? And how his brothers' stories are parallel to ours? And how the story of the reunion of Joseph with his brothers is also therefore a story of our reunion with the Lord? And how that story will stir your soul when you see it?
>
> Joseph is as relevant today as ever. After all, he dreamed about us.

Seventeen-year-old Joseph, the eleventh of Israel's twelve sons, was beloved by his father. The scriptures tell us that "Israel loved Joseph more than all his children."[1] Seeing "that their father loved him more than all his brethren," Joseph's ten older brothers "hated [Joseph], and could not speak peaceably unto him."[2]

United in envy, Joseph's brothers fanned the fires of hate. One day, as they saw Joseph approaching from "afar off," they conspired to kill him.[3] "Behold, this dreamer cometh," they said to each other,[4] apparently referring to two dreams Joseph had recently recounted to them.[5] Then, after devising a plan to slay him (a plan they later revised, settling instead for selling him into slavery), they exclaimed with a collective sneer: "We shall see what will become of his *dreams*."[6]

What becomes of his dreams is a majestic parallel fulfillment that spans the centuries from Joseph's day to the present.

This is how Joseph described his first dream: "And he said unto [his brothers], Hear, I pray you, this dream which I have dreamed: For behold, we were binding sheaves in the field, and, lo, my sheaf arose, and also stood upright; and, behold, your sheaves stood round about, and made obeisance to my sheaf."[7] His brothers took offense at his telling: "Shalt thou indeed reign over us? or shalt thou indeed have dominion over us? And they hated him yet the more for his dreams, and for his words."[8]

In the very next verse, Joseph related his second dream: "And [Joseph] dreamed yet another dream, and told it his brethren, and said, Behold, I have dreamed a dream more; and, behold, the sun and the moon and the eleven stars made obeisance to me."[9] At report of this dream, Jacob rebuked his son: "Shall I and thy mother and thy brethren indeed come to bow ourselves to thee to the earth?"[10] But the text suggests that Jacob's reaction changed as he pondered the dream: For "his brethren envied him; *but his father observed the saying.*"[11]

What are we to make of these two dreams? On one level, the interpretations appear obvious: Both imply that the family would bow before Joseph. But why *two* dreams? And if two dreams, why two *different* dreams? What meaning might there be in their similarities and differences?

While both dreams imply that Joseph's family would bow to him, the dreams are different in at least two significant ways. Only the second dream implies, for example, that those paying obeisance to Joseph would include his mother and father. And secondly, the dream elements changed significantly from the first to the second dream: instead of sheaves of grain, in the second dream Joseph saw heavenly bodies—the sun, the moon, and the stars.

What might be implied by these differences? Consider this possibility: Perhaps by these two dreams the Lord was communicating related but different points. The earthly elements of the first dream imply that Joseph would in some sense rule over his family temporally; the otherworldly elements of the second dream imply that Joseph would in some sense rule over his family spiritually. The possibility of a spiritual interpretation to the second dream that reaches beyond the temporal is supported by Jacob's expressed interpretation that Joseph's mother, *who had died a few years earlier,* would bow to Joseph.

So the dreams may suggest that Joseph would be instrumental in bringing both temporal *and* spiritual deliverance or salvation to his family. If so, the parallel structure of the two dreams suggests that however events transpired, the temporal and spiritual salvation stories would unfold in parallel ways.

THE STORY OF TEMPORAL DELIVERANCE: A PATTERN OF DELIVERANCE

Ironically, the story of Joseph's role in saving the house of Israel from physical death begins with a plan by the children of Israel to kill him. After first conspiring to kill him, his jealous older brothers threw him into a pit and then sold him to Ishmeelite merchants who were passing by. At the time, Joseph must have wondered if he would ever see his family again. This is the first element of the story of temporal salvation at the hand of Joseph: *He was broken off to a place apart from the house of Israel.*

Joseph's captors took him to Egypt, where they sold him to Potiphar, "an officer of Pharaoh, captain of the guard, an Egyptian."[12] He would reside in Egypt for two decades without his family's knowledge, and would remain in Egypt until his death at the age of 110.[13] This is the second element of the story of temporal salvation: *Joseph resided in a distant land, unknown to his family.*

Potiphar soon noticed that "the Lord made all that [Joseph] did to prosper in his hand,"[14] and he made Joseph "overseer in his house, and over all he had."[15] While in Potiphar's service, Joseph resisted the advances of Potiphar's wife,[16] who then bore false witness against him and caused that he be thrown into prison.[17] Joseph spent the next several years in that prison. If not for his interpretation of the dreams of two fellow prisoners, he might have died there.

Two years after Joseph had correctly interpreted the dreams of his fellow inmates, he was summoned to interpret two dreams that were troubling Pharaoh. Joseph was able to interpret their meaning: seven years of famine would follow seven years of plenty.[18] Joseph then suggested a plan of action to store up food against the terrible years that were coming.[19] So pleased was Pharaoh at the wisdom and discretion of Joseph that he placed Joseph over his entire house and kingdom![20] Joseph then began preparing Egypt against the coming years of famine, storing up grain and other necessary items in a massive, seven-year effort.[21]

After the seven years of plenty passed, the seven years of famine bore down upon them. "And the dearth was in all lands."[22] Because of Joseph's storage campaign in Egypt, however, "in all the land of Egypt there was bread."[23] "And all countries came into Egypt to Joseph for to buy corn; because that the famine was so sore in all lands."[24] These events comprise the third element of the story of temporal salvation: *Joseph's experiences in the distant land prepared the way for the salvation of Israel.*

The famine raged in Canaan, and Jacob feared for the survival of his family.[25] When Jacob heard that there was corn in Egypt, he sent his sons to buy some, so that the family "may live, and not die."[26] The scriptural scene then moves to Egypt: "And the sons of Israel came to buy corn among those that came: for the famine was in the land of Canaan. And Joseph was the governor over the land, and he it was that sold to all the people of the land."[27]

Seeing his brothers, "Joseph knew [them], but they knew him not."[28] After a series of events spanning chapters 42 through 45 of Genesis, they would come to know him. And after coming to know him, they and their families would be rescued from the remaining years of the famine. Had Jacob not heard that there was corn in Egypt, the house of Israel likely would have perished. Therefore, the information about corn in Egypt was the beginning of temporal salvation for Israel. And though they didn't yet know it, information about corn in Egypt was also the beginning of knowledge concerning their lost brother—for the story of corn in Egypt was *his* story. Accordingly, the fourth element of the temporal salvation story is that *Israel began to be saved when they learned of Joseph, who was separated.*

When Joseph's brothers came to Egypt for food, we are told that they "came, and bowed down themselves before him with their faces to the earth."[29] Seeing this, and recognizing his brothers, "Joseph remembered the dreams which he dreamed of them,"[30] and he recognized the significance of the bow. *This bow was the fulfillment of the final element in the prophecy of the story of temporal salvation.*

After Jacob came down to Egypt with his family, he confirmed the significance of the event in tender words to Joseph: "Therefore, O my son, he hath blessed me in raising thee up to be a servant unto me, in saving my house from death; In delivering my people, thy brethren, from famine which was sore in the land. . . . *Thou hast prevailed, and thy father's house hath bowed down unto thee, even as it was shown unto thee, before thou wast sold into Egypt by the hands of thy brethren.*"[31]

Jacob recognized that Joseph's role in providing food to the house of Israel and saving them from death was a direct fulfillment of the prophecy communicated in Joseph's dreams. But Jacob also recognized, as Joseph's dual dreams suggested, that there would be yet a future deliverance at Joseph's hand—this one a spiritual deliverance: "Thy brethren *shall* bow down unto thee, from generation to generation," he declared, "unto the fruit of thy loins for ever; For thou *shalt be* a light unto my people, *to deliver them in the days of their captivity, from bondage; and to bring salvation unto them, when they are altogether bowed down under sin.*"[32]

The parallel nature of Joseph's dreams suggests that this future spiritual deliverance would parallel the pattern of deliverance established in Egypt. This pattern was as follows:

1. Joseph was broken off to a place apart from the rest of the house of Israel.
2. Joseph resided in a distant land, unknown to his family.
3. The experiences of Joseph in the distant land prepared the way for the salvation of Israel.
4. Israel began to be saved when they learned of Joseph who was separated.
5. The house of Israel bowed before Joseph.

As we shall see, Israel's spiritual deliverance unfolds in precisely the same way.

SPIRITUAL DELIVERANCE THROUGH JOSEPH:
FOLLOWING THE PATTERN OF THE TEMPORAL
DELIVERANCE IN EGYPT

Just before his death, Joseph prophesied that history would repeat itself. A branch of his posterity would be broken off and separated from the house of Israel, just as he had been broken off and separated from his father's house: "And it shall come to pass that [Israel] shall be scattered again; and *a branch [of the fruit of the loins of Joseph] shall be broken off, and shall be carried into a far country.*"[33]

This prophecy is fulfilled in the story of Lehi, a descendant of Joseph,[34] who was led away from the land of Israel to a land apart. Moroni confirms the historical parallelism: "For as Joseph brought his father down into the land of Egypt . . . the Lord brought a remnant of the seed of Joseph, that they should perish not, even as he was merciful unto the father of Joseph, that he should perish not."[35]

Accordingly, the story of Israel's spiritual salvation began just as the story of their temporal salvation did, with Joseph being broken off to a place apart from the rest of the house of Israel.

The second parallel element is introduced in the blessing Moses pronounced upon the tribe of Joseph: "Blessed of the Lord be *his land,* for the precious things of heaven, for the dew, and for the deep that coucheth beneath, And for the precious fruits brought forth by the sun, and for the precious things put forth by the moon, And for the chief things of the ancient mountains, and for the precious things of the lasting hills."[36]

That Moses confirms a land upon the tribe of Joseph is interesting in light of the fact that the tribe of Joseph itself was not given a land inheritance when the Israelites entered Canaan.[37] Joseph's sons, Ephraim and Manasseh, received land inheritances in Canaan,[38] so Moses' blessing of land to Joseph may be in reference to the lands to be given to his sons. However, the Book of Mormon suggests a different interpretation. Lehi's son Nephi was promised that his family would be led to a land that had been prepared as a land of promise for his father's posterity: "And inasmuch as ye shall keep my commandments, ye . . . shall be led to a land of promise; yea even a land which I have prepared for you; yea a land which is choice above all other lands."[39]

In the book of Ether we learn that the land inherited by Lehi's family was precisely the land that had been set apart for Joseph: "And [Ether] spake also . . . that a New Jerusalem should be built up upon this land, unto the remnant of the seed of Joseph, for which things there has been a type. For as Joseph brought his father down into the land of Egypt, even so he died there; wherefore, the Lord brought a remnant of the seed of Joseph out of the land of Jerusalem, that he might be merciful unto the seed of Joseph that they should perish not, even as he was merciful unto the father of Joseph that he should perish not. *Wherefore, the remnant of the house of Joseph shall be built upon this land; and it shall be a land of their inheritance;* and they shall build up a holy city unto the Lord, like unto the Jerusalem of old."[40]

So we see that Lehi was led away by the hand of the Lord into a land that had been prepared as an inheritance for his seed—the seed of Joseph. Their inheritance was the land of "ancient mountains" and "[ever]lasting hills"—the American continent. As it was with Joseph anciently, those who remained behind in the original promised land knew nothing of the whereabouts or life of their separated brother: "And behold, this is the land of your inheritance," the Savior announced to the seed of Joseph in the Americas, "and the Father hath given it unto you. And not at any time hath the Father given me commandment that I should tell it unto your brethren at Jerusalem."[41] They "know not of you."[42] Once again, Joseph resided in a distant land, unknown to his brethren—so the *second* parallel element to the temporal salvation story is fulfilled in the story of Lehi.

The experiences of the remnant of the house of Joseph in the new land are recorded in the Book of Mormon. Joseph prophesied that this book, the book to be written by his seed, would come forth and join the book written by the seed of Judah: "Wherefore the fruit of [the loins of Joseph] shall write, and the fruit of the loins of Judah shall write; and that which shall be written by the fruit of [the loins of Joseph], and also that which shall be written by the fruit of the loins of Judah, shall grow together."[43] Ezekiel made the same prophecy: "Moreover, thou son of man, take thee one stick, and write upon it, For Judah, and for the children of Israel his companions: then take another stick, and write upon it, For Joseph, the stick of Ephraim, and for all the house of Israel his companions: And join them one to another into one stick; and they shall become one in thine hand."[44]

So the recorded history of the seed of Joseph in the distant land would join with the recorded history of the seed of Judah. But to what effect? Here the *third* element of Joseph's story has a spiritual parallel: According to prophecy, the recorded new-world experiences of the seed of Joseph would prepare the way for the salvation of the house of Israel.[45] The events in the new land would have power to deliver Israel. So the third parallel element—that the experiences of Joseph in the distant land shall prepare the way for salvation for the house of Israel—is fulfilled in the story of the Book of Mormon, the book written by the descendants of Lehi and Joseph.

In the story of temporal salvation, deliverance came when the members of the house of Israel came to the knowledge of their brother Joseph in Egypt. The parallelism we are exploring suggests that spiritual salvation likewise will come to the house of Israel when they come to the knowledge of the separated seed of Joseph through the Book of Mormon. This is precisely the sign of salvation revealed by the Savior: "And verily I say unto you, I give unto you a sign, that ye may know the time when these things shall be about to take place—that I shall gather in, from their long dispersion, my people, O house of Israel, and shall establish again among them my Zion. . . . And when [Israel] shall begin to know [the record of the seed of Joseph]—it shall be a sign unto them, that they may know that the work of the Father hath already commenced unto the fulfilling of the covenant which he hath made unto the people who are of the house of Israel."[46] In the ancient story, the gentiles knew of Joseph before his brethren did. In addition, it was the work of the gentile Egyptians in gathering food at Joseph's direction that would ultimately provide deliverance to Israel. The salvation that would save Israel in Egypt also saved the gentiles in and around Egypt.

The ancient story was in similitude of the salvation then future: Just as knowledge of Joseph saved ancient Israel from death, so knowledge of Joseph will save *latter-day* Israel from death—the first salvation physical, and the second spiritual. As in the ancient story, the gentiles in the later story would be the first to learn of and enjoy the deliverance, and it would be by the efforts of the gentiles that deliverance for Israel would be possible:

> For after [the Book of Mormon] shall come forth, and be written unto the Gentiles, and sealed up again unto the Lord, there shall be many which shall believe the words which are written; and they shall carry them forth unto the remnant of our seed. And then shall the remnant of our seed know concerning us, how that we came out from Jerusalem, and that they are descendants of the Jews. And the gospel of Jesus Christ shall be declared among them; wherefore, they shall be restored unto the knowledge of their fathers, and also to the knowledge of Jesus Christ, which was had among their fathers. And then shall they rejoice; for they shall know that it is a blessing unto them from the hand of God; and their scales of darkness shall begin to fall from their eyes; and many generations shall not pass away among them, save they shall be a pure and a delightsome people. And it shall come to pass that the Jews which are scattered also shall begin to believe in Christ; and they shall begin to gather in upon the face of the land; and as many as shall believe in Christ shall also become a delightsome people.[47]

The knowledge of Joseph recorded in the Book of Mormon is the beginning of the deliverance prepared for Israel. Accordingly, Israel will be saved as they come to a knowledge of Joseph through the book, so the *fourth* parallel element is fulfilled in the spiritual gathering occasioned through the Book of Mormon.

This record of Joseph—the Book of Mormon—was revealed to the world through the hands of a descendant bearing the same name, just as Joseph of Israel prophesied anciently.[48] Joseph Smith was of the lineage of Joseph of Israel through Ephraim, the holder of the birthright in Israel; "[he] was a pure Ephraimite."[49] The gospel was restored to a barren earth through an Ephraimite, and the gathering of the Saints in the latter days has to this point been largely a gathering of members of the tribe of Ephraim—who, as holders of the birthright in Israel, are to restore the remaining tribes to the blessings in the gospel.[50]

Latter-day revelation reveals that Israel will come to Zion, or the New Jerusalem, which is to be built by Joseph/Ephraim on the American continent, and there bow down and be crowned with the blessings of spiritual deliverance: "And [the house of Israel] shall bring forth their rich treasures unto the children of Ephraim, my servants. And the boundaries of the everlasting hills shall tremble at their presence. *And there shall they fall down and be crowned with glory,* even in Zion, by the hands of the servants of the Lord, even the children of Ephraim. And they shall be filled with songs of everlasting joy."[51]

The event so prophesied is the fulfillment of the *fifth and final* element of the parallel stories of salvation. Just as foreshadowed by their bow before Joseph in Egypt, the house of Israel will bow to him in a spiritual sense as well: They will come to Joseph—the restored Church—to receive the blessings and ordinances of salvation. As Jacob prophesied regarding the parallel spiritual deliverance, "Thy brethren shall bow down unto thee, from generation to generation, unto the fruit of thy loins for ever."[52]

Joseph's brothers, filled with envy and hate, were unable to see that this bow would be a bow of gratitude. By bowing to Joseph, they would be "crowned with glory" and "filled with songs of everlasting joy." The temporal deliverance obtained when they discovered their brother millennia earlier pales in comparison with the spiritual deliverance obtained through the discovery of their brother in these latter days.

JOSEPH AS TEMPORAL AND SPIRITUAL DELIVERER: A TYPE AND SHADOW

Consider the majesty of Joseph's deliverance: He saved Israel from physical death, and *will* save Israel from spiritual death. In overcoming the two deaths, the beloved son of Israel is in similitude of the Beloved Son of the Father.

This deep similitude is but the last in a life that was in nearly every respect parallel to the Master's. As the chosen instrument of temporal and spiritual deliverance, Joseph's path of preparation points in striking similitude to the path of paths—the solitary way of the Savior of all. The following are true both of Joseph and the Lord:

- He is the beloved son.[53]
- He reveals that he will rule over Israel.[54]
- The children of Israel reject him out of jealousy and hate.[55]
- Notwithstanding their mistreatment of him, he seeks out his brethren on behalf of his father.[56]
- When they cannot be found where they were thought to be, he goes farther. He will go wherever he needs to go to do the work of his father.[57]
- But the children of Israel conspire to kill him.[58]
- He is betrayed by the hand of Judah—or, in the Greek, Judas.[59]
- He is sold for the price of a slave of his age.[60]
- This very attempt to destroy him sets in motion events that will eventually save the house of Israel from death.
- He resists temptation perfectly.[61]
- He begins his public mission of preparing salvation for Israel at the age of thirty.[62]
- He provides bread for Israel, saving them from death.[63]
- He offers that bread without price.[64]
- In the offering of that bread, he offers the opportunity to repent.[65]

The extent of the parallelism is remarkable. When we understand that Joseph is a similitude of the Savior, the relationship with his brothers suddenly takes on a very personal significance. For, in an important way, Joseph's brothers are in similitude of *us*. Through our sins, we, in effect, have thrown the Savior into the pit. *We* are the cause of his suffering—suffering that has a type in Joseph. In this light, the following episode in Joseph's story is unspeakably moving. It is the story of the Savior's offering to *us*:

> Then Joseph could not refrain himself before all them that stood by him; and he cried, Cause every man to go out from me. And there stood no man with him, while Joseph made

himself known unto his brethren. *And he wept aloud:* and the Egyptians and the house of Pharaoh heard.

And Joseph said unto his brethren, I am Joseph; doth my father yet live? And his brethren could not answer him; for they were troubled at his presence.

And Joseph said unto his brethren, Come near to me, I pray you. And they came near. And he said, I am Joseph your brother, whom ye sold into Egypt. Now therefore be not grieved, nor angry with yourselves, that ye sold me hither: for God did send me before you to preserve life. For these two years hath the famine been in the land: and yet there are five years, in the which there shall neither be earing nor harvest. And God sent me before you to preserve you a posterity in the earth, and to save your lives by a great deliverance.

So now it was not you that sent me hither, but God: and he hath made me a father to Pharaoh, and lord of all his house, and a ruler throughout all the land of Egypt. . . .

And he fell upon his brother Benjamin's neck, and wept; and Benjamin wept upon his neck. Moreover he kissed all his brethren, and wept upon them: and after that his brethren talked with him.[66]

Like Joseph before his brethren, the Savior stands before us. He weeps for us—not for the pain we have caused him, but because we hold ourselves back from him out of guilt over the pain we have caused him. Each of our sins has been an offense against him, a failure to love him. And now the damning weight of those sins keeps us slinking in the shadows. "We are verily guilty concerning our brother," we say with Joseph's kin, "in that we saw the anguish of his soul, when he besought us, and we would not hear."[67] Pained by our sins, we cannot bear to look upon him who was pained on account of our sins. Embarrassed, afraid, feeling unworthy, we cannot go to him. And so he weeps—for the separation that we maintain even when he is before us.

But he calls to us, ever lovingly. *"Come near to me, I pray you."* Only in coming to him can we be relieved of the pain caused and maintained by our continued refusal to come to him. Our sin was our flight from him. Repentance is our return. And so he calls, and prays that we might come again.

Who can fathom this love?

We learn of this love through the similitude of Joseph. Temporal and spiritual salvation is in him of whom Joseph is a type. For "God did send [him] before [us] to preserve life." Through Joseph and his sin-bound brothers, the Lord's salvation is made clear. If there was hope for them, there is hope also for us.

CHAPTER 8

THE EXODUS: DELIVERANCE THROUGH THE DELIVERER

I Will Bring You Out . . . I Will Free You . . . I Will Redeem You

"Much as I like the Moses story, I don't see what it has to do with me."

What if Egypt (the great world power to the west from which Israel goes forth to the world) has a latter-day parallel—the United States (the great world power in the West from which the gospel is going forth to the world)? And what if we in the latter days are in bondage, just as the Israelites were in bondage in Egypt? What if we too, like the Israelites from Egypt, need an exodus? From what bondage might we need to escape?

Oh, and what was with all those plagues in Egypt, anyway? Why did the Lord go to all that trouble? And do the plagues have anything to do with us today?

After years of Israel's hospitable residence in Egypt, "there arose up a new king over Egypt, [who] knew not Joseph."[1] Joseph and the rest of the immediate children of Israel had died. (They lived long lives—Joseph, for example, to age 110, and his brother Levi to age 137.) During these many years, the house of Israel had "increased abundantly, and multiplied, and waxed exceeding mighty; and the land was filled with them."[2] Out of fear, the new pharaoh had the Israelites enslaved. From that point forward, Israel's life in Egypt was bitter—made difficult by hard bondage.[3]

The Bible is ambiguous as to the length of the Israelites' stay in Egypt. On the one hand, in what appears to be a clear and definitive statement, Exodus 12:40–41 says that the period they lived in "Egypt, was [430] years," and that it was "at the end of the [430] years, [to the very day,] that all the hosts of the Lord went out from the land of Egypt." On the other hand, the genealogy supplied in the sixth chapter of Exodus, if complete, couldn't possibly support such a length of time, but suggests a sojourn of no more than 220 years between Israel's entry into Egypt and its exodus.[4]

Whether the Israelites spent 200 or 400 years in Egypt, one can imagine the impact such a stay would have had on their cultural and religious beliefs. Egypt was the premiere power in the world, and had been for some time. The pyramids had been standing for some 1,000 years as a testament to the preeminence and power of the Egyptian culture. To the young of a relatively small band of people, a people who were enslaved, who were compelled to build up Egyptian shrines and treasure cities,[5] the Egyptian splendor and success must have been impressive—perhaps in some ways even intoxicating.

The Egyptians worshipped many gods. Among these were Hopi (the god of the Nile/water), Heqt (the goddess in whom the frog had been deified), the bull gods Apis and Mnevis, the cow god Hathor, the ram god Khnum, the sun god Ra (or Re), and Pharaoh, who was himself considered a god. In the context of the overpowering might of Egypt, these gods must have looked powerful to Egyptians and non-Egyptians alike. To the generations of Israel born in Egypt, Egyptian success must have made the Egyptian culture and gods alluring. (Witness, for example, Israel's quick slide into idol worship after the miraculous exodus.[6])

In light of their enslavement, the Israelites had a real problem: They were kept from the covenant land that had been promised to their fathers Abraham, Isaac, and Jacob. Somehow, in order to fulfill prophecy, Israel had to be taken out of Egypt. But, as we have discussed in earlier chapters, the covenants made to Abraham, and renewed through Isaac and Jacob, were spiritual as well as temporal. Or, more precisely, the temporal aspects of those covenants were types and shadows of the greater spiritual blessings. The biggest problem for the Israelites was not that they were stuck in Egypt. The biggest problem was that Egypt had become stuck in them. In order to fulfill prophecy, Egypt—including the allure of Egypt—had to be taken out of Israel. Unless Israel could be reoriented to Christ, the blessings pronounced upon Abraham, Isaac, and Jacob would be for naught.

Our situation is analogous. We too are separated from our promised land—that is, we are separated from God and are not of ourselves worthy to enter into his presence. That is our problem. But we have a bigger problem: *We have come to enjoy the things that will keep us separated from God.* As with the Israelites, our hearts are not fully turned to the Savior.

There is another way in which our latter-day situation mirrors the story of the Israelites in Egypt. Considering the fact that Egypt was by far the dominant power in the world at the time—a country in the "West," in which Israel was nourished by a prophet named Joseph, and from which Israel would then spread to fill the earth—we are living in a latter-day parallel universe. For, beginning in the preeminent Western power in the modern world, the United States, the house of Israel has again been nourished by a prophet named Joseph, and Israel is now going forth to fill the world. Isaiah himself appears to use the name *Egypt* to describe the latter-day United States,[7] and, like ancient Israel, latter-day Israel is in danger of becoming intoxicated by the power of the modern culture—the gods, for example, of entertainment, technology, and commerce. If the gods of our culture have captivated us to any degree, then we too, like the ancient Israelites, are in bondage in Egypt.

Given the similitudes, the Israelite story is *our* story, and their predicament is *our* predicament. This means that their exodus must be *our* exodus as well, and the key to their deliverance is likely to be the way to our own.

The heart and soul of the Exodus story—and our story—is found in Exodus 6:6–8: "I am the Lord, and I will bring you out from under the burdens of the Egyptians, and I will rid you out of their bondage, and I will redeem you with a stretched out arm, and with great judgments: And I will take you to me for a people, and I will be to you a God. . . . And I will bring you in unto the [promised] land . . . I am the Lord."

Those promises reflect both a physical and spiritual deliverance. Significantly, each promise begins with the words "I will." If we are to be brought out from under our burdens, or freed from bondage, or redeemed, or accounted children of God, or awarded a place in the eternities, it will be because Christ has affirmatively reached out to us with "a stretched out arm." Without him there is no promise, for he *is* the promise.

Christ's centrality is emphasized throughout the exodus story through three elements: the manner of Moses' call as deliverer, the nature of the deliverance itself, and the nature of the deliverer.

THE MANNER OF MOSES' CALL AS DELIVERER

For forty years after his escape from Egypt, Moses lived in the land of Midian with his father-in-law, Jethro, the priest of Midian. It seems fitting, given that Moses would end up delivering Israel from bondage in similitude of the Savior's deliverance, that he spent these years tending Jethro's flocks.[8] Like the Great Shepherd, Moses too knew what it meant to care for his sheep.

On one such occasion, Moses "led the flock to the backside of the desert, and came to the mountain of God."[9] There, the Lord appeared to him in a flame of fire. The Joseph Smith Translation says: "And *again,* the presence of the Lord appeared unto him, in a flame of fire in the midst of a bush."[10] Apparently this was not the first time the Lord had appeared to Moses—perhaps not even the first time on that mountain. Nor would it be the last.

Moses' mountain of God was no ordinary mountain; the Lord declared it to be "holy ground."[11] Anciently, mountains were symbolic of the temple. Where there was no temple, the Lord would make use of mountains for his divine purposes.[12] According to Joseph Smith, Moses received the endowment on a high mountain.[13] Joseph Fielding Smith made a similar statement: "No man can get the fulness of the priesthood outside of the temple of the Lord. There was a time when that could be done, for the Lord could give these things on the mountain tops—no doubt that is where Moses got it."[14]

It seems likely that Moses received his full endowment of the priesthood on the mountain, at the hand of the Lord himself. And what would that have involved? Concerning temple ordinances, Brigham Young stated: "Your endowment is, to receive all those ordinances in the house of the Lord, which are necessary for you, after you have departed this life, to enable you to walk back to the presence of the Father, passing the angels who stand as sentinels, being enabled to give them the *key words,* the *signs* and *tokens,* pertaining to the holy Priesthood, and gain your eternal exaltation in spite of earth and hell."[15] On the mountain of God, Moses received pre-cisely these elements—all of which point to the Savior.

The Lord revealed a token

The Lord called to Moses from the flame of fire: "Behold, the cry of the children of Israel is come unto me: and I have also seen the oppression wherewith the Egyptians oppress them. Come now therefore, and I will send thee unto Pharaoh, that thou mayest bring forth my people the chil-dren of Israel out of Egypt."[16]

Moses, an Egyptian by upbringing, a fugitive from justice, forty years removed from Egypt, and poorly received by the Israelites even when he had tried to help them,[17] was being told to return to Pharaoh and demand the release of the Israelites. "Who am I," he replied, "that I should go unto Pharaoh, and that I should bring forth the children of Israel out of Egypt?"[18] In other words, "Why would Pharaoh or the Israelites hearken to me?" Moses wondered. "How could I ever have the power to do what you are requesting?"

Because, the Lord responded, "I will be with thee."[19] And then the Lord revealed a token: "Certainly I will be with thee; and this shall be a token unto thee, that I have sent thee: When thou hast brought forth the people out of Egypt, ye shall serve God upon this mountain."[20]

The token given to Moses, therefore, was the Lord himself. *He* would be with Moses. Moses and the Israelites would successfully escape because of *his* presence and would therefore worship *him* as instructed. The token was their successful deliverance, and that deliverance would be possible be-cause of *him*.

The Lord revealed a name

"I will be with thee" is a comforting response from Moses' perspective, depending on who "I" is. Moses was raised in an Egyptian household, and likely was taught from an early age to trust in the Egyptians' panoply of gods. For perhaps this and other reasons, Moses responded cautiously to the Lord's token: "Behold, when I come unto the children of Israel, and shall say unto them, The God of your fathers hath sent me unto you; and they shall say to me, What is his name? What shall I say unto them?"[21]

To this, the Lord responded, famously: "I AM THAT I AM. . . . Thus shalt thou say unto the children of Israel, I AM hath sent me unto you."[22]

The Hebrew term translated here as "I am" is the first-person-singular form of the "to be" verb, more accurately translated as "I will be" or "I will become." The third-person-singular form of the same word is "Yahweh"— the Hebrew spelling of the name "Jehovah." So Jehovah—the name of the premortal Christ—means, literally, "He will be." Think about the significance of that as a reference to the Savior: Yahweh is who he is precisely because of who he will be in the meridian of time. Even the Lord's very name points to his great and last sacrifice.

It is entirely reasonable that the Lord, when speaking of himself, would use the first-person form of "Yahweh," which is the third-person term others use when speaking of him. Therefore, it is as if the Lord told Moses: "I am (or I will be) 'He will be,'" or "I am the God known to Israel as Yahweh"—that is, "I am He who will come in the meridian of time to redeem mankind."

With this understanding of the connection between the term "I am" and the name "Yahweh," the next verse after the Lord's declaration follows naturally from the I AM statement. Indeed, the next verse is a continuation of the same thought: "Thus shalt thou say unto the children of Israel, The Lord God of your fathers, the God of Abraham, the God of Isaac, and the God of Jacob [i.e., Yahweh], hath sent me unto you: this is my name for ever."[23]

As with the token revealed earlier, the name revealed by the Lord points to the Savior's redeeming mission and saving power.

The Lord revealed a sign

Having been promised the Lord's presence, and knowing the identity of the Lord, Moses asked, in essence, What if the Israelites don't believe me? "But behold," he objected, "they will not believe me, nor hearken unto my voice: for they will say, [Yahweh] hath not appeared unto thee."[24]

In response, the Lord gave Moses a sign: He commanded Moses to cast down his staff, which immediately turned into a serpent. He then instructed Moses to take the serpent by the tail. When Moses took hold of the tail as commanded, the serpent turned back into a staff.[25] Next, the Lord commanded Moses to "put his hand into his bosom."[26] (The New International Version of the Bible translates the Lord's instruction as: "Put your hand inside your cloak."[27]) When Moses took his hand back out of his cloak, it was "leprous as snow."[28] The Lord then commanded Moses to put his hand back into his cloak. After he had done so, Moses' hand was healed completely.[29] The Lord told Moses that he gave him these signs "that they [Israel] may believe that the Lord God of their fathers, the God of Abraham, the God of Isaac, and the God of Jacob, hath appeared unto thee."[30]

But what is it about these signs that would establish that *Yahweh,* and not some other god, had sent Moses? Let's consider the signs. Both of the signs have two parts to them: Moses' staff was turned into a serpent and then back into a staff, and Moses' hand was turned leprous and then healed. Why two parts? Wouldn't it have been enough to turn the staff into a serpent and to make a hand diseased? Wouldn't such signs of power have convinced the Israelites of Moses' divine calling? What is the significance of the second part to both of these signs? Consider this as a possibility: The purpose for the signs was not to show mere power, but to demonstrate the power to *save.* The signs demonstrated that Moses had not only acquired power, he had acquired power from *Yahweh*—he who is and will be the Savior of mankind. The signs, therefore, were themselves signs of his redemption.

The Lord drove this point home with a third sign: "If [Israel] will not believe . . . these two signs, neither hearken unto thy voice, . . . thou shalt take of the water of the river, and pour it upon the dry land: and the water which thou takest out of the river shall become blood upon the dry land."[31] This final sign points to the blood of the Lamb of God, which would be spilt for sins. Israel would recognize in the spilt blood the typifying of Yahweh, for sacrificial blood was made "a similitude of the sacrifice of the Only Begotten" among the fathers from the beginning.[32]

The message of these signs to Moses and to Israel is clear: I am the Redeemer, the only God with the power of deliverance, the only name whereby man can be saved. Everything shown to Moses—the token, the name, and the sign—pointed to the Savior and prepared Moses to turn Israel toward His redeeming blood.

The Lord showed Moses the Creation and the events
before and after the Fall, and taught Moses that the
Savior was the source of creation and redemption

The book of Moses reveals the glorious visions and experiences the Lord shared with Moses during a session on a mountain. Moses beheld the creation of the earth. He learned that the Savior was the creator of this earth and worlds without number.[33] He witnessed Adam and Eve in the garden, and learned of their Fall, and of the plan set in motion for their deliverance. He saw messengers sent to teach them the gospel. The Lord taught Moses that deliverance is only in and through the Savior: "Wherefore, thou shalt do all that thou doest in the name of the Son, and thou shalt repent and call upon God in the name of the Son forevermore."[34] He learned of the Holy Ghost, "which beareth record of the Father and the Son, saying: I am the Only Begotten of the Father from the beginning, henceforth and forever, that as thou hast fallen thou mayest be redeemed, and all mankind, even as many as will."[35] He learned that Jesus Christ is "the only name which shall be given under heaven, whereby salvation shall come unto the children of men."[36] He learned of ordinances that are symbolic of Christ.[37] Indeed, he was taught that all things bear record of the Savior.[38]

Having become a son of God,[39] with all that implies (see chapter 3),[40] and having received the sanctifying ordinances necessary to enter into the rest of the Lord (see Appendix B), Moses was admitted into the Lord's presence.[41] For Moses, this preparation was essential, as he was to prepare Israel for the same blessings.[42]

Moses was now ready to fulfill his mission. He had been endowed with the power of the Lord. He was prepared to be an instrument in the Lord's hands in returning Israel fully to the Savior. In similitude of the Savior, he was to "deliver [the Lord's] people from bondage, even Israel [the Lord's] chosen."[43] He once fled Egypt to escape death.[44] Now he would return as a bearer of the gospel of life.

THE NATURE OF THE DELIVERANCE FROM EGYPT

The plagues: exposing all other gods as powerless to save

When Moses returned to Egypt, the Israelites accepted the signs and believed that he had been sent as a representative of Yahweh. Consequently, they bowed down and worshipped the Lord.[45] However, their faith in the Savior failed them both before and after the Exodus, showing the power Egypt still held over their hearts.[46] The earliest example of this was their reaction when Pharaoh scoffed at Moses' demand for the Israelites' release and increased their burdens.[47]

As Pharaoh repeatedly hardened his heart and refused to let Israel go, the Lord had Moses inflict Egypt with ten great plagues:

1. The river turned to blood.[48]
2. Frogs infested the land, including Pharaoh's house.[49]
3. Lice/gnats infested the land.[50]
4. Flies swarmed the land, and Pharaoh personally, and his house.[51]
5. Livestock in the field were afflicted with a great plague.[52]
6. Boils afflicted man (including those close to Pharaoh) and beast.[53]
7. Hail beat down the crops and killed every man and beast in the field.[54]
8. Locusts covered the face of the land (even filling the house of Pharaoh) and ate what remained in the fields after the hail.[55]
9. Darkness covered Egypt for three days.[56]
10. The firstborn of Egypt (and noncompliant Israel) were killed.[57]

Despite their efforts, the Egyptian magicians could not deliver Egypt from any of these plagues. They could duplicate the first two plagues, but could not put an end to them.[58] "This is the finger of God," the magicians exclaimed as they realized their own powerlessness.[59] Only Moses, calling upon the Lord, could deliver Egypt from the plagues.[60] What is the significance of the inability of the Egyptian magicians to deliver Egypt from these calamities? And in light of that, what is the significance of Moses' ability to deliver the people from the plagues? And even more fundamentally, why the plagues at all?

The Lord gave us an important insight into the meaning and purpose of these plagues when he said: "Against all the gods of Egypt I will execute judgment."[61] This is a curious statement. In what ways are these plagues judgments against the gods of Egypt? Thinking back to the list of Egyptian gods, you will notice that each of these plagues is directed toward one or more of those gods, and was designed to expose the god as powerless:

THE PLAGUES ON THE GODS OF EGYPT	EGYPTIAN GOD EXPOSED AS POWERLESS
River to blood	river/water god (Hopi)
Darkness	sun god (Re/Ra)
Plague on livestock in the field	livestock gods (Apis, Mnevis, Hathor, Khnum)
Hail	livestock gods
Boils	livestock and Pharaoh
Frogs	frog god (Heqt) and Pharaoh
Locusts	Pharaoh
Lice/gnats	Pharaoh
Flies	Pharaoh
Death of the firstborn	Pharaoh

Why might it have been important for the gods of Egypt to be exposed as powerless? "That thou mayest know that there is none like me in all the earth,"[62] the Lord answered. "If thou wilt diligently [keep the] commandments," he told Israel, "I will put none of these diseases upon thee, which I have brought upon the Egyptians: *for I am the Lord that healeth thee.*"[63] Once again, the point is clear: The Israelites' belief and inclination toward Egypt's salvationless gods had to be rooted out of their hearts and minds.

Unlike the Egyptian people, who began to support and revere the Israelites and their God in the face of the plagues,[64] Pharaoh—himself a god in Egypt—would not open his heart. He had become a god unto himself, which is the greatest plague of all. He "exaltest . . . [himself] that he [would] not let [Israel] go."[65] Perhaps this explains why so many of the plagues had to be directed at Pharaoh himself. He, unlike Hopi, Heqt, Apis, Mnevis, Hathor, Khnum, Ra, and the rest, had actual power and could have freed the Israelites. But he was turned unto himself and would not respond to the "stretched out arm" of the Savior. By refusing to turn to the true God and free Israel, Pharaoh simultaneously refused to free himself from spiritual bondage and condemned himself and his house to literal destruction.

The cure to every plague was given in the signs that Moses received on the mountain of God: Only "He will be," the Lamb of God, has power to deliver and redeem—including from the plague of hard-hearted self-exaltation. Deliverance was available to all, even to Pharaoh, if they would look to the deliverance of the Savior.

The Passover: deliverance from the plague of death by the blood of the Lamb

The children of Israel were spared the harm of many, if not all, of the first nine plagues.[66] They appear to have been spared these calamities simply by their identity as Israelites. However, in order to escape the judgment of the tenth plague—the death of all the firstborn males—Israel had to comply strictly with the commandments of the Lord. Life was granted only through obedience to his word.

To Moses, the Lord said: "Yet will I bring one plague more upon Pharaoh, and upon Egypt. . . . About midnight will I go out into the midst of Egypt: And all the firstborn in the land of Egypt shall die, from the firstborn of Pharaoh that sitteth upon his throne, even unto the firstborn of the maidservant that is behind the mill; and all the firstborn of beasts."[67]

To Israel, the Lord provided an outward ordinance that provided a way of deliverance from this death:

1. The calendar was to be changed—the month of deliverance was to be regarded the first month of the year.[68]
2. Take a male lamb without defect.[69]
3. Take care of the lamb for five days.[70]
4. The bones of the lamb must not be broken.[71]
5. Spill the blood of the lamb—all of us, together.[72]
6. Take some of the blood and put it on the top and both sides of the door frame to the household.[73]
7. Eat the flesh of the lamb.[74]
8. Remove all yeast from the house.[75]
9. Eat unleavened bread, or bread without yeast.[76]
10. Also eat bitter herbs.[77]
11. Remain ready to act at a moment's notice on the Lord's instructions.[78]
12. Keep the Lord's Passover in remembrance and teach it to children through the generations.[79]
13. Obey this ordinance with exactness—doing *just* what is commanded.[80]
14. The lamb saves Israel by saving each family.[81]

This list of instructions is worth pondering for a lifetime. We must ask: What is it about this list of instructions that saves us from death? And what salvation do the elements point to? Let's briefly consider a few of the elements.

What is the significance of the change to the calendar? Certainly the rest of the elements of the Lord's Passover could have been instituted without changing the calendar. But consider how such a change oriented Israel to the Lord: the beginning of every new year points to the Lord's deliverance. The very calendar tells Israel that their time on this earth should be directed toward him.

The symbolism of the second element—selecting for sacrifice a male lamb, without defect—is obvious: The Lord is the Lamb of God—perfect, sinless—and it is *his* perfect, sinless sacrifice that creates the way for our escape from that "awful monster . . . death and hell."[82]

What is the significance of the command to take care of the lamb for a period of days? Why didn't the Lord command the Israelites simply to select a lamb and then kill it in his similitude? Why must Israel *take care of* the lamb before it is sacrificed? Perhaps this emphasizes that the death of the Lamb alone is not sufficient to save us. We must come to *know* the Lamb of God. We must regard him as our Lord and Savior, and live accordingly, in order for that sacrifice to have exalting effect in our own lives. With respect to the emblems of the Lord's supper, for example, this command to take care of the lamb suggests that the sacrament will have renewing and cleansing impact in our lives only as we orient our lives toward the Savior each and every day and week. The ordinance alone will not save us.

We—together—spill the blood of the sacrificial lamb perhaps in similitude of the way each of us, through sin, has caused the blood to spill from the Lamb of God. He was slain "*for* the sins of the world"[83]—that is, he was crucified because of, and in order to provide deliverance from, our sins. He has purchased every one of us with his blood.

After sacrificing the lamb, each of the families of Israel were to take some of the blood of the lamb and put it on the top and both sides of the door frame to the household. The Lord then passed over the houses where this blood was around the door frame, sparing them from the plague of death.[84] Why the door frame?

Perhaps the blood around the door signifies the absolute devotion to the Lord that is necessary for salvation. When we enter and leave our homes, we do so in the name of the Lord, whose blood will save the house. Perhaps it is significant in this regard that in commemoration of the Passover through the generations, the Israelites sprinkled the blood of the lamb on the altar of the temple—signifying that our homes are as altars and temples to the Lord. When we enter our homes, framed as they are by the blood of the Lamb, we are to understand that we are entering a holy place, a place that he has looked upon, set apart, and saved, a house of the Lord. No unclean thing shall enter the home—and, perhaps even more important, nothing that leaves the home should have become corrupted in any way while there. In both our entering and leaving, we should keep the Lord in remembrance and worship him.

Before the evening of the Passover, the Israelites were to remove all the leaven or yeast from their houses. Then, during the Passover meal, they were to eat unleavened bread. What might be the significance of the removal of the yeast? Anciently, yeast was viewed as a corruptible agent.[85] It is true that yeast makes the bread rise, but it also leads to fermentation. So one way to look at the removal of the yeast is that it signifies the requirement that we remove all corruption from our lives. And again, the Savior points the way: He, by his life, shows us clearly the corruption in our own. A very different way to think of the yeast is to see it as a representation of man's inability to rise from the corruption of sin save for the Atonement of the risen Lord. For it is only in the Savior that we rise. He is, in that sense, the leaven of mankind—not leaven in terms of corruption, but in this case leaven in terms of salvation. Alone, we are as unleavened bread, never to rise.[86]

It is worth pondering the significance of the command that each family or household partake of the Passover meal in the family unit, and that the Lord thereby passed over Israel by passing over each Israelite *household*. As was made clear to Abraham, Isaac, and Jacob, and to the fathers from the beginning, the family unit is central to our exaltation in the eternities. We are saved together or we are not saved.

Every element comprising the Passover points to a salvation far more important than the mere removal of Israel from Egypt. The combined elements point to the Savior—to his great and last sacrifice, to his power to save, to his infinite Atonement. The ordinance that was critical in the temporal salvation of Israel was a type of the spiritual salvation that awaits us if we turn fully to the Lamb of God. So Israel was taken out of Egypt in similitude of the way that Egypt must be taken out of Israel—by the saving grace and power of the blood of the Lamb. The death of the firstborn removed Israel from temporal bondage, just as the death of the Firstborn—and obedience to the laws and ordinances pertaining to Him—can remove us from spiritual bondage.

THE NATURE OF THE DELIVERER

As we have seen, Moses' call as deliverer and the nature of the deliverance itself point to the Savior. It should not be surprising, then, to discover that Moses is himself in similitude of the Savior. The Lord himself informs us of this: "Thou art in the similitude of mine Only Begotten," he said to Moses on the mount.[87]

Consider, for example, the following key similarities between Moses and Christ:

- Their births and missions as deliverers of Israel were prophesied.[88]
- The kings at the time of their births commanded that the children of their age be put to death.[89]
- Both escaped this sentence of death by being, as it were, "sent into Egypt."[90]
- Both spent forty days fasting and communing with God before bringing the gospel to Israel.[91]
- Both resisted Satan's temptations in nearly parallel experiences and rebuked him using similar words.[92]
- Both performed many miracles.
- Both had power over the waters.[93]
- Both would have preferred not to drink from the bitter cup, but fulfilled the will of God.[94]
- Both delivered Israel from bondage.[95]
- Both were mediators of the covenant—Moses of the old and Christ of the new.[96]

The Lord prepared Moses, on a mountaintop, to be a deliverer of Israel—a deliverer who would be in the Lord's own likeness. That Moses, in his role as the deliverer of Israel, would be in the similitude of the Savior tells us something about the nature of his mission of deliverance. As great as the story of the Exodus was, it is first and foremost a type and shadow of the deliverance that can be ours through Christ. Now as then, to be truly brought out, freed, and redeemed, Israel must look to Him whom Moses foreshadows.

CHAPTER 9

THE TEMPLE AS THE WAY OF ESCAPE AND RETURN

In the Temple I Will Meet Thee

"What can the Old Testament teach me about the temple that is relevant today?"

As we discussed in the previous chapter, the biggest problem for the Israelites was not that they were stuck in the Egypt but that Egypt was stuck in them—a predicament that mirrors our own. The Lord revealed to Moses the antidote for this problem, and that antidote was and is the temple. Through a series of surprising similitudes, the temple is revealed to be the means of escape from the bondage of the world, a space set apart for the sanctification of man so that, once purified, we can again stand in the presence of God.

Three months into their trek in the wilderness, the Israelites came to the mountain of God, called Horeb or Sinai. As we have discussed, here Moses had previously been taught and endowed with power by God, and here, as instructed by God, Moses had brought the children of Israel to participate in those same blessings. Moses ascended the mount and communed with God yet again. There, the Lord told him: "Ye have seen what I did unto the Egyptians, and how I bare you on eagles' wings, and brought you unto myself. Now therefore, if ye will obey my voice indeed, and keep my covenant, then ye shall be a peculiar treasure unto me above all people: for all the earth is mine: And ye shall be unto me a kingdom of priests, and an holy nation."[1]

Moses descended from the mountain and laid before the elders of the people "all these words which the Lord commanded him."[2] To which "all

97

the people answered together, and said, All that the Lord hath spoken we will do."³ Moses then ascended the mount again, reporting the people's words to the Lord.⁴ After returning twice to the people, commanding them to sanctify themselves in preparation for the Lord's presence,⁵ Moses again communed with God on the mount. On this occasion, he received the Ten Commandments and outward laws that follow from those commandments.⁶ Moses then descended the mount and "told the people all the words of the Lord, and all the judgments."⁷ As before, "all the people answered with one voice, and said, All the words which the Lord hath said will we do."⁸ "And Moses wrote all the words of the Lord [the Ten Commandments recorded in Exodus chapter 20, and the additional laws the Lord revealed, beginning in Exodus 20:22 and continuing in chapters 21, 22, and 23 of Exodus], and rose up early in the morning, and builded an altar," and there by sacrifice Moses entered the people into covenant to keep their word to the Lord.⁹

After the Israelites had covenanted to obey the basic laws the Lord had revealed, Moses was called to the mount again.¹⁰ This visit with the Lord, which lasted forty days,¹¹ appears to have been devoted largely to the subject of the temple: "And the Lord spake to Moses, saying . . . let them make me a sanctuary; that I may dwell among them. According to all that I shew thee, after the pattern of the tabernacle, and the pattern of all the instruments thereof, even so shall ye make it. . . . And there I will meet with thee, and I will commune with thee from above the mercy seat."¹²

Notice the Lord's stated purpose for construction of the sanctuary: "that [He] may dwell among them," and "meet with" them. He desired for Israel to enter into his presence, and this was to happen in the temple. "Now this Moses plainly taught to the children of Israel in the wilderness," we are told elsewhere, *and sought diligently to sanctify his people that they might behold the face of God.*"¹³

THE TEMPLE AS THE MEANS OF SPIRITUAL DELIVERANCE

In chapters 25 through 31 of Exodus, the Lord explained in detail the construction of each of the elements that were to comprise the temple. These instructions were followed in chapters 35 through 40 of Exodus, and the Israelites constructed a portable tabernacle after the form shown in the figure below.

The Tabernacle/Temple of Israel

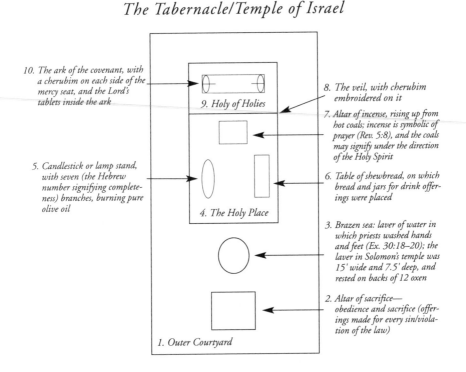

10. The ark of the covenant, with a cherubim on each side of the mercy seat, and the Lord's tablets inside the ark

9. Holy of Holies

8. The veil, with cherubim embroidered on it

7. Altar of incense, rising up from hot coals; incense is symbolic of prayer (Rev. 5:8), and the coals may signify under the direction of the Holy Spirit

5. Candlestick or lamp stand, with seven (the Hebrew number signifying complete-ness) branches, burning pure olive oil

4. The Holy Place

6. Table of shewbread, on which bread and jars for drink offer-ings were placed

3. Brazen sea: laver of water in which priests washed hands and feet (Ex. 30:18–20); the laver in Solomon's temple was 15' wide and 7.5' deep, and rested on backs of 12 oxen

2. Altar of sacrifice—obedience and sacrifice (offer-ings made for every sin/viola-tion of the law)

1. Outer Courtyard

Notice how the elements of the revealed temple bear striking similar-ity to the elements of Israel's escape from Egypt. For example, the outer courtyard could be compared to Egypt, and the altar considered a symbol of the sacrifices of the lambs on the eve of the Passover, which delivered the Israelites from the plague of death. Continuing the similitude, the brazen sea signifies the sea of water through which the Israelites then passed. Having passed through the sea of water, Israel then entered the wilderness, where they took upon themselves significant covenants, as just discussed. The wilderness corresponds nicely (both as a matter of order of progression and as a matter of content) to the Holy Place in the taber-nacle. In the wilderness, Israel witnessed and was led by the light of the Lord.[14] Just so, the candlestick or lamp stand, with seven branches filled with pure olive oil, lit the interior of the Holy Place. Also in the Holy

Place was the table of shewbread on which were placed bread and jars for drink offerings, parallel to the manna and water from heaven that sustained Israel throughout their sojourn in the wilderness.[15] The final element in the Holy Place was the altar of incense, placed directly in front of the veil separating the Holy Place from the Holy of Holies (or, the Most Holy Place). The hot coals on this altar lifted incense heavenward, possibly in representation of prayer.[16] Perhaps this corresponds to the prayers of Moses, which saved the Israelites from death[17] and thereby allowed Israel the opportunity to prepare and come to the borders of the Promised Land—signified by the veil.

On the other side of that border was the Promised Land—the land promised by the Lord as an inheritance to Abraham, Isaac, and Jacob. The Israelites had marched to the border and were preparing to enter. The Lord instructed Moses to send twelve spies, one from each of the landed tribes of Israel, to scout the land and return and report.[18] After forty days they returned from their expedition, reporting a land "[flowing] with milk and honey."[19] However, ten of the twelve reported that "we be not able to go up against the people; for they are stronger than we."[20] Despite the faithful exhortation by the other two spies—Caleb (of the tribe of Judah) and Joshua (of the tribe of Ephraim)—that "if the Lord delight in us, then he will bring us into this land, and give it us,"[21] the ten faithless representatives stirred fear in the people. "And all the children of Israel murmured against Moses and against Aaron: and the whole congregation said unto them, Would God that we had died in the land of Egypt! Or would God we had died in this wilderness!"[22]

After this faithless rejection, the Lord swore that, other than Caleb and Joshua, none of the men of Israel who were over twenty years of age at the time of the Exodus would be permitted to enter the Promised Land.[23] For forty years the Israelites then toiled in the wilderness, not being allowed to enter the land. It was only after the last of these men had died that the remainder of the people were allowed entrance. Only the pure and innocent were able to pass into the Promised Land.

Similarly, after the tabernacle was constructed, due to the rebellion of the people when they began to worship the golden calf in Moses' absence[24] (a violation of the first two of the Ten Commandments they had previously covenanted to keep), the Lord strictly limited entrance into the Holy of Holies. In fact, from that time forward, only the High Priest of Israel was allowed to enter the Holy of Holies, and then only once a year on the Day of Atonement, in sacred similitude of the Savior.[25] This is in contrast to the Lord's original intention for the temple—that by virtue of the sanctifying ordinances to be administered there,[26] the *entire* people would become unto him "a kingdom of priests, and an holy nation,"[27] so that he would be able to meet with them in the Holy of Holies, speaking with them from above the mercy seat.[28] Had it not been for the rebellion of the people, and their rejection of the covenants they had made, the righteous of Israel would have been able to enter the Holy of Holies, much as worthy Church members today enter the celestial room in latter-day temples. This right, and the ordinances of the holy priesthood that would have made it possible, were taken from Israel because of transgression.[29] (For a discussion of how the rights removed from Israel in the wilderness have been restored in the latter days, see Appendix B.)

Had the congregation of Israel been allowed entrance into the Holy of Holies, they would have seen that its only article of furniture was the ark of the covenant, which held the tablets containing the law of God. On either side of the ark were cherubim, and between them, on top of the ark, was the "mercy seat," or throne of God—the place from which the Lord had desired to meet with and speak to his people.

Putting these elements together in illustration, the temporal deliverance of Israel can be depicted as exactly parallel to the tabernacle of Israel. Consider the following parallelisms:

ELEMENTS OF THE TEMPLE	PARALLEL ELEMENTS OF THE EXODUS
1. The outer courtyard	1. Egypt
2. The altar	2. The sacrifices of the lambs on the eve of the Passover, which delivered the Israelites from the plague of death
3. The brazen sea	3. The sea through which the Israelites passed
4. The Holy Place	4. The wilderness beyond the Red Sea, where Israel entered sacred covenants
5. The candlestick/lamp stand	5. The light of the Lord that led Israel to Sinai
6. The table of shewbread with bread and jars for drink offerings	6. The manna and water from heaven that sustained Israel throughout their sojourn in the wilderness
7. The altar of incense, which lifted incense heavenward	7. The prayers of Moses, which saved the Israelites from death (see, e.g., Ex. 32:9–14; Num. 14:11–23)
8. The veil, with embroidered cherubim	8. The border of the Promised Land, over which only the sanctified of Israel could pass. The unrighteous who tried to pass over the border into the Promised Land were immediately destroyed (see Num. 14:39–45)
9. The Holy of Holies	9. The Promised Land that could be entered by the pure and the innocent only after the rebellious generation had passed away
10. The mercy seat and ark of the covenant, with the stone tablets containing the Ten Commandments	10. Israel's appointed position as "a kingdom of priests, and an holy nation" unto the Lord (Ex. 19:6), ruled by the laws of God

The Lord revealed that the temple's purpose was to sanctify man to meet with God, and then directed that the sanctuary be an exact representation of Israel's temporal salvation from Egypt. Thus he emphasized again the spiritual significance of the temporal events Israel was experiencing. The Exodus from Egypt was never merely a physical salvation. Rather, it was a physical salvation that pointed with dramatic clarity to the spiritual salvation offered through the Savior of mankind. The temple in Israel's midst would serve as a continual reminder that the real exodus—the exodus to be found through *him*—was a continuing process. Both the temple and the deliverance it memorialized pointed Israel to the hope of *spiritual* deliverance available through the temple, as considered in the third column of the following chart:

ELEMENTS OF THE TEMPLE	PARALLEL ELEMENTS OF THE EXODUS	PARALLEL ELEMENTS OF SPIRITUAL DELIVERANCE
1. The outer courtyard	1. Egypt	1. The world
2. The altar	2. The sacrifices of the lambs on the eve of the Passover, which delivered the Israelites from the plague of death	2. Sacrifice of a broken heart and contrite spirit (Ps. 51:17; 2 Ne. 2:7)
3. The brazen sea	3. The sea of water through which the Israelites passed	3. Baptism
4. The Holy Place	4. The wilderness beyond the Red Sea, where Israel entered sacred covenants	4. The strait and narrow path (2 Ne. 31:17–18)
5. The candlestick/lamp stand	5. The light of the Lord that led Israel to Sinai	5. The gift of the Holy Ghost
6. The table of shewbread with bread and jars for drink offerings	6. The manna and water from heaven that sustained Israel throughout their sojourn in the wilderness	6. The sacrament of the Lord's body and blood

ELEMENTS OF THE TEMPLE	PARALLEL ELEMENTS OF THE EXODUS	PARALLEL ELEMENTS OF SPIRITUAL DELIVERANCE
7. The altar of incense, which lifted incense heavenward	7. The prayers of Moses, which saved the Israelites from death (see, e.g., Ex. 32:9–14; Num. 14:11–23)	7. Sacred ordinances, culminating in the holy order of prayer
8. The veil, with embroidered cherubim	8. The border of the Promised Land, over which only the sanctified of Israel could pass. The unrighteous who tried to pass over the border into the Promised Land were immediately destroyed (see Num. 14:39–45)	8. The veil separating us from the Lord's presence, through which only the sanctified can pass
9. The Holy of Holies	9. The Promised Land that could be entered by the pure and the innocent only after the rebellious generation had passed away	9. Eternal life in the celestial kingdom
10. The mercy seat and ark of the covenant, with the stone tablets containing the Ten Commandments	10. Israel's appointed position as "a kingdom of priests, and an holy nation" unto the Lord (Ex. 19:6), ruled by the laws of God	10. The throne of God in the middle of kings and queens, priests and priestesses

So we see that the temple is both the means of making spiritual covenants that will prepare us to live with the Lord, *and* the exact similitude of the path we must walk to reenter his presence. As Aaron "stood between the dead and the living" in order to stay the plague that was spreading though Israel,[30] so the temple (along with the ordinances therein) stays our own plague of spiritual death by bringing the Lord's holy presence—and the means to enter into that presence—to us.[31]

In this way, the temple is itself a likeness of the Savior, who came into our presence in mortality so that we might become reconciled to God. Looking at each element of the temple's path to spiritual salvation, we see that the temple is a similitude of Christ.

Christ As the Temple of God

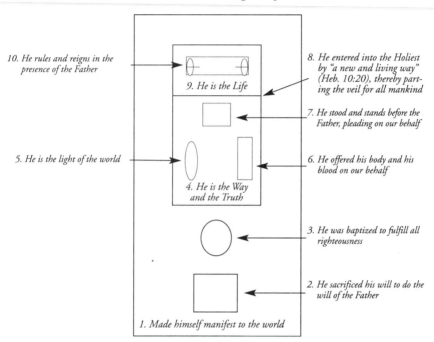

10. He rules and reigns in the presence of the Father

9. He is the Life

8. He entered into the Holiest by "a new and living way" (Heb. 10:20), thereby parting the veil for all mankind

7. He stood and stands before the Father, pleading on our behalf

5. He is the light of the world

6. He offered his body and his blood on our behalf

4. He is the Way and the Truth

3. He was baptized to fulfill all righteousness

2. He sacrificed his will to do the will of the Father

1. Made himself manifest to the world

Christ is "the way, the truth, and the life."[32] He made himself manifest to the world. He sacrificed his will. He was baptized to "fulfill all righteousness."[33] He was and is the light of the world. He offered his body and blood. He stood and stands before the Father pleading on our behalf. He entered into the "holiest" by "a new and living way."[34] He rules and reigns in the presence of the Father.

If we are to become his sons and his daughters, we must follow in his merciful footsteps. Those footsteps lead us to the temple, and the temple leads us into his presence.

The Temple As the Means of Reversing the Effects of the Fall

In addition to its metaphorical message regarding Christ and the escape from spiritual Egypt, the ancient temple can also be seen as a physical representation of both the fall and the redemption of man. Let us look at the ancient temple again, this time with the temple situated, as the garden of Eden was, with its entrance on the east side. The letters *A* through *I* show how a move from the Holy of Holies, step-by-step, to the east through the temple parallels Adam and Eve's move from the garden.

The Holy of Holies, with the ark of the covenant and throne of God (similar to celestial room)

The Holy Place, with menorah and other elements (similar to terrestrial room)

The bronze basin of water (in Solomon's temple was 15' wide and 7.5' deep and rested on the backs of 12 oxen)

The altar of sacrifice

A | B   C   D   E   F | G   –H–   I

W ← → E

The outer courtyard (similar to telestial room)

The Holy of Holies (element A) can be thought to represent Adam and Eve when they were in the presence of God and the tree of life in the garden. When they transgressed, we are told that cherubim were placed to guard the way of the tree of life (element B). Similarly, cherubim were embroidered on the veil that separated the Holy of Holies from the Holy Place.[35] Just as the garden of Eden was filled with trees and other beautifying elements, so too the Holy Place was the sanctuary for the tree-shaped candlestick or menorah (element C).[36] (The temple of Solomon had ten menorah in the Holy Place, and on the walls were carved palm trees and open flowers.[37]) While still in the garden, Adam and Eve received instruction from the Lord (element D).[38] The Lord also clothed them in garments (element E).[39] They then were cast out of the garden, and cherubim were placed at the east entrance to the garden to prevent their unauthorized return (element F).[40] They were driven eastward out of the garden (element G), where they built an altar and offered sacrifice[41] and were baptized (element H),[42] actions symbolized in the temple by the altar[43] and basin of water.[44] They then lived among a world in sin (element I).[45]

Consider how we reverse these elements and walk from a world in sin into the presence of God as we observe temple worship: We live among a world in sin (element I). Before entering the temple, we must first offer sacrifice (of a broken heart and contrite spirit) and get baptized (element H). The entrance to the temple is at the east of the structure (the angel Moroni is usually facing the east on our latter-day temples), so we travel west when we enter and progress through the temple (element G). When we pass through the eastern entrance of the temple, we must pass by "cherubim" who are set to guard the way (element F). There is special clothing for those who enter into the Holy Place or temple (element E). Once in the temple, we receive instruction from the Lord (element D). Anciently, in the Holy Place there were menorah (candlestick like a tree with seven branches—ten in Solomon's Temple), along with many other beautifying elements, just as modern-day temples are beautified. In addition, each branch of the menorah can be thought to signify the various covenants we make in the temple (together, element C). The Holy Place where instruction is received is separated from the Holy of Holies (or Most Holy Place) by a veil—anciently, there were cherubim embroidered on the veil; in latter-day temples, "cherubim" guard the way (element B). Beyond the veil, we enter into the place dedicated to the glory and presence of God (element A).

Putting both the Adam and Eve story and our own experience in the temple beneath a depiction of the ancient temple, we see that the temple was (and is) itself a representation of the path of man's fall and redemption.

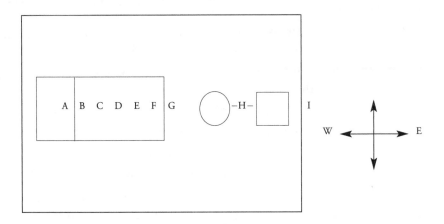

Adam and Eve Leaving the Garden

A They were in the presence of God in the garden.

  B When Adam and Eve transgressed, cherubim were placed to guard the way of the tree of life.

    C The garden had been filled with trees (including the tree of knowledge of good and evil) and other beautifying elements.

      D Adam and Eve received instruction from the Lord.

        E The Lord clothed them in garments of coats of skins.

          F Cherubim were placed at the east of the garden to prevent the fallen couple from an unauthorized return to the garden (suggests an eastern entrance into the garden).

            G They were driven eastward out of the garden.

              H They built an altar and offered sacrifice and were baptized.

                I They lived among a world in sin.

Progression of Temple Patrons Back into Presence of God

                I' We live among a world in sin.

              H' We first offer sacrifice (of a broken heart and contrite spirit) and get baptized.

            G' The entrance to the temple is at the east, so we travel west when entering and progressing through the temple.

          F' We pass through the eastern entrance of the Holy Place through doors with cherubim, set to guard the way.

        E' Special clothing is donned by those who enter into the Holy Place.

      D' We receive instruction from the Lord.

    C' Anciently, in the Holy Place there were menorah (candlestick like a tree with seven branches), along with many other beautifying elements.

  B' The Holy Place is separated from the Holy of Holies by a veil on which cherubim are embroidered.

A' We enter the presence of God on the throne in the Most Holy Place.

So we see that the temple (both ancient and modern), in its overall structure, and in the order of its elements, is a rich representation both of the fall of man and of the process required to reverse its effects. When ancient Israel entered into the temple, and when we enter into it today, we are stepping backwards—our hearts "turned toward the west"—to the presence of God that man left when Adam and Eve were cast out of the garden. And when we turn to the temple and the Lord in this way, we begin a journey, parallel to the journey of the children of Israel when they escaped the bondage of Egypt. This journey offers us the opportunity to escape the bondage of our times—the darkened desires and habits that hold us fast. Like Israel of old, when we trace the steps of the Exodus as we progress through the temple, we learn that the temple, like the Exodus, exists not so much to get us out of the world as to get the world out of us.

We need an exodus as much as Israel of old, and that exodus happens, in its fulness, through the temple.

CHAPTER 10

UNDERSTANDING THE
LAW OF MOSES

Every One That Is Bitten, When He Looketh upon It, Shall Live

> *"I'm sure glad we don't have to live by the law of Moses today."*
>
> Actually, we are commanded to live by a set of laws that is even more difficult. The law of Moses set forth detailed, outward laws that Israel couldn't fully keep. Our situation today is analogous, as we are under obligation to live by inward laws (for example, to be merciful and pure in heart) that we too don't fully keep. It might strike you as odd that the Lord would demand compliance to a set of laws that we, of ourselves, can't fully live. But that inability to fully live the law is at the heart of one of the key purposes of the law—both anciently and today. Perfectionists, beware: The law is designed to expose our imperfection. And therefore to turn us to the only One who is perfect.

As mentioned in chapter 9, at the very moment that Moses was receiving detailed instructions from the Lord about the temple, the Israelites reverted to idol worship in Moses' absence.[1] By this rebellion, the Israelites "turned aside quickly"[2] and broke the covenant they had made to keep the Ten Commandments, the first two of which specifically prohibited such practices.[3]

Because of this rebellion, "the Lord in his wrath . . . swore that [the Israelites] should not enter into his rest while in the wilderness, which rest is the fulness of his glory."[4] "And he said unto Moses . . . there shall no man among them see me at this time, and live, for they are exceeding sinful. And no sinful man hath at any time, *neither shall there be any sinful man at any time, that shall see my face and live.*"[5]

So everything was now changed. It had been the Lord's intention to prepare the Israelites to enter into his presence through the sanctification enabled by the covenants and ordinances of the temple.[6] Now, however, that wouldn't be possible. As discussed in chapter 3, only those who are born again in Christ through a broken heart and contrite spirit (symbolized by the altar in the temple) are able to enter the Holy Place and receive the ordinances that enable man to abide the presence of the glorified Lord. Having "hardened their hearts" and turned from Christ, they "could not endure his presence"; the ordinances that would have enabled the people to be prepared for a fulness of glory were removed from Israel.[7]

This situation is akin to the situation Adam and Eve were in after transgressing in the garden. "For behold, if Adam had put forth his hand immediately, and partaken of the tree of life, he would have lived forever, according to the word of God, having no space for repentance."[8] Just as a fallen Adam and Eve would have been condemned forever had they partaken of the tree of life, so the sinful children of Israel would have been destroyed in their sins had they entered into the Lord's presence without having been sanctified.

As a result of this unworthiness, the Lord told Moses: "Hew thee two other tables of stone, like unto the first, and I will write upon them also, the words of the law, according as they were written at the first on the tables which thou brakest; but it shall not be according to the first, for *I will take away the priesthood out of their midst; therefore my holy order, and the ordinances thereof, shall not go before them; for my presence shall not go up in their midst, lest I destroy them.*"[9]

This meant that the power and authority to conduct the holy ordinances that would have been available to the Israelites in the temple were removed from Israel.[10] The Lord "took Moses out of their midst, and the Holy [Melchizedek] Priesthood also."[11] Without the authority to conduct the holy ordinances of the temple, no one would be qualified to enter into the Holy of Holies. From this time forward, only the *priests* of Israel, and not the people as a whole, were allowed to enter into the Holy Place. Furthermore, while there, the ordinances they might otherwise have received, and the sanctifying covenants that attend them, would not be made available to them. As a result, the Holy of Holies, on the other side of the veil, was made off-limits to them. Only the High Priest of the people could enter the Holy of Holies—and even he could enter only once a year, and then only to offer the blood of the sin offering for the people, in similitude of the Savior's ultimate offering.[12] This arrangement did not reflect what the fulness of the gospel offered, which, as the Lord expressed, was that he would be able to meet in glory with all of his people within the tabernacle.[13] Because of transgression, "the way into the [Holy of Holies—and thus into the presence of the Lord] was *not yet* made manifest."[14]

Israel would spend more than a millennium after this time preparing to receive what they might have received in the tabernacle at Sinai. The time between the rejection of the Lord at the mountain of God and the Lord's mortal birth would be a preparatory time for Israel—a time granted for repentance in order to become worthy of the presence of the Lord. "And thus we see, that there was a time granted unto man to repent, yea a probationary time, a time to repent and serve God."[15] During this probationary time, the Lord instituted a preparatory law—a law whose sole purpose was to bring Israel to Christ. This law is known as the law of Moses.

In Doctrine and Covenants section 84, the Lord explains the authority that remained with Israel after the Melchizedek Priesthood was taken away from the people as a whole: "And the lesser [Aaronic] priesthood continued, which priesthood holdeth the key of the ministering of angels and the preparatory gospel."[16] And what is the "preparatory gospel"? It is "the gospel of repentance and of baptism, and the remission of sins, and the law of carnal commandments, which the Lord . . . caused to continue with the house of Aaron among the children of Israel until John, whom God raised up, being filled with the Holy Ghost from his mother's womb."[17]

This is significant. The gospel that remained in Israel held the keys pertaining to repentance, baptism, and the remission of sins. This same gospel is fundamental today. These elements form the basic building blocks of the gospel. However, without the ordinances of the holy Melchizedek Priesthood, the Israelites were unable to enjoy the baptism of fire and of the Spirit through the gift of the Holy Ghost, or any other Melchizedek Priesthood ordinances. (In contrast, the righteous branch of

Israel that was split off to the new world appears to have been blessed with the Melchizedek Priesthood.[18]) Having rejected the Lord's lead in the wilderness, Israel was unprepared for the gift of the Holy Ghost, which is precisely the Lord's lead in each of our lives. They were left largely to their own counsel so that they might learn, as they failed to learn in the wilderness, that they cannot be saved without the Lord. The priesthood that remained with them had the power and authority to prepare them to abide the presence of angels, but the greater priesthood, which holds the authority and power to prepare man to abide the presence of God, was taken from them.[19]

Of the preparatory law that remained, the prophet Abinadi stated: "And now I say unto you that it was expedient that there should be a law given to the children of Israel, yea, even a very strict law; for they were a stiffnecked people, quick to do iniquity, and slow to remember the Lord their God; Therefore there was a law given them, yea, a law of performances and of ordinances, *a law which they were to observe strictly from day to day, to keep them in remembrance of God and their duty towards him.*"[20]

How the Law of Moses Was Designed to Turn Israel to the Savior

The law of Moses was designed to turn Israel to the Savior. It did this in at least three ways: first, through the impossibility of the law, which made all men condemned under the law and created remorse of conscience[21]; second, by the law's requirement of vicarious atonement sacrifice for all transgressions[22]; and third, through the obvious insufficiency of animal sacrifices to purge man of sin, which then pointed Israel beyond the law to the need for a Savior.[23] "And behold, this is the whole meaning of the law," Amulek declared, "every whit pointing to that great and last sacrifice; and that great and last sacrifice will be the Son of God, yea, infinite and eternal."[24]

A little-known application of a well-known experience during Israel's wanderings in the wilderness illustrates how the law of Moses was designed to bring Israel to Christ. On an occasion in the wilderness when the Israelites started complaining against Moses because of the difficulty of the way, "the Lord sent fiery serpents among the people, and they bit the people; and much people of Israel died."[25] The people then came to Moses in the spirit of repentance and begged him to intercede for them before the Lord.[26] Moses did so, and the Lord instructed him to make a fiery serpent out of brass, and to set it on a pole. He was then instructed to command Israel to look upon the serpent of brass. All those who looked upon the serpent lived.[27]

The scriptures confirm what one suspects when reading this story—the brass serpent was a type of the Savior: "Behold, [the Savior] was spoken of by Moses," Alma taught, "yea, and behold a type was raised up in the wilderness, that whosoever would look upon it might live."[28] John, speaking of the same event, added, "as Moses lifted up the serpent in the wilderness, even so must the Son of man be lifted up: That whosoever believeth in him should not perish, but have eternal life."[29]

Here is a question that illuminates the role of the law of Moses: If the brass serpent is a type of the Savior, of what might the fiery serpents be a type? Consider this possibility: that the fiery serpents are a type of the law of Moses.

The chart on the opposite page illustrates the parallels between the fiery serpents and the law of Moses. Israel was given "a law of performances and of ordinances, a law which they were to observe strictly from day to day, to keep them in remembrance of God and their duty towards him."[30] Like the fiery serpents, the law of Moses was given to Israel to turn them to Christ. The law, like each serpent, was designed to continually "bite" Israel by reminding them of their sins and requiring them to seek atonement for them. Just as salvation from the poison of the fiery serpents required Israel to look to the representation of Christ that Moses raised on the pole, so salvation from transgressions under the law required them to look to the Lord himself. The fiery serpent episode was a living representation of the law of Moses and its role for Israel.

ELEMENT	FIERY SERPENT	LAW OF MOSES
The people sinned	"And the people spake against God, and against Moses, Wherefore have ye brought us up out of Egypt to die in the wilderness?" (Num. 21:5)	The people rejected the Lord and turned back to idolatry (see Ex. 32:1–6), thereby violating the covenant they had made (see Ex. 24:3–8)
The Lord created a condition to "bite" them	"And the Lord sent fiery serpents among the people, and they bit the people; and much of the people of Israel died" (Num. 21:6)	"The law was added because of transgressions" (JST, Gal. 3:19). "Now, how could a man repent except he should sin? How could he sin if there was no law? How could there be no law save there was a punishment? Now, there was a punishment affixed, and a just law given" (Alma 42:17–18) "that . . . all the world may become guilty before God" (Rom. 3:19)
This condition awakened the people to their sins	"Therefore the people came to Moses, and said, We have sinned, for we have spoken against the Lord, and against thee; pray unto the Lord, that he take away the serpents from us" (Num. 21:7)	This punishment and law "brought remorse of conscience unto man. . . . [By this means there was] a repentance granted" (Alma 42:18, 22), "for by the law is the knowledge of sin" (Rom. 3:20)
The thing which awakened Israel to their sins was prepared also to be the way through which they could be healed from the effect of their sins	"And the Lord said unto Moses, Make thee a fiery serpent, and set it upon a pole: and it shall come to pass, that every one that is bitten, when he looketh upon it, shall live" (Num. 21:8)	"It was expedient that there should be a law given to the children of Israel, yea, even a very strict law; for they were a stiffnecked people, quick to do iniquity, and slow to remember the Lord their God; Therefore there was a law given them, yea, a law of performances and of ordinances, a law which they were to observe strictly from day to day, to keep them in remembrance of God and their duty towards him" (Mosiah 13:29–30)
The means of deliverance could not of itself save spiritually, but pointed to the Savior as the source of salvation	"Behold, [the Savior] was spoken of by Moses; yea, and behold a type was raised up in the wilderness, that whosoever would look upon it might live" (Alma 33:19). "And as Moses lifted up the serpent in the wilderness, even so must the Son of man be lifted up: That whosoever believeth in him should not perish, but have eternal life" (John 3:14–15)	"For the law having a shadow of good things to come, and not the very image of the things, can never with those sacrifices which they offered year by year continually make the comers thereunto perfect" (Heb. 10:1). "And behold, this is the whole meaning of the law, every whit pointing to that great and last sacrifice; and that great and last sacrifice will be the Son of God, yea, infinite and eternal" (Alma 34:14). "Wherefore the law was [the] schoolmaster to bring [Israel] to Christ" (Gal. 3:24)
Those who looked to the temporal type of spiritual salvation were blessed with life, while those who didn't were cursed with death	"Behold, he was spoken of by Moses; yea, and behold a type was raised up in the wilderness, that whosoever would look upon it might live. And many did look and live. . . . But there were many who were so hardened that they would not look, therefore they perished. Now the reason they would not look is because they did not believe that it would heal them" (Alma 33:19–20)	"And the Lord commanded us to do all these statutes, to fear the Lord our God, for our good always, that he might preserve us alive, as it is at this day. And it shall be our righteousness, if we observe to do all these commandments before the Lord our God, as he hath commanded us" (Deut. 6:24–25)

This parallelism helps to explain the otherwise curious fact that the Lord told Moses to create, in effect, an image of worship, which appears to violate the commandment against graven images, and that the image was in the form of a serpent, which is usually associated in the scriptures with evil.[31] Confusion on this matter comes when we fail to see what the fiery serpents were representing, and think that Israel simply needed to be delivered from the plague of those serpents. That which the children of Israel thought to be evil—the fiery serpent that bit them—was in fact for their benefit. The Lord tried to emphasize this point for Israel by directing that the source of salvation be an image of the very thing that was biting them.

As with the fiery serpents, the strictness of the law—its "bite"—was for the purpose of prodding Israel toward the Lord.

THE LAW TODAY: THE SAME PURPOSE

The commandments we are to live by today have the same purpose. Their intent is to bring us to Christ. But how do they do this? Not in the way we usually think they do.

To the Nephites, the Savior revealed one of the key purposes for the commandments: "And behold, I have given you the law and the commandments of my Father, . . . *that ye shall repent of your sins, and come unto me with a broken heart and a contrite spirit.*"[32] Notice: The law is designed not to make us perfect but rather to reveal our imperfections, and therefore to turn us more fully to the perfected Christ. The law leads us to repentance by creating within us a broken heart and contrite spirit—the very "remorse of conscience" the law of Moses was designed to create. How does the law do this? The same way it did for the ancient Israelites: by requiring a level of living that we cannot of ourselves perfectly achieve, thereby creating the need to repent, which need awakens us to our complete and utter need for the Savior. "By the deeds of the law," Paul wrote, "there shall no flesh be justified in his sight: for by the law is the knowledge of sin."[33] In fact, he taught, the law was created, at least in part, "that every mouth may be stopped, and all the world may become guilty before God."[34]

While the law we are now commanded to live may be less outwardly demanding than the law of Moses was, it is far more inwardly demanding. Consider the Lord's words to the Nephites: "Ye have heard that it hath been said by them of old time . . . that thou shalt not kill."[35] That was the outward law—a relatively easy commandment to keep for most of us. But then the Savior taught that we are required to live by a deeper, inward law: "I say unto you, that whosoever is angry with his brother shall be in danger of [the] judgment."[36]

I may be able to keep perfectly the commandment not to kill, but the commandment not to get angry? That one I am sure to break—sometime, somewhere. The Savior continued: "Behold, it is written by them of old time, that thou shalt not commit adultery; But I say unto you, that whosoever looketh on a woman, to lust after her, hath committed adultery already in his heart. Behold, I give you a commandment, that ye suffer none of these things to enter into your heart."[37] Continuing his discourse on the inward law, the Savior explained that we are to be "meek,"[38] merciful,"[39] and "pure in heart,"[40] with "bowels . . . full of charity towards all men."[41] If the ancient Israelites were bound to stumble by the strictness of their outward law, we are even more certain to stumble by the strictness of this inward law—what Jesus called the "weightier matters of the law."[42]

The fact that we are now commanded to live to this level of inward righteousness, coupled with the fact that we are almost certain to fail to live to this level of inward righteousness, creates within us an ongoing need for repentance, which requires us frequently to be coming to Christ. So what was true for the Israelites regarding the law of Moses is true as well for us regarding the law we have been commanded to live. We, of ourselves, can't do it perfectly. That, in fact, is the point of it: "If men come unto me," the Savior taught, "I will show unto them their weakness . . . that they may be humble."[43] If we could live perfectly in and of ourselves, then we would feel no need for the Savior, and we would never come to him to be purified, made holy, and saved.

The law does not perfect us. That is not its purpose. Rather, it "bites" us, and requires that we look to the being raised on the pole for deliverance.

"Come unto Christ, and be perfected in him,"[44] Moroni wrote, which is to say that we are perfected, if at all, only in Christ. The commandments are designed to get us to realize how fully we need the purity and perfection that are available only *in him*.

CHAPTER 11

DISCOVERING DEUTERONOMY

Rejoice, for He Shall Make Atonement for His Land and People

"Sorry, when I get to Deuteronomy, I hit the snooze button."

Okay, but before you do, could you do me a favor? Could you learn a song? Not just any song, mind you, but a song that the Lord has given us—a song that, among other things, reveals how the Church and priesthood would be established in the latter days, in the land of "everlasting hills." A song that tells of our history and future, and what we must do to cross into our own promised land.

The lyrics are in the thirty-second chapter of Deuteronomy.

Who can comprehend the greatness of Moses? Raised a prince, he chose the shepherd's life. He had come to the defense of a slave, and it cost him his home, his future, his glory. He fled for his life, across sea and desert, and settled as a stranger in a faraway land. For forty years he toiled there, raised a family, tended sheep. Eighty-year-old Moses—raised in the palace of Pharaoh—became a man in the deserts of Arabia.

But he became so much more than a man. In the desert a prophet was born. There he communed with Jehovah. The man who as a boy had learned of many gods, as a man was taught by the one true God. Through Moses the world knows of the Creation and the Fall. From his hand we learn of our first parents, and how they were taught the gospel from on high. From Moses' account of their lives we first learn of the joy of the Lord's redemption—for having been "filled" with the spirit of the Holy Ghost upon learning of "the sacrifice of the Only Begotten of the Father," they "blessed . . . the name of God" and were "glad."[1]

119

He witnessed the panorama of human history, and was set apart to share it with us.[2] How else would we have known? He saw the fathers from Adam down through the generations. Through Moses we learn that the new and everlasting covenant was never "new," only restored. And all "which was in the beginning, shall be in the end of the world also,"[3] "all things . . . confirmed . . . by an holy ordinance."[4] Who can imagine what it must have been like to witness the glory of Zion, the finality of the flood, the righteousness of Melchizedek, and the faith of Abraham? Perhaps he stood at the side of the Only Begotten as he witnessed—in order to record for us—the sacrificial journey of Abraham and *his* "only begotten." Having had his own experiences with the Savior, Moses would have understood well Jacob's experience with the Lord at Bethel, where the Savior himself renewed the holy covenant in Jacob and taught him the steps to salvation.[5] And how he must have related to Joseph, who was alternately a ruler and an outcast in Egypt, and became the means of salvation to his brethren.

How could we have understood the Lord's Atonement without Moses? How much do we owe the humble prince of Egypt? How could we gather to the Lord without the understanding that the Lord revealed through him? Truly, as the Lord told him, Moses was called to "deliver my people from bondage, even Israel my chosen."[6] And perhaps the extent of that deliverance is broader than we might at first think. For his words remain instrumental in bringing the world to the truth.

Imagine the love and frustration Moses knew in the desert of Sinai as he toiled to remove Egypt from the Israelites. In the face of rejection and betrayal, he remained ever faithful—to the Lord and to his people. Forty years in barren wilderness, because of the sins of others. How many of us would have left, given up, gone it alone, become embittered? But he loved his people. He taught. He toiled. He pled for their lives and stayed the hand of death.[7]

Forty years after the Exodus, Moses and his people were encamped on the border of the land of promise. Only the Jordan separated them from Abraham's inheritance. Alas, Moses, "man of God,"[8] "servant of the Lord,"[9] "similitude of [the] Only Begotten,"[10] would not be crossing with them. His promised land lay heavenward. One more journey up a mountain and he would commune again with the Lord—this time for eternity.[11]

In the days before his final journey, there on the banks of the Jordan, the prophet had occasion to teach his people for the final time. Imagine the emotion. Imagine the hope. Imagine the love. Whatever he chose to teach his people in his last days with them would be precious beyond measure. His words on these occasions are recorded in the book of Deuteronomy.

As a record of speeches about the law, Deuteronomy is more dense than most other books of scripture. But it contains within it a wonderful key to unlocking its meaning. The key was revealed by the Lord to Moses. The key is a song.

In chapter 31, after revealing to Moses that Israel would break their covenant with the Lord and "go a whoring after the gods of the strangers of the land,"[12] the Lord teaches Moses a song and commands him to teach it to the Israelites:

> Now therefore write ye this song for you, and teach it [to] the children of Israel: put it in their mouths, that this song may be a witness for me against the children of Israel. For when I shall have brought them into the land which I sware unto their fathers, that floweth with milk and honey; and they shall have eaten and filled themselves, and waxen fat; then will they turn unto other gods, and serve them, and provoke me, and break my covenant. And it shall come to pass, when many evils and troubles are befallen them, that this song shall testify against them as a witness; for it shall not be forgotten out of the mouths of their seed. . . .
>
> Moses therefore wrote this song the same day, and taught it the children of Israel.[13]

Over 43 verses in chapter 32, the song—known as "the Song of Moses"—summarizes the material contained in Deuteronomy. Consider the significance of a song revealed word by word by the Lord. It demands our attention. And the song's structure, topics, and sequence illuminate the meaning of the book's message. The Lord has provided us a key for understanding Moses' last words to Israel. We should pay attention. After all, we are Israel, for whom "this song shall testify against them as a witness."

THE LORD'S KEY TO DEUTERONOMY:
THE SONG OF MOSES

On the following pages, I lay out the Song of Moses in verse form. I have chosen to use the highly regarded New International Version of the Bible for these verses, as its translation is slightly easier to read than the King James Version, and I find it to be slightly clearer through these verses. I suggest that you read the song before moving to the discussion that will follow. You will notice as you do so that I list numbers 1 through 8 next to certain highlighted elements of the text. These elements will be key in the discussion that follows, so I mark them in the text in order to easily reference them later.

> Deuteronomy 32
> 1. Listen, O heavens, and I will speak;
> hear, O earth, the words of my mouth.
> 2. Let my teaching fall like rain
> and my words descend like **dew, (1)**
> like showers on new grass,
> like abundant rain on tender plants.
>
> 3. I will proclaim the name of the Lord.
> Oh, praise the greatness of our God!
> 4. He is the **Rock,** his works are perfect, **(2)**
> and all his ways are just.
> A faithful God who does no wrong,
> upright and just is he.
>
> 5. They have acted corruptly toward him;
> to their shame they are **no longer his children, (3)**
> but a warped and crooked generation.
> 6. Is this the way you **repay** the Lord, **(4)**
> O foolish and unwise people?

Is he not your Father, your Creator,
who made you and formed you?
7. Remember the days of old;
consider the generations long past.
Ask your father and he will tell you,
your elders, and they will explain to you.
8. When the most high gave the nations their
inheritance, when he divided all mankind,
he set up boundaries for the peoples
according to the number of the sons of Israel.
9. For the Lord's portion is his people,
Jacob his allotted inheritance.

10. In a desert land he found him,
in a barren and howling waste.
He shielded him and cared for him;
he guarded him as the apple of his eye,
11. like an eagle that stirs up its nest
and hovers over its young,
that spreads its wings to catch them
and carries them on its pinions.
12. The Lord alone led him;
no foreign god was with him.

13. He made him ride on the heights of the land
and fed him with the fruit of the fields.
He nourished him with honey from the rock,
and with oil from the flinty crag,
14. with curds and milk from herd and flock
and with fattened lambs and goats,
with choice rams of Bashan
and the finest kernels of wheat.
You drank the foaming blood of the grape.

15. Jeshurun **grew fat and kicked; (5)**
filled with food,

he became heavy and sleek.
He abandoned the God who made him
and rejected the Rock his Savior.
16. They made him jealous with their foreign gods
and angered him with their detestable idols.
17. They sacrificed to demons, which are not God—
gods they had not known,
gods that recently appeared,
gods your fathers did not fear.
18. You deserted the Rock, who fathered you;
you forgot the God who gave you birth.

19. The Lord saw this and rejected them
because he was angered by his sons and daughters.
20. "I will hide my face from them," he said,
"and see what their end will be;
for they are a perverse generation,
children who are unfaithful.
21. They made me jealous by what is no god
and angered me with their worthless idols.
I will make them envious by those who are not a people;
I will make them angry by a nation
that has no understanding.
22. For a fire has been kindled by my wrath,
one that burns to the realm of death below.
It will devour the earth and its harvests
and set afire the foundations of the mountains.

23. "I will heap calamities upon them
and spend my arrows against them.
24. I will send wasting famine against them,
consuming pestilence and deadly plague;
I will send against them the fangs of wild beasts,
the venom of vipers that glide in the dust.
25. In the street the sword will make them childless;

in their homes terror will reign.
Young men and young women will perish,
infants and gray-haired men.
26. **I said I would scatter them (6)**
and blot out their memory from mankind,
27. but I dreaded the taunt of the enemy,
lest the adversary misunderstand
and say 'Our hand has triumphed;
the Lord has not done all this.'"

28. They are a nation without sense,
there is no discernment in them.
29. If only they were wise and would understand this
and discern what their end will be!
30. How could one man chase a thousand,
or two put ten thousand to flight,
unless their Rock had sold them,
unless the Lord had given them up?
31. For their rock is not like our Rock,
as even our enemies concede.
32. Their vine comes from the vine of Sodom
and from the fields of Gomorrah.
Their grapes are filled with poison,
and their clusters with bitterness.
33. Their wine is the venom of serpents,
the deadly poison of cobras.

34. "Have I not kept this in reserve
and sealed it in my vaults?
35. It is mine to avenge; I will repay.
In due time their foot will slip;
their day of disaster is near
and their doom rushes upon them."

36. **The Lord will judge his people**
and have compassion on his servants (7)

when he sees their strength is gone
and no one is left, slave or free.
37. He will say: "Now where are their gods,
the rock they took refuge in,
38. the gods who ate the fat of their sacrifices
and drank the wine of their drink offerings?
Let them rise up to help you!
Let them give you shelter!

39. "See now that I myself am He!
There is no other god besides me.
I put to death and I bring to life,
I have wounded and I will heal,
And no one can deliver out of my hand.
40. I lift my hand to heaven and declare:
As surely as I live forever,
41. when I sharpen my flashing sword
and my hand grasps it in judgment,
I will take vengeance on my adversaries
and repay those who hate me.
42. I will make my arrows drunk with blood,
while my sword devours flesh:
the blood of the slain and the captives,
the heads of the enemy leaders."

43. Rejoice, O nations, with his people,
for he will avenge the blood of his servants;
he will take vengeance on his enemies
and **make atonement for his land and people. (8)**

PONDERING THE SONG OF MOSES

1. The "dew" from heaven

The Lord begins the song with a call to all of heaven and earth:
"Listen, O heavens, and I will speak; hear, O earth, the words of my

mouth. Let my teaching fall like rain and my words descend like *dew,* like showers on new grass, like abundant rain on tender plants."[14] The Lord here establishes the dew and the rain as a matter of life and death. He emphasizes this by referring to "new grass" and "tender plants." Unlike more mature vegetation, which might have root systems that can sustain life through extended periods without moisture, new growth is absolutely dependent on the moisture from the heavens. Without it, the new grass and tender plant will quickly wither and die.

Given that in verse 10 the Lord states that he found Israel in "a barren and howling waste," the new grass and tender plant would appear to be a reference to Israel itself—a people chosen by the Lord for special nourishment. He "shielded" them and "cared for" them, thus allowing the grass to take root and the tender plant to grow. They—Israel—were to be fed by the dews from heaven.

Given the Israelites' experiences in the wilderness, the reference to "dew" would have had an immediate and personal meaning: "In the morning the dew lay round about the host. And when the dew that lay was gone up, behold, upon the face of the wilderness there lay a small round thing, as small as the hoar frost on the ground. And when the children of Israel saw it, they said one to another, It is manna: for they wist not what it was. And Moses said unto them, This is the bread which the Lord hath given you to eat."[15]

This miracle of physical salvation points to the miracle of spiritual salvation,[16] a miracle that is administered through the power of the holy priesthood—the doctrine of which descends, we are told, like manna descended, "as the dews from heaven."[17]

It is interesting that in the chapter immediately following the Song of Moses, only one tribe is blessed with the dews from heaven: the tribe of Joseph. "And of Joseph he said, Blessed of the Lord be his land, *for the precious things of heaven, for the dew.*"[18] (The NIV translation of this verse reads: "May the Lord bless his [Joseph's] land with the precious dew from heaven above."[19])

So, while in verses 1 and 2 the Lord expresses his desire that all of Israel would receive the dews of heaven, in the blessings that follow a chapter later, only one tribe—Joseph—receives a blessing that explicitly promises such dew. We will return to the significance of this shortly.

2. The Lord is "the Rock"

The term *Rock* plays a prominent role in the Song of Moses, appearing as a name for the God of Israel in verses 4, 15, 18, 30, and 31. In order to understand what the Israelites might have understood by this title, let's consider the use of the term *rock* (or similar references like stone) in earlier scriptures.

a. The Rock as "the stone of Israel"

In Genesis 49:24, the Savior is referred to as "the stone of Israel." The Lord uses the same expression to refer to himself in D&C 50:44. Neither scripture provides obvious context for the title, but an event in Genesis 28 may help to explain the initial use of this title. In Genesis 28, Jacob (or "Israel"), as he lay sleeping in Bethel, saw a vision of the Lord. The vision has become known as "Jacob's ladder," for he saw "a ladder set up on the earth, and the top of it reached to heaven: and behold the angels of God ascending and descending on it."[20] Then Jacob saw the Lord, standing above it, and the Lord then renewed in Jacob the covenant he had made with Abraham and Isaac.[21] Marion G. Romney taught that Jacob here received a temple experience.[22]

The next morning, Jacob "took the stone that he had put for his pillows, and set it up for a pillar, and poured oil upon the top of it."[23] Jacob then "vowed a vow," covenanting with the Lord over the stone altar he constructed. At the close of this event, Jacob said, "And this stone, which I have set for a pillar, shall be God's house,"[24] for "surely the Lord is in this place."[25]

This stone altar that Israel called the house of God may well illuminate the original use of the title "the stone of Israel." If so, that term, as originally used, pointed Israel to the Savior, and to the covenants made in his house.

b. The Rock as the source of life-sustaining water

Certainly a reference to *Rock* in the Song of Moses would have reminded Israel of the nourishment they received from rocks while in the desert: "Behold, I will stand before thee there upon the rock in Horeb; and thou shalt smite the rock, and there shall come water out of it, that the people may drink. And Moses did so in the sight of the elders of Israel."[26]

The Apostle Paul taught that these water-giving rocks were symbolic of the Savior: "Moreover, brethren, I would not that ye should be ignorant, how that all our fathers . . . did all drink the same spiritual drink: for they drank of that spiritual Rock that followed them [in the wilderness]: and that Rock was Christ."[27]

c. The Rock as the law and the covenant

The reference to *Rock* in this song also would have reminded the Israelites of another important event in their history: "When I was gone up into the mount to receive the tables of stone, even the tables of the covenant which the Lord made with you, then I abode in the mount forty days and forty nights, I neither did eat bread nor drink water: and the Lord delivered unto me two tables of stone written with the finger of God . . . even the tables of the covenant."[28]

So the Israelites received the law on the "stone tables of the covenant"—which were delivered to Moses by the One who was himself the law.[29] These very stone tablets were resting in the ark of the covenant within the Holy of Holies in the tabernacle when Moses received this song for Israel. Any reference to rock likely would have reminded Israel of the Lawgiver who had extended his finger and written the law they were to live upon these tablets of stone.

d. The Rock as our sure foundation

All of the parallels between rocks and Christ that we have discussed so far were available for the Israelites' consideration before Moses revealed the Lord's song to them. In each case, these stories of rocks were central to their history as a people, and should have therefore informed their understanding of the identity of the "Rock."

The references to Rock as a title for God after Deuteronomy most often refer to rock in terms of a foundation upon which we must build.[30] The Apostle Paul taught that these references to foundation are references to Christ: "For other foundation can no man lay than that is laid, which is Jesus Christ."[31] Likewise, Helaman exhorted his sons to "remember that it is upon the rock of our Redeemer, who is Christ, the Son of God, that ye must build your foundation."[32]

3. "No longer his children"

After establishing that the Lord is the Rock, verse 5 of the Song of Moses states: "They have acted corruptly toward him; to their shame they are no longer his children, but a warped and crooked generation."[33] Children of a physical father do not become "no longer his children." So there must be more to the familial reference here than mere membership in a physical family. The reference is to membership in Christ's family, as discussed in depth in chapter 3 herein.

As the Savior said, "Ye do the deeds of your father."[34] Verses 4 and 5 of the Song of Moses make clear that the deeds of the Israelites were far from the deeds of the Savior: The Rock is described as one who "does no wrong," who is "upright" and "just,"[35] while the Israelites are described as having "acted corruptly," and as being "warped" and "crooked."[36] Moses was a "son of God" because his life was in similitude of the Savior's[37]; the Israelites would become "no longer his children" because they would fail to follow in the Lord's ways.

4. "Is this the way you repay the Lord?"

After recounting the failure of Israel to qualify as children of the Lord, the Lord says: "Is this the way you repay the Lord?"[38] The word *repay* implies that we owe the Lord something. We are in his debt. Verse 6 in the King James Version makes this debt explicit: "Is not he thy father that hath bought thee?"

What is the extent of our debt to the Lord? Verses 10 through 14 make our debt clear: *"He"* found Israel. *"He"* shielded Israel. *"He"* cared for Israel. *"He"* guarded Israel. *"He"* led Israel. *"He"* made Israel to ride on the heights. *"He"* fed Israel. *"He"* nourished Israel. Israel was likened to a baby eagle dependent for everything on the parent that "hovers over its young, that spreads its wings to catch them and carries them on its pinions."[39] The message is clear: What do we owe the Lord? *Everything.* Nothing we have is ours. Everything is a gift of his good grace.

Many of the laws given to Israel in Deuteronomy would, if kept, create in them a generous spirit. For if everything we have is a free gift, then we must freely share our blessings with others. To hold tight to what we have been given is a sin of the highest order; it is to deny our debt to the Lord.

The following is a partial list of the commandments in Deuteronomy that are designed to develop within us this generous spirit:

- Pay tithing (14:22–29)
- Extend the Lord's release (every seven years, the Israelites were to forgive all debts of their fellow Israelites) (15:1)
- Freely lend to the poor, even if the seventh year is at hand (15:7–11)
- Must free servants in the seventh year, with abundant supplies (15:12–15)
- Consecrate firstborn animals (15:19–23)
- Consecrate firstfruits (26:2–3, 8–11)
- Hold Passover, Feast of Weeks, and Feast of Tabernacles commemorating generosity of the Lord (16:10–17)
- Take care of others' stray property until they come to claim it (22:1–3)
- Keep homes safe for others (22:8)
- Let any escaped slave take refuge with you (23:15–16)
- Do not charge any fellow Israelite interest (23:19–20)
- Must allow others to eat freely of your fields (23:24–25; 24:19–22)
- Never take advantage of the poor and needy (24:14–15)
- Do not deprive the disadvantaged of justice (24:17)

Every blessing carries the following risk: that we will think we *deserve* it. All of the commandments listed above are designed to help us remember that nothing we have is ours. We owe the Lord everything.

5. Israel "grew fat and kicked"

After listing in verses 10 through 14 the great blessings the Lord had given Israel, the very next verse begins: "Jeshurun [i.e., Israel] grew fat and kicked."[40] What might be meant by "grew fat"?

Appearing, as it does, immediately following the abundant blessings from the Lord to Israel—and especially the blessings in verses 13 and 14 of "fruit of the fields," "honey from the rock," "oil," "curds and milk," "fattened lambs and goats," "choice rams," "finest kernels of wheat," and "foaming blood of the grape"—growing fat implies that Israel would come to gorge itself on those blessings, taking them for granted, with no exercise of thanksgiving or faith.

Moses warned Israel of just such a sin:

> Beware that thou forget not the Lord thy God . . . lest when thou hast eaten and art full, and hast built goodly houses, and dwelt therein; and when thy herds and thy flocks multiply, and thy silver and thy gold is multiplied, and all that thou hast is multiplied; then thine heart be lifted up, and thou forget the Lord thy God . . . and thou say in thine heart, My power and the might of mine hand hath gotten me this wealth. But thou shalt remember the Lord thy God: for it is he that giveth thee power to get wealth, that he may establish his covenant which he sware unto thy fathers.[41]

Failing to heed Moses' warning, Israel would come to feel that the blessings of the Lord were theirs by right—that they had earned them, that they were *entitled*. In so thinking, they "kicked" against the Lord. Verses 15 through 18 suggest that the word *kick* as used here means that Israel "rejected the Rock," turned to "foreign gods," "abandoned the God who made [them,]" and "deserted the Rock, who fathered [them]."[42]

6. The Lord will "scatter" his people

This rejection of the Lord would bring upon Israel the curses that had been set forth by Moses for disobedience to the law.[43] Of these curses, two stand out and are emphasized in the Song of Moses: (a) "I will hide my face from them"[44]; and (b) "I said I would scatter them."[45]

Having rejected the Lord, Israel was warned that the Lord would hide his face from them "and see what their end will be."[46] In other words, if the people of Israel think they are themselves responsible, through their industry or otherwise, for their great blessings, the Lord will leave them to produce for themselves. Then they will discover just what they deserve of themselves.

As a result of being left unto their own power, they would be scattered: "The Lord shall scatter you among the nations, and ye shall be left few in number among the heathen, whither the Lord shall lead you. And there ye shall serve gods, the work of men's hands, wood and stone, which neither see, nor hear, nor eat, nor smell."[47]

So we see that Israel would be scattered physically after they scattered themselves spiritually by rejecting the Lord. The physical scattering followed the spiritual scattering.

7. The Lord will have compassion on Israel "when he sees their strength is gone"

The Lord says that although these curses (including scattering) would take a terrible toll on Israel, Israel would not be utterly destroyed.[48] Although broken, destitute, and weak, they would survive. When they are in just such a state, the Lord says he will call to them, pointing out the powerlessness of the gods they had followed: "Now where are their gods, the rock they took refuge in, the gods who ate the fat of their sacrifices and drank the wine of their drink offerings? Let them rise up to help you! Let them give you shelter!"[49] Their state of desolation would expose the powerlessness of the gods they had chosen over the Lord: "See now that I myself am He [who helps and gives shelter]! There is no other god besides me. I put to death and I bring to life, I have wounded and I will heal, and no one can deliver out of my hand."[50]

Then, *"when he sees their strength is gone,"*[51] his compassion will be moved toward them. They will be given strength once more when they look again to the one source of strength: "If from thence thou shalt seek the Lord thy God, thou shalt find him, if thou seek him with all thy heart and with all thy soul. When thou art in tribulation, and all these things are come upon thee, even in the latter days, if thou turn to the Lord thy God, and shalt be obedient unto his voice . . . he will not forsake thee, neither destroy thee, nor forget the covenant of thy fathers which he sware unto them."[52]

8. "He will . . . make atonement for his land and people"

Fittingly, the last stanza of Moses' song begins, "Rejoice." After calamities, arrows, famine, pestilence, plague, fangs, venom, swords, terror, and scattering, "Rejoice"!

Why rejoice? Because, we are told, "[the Lord] will . . . make atonement for his land and people."[53] "When all these things are come upon thee," the Lord said, "and [thou] shalt return unto the Lord thy God, and shalt obey his voice according to all that I command thee this day, thou and thy children, with all thine heart, and with all thy soul . . . then the Lord thy God will turn thy captivity, and have compassion upon thee, and will return and gather thee from all the nations, whither the Lord thy God hath scattered thee."[54]

So Israel will be gathered as they turn again to the Lord and his strength for nourishment.

BUT WHO SHALL GATHER ISRAEL TO THE LORD?

The holy priesthood, with its power to seal us up unto the Lord, was taken from Israel when they rebelled against the Lord.[55] So who is to lead the gathering of Israel? Moses' blessings to the tribes of Israel give a clue.

As discussed above, to Joseph—and Joseph only—Moses promised "the precious dew from heaven above."[56] Section 121 of the Doctrine and Covenants uses the "dews from heaven" as a metaphor for the doctrine of the fulness of the priesthood.[57] The exclusivity of this blessing of dew to Joseph juxtaposed against the Lord's call in the prior chapter for all heaven and earth to receive the dew[58] suggests that: (a) at least initially, the tribe of Joseph would be the only tribe to receive the fulness of the priesthood or dew from heaven; and (b) Joseph, as the possessor of that priesthood, would be instrumental in administering the message of the Lord's joy and Atonement to all of Israel.

So Joseph, as the bearer of the Lord's holy priesthood, is to be the instrument through whom the Lord will gather Israel in the latter days: "Let the blessing come upon the head of Joseph, and upon the top of the head of him that was separated from his brethren. His glory is like the firstling of his bullock, and his horns are like the horns of unicorns: with them he shall push the people together to the ends of the earth."[59]

As discussed in detail in chapter 7, this is precisely what is unfolding in the present day, with Ephraim, the birthright son of Joseph, leading the way in these latter days.

MOSES' INSTRUCTION FOR RECEIVING THE JOY OF THE LORD'S ATONEMENT

And so Moses, righteous Moses, saw not only the beginning, but the end: the Creation, the Fall, the covenant, the rejection of the covenant, the scattering, the new covenant, the gathering, the joy. These were his topics as he counseled the Israelites on the banks of the Jordan. His words, summarized by the Lord in song, "testify against [us] as a witness."[60]

These words reveal what Moses thought was crucial for the people to know on their way to the promised land. We also sit, at least metaphorically, on the banks of the Jordan, and must follow his words to make it to the promise of the Lord's presence. Moses' song was not only about Israel in ancient days but about the house of Israel in latter days as well.

The rest of the Lord awaits—for us, as well as for them. "Rejoice!" we are told. For the Lord has made atonement for his land and people.

CHAPTER 12

EARLY YEARS IN THE PROMISED LAND: THE PATTERN OF FALL AND REDEMPTION

The Lord Raised Up a Deliverer

Some people think the God of the Old Testament seems harsh, citing examples of punishments under the law (death to transgressors by stoning, for example), and the commandment for the Israelites to kill every person who lived in the promised land when they finally crossed into the land to occupy it. However, if you think of the body of Israel not as a collection of individuals, but as a representation of a single person—one who is to be a follower of Christ—all of these apparent harsh contradictions make divine sense, and Old Testament books like Joshua and Judges suddenly become illuminating guides to repentance and sanctification. We truly do need to wipe out all the temptations around us and stop dabbling in sin. Through an amazing repeating pattern, Joshua and Judges show us how.

Because Egypt, as it were, was still within the Israelites,[1] they were not allowed to cross into the promised land for forty years. As a body, they had to become sanctified. For the Israelites, this meant that all males of the older generation (twenty years old and up) who doubted the Lord's ability to deliver the land into their hands—which was everyone but Joshua and Caleb—had to die before the rest of Israel would be allowed to enter.[2]

One might wonder why all the people had to wait for the purification of the whole before they were allowed to enter into the promised land. Why couldn't some have entered sooner on their own—when they, themselves, were ready? But this isn't the only, or even the most difficult, question raised by this story. Consider the commandment, announced through

Moses, concerning how the Israelites were to treat those who presently occupied the land.

> Of the cities of these people, which the Lord thy God doth give thee for an inheritance, [Moses told the people,] thou shalt save alive nothing that breatheth: But thou shalt utterly destroy them; namely, the Hittites, and the Amorites, the Canaanites, and the Perizzites, the Hivites, and the Jebusites; as the Lord thy God hath commanded thee.[3]

> Thou shalt smite them, and utterly destroy them; thou shalt make no covenant with them, nor shew mercy unto them: Neither shalt thou make marriages with them; thy daughter thou shalt not give unto his son, nor his daughter shalt thou take unto thy son.[4]

So we encounter two puzzling issues at this point of the Israelites' story. The first is, Why could the Israelites enter the promised land, if at all, only as a sanctified whole? The second is, Why would the Lord command Israel to destroy all other peoples from the land after they entered— a command, after all, that seems to contradict the commandment not to kill? A possible answer to both questions is implied in words Moses was instructed to speak to Pharaoh: "And thou shalt say unto Pharaoh, Thus saith the Lord, Israel is my son, even my firstborn: And I say unto thee, Let my son go, that he may serve me: and if thou refuse to let him go, behold, I will slay thy son, even thy firstborn."[5] Notice how the Lord here characterizes a whole collection of individuals as a single person—as his son, his firstborn. If we think of the body of Israel metaphorically as a single person, then it makes sense that all of the impure elements within that person must be cleansed or expunged before the person can be allowed into the place that is most holy. Under this view, the story of the Exodus isn't merely, or even primarily, intended to be read as a story about many different individuals, some of whom make it into the promised land and some of whom do not. Rather, it can be read, metaphorically, as an illustration of how a single person can make it into the promised land of the celestial kingdom.

This reading of the story is supported further by the Lord's explanation for why Israel was to remove all of the inhabitants from the land. Here again, the Lord refers to the Israelites as a single person: "For [these other peoples] will turn away thy son from following me, that they may serve other gods: so will the anger of the Lord be kindled against you, and destroy thee suddenly. But thus shall ye deal with them; ye shall destroy their altars, and break down their images, and cut down their groves, and burn their graven images with fire. For thou art an holy people unto the Lord thy God."[6]

The scriptural passages that require the deaths of those within and without the body of Israel have caused some to complain that the God of the Old Testament is a harsh judge and, in some cases, a biased respecter of persons. However, if we think of the body of Israel as a *single person* who is to be a follower of the Lord—as God's own words invite us to do—the story takes on a different and divine meaning. All that is ungodly within each of us truly must be put to death or we will not be able to enter into the presence of the Lord. Furthermore, in order to become holy, we really do need to overcome all the temptations around us and stop dabbling in sin. "Go ye out of Babylon," the Lord has instructed.[7] If we are content to surround ourselves with unholiness, we, too, will become unholy and will therefore remain separated from the Lord, which, in the language of the scriptures, is death—spiritual death.

It is vitally important, and not unkind, for the Lord to teach us these truths. We ought to be inspired and instructed, rather than repulsed or confused, by the condition that all the unfaithful and unbelieving within Israel had to die before Israel was allowed to pass into the promised land. Likewise, although certainly disastrous for the mortal prospects of the inhabitants of the land of Canaan, one way to read these passages is that their physical death was commanded in order to emphasize for all time how serious a matter spiritual death is. The destination for Israel was no random piece of wilderness, but a land set apart as holy, a representation of the Lord's presence on earth. Symbolically, the land had the status of heaven itself—the celestial kingdom. Anything impure rendered the land unholy and therefore unheavenly. This applied equally to Israelites and non-Israelites. The Lord's intention during the time of Joshua and the rest of the period of the judges was to give the land the metaphorical and in-spirational status as His kingdom. The land had to be clean, and his child—the body of Israel—had to remain clean himself in order to remain there. This required a cleansing of the land and of Israel itself.

This cleansing of the land points to the cleansing that will occur at the second coming of the Savior.[8] It is perhaps no accident that the name of the person who led this cleansing, Joshua, is the Hebrew form of the Greek name Jesus, and is likely the name by which Jesus was called by his con-temporaries. The name means "God saves," and the story of Joshua re-minds us that God does not save us in our sins but from our sins.[9] God saves by purifying us from all ungodliness.

After Moses ascended into heaven, Joshua led Israel across the Jordan and into the promised land of Canaan. The scriptures tell us that he set out to cleanse the land and "left nothing undone of all that the Lord com-manded Moses."[10] First, after he laid siege to Jericho and marched the chil-dren of Israel around the city with the ark of the covenant once a day for six days and seven times on the seventh, the walls came tumbling down at the blast of the trumpets of rams' horns.[11] Then, according to the Lord's command, the children of Israel destroyed all of the city's inhabitants,[12] ex-cept for the inhabitants of the house of the harlot Rahab, who had pro-tected two men that Joshua had sent to scout the city.[13]

After destroying Jericho, the Israelites proceeded to purge the inhabi-tants of Ai,[14] then Jerusalem, Hebron, Jarmuth, Lachish, Eglon, Makkedah, Libnah, Gezer, Debir, and "all the country of the hills, and of the south, and of the vale, and of the springs," from Kadesh-barnea even unto Gaza, and all the country of Goshen, even unto Gibeon.[15] Then Israel took all the land of "the valley, and the plain, and the mountain of Israel, and the valley of the same; even from the mount Halak, that goeth up to Seir, even unto Baak-gad in the valley of Lebanon under mount Hermon"[16] until "Joshua took the whole land, according to all that the Lord said unto Moses,"[17] as listed in chapter twelve of the book of Joshua.

By this time, Joshua was "old and stricken in years,"[18] and although he had been ever faithful in acquiring the lands for Israel's inheritance, there still remained "much land to be possessed."[19] It would be left to those Joshua had so faithfully led to complete their compliance with the Lord's

commands. The land of their inheritance was divided among the tribes of
Israel,[20] and Joshua died after exhorting Israel for a final time to complete
the task set forth through Moses:

> And the Lord your God, he shall expel [the remaining na-
> tions] from before you, and drive them from out of your sight;
> and ye shall possess their land, as the Lord your God hath
> promised unto you. . . .
>
> [But] if ye do in any wise go back, and cleave unto the rem-
> nant of these nations, even these that remain among you, and
> shall make marriages with them, and go in unto them, and they
> to you: Know for a certainty that the Lord your God will no
> more drive out any of these nations from before you; but they
> shall be snares and traps unto you, and scourges in your sides,
> and thorns in your eyes, until ye perish from off this good land
> which the Lord your God hath given you.[21]

Unfortunately for Israel, they failed to expel the remaining nations.
That failure was a sign of their failure to keep the commandment that had
been given them. It was also a sign of Israel's failure to serve the Lord to
the degree necessary to have him drive those nations from before them.

> Judah . . . could not drive out the inhabitants of the valley.[22]

> And the children of Benjamin did not drive out the
> Jebusites that inhabited Jerusalem; but the Jebusites dwell with
> the children of Benjamin in Jerusalem unto this day.[23]

> Neither did Manasseh drive out the inhabitants of Beth-
> shean and her towns, nor Taanach and her towns, nor the in-
> habitants of Dor and her towns, nor the inhabitants of Ibleam
> and her towns, nor the inhabitants of Megiddo and her towns;
> but the Canaanites would dwell in that land.[24]

> Neither did Ephraim drive out the Canaanites that dwell
> in Gezer; but the Canaanites dwelt in Gezer among them.[25]

Neither did Zebulun drive out the inhabitants of Kitron, nor the inhabitants of Nahalol; but the Canaanites dwelt among them.[26]

Neither did Asher drive out the inhabitants of Accho, nor the inhabitants of Zidon, nor of Ahlab, nor of Achzib, nor of Helbah, nor of Aphik, nor of Rehob: But the Asherites dwelt among the Canaanites, the inhabitants of the land: for they did not drive them out.[27]

Neither did Naphtali drive out the inhabitants of Beth-shemesh, nor the inhabitants of Bethanaath; but he dwelt among the Canaanites, the inhabitants of the land.[28]

And the Amorites forced the children of Dan into the mountain: for they would not suffer them to come down to the valley.[29]

Having failed to remove the ungodly elements around them, the Israelites condemned themselves to certain sin and left the promised land well short of its metaphorical status as God's holy kingdom.

The period of Israel's history between Joshua's singular leadership and Saul's establishment as king is known as the period of the judges—a period during which the individual tribes of Israel governed their own affairs but did so among the influence of heathen peoples who led them to sin.

The period of the judges provides a sustained lesson in the cycle of sin. In addition, perhaps more than any other book of scripture, the book of Judges points in its structure to the One who delivers from sin. Throughout this period, deliverers were raised up to save the tribes of Israel from their sins—deliverers who were in similitude of the Great Deliverer. Six major deliverers emerge, and many lesser ones. The major deliverers were Othniel, Ehud, Deborah, Gideon, Jephthah, and Samson. Their stories are parallel to each other and to the Master's. You can compare their stories on the accompanying chart.

THE CYCLE OF THE PERIOD OF THE JUDGES

	OTHNIEL	EHUD	DEBORAH
Sin	"And the children of Israel **did evil in the sight of the Lord,** and forgat the Lord their God, and served Baalim and the groves." (Judges 3:7)	"And the children of Israel **did evil again in the sight of the Lord.**" (3:12)	"And the children of Israel again **did evil in the sight of the Lord.**" (4:1)
Consequences of sin	"Therefore the anger of the Lord was hot against Israel, and **he sold them into the hand of [the king of] Mesopotamia;** and the children of Israel served [him] eight years." (3:8)	"And **the Lord strengthened [the Moabites] against Israel,** because they had done evil in the sight of the Lord. . . . So the children of Israel served [Moab] eighteen years." (3:12–14)	"And **the Lord sold them into the hand of Jabin king of Canaan** . . . the captain of whose host was Sisera." (4:2) "And twenty years [Jabin] mightily oppressed the children of Israel." (4:3)
Repentance	"And . . . the children of Israel **cried unto the Lord.**" (3:9)	"The children of Israel **cried unto the Lord.**" (3:15)	"And the children of Israel **cried unto the Lord.**" (4:3)
Means of deliverance	"The Lord **raised up a deliverer** to the children of Israel, who delivered them, even Othniel the son of Kenaz, Caleb's younger brother. And the Spirit of the Lord came upon him, and he judged Israel, and went out to war." (3:9–10)	"The Lord **raised them up a deliverer,** Ehud the son of Gera, a Benjamite, a man left-handed." (3:15)	"And Deborah, **a prophetess** . . . judged Israel at that time . . . and the children of Israel came up to her for judgment" (4:4–5). "And Deborah said unto Barak, Up; for this is the day in which the Lord hath delivered Sisera into thine hand: is not the Lord gone out before thee? So Barak went down from mount Tabor, and ten thousand men after him." (4:14)
Deliverance	Israel followed Othniel into war, "and **the Lord delivered** [the] king of Mesopotamia into [Othniel's] hand; and his hand prevailed against [him]." (3:10)	"And [Ehud] said unto them, Follow after me: for **the Lord hath delivered** your enemies the Moabites into your hand . . . So Moab was subdued that day under the hand of Israel." (3:28, 30)	Following Deborah's command, Barak and the army routed Sisera, who was then killed by a woman, Jael (4:15, 21). "So **God subdued** on that day Jabin the king of Canaan" (4:23)
Peace	"And **the land had rest** forty years." (3:11)	"And **the land had rest** [80] years." (3:30)	"And **the land had rest** forty years." (5:31)

The Cycle of the Period of the Judges

Gideon	Jephthah	Samson
"And the children of Israel **did evil in the sight of the Lord.**" (6:1)	"And the children of Israel **did evil again in the sight of the Lord,** and served Baalim, and Ashtaroth, and the gods of Syria, and the gods of Zidon, and the gods of Moab, and the gods of the children of Ammon, and the gods of the Philistines, and forsook the Lord, and served not him." (10:6)	"And the children of Israel **did evil again in the sight of the Lord.**" (13:1)
"And **the Lord delivered them into the hand of Midian** seven years. And the hand of Midian prevailed against Israel . . . And Israel was greatly impoverished because of the Midianites." (6:1–2, 6)	"And the anger of the Lord was hot against Israel, and **he sold them into the hands of the Philistines, and into the hands of the children of Ammon.** And . . . they vexed and oppressed the children of Israel . . . eighteen years . . . so that Israel was sore distressed." (10:7–9)	"And **the Lord delivered them into the hand of the Philistines** forty years." (13:1)
"And the children of Israel **cried unto the Lord** . . . because of the Midianites." (6:6–7)	"And the children of Israel **cried unto the Lord,** saying, We have sinned against thee, both because we have forsaken our God, and also served Baalim." (10:10) "And the children of Israel said unto the Lord, We have sinned: do thou unto us whatsoever seemeth good unto thee; deliver us only, we pray thee, this day. And they put away the strange gods from among them, and served the Lord; and his soul was grieved for the misery of Israel." (10:15–16)	*No mention of Israelites crying unto the Lord.*
"And the Lord looked upon [Gideon], and said, Go in . . . thy might, and thou shalt save Israel from the . . . Midianites: have not I sent thee? And [Gideon] said unto him, Oh my Lord, wherewith shall I save Israel? Behold, my family is poor in Manasseh, and I am the least in my father's house. **And the Lord said . . . Surely I will be with thee, and thou shalt smite the Midianites as one man.**" (6:14–16)	"Jephthah . . . was a mighty man . . . and the son of an harlot." (11:1) "When the children of Ammon made war against Israel, the elders of Gilead went to fetch Jephthah out of the land of Tob: And they said unto Jephthah, Come, and be our captain. . . . And Jephthah said unto [them], If ye bring me home again to fight against the children of Ammon, and the Lord deliver them before me, shall I be your head? And the elders of Gilead said unto Jephthah, The Lord be witness between us, if we do not so according to thy words. Then Jephthah went with [them], **and the people made him head and captain over them.**" (11:5–11)	"And there was a certain man . . . of the Danites, whose name was Manoah; and his wife was barren, and bare not. And the angel of the Lord appeared unto the woman, and said unto her, Behold now, thou art barren, and bearest not: but thou shalt conceive, and bear a son. Now therefore beware, I pray thee, and drink not wine nor strong drink, and eat not any unclean thing: For, lo, thou shalt conceive, and bear a son; and no razor shall come on his head: for the child shall be a Nazarite unto God from the womb: **and he shall begin to deliver Israel** out of the hand of the Philistines." (13:2–5)
The Lord reduced Israelite army to 300 men, who followed Gideon's lead and defeated the Midianites by blowing trumpets and shouting. (7:1–25) "**Thus was Midian subdued** before . . . Israel, so that they lifted up their heads no more." (8:28)	After making Jephthah head and captain over them, the Israelites, following Jephthah, "passed over unto the children of Ammon to fight against them; and **the Lord delivered** them into his hands. . . . Thus the children of Ammon were subdued before the children of Israel." (11:32–33)	*The Philistines are not subdued, but Samson afflicts them* (14:19; 15:3–5, 14–15; 16:28–30), for "the Lord . . . sought an occasion against the Philistines." (14:4)
"And **the country was in quietness** forty years." (8:28)	*No peace mentioned.* (Still fighting the Philistines, and had civil war with Ephraimites—see 12:1–7)	*No peace mentioned.*

To begin with, consider the state of the people at the time just before each of these deliverers emerges. In the Othniel story, we are told, "And the children of Israel did evil in the sight of the Lord, and forgat the Lord their God, and served Baalim and the groves."[30] The Ehud story begins, "And the children of Israel did evil again in the sight of the Lord."[31] Likewise, in the Deborah story, "the children of Israel again did evil in the sight of the Lord."[32] The Gideon story begins the same way, "And the children of Israel did evil in the sight of the Lord,"[33] as does the Jephthah story, where "the children of Israel did evil again in the sight of the Lord, and served Baalim, and Ashtaroth, and the gods of Syria, and the gods of Zidon, and the gods of Moab, and the gods of the children of Ammon, and the gods of the Philistines, and forsook the Lord, and served not him."[34] The Samson story repeats the pattern: "And the children of Israel did evil again in the sight of the Lord."[35]

Each story then continues with a parallel second element: oppression at the hands of the non-Israelites in their midst. In the Othniel story, as a result of Israel's sin, we are told that the Lord "sold them into the hand of [the king of] Mesopotamia: and the children of Israel served [him] eight years."[36] When Israel rebelled again at the beginning of the Ehud story, "the Lord strengthened [the Moabites] against Israel . . . [so] the children of Israel served [Moab] eighteen years."[37] After rebelling again at the beginning of the Deborah story, "the Lord sold [Israel] into the hand of Jabin king of Canaan . . . [and] twenty years [Jabin] mightily oppressed the children of Israel."[38] Likewise in the Gideon story, "the Lord delivered them into the hand of Midian seven years."[39] In the Jephthah story, "the anger of the Lord was hot against Israel, and he sold them into the hands of the Philistines, and into the hands of the children of Ammon. And . . . they vexed and oppressed the children of Israel . . . eighteen years . . . so that Israel was sore distressed."[40] In the Samson story, "the Lord delivered [Israel] into the hand of the Philistines forty years."[41]

The third parallel element in each of the stories of deliverance is the Israelites' cry to the Lord for deliverance. Each story but one, the Samson story, contains the phrase, "and the children of Israel cried unto the Lord."[42] As we shall discover, the absence of this element in the Samson story is significant.

In each of the stories besides the Samson story, a deliverer was raised up *after* the Israelites cried to the Lord.[43] As the Israelites followed these deliverers, the Lord then delivered Israel out from the oppression of their captors.[44] The result of these deliverances was peace.[45]

Where detail of these deliverers is given, in their humble beginnings as well as their missions of deliverance, they point to the Deliverer who was yet to come. Deborah and Jael (who figured prominently in that story of deliverance[46]) were women—in outward appearance hardly what those in ancient Israel would have expected in a deliverer. Gideon was "the least in [his] father's house"—a house that was "poor in Manasseh."[47]

The story of Jephthah is perhaps the most beautiful of the Messianic parallels among the judges. The circumstances of Jephthah's birth brought him great persecution. He was "the son of an harlot,"[48] for which he was persecuted and finally cast out from among his people.[49] But he "was a mighty man of valour,"[50] and when the children of Ammon came against Israel, the elders of the people went to fetch Jephthah and to beg him to come and deliver them. Consider in the following passage how we, who effectively cast the Savior out from us through our sin, return to him in time of need the same way the elders returned to Jephthah. And consider as well how the Savior forgives and delivers us, just as Jephthah did his people, and upon the same conditions:

> When the children of Ammon made war against Israel, the elders of Gilead went to fetch Jephthah out of the land of Tob: And they said unto Jephthah, Come, and be our captain. . . . And Jephthah said . . . , Did not ye hate me, and expel me out of my father's house? and why are ye come unto me now when ye are in distress? And [they] said unto Jephthah, Therefore we turn again to thee now, that thou mayest . . . fight against the children of Ammon, and be our head over all the inhabitants of Gilead. And Jephthah said unto [them], If ye bring me home again to fight against the children of Ammon, and the Lord deliver them before me, shall I be your head? And the elders of Gilead said unto Jephthah, The Lord be witness between us, if we do not so according to thy words. Then Jephthah went with

[them], and the people made him head and captain over them.[51]

Jephthah, in similitude of the Savior's promise to us, delivered Israel when they made him head and captain over them.

Samson was also largely in similitude of the Savior, although Samson's deliverance is different from the deliverance supplied by the other deliverers in Judges. Like the Savior, Samson was the product of a miraculous birth. His mother was barren, and "the angel of the Lord appeared unto the woman, [saying] . . . thou shalt conceive, and bear a son . . . and he shall begin to deliver Israel out of the hand of the Philistines."[52]

As mentioned earlier, the children of Israel did *not* cry for deliverance before Samson was raised up as a deliverer. By this time, Israel apparently had become so entwined with its heathen neighbors that the Israelites no longer felt oppressed by their condition. They had become assimilated into sin to such a degree that they had become blind to their iniquity. It was into this spiritual malaise that Samson was born, and Samson's wild and lone antics against the Philistines[53] can be seen as an attempt to set again enmity between Israel and its sinful partners, so as to awaken Israel to the danger in its alliances. Samson's deliverance was not so much deliverance from oppressors as it was deliverance from comfort in oppression. He afflicted the Philistines because "the Lord . . . sought an occasion against the Philistines"[54]—an occasion that would provoke the Philistines against Israel, thereby awakening Israel from what had become a deep slumber in sin.

Like the Savior, Samson would not bring temporal freedom to ancient Israel. Rather, he would set in motion spiritual events that would lead to eventual temporal and spiritual freedom. And like the Savior, in his death, Samson would bring down the house of evil.

Unlike the Savior, however, Samson ultimately became a tragic figure, breaking key vows just as Israel as a whole had done. In this respect, Samson is in similitude of ancient Israel and in particular Israel during the period of the judges—a chosen vessel, called for the purpose of deliverance, who ultimately fell among the heathen.

CHAPTER 13

⌒

SAMUEL AND THE MESSIANIC KINGDOM

The Lord Your God Is Your King

> The book of First Samuel contains a hidden prophecy of the great apostasy and restoration that is as comprehensive and majestic as any in scripture. When we see it, we gain a new and awesome sense of the "bigness" of the restoration of which we are a part.
>
> And when we see how closely Samuel's life parallels the Savior's, and what that parallelism implies, we gain a greater understanding of the history of Israel and see more clearly how we fit into that history and the coming future.

The prophet Samuel was the last of the judges. The book of First Samuel begins with a look into the heart of his mother—a woman, still barren, who could not have children. Year after year righteous Hannah prayed at the temple for the blessing of motherhood. Still, she remained childless. "And she was in bitterness of soul," we are told, "and prayed unto the Lord, and wept sore."[1] This emphasis on Hannah's condition in the first sixteen verses of First Samuel leaves us without doubt: This was no temporary condition; Hannah could not have children. When she does conceive and have a child, then, we know that it was through the intervention and power of God.[2]

In this way, beginning with the miraculous circumstances of his birth, Samuel, the firstborn of Hannah and Elkanah, reminds us of the Savior. Filled with joy, Hannah offered a song of praise and thanksgiving that prefigures the song offered under similar circumstances by blessed Mary.[3]

Samuel was then dedicated to the Lord for life,[4] just as Jesus was set apart to "reign over the house of Jacob forever."[5]

The similarities continue in the description of their youthful experiences at the temple:

> And [Samuel's parents] brought him unto the house of the Lord in Shiloh: and the child was young. . . . And [his parents] went to Ramah to [their] house. [But] the child [remained at the temple and] did minister unto the Lord.[6]

> And when [Jesus] was twelve years old, they went up to Jerusalem. . . . And when they had fulfilled the days, as they returned, the child Jesus tarried behind in Jerusalem . . . in the temple, sitting in the midst of the doctors, both hearing them, and asking them questions.[7]

The description of their development is nearly identical as well: Samuel "continued to grow in stature and in favor with the Lord and with men,"[8] just as Jesus "increased in wisdom and stature, and in favour with God and man."[9] Both matured in Israel at a time when the religious leaders had become corrupt,[10] and they were each called to deliver the word of God to Israel.[11] Just as "the fame of [Jesus] went out into every place of the country round about,"[12] so too "all Israel from Dan even to Beer-sheba knew that Samuel was established to be a prophet of the Lord."[13]

But the most dramatic similarity remains—a similarity they share in silence.

The Loss and Restoration of the Ark of the Lord

Throughout the first three chapters of First Samuel, the narrative builds in crescendo with Samuel's life, until at the end of chapter 3 he is known throughout *all* of Israel, and *all* of Israel receives the Lord's word through him. But then there is a sudden change. Just when we catch the momentum of Samuel, the Lord's prophet, and at the point where the text emphasizes his fame and importance to Israel, his name disappears from the record. Beginning in the last half of the first verse of chapter 4 and continuing for three chapters, no mention is made of him. He reappears as the narrative's central figure in chapter 7.

What are we to make of chapters 4 through 6? What could be of such importance that it completely interrupts the story of Samuel? And what might this silence have to do with Christ as well? The answers to these questions open vistas of meaning. In a way that will become clearer as we go, chapters 4 through 6 are more fully about Samuel—and Christ—than any other chapters in First Samuel. In order to see how that might be the case, and of what significance it might be, we need to get beneath the story in these chapters.

First Samuel, chapter 4, begins with a Philistine victory against the Israelites. Israel was rocked by this loss. Lamenting their defeat, they wondered aloud, "Wherefore hath the Lord smitten us to day before the Philistines?"[14] Perhaps reflecting on the miracle at Jericho, where the walls of that city crumbled as Israel carried the ark of the covenant around it,[15] they trusted that the ark might once again be instrumental in delivering a military victory. So the people said, "Let us fetch the ark of the covenant of the Lord out of Shiloh unto us, that, when it cometh among us, it may save us out of the hand of our enemies."[16]

The presence of the ark in the camp of Israel raised their spirits, and "all Israel shouted with a great shout, so that the earth rang again."[17] The Philistines wondered at this show of confidence, and feared.[18] Nevertheless, "the Philistines fought, and Israel was smitten, and they fled every man into his tent: and there was a very great slaughter; for there fell of Israel thirty thousand footmen."[19] Israel had made a grave mistake. The Lord had commanded them to carry the ark around Jericho. Here, they had taken it upon themselves, and they were routed. The unthinkable had happened: the sacred "ark of God was taken" by the Philistines.[20]

A man ran from the army, clothes rent and dust on his head, to bear the terrible news. To Eli, who had been waiting anxiously on the wayside for news of the battle, he panted, "Israel is fled before the Philistines, and there hath been also a great slaughter among the people, and thy two sons also . . . are dead, and the ark of God is taken."[21]

Eli had lost his two sons, who had been the bearers of the ark, and his people had been defeated, but he focused on neither of these two facts.

Rather, his "heart trembled [out of worry] for the ark of God," and at the mention of its loss, he recoiled in horror, "fell from off the seat backward by the side of the gate, and his neck brake, and he died."[22] And "all the city cried out."[23] With the loss of the ark, the essence of the temple had been taken from Israel.

Reveling in their victory, the Philistines took the spoils back to their cities. "And [they] took the ark of God, and brought it . . . unto Ashdod."[24] At Ashdod, they "brought it into the house of Dagon [a temple erected for Dagon, the chief of the Philistines' gods], and set it by Dagon."[25] So the ark of God was placed in a false temple, before a false god.

The next morning, the Philistines awoke to an unexpected sight: "Dagon was fallen . . . before the ark of the Lord."[26] Puzzled, but perhaps thinking it a coincidence, the Philistines "took Dagon, and set him in his place again."[27] But the next morning, mere coincidence was exposed as a lie: "And when they arose early on the morrow morning, behold, Dagon was fallen upon his face to the ground before the ark of the Lord; and the head of Dagon and both the palms of his hands were cut off upon the threshold; only the stump of Dagon was left to him."[28] The god of the Philistines fell before the ark of the Lord.

In addition to exposing the powerlessness of false gods, the presence of the ark brought affliction upon the Philistines: "The hand of the Lord was heavy upon them of Ashdod, and he destroyed them, and smote them with [tumors or boils]."[29] The same fate befell the inhabitants of Gath and Ekron when the ark was moved to those locations. By the time the Philistines had moved the ark to Ekron, the people had come to believe in its power: "And it came to pass, as the ark of God came to Ekron, that the Ekronites cried out, saying, They have brought about the ark of the God of Israel to us, to slay us and our people."[30]

Believing in the power of the ark of the God of Israel, the people "sent and gathered together all the lords of the Philistines, and said, Send away the ark of the God of Israel, and let it go again to his own place."[31] And then the priests and diviners among the Philistines said, "If ye send away the ark of the God of Israel, send it not empty; but in any wise return him a trespass offering: then ye shall be healed, and it shall be known to you why his hand is not removed from you."[32] Under the law of Moses, trespass offerings were offered in atonement for a sin or trespass against a person.[33] In offering a trespass offering, the Philistines were, in effect, repenting of sin!

Seven months after the Philistines had captured the ark,[34] they laid it upon a cart "and put the jewels of gold, which [they] return[ed] him for a trespass offering, in a coffer by the side thereof."[35] They hitched two cows to the cart, and the cows "took the straight way to the way of Beth-shemesh [an Israelite town] . . . and the lords of the Philistines went after them unto the border of Beth-shemesh."[36]

What a moment this must have been—the Philistine rulers walking along with the ark of the God of Israel, returning the ark to the Israelites! The cows, "lowing as they went," turned neither to the right nor to the left, and steadily made their way back to Israel.[37]

The Israelites "were reaping their wheat harvest in the valley" when the ark crested the hill, "and they lifted up their eyes, and saw the ark, and rejoiced to see it."[38] Many of the Israelites in Beth-shemesh then "looked into the ark of the Lord,"[39] in violation of the commandment.[40] As a result, "the Lord [smote] many of the people with a great slaughter,"[41] and the ark was taken to others of the Israelites, who "fetched up the ark of the Lord, and brought it into the house of Abinadab in the hill, and sanctified Eleazar his son to keep the ark of the Lord."[42] The ark abode in Abinadab's house—not the tabernacle—for twenty years. "And all the house of Israel lamented after the Lord."[43] The New International Version of the Bible translates *lamented* as "mourned and sought after."

It was at this point—when Israel was again beginning to seek after the Lord—that Samuel reentered the story: "And Samuel spake unto all the house of Israel, saying, If ye do return unto the Lord with all your hearts, then put away the strange gods . . . from among you, and prepare your hearts unto the Lord, and serve him only . . . he will deliver you out of the hand of the Philistines."[44] In response to Samuel's instruction, "the children of Israel did put away Baalim and Ashtaroth, and served the Lord only."[45] And Samuel said, "Gather all Israel to Mizpeh, and I will pray for you unto the Lord."[46] "And they gathered together to Mizpeh, and drew water, and poured it out before the Lord, and fasted on that day, and said there, We have sinned against the Lord."[47]

When the Philistines heard that the children of Israel were gathered to Mizpeh, "the lords of the Philistines went up against Israel."[48] The children of Israel were afraid when they heard it, but they turned to Samuel, and said: "Cease not to cry unto the Lord our God for us, that he will save us out of the hand of the Philistines."[49] At this plea, Samuel "offered . . . a burnt offering wholly unto the Lord: and . . . cried unto the Lord for Israel; and the Lord heard him."[50] As Samuel was offering up the burnt offering, the Philistines drew near to battle against Israel. But "the Lord thundered with a great thunder on that day upon the Philistines, and discomfited them; and they were smitten before Israel."[51]

After the Lord smote the Philistines, the elders of Israel came to Samuel and said, "Now make us a king to judge us like all the nations . . . that we also may be like all the nations; and that our king may judge us, and go out before us, and fight our battles."[52]

Think about it: In response to the miraculous intercession by their heavenly king, the Israelites clamored for a mortal king—one who would bring them temporal protection and victory. Their blind desire for a temporal king is a theme we must follow, as it shapes Israel from this point forward. To do that, however, we need to consider a pattern in the story of the ark's loss and return.

THE ARK STORY AS A TYPE AND SHADOW

In the following chart, I list the elements of the ark story on the left. On the right, I list the same elements, with minor word changes. (For example, I substitute gospel for ark and Gentiles for Philistines, changes indicated in boldface in the right-hand column.) Looking at these events in this parallel form, we can see that the ark story bears striking resemblance to a much larger story—a story that is not obvious on the surface. There may be more going on in First Samuel 4 through 6 than at first meets the eye. . . .

LOSS AND RETURN OF THE ARK	LOSS AND RETURN OF THE GOSPEL
1. Israel looks to the ark as a power that will deliver a political/military victory	1. Israel looks for **a Messiah** who will deliver a political/military victory
2. The ark is lost from Israel	2. The **gospel** is lost from Israel
3. The temple is therefore lost from Israel	3. The temple is therefore lost from Israel
4. The ark of the God of Israel overcomes the gods of the Philistines	4. The **gospel** of the God of Israel overcomes the gods of the **Gentiles**
5. The ark afflicts the Philistines	5. The **gospel** afflicts the **Gentiles**
6. The Philistines come to believe in the power of the God of Israel	6. The **Gentiles** come to believe in the power of the God of Israel
7. The Philistines repent of their wrongdoing	7. The **Gentiles** repent of their wrongdoing
8. The Philistines take the ark back to Israel	8. The **Gentiles** take the **gospel** back to Israel
9. The Israelites who don't treat the ark with proper respect lose the ark again and are destroyed	9. The Israelites who don't treat the **gospel** with proper respect lose the **gospel** again and are destroyed
10. The return of the ark leads the Israelites to mourn and seek after the Lord	10. The return of the **gospel** leads the Israelites to mourn and seek after the Lord
11. The Israelites repent and put away false gods	11. The Israelites repent and put away false gods
12. The Israelites put their trust in the Lord when being attacked by their enemies	12. The Israelites put their trust in the Lord when being attacked by their enemies
13. The Lord provides a military victory	13. The Lord provides a military victory
14. Israel looks for a temporal king	14. **The Lord** is established as King over Israel

Seen this way, the ark story becomes a "type" of a much larger story: It can be viewed as a grand prophecy of the loss of the gospel from Israel and the latter-day restoration of that gospel through the Gentiles.

Just as the Israelites looked to the ark for political or military deliverance and missed the spiritual dimension of the ark and its source of power, so too at the time of Christ "they were too busy staring in search of a political liberator and missed the Messiah."[53] In missing the Messiah, they missed his gospel, and without that gospel, the fulness of the priesthood and the ordinances of the temple remained hidden from them.

Just as the ark became possessed by the Philistines, after Israel's rejection of the Lord, the gospel was revealed to the Gentiles. "For thus it behooveth the Father that it should come forth from the Gentiles, that he may show forth his power unto the Gentiles."[54] Just as the ark overcame the gods of the Philistines, the restored gospel will overcome the gods of the Gentiles, rolling forth as a stone cut out of a mountain without hands.[55] One by one, men will be brought by that gospel to a knowledge of their sins—and it will afflict them the way the ark afflicted the Philistines.

As discussed in chapters 7 and 11 of this book, after the Gentiles in the latter days come to the knowledge of the gospel and turn to Christ, they will be the instruments through whom the Lord restores the fulness of the gospel to the house of Israel: "In the latter days . . . shall the fulness of the gospel of the Messiah come unto the Gentiles, and from the Gentiles unto [Israel]."[56] "And the last shall be first, and the first shall be last."[57] Just as the Philistines brought the ark back to Israel, so too in the latter days the Gentiles will bring the gospel back to Israel.

As in the ark story, when the gospel is restored to Israel, "as many of the Jews as will not repent shall be cast off."[58] Nevertheless, the restoration will lead many Israelites to mourn and seek after the Lord,[59] and then to repent and put away false gods.[60] After they repent they will turn to the Lord for deliverance.[61] And when they do, the Lord will provide them a great military victory: "Then shall the Lord go forth, and fight against those nations, as when he fought in the day of battle. And his feet shall stand in that day upon the mount of Olives, which is before Jerusalem on the east, and the mount of Olives shall cleave in the midst thereof toward the east and toward the west, and there shall be a very great valley; and half of the mountain shall remove toward the north, and half of it toward the south. And ye shall flee to the valley of the mountains . . . and the Lord my God shall come, and all the saints with thee."[62]

Completing the parallelism, after this great victory, "the Lord shall be king over all the earth."[63]

We can see that from start to finish, the ark story matches the larger gospel story. The parallelism is striking. This raises the question: Besides providing a prophecy concerning the coming forth of the gospel in the latter days, is there any other reason why this particular parallelism appears where it does in First Samuel? I submit that the answer to this question is yes. The question and its answer bring us back to the issue of a king in Israel.

THE ARK/GOSPEL PARALLELISM AND THE QUESTION OF A KING FOR ISRAEL

With the possible exception of Melchizedek, who was referred to as "the king of Salem,"[65] since the fall of Adam the people of God had never had a king. However, the children of Israel began clamoring for one during the period of the judges. After Gideon had been an instrument in the Lord's hands in bringing a dramatic victory to Israel, for example, the people pressed him to be their king: "Rule thou over us, both thou, and thy son," they said, "and thy son's son also: for thou hast delivered us from the hand of Midian."[66] This might have been an intoxicating request for many, but not for Gideon. He was unwavering in his rejection of the idea, and prophetically clear as to why: "I will not rule over you," he answered, "neither shall my son rule over you: *the Lord shall rule over you.*"[67] The Israelites' failure to look to the Lord as their king is emphasized in the last verse of Judges: "In those days there was no king in Israel: *every man did that which was right in his own eyes.*"[68]

Doing "that which was right in [their] own eyes," the Israelites failed to keep their covenants in a way that would have brought them power and protection from the King of Heaven. Their spiritual unworthiness made them vulnerable, and, feeling vulnerable, they added to their sin by clamoring for temporal power and protection. By the time of Samuel, the clamor for a mortal king had reached a crescendo: "Then *all the elders* of Israel gathered themselves together, and came to Samuel unto Ramah, and said unto him, Behold, thou art old, and thy sons walk not in thy ways: now make us a king to judge us like all the nations."[69]

Samuel, like Gideon, knew what was at stake in this request. He was sorely displeased,[70] and warned them of the dangers of a king.[71] But the people dismissed the warning out of hand. "Nay; but we will have a king over us," they said, "that we also may be like all the nations; and that our king may judge us, and go out before us, and fight our battles."[72] And they insisted on this, you will recall, soon after the Lord had delivered them from the Philistines. This is why, upon the people's request for a temporal king, the Lord told Samuel: "[The people] have not rejected thee [Samuel], but they have rejected me. . . . [As] they have forsaken me, and served other gods, so do they also unto thee."[73]

The Lord said to Samuel, "Hearken unto their voice, and make them a king."[74] And Samuel anointed Saul to be king, according to the Lord's direction.[75] Israel received what they thought they wanted—a king they believed would deliver temporal victory.

Notice that this desire for a temporal king is both the final element of the ark story and the first element of the gospel story. So the story of the loss of the ark does more than merely point to the larger story of the loss of the gospel. It is itself the beginning of that story. The Lord, through the ark story, is warning Israel of the terrible consequences of trusting in man rather than in the Lord. By desiring a temporal deliverer and king, they risked losing the gospel itself, just as they had lost the ark.

Which brings us back to Samuel.

THE INTERSECTION OF THE ARK/GOSPEL AND SAMUEL/CHRIST PARALLELISMS

Seeing that the elements of Samuel's early life point to the Savior's early life, we should not be surprised that Israel completely ignored him when they became fixated on political and military victory in chapters 4 through 6 of First Samuel. As a type of the Savior, he was overlooked by the people just as they would later look past the Lord.

Likewise, perhaps it is no coincidence that, as a type of the Savior, Samuel reemerges in the story at the moment the people "mourn and seek" after the Lord.[76] In similitude of the Savior, when Israel looks to Samuel, he exhorts them to repentance;[77] when they repent, he intercedes with God on their behalf;[78] and when they look to him as their leader, he delivers them from death.[79]

Just when the parallelism might leave us despairing for Israel, however, as it appears that they have rejected both the Lord and his prophet, it offers hope: Samuel went before the people and dramatically demonstrated that Israel's insistence on a temporal king was a sin of the highest order,[80] and Israel repented of what they had done: "Pray for thy servants unto the Lord thy God," the people begged Samuel, "that we die not: for we have added unto all our sins this evil, to ask us a king."[81]

Now humble, they were open to being taught. "If ye will fear the Lord," Samuel declared, "and serve him, and obey his voice, and not rebel against the commandment of the Lord, then shall both ye and also the king that reigneth over you continue following the Lord. God forbid," he continued, "that I should [cease] to pray for you: but I will teach you the good and the right way."[82]

From this more humble place, Israel could now be taught the truth about the kingship in Israel: "Behold, the *Lord* hath set a king over you,"[83] Samuel exclaimed, teaching them that the king had been established not by man but by God. Furthermore, by establishing the Israelite monarchy at the hand of a prophet who was the very likeness of the Savior, the Lord put Israel on notice that He was the Monarch over the monarchy. Understood in this spiritual dimension, the theocratically established monarchy in Israel actually *pointed* to the Savior.

Under this system, it was the Lord, not the mortal king, who was recognized as sovereign. The king was as bound to the laws and covenants of the Lord as the people were. As we shall see in the next chapter, Saul lost his right to the kingship because he violated the laws of God, and Samuel anointed another in his stead.

In the years from Saul to the coming of Christ in the flesh, Israel and their kings would prosper only to the extent that they bowed before the throne of heaven. The kings and the people would be blessed, or cursed, based on their obedience to the laws of the King of Heaven.[84] This is what Samuel taught Israel when he—the Lord's likeness and prophet—"told the people the manner of the kingdom, and wrote it in a book, and laid it up before the Lord."[85]

CHAPTER 14

DAVID, SAUL, JONATHAN, AND THE ALLEGORY OF SALVATION

Upon Me Let This Iniquity Be

What I learned pondering the last half of First Samuel changed my life and became the impetus for my earlier book *The Peacegiver.* There is no more beautiful character in all the words ever written than the peacegiver Abigail. Her words and actions change everything—every interaction, every relationship, every feeling, every thought. They change everything because they teach us something extraordinary about the Lord's Atonement.

Those who see Abigail's offering never see life the same way again. David and Jonathan saw it. Unfortunately, Saul never did. The question is, will *we* see it?

Saul was anointed the first king of Israel when he "wast little in [his] own sight"[1]—an interesting comment that foreshadowed the problems soon to come. Saul reigned for several decades,[2] and he proved to be an effective and courageous leader. After his first great military victory, he humbly ascribed the triumph to the Lord: "To day the Lord hath wrought salvation in Israel."[3] Humble before the Lord, he frankly dismissed the suggestion by some in Israel to put to death those who had formerly opposed his kingship.[4]

However, Samuel's statement to Saul, "when thou wast little in thine own sight," is a biting accusation of what he became, for it reveals that Saul lost his humility during the course of his reign. He whose initial response to Samuel had been, "Am I not a Benjamite, of the smallest of the tribes of Israel? and my family the least of all the families of the tribe of

Benjamin?"⁵ presumed later to take upon himself priestly functions in the stead of the prophet Samuel.⁶ He then explicitly overrode a command of the Lord, choosing a course of action he found more agreeable than the directives Samuel had given him.⁷ For his impetuousness, the blessing of kingship was removed from Saul's house: "The Lord hath rejected thee from being king over Israel," Samuel told him, "[he] hath rent the kingdom of Israel from thee this day, and hath given it to a neighbor of thine, that is better than thou."⁸

As a result of sin, Saul lost the blessing of the anointing he had received at Samuel's hand. The scepter would be lost from his house. This meant not only that Saul would eventually lose the kingship but that his heir—Jonathan—also would be denied the throne.

The "neighbor" to whom the kingdom was to be committed was David, the youngest son of Jesse of Bethlehem. We meet David in chapter 16 of First Samuel, where Samuel anoints him to become king "in the midst of his brethren."⁹ The balance of First Samuel through the first chapter of Second Samuel is almost entirely a record of the relationships of these three men—Saul and Jonathan, who are both to lose their positions on the throne of Israel, and David, the chosen of the Lord who is to reign in their stead. Over this period, Saul (who at the beginning of his reign refused to execute those who had opposed his rule¹⁰) spent most of the last ten years of his reign seeking to exterminate the one—David—who had been chosen by God to rule in his place.

In terms of pure emotion and drama, the saga of the relationship of these three men is unmatched anywhere in scripture, and perhaps anywhere in literature. The verse-by-verse juxtapositions of love and envy, commitment and betrayal, courage and cowardice, compassion and vengeance, humility and pride, life and death, and righteousness and sin place the reader in the middle of a high-stakes morality play. But this is no play.

THE RELATIONSHIPS OF SAUL, DAVID, AND JONATHAN

We pick up the story after David's victory over Goliath.¹¹ His courageous feat brings him instant fame throughout Israel. Saul, who apparently doesn't yet know that David is the Lord's chosen replacement, is astonished by the boy's feat. "Whose son art thou, thou young man?" he asked. David answered, "I am the son of thy servant Jesse the Beth-lehemite."[12]

Then we read this beautiful passage:

> And it came to pass, when [David] had made an end of speaking unto Saul, that the soul of Jonathan was knit with the soul of David, and Jonathan *loved him as his own soul.* . . . Then Jonathan and David made a covenant, because he loved him as his own soul. And Jonathan stripped himself of the robe that was upon him, and gave it to David, and his garments, even to his sword, and to his bow, and to his girdle.[13]

What significance might there be in Jonathan giving to David the outward symbols of Jonathan's power and position as the heir of Saul? The implication is that Jonathan knew David was to be the next king and that the covenant mentioned here between David and Jonathan was precisely Jonathan's covenant to embrace and support David's call in his stead. This possibility is supported by verse 17 of chapter 23, where Jonathan says: "Fear not: for the hand of Saul my father shall not find thee; and thou shalt be king over Israel, and I shall be next unto thee; and that also Saul my father knoweth. And they two made a covenant before the Lord."[14] So Jonathan, loving David "as his own soul," willingly gave up the kingdom. And this he did without grudge or envy, for he "delighted much in David."[15]

This story of Jonathan's love for one who was designated "neighbour"[16] illuminates what might be at the heart of the second great commandment, to "love thy neighbour as thyself"[17] (or as stated on this occasion, to "love as one's own soul"). If I love another as my own soul, then my heart makes no distinction between myself and others. At the success of another, I rejoice. My joy is the same as it would be had I experienced the success myself—for the other is "as myself." Loving David as his own soul, Jonathan felt no envy at David's call to kingship. His heart was knit with David's. They were one.

Unfortunately, Saul reacted differently:

> And it came to pass as they came, when David was re-
> turned from the slaughter of the Philistine, that the women
> came out of all cities of Israel, singing and dancing, to meet
> king Saul. . . . And the women answered one another as they
> played, and said, Saul hath slain his thousands, and David his
> ten thousands. And Saul was very wroth, and the saying dis-
> pleased him; and he said, They have ascribed unto David ten
> thousands, and to me they have ascribed but thousands: and
> what can he have more but the kingdom? And *Saul eyed David
> from that day and forward.*[18]

By now, loving nothing so much as his own soul, Saul was riddled
with envy. He was on the lookout for difference. He was as far from delight as he could be. He was afraid—"afraid of David, because the Lord
was with him, and was departed from Saul."[19] Failing to love David as his
own soul, Saul actually put his own soul in jeopardy.

These stark differences between the reactions of Jonathan and Saul to
David build throughout the narrative of First Samuel. On the one hand,
Jonathan (faced with losing the kingdom to David) freely gave David
everything that would have been his, even promising to do for David
"whatsoever [David's] soul desireth."[20] Hearts knit together, a gain to one
was a gain to both. As a result, Jonathan protected David, invited others to
do right by David, defended David even at the risk of his own life, and
strengthened David in the Lord.[21]

Saul, on the other hand, was bloated with envy. He viewed David's
gain as his own loss. He lived in fear and blindly sought to destroy his adversary, the Lord's chosen. At least twice he tried to smite David with his
own javelin,[22] and many more times commanded others to do the same.[23]
Those who helped David fell victim to Saul's fearful rage.[24] He was bent
on protecting what was no longer his, and became blind to the will of the
Lord.

As a result of Saul's rage, David was forced to live the life of a fugitive.
When others were able to go back to their homes, David had to remain
"in the wood."[25] He was separated from his family,[26] kept from his home,
and forced to live among the Philistines.[27] He hid amidst the hills and

caves of the desert with a band of men comprised of debtors, the distressed, and the discontented.[28] How is one to react to such vile injustice and mistreatment? If ever there was someone who had reason for revenge and justification for vengeance, it was David.

The opportunity for vengeance came as Saul rested from his pursuit of David in the very cave David and his men were using for cover: "Then Saul took three thousand chosen men . . . and went to seek David and his men. . . . And he came to . . . a cave; and Saul went in to cover his feet: and David and his men remained in the sides of the cave. And the men of David said unto him, Behold [this is] the day of which the Lord said unto thee, Behold, I will deliver thine enemy into thine hand, that thou mayest do to him as it shall seem good unto thee."[29]

David's adversary was delivered into his hands. With one thrust of his spear, David could have been rid of Saul and the discomforts of life that Saul had caused him. His men urged him to do it. But he wouldn't. Instead, he stealthily cut off a corner of Saul's robe,[30] and then, when Saul had left the cave, cried out to him, "My lord the king."[31]

Saul turned toward David's voice, and "David stooped with his face to the earth, and bowed himself."[32] And David said to Saul, "Wherefore hearest thou men's words, saying, Behold, David seeketh thy hurt? Behold, this day thine eyes have seen how that the Lord had delivered thee to day into mine hand in the cave: and some bade me kill thee: but . . . I said, I will not put forth mine hand against my lord; for he is the Lord's anointed. Moreover . . . see the skirt of thy robe in my hand: for in that I cut off the skirt of thy robe, and killed thee not, know thou and see that there is neither evil nor transgression in mine hand, and I have not sinned against thee."[33]

Nearly the same scenario repeated itself two chapters later: Saul came down against David with 3,000 of his troops. At night, when they were sleeping, David and one of his men snuck into Saul's camp and came to Saul's side. David's companion urged him to take up Saul's spear and thrust it through him, to put an end to the misery Saul had been causing him. But David wouldn't. "The Lord forbid that I should stretch forth mine hand against the Lord's anointed," he answered (in a whisper, no doubt), "but, I pray thee, take thou now the spear that is at his bolster, and the cruse of water, and let us go. So [they] took the spear and the cruse of water from Saul's bolster; and they gat them away, and no man saw it, nor knew it, neither awaked."[34]

Once again, David cried out to Saul from afar off, holding up Saul's spear and cruse of water: "See where the king's spear is, and the cruse of water that was at his bolster. . . . Wherefore doth my lord thus pursue after his servant? for what have I done? or what evil is in mine hand? . . . Now therefore, let not my blood fall to the earth before the face of the Lord: for the king of Israel is come out to seek a flea, as when one doth hunt a partridge in the mountains."[35]

David's response in each of these situations fills me with wonder. How is such a response possible? How can we not only resist vengeance toward those who have harmed us but apparently feel no desire for it? David's response at the news of Saul's death in Second Samuel chapter 1 makes this question even more salient, for when he heard that both Saul and Jonathan had been killed in battle, he wept for Jonathan and Saul alike: "Then David took hold on his clothes, and rent them . . . and wept, and fasted until even, *for Saul, and for Jonathan his son.* . . . And David lamented with this lamentation *over Saul and over Jonathan his son.* . . . *Saul and Jonathan* were lovely and pleasant in their lives, and in their death they were not divided: they were swifter than eagles, they were stronger than lions. . . . How are the mighty fallen . . . !"[36]

What is striking about David's response here is that there is almost no difference in his expressed feelings for Saul and for Jonathan. He is devastated by both of their deaths. One would expect him to feel that way about Jonathan, but Saul? How could David's feelings for one who tried to destroy him be so similar to the feelings he had for one who loved him as his own soul?

Accordingly, the last half of First Samuel presents us with two intriguing questions: How is it possible that two men, Saul and Jonathan, could respond so differently to their loss of the throne? And how is it possible that one man, David, could respond with the same loving attitude toward two men, Saul and Jonathan, whose treatment of him was so different? What makes such responses possible?

Few questions are more pertinent to our lives, for who has not felt envious, angry, or embittered toward others? Such feelings seem to haunt our lives, but Jonathan and David suggest that they don't have to. Their lives testify of a better way.

How do we find that better way?

A beautiful and largely overlooked story, sandwiched between the two occasions where David spared Saul's life, provides an answer.

NABAL AND SAUL: A PARALLELISM

In verses 2 and 3 of chapter 25, we are introduced to a man who "was very great." "He had three thousand sheep, and a thousand goats." The man is described in kingly terms, as "he held a feast in his house, like the feast of a king."[37] His name was Nabal, which means, oddly, "fool."[38] While David and his men were hiding from Saul in the wilderness, they performed a great service for Nabal by protecting and preserving his men and possessions. "They were a wall unto [Nabal's men and possessions] both by night and day," and "were very good unto [them]," so that they "were not hurt, neither missed . . . any thing" as long as David's men were around them.[39]

Still forced to reside in the wilderness, David sent a few of his servants to Nabal to ask for provisions in light of the service they had performed him.[40] But Nabal flatly refused, saying: "Who is David? and who is the son of Jesse? . . . Shall I then take my bread, and my water, and my flesh that I have killed for my shearers, and give it unto men, whom I know not whence they be?"[41]

A few aspects of this story may ring familiar. First of all, Nabal, being "very great" in possessions, reminds us of the other man of great possessions through these chapters: Saul. The description of Nabal in kingly terms adds to the possibility of a similitude between the two men. David's relationship to the two men also is similar, for he protected both of their "kingdoms" (in the case of Saul, through his military conquests against the Philistines, and in the case of Nabal, through protecting his possessions from others). Nevertheless, both Nabal and Saul ignored David's service and imputed evil to him. Both refused to listen to the appeals of others, and denied that David had any legitimate claim on their kingdoms.[42]

Interestingly, in the chapter after the Nabal story, Saul said that he had "played *the fool*"[43] in his actions toward David, thus establishing a link between Saul and the very name of Nabal. Given the striking nature of these similarities, perhaps the Nabal story is not only about Nabal.

After hearing how Nabal refused to provide them supplies, "David said unto his men, Gird ye on every man his sword. And they girded on every man his sword; and David also girded on his sword: and there went up after David about four hundred men."[44] David mused bitterly, "Surely in vain have I kept all that this fellow hath in the wilderness, so that nothing was missed of all that pertained unto him: and he hath requited me evil for good."[45]

So here we have a man, Nabal, who is the likeness of Saul. He, like Saul, mistreated David, although certainly less severely. His story is placed between two stories of how David refused to take vengeance against Saul. But in contrast to the Saul stories, in this story David set out to destroy the one who had mistreated him. What is going on here? Why vengeance against Nabal but not Saul? And even more importantly, if Nabal is the likeness of Saul, how does David's vengeance toward Nabal fit into the picture?

Although the Nabal story begins with vengeance, it doesn't end with it. David encounters someone who changes his heart and saves him from the sin of vengeance—a little-known character whose story is one of the most beautiful in all of scripture.

ABIGAIL AND THE ALLEGORY OF SALVATION[46]

After we learn of Nabal's sin against David, and David's vengeful reaction to that sin, the narrative tells us that one of Nabal's servants went and told Abigail, Nabal's wife, of Nabal's ungrateful act. Abigail then "made haste, and took two hundred loaves, and two bottles of wine, and five sheep ready dressed, and five measures of parched corn, and an hundred clusters of raisins, and two hundred cakes of figs, and laid them on asses."[47] And then she and her servants set off on the road to take these offerings to David and his men. We then encounter one of the most beautiful passages in scripture:

And it was so, as she rode on the ass, that she came down
by the covert of the hill, and, behold, David and his men came
down against her; and she met them. . . .

And when Abigail saw David, she hasted, and lighted off
the ass, and fell before David on her face, and bowed herself to
the ground,

And fell at his feet, and said, *Upon me, my lord, upon me let
this iniquity be.* . . .

Let not my lord, I pray thee, regard this man of Belial, even
Nabal: for . . . folly is with him. . . .

I pray thee, *forgive the trespass of thine handmaid:* for the
Lord will certainly make my lord a sure house; because my lord
fighteth the battles of the Lord, and evil hath not been found
in thee all thy days. . . . That this shall be no grief unto thee,
nor offence of heart unto my lord, either that thou hast shed
blood causeless, or that my lord hath avenged himself.[48]

What amazing grace! Upon hearing of the wrong committed by another, Abigail raced to gather what the aggrieved—David and his men—
had been denied by Nabal's mistreatment. She then sought out David with
her gift—to save him from avenging himself, wherewith he would begin
to fight his own battles rather than the Lord's, and commit an "offence of
heart" that would keep him from receiving "all the good that [the Lord
had] spoken concerning [him]."[49]

Upon delivering to David all that he needed and more, thereby atoning for Nabal's sin, she then took Nabal's sin on her own head when she
pleaded, "upon me let this iniquity be."[50] And then, incredibly to me, in an
utterance that teaches us just what it means to take upon oneself the sins of
another, she pleaded, "forgive the trespass of thine handmaid."[51] Think of
it: The one who had done no wrong[52] asked for the mistreated person to
forgive *her*—not Nabal, the actual perpetrator of the wrong, but *her!* In
her mind, as she knelt before David, Nabal's sin was now hers. She had
taken it upon her, claiming it as her own.

"Forgive the trespass of thine handmaid." No purer words have ever been spoken—except, that is, by Him in whose similitude she uttered them. Consider how closely Abigail's story parallels the Savior's:

- She atoned for the wrong committed by another.
- She provided all that was needed to him who was harmed.
- She took the sinner's iniquity on her own head, even though she herself had done no wrong.
- She pled for the avenger to give up vengeance.
- And, as we will discover shortly, she was the means of delivering peace.

When we think of the Atonement, we most often think about how the Savior filled in the gaps for our *own* sins, which he surely did. That is, we are all sinners, and someone had to bridge for each of us the otherwise impassable chasm between us and eternal life that we have created through sin. So normally we think of the Atonement as something that Christ has done for *us*—for *ourselves*. But Abigail invites us to look at the Atonement from a different angle—not from the perspective of how Christ has atoned for our own sins, but rather from the equally true perspective that he has atoned for the sins of others. And part of that Atonement, Abigail suggests, is the idea that the Lord offers to those who have been harmed or potentially harmed by the sins of others the help and sustaining they need to be made whole. Those deprived of love can receive his love. The companionless can find a companion in *him*. Those with a cross to bear can find another who carries and makes it light.

With their burdens lifted in this way, the sinned-against are saved from the provocation to sin—provocation to anger, for example, or resentment, or despair, all of which are feelings we are commanded not to harbor[53]—and are therefore redeemed from their own sins.

Abigail's offering, and her plea for forgiveness in the stead of Nabal, helps to illuminate one of the most challenging of scriptures: "Ye ought to forgive one another," the Lord taught, "for he that forgiveth not his brother his trespasses standeth condemned before the Lord; for there remaineth in him the greater sin."[54] On its face, the idea that failing to forgive others for their mistreatment of us is a greater sin than the mistreatment itself sounds unduly harsh, as if it must be a case of hyperbole that couldn't really be true. But it is true, and the scriptures are clear as to why:

"The Lord shall . . . measure to every man according to the measure which he has measured to his fellow man."[55]

"He shall have judgment without mercy, that hath shewed no mercy."[56]

"For with what judgment ye judge, ye shall be judged: and with what measure ye mete, it shall be measured to you again."[57]

"If ye forgive men their trespasses, your heavenly Father will also forgive you: But if ye forgive not men their trespasses, neither will your Father forgive your trespasses."[58]

"Forgive, and ye shall be forgiven."[59]

The Lord is clearly warning us that eternity itself depends on our willingness to forgive. If we ourselves are not merciful toward others, and fail to forgive them "from [our] hearts,"[60] we will be delivered to "the tormenters," as was the unmerciful servant in the Lord's parable.[61] Since our only hope for salvation is the Lord's mercy, we fail to extend mercy at our own peril.

Here, the Abigail story shines the brightest, as it teaches us how the Lord helps us to do what we most need to do—forgive. David might have felt justified in withholding forgiveness from Nabal, however sinful such withholding might have been, but from Abigail? No, her offering on behalf of another obliterated every justification David might otherwise have had:

"And David said to Abigail, Blessed be the Lord God of Israel, which sent thee this day to meet me: And blessed be thy advice, and blessed be thou, which hast kept me this day from coming to shed blood, and from avenging myself with mine own hand. . . .

"So David received of her hand that which she had brought him, and said unto her, Go up in peace to thine house; see, I have hearkened to thy voice, and have accepted thy person."[62]

By her atonement offering, Abigail freed David from the blind comfort of his grudges. Through her merciful act, she created for David the most forgiveness-friendly environment that could possibly be created.

David was never more able to do what he needed most to do—forgive, or, more precisely, repent of his failing to forgive—than when the request for forgiveness was made by one who had atoned in full for the sin David was raging against.

The Lord, by taking the sins of our Nabals upon his head, extends us the same mercy. "Upon me let this iniquity be," he pleads. "Let me deal with it if there is any dealing to be done. But you, my dear son or dear daughter, let it go. Let me take it, as I already have done. Forgive."

Although the Lord doesn't actually ask us to forgive *him,* the effect of the Atonement is such that it's *as if* that is what he is asking. "Inasmuch as ye have done it [or done it not] unto one of the least of these," the Savior taught, "ye have done it [or done it not] unto me."[63] When we withhold forgiveness from others, we are in effect saying that the Atonement alone was insufficient to pay for this sin. We are holding out for more. We are finding fault with the Lord's offering. We are, in essence, demanding that the Lord repent of an insufficient atonement. So when we fail to forgive another, it is as if we are failing to forgive the Lord—who, of course, needs no forgiveness.

Consider the miracle of this story: The vengeance David felt toward Nabal was swallowed up through the intervention of Abigail. One who set out for revenge turned back in peace. He spared Nabal the same way he spared Saul, and the Abigail story reveals the key to his loving response in both cases: hearkening to the voice of the Lord and accepting his Atonement.

Those who hearken to the Lord and accept his Atonement become themselves saviors on Mount Zion, for they, like Abigail, invite others to come to the Lord. Jonathan was such a person. Like Abigail, he intervened between David and a family member. Like Abigail, he strengthened David in the Lord. Like Abigail, who freely gave of her house to David, Jonathan freely submitted the throne of his house to David. Accepting the gift of the Lord—directly, and indirectly through Jonathan and Abigail—David also extended forgiveness in the way *he* lived. Even Saul was affected by the love of the Savior that he felt through David:

> And it came to pass, when David had made an end of
> speaking these words unto Saul, that Saul said, Is this thy voice,

my son David? And Saul lifted up his voice, and wept. And he said to David, Thou art more righteous than I: for thou hast rewarded me good, whereas I have rewarded thee evil. And thou hast shewed this day how that thou hast dealt well with me: forasmuch as when the Lord had delivered me into thine hand, thou killedst me not. For if a man find his enemy, will he let him go well away? wherefore the Lord reward thee good for that thou hast done unto me this day. And now, behold, I know well that thou shalt surely be king, and that the kingdom of Israel shall be established in thine hand.[64]

Then said Saul, I have sinned: return, my son David: for I will no more do thee harm, because my soul was precious in thine eyes this day: behold, I have played the fool, and have erred exceedingly.[65]

The Savior's love can pierce the darkest sky. His Atonement is the answer to every bit of turmoil in our souls. Envy, vengefulness, anger, bitterness, callousness—all are swallowed up in him whom we have mistreated the most. Whatever we may see in others that troubles us, he calls: "Upon me let this iniquity be."[66] In his call is love. In his call is forgiveness. In his call is peace.

CHAPTER 15

THE HOUSES OF THE KINGS AND THE HOUSE OF THE LORD

I Will Make Thee an House

> I never really understood the significance of the temple until I noticed an amazing pattern in the history of the kings of the Northern and Southern Kingdoms of Israel—a pattern that unfolds the central importance of the temple not just in their lives but also in ours.
>
> Here's a hint: The success or failure of the "houses" (or families) of each of the forty kings in these kingdoms depended entirely on one thing: their attitude regarding the house of the Lord.
>
> What might that mean for us and our "houses" today?

The reign of Saul's house over Israel ended at one generation. Upon Saul's death, David was anointed king over the house of Judah.[1] Abner, captain of Saul's armies, attempted to install Saul's son Ish-bosheth as king,[2] and a battle raged for control in Israel.[3] However, some seven years after Saul and Jonathan were slain, David became king of a united Israel.[4] Shortly after becoming king of Israel, David moved the ark of the covenant from the house of Abinadab in Gibeah (where it had resided since its return by the Philistines) to Jerusalem.[5] There David "set it . . . in the midst of the tabernacle that [he] had pitched for it."[6]

In comparison to his own "house of cedar," David began to feel that the ark's cloth sanctuary was inadequate and expressed to Nathan the prophet his desire to build a permanent sanctuary for the ark. That night, the Lord delivered to Nathan a message for David, a message known as the "Davidic Covenant":

Thus saith the Lord, Thou shalt not build me an house to dwell in: For I have not dwelt in an house since the day that I brought up Israel unto this day; but have gone from tent to tent, and from one tabernacle to another. Wheresoever I have walked with all Israel, spake I a word to any of the judges of Israel . . . saying, Why have ye not built me an house of cedars?[7]

Furthermore I tell thee that the Lord will build thee an house. And it shall come to pass, when thy days be expired that thou must go to be with thy fathers, that I will raise up thy seed after thee, which shall be of thy sons; and I will establish his kingdom. He shall build me an house, and I will stablish his throne for ever. I will be his father, and he shall be my son: and I will not take my mercy away from him, as I took it from him that was before thee: But I will settle him in mine house and in my kingdom for ever: and his throne shall be established for evermore.[8]

The Lord's words to David were partially fulfilled in David's son Solomon who, after David's death, built a magnificent temple to house the ark. The Lord accepted the house and in so doing communicated the requirements that Solomon and the rest of the house of Israel would have to meet in order to enjoy for themselves the blessings of the Davidic Covenant:

If thou wilt walk before me . . . in integrity of heart, and in uprightness, to do according to all that I have commanded thee, and wilt keep my statutes and my judgments: Then I will establish the throne of thy kingdom upon Israel for ever, as I promised to David thy father. . . . But if ye shall at all turn from following me, ye or your children, and will not keep my commandments and my statutes which I have set before you, but go and serve other gods, and worship them: Then will I cut off Israel out of the land which I have given them; and this house, which I have hallowed for my name, will I cast out of my sight; and Israel shall be a proverb and a byword among all people.[9]

The Davidic Covenant was much more than a promise of a physical house for the Lord, built by a son of David. Solomon's construction of the physical temple was but a type and shadow of the covenant's deeper promise, which is revealed as one ponders the dual meaning of the word *house.*

When the Lord said that he would make David a house, he did not mean that he would construct a physical structure for David to dwell in. After all, David already dwelt in a splendid home of cedar. Rather, the Lord was making a promise regarding the "house of David"—that is, the *family* of David. The promise was precisely this: that among David's posterity, a son of God would be raised up who would build the Lord's house in the eternities and there rule forevermore. This deeper promise was fulfilled in Christ, who, by his Atonement, built not a physical structure but a *family* structure—a house of *people* who through him would inherit all that the Father hath.[10] These are they of whom Paul declared, "Ye are God's building"[11]—the house of Christ.[12] In this respect, the Davidic Covenant was not a new covenant, but a renewal of the covenant made to Abraham and the fathers before him.[13]

When we consider the duality in the Davidic Covenant through the dual meaning of the word *house,* the covenant's parallel prophecies draw together into one. For it is only through entering into the sacred covenants administered by priesthood authority in the physical structure of the Lord's house that we qualify to be made part of the Lord's house—the Lord's family—in the eternities.

With the establishment by covenant of a permanent dwelling place for the Lord in Jerusalem—a place where, when the fulness of the priesthood is present, *our* houses or families can be made part of his—from this point forward, the fate of the house of Israel, and each of the families that comprised it, depended entirely on their regard for the house of the Lord that was in their midst. Each turn away from the temple was a turn away from him who is the temple.[14] By disregarding his house, they disregarded him—the only one who could establish *their* houses forevermore.

The centuries that followed the revelation of the Davidic Covenant were perhaps the darkest in the history of Israel. This descent began when David's son, Solomon, eventually "turned away his heart after other gods."[15] For this sin the Lord told Solomon, "I will surely rend the kingdom from thee, and will give it to thy servant."[16] This prophecy was fulfilled in Jeroboam, a "mighty man of valour" who was the son of one of Solomon's servants.[17] The prophet Ahijah prophesied to Jeroboam that the Lord would "rend the kingdom out of the hand of Solomon," and would "give ten tribes to thee,"[18] and "build thee a sure house" so long as Jeroboam would hearken unto all of the Lord's commandments.[19]

Upon Solomon's death, his son Rehoboam assumed the throne. However, the people revolted against Rehoboam when he petulantly decreed that he would increase the burdens that they had felt under Solomon.[20] At that day, all of the tribes of Israel but Judah and Benjamin declared their independence from Judah and formed their own kingdom. Jeroboam, in fulfillment of Ahijah's prophecy, was made king over these ten tribes. This new kingdom became known as the "Northern Kingdom," or the "Kingdom of Israel." Rehoboam ruled only over the "Southern Kingdom," or "Kingdom of Judah." This split of the kingdoms occurred in 930 B.C.

The Kingdom of Israel—or Northern Kingdom—continued until 721 B.C., when it was overrun and destroyed by the Assyrians, who led the ten tribes of the Northern Kingdom into captivity. (A repentant subset of this group, sometimes referred to as "the lost ten tribes," may have been led by the Lord out of Assyrian captivity and into the north countries.[21]) From the beginning of Jeroboam's reign in 930 B.C. to the fall of the kingdom in 721 B.C., the Northern Kingdom experienced twenty monarchs from five different family dynasties or "houses." Without exception, those monarchs were wicked.

The Kingdom of Judah continued until 587 B.C., when it fell to the Babylonians. Like the Kingdom of Israel, the Kingdom of Judah was ruled by twenty successive monarchs before its demise. In contrast to Israel, however, each of the monarchs in the Kingdom of Judah came from one house—the house of David. Of Judah's twenty monarchs, only four could be characterized as righteous—Asa (910–869 B.C.), Jehoshaphat (872–848), Hezekiah (715–686), and Josiah (640–609).

There emerges in the histories of both kingdoms a clear and distinct pattern—a common cause of their incessant difficulties and ultimate destruction. The cause of their destruction was their failure to honor the Davidic Covenant. The houses of both kingdoms fell because they failed to honor the house of the Lord.

THE FALL OF THE RULING HOUSES
IN THE KINGDOM OF ISRAEL

After leading the revolt against the ruling house of Judah, the king of the newly formed Kingdom of Israel, Jeroboam, worried that he would lose his kingdom to Rehoboam if his people returned to the house of the Lord at Jerusalem to offer up sacrifices according to their law.[22] (Jerusalem was located within the boundaries of the Southern Kingdom or Kingdom of Judah.) So Jeroboam "took counsel, and made two calves of gold, and said unto [those in the Northern Kingdom], It is too much for you to return to Jerusalem: behold thy gods, O Israel, which brought thee up out of the land of Egypt. And he set one in Beth-el, and the other put he in Dan."[23]

The next verse says that "this thing became a sin."[24] It was a grave sin indeed, for Jeroboam turned the Kingdom of Israel away from the house of the Lord. Thereafter, the descriptions of nearly all of the Northern Kingdom rulers include a reference to the sins of Jeroboam, which were repeated by each successive monarch. Notice how each house of rulers in the Northern Kingdom was destroyed because they walked in the sins of Jeroboam and failed to honor the house of the Lord:

The House of Jeroboam

Jeroboam (930 B.C.–909 B.C.): He created pagan temples in place of the house of the Lord at Jerusalem so as to save his own house.

Nadab (909–908): "And he did evil in the sight of the Lord, and **walked in the way of his father [Jeroboam],** and in his sin wherewith he made Israel to sin" (1 Kings 15:26). Nadab was assassinated by Baasha in a military revolt, and all of the members of the house of Jeroboam were executed because of the sins he committed and caused Israel to commit (1 Kings 14:14–16; 15:29–30).

The House of Baasha

Baasha (908–886): "And he did evil in the sight of the Lord, and **walked in the way of Jeroboam,** and in his sin wherewith he made Israel to sin" (1 Kings 15:34).

Elah (886–885): "Elah . . . sinned, and . . . made Israel to sin" (1 Kings 16:13).

<u>Zimri (885, seven days)</u>: "[He] sinned in doing evil in the sight of the Lord, in **walking in the way of Jeroboam,** and in his sin which he did, to make Israel to sin" (1 Kings 16:19).

<u>Tibni (885–880)</u>: Not much mention made of him; he died in struggle for power against Omri. The house of Baasha was destroyed because they walked in the ways of Jeroboam. See 1 Kings 16:1–4, 11–13.

The House of Omri

<u>Omri (885–874)</u>: "[He] **walked in all the way of Jeroboam** . . . , and in his sin wherewith he made Israel to sin" (1 Kings 16:25–26).

<u>Ahab (874–853)</u>: "[He] did evil in the sight of the Lord above all that were before him. And it came to pass, as if it had been a light thing for him to **walk in the sins of Jeroboam**" (1 Kings 16:30–31).

<u>Ahaziah (853–852)</u>: "[He] did evil in the sight of the Lord, and **walked in** the way of his father, and in the way of his mother, and in **the way of Jeroboam** . . . who made Israel to sin" (1 Kings 22:52–53).

<u>Jehoram (852–841)</u>: "[He] wrought evil in the sight of the Lord; . . . [he] **cleaved unto the sins of Jeroboam** . . . which made Israel to sin; he departed not therefrom" (2 Kings 3:2–3). The entire house of Ahab was destroyed on account of Ahab's wickedness (see 1 Kings 21:20–24).

The House of Jehu

<u>Jehu (841–814)</u>: "[He] **departed not from the sins of Jeroboam,** which made Israel to sin" (2 Kings 10:31).

<u>Jehoahaz (814–798)</u>: [He] did that which was evil in the sight of the Lord, and **followed the sins of Jeroboam** . . . which made Israel to sin; he departed not therefrom" (2 Kings 13:2).

<u>Jehoash (798–782)</u>: "[He] did that which was evil in the sight of the Lord; he **departed not from all the sins of Jeroboam** . . . who made Israel sin: but he walked therein" (2 Kings 13:11).

<u>Jeroboam II (782–753)</u>: "[He] did that which was evil in the sight of the Lord: he **departed not from all the sins of Jeroboam** . . . who made Israel to sin" (2 Kings 14:24).

<u>Zachariah (753, six months)</u>: "[He] did that which was evil in the sight of the Lord . . . he **departed not from the sins of Jeroboam** . . . who made Israel to sin" (2 Kings 15:9).

Shallum (752, one month): Reigned as king for only one month before being assassinated. *The house of Jehu was destroyed.*

The House of Menahem

Menahem (752–742): "[He] did that which was evil in the sight of the Lord: he **departed not all his days from the sins of Jeroboam** . . . who made Israel to sin" (2 Kings 15:18).

Pekahiah (742–740): "[He] did that which was evil in the sight of the Lord: he **departed not from the sins of Jeroboam** . . . who made Israel to sin" (2 Kings 15:24).

Pekah (740–732): "[He] did that which was evil in the sight of the Lord: he **departed not from the sins of Jeroboam** . . . who made Israel to sin" (2 Kings 15:28).

Hoshea (732–721): "[He] did that which was evil in the sight of the Lord, but not as the kings of Israel that were before him" (2 Kings 17:2). *The Kingdom of Israel was destroyed and carried off captive by Assyria because they departed not from the sins of Jeroboam* (see 2 Kings 17:7–23).

As we can see, the failure of each of the "houses" of the kings in the Northern Kingdom was bound up in their continuation of the "sins of Jeroboam"—that is, their continued rejection of the house of the Lord. So the tragic history of the Northern Kingdom testifies of the importance of the temple, a truth that is made even more clear by the history of the Southern Kingdom.

THE FALL OF THE RULING HOUSE IN THE KINGDOM OF JUDAH

From 930 B.C. to Judah's destruction at the hands of the Babylonians in 587 B.C., only four of the twenty kings in Judah were righteous, and their righteousness consisted in their breaking down altars of false gods and returning their people to the house of the Lord.

The first of the righteous kings in Judah was Asa, who ruled from 910 B.C. until 869 B.C. We are told that he "did that which was good and right in the eyes of the Lord his God: For he took away the altars of the strange gods, and the high places, and brake down the images . . . And commanded Judah to seek the Lord God of their fathers, and to do the law and the commandment."²⁵ "And he brought into the house of God the things that his father had dedicated, and that he himself had dedicated."²⁶

Asa's son Jehoshaphat, who ruled Judah from 872 B.C. to 848 B.C., continued in his father's righteous ways. He had the people throughout Judah taught from "the book of the law of the Lord,"²⁷ and he "stood in the congregation of Judah and Jerusalem, in the house of the Lord, [and prayed to the Lord on behalf of the people.]"²⁸

Joash, who ruled Judah from 835 B.C. to 796 B.C., ruled righteously in his early years, minding to the repair of the house of the Lord,²⁹ but he ultimately "left the house of the Lord . . . and served groves and idols: and wrath came upon Judah and Jerusalem for this their trespass."³⁰ So from the time of Jehoshaphat, nine monarchs and 133 years came and went before Judah again enjoyed a righteous king—Hezekiah, who turned them again to the temple.

In the first year of his reign, Hezekiah, who ruled Judah from 715 B.C. to 686 B.C., "opened the doors of the house of the Lord, and repaired them," and he gathered and commanded the priests and Levites to sanctify themselves, "and sanctify the house of the Lord God . . . and carry forth the filthiness out of the holy place. For," he told them, "our fathers have trespassed, and done that which was evil in the eyes of the Lord our God, and have forsaken him, and have . . . turned their backs." He declared that they must "make a covenant with the Lord God of Israel, that his fierce wrath may turn away from us." Hearing Hezekiah, the priests and Levites he had gathered "sanctified themselves, and came, according to the commandment of the king, by the words of the Lord, to cleanse the house of the Lord. . . . Then Hezekiah . . . rose early, and gathered the rulers of the city, and went up to the house of the Lord."³¹

Judah's last righteous king before the Babylonian captivity—Josiah— turned them back to the temple one final time, after the two kings who followed Hezekiah did evil by forsaking the house of the Lord. Josiah renovated and restored the temple and purged it of all the unholy elements that had been introduced by his predecessors.³² Unfortunately, after Josiah, the rulers and people of Judah once again turned their backs to the temple, and within another twenty years or so the Kingdom of Judah fell to foreign powers just as the Kingdom of Israel had fallen some 130 years earlier.

THE TEMPLE AS THE MEANS OF MEMBERSHIP
IN THE LORD'S HOUSE

The histories of the Kingdoms of Israel and Judah clearly demonstrate the direct relationship between the physical house that was to be built up by a son of David and the spiritual house that would be built up by another of David's sons—the Savior. Those who failed to honor the physical house of the Lord failed as well to realize the promise of the spiritual house that lasted forever. It is no coincidence that in the Davidic Covenant the Lord's promise of thrones and kingdoms comes *after* the prophecy that a son of David would build a house for the Lord's name. For we can be made part of the Lord's house in the eternities only by honoring his house in mortality.

So the temple is not only the great symbol of our membership in the Church, it is also the barometer of our membership in the family of God. The history of the kings in Israel and Judah shows that at any given moment we can know where we are in relation to the Lord by reference to where we are in relation to the temple. The Lord makes us "an house" as we fully turn to *his* house.

~⌒

CHAPTER 16

ELIJAH AND THE FOUR GREAT SEPARATIONS

Therefore Ye Sons of Jacob Are Not Consumed

"I know Elijah is important. Could you tell me why?"

I can try. There are four great separations that doom mankind to destruction. Elijah was a prophet who lived in Israel during a period when each of these separations was at its height. Whether for this or for other reasons, he is the prophet to whom the Lord entrusted the keys of the binding together—or sealing—of these separations. This is his mission.

Now, why should we care? Because we suffer from these separations as much as the ancient Israelites did. If we are to overcome them (which we must), we too must undergo a "binding together" of the separations.

So how do we receive this binding together or sealing? That is the question.

Of the twenty kings who ruled the Northern Kingdom of Israel before its destruction, the scriptures tell us that Ahab, the eighth king, was the worst of all. "And Ahab . . . did evil in the sight of the Lord above all that were before him."[1] "[He] did more to provoke the Lord God of Israel to anger than all the kings of Israel that were before him."[2] No such comment was made about any later king, as bad as they uniformly were.

The time of Ahab was perhaps the tragic height of four great (and self-imposed) separations in Israel. The first separation was the separation of the people from the temple, which was the central "sin of Jeroboam" wherewith "he made Israel to sin"[3]—a sin that (as we discussed in chapter 15) was repeated by every king in the Northern Kingdom.

To this first separation was added another: man's separation from each other. This separation was illustrated by the separation of the ten tribes of the Northern Kingdom from the tribes in the Southern Kingdom—a separation of the family of Israel. In the day of Ahab, the children of Israel were divided one from another. They did not stand together as a family.

The third separation, illustrated plainly and painfully by the houses of the kings in the Northern Kingdom, was the separation of father and mother from a continuation of their family. Each of the five "houses" of the kings of Israel was destroyed. The day of Ahab was a day of the discontinuation of the seed.

Finally, the day of Ahab was a day of separation from God and his power. This separation is most clearly illustrated by the powerlessness of the priests of Baal, who served at Ahab's will and pleasure and who, in their famous showdown with Elijah, were shown to have no access to power from the heavens.[4]

Elijah was a prophet in the Northern Kingdom of Israel from 870 to 850 B.C. This made his period of service roughly concurrent with Ahab's—he appeared on the scene as prophet roughly four years after Ahab began his reign, and continued in his mortal calling for twenty years, until some three years after Ahab's death. He lived at the time in his dispensation when these separations—the separation from the temple, from each other, from the continuation of the family, and from the power of God—were the greatest, and witnessed firsthand the curse that falls on mankind when these separations are not overcome. His mortal ministry was an indictment of Israel's persistence in these separations, and perhaps no prophet who ever lived knew more fully the devastation that results from the failure to overcome them. Should it surprise us, then, that it was to Elijah that the Lord entrusted the keys of the overcoming of separation—otherwise known as the powers of "binding together" or "sealing"? The keys held by Elijah, and conferred upon Joseph Smith as foretold in Malachi 4:5–6, are keys that enable our overcoming each of the four great separations.

Consider the words of Moroni[5] on the occasion of his first appearance to the Prophet Joseph Smith: "Behold, I will send my messenger, and he shall prepare the way before me: and the Lord, whom ye seek, shall suddenly come to his temple, even the messenger of the covenant, whom ye delight in: behold, he shall come, saith the Lord of hosts. But who may abide the day of his coming? and who shall stand when he appeareth? For he is like a refiner's fire, and like fullers' soap: And he shall sit as a refiner and purifier of silver."[6]

In this opening statement, Moroni announced the predicament the world will face when the Lord comes in his glory. As discussed in chapter 3 and Appendix B, those who are unworthy will not be able to abide his presence, and will be destroyed when he comes. That is, many will face the predicament of separation from the power of God—a separation that will not allow them to withstand the Lord in his glory. So Moroni asked, with Malachi, "Who shall stand when he appeareth? for he is like a refiner's fire."[7]

Continuing with the words of Malachi, Moroni explained how the Lord would prepare his people to abide his presence: "And he shall purify the sons of Levi, and purge them as gold and silver, that they may offer unto the Lord an offering in righteousness. Then shall the offering of Judah and Jerusalem be pleasant unto the Lord, as in the days of old, and as in former years. . . . Therefore ye sons of Jacob are not consumed. Even from the days of your fathers ye are gone away from mine ordinances, and have not kept them. Return unto me, and I will return unto you, saith the Lord of hosts."[8]

The first line in this passage is interesting; it says that "he shall purify the *sons of Levi*."[9] Who are the sons of Levi? They were the priesthood bearers in Israel—those who were authorized to work in the temple and perform the rites and offerings of the Lord's house. So the Lord is saying that his people—chosen Israel, whom he refers to as the "sons of Jacob"[10]—would not be consumed when those who work in the temple are purified and once again make an "offering in righteousness . . . as in the days of old, and as in former years."

What is the "offering" he is referring to "as in days of old" that must be offered in righteousness? The passage itself answers the question: "Even from the days of your fathers [i.e., "days of old"] ye are gone away from mine ordinances, and have not kept them,"[11] the Lord says. The "offering" that must be made in righteousness, as in days of old, refers to the offering of the ordinances of the temple that Israel had turned from, "even from the days of [their] fathers."[12] The ordinances being performed in Malachi's day—the standard ordinances of the tabernacle that had been in Israel since their rebellion before Sinai—were not sufficient. In order to withstand the coming of the Lord in his glory, Israel once again had to receive a fulness of the ordinances pertaining to the temple[13]—the ordinances and covenants with which the Lord had desired to endow Israel through Moses before their rebellion, ordinances that had been among men since the days of Adam.[14] "Return unto me [that is, return unto mine ordinances]," Moroni said, speaking for the Lord, "and I will return unto you."[15] So the required ordinances of the holy temple and the priesthood must be restored in order for Israel not to be consumed at the Lord's coming. (Again, see Appendix B for a discussion of the restoration of this authority and these ordinances in the latter days.)

Moroni then continued with his recitation from Malachi, revealing what must happen in order for the temple ordinances and priesthood from "former years" to be restored:

> For behold, the day cometh that shall burn as an oven, and all the proud, yea, and all that do wickedly shall burn as stubble; for they that come shall burn them, saith the Lord of Hosts, that it shall leave them neither root nor branch. . . .
>
> Remember ye the law of Moses my servant, which I commanded unto him in Horeb for all Israel, with the statutes and judgments.
>
> Behold, I will reveal unto you the Priesthood, by the hand of Elijah the prophet, before the coming of the great and dreadful day of the Lord. And he shall plant in the hearts of the children the promises made to the fathers, and the hearts of the children shall turn to their fathers. If it were not so, the whole earth would be utterly wasted at his coming.[16]

The first paragraph in the above quotation adds a further detail to the burning that will happen at the Lord's coming in glory. In this burning, the wicked—those who are without the protection of the Lord's power that has been received in the temple—will be left with "neither root nor branch."[17] This reference to "root" and "branch" is symbolic of our progenitors and posterity. The burning at the Lord's coming will consume not only all those who have not come to the Lord as best as they are able in mortality, it will also consume the links that bind mankind into family units. Only those links that are sealed together by the power of God will survive the end of mortality.

And how can they be so sealed together? Consider the second and third paragraphs just quoted. In the second paragraph, Moroni, again quoting Malachi, said to "Remember . . . the law of Moses my servant, which I commanded unto him in Horeb for all Israel, with the statutes and judgments."[18] Why remember the law of Moses? The third paragraph reveals the answer: "Behold, I will reveal unto you the Priesthood, by the hand of Elijah the prophet."[19] That is, we must remember the law of Moses, with its statutes and judgments that were revealed after Israel's rebellion at Horeb, because then we will remember that Israel failed at the time to receive the fulness of the priesthood that the Lord stood willing to give. (See chapters 9 and 10 and Appendix B herein.) By saying, "I will reveal unto you the Priesthood," the Lord is saying that what ultimately was given at Horeb was not sufficient; it was not a fulness. There needed to be a restoration of the priesthood—that is, of the "promises made to the fathers,"[20] the priesthood given to Adam and to all the patriarchs down to Abraham, Isaac, and Jacob. When the promises made to *the* fathers are planted in our hearts—that is, when we receive the priesthood blessings of the Abrahamic covenant that were conferred upon the ancient fathers or patriarchs[21]—then our hearts will be turned to *our own* fathers, which is to say that we will then become bound through the sealing powers of the priesthood to our progenitors and posterity. For those who receive the restored ordinances of the holy temple, and the sealing that binds those promises and relationships beyond the grave, their "roots" and "branches" will survive the Lord's coming, and their houses will not be "utterly wasted" at his coming. This was the priesthood that was "revealed" by Elijah to the Prophet Joseph Smith.[22] The ordinances that the children of Israel had "gone away from"[23] were restored in the latter days, according to the prophecy made by Malachi and reiterated by Moroni. Accordingly, we are now in a position to "return unto [the Lord],"[24] "as in days of old, and as in former years."[25] The latter-day sons of Levi are offering up an of-fering in righteousness in the Lord's house, and all who come and are faith-ful in the ordinances they receive and covenants they make there will not be "consumed" at the Lord's coming. They shall remain bound together in family relationships in the eternities—their roots and branches intact and increasing.[26]

In light of all this, consider how the mission of Elijah was and is to overcome the four great separations that keep us isolated from one another and from God:

He came in the latter days, in fulfillment of prophecy, to reveal the priesthood that pertains to the temple. So, through Elijah, man's separa-tion from the temple was overcome.

Consider as well the effect of his mission upon the second great separation—the separation of man from one another and family. Through the ordinances of the temple, men and women can become sealed to one another in family units.

This is the means by which the third great separation is overcome as well—the separation of man from a continuation and increase of his fam-ily. Through the ordinances of the temple, men and women receive the promises made to Abraham, including the promise of family and increase into the eternities. (See chapter 4 herein.) Whereas each of the houses of the kings of the Northern Kingdom was utterly destroyed, the "houses" of those who enter the house of the Lord will never end.

Finally, of course, it is through the priesthood restored by Elijah that man receives the highest power of the heavens—the power to overcome the separation between God and man and be restored into the presence of God, able to survive his glory. This is the "key of the knowledge of God"[27] spoken of by the Lord—the power to "enjoy the communion and presence of God the Father, and Jesus the mediator of the new covenant,"[28] which comes with the holy priesthood.[29]

Elijah, the prophet during a period when the four great separations were particularly acute, was the prophet the Lord entrusted with the keys of overcoming these separations—the keys of binding together or sealing. Through Elijah's ministry, the sins of Jeroboam have been overcome, the temple is again in our midst, and the ordinances and covenants that were had before the rebellion at Horeb are had again among men. Through the priesthood power pertaining to the restored temple, the separations of man from man, man from his family, and man from God have been surmounted. Through Elijah, the four great separations have been bound together and overcome.

CHAPTER 17

THE LORD'S QUESTION TO JONAH[1]

Should Not I Spare Nineveh?

> The little book of Jonah contains a really big message, with present-day application that is direct and immediate. To see the message, we must first understand the context, and then notice an interesting structure in the book itself—a structure that makes the book a direct communication from the Lord to us. That communication is in the form of a question—a question that each of us is answering every moment of every day.
>
> Why is this important? Because happiness itself depends on how we are answering the Lord's question.

Jonah was a prophet in the Northern Kingdom, or Kingdom of Israel, some 100 years after Elijah. The historical record places the beginning of his ministry at approximately 765 B.C. The Kingdom of Israel was completely destroyed by the Assyrians in 721 B.C., or no more than forty-four years after the events recorded in Jonah. The beginning of Assyria's brutal military campaigns against Israel would occur some twenty years earlier than that. Jonah, as a prophet of God, would have been familiar with the prophecies throughout the ages concerning the fall and scattering of Israel at the hand of Gentile nations.[2] He also would have been familiar with the prophecies of his contemporaries, Amos and Hosea, who warned the inhabitants of Israel of the pending destruction of the kingdom. Amos didn't mention the name of the enemy that would destroy Israel, but Hosea did: Assyria would be the conquering enemy.[3] This is relevant to Jonah's feelings regarding Nineveh—for Nineveh was the capital of the Assyrian empire.

Jonah may well have desired the destruction of Nineveh because he recognized that Assyria would soon bring tremendous hardship and suffering to his country, completely destroying it within forty or so years. Anyone who would do that, he might have thought, doesn't deserve to be saved.

Into this context came the voice of the Lord to Jonah: "Arise, go to Nineveh, that great city, and cry against it; for their wickedness is come up before me."[4] But Jonah didn't go. Instead, he "rose up to flee unto Tarshish from the presence of the Lord."[5]

Tarshish was, in Jonah's day, a city on the southwestern tip of what is today known as Spain. For all intents and purposes, it was the westernmost point of the known world, and the farthest place from Nineveh (which lay to the east of him) that Jonah could find. He fled before the Lord because he did not want to help the very country that would soon destroy his own people.

Jonah "went down to [the Jewish port] Joppa; and he found a ship going to Tarshish: so he paid the fare thereof, and went down into it, to go with them unto Tarshish from the presence of the Lord."[6] The ship was most likely a Phoenician merchant vessel, as the Phoenicians were the lords of shipbuilding and maritime commerce during the period.

A great storm arose as they sailed westward on the Mediterranean. The crew threw everything they could spare over the side of the ship to save their vessel and their lives, but it was no use. Finally convinced that the impending disaster must be God's response to the sins of someone on board, they cast lots to see who was responsible.[7] The lot fell upon Jonah. He confessed that the tempest was on his account and urged the men to take him up and cast him overboard in order to save themselves.[8] But they wouldn't do it. Only after trying all that they could do to save the ship without casting Jonah out did they finally relent and, with a heartfelt prayer for the Lord's pardon, cast Jonah into the sea.[9]

Jonah would have drowned, of course, but for the Lord's act of mercy in sending a large fish that took Jonah into its belly.[10] After Jonah's sore repentance over three days,[11] "the Lord spake unto the fish, and it vomited Jonah upon the dry land."[12] Jonah—finally repentant—had been saved.

"And the word of the Lord came unto Jonah the second time," we are told, saying, "Arise, go unto Nineveh, that great city, and preach unto it the preaching that I bid thee."[13] Having learned his lesson, this time Jonah obeyed. The record says matter-of-factly, "So Jonah arose, and went unto Nineveh."[14]

He cried repentance unto the inhabitants of the city for forty days and then retired to a hillside overlooking the city to watch its destruction. However, the destruction didn't come, for "God saw their works, that they turned away from their evil way and repented; and God turned away the evil that he had said he would bring upon them."[15]

This "displeased Jonah exceedingly, and he was very angry."[16] He had preached to the Ninevites as the Lord commanded, but he had never given up hope for their destruction. He didn't want them to repent. And if they did, he didn't want the Lord to save them. In fact, he worried that the Lord might "repent" of his intent to destroy Nineveh[17] because he was, in Jonah's words, "a gracious God, and merciful, slow to anger, and of great kindness."[18] So he sat beneath a sweltering sun, in a makeshift shelter, demanding that the Lord deliver his threatened destruction.

As Jonah sat stewing in his anger, the Lord asked him a question. Curiously, the book of Jonah ends with the Lord's question hanging in the air over Nineveh. We don't know how Jonah answered it. The question the Lord asked of Jonah was, "Should not I spare Nineveh?"[19]

What are we to make of such an ending to the book of Jonah? Why would it end with a question? And why wouldn't we be told how Jonah answered it? Isn't the answer important?

In order to answer these questions, we need to notice something about the book of Jonah. Consider how the story unfolds:

A The Lord commands Jonah to preach against the wicked
   Nineveh (Jonah 1:1–2)
  B Jonah sins, not wanting Nineveh to be saved (Jonah 1:3–17)
    C Jonah repents, and the Lord saves Jonah (Jonah 2:1–10)
    C' Nineveh repents, and the Lord saves Nineveh (Jonah
       3:1–10)
  B' Jonah sins, not wanting Nineveh to be saved (Jonah 4:1–10)
A' The Lord asks Jonah a question: Should not I spare Nineveh?
   (Jonah 4:11)

The book of Jonah is a chiasm—an ancient literary structure, developed in its most intricate forms by the Hebrews, in which the elements of a passage repeat themselves in reverse order.[20] The chiastic structure transforms the normal flow of ideas in a text. Where we are accustomed to ideas developing in linear fashion, each idea building on the one before it, in a chiasm, the ideas point inward. The end of a chiasm is not the end in the normal sense. Likewise, the beginning is not merely a beginning. There is a sense in which the beginning is the end and the end is the beginning (to use a chiasmus to explain chiasmus). And together, the frames formed by like elements at the beginning and end point toward the middle of the chiasm, where key elements typically appear.

The chiastic form is of far more than mere literary interest. To fully understand a chiastic text, we need to recognize its structure, for a linear reading of a nonlinear text will not reveal its nonlinear meaning. In a chiastic text, for example, the end is not so much the end as it is an invitation to consider the center anew.

With that in mind, let's reconsider the final element of the Jonah chiasm—the Lord's question to Jonah, "Should not I spare Nineveh?"—by looking at the center elements of the chiasm:

C Jonah repents, and the Lord saves Jonah (Jonah 2:1–10)
C' Nineveh repents, and the Lord saves Nineveh (Jonah 3:1–10)

At the center of the chiasm, Jonah and Nineveh were each spared by the Lord after they had repented. They were saved alike, on the same terms, and by the same mercy. Consider the relevance, then, of the Lord's question, "Should not I spare Nineveh?" If Jonah were to answer "No, Nineveh should not be saved, notwithstanding their repentance," by implication, Jonah also would be saying that he himself should not be saved. When the Lord asks Jonah his question, he isn't really asking whether Nineveh will be saved. The Lord had already spared them. The mercy in question is not mercy for Nineveh, but mercy for Jonah. If Jonah insists that mercy should not be extended to Nineveh, he implies that he himself should not receive the Lord's saving mercy. The Lord, by asking the question, and by unfolding the story as he does, is mercifully giving Jonah the opportunity to see the hard-hearted folly in his position.

It is no accident that the very center statement of the book of Jonah, which appears in the middle of the center elements of the chiasm, with twenty-four verses preceding it and twenty-three verses following, reads: "They that observe lying vanities forsake their own mercy."[21] As Jonah sits baking under the sticks, waiting for Nineveh's destruction, he is "observing lying vanities," and because he is, he is in danger of forsaking his own mercy.

What are the lying vanities that hold him fast? Consider: Jonah's primary objections to the salvation of Nineveh would appear to be that Nineveh doesn't deserve to be saved because: (1) Nineveh is sinful, and (2) Nineveh threatens others—namely Israel—with destruction. His demand that Nineveh be destroyed for these reasons is a "lying vanity" because he is failing to recognize how he is exactly like Nineveh in both respects.

As for Jonah's first objection, by running from the Lord rather than doing what he had been commanded to do, Jonah was himself sinful. Jonah, in that sense, was just like Nineveh. If Nineveh's sinfulness precluded the opportunity for repentance and salvation, then so must Jonah's. By extending *Jonah* the opportunity to repent by sending a fish to save him from destruction in his sins, the Lord demonstrated that he would offer the sinner opportunity to repent. If sin were to wipe out the opportunity for repentance, as Jonah wanted it to do for Nineveh, then Jonah and the rest of us would drown in the sea.

Jonah's second objection is more subtle. What about people who make life difficult for others? In particular, what about people who make life difficult *for me?* In Jonah's mind, saving Nineveh would facilitate the destruction of Israel. Surely in such a case one cannot be expected to extend mercy!

But consider Jonah's own story: As a result of his sinful flight from the Lord, he exposed a completely innocent group of mariners to the wilds of the angry sea. They threw their possessions overboard in an effort to save themselves,[22] struggled to save a ship that "was like to be broken,"[23] and feared that they would soon perish.[24] When they drew lots to see who was responsible for "this evil," and the lot fell on Jonah, what did the mariners do? One would expect them to throw him immediately overboard. After all, *he* had caused the trouble. *He alone* was responsible for the evil. They were the innocent victims of *his* sin. Under the circumstances, surely the mariners would be justified in jettisoning what otherwise would be the cause of their deaths. *"Nevertheless,"* the scripture says, *"the men rowed hard to bring it to the land;* but they could not: for the sea wrought, and was tempestuous against them."[25] They ended up casting Jonah overboard as he had instructed them to do, but only after doing everything in their power to save him.

To the mariners in this story, Jonah presented precisely the same threat as Nineveh posed to Israel. Like Nineveh, Jonah threatened others with destruction. The mariners' merciful reaction to Jonah was a rebuke of the merciless grudge Jonah held toward the Ninevites.

So Jonah, who objected to the sin and destructive threat of Nineveh, was *himself* sinful and dangerously destructive. In every respect he was just as "Ninevitish" as the Ninevites. Yet in his grudge, he was blind to his own "Ninevehness": He had forgotten *his* prior sin; he had forgotten the mercy extended to him by the mariners; and he had forgotten the ultimate mercy of the Lord, who had delivered him from certain death. And so at the end of the story Jonah is blind to the fact that he is just like Nineveh. Fancying himself different, he feels he deserves something that others like him do not deserve. He is wrapped up in vanity.

But his eyes and feelings lie to him. No one *deserves* mercy. Mercy is mercy precisely because it is *un*deserved. Jonah's hypercritical view of Nineveh is a lying vanity. Holding to it, Jonah is in danger of forsaking his own mercy.

Although we can do nothing of ourselves to *merit* mercy, the Jonah story suggests that we *can* disqualify ourselves from it. As the Lord taught in the parable of the unmerciful servant, foremost among the ways we can forsake mercy is our own failure to extend it: "Then his lord, after that he had called him, said unto him, O thou wicked servant, I forgave thee all that debt, because thou desiredst me: *Shouldest not thou also have had com-passion on thy fellowservant, even as I had pity on thee?*"[26]

The lord's question to the servant in this parable is the same question the Lord asks Jonah: "Should not I spare Nineveh?" For the servant, for Jonah, and for us, everything depends on our answer to this question, as the fate of the unmerciful servant illustrates: "And his lord was wroth, and delivered him to the tormentors, till he should pay all that was due unto him. So likewise shall my heavenly Father do also unto you, if ye from your hearts forgive not every one his brother their trespass."[27]

Forgive every one his brother their trespass? Yes! Even sinners? Yes! Even those who are out to destroy us? Yes! Even Nineveh? Yes! And not just in an obligatory way. We are to forgive Nineveh *"from [our] hearts."*[28] It is in so forgiving that we can be forgiven. For we *are* Nineveh.

We are now in a position to consider why the book of Jonah ended without an answer from Jonah to the Lord's question. Perhaps it is because the question is really a question for us. Our position in the eternities, like Jonah's, will depend on whether we give up our own lying vanities— whether we let ourselves be troubled only by our *own* sins,[29] and whether we extend mercy to the Ninevites in our own lives. That is the Lord's question, not only to Jonah but to us. He doesn't let us off the hook by providing Jonah's answer to the question, which might mislead us into thinking that this was simply a question for Jonah. No, it is a question to mankind, and to each of us individually. What will be our answer—and therefore our fate? That is the question.

ISRAEL AND THE BOOK OF JONAH

As we have seen, the book of Jonah's chiastic structure reveals a powerful message regarding repentance and personal salvation. But another look at the chiasm reveals at least another layer of meaning. Jonah is also a revelation, prophecy, and warning to the house of Israel.

Consider, for example, how the following elements from the first chapter of Jonah were true both of Jonah and of Israel:

- Knew the Lord[30]
- Turned from God[31]
- Great hardship resulted from sin[32]
- Asleep to sins[33]
- Messenger(s) sent to awaken him[34]
- "Hebrew"[35]

- "Cast . . . into the sea" by Gentiles[36]
- Life preserved by the Lord in the sea[37]

These elements from chapter 1 of the book of Jonah tell the story of the calling, sin, and scattering of Israel. If Jonah, in addition to being a story of personal sin and repentance, is an allegory for the national sin and repentance of the house of Israel, we would expect the rest of the story to continue the similitude. Let's see what we find.

At the beginning of chapter 2, Jonah is being preserved in the sea by the hand of the Lord. Perhaps this corresponds to the Lord's preservation of scattered Israel among the Gentile nations. Jonah then cries to the Lord "by reason of [his] affliction,"[38] just as Israel would cry out in affliction after they had been scattered.

Things began to turn for Jonah in chapter 2 when he resolved to "look again toward [the Lord's] holy temple."[39] Similarly, the beginning of the first gathering of Israel was marked by a return to the temple. The Kingdom of Judah fell to the Babylonians in 587 B.C., and the people were led away into captivity. Over a century later, Babylon was conquered by Persia, led by Cyrus the Great. Cyrus allowed the Israelites to return to Jerusalem *to rebuild the temple:* "Thus saith Cyrus king of Persia, All the kingdoms of the earth hath the Lord God of heaven given me; and he hath charged me to build him an house in Jerusalem, which is in Judah. Who is there among you of all his people? The Lord his God be with him, and let him go up."[40]

Led by Haggai and Zechariah, and some seventy years later by Ezra and Nehemiah, the gathering of the Jews to Jerusalem occurred as the people looked again to the Lord's holy temple. Chapter 2 ends with Jonah emerging from the sea/fish onto dry land after he looked to the temple, just as the Israelites gathered again to their land after they looked to the temple.

In chapter 4, Jonah commits the same sin he committed at the beginning of the book. This earlier sin resulted in his being cast into the sea. Jonah's fate after his sinful repeat in chapter 4 is unknown. However, the implication is that should he answer "no" to the Lord's question, he would suffer a fate similar to the fate he suffered before—namely, destruction and expulsion. Destruction was precisely the fate Nineveh faced in chapter 3, but the people escaped destruction because they hearkened to the words of the Lord through Jonah. By listening to Jonah, their political enemy, the Ninevites answered the Lord's question, in effect, with a collective "yes." Jesus revealed that the Israelites would be condemned unless they hearkened to the Lord as Nineveh did—when the Jews asked him for a sign of his divinity, Jesus scolded:

> Yea rather, blessed are they that hear the word of God, and keep it. And when the people were gathered thick together, he began to say, This is an evil generation: they seek a sign; and there shall no sign be given it, but the sign of Jonas the prophet. *For as Jonas was a sign unto the Ninevites, so shall also the Son of man be to this generation. . . . The men of Nineve[h] shall rise up in the judgment with this generation, and shall condemn it: for they repented at the preaching of Jonas; and, behold, a greater than Jonas is here.*[41]

Just as the Savior's words suggested, most of the Jews would reject his preaching. As a result, they were scattered again amongst the nations, just as the Jonah chiasm would predict. In the latter days, the people of Israel find themselves as Jonah was in chapter 4—separated from their homeland, alone, and perhaps feeling superior. The way for deliverance from their condition is revealed, as it was for Jonah, at the center of the Jonah chiasm. Deliverance for Israel will come as it came for Jonah: by remembering the Lord and his covenants.[42] And that remembrance will come just as it came to Nineveh—through the preaching of the word of the Lord. And just as Nineveh had to receive that preaching from a foreigner, so Israel in the latter days will have to receive that preaching from the Gentiles. Hope for the Israelites will depend on their ability to listen humbly to the Lord's representatives from the Gentile nations.

ANOTHER LOOK AT THE CENTER: JONAH, ISRAEL, AND CHRIST

In Matthew, the Lord drew a connection between himself and Jonah when he stated:

"An evil and adulterous generation seeketh after a sign; and there shall no sign be given to it, but the sign of the prophet Jonas: *For as Jonas was three days and three nights in the whale's belly; so shall the Son of man be three days and three nights in the heart of the earth.*"[43]

Jonah's burial within the fish was in similitude of the Lord's burial in the earth, a parallelism known as "the sign of Jonah." Besides the similarity in the span of time they were "buried," Jonah's experience while buried in the "whale's belly" reveals something as well about the Lord. For in Jonah's struggle to repent, we hear echoes of the burdens the Savior must have carried when he took upon himself the sins of mankind. Consider Jonah's words:

"Out of the belly of hell cried I, and thou heardest my voice."[44]

"I went down to the bottoms of the mountains; the earth with her bars was about me for ever."[45]

"For thou hadst cast me into the deep, in the midst of the seas."[46]

"The depth closed me round about, the weeds were wrapped about my head."[47]

"And the floods compassed me about: all thy billows and thy waves passed over me."[48]

"The waters compassed me about, even to the soul."[49]

With the full anguish of our sins upon him, consider how these words of Jonah foreshadow the words of the Lord in his final moments in mortality:

"Then I said, I am cast out of thy sight;"[50]

    ("My God, my God, why hast thou forsaken me?"[51])

"yet I will look again toward thy holy temple."[52]

    ("Father, into thy hands I commend my spirit."[53])

The perfect Lord is at the center of the story of Jonah and Israel. *He* suffered that Jonah, Israel, and Nineveh might be delivered from suffering. His deliverance makes our repentance possible. Only the pure Lord, separated from the Father by the weight of the world's sins, could nevertheless step again into his presence and look upon his holy temple. Because he did so, we whose sins he swallowed can step with him—if we remember him, and pay all that we have vowed.[54] *And* only if we rejoice in the ability of others to do the same thing and to receive the same mercy.

Jonah's burial in the sea, the Israelites' burial in the nations, and the Ninevites' burial of their sins, all are types and shadows of the burial established to bring us forth from death. The Savior's mercy is extended to all mankind—to Israelite and Ninevite. Should not the Lord save Nineveh? Should not the Lord save Israel? The questions are the same. The Savior, through his suffering, says "Yes!"

Our answer must echo his—for he himself is the answer. Answer differently, and we forsake our own mercy.

CHAPTER 18

THE HOUSE OF ISRAEL AS A TYPE
AND SHADOW

My Righteous Servant

Now we're to the point in the Old Testament that I used to fear most: Isaiah. Thankfully, my fear is now gone, replaced by wonder. Isaiah wrote as a musician writes music—in chords. Which is to say, there is always more than one level in his writing, and his words usually have at least two, if not multiple, fulfillments. So when you read Isaiah, don't just listen for the melody. Become immersed in the chords of his writing—in its multiple, harmonious applications.

In this chapter, I don't take on the whole symphony of Isaiah, but one of its most beautiful and personally relevant chords—a chord that links ancient Israel with Joseph Smith, and both of them with the Savior. It is a story we are now living.

To introduce it, I need to introduce yet another metaphor. . . .

Isaiah is like an immense river of verdant blues and greens, moving in powerful unison around forested bends. The water moves swiftly on—calm, constant, determined. Although apparently devoid of rapids, the river's pace and sheer size inspire awe. Swirls on its surface reveal a submerged world somehow powerful enough to shape its currents. Standing on its banks, we feel its vitality and power and know that we are no match for the river.

Unlike every other river, perhaps, this river has no shallows. And even if it did, its power would make wading impossible. Those looking for a place to frolic turn to gentler and shallower streams. But for those desiring knowledge of the heart of the countryside, this river can take them where no other can. However, it can do that only if they immerse themselves in it.

Of course, most never do. The current seems too strong; to those on the bank it makes the river foreboding. But those who dive in discover that the water no longer tears at them as it did when they kept one foot on shore. Having joined the river, they become one with it.

The river itself is one entity, stretching forward and back, each location within it dependent on and implied by the others, every part of the river speaking to every other part, warning of things to come by speaking of things past. Those who have joined the river join the river's conversation as well. Immersed in the conversation, they gain an intuitive feel for the river, and for the submerged terrain that shapes it. They perceive patterns in the water, and come to anticipate and feel rocks as the river rushes over them, not because they see or brush against them but because they recognize subtle shifts in the flow around them.

Part of the intuition that we develop as we float the river of Isaiah is that most of his prophecies have ancient *and* modern fulfillment, and sometimes more than one instance of each. Jacob may have been referring to the dualistic nature of Isaiah's prophecies when he wrote: "And now, behold, I would speak unto you concerning *things which are, and which are to come;* wherefore, I will read you the words of Isaiah."[1] The Savior's description of Isaiah's words implies that same dualism: "And all things that he spake *have been and shall be,* even according to the words which he spake."[2]

Isaiah himself wrote that the Lord declares "the end from the beginning, and from ancient times the things that are not yet done."[3] One possible reading of this verse is that the Lord reveals all things, from the beginning to the end. However, it may also mean that the Lord reveals the end by revealing the beginning. This latter reading implies a parallel structure to history itself, at least to the world's *spiritual* history (a possibility explored more fully in the next chapter). Support for this idea is found in Isaiah 44:7, where the Lord says, "things that are coming, and shall come, let [my ancient people] shew unto them." Perhaps the nature of the spiritual history of the world is such that we can know of things to come by observing what happened anciently to the Lord's chosen people.

Keeping Isaiah's dualistic structure in mind, let's consider the significance of a repeating word pattern that emerges in chapters 41 through 53 of Isaiah. Consider the following excerpts from those chapters (emphasis added):

"But thou, Israel, art *my servant* . . ." (Isaiah 41:8).

"Thou art *my servant;* I have chosen thee, and not cast thee
away" (Isaiah 41:9).

"Behold *my servant,* whom I uphold . . ." (Isaiah 42:1).

"I will send *my servant* unto you . . ." (JST, Isaiah 42:19).

"Ye are . . . *my servant* whom I have chosen . . ." (Isaiah 43:10).

"Yet now hear, O Jacob *my servant* . . ." (Isaiah 44:1).

"Fear not, O Jacob, *my servant* . . ." (Isaiah 44:2).

"Remember these, O Jacob and Israel; for thou art *my servant*
. . ." (Isaiah 44:21).

"That confirmeth the word of *his servant* . . ." (Isaiah 44:26).

"The Lord hath redeemed *his servant* Jacob" (Isaiah 48:20).

"Thou art *my servant,* O Israel . . ." (Isaiah 49:3).

"And now, saith the Lord that formed me from the womb to be
his servant . . ." (Isaiah 49:5).

"Thou shouldest be *my servant* . . ." (Isaiah 49:6).

"Thus saith the Lord . . . to *a servant* of rulers . . ." (Isaiah 49:7).

"Who is among you . . . that obeyeth the voice of *his servant* . . ."
(Isaiah 50:10).

"Behold, *my servant* . . ." (Isaiah 52:13).

"By his knowledge shall *my righteous servant* justify many . . ."
(Isaiah 53:11).

THE IDENTITY OF THE SERVANT

A number of these verses plainly say that the servant is the house of Israel. For example, in Isaiah 44:21 we read: "Remember these, O Jacob and Israel; for thou art my servant: I have formed thee; thou art my servant: O Israel, thou shalt not be forgotten of me." Similarly, Isaiah 49:3

says: "Thou art my servant, O Israel, in whom I will be glorified." So the title "servant" in these chapters would appear to refer to the house of Israel.

But if the servant is Israel, what are we to make of Isaiah's reference just two verses later, where he says that the servant is one who will *gather* Israel? "*And now, saith the Lord that formed me from the womb to be his servant, to bring Jacob again to him,* Though Israel be not gathered, yet shall I be glorious in the eyes of the Lord, and my God shall be my strength. *And he said, It is a light thing that thou shouldest be my servant to raise up the tribes of Jacob, and to restore the preserved of Israel: I will also give thee for a light to the Gentiles, that thou mayest be my salvation unto the end of the earth.*"[4]

Again, if the servant is Israel, how can he also be one who is raised to gather Israel? Either the passage is unnecessarily misleading, or Isaiah is using the term "servant" to describe more than one person or group. Luke's description of Simeon's reaction upon handling the babe Jesus calls to mind this particular description of the servant, suggesting that the term "servant" in Isaiah may also be a reference to Christ: "Lord, now lettest thou [me] depart in peace, according to thy word: For mine eyes have seen thy salvation, Which thou hast prepared before the face of all people; *A light to lighten the Gentiles, and the glory of thy people Israel.*"[5]

Matthew clearly regarded Isaiah's "servant" to be prophetic of the Savior (compare to Isaiah 42:1–4): "That it might be fulfilled which was spoken by Esaias the prophet, saying, Behold my servant, whom I have chosen; my beloved, in whom my soul is well pleased: I will put my spirit upon him, and he shall shew judgment to the Gentiles. He shall not strive, nor cry; neither shall any man hear his voice in the streets. A bruised reed shall he not break, and smoking flax shall he not quench, till he send forth judgment unto victory. And in his name shall the Gentiles trust."[6]

Support for the idea that Isaiah's servant prophecies apply to Christ is supplied as well by Elder Bruce R. McConkie: Isaiah described the servant as one whose "visage was so marred more than any man, and his form more than the sons of men."[7] Elder McConkie stated that this "prophecy . . . is clearly Messianic and applies to Jesus who was crucified and rose from the dead."[8]

It would appear, then, that Isaiah uses the term "servant" to describe not only Israel, but Christ.

However, if the application is limited to Israel and Christ, what are we to make of the Lord's quotation of Isaiah's marred servant prophecy when he appeared to the descendants of Lehi? After quoting verses 12 through 15 from Isaiah 52 regarding the marred servant, the risen Lord said, "Verily, verily, I say unto you, all these things *shall surely come*."[9] He then proceeded to identify the marred servant as a man yet to come, who would declare a "great and a marvelous work" among men,[10] who would be given power to bring forth the words of the Lord unto the Gentiles,[11] and through whom the gathering of Israel would then commence.[12]

So on the one hand it appears that Isaiah's marred servant prophecy applies to the Savior. But then the Savior himself uses it to describe another—a person yet to come who will bring forth a "marvelous work and a wonder," a person whose mission resembles the latter-day mission of Joseph Smith. So who is the marred servant—Christ, Joseph Smith, or still someone else? The answer, according to Elder McConkie, is that the prophecy, like Isaiah's prophecies generally, is dualistic. It applies to the Savior *and* to Joseph Smith, and perhaps to others as well: "In this whole discourse [to the Nephites in 3 Nephi 20:10–22:17], Jesus is applying the prophetic word to the latter days, meaning that, as with many prophecies, the divine word has dual fulfillment. In this setting, we may properly say that Joseph Smith—whose voice declared the word for this dispensation— was marred, as his Lord had been."[13]

The servant references in Isaiah would appear to apply, then, not only to Israel, but also to the Savior and to Joseph Smith.

SIGNIFICANCE OF THE TRIFOLD PROPHECY

Isaiah's servant prophecies can be grouped roughly into nine characteristics of the servant:

1. God's chosen
2. Raised from humble, plain beginnings
3. Found refuge in "Egypt"[14]

4. Possessor of the law through whom salvation comes to the world
5. Smitten and held in scorn and derision
6. Experienced suffering and cruel death
7. Lifted up and restored
8. Will obtain victory over enemies
9. Shall receive an inheritance of seed innumerable

We have discovered in our study of the Old Testament that many of the characters and elements in the Bible are types and shadows of Christ. These parallelisms establish, reestablish, and confirm the divinity of the Lord Jesus Christ as the Savior of the world. They reveal the Old Testament to be a sustained testimony of his life and mission. (For more on this, see chapter 22 and Appendix A herein.) Through the servant metaphor, and the characteristics of the servant listed above, Isaiah introduces what is perhaps the grandest similitude of all: that the story of the house of Israel, which is almost entirely the focus of the Old Testament, is itself in similitude of the Savior. Recognizing this grand parallelism, the Old Testament becomes, both in its entirety and in its particulars, a record of the Master.

As grand and significant as the house of Israel/Savior parallelism is, however, alone it fails to capture the entire majesty of Isaiah's servant prophecies. For, as we have seen, those prophecies reveal at least one additional parallel figure: the Prophet Joseph Smith. Which raises the question, why? Why does the Prophet of the Restoration appear to be included in this trifold prophecy? And why the trifold prophecy at all? Wouldn't it have been enough to show the parallelism between the house of Israel and Christ?

Among perhaps many reasons is this one: Without Joseph Smith, the story of the house of Israel *could not* be parallel to the Savior. This is because without a restoration, the story of the house of Israel ends in death, and no story that ends in a final, lasting death is the Savior's story. The Prophet of the Restoration was the agent through whom the gospel of life was restored to the world. As the children of Israel gather to that gospel, they are resurrected to the truth. In other words, it was through the restoration (or resurrection) of the gospel that the restoration (or resurrection) of Israel would be wrought. The Prophet brought about that resurrection. Without him, Israel could not have been raised again to the Lord.

Ezekiel made this connection explicit. In verses 1 through 14 of chapter 37, he detailed a remarkable vision regarding the resurrection. After witnessing a valley full of dry bones, he described how at the Lord's direction the bones came together, sinews and flesh came upon them, and the spirits entered the bodies, bringing them to life. By the context of the vision, we know that in addition to being a prophecy of the resurrection of man, it is also a parallel prophecy of the restoration of the house of Israel. For the Lord told Ezekiel: "these bones are the whole house of Israel."[15] "Behold, O my people," the Lord continued, "I will open your graves, and cause you to come up out of your graves, and bring you into the land of Israel. . . . And shall put my spirit in you, and ye shall live. . . . Then shall ye know that I the Lord have spoken it, and performed it."[16]

After connecting the house of Israel and the Savior through the image of the resurrection, Ezekiel then connected them both to the Prophet Joseph. For immediately following the vision of the gathering of the bones in the resurrection, Ezekiel was told by the Lord that the gathering of Israel's bones into one body would happen immediately following the gathering of two sticks—one for Judah and one for Joseph.[17] These sticks would be gathered into one, to be in the hands of the prophet before Israel.[18] Only then would the Lord "take the children of Israel from among the heathen" and "gather them on every side, and bring them into their own land,"[19] as the Lord had shown Ezekiel would happen in the vision of the resurrection. The two sticks, of course, are the Bible and the Book of Mormon,[20] and the Prophet Joseph was the prophet through whom those sticks became joined, precipitating the restoration (or "resurrection") of the house of Israel. The Prophet Joseph, then, makes possible the unity between the house of Israel and the Savior. Through his mission, Israel is raised up and brought back into the presence of the Lord.

By demonstrating a parallelism between the house of Israel and the Savior, Isaiah and Ezekiel at once direct Israel to look to Christ and to the restoration. To Christ because the parallelism demands that they be one with Christ. To the restoration because they can be one with Christ only as they are resurrected unto the truth that was restored through Joseph Smith. Of Joseph, Isaiah prophesied, "and [the Lord] shall send them a saviour, and a great one, and he shall deliver them."[21] It is fitting that the servant through whom the resurrection of the house of Israel would be wrought was himself in similitude of Him who was resurrected.

CHAPTER 19

THE DISPENSATIONS OF
THE LORD'S PEOPLE

The First Shall Be Last and the Last Shall Be First

> A recurring pattern in the scriptures is embedded into the fabric of history itself. This pattern illuminates the arch of the gospel throughout history—including its latter-day restoration—in clear and surprising ways. This pattern, once seen, reinforces and strengthens one's conviction and testimony of the latter-day mission of the Church.

From Isaiah, we see that scriptural references often foreshadow multiple events. It is interesting that the literary form of the scriptures, which is characterized by parallelism and repetition (and by more complicated literary structures of repetition such as chiasmus[1]) embodies what the scriptural message is often trying to say: "all things have their likeness."[2] History—temporal and spiritual—repeats. Events past foreshadow events to come. Characters and events in the scriptures testify of Christ.

The Lord is speaking of this grand pattern of repetition when he declares that "the last shall be first, and the first shall be last."[3] This, as we discussed in chapter 17 about Jonah, is both an example and a description of the literary form known as chiasmus. This particular scripture is used to describe how the Jews, who were first to receive the gospel in olden times, and the Gentiles second, will in the latter days be last to receive the gospel, while the Gentiles will be first.[4] However, another passage that uses this same language offers a second interpretation: The Lord says that all things were created first spiritually, and then temporally, and that he then has commanded man first temporally, and then spiritually—that is, that all his temporal commands have also been spiritual.[5] I would propose at least a third interpretation of this chiasm: That it rightfully describes the spiritual history of the earth as that entire history unfolds (and refolds) as a chiasm. Consider the following:

THE CHIASTIC HISTORY OF THE EARTH

A We lived with the Father and the Son
  B Satan and his followers were cast out
    C Creation of glorified earth
      D Man received an immortal body
        E There was peace on the earth among all creation
          F The Lord was present on the earth
            G Man fell due to sin and was cast out of the Lord's presence (spiritual and physical death)
              H The gospel was given to man, and preached throughout the earth
              I A chosen people
                J There was gross wickedness among man
                  K The fulness of the gospel was taken from the earth
                  L Christ loosed the bands of spiritual death
                  L' Christ loosed the bands of physical death
                K' The fulness of the gospel was taken from the earth
                J' There was gross wickedness among man
              I' A chosen people
            H' The gospel was given to man, and preached throughout the earth
          G' Men who, due to sin, will not be able to endure his presence, are destroyed
        F' The Lord comes again to the earth
      E' There is peace on the earth among all creation
    D' Man receives an immortal body
   C' The earth receives its paradisiacal glory
  B' Satan and his followers are cast out forever
A' We live with the Father and the Son

Notice that Christ is "the first and the last," the "Alpha and Omega,"[6] in this grand history. He also came to the earth at the center of the earth's chiastic history, in the "meridian of time."[7] By looking at this chiasm, we see that the scriptures about the first being last and the last first also find fulfillment in Christ. He is the first and the last in the first half of the chiasm, and then the last and the first in the second half.

This pattern of repetition, and of chiasmus, repeats itself as well in the history of God's people throughout the ages of the earth. Consider, for example, the Apostle Paul's well-known prophecy to the Thessalonians that there would be an apostasy—a "falling away"—before the second coming of the Lord: "Let no man deceive you by any means: for that day shall not come, except there come a falling away first."[8] Latter-day Saints are well aware of the falling away that required a restoration of the gospel to Joseph Smith. What they and others are may not be as well aware of, however, is that this falling away after Christ's coming was simply the last of many instances of falling away throughout the ages.

Consider, for example, the falling away that happened among the family of Adam. When man was placed on the earth, all who were on the earth—that is, Adam and Eve—were followers of Christ. However, Satan came among their children to tempt them, and we are told that the sons and daughters of Adam and Eve "loved Satan more than God. And men began from that time forth to be carnal, sensual, and devilish."[9] So complete was this first falling away that the Lord destroyed all who walked the earth, save Noah's family only.[10]

Likewise, when Noah and his family exited the ark, the world again was populated only by those who were followers of Christ. But again there was a falling away from the truth, so that by Abraham's day only Melchizedek and his people appear to have had a fulness of the gospel. As mentioned in chapter 4 herein, there is an interesting argument to be made that Melchizedek and his city were translated, as the city of Enoch before them, so that only Abraham remained on the earth as the head of a new gospel dispensation.

But of course, the children of Israel, after years in Egypt, fell away from a fulness as well. Moses was called to restore them to the truth. However, as discussed in chapter 9 herein, they rebelled at Sinai or Horeb, and were unable to receive the fulness of the gospel. The next restoration was through the Savior himself. The fulness of the gospel that had been restored multiple times already, due to repeated apostasy among the children of men, was restored to the people, and the priesthood keys of administering that fulness were conferred upon Peter, James, and John.[11] This set the stage for the final falling away that would require the restoration of the gospel through Joseph Smith in the "dispensation of the fulness of times"[12]—the "times of refreshing," when there would be a "restitution of all things."[13] This final dispensation is the time when all things will be gathered together as one in Christ.[14] It is the time when things which have been kept hidden from the beginning will be revealed, when the keys and glories from Adam to the present will be restored, and when all of the dispensations from the beginning will be welded together.[15]

With this broad history, consider the following:

A At the beginning of the dispensation of Adam, all who walked the earth had a fulness of the gospel.

  B At the end of the dispensation of Adam, none who walked the earth had a fulness of the gospel.

  B' At the beginning of the dispensation of the fulness of times, none who walked the earth had a fulness of the gospel.

A' At the end of the dispensation of the fulness of times, all who walk the earth will have a fulness of the gospel.

The bookend dispensations of the gospel repeat the core chiasm that "the first shall be last, and the last shall be first." As in the beginning, when all the earth (at that time, Adam and Eve) were followers of Christ, so too at the end of time, only those who are followers of Christ will be able to abide his glory at his coming (see chapter 3 and Appendix B herein for discussions of why this is the case). All in the end must return to how it was in the beginning. This is the doctrine of the redemption from the Fall, and this doctrine is present in all of the patterns of history—even in the very structure of scriptural writings—so that we will not miss the point. In fact, chiastic structure could not be avoided by scriptural writers even had they wanted to avoid it, as the story of man's fall and redemption (both individually and as a race) is itself chiastic. In form and structure, as well as in content, the scriptures testify of Christ—of the redemption of man from the Fall through the Savior's central atoning act.

Between the first and last dispensations, the pattern of fall and redemption, or apostasy and restoration, repeats itself anew numerous times, as discussed previously. This pattern of apostasy and restoration is depicted on the accompanying diagram of the various dispensations of the gospel down through time. (See the diagram on the next page.)

To begin with, the word *dispensation* in the Bible is translated from the Greek word *oikonomia,* which is translated half the time as "stewardship." This is significant, as a new gospel dispensation begins whenever the Lord entrusts or restores to a prophet on the earth keys of the fulness of the gospel that have been lost from among the people. In other words, each new dispensation begins with a sacred stewardship entrusted to man.

The main dispensations of man can be thought of as the dispensations of Adam, Noah, Abraham, Moses, Jesus, and Joseph Smith. Enoch is sometimes said to head a dispensation, and I believe he does. However, I believe he is more accurately characterized as the head of what might be considered a secondary dispensation in the sense that it is a dispensation that was removed out of the central spiritual history of the earth. Such dispensations that are "led apart" differ from the central dispensations down through history, both because they are led apart from the central history of the earth and also because they do not necessarily follow total apostasy but are rather ways to preserve the righteous before total apostasy has taken hold and the true gospel is completely lost.

The characteristics of each gospel dispensation include the following: (1) There is always a falling away from a fulness—an "apostasy"—before a new dispensation is started (as stated above, this is different in the case of dispensations entrusted to those who are led apart); (2) a new dispensation begins when the Lord institutes a restoration of truths and fulness of priesthood authority that have been lost or entrusts the same to a lone prophet who remains when the other saints are led apart and/or taken up into heaven (such as with Noah, when Enoch and his people were taken; and with Abraham, when Melchizedek and his people were likely taken); (3) the head of each new dispensation is visited by the Savior himself; and

	HEADS OF CENTRAL GOSPEL DISPENSATIONS ON EARTH *(Each dispensation but the last one ends in darkness and apostasy, which is what necessitates a new dispensation)*
Year	
Beginning of Time	**ADAM** *Stewardship over all of mankind on the earth granted Adam by Jehovah/Christ*
	APOSTASY
Time of the Great Flood	**NOAH (THE "SECOND ADAM")** *Stewardship over all of mankind on the earth from this dispensation onward (held subordinate to Adam)*
	APOSTASY
2000 B.C.	**ABRAHAM** *Stewardship over a particular covenant family from this dispensation onward. Covenants renewed through Isaac and Jacob/Israel*
	APOSTASY
1570 B.C.	**MOSES** *Stewardship of gathering the covenant family to the Lord*
	APOSTASY
30 A.D.	**JESUS (PETER/JAMES/JOHN)** *Stewardship for delivering salvation to the world—for bringing all into the divine covenant family*
	APOSTASY
1820 A.D.	**JOSEPH SMITH** *The collective stewardship of all the dispensations of the earth (delegated by the holders of those stewardships), with the responsibility of delivering salvation to the living and to the dead of each of the dispensations—thus, "the Dispensation of the Fulness of Times." Keys passed to subsequent prophets.*

HEADS OF DISPENSATIONS LED APART

(Dispensations separated either from the earth or from the main body of believers, requiring their own sets of keys)

ENOCH

Enoch and his City of Holiness were translated—taken up into heaven without tasting death—to return with the Lord at his coming (Moses 7:63, 69)

BROTHER OF JARED

MELCHIZEDEK?

After Abraham received the priesthood from Melchizedek, there is no more mention of Melchizedek in the scriptural record. The scriptures tell us that he was attempting to create another Zion that would join Enoch's people in heaven. The scriptures suggest he may have been successful and that his people were translated as Enoch's were, leaving Abraham to lead a new dispensation, as Noah was left behind after Enoch to lead a new dispensation. (See JST Gen. 14:32–36; JST Gen. 14:37–39; Heb. 7:8)

A LEADER FROM A REMNANT OF "THE LOST TRIBES"?

A subset of the ten tribes led away by Assyria are said (in Aprcrypha) to have sought the Lord in repentance, who then led them to a land apart, to return again at his coming. Some statements (including scriptures in Isaiah and 3 Nephi) imply a literal coming of a body of the ten tribes who have been preserved by the Lord; other authorities suggest these refer to the gathering of the scattered elect from the nations.

LEHI/NEPHI

Keys pass to subsequent prophets until Moroni around 400 A.D., who was the last to hold the keys of the stick of Ephraim (JS–H 1:30–49)

(4) the work of each dispensation is to save all those who lived during the dispensation by preaching the gospel and delivering to mankind the saving ordinances of the fulness of the gospel. (In a moment, I will add one additional feature to this list, a feature that applies only to the last two dispensations of the earth.)

Each dispensation attempts to spread the light of the gospel to the inhabitants of the earth. In all but the final dispensation, these efforts ultimately fail, and the world returns to darkness and apostasy. There are people in each dispensation who failed to receive the gospel and its saving ordinances in that dispensation. (In the case of the dispensation led by Moses, almost no one received the saving ordinances, as the authority of the greater or Melchizedek Priesthood was removed from Israel for a time. It should be noted, however, that the Melchizedek Priesthood was had among the descendents of Lehi and Nephi during part of this period.[16]) All of those persons will be left with no way to abide the Lord's presence at his coming,[17] nor will they be sealed together in family units in the eternities, unless the saving ordinance work is performed for them by proxy.

This is a fifth facet of the work of dispensations that applies only to the messianic dispensation and the dispensation of the fulness of times. Before the Atonement of Christ, the dead who had not received these saving ordinances while living remained locked in "prison."[18] After the Lord's death, he organized the preaching of the gospel to these spirits in prison,[19] and the way was opened for them to receive the gospel in the hereafter. After the Lord's death and resurrection, the saints began the practice of vicarious work for the dead.[20] This work stopped when the authority to perform it was taken from the earth as the people fell away from the truth. With the final restoration in the latter days, this work has been restored to the earth. The final gospel dispensation of the world's history is called the "dispensation of the fulness of times" largely because it is the dispensation during which the work for the dead must be performed for all dispensations. Joseph Smith taught:

> Now the thing to be known is, what the fulness of times
> means, or the extent and authority thereof. It means this, that
> the dispensation of the fulness of times is made up of all the

dispensations that ever have been given since the world began, until this time.[21]

The earth will be smitten with a curse unless there is a welding link of some kind or other between the fathers and the children, upon some subject or other—and behold what is that subject? It is the baptism for the dead. For we without them cannot be made perfect; neither can they without us be made perfect. Neither can they nor we be made perfect without those who have died in the gospel also; for it is necessary in the ushering in of the dispensation of the fulness of times, which dispensation is now beginning to usher in, that a whole and complete and perfect union, and welding together of dispensations, and keys, and powers, and glories should take place, and be revealed from the days of Adam even to the present time.[22]

In light of all of this, consider the Prophet Joseph Smith, and how he alone claims that the events required to usher in the prophesied final dispensation of the fulness of times have occurred:

- Who else has declared that there was a falling away after Christ, as was prophesied would be the case?
- Who else has declared that a new dispensation was started, as required by scripture and implied by the entire historical record?
- Who else has declared that the Savior appeared to him, as is apparently required for a new dispensation to open?
- Who else has declared that Elijah has returned, as required by scripture and as also required as part of a restoration of keys that must occur at the start of a new dispensation?
- Who else has declared to have received the priesthood keys necessary to preside over the ordinances of the fulness of the gospel?
- Who else has instituted a gospel with all of the ordinances practiced anciently?
- Who else declares the restitution of all things, as required by scripture?

- Who else is engaged in saving all the people of all the dispensations of the earth, which is the singular mission of the dispensation that was promised in the last days—the dispensation of the fulness of times?

This last dispensation, with Joseph Smith as its head steward, is not something new, but the culmination of all that has gone before. All of the patterns of past dispensations have been repeated anew in this one. The falling away that preceded this last dispensation, while longer than those preceding it (perhaps because of the political, economic, and technological advances that had to happen before the work of the last dispensation could go forth), was nevertheless just another apostasy in a history of apostasies. The Restoration likewise was simply a final restoration after many previous restorations.

The language of the earth's spiritual history, as the language of the scriptures, is the language of parallelism and repetition, and the repetitions of history bear witness of the truth of the repetition known as the latter-day Restoration.

PART FOUR

CHRIST AND
THE WRITINGS

〜⌒〜

CHAPTER 20

JOB, DAVID, AND THE SUFFERING
OF THE LORD

I Looked for Some to Take Pity, but There Was None

> On account of our sins and in order to bring to pass the resur-
> rection, the Savior suffered in both body and spirit. Two stories in
> the scriptures—one heartbreaking, the other body-breaking—give us
> a glimpse into what that suffering might have been like.
> The glimpse may surprise you.

According to the book of Job, there came a day when Satan presented himself before the Lord and challenged the piety of one—Job—whom the Lord had touted as "perfect" and "upright," and unlike anyone in the earth.[1] "Hast not thou made an hedge about him," Satan complained, "and about his house, and about all that he hath on every side? . . . Put forth thine hand now," he continued, "and touch all that he hath, and [Job] will curse thee to thy face."[2]

At this, the Lord gave Satan leave to destroy all that Job had. "Only upon himself put not forth thine hand," he said.[3] With this permission, save the one limitation only, Satan landed in fury upon Job's house. In the span of seven verses, Job lost his oxen, his asses, his sheep, his camels, his servants, his sons, and his daughters.[4]

"Then Job arose," we are told, "and rent his mantle, and shaved his head, and fell down upon the ground, and worshipped. And said, Naked came I out of my mother's womb, and naked shall I return thither: the Lord gave, and the Lord hath taken away; blessed be the name of the Lord."[5] "In all this," the author tells us, "Job sinned not."[6]

Satan came and complained again to the Lord that the only reason Job had been able to refrain from sin was because the Lord had prohibited Satan from harming Job physically. "Put forth thine hand now, and touch his bone and his flesh, and he will curse thee to thy face."[7]

The Lord then gave Satan leave to devastate Job's body, with the only limitation being that he couldn't take his life.[8] Immediately thereafter, Satan "smote Job with sore boils from the sole of his foot unto his crown."[9] So devastating was the affliction that his friends, when they looked on him, "knew him not."[10] They "lifted up their voice, and wept; and they rent every one his mantle, and sprinkled dust upon their heads toward heaven."[11] For seven days and seven nights they sat in silence with Job, "for they saw that [Job's] grief was very great."[12]

Like many of the figures we have encountered in the Old Testament, Job is in similitude of the Savior. Consider:

- He was perfect and upright (Job 1:8).
- There was none like him in all the earth (Job 1:8).
- Satan desired to destroy him (Job 1:9–19; 2:4–7).
- He suffered immeasurably for no wrong or fault of his own (Job 1:12–2:8).
- He was mocked and scorned by his "friends" (see, for example, Job 16:20; 17:2).
- He remained absolutely steadfast (see, for example, Job 13:15).
- He endured all the sufferings without murmuring (see, for example, Job 1:21–22; 2:10).
- As a result of his faithfulness, sinners can be accepted before the Lord through him and do not have to suffer for their own sins (Job 42:7–10).
- He gained everything after he endured the sufferings (Job 42:10–13).

When seen as an archetype of the Savior, the story of Job takes on tremendous significance. For example, the parallelism suggests that if Satan was allowed to wreak havoc on the physical life of the upright man Job, he certainly would have wanted to do the same to the Savior, thereby hoping, as he hoped with Job, to lead the Savior to sin. The story of Job, parallel as it is to the Savior, suggests that Satan was allowed to wreak havoc in Jesus' life—on his belongings, for example, and most especially on his body. That possibility illuminates the following scriptures:

> And he shall go forth, *suffering pains and afflictions* and temptations *of every kind;* and this that the word might be fulfilled which saith *he will take upon him the pains and the sicknesses of his people.* . . . *And he will take upon him their infirmities,* that his bowels may be filled with mercy, according to the flesh, that he may know according to the flesh how to succor his people according to their infirmities.[13]

> For behold, *he suffereth the pains . . . of every living creature,* both men, women, and children, who belong to the family of Adam. And he suffereth this that the resurrection might pass upon all men, that all might stand before him at the great and judgment day.[14]

When we think of Christ's suffering for us, most often we think of his suffering for our *sins*—suffering so horrific that it caused him, "even God, the greatest of all, to tremble because of pain, and to bleed at every pore."[15] But the Job parallelism and the scriptures cited above suggest a second kind of suffering as well—or rather, a *prior* kind of suffering. This prior suffering was not necessarily focused in the narrow band of time between Gethsemane and Calvary, when the weight of the world's sins was upon the Lord. Rather, it was pain that he suffered, in the words of Alma, as he went forth—ongoing, day-to-day, long-term affliction and pain.[16]

Perhaps he could relate well to the blind man about whom his disciples asked, "Master, who did sin, this man, or his parents, that he was born blind?"[17] for Isaiah described that the Savior's physical afflictions would cause many to accuse him similarly:

> *His visage was so marred more than any man, and his form more than the sons of men.* . . . He hath no form nor comeliness; and when we shall see him, there is no beauty that we should desire him. He is despised and rejected of men; a man of

sorrows, and acquainted with grief: and we hid as it were our faces from him; he was despised, and we esteemed him not. Surely he hath borne our griefs, and carried our sorrows: *yet we did esteem him stricken, smitten of God, and afflicted.*[18]

Like Job, whose friends esteemed him stricken of God after viewing his marred body, the Savior—whose visage, according to Isaiah, was marred more than any man—knew rejection, sorrow, and grief on account of his afflictions. Jesus alluded to his own physical trials, and to the rejection he would receive because of them, when he said to those in Nazareth, after fame from his miracles had begun to spread, "Ye will surely say unto me this proverb, *Physician, heal thyself.*"[19]

If Jesus suffered physical "pains and afflictions" of every kind over the course of his life, as the Job story and the scriptures we have considered suggest, one must ask, Why would the Father have allowed it to be so? The scriptures suggest at least three reasons.

Alma reveals that such physical pain and suffering was necessary so that the Savior would "know according to the flesh how to succor his people according to their infirmities."[20] Having taken upon himself the pains of every living creature, he knew well, for example, the pain and suffering that led the Prophet Joseph to cry, "O God, where art thou? And where is the pavilion that covereth thy hiding place?"[21] Because he knew Joseph's pain, he was able to succor Joseph through it and bring peace to his soul.[22] Interestingly, the Lord reminded Joseph of Job on this occasion: "Thou art not yet as Job,"[23] he said, and later added: "The Son of Man hath descended below them all. Art thou greater than he?"[24] If the Son of Man has descended below them all, then he descended below Job as well. The suffering that Joseph was experiencing, as the pains of Job, were familiar to the Lord, for he too had suffered them. And because he had, he could succor Joseph and Job through them.

Jacob suggests another critical reason why the Lord had to suffer in the flesh for our bodily pains and afflictions: "He suffereth the pains of all men . . . that the resurrection might pass upon all men."[25] Jacob here suggests that in order for mortality to be overcome through the resurrection, all of the infirmities of mortality had to be heaped upon the body of Him who would be resurrected. That is, Christ's Resurrection would enable the resurrection of "all men" only if all of mankind's infirmities were present in the body that was then lifted to immortality. If the One who overcame his own mortality did not, in so doing, overcome the mortality of each of us, mortality would still hold us captive. Jacob explained further, "Save it should be an infinite atonement this corruption could not put on incorruption. . . . And if so, this flesh must have laid down to rot and to crumble to its mother earth, to rise no more."[26]

In this respect, the two grand parts of the Atonement—the overcoming of physical death through the Resurrection, and the overcoming of spiritual death through Christ's taking upon himself the sins of mankind—may be parallel in a way we don't normally consider. As discussed in chapter 2 herein, the miracle of the new heart that is made possible by Christ's suffering for our sins is accessible only because Christ, in proxy for us, took upon himself the sinfulness of each and every one of us, so that each of us could be freed from the chains of sinfulness that hold us bound. Jacob's comment in 2 Nephi 9:21 seems to imply that the miracle of the resurrection required on the physical side just what was required for sins on the spiritual side—a proxy who would take upon himself the mortal pains and infirmities of all men, so that through his resurrection, all of us would be freed from the infirmities that otherwise would cause our bodies to "rot and to crumble to [their] mother earth, to rise no more."

Finally, Job suggests a third reason for Jesus' physical suffering: As part of the infinite Atonement, if the Savior was to save us from the adversary, there could be no hedge about him to protect *him* from the adversary. Satan knew who the Savior was. He knew well that if he could cause the Savior to sin, the great plan of happiness would be destroyed.[27] And he knew that long, drawn-out physical pain can drag men down into depression and darkness. Since the Savior had to descend below all, including Job, the story of Job suggests that the fury of hell was constantly beating upon the Savior to do just that—to depress his spirit so that Satan could then more easily provoke him to sin. He may have never known a step without pain. The offering of his body may well have been an offering he made every step of his life—an offering that caused him to be "marred more than any man."[28]

The second (and perhaps parallel) offering he made for us—the offering of his blood—was made "for the remission of sins."[29] This was the unfathomable suffering of Gethsemane and Calvary—the anguish and despair of spirit on account of the sins of mankind that caused the Lord to bleed from every pore.[30] Although there is no way to comprehend the weight of the aggregated sins that pressed upon the Lord's spirit in this hour, the Old Testament provides us with a most poignant example of the anguish suffered by *one* person because of his sins: David.

As discussed in chapter 14, David was a magnificent human being. Loving toward both Saul and Jonathan, David persevered in righteousness through tremendous trial and suffering to become the greatest earthly king Israel has ever known. In these respects, David's life largely paralleled the Savior's:

- He was born in Bethlehem (1 Samuel 16:1).
- He was the anointed one (1 Samuel 16:13).
- His outward appearance was not necessarily what one would expect it to be (1 Samuel 16:6–7).
- Some of the Israelite people loved and followed him, but he was despised as a threat by the Israelite leaders (1 Samuel 20:30–31).
- The Israelite leaders desired to kill him (see, for example, 1 Samuel 18:11, 21–29; 19:10–11; 20:31; 23:8).
- He was a man after God's own heart (1 Samuel 13:14).
- He spent his time feeding his father's sheep (1 Samuel 17:15).
- He endured tremendous trials, suffering, and persecution.
- He never raised his hand against the Israelites who were trying to kill him (1 Samuel 24:2–15; 26:2–20).
- He would not allow those with him to exact revenge against those who would have him killed (1 Samuel 24:2–15; 26:2–20).
- He loved saint and sinner alike (2 Samuel 1:2–27).
- He was the king of Israel.
- He united Israel.
- He was promised the throne forever (2 Samuel 7:13, 16).
- He suffered incredible anguish for sins (see Psalms).

But David fell. He committed adultery and then tried to cover his sin with murder.[31] Perhaps no one in all of history has fallen so far. In anguished remorse for his sins, as recorded in Psalms, David becomes parallel to the Savior in one final way: He is an archetype of the Savior in his suffering for sin.

The Savior, of course, suffered for the sins of others, while David suffered for his *own* sins. In that respect they couldn't be more different. However, the Savior's suffering for others' sins consisted in his suffering for sins in precisely the same way that David suffered for his own, only many times over—for David, and for each of us as well. In this respect, David's suffering for sin—which, given the depth of his fall, probably was as great as any anguish felt by mortal man—gives us a glimpse of a miniscule fraction of the Savior's suffering.

So when David says, "Save me, O God; for the waters are come in unto my soul,"[32] we learn a little of the Savior, who desired that he "might not drink the bitter cup, and shrink."[33] David's lament, "Reproach hath broken my heart; and I am full of heaviness: and I looked for some to take pity, but there was none; and for comforters, but I found none,"[34] foreshadowed what the Lord would later experience as well: "And he took with him Peter and the two sons of Zebedee, and began to be sorrowful and very heavy. Then saith he unto them, My soul is exceeding sorrowful, even unto death: tarry ye here, and watch with me. And he went a little further, and fell on his face, and prayed. . . . And he cometh unto the disciples, and findeth them asleep, and saith unto Peter, What, could ye not watch with me one hour?"[35]

Elsewhere, David cried heavenward, as the Savior would echo centuries later, "My God, my God, why hast thou forsaken me? why art thou so far from helping me, and from the words of my roaring?"[36] "I am weary of my crying: my throat is dried,"[37] David grieved, his "strength . . . dried up like a potsherd; and [his] tongue cleav[ing] to [his] jaws,"[38] in similitude of the Savior, who in great pain uttered simply, "I thirst."[39] Throughout the Psalms, the Savior's infinite suffering is revealed through a single man whose suffering for his own sins nearly crushed him:

- He who ate of his bread, in whom he trusted, lifted his heel against him (Psalm 41:9).
- He looked for some to take pity, but there was none (Psalm 69:20).
- He opened not his mouth (Psalm 38:13).
- They pierced his hands and feet (Psalm 22:16).
- His throat was dry (Psalm 69:3).
- They gave him gall to eat and vinegar to drink (Psalm 69:21).
- Others mocked him, saying that the Lord in whom he trusted should deliver him (Psalm 22:7–8).
- They parted his garments among them (Psalm 22:18).
- He said, "My God, my God, why hast thou forsaken me?" (Psalm 22:1).
- He said, "Into thine hand I commit my spirit" (Psalm 31:5).

So we see that two figures in the Old Testament are archetypes that teach us about the extent and depth of the Savior's suffering on our behalf. Through Job, we learn of the Savior's bodily offering—the pain, affliction, and the physical torment that likely accompanied his every mortal step in ransom for our own immortality. And through the tragic story of David, and his struggles to repent of grievous sins, we learn of the suffering of our Lord in payment for our sins—a suffering that was infinitely greater than David's.

◡

CHAPTER 21

THE WISDOM OF THE SCRIPTURES

Whoso Findeth Me Findeth Life

> On the surface, Proverbs is an odd book, as it seems almost to deify the virtue of "wisdom." But what if that deification is itself a clue? What if, when Proverbs is talking about "wisdom," it really isn't talking about wisdom at all, but something (or rather, someone) else? Then Proverbs reveals itself in a most stunning and inspiring way, and resurrects hope in those of us who know we're not that wise.
>
> For those who might think they're wise, it's a different, and perhaps painful, story—a story that includes the most poignant depiction and description of temptation in all of scripture, and practical advice for avoiding the clutches of sin.

In the first several verses of Proverbs, Solomon identifies four purposes for the book:

- "To know wisdom and instruction;
     to perceive the words of understanding."[1]
- "To receive the instruction of wisdom,
     justice, and judgment, and equity."[2]
- "To give subtilty to the simple,
     to the young man knowledge and discretion.
     A wise man will hear, and will increase learning;
     and a man of understanding shall attain unto wise counsels."[3]
- "To understand a proverb, and the interpretation;
     the words of the wise, and their dark sayings."[4]

Like most of Proverbs, these statements of purpose are written in poetic verse. In each stanza, the idea expressed in the indented second line is parallel with the idea expressed in the line before it. Although the second line adds dimension to the first, the two lines together can be regarded as one entire idea. I have included the statement "a wise man will hear . . ." with the stanza before it because together the four lines express the single idea of an increase in wisdom.

According to Solomon, then, Proverbs is primarily a book about wisdom: The book is to help us (1) *know* wisdom, (2) *receive* wisdom, and (3) *increase in* wisdom. The final and fourth purpose Solomon gives for Proverbs is that it is intended to help us "understand a proverb, and the interpretation." This is an interesting statement. If the book's purpose is to help us "understand a proverb, and the interpretation," then the book of Proverbs must be more than a collection of proverbs with transparent meaning. The implication is that the proverbs have hidden depth, and that something about the book reveals how we are to read the proverbs so that they will be understood.

In this regard, what are we to make of the second line in the fourth stanza: "the words of the wise, and their dark sayings"? What are "dark sayings"? Although the English translation makes the term sound sinister, the Hebrew word translated as "dark sayings"—*chiydah*—means "riddles." *Dark* in this context therefore means "hidden" or "unknown." The implication of this line for the line before it is that proverbs are in a sense riddles. In other words, they contain hidden meaning, and one's interpretation of a proverb is correct only when it uncovers that meaning. If this is correct, then something about Proverbs must reveal the key to the riddle of the proverbs.

In other words, there may be more to understanding Proverbs than meets the eye. Perhaps, as Solomon suggests, Proverbs itself hints at a reading that reveals "hidden" meaning in the proverbs. And perhaps we "understand a proverb, and the interpretation" only when that hidden meaning comes to light.

"Wisdom"

Solomon makes the following bold claim about wisdom: "Wisdom is the principal thing; therefore get wisdom: and with all thy getting get understanding."[5]

Is wisdom truly the *principal* thing? Is nothing more important? At first such a statement seems mistaken. What about charity, for example, which is "the greatest of all"?[6] Or humility? Or purity? Or faith? Certainly Solomon's life is a testimony that wisdom is not the principal thing, since he sinned greatly[7] despite being blessed with "a wise and an understanding heart; so that there was none like [him] before . . . neither after."[8]

Add to this Solomon's very different expressions about wisdom in Ecclesiastes:

> I communed with mine own heart, saying, Lo, I am come to great estate, and have gotten more wisdom than all they that have been before me in Jerusalem: yea, my heart had great experience of wisdom and knowledge. And I gave my heart to know wisdom, and to know madness and folly: I perceived that this also is vexation of spirit. For in much wisdom is much grief: and he that increaseth knowledge increaseth sorrow.[9]

> And I turned myself to behold wisdom, and madness, and folly. . . . Then I saw that wisdom excelleth folly, as far as light excelleth darkness. The wise man's eyes are in his head; but the fool walketh in darkness: and I myself perceived also that one event happeneth to them all. Then said I in my heart, As it happeneth to the fool, so it happeneth even to me; and why was I then more wise? Then I said in my heart, that this also is vanity. For there is no remembrance of the wise more than of the fool for ever; seeing that which now is in the days to come shall all be forgotten. And how dieth the wise man? as the fool. Therefore I hated life; because the work that is wrought under the sun is grievous unto me: for all is vanity and vexation of spirit.[10]

In these statements, Solomon seems to be despairing of wisdom. Perhaps the wisdom he is talking about in these verses is not so "principal" after all.

Nevertheless, Proverbs is consistent in its view that wisdom is primary. "All the things that may be desired are not to be compared to [wisdom]," wrote Solomon.[11] Consider the following descriptions of wisdom's power:

- "Whoso hearkeneth unto [wisdom] shall dwell safely, and shall be quiet from fear of evil."[12]
- "Length of days is in [wisdom's] right hand; and in her left hand riches and honour."[13]
- "[Wisdom] is a tree of life to them that lay hold upon her."[14]
- "[Wisdom] shall give to thine head an ornament of grace: a crown of glory shall she deliver to thee."[15]
- "Riches and honor are with [wisdom]; yea, durable riches and righteousness."[16]
- "Whoso findeth [wisdom] findeth life."[17]
- "For by [wisdom] thy days shall be multiplied, and the years of thy life shall be increased."[18]

This list is intriguing. What does it mean, for example, that wisdom is a "tree of life"? Or that wisdom has the power to multiply the days of one's life—holding life itself, as it were, in its right hand? Or what about the description of wisdom as dispensing grace and glory? Or wisdom as the key to durable riches and righteousness? Each of these descriptions describes wisdom in much more powerful terms than one normally would use. This must mean either that as a culture we misunderstand the importance and power of wisdom, or that what is meant by "wisdom" in these passages is different from what we normally mean.

What, then, are we to make of wisdom in Proverbs? And how can we reconcile the Proverbs position that wisdom is primary with the Ecclesiastes position that wisdom is "vanity and vexation of spirit."[19] Can wisdom do all that Proverbs suggests it can do? In order to answer these questions, we must get beneath the meaning of wisdom in Proverbs.

BENEATH THE MEANING OF "WISDOM" IN PROVERBS

A curious feature of Proverb's treatment of wisdom is that through the first nine chapters, wisdom is often personified. This happens first in chapter 1:

"Wisdom crieth without;
> she uttereth her voice in the streets:
She crieth in the chief place of concourse,
> in the openings of the gates: in the city she uttereth her words."[20]

Through the voice of personified Wisdom, we begin to gain an understanding into what is meant in Proverbs by "wisdom." Consider the following characteristics of the person Proverbs calls "Wisdom":

- The source of happiness.[21]
- Holds the power of life.[22]
- All paths are peace.[23]
- A tree of life.[24]
- The power by which the earth and the heavens were established.[25]
- Will pour out the spirit upon us if we obey.[26]
- Those who don't hearken unto Wisdom will be destroyed.[27]
- Slow to hearken to those who have persisted in disobedience.[28]
- Promotes and brings honor to those who embrace.[29]
- Bestows grace and glory.[30]
- Calls and cries to us all.[31]
- Speaks only truth and righteousness.[32]
- A being characterized by "counsel."[33]
- Loves those who love.[34]
- Those who seek shall find.[35]
- Set up from before the world was.[36]
- With God when the heavens and earth were prepared.[37]
- Calls us children.[38]
- Those who keep ways are blessed.[39]
- Those who find Wisdom find life.[40]

- Offers us bread and drink.[41]
- Holds the power to multiply and increase our lives.[42]

As the description of wisdom builds in Proverbs, a picture begins emerging. Who is the source of happiness? Who holds the power of life? Whose paths are peace? Who is a tree of life? Who is the power by which the earth and the heavens were established? Who will pour out the spirit on us if we obey? Who destroys those who fail to hearken? Who is slow to hear the disobedient? Who promotes and brings honor? Who bestows grace and glory? Who calls and cries to all? Who speaks only truth and righteousness? Who is characterized as a being of "counsel"? Who loves those who love? Whom do we find when we seek? Who was set up from before the world was? Who was with God when the heavens and earth were prepared? Who calls us "children"? Whose ways are blessed? Who is life to those who find? Who offers us bread and drink? Who holds the power to multiply and increase our lives?

These descriptions of the personage Wisdom reveal the key for "understand[ing] a proverb, and the interpretation": The descriptions of wisdom in Proverbs are descriptions of Christ. Wisdom is the "principal thing" because Wisdom is Christ.

The Apostle Paul explicitly equates Christ to wisdom in his letter to the Corinthians: "Hath not God made foolish the wisdom of this world? For after that in the wisdom of God the world by wisdom knew not God, it pleased God by the foolishness of preaching to save them that believe. For the Jews require a sign, and the Greeks seek after wisdom: But we preach Christ crucified, unto the Jews a stumblingblock, and unto the Greeks foolishness; But unto them which are called, both Jews and Greeks, *Christ the power of God, and the wisdom of God.*"[43]

As Paul explains, it was the wisdom of God that by wisdom we cannot know God. So how do we know God if not by wisdom? The answer: through Christ, who is revealed as the power and wisdom of God to all who believe, whether Jew or Greek/Gentile. And notice that belief in Christ is not accomplished by wisdom, but by believing "the foolishness of preaching." Only those who believe what is "foolishness," according to the world's wisdom, and who see, as Solomon did in Ecclesiastes, that wisdom of the flesh is "vanity and vexation of spirit,"[44] avoid the haughty damnation of the wise:

> For ye see your calling, brethren, how that not many wise men after the flesh, not many mighty, not many noble, are called: But God hath chosen the foolish things of the world to confound the wise; and God hath chosen the weak things of the world to confound the things which are mighty; And base things of the world, and things which are despised, hath God chosen, yea, and things which are not, to bring to nought things that are: That no flesh should glory in his presence. *But of him are ye in Christ Jesus, who of God is made unto us wisdom,* and righteousness, and sanctification, and redemption: That, according as it is written, *He that glorieth, let him glory in the Lord.*[45]

The wise glory in themselves, and are thus damned. Those who are made "of him" are those who realize that there is nothing to glory in themselves. We are "of him" only if we are made so "in Christ Jesus." Accordingly, there is no wisdom but Christ. All else is vanity and vexation of spirit. So "he that glorieth, let him glory in the Lord."

A REMAINING RIDDLE

But if wisdom is Christ, there remains a perplexing riddle. Why does Solomon personify Wisdom as female instead of male? "*She* crieth at the gates, at the entry of the city," Solomon tells us.[46] "*She* is a tree of life."[47] "*She* shall give to thine head an ornament of grace."[48] "All *her* paths are peace."[49] Why, if wisdom is Christ, would Solomon characterize Wisdom in these ways as female?

Perhaps the answer to this question lies primarily in the attributes of the power Solomon characterizes as opposing Wisdom. Wisdom's opposite in Proverbs is a seductive adulteress or prostitute Solomon identifies as the "foolish woman," or "the woman Folly."[50] The seductive woman Folly is described in numerous passages through the first nine chapters of Proverbs.[51] The following passage from chapter 7 illustrates well her strategies. In verses 1 through 5, Solomon has given his son instruction for avoiding the woman Folly. The primary defense against her is to store up the commands he has given regarding Wisdom. "Write them upon the table of thine heart," he instructs his son, and then commit yourself to Wisdom as if she were family.[52] Then he tells the following story of one who set out after Wisdom, but was sidetracked and destroyed by Folly. (The lines are set poetically, as they may have been in the original text, and comprise verses 6 through 27 of Proverbs, chapter 7.)

> For at the window of my house
>   I looked through my casement,
> And beheld among the simple ones,
>   I discerned among the youths,
>   a young man void of understanding,
> Passing through the street near her [i.e., Wisdom's] corner;
>   and he went the way to her house,
> In the twilight, in the evening,
>   in the black and dark night:
>
> And, behold, there met him a woman
>   with the attire of an harlot, and subtil of heart.
> (She is loud and stubborn;
>   her feet abide not in her house:
> Now is she without, now in the streets,
>   and lieth in wait at every corner.)
> So she caught him, and kissed him,
>   and with an impudent face said unto him,
>
> I have peace offerings with me;
>   this day have I payed my vows.
> Therefore came I forth to meet thee, diligently to seek thy face,
>   and I have found thee.
> I have decked my bed with coverings of tapestry,
>   with carved works, with fine linen of Egypt.
> I have perfumed my bed
>   with myrrh, aloes, and cinnamon.

Come, let us take our fill of love until the morning:
    let us solace ourselves with loves.
For the goodman is not at home,
    he is gone a long journey:
He hath taken a bag of money with him,
    and will come home at the day appointed.

With her much fair speech she caused him to yield,
    with the flattering of her lips she forced him.
He goeth after her straightway,
    as an ox goeth to the slaughter,
    or as a fool to the correction of the stocks;
Till a dart strike through his liver;
    as a bird hasteth to the snare,
    and knoweth not that it is for his life.

Hearken unto me now therefore, O ye children,
    and attend to the words of my mouth.
Let not thine heart decline to her ways,
    go not astray in her paths.
For she hath cast down many wounded:
    yea, many strong men have been slain by her.
Her house is the way to hell,
    going down to the chambers of death.

The woman Folly dresses so as to entice us.[53] She lies in wait everywhere, "at every corner" or place of choice,[54] trying to divert us from meeting with Wisdom. She is ever persistent.[55] Once one begins to feel enticed by her, she drowns out other influences by the volume of her appeals.[56] She dulls the desire for Wisdom by offering pleasures,[57] riches,[58] and the promise of harmlessness[59]—a promise that would have been transparently false had the subject not already "declined"[60] toward her beauty: "With her much fair speech she caused him to yield, with the flattery of her lips she forced him. He goeth after her straightway, as an ox goeth to the slaughter."[61]

Folly's objective is clear: to keep us from the house of Wisdom. Her objective is purely negative. It matters not to her *where* she leads us so long as it is *away* from Wisdom. And so, in Solomon's example, she "came forth" to Wisdom's very doorstep. Through her subtle deceit she captured one who had set out for Wisdom's door. From there, she led him "after her straightway."[62] "Let not thine heart decline to her ways," Solomon warns, "go not *astray* in her paths."[63] Every other house but Wisdom's is a house of Folly. And Folly's house "is the way to hell."[64]

With 700 wives and 300 concubines,[65] Solomon perhaps knew as much as anyone about the influence of different kinds of women. He married foreign women in defiance of the law of the Lord.[66] And when he "was old," these women "turned away his heart after other gods: and his heart was not perfect with the Lord his God."[67] So Solomon knew through personal experience and tragedy the story of enticement that he detailed for his son. He knew what it meant to "decline" to the ways of those he felt enticed by. He knew what it felt like to be led astray as a consequence— going willingly, as an "ox goeth to the slaughter."[68] In constructing Proverbs, he drew upon his own painful experiences.

His metaphor of Folly as the evil adulteress captures as perhaps no other metaphor can the seductive characteristics and strategies of the evil one. Those who decline toward darkness slide away from the light as if led by hormonal influences beyond their control—"holden with the cords of [their] sins."[69] In this respect, nothing captures the damning enticement and consequences of sin quite so well as the image of the seductive adulteress. By casting "Wisdom" as a woman, Solomon was able to preserve the instructive metaphor of Wisdom's opposite—"Folly"—as the evil adulteress. In Solomon's experience, there probably was no more enlightening way to contrast the difference between the influences of the Prince of Peace and the prince of darkness than to contrast the ways of righteous and evil women.

And so, Solomon pleads: "Hear me now therefore, O ye children, and depart not from the words of my mouth. Remove thy way far from [Folly], and come not nigh the door of her house."[70] "Lust not after her beauty in thine heart."[71] "[Her] house inclineth unto death, and her paths unto the dead. None that go unto her return again, neither take they hold of the paths of life."[72]

In contrast, about Wisdom he says: "Exalt her, and she shall promote thee: she shall bring thee to honour, when thou dost embrace her. She shall give to thine head an ornament of grace: a crown of glory shall she deliver to thee. Hear, O my son, and receive my sayings; and the years of thy life shall be many."[73]

Satan stands in opposition to the Savior and his work just as Folly stands in opposition to Wisdom. We can incline either to one or to the other—if toward Christ, we find life; if toward Satan, we suffer death. And so, Wisdom cries to us: "For whoso findeth me findeth life. . . . But he that sinneth against me wrongeth his own soul: all they that hate me love death."[74]

PROVERBS REVISITED

Consider the irony of Proverbs. On its face it appears to be a book glorifying wisdom and the wise. But in its depths, it is a scathing rebuke of wisdom and the wise. On the surface, there is no explicit mention of Christ—as there wouldn't be if it were merely a book about "wisdom." But ponder the book and its descriptions of wisdom, and Christ suddenly appears in every verse—as he would if it were really a book about him who is Wisdom.

Far from a collection of loosely related maxims, Proverbs shouts in unified voice: Everything but the effort to obtain Wisdom—who is Christ—is foolishness. "Vanity of vanities, saith the preacher; all is vanity."[75] All, that is, but Christ. And so, the "conclusion of the whole matter," according to Solomon in Ecclesiastes, is to "fear God, and keep his commandments: for this is the whole duty of man."[76]

Ecclesiastes ends where Proverbs begins: "The fear of the Lord is the beginning of knowledge,"[77] Solomon says. He later adds: "Trust in the Lord with all thine heart; and lean not unto thine own understanding. In all thy ways acknowledge him, and he shall direct thy paths. Be not wise in thine own eyes: fear the Lord, and depart from evil."[78]

So we see that Proverbs communicates through biting irony that the task of life is not to become "wise," as the world thinks of the term, but to become one with him who is Wisdom. There is no wisdom apart from him who is "made unto us wisdom."[79] He alone dispenses life. All else is death. "Wisdom, and righteousness, and sanctification, and redemption"[80] are in him, and him alone.

CHAPTER 22

⌒〜⌒

THE OLD TESTAMENT'S UNIFIED TESTIMONY

All Things Are the Typifying of Him, and Testify of His Work and Glory

> The Old Testament is a marvel. In its individual parts, it teaches like no other book. And then, in its whole, it delivers a message so integrated, so powerful, and so prophetic, it would bring the entire world to its knees if the world just knew what it said. For those who read beneath the surface, "every knee shall bow and every tongue confess" that Jesus is the Christ—the Messiah long promised who will come yet again.
>
> The *reason* every knee would bow and every tongue confess is that when we put the book's stories together, this is what we find. . . .

We have discovered throughout this study that many of the central and lesser characters in the Old Testament are in similitude of Christ. (For a listing of these characters, and the elements of their lives that are a type and shadow of the Lord, see Appendix A.) Although these individuals prefigure the life of Christ, no one life can capture his, of course. Put the lives of these figures together, however, and the Old Testament reveals Jesus' life in majestic detail. Drawing upon the ideas we have discussed and on the parallelisms listed in Appendix A (elements of which I recount below, along with the identities of the corresponding Old Testament figures from which these elements are drawn), we discover the Savior's story beneath the stories of the Old Testament:

He was set up from before the foundation of the world (Wisdom). He was the Firstborn (Adam, Samuel, the house of Israel)—the beloved, chosen son (Seth, Joseph, the house of Israel). He was near unto God (Isaiah), and none were greater (Melchizedek). He was preferred above all because an excellent spirit was in him (Daniel), speaking only truth and righteousness (Wisdom).

He was like unto his father in all things (Seth). Even in appearance he was the express likeness of his father (Seth). He was the anointed one (David)—known, sanctified, and ordained from before his birth (Jeremiah). In his calling he was set up to be at the head of mankind (Adam). He is known as the "prince of peace," the "king of heaven," and the "king of peace" (Melchizedek). The holy priesthood was named after him (Melchizedek).

God asked, "Whom shall I send, and who will go for us?" (Isaiah). In response, he said, "Here am I, send me" (Isaiah). He was prepared as the means of deliverance from certain death (brazen serpent), and chose to leave the presence of God to fulfill the plan of salvation (Adam). He was the power by which the earth and the heavens were established (Wisdom), and came to earth to preach repentance (Isaiah) and to deliver the house of Israel from bondage (Moses, Gideon). His birth and mission as a deliverer of Israel was prophesied (Moses), his birth—to a virgin (Maher-shalal-hash-baz)—foretold by an angel (Isaac). His name also was foretold (Isaac, Maher-shalal-hash-baz).

There was a long wait before his birth (Isaac). An angel appeared to his mother, telling her that she would bring forth a son (Samson). She then conceived miraculously (Isaac, Samson, Samuel), and upon the boy's birth sang a song of praise and thanksgiving (Samuel). He was born in Bethlehem (David) to a poor, nondescript family in humble and plain circumstances (Gideon, the house of Israel). He was the "only begotten son" (Isaac), a child of no blemish (Daniel).

He came to Israel in the day of Israel's captivity (Eliakim), when Israel had become corrupted by heathen neighbors (Samson). His birth was a sign that the land of Israel was soon to be forsaken, and that the Israelites would soon be carried off from their land (Maher-shalal-hash-baz). The king at the time of his birth commanded that the children of his age be put to death (Moses). His parents saved him from death by sending him into Egypt (Moses), where he found refuge (the house of Israel).

He was sanctified to God for life (Samuel), and communed with God from an early age (Samuel). He remained at the temple at an early age (Samuel), and grew in favor with God and man (Samuel). He was greater in wisdom than all the wise at a young age (Daniel).

He began his ministry of preparing salvation for Israel when he was thirty years old (Joseph). He was baptized (the house of Israel), and then spent forty days fasting and communing with God (Moses, Elijah). Satan desired to destroy him (Job), but he resisted temptation perfectly (Joseph) and rebuked Satan (Moses). He then sought out his brethren on behalf of his father (Joseph), and spent his time feeding his father's sheep (David). God revealed himself to him, and through him to Israel (Samuel). He was the mouthpiece of God to his people (Samuel).

His outward appearance was not necessarily what one would have expected it to be (David, servant from Isaiah), perhaps even marred more than any man (servant). But he was a man after God's own heart (David)—in similitude of, and one with, his father (Isaac)—just, perfect, and upright (Seth, Noah, Job). There was none like him in all the earth (Job).

He loved saint and sinner alike (David), and exhorted Israel to repentance (Samuel). He declared that he would be the ruler over the children of Israel (Joseph), and preached tirelessly to the people (Noah). He performed many miracles (Moses), and had power over the waters (Moses). The elements obeyed his every word (Elijah). He multiplied a meager ration of food to feed the faithful (Elijah). He raised a child from the dead (Elijah). He observed that the temple had become "a den of robbers" (Jeremiah), and prophesied regarding its destruction (Jeremiah).

Some of the Israelite people loved and followed him (David), and he established righteousness among them (Melchizedek). He passed his authority to those who followed him (Elijah), and with a small band of men he defeated the enemy (Gideon). However, the priests at the time had grown corrupt (Samuel), and he was largely rejected by the people (Noah). Many ignored him because he was not a political or military leader (Samuel). Others saw him as taking authority over them and rejected and hated him (Joseph). Many of the Israelite leaders despised him as a threat (David) and sought to kill him (Noah, David).

He was mocked and scorned by his "friends" (Job), and endured tremendous trials, suffering, and persecution (Job, David). He was grieved by the sins of the people (Noah).

He traveled to Jerusalem on a donkey (Isaac), and the children of Israel conspired to kill him (Joseph). Judas betrayed him (Joseph); he who ate of his bread, in whom he trusted, lifted his heel against him (the Psalmist). He was sold for the price of a slave of his age, in pieces of silver (Joseph). This attempt to destroy him set in motion events that saved man from death (Joseph).

Those with him were asked to wait while he went yonder to worship/pray (Isaac). He looked for some to take pity, but there was none (the Psalmist). He preferred not to have to do what he was to do, but submitted to the will of God (Moses), voluntarily submitting to the will of his father (Isaac). He atoned for the wrongs of others (Abigail), taking the sinners' iniquity on his own head, even though he had done no wrong (Abigail). He suffered immeasurably for no wrong or fault of his own (Job), suffering immensely for sin (Jonah, the house of Israel). He descended to the depths (Jonah), and in so doing interceded with God for Israel (Samuel). He remained absolutely steadfast (Job) and endured all the sufferings without murmuring (Job).

He never raised his hand against the Israelites who were trying to kill him (David), and would not allow those with him to exact revenge against those who would have him killed (David).

He was taken captive (Joseph, Jeremiah, the house of Israel), smitten, and held in scorn and derision (the house of Israel). Those jealous of his power sought occasion under the law against him, but could find none (Daniel). And so these leaders sought occasion to entrap him (Daniel). But he continued in righteousness notwithstanding the threat (Daniel).

He was condemned to death (Daniel), but opened not his mouth (the Psalmist). No error or fault was found in him, so the ruler sought to have him released (Daniel). But the people would not allow it (Daniel). The religious leaders asserted to the political leaders and to the people that he was "worthy to die" (Jeremiah). The presiding political authority washed his hands of the decision regarding him, committing him to the hands of the people (Jeremiah).

And so he was hated and expelled by his people (Jephthah). He was like "a lamb that is brought to the slaughter" (Jeremiah).

He was to be sacrificed on a hill in the area of Moriah (Isaac), and carried the wood to be instrumental in his death (Isaac). They pierced his hands and feet (the Psalmist), and raised him up on a pole (the brazen serpent). His throat was dry (the Psalmist), and they gave him gall to eat and vinegar to drink (the Psalmist). They parted his garments among them (the Psalmist). Observers mocked him, saying that the Lord in whom he trusted should deliver him (the Psalmist). But they missed the point that he allowed himself to be cast to certain death in order to save others, taking death upon himself so that all might live (Adam, Jonah). He nevertheless forgave those who had caused him to suffer (Joseph), and did all that the Lord commanded him (Noah).

In this moment, he felt forsaken by the Lord (Jonah). He said, "My God, my God, why hast thou forsaken me?" (the Psalmist). But in this moment of utter aloneness, he nevertheless looked to God (Jonah), saying, "Into thine hand I commit my spirit" (the Psalmist).

The den of death was sealed with a stone (Daniel), and he was swallowed up for three days (Jonah). Rising early in the morning, the believers came to the place to see him (Daniel). They assumed him to be dead (Daniel), but he had been raised up and restored (the house of Israel)—delivered from death because "before [God] innocency was found in [him]" (Daniel). He had come forth alive after those three days (Jonah), in perfect condition (Daniel).

He ascended miraculously into heaven in the sight of those who had followed him (Elijah). All of his words were fulfilled (Samuel). His message, however, was largely rejected (Isaiah), and the temple was soon lost from them (Samuel) and the nation scattered (Isaiah). Nevertheless, as a result of his miraculous deliverance, the gospel of the Lord's deliverance is being published throughout all the nations of the earth (Daniel).

And this is that gospel:

He is the great high priest (Melchizedek), possessor of the law through whom salvation comes to the world (the house of Israel), the mediator of the covenant between God and man (Moses), and the bestower of grace and glory (Wisdom).

Being delivered from death, he constructed the means of saving all mankind (Noah), and therefore reigns as our father forever (Adam). He holds the power of life (Wisdom), and offers us life through the offering of his bread and water (Joseph, Wisdom). He offers that bread and water without price (Joseph), and in its offering, he offers the opportunity to repent (Joseph). Through him, sinners are accepted before God and do not have to suffer for their own sins (Job). He pours out his spirit upon those who obey (Wisdom). He brings peace to those who follow him (Gideon, Abigail), and when they follow, he becomes their deliverer (Jephthah)— subduing the enemy on behalf of all who make him head and captain over them (Jephthah, Samuel) and saving them from death (Noah). Hence, his message to those who seek him is "live forever" (Daniel). All those who look to him shall live (the brazen serpent).

His return is promised (Elijah). And when he returns, those who fight against him shall die (Daniel). He shall unite Israel (David) and deliver it from bondage (Moses). He shall obtain victory over all his enemies (the house of Israel), and shall be the king of Israel (David) and the father to the inhabitants of the holy city (Eliakim), inheriting the throne promised him forever (David).

The government is placed in his hand (Eliakim). The key to the house of David rests upon his shoulder (Eliakim). He occupies the glorious throne in his father's house (Eliakim), and determines entrance into that house (Eliakim). He is the nail fastened in a sure place (Eliakim) on whom all the glory of his father's house rests, including the offspring and issue (Eliakim). Those who accept the gospel shall become his seed—his sons and daughters (Isaac), whom he will call his children (Wisdom). For only those who are his family are saved (Noah).

CONCLUSION

The Old Testament shouts in unified testimony: Jesus of Nazareth was and is the promised Messiah. The testimony of his life and mission is hidden below the surface of the Old Testament at a level where it would survive the loss of every plain and precious thing.[1] This is why the Lord had to "open" the scriptures to his disciples. What he opened to them were "the things concerning himself."[2]

The history of the Lord's people and of his Church is also revealed by the Old Testament, as it is through the Lord's Church that the fulness of these truths will be delivered to the world. Consider what the testament hidden below the surface of the Old Testament reveals about the history of Israel in both ancient and latter days (references in parentheses are to similitudes discussed in earlier chapters):

A branch of Joseph will be broken off to a place apart from the rest of the house of Israel (Joseph). This branch of Joseph will reside in a distant land, unknown to his family (Joseph)—a land set apart as an inheritance for Joseph (Joseph, Deuteronomy "dew" prophecies). The experiences in the distant land shall prepare the way for the salvation of Israel (Joseph).

Meanwhile, Israel will look for a messiah who will deliver a political/military victory, and will therefore miss the Savior (the ark of the covenant story in 1 Samuel). The gospel will thereafter be lost from Israel (ark), and Israel will then be scattered, as if thrown into the sea (Jonah). They will be smitten and held in scorn and derision (servant). They will experience suffering and cruel death (servant).

The gospel will then be revealed to the Gentiles (ark). A prophet named Joseph will nourish the Gentiles in the Gentile nations (Egypt parallelism and Joseph) in a country that is the most powerful of its era (Egypt). The gospel will then come forth from that country to fill the earth (Egypt).

The gospel will overcome the gods of the Gentiles (ark), and show those gods to be powerless (exodus parallelism). It will afflict the Gentiles unto repentance (ark), and the Gentiles will come to believe in the power of the God of Israel (ark). The gospel will then be returned by the Gentiles back to Israel (ark), who will be in bondage to false gods (Egypt).

Israel will then learn about the branch of Joseph that had been separated (Joseph) by listening to the preaching of foreigners or Gentiles (Jonah). This work of gathering will be led by the house of Joseph (Joseph), which will be blessed with the precious dew from heaven, even the priesthood (Deuteronomy), and be entrusted with the mission of gathering the children of Israel together throughout the ends of the earth

(Deuteronomy). These gatherers will be carrying in their hands two sticks joined into one—the stick of Judah and the stick of Joseph/Ephraim (Ezekiel resurrection vision)—the stick of Joseph being the history of the branch of Israel that had been broken apart (Ezekiel and Joseph). Israel will begin to be saved as they learn about Joseph who had been separated from them (Joseph). Upon reading this united history, Israel will be resurrected from the nations (Ezekiel), and the Lord will preserve the life of scattered Israel (Jonah). They will be lifted up (servant), and then gather to the gospel (ark), repent, put away false gods (exodus, ark), and bow down before Joseph (Joseph), who will be leading the Church in the latter days (Joseph, Deuteronomy).

The church led by Joseph will be endowed with the promises made to the fathers (Malachi's Elijah prophecies)—the ordinances of the holy priesthood "as in days of old" (Malachi), which will be restored by Elijah (Malachi). It will then administer those ordinances to Israel (Malachi), sanctify them through the temple (Malachi and temple metaphors), and prepare the people for the coming of the Lord in his glory (Malachi). The Lord will then come in power in defense of his people, and provide a great military victory (ark, servant). The Lord will then be established as king over Israel forever (ark), and Israel shall receive an inheritance of seed innumerable (servant).

So we see that the scriptures declare the works of God—both his nature and his works among the children of men. Beneath the surface of the Old Testament lies a hidden testament that declares that Jesus is the Christ, and that his Church has been restored in the latter days.

However, we live in a world filled with doubt. Faith has become unfashionable. Many today walk their own roads to Emmaus, and, as with those humble disciples of olden time, their faith is shaken. To us, as to them, the Lord asks, "Why are ye troubled?"[3] For all has been revealed in the scriptures. "All things which have been given of God from the beginning . . . are the typifying of [Christ]."[4] And all his works are known—"the end from the beginning."[5]

To all with ears to hear, the Old Testament proclaims his life, his identity, his divinity, and his gospel. He walked to Moriah as did Isaac. He died for us as did Adam. He is risen as the house of Israel. And his people too are now rising back to a knowledge of the truth. The truths regarding the house of Joseph in the book referred to as "Another Testament of Jesus Christ" have come together with the record of Judah as "one in [our] hand,"[6] and are being delivered to the world, as Old Testament prophets testified would happen.

The story of Christ's life and the history of his gospel speak to us from every verse of scripture. This is the hidden testament of Christ: that he lives, and that he has prepared the way that we might live as well. May we, like the disciples of old, discover his life and gospel more fully, so that we might come more fully to him, and be blessed with life and the "great joy"[7] he promises to those who follow him.

KEY CHRIST SIMILITUDES IN THE OLD TESTAMENT

Adam

1. The Firstborn (Moses 3:7)
2. Created in the Father's image (Gen. 1:27)
3. Chose to leave the presence of God to fulfill the plan of salvation
4. Chose to partake of bitterness in a garden
5. Took upon himself death so that all might live
6. The person through whom the gospel was delivered to all mankind (Moses 5:12)
7. Set up to be at the head of mankind (D&C 107:55)
8. Reigns as our father forever (Abr. 1:3; D&C 107:53–56)

Seth

1. The chosen son (D&C 107:42)
2. A perfect man (D&C 107:43)
3. His likeness was the express likeness of his father (D&C 107:43; Moses 6:10)
4. Was like unto his father in all things (D&C 107:43)

Noah

1. Preached tirelessly to people who largely rejected him (Moses 8:19–21, 23)
2. He was grieved by the sins of the people (Moses 8:25)

3. He was just, and perfect in his generation (Moses 8:27; Gen. 6:9)

4. He was mocked by the people (Moses 8:21)

5. He did all that the Lord commanded him (Gen. 6:22; 7:5)

6. People sought to kill him (Moses 8:18)

7. He constructed the means of saving all mankind (Gen. 6:18)

8. Those who followed him were saved from death (Gen. 6:18)

9. Only those who were his family were saved (Gen. 7:1, 7)

10. His salvation also saved the animals from death (Gen. 7:1–4)

Melchizedek

1. A great high priest (D&C 107:2)

2. None were greater (Alma 13:19)

3. Offered the Lord's Supper (Gen. 14:18–20; JST, Gen. 14:17–20)

4. Established righteousness among his followers (JST, Gen. 14:33–34)

5. Known as the "prince of peace" (JST, Gen. 14:33)

6. Known as the "king of heaven" (JST, Gen. 14:36)

7. Known as the "king of peace" (JST, Gen. 14:36)

8. The holy priesthood was named after him (D&C 107:2–4)

Abraham

1. Known as the father of the faithful (D&C 138:41)

2. All nations of the earth blessed through him (Abr. 2:9)

3. Mediator between God and man (Gen. 18:20–33)

4. Believers are known as his children or seed (Gal. 3:29)

5. Offered by his father as a sacrifice (Abr., Fac. 1)

6. Comforted by an angel in his greatest hour of need (Abr. 1:15)

7. Shares the blessings of his covenant with all who accept the gospel (Gen. 11:31; 17:18; Abr. 2:15)

Isaac

1. Long wait for his birth (Gen. 17:17)

2. His name and birth were foretold by an angel (Gen. 17:16, 19)

3. His mother conceived miraculously and brought forth a son (Gen. 21:2, 6–7)
4. He was called the "only begotten son" (Heb. 11:17)
5. Traveled to Jerusalem with a donkey (Gen. 22:3)
6. Those with him were asked to wait while he went yonder to worship/pray (Gen. 22:5)
7. Was to be sacrificed on a hill in the area of Moriah (Gen. 22:2)
8. Carried the wood to be instrumental in his death (Gen. 22:6)
9. Was one with his father (Gen. 22:6, 8)
10. Was in similitude of his father (Abr. 1:5–16; Gen. 26:1–4, 24)
11. Voluntarily submitted to the will of his father (Gen. 22:8–9)
12. Those who accept the gospel become his seed—his sons and daughters (Abr. 2:10; Gen. 26:1–4, 24)

Jacob

1. His brother lost his birthright
2. His brother hated him and sought to destroy him (Gen. 27:41)
3. Overcame his brother (Gen. 27:37–40)
4. Was promised that his followers would be stronger than those of his brother (Gen. 25:23)
5. The chosen son
6. A plain man (Gen. 25:27)

Joseph

1. The beloved son (Gen. 37:3)
2. Declared that he would be the ruler over the children of Israel (Gen. 37:6–11)
3. The children of Israel saw him as taking authority over them and rejected and hated him (Gen. 37:8, 11)
4. Sought out his brethren on behalf of his father (Gen. 37:12–17)
5. The children of Israel conspired to kill him (Gen. 37:18–20)
6. Judah (in Greek, *Judas*) betrayed him to the Gentiles (Gen. 37:25–28)

7. Sold for the price of a slave of his age, in pieces of silver (Gen. 37:25–28; Lev. 27:5)

8. The attempt to destroy him set in motion events that saved the children of Israel from death

9. Was taken captive and placed under the dominion of an officer of the strongest army of the world

10. Resisted temptation perfectly (Gen. 39:7–12)

11. Was falsely accused (Gen. 39:16–19)

12. Was given the name of Zaphnath-paaneah, which means Savior (Gen. 41:45)

13. Began his ministry of preparing salvation for Israel when thirty years old (Gen. 41:46)

14. Provided bread and water to Israel and saved them from death (Gen. 42:25)

15. Offers that bread without price (Gen. 42:25; 44:1)

16. In offering that bread, he offers the opportunity to repent (Gen. 42:25; 44:1)

17. Forgave those who had caused him to suffer and offered them opportunity to repent (Gen. 45:1–5, 14–15)

18. Was recognized and accepted by his people only the second time they met (Gen. 45)

19. All bowed to him (Gen. 43:26–28)

Moses

1. His birth and mission as a deliverer of Israel was prophesied (JST, Gen. 50:24, 29)

2. The king at the time of his birth commanded that the children of his age be put to death (Ex. 1:15–16, 22)

3. His parents saved him from death by sending him into Egypt (Ex. 2:1–5)

4. Spent forty days fasting and communing with God before bringing the gospel to Israel (Ex. 24:18; 34:28)

5. Was rejected when he first came to Israel (Ex. 2:13–14)

6. He resisted and rebuked Satan (Moses 1:20–21)

7. Performed many miracles

8. Had power over the elements (Moses 1:25; Ex. 14:21–29)
9. Preferred not to have to do what he was to do, but submitted to the will of God (Ex. 3:11; 4:13–18)
10. Fed his followers with bread from heaven (Ex. 16; Deut. 8:3)
11. Brought a "new law" (Ex. 20–24; 31–34)
12. Delivered Israel from bondage (Moses 1:6, 26)
13. Mediator of the covenant between God and man (JST, Gal. 3:19–20)

Ancient Temple

1. The courtyard, signifying presence in the world
2. The altar, signifying sacrifice to do the will of the Father
3. The laver of water, signifying baptism
4. The candlesticks, signifying the light supplied to the world
5. The water and bread, signifying the offering of body and blood
6. The incense before the veil, signifying the pleading cries before the Father on our behalf
7. The veil, signifying the barriers of sin and death that were overcome
8. Entry through the veil, which signifies the way created back to the Father
9. The mercy seat and throne in the Most Holy Place, signifying merciful judgment and rule

Brazen Serpent

1. Was prepared as the means of deliverance from certain death (Num. 21:8)
2. Was raised up on a pole (Num. 21:9)
3. All those who look to him live (Num. 21:8; Alma 33:19)

Gideon

1. Was raised up in poor, nondescript family (Judg. 6:15)
2. God sent him to deliver the Israelites from bondage (Judg. 6:14)

3. With a small band of men, he defeated the enemy (Judg. 7:7, 16–22)

4. He brought peace to those who followed him (Judg. 8:28)

Jephthah

1. He was hated and expelled by his people (Judg. 11:2)

2. The people turned to him when they were in distress (Judg. 11:5–10)

3. When the people turned to him, he became their deliverer (Judg. 11:11)

4. He subdued the enemy on behalf of the people who had made him head and captain over them (Judg. 11:12–33)

Samson

1. Israel had become corrupted by heathen neighbors

2. Angel appeared to his mother, telling her that she would conceive and bring forth a son (Judg. 13:3)

3. Prophesied that he would deliver Israel out of bondage (Judg. 13:5)

4. Mother conceived miraculously and brought forth a son (Judg. 13:24)

5. Had great strength to do miracles

6. Was sent to awaken Israel to their sins

7. Did not bring temporal freedom to Israel, but set in motion spiritual events that would lead to eventual temporal and spiritual freedom

8. By his death, brought down the house of evil

Samuel

1. His mother conceived miraculously and brought forth a son (1 Sam. 1:17–20)

2. The firstborn (1 Sam. 2:5, 20–21)

3. Upon his birth his mother sang a song of praise and thanksgiving (1 Sam. 2:1–10)

4. He was sanctified to God for life (1 Sam. 1:28)

5. Communed with God from an early age
6. Remained at the temple at an early age (1 Sam. 1:24; 2:11)
7. At early age, he grew in favor with God and man (1 Sam. 2:26)
8. The priests at the time had grown corrupt (1 Sam. 2:12, 17; 3:13)
9. Was the mouthpiece of God to his people (1 Sam. 3:21–4:1)
10. God revealed himself to him, and through him to Israel (1 Sam. 3:21–4:1)
11. All of his words were fulfilled (1 Sam. 3:19)
12. Was ignored because he was not a political or military leader (1 Sam. 4:1–11)
13. When people ignored him, the power of the Lord was lost from them (1 Sam. 4:11)
14. Exhorted Israel to repentance (1 Sam. 7:3)
15. Interceded with God for Israel (1 Sam. 7:5, 8)
16. Delivered the people after they turned to him as their leader (1 Sam. 7:4, 8–10, 13)

David

1. Born in Bethlehem (1 Sam. 16:1)
2. The "anointed one" (1 Sam. 16:13)
3. His outward appearance was not necessarily what one would expect it to be (1 Sam. 16:6–7)
4. Loved by many of the Israelite people
5. Despised as a threat by the Israelite leaders (1 Sam. 20:30–31)
6. Israelite leaders desired to kill him (1 Sam. 18:11, 21–29; 19:10–11; 20:31; 23:8)
7. A man after God's own heart (1 Sam. 13:14)
8. Spent his time feeding his father's sheep (1 Sam. 17:15)
9. Endured tremendous trials, suffering, and persecution
10. Never raised his hand against the Israelites who were trying to kill him (1 Sam. 24:2–15; 26:2–20)
11. Would not allow those with him to exact revenge against those who would have him killed (1 Sam. 24:2–15; 26:2–20)
12. Loved saint and sinner alike (2 Sam. 1:2–27)
13. Became the king of Israel

14. United Israel
15. Was promised the throne forever (2 Sam. 7:13, 16)

The Psalmist

1. He who ate of his bread, in whom he trusted, lifted his heel against him (Ps. 41:9)
2. Looked for some to take pity, but there was none (Ps. 69:20)
3. He opened not his mouth (Ps. 38:13)
4. They pierced his hands and feet (Ps. 22:16)
5. Throat was dry (Ps. 69:3)
6. They gave him gall to eat and vinegar to drink (Ps. 69:21)
7. Others mocked him, saying that the Lord in whom he trusted should deliver him (Ps. 22:7–8)
8. They parted his garments among them (Ps. 22:18)
9. He said, "My God, my God, why hast thou forsaken me?" (Ps. 22:1)
10. He said, "Into thine hand I commit my spirit" (Ps. 31:5)

Abigail

1. Atoned for a wrong by another (1 Sam. 25:14–24)
2. Provided all that was needed to him who was harmed (1 Sam. 25:14–24)
3. Took the sinner's iniquity on own head, even though did no wrong (1 Sam. 25:24–25)
4. Pled for the avenger to give up vengeance (1 Sam. 25:28–31)
5. Was the means of delivering peace (1 Sam. 25:32–35)

Elijah

1. The elements obeyed his every word (1 Kgs. 17:1)
2. He multiplied a meager ration of food to feed the faithful (1 Kgs. 17:9–16)
3. Raised a child from the dead (1 Kgs. 17:17–24)
4. Fasted forty days and nights (1 Kgs. 19:8)

5. Passed his authority to one who followed him (1 Kgs. 19:19–21)

6. Ascended miraculously into heaven, in the sight of those who had followed him (2 Kgs. 2:11)

7. His return was promised (Mal. 4:5–6)

Job

1. He was perfect and upright (Job 1:8)

2. None like him in all the earth (Job 1:8)

3. Satan desired to destroy him (Job 1:9–19; 2:4–7)

4. Suffered immeasurably for no wrong or fault of his own (Job 1:12–2:8)

5. Was mocked and scorned by his "friends" (Job 16:20; 17:2)

6. Remained absolutely steadfast (see, e.g., Job 13:15)

7. He endured all the sufferings without murmuring (see, e.g., Job 1:21–22; 2:10)

8. Offered sacrifice for and prayed for those who had rejected him (Job 42:8)

9. Sinners can be accepted before God through him and do not have to suffer for their own sins (Job 42:7–10)

10. He gained everything after he endured the sufferings (Job 42:10–13)

Jonah

1. Allowed himself to be cast to certain death in order to save others (Jonah 1:12)

2. Descended to the depths (Jonah 2:3–6)

3. Suffered immensely for sin (Jonah 2:1–6)

4. Felt forsaken by the Lord (Jonah 2:4)

5. In moment of utter aloneness, nevertheless looked to the Lord (Jonah 2:4, 7)

6. Was swallowed up for three days (Jonah 1:17)

7. Came forth alive after three days (Jonah 2:10)

Isaiah

1. He was near unto God (Isa. 6:1–4)
2. God asked, "Whom shall I send, and who will go for us?" (Isa. 6:8)
3. In response, he said: "Here am I, send me." (Isa. 6:8)
4. He then came and preached repentance to Israel
5. His message was largely rejected, and the nation was soon scattered

Maher-shalal-hash-baz

1. His birth and name were foretold (Isa. 7:14; 8:1–3)
2. Was prophesied that he would be born of a "virgin" (this may have been in reference to a virgin that was soon to be Isaiah's wife) (Isa. 7:14)
3. His mother conceived and brought forth a son (Isa. 8:3)
4. He was named according to the prophecy (Isa. 8:3)
5. His birth was a sign that the land of Israel was soon to be forsaken (Isa. 7:16–25; 8:4)
6. His birth was a sign that the Israelites would soon be carried off from their land (Isa. 8:4–8)

Eliakim

1. The Lord's servant in the day of Israel's captivity (Isa. 22:17–20)
2. The government was placed in his hand (Isa. 22:21)
3. He was father to the inhabitants of the holy city (Isa. 22:21)
4. The key of the house of David rested upon his shoulder (Isa. 22:22)
5. He determined entrance into his father's house (Isa. 22:22)
6. Fastened as a nail in a sure place (Isa. 22:23)
7. He occupied a glorious throne in his father's house (Isa. 22:23)
8. All the glory of his father's house rested on him, including the offspring and issue (Isa. 22:24)

Jeremiah

1. Was known, sanctified, and ordained from before his birth (Jer. 1:5)
2. Observed that the temple had become "a den of robbers" (Jer. 7:11)
3. Prophesied regarding the destruction of the temple (Jer. 7:12, 14)
4. Was taken captive
5. The religious leaders asserted to the political leaders and to the people that he was "worthy to die" (Jer. 26:11)
6. Was like "a lamb . . . that is brought to the slaughter" (Jer. 11:19)
7. The king washed his hands of the decision regarding him, committing him to the hands of the people (Jer. 38:5)

Daniel

1. A child of no blemish (Dan. 1:4)
2. Had wisdom more than all the wise at a young age (Dan. 1:20)
3. Was preferred above all because an excellent spirit was in him (Dan. 6:3)
4. No error or fault was found in him (Dan. 6:4)
5. Those jealous of his power sought occasion under the law against him, but could find none (Dan. 6:4)
6. So these leaders sought occasion to entrap him (Dan. 6:5–9)
7. Continued in righteousness notwithstanding the threat (Dan. 6:10–11)
8. Was condemned to death (Dan. 6:12–13)
9. The ruler sought to have him released (Dan. 6:14)
10. But the people would not allow it (Dan. 6:15)
11. The den of death was sealed with a stone (Dan. 6:17)
12. Rising early in the morning, the believer(s) came to the place to see him (Dan. 6:19)
13. Those who believed in him assumed he was dead (Dan. 6:20)
14. Being delivered from death, his message to those who seek him is "live for ever" (Dan. 6:21)

15. Was delivered from death because "before [God] innocency was found in [him]" (Dan. 6:22)
16. Came forth in perfect condition (Dan. 6:23)
17. Those who fight against him shall die (Dan. 6:24)
18. As a result of his miraculous deliverance, the gospel of the Lord's deliverance was published throughout all the earth (Dan. 6:25–27)

House of Israel

1. God's chosen, his "firstborn" (Ex. 4:22)
2. Raised from humble, plain beginnings
3. Found refuge in Egypt
4. Was baptized (1 Cor. 10:1–2)
5. Possessor of the law through whom salvation comes to the world
6. Smitten and held in scorn and derision
7. Was taken captive
8. Experienced suffering and death
9. Will be raised up and restored
10. Obtains victory over enemies

"Wisdom"

1. Set up from before the world was (Prov. 8:23–26)
2. Was with God when the heavens and earth were prepared (Prov. 8:27–31)
3. The power by which the earth and the heavens were established (Prov. 3:19)
4. Speaks only truth and righteousness (Prov. 8:7–8)
5. A being characterized by "counsel" (Prov. 8:14)
6. Calls and cries to us all (Prov. 8:1)
7. Offers us bread and drink (Prov. 9:5)
8. Will pour out the spirit upon us if we obey (Prov. 1:23)
9. Those who seek shall find (Prov. 8:17)
10. Bestows grace and glory (Prov. 4:9)
11. Calls us children (Prov. 8:32)

12. Holds the power of life (Prov. 3:16)
13. Those who find, find life (Prov. 8:35)
14. Those who keep ways are blessed (Prov. 8:32)
15. Holds the power to multiply and increase our lives (Prov. 9:11)
16. The source of happiness (Prov. 3:13)
17. Is slow to hearken to those who have persisted in disobedience (Prov. 1:28–31)
18. Those who don't hearken will be destroyed (Prov. 1:24–27)

THE LATTER-DAY RESTORATION OF THE LOST TEMPLE ORDINANCES

A Structural Analysis of the Oath and Covenant of the Priesthood

The latter-day restoration of the fulness of the gospel of the temple teaches us what the children of Israel in Moses' day missed when they qualified only for the preparatory priesthood. In this regard, let us consider the 84th section of the Doctrine and Covenants, with its "oath and covenant of the priesthood"—an oath and covenant that has to do with the priesthood that was taken from Israel when they sinned before the Lord.

The full revelation we know as section 84 was received by the Prophet Joseph Smith over a two-day period in the fall of 1832. The occasion was a gathering of priesthood leaders, recently returned from preaching the gospel in the Eastern States. The scriptural passage widely referred to as "the oath and covenant of the priesthood" spans verses 33 through 40 of that section.

In the *History of the Church,* the Prophet prefaced his presentation of this section with these words: "And while together in these seasons of joy, I inquired of the Lord, and received on the 22nd and 23rd of September, the following revelation on Priesthood."[1] By these words, the Prophet signaled that he viewed section 84 to be an integrated whole—a "revelation" (not "revelations") on priesthood. It follows from this that our understanding of the portion of these verses we call "the oath and covenant of the priesthood" will depend, among other things, on our understanding of the passages that precede and follow it.

With this in mind, let us take a bird's-eye look at the structure of section 84, and then discuss what we learn from this view of the revelation. I quote verses 1 through 40 (the subheads and emphasis are my own addition):

A revelation of Jesus Christ unto his servant Joseph Smith, Jun., and six elders, as they united their hearts and lifted their voices on high.

Establishment of Zion and the temple at the New Jerusalem in Jackson County, Missouri (verses 2–5)

Yea, the word of the Lord concerning his church, established in the last days for the restoration of his people, as he has spoken by the mouth of his prophets, and for the gathering of his saints to stand upon Mount Zion, which shall be the city of New Jerusalem. Which city shall be built, beginning at the temple lot, which is appointed by the finger of the Lord, in the western boundaries of the State of Missouri, and dedicated by the hand of Joseph Smith, Jun., and others with whom the Lord was well pleased. Verily this is the word of the Lord, that the city New Jerusalem shall be built by the gathering of the saints, beginning at this place, even the place of the temple, which temple shall be reared in this generation. For verily this generation shall not all pass away until an house shall be built unto the Lord, and a cloud shall rest upon it, which cloud shall be even the glory of the Lord, which shall fill the house.

Abiding the Lord's presence when he comes to his temple (verses 6–32)

And **the sons of Moses,**

> **according to the Holy Priesthood**

>> which he received under the hand of his father-in-law, Jethro; And Jethro received it under the hand of Caleb; And Caleb received it under the hand of Elihu; And Elihu under the hand of Jeremy; And Jeremy under the hand of Gad; And Gad under the hand of Esaias; And Esaias received it under the hand of God. Esaias also lived in the days of Abraham, and was blessed of him—Which Abraham received the priesthood from Melchizedek, who received it through the lineage of his fathers, even till Noah; And from Noah

till Enoch, through the lineage of their fathers; And from Enoch to Abel, who was slain by the conspiracy of his brother, who received the priesthood by the commandments of God, by the hand of his father Adam, who was the first man—

Which priesthood continueth in the church of God in all generations, and is without beginning of days or end of years.

And the Lord confirmed a priesthood also upon Aaron and his seed, throughout all their generations, which priesthood also continueth and abideth forever with the priesthood which is after the holiest order of God.

And this greater priesthood administereth the gospel and holdeth the key of the mysteries of the kingdom, even the key of the knowledge of God. Therefore, in the ordinances thereof [i.e., the ordinances of the temple], the power of godliness is manifest. And without the ordinances thereof, and the authority of the priesthood, the power of godliness is not manifest unto men in the flesh; For without this no man can see the face of God, even the Father, and live.

Now this Moses plainly taught to the children of Israel in the wilderness, and sought diligently to sanctify his people that they might behold the face of God; But they hardened their hearts and could not endure his presence; therefore, the Lord in his wrath, for his anger was kindled against them, swore that they should not enter into his rest while in the wilderness, which rest is the fulness of his glory. Therefore, he took Moses out of their midst, and the Holy Priesthood also;

And the lesser priesthood continued, which priesthood holdeth the key of the ministering of angels and the preparatory gospel; Which gospel is the gospel of repentance and of baptism, and the remission of sins, and the law of carnal commandments, which the Lord in his wrath caused to continue with the house of Aaron among the children of Israel until John, whom God raised up, being filled with the Holy Ghost from his mother's womb. For he was baptized while he was yet in his childhood, and was ordained by the angel of God at the time he was eight days old unto this power, to overthrow the kingdom of the Jews, and to make straight the way of the Lord before the face of his people, to prepare them for the coming of the Lord, in whose hand is given all power.

And again, the offices of elder and bishop are necessary appendages belonging unto the high priesthood. And again, the offices of teacher and deacon are necessary appendages belonging to the lesser priesthood, which priesthood was confirmed upon Aaron and his sons.

Therefore, as I said concerning the sons of Moses—for the sons of Moses and also the sons of Aaron shall offer an acceptable offering and sacrifice in the house of the Lord, which house shall be built unto the Lord in this generation, upon the consecrated spot as I have appointed—And the sons of Moses and of Aaron shall be filled with the glory of the Lord, upon Mount Zion in the Lord's house, whose sons are ye; and also many whom I have called and sent forth to build up my church.

The oath and covenant of the priesthood (verses 33–40)

For whoso is faithful unto [a] the **obtaining** these two priesthoods of which I have spoken, and [b] the magnifying their calling, are sanctified by the Spirit unto the renewing of their bodies. They become the sons of Moses and of Aaron and the seed of Abraham, and the church and kingdom, and the elect of God.

And also all they who **receive** this priesthood **receive** me, saith the Lord; For he that **receiveth** my servants **receiveth** me; And he that **receiveth** me **receiveth** my Father; And he that **receiveth** my Father

receiveth my Father's kingdom; therefore all that my Father hath shall be given unto him.

And this is according to the oath and covenant which belongeth to the priesthood. *Therefore, all those who* **receive** *the priesthood,* **receive** *this oath and covenant of my Father,* which he cannot break, neither can it be moved.

Punishment for breaking the covenant (verses 41–42)
Instructions regarding worthiness (verses 43–62)
Command and instruction to take gospel to the world
before Lord comes in glory (verses 62–120)

AN ASIDE ON PRIESTHOOD

Two curious textual features leap from the verses of section 84. The first of these is implied by verse 31, which begins with these words: "Therefore, as I said concerning the sons of Moses . . ." The Lord here refers to an earlier mention of the sons of Moses (that is, the holders of the priesthood), which appears way back in verse 6. This means there is a 25-verse aside or parenthetical discussion between these two references to the sons of Moses—a parenthetical that turns out to be a major discourse on the priesthood. That raises the question: Why did the Lord interrupt his comments regarding the sons of Moses to provide this discourse on the priesthood?

In order to answer that, let's begin by placing the discourse on priesthood in context—that is, by understanding what immediately precedes and follows it.

The first four verses of section 84 are a declaration by the Lord that the New Jerusalem would be built in "the western boundaries of the State of Missouri," and that the city would feature the Lord's holy temple. Verse 5—the verse immediately preceding the first reference to "the sons of Moses"—then reads: "For verily this generation shall not all pass away until an house shall be built unto the Lord, and a cloud shall rest upon it, which cloud shall be even the glory of the Lord, which shall fill the house." Interestingly, this reference to the glory of the Lord in the temple is echoed in verses 31 and 32, immediately following the later reference to the sons of Moses. Consider verse 32, which reads: "And the sons of Moses and of Aaron shall be filled with the glory of the Lord, upon Mount Zion in the Lord's house . . ."

What significance might there be to the ordering of these elements in section 84? (1) The Lord will come in glory to the temple, (2) a discourse on priesthood, (3) and then a declaration that the sons of Moses will join the Lord in the temple and be filled with his glory. In order to answer this question, we need to consider the content of the intervening discourse on the priesthood.

That discourse begins with a recitation of the line of authority of the holy priesthood from Moses back to Adam.[2] The key doctrinal verses in this discourse regarding this priesthood are verses 19 through 22, where the Lord reveals three glorious truths regarding the holy priesthood: (1) it holds the key of the knowledge of God;[3] (2) when its authority is on the earth, the power of godliness is manifest unto man only by virtue of its ordinances;[4] and (3) without these ordinances, no one can see the face of God (that is, a fulness of the glory of God) and live.[5]

After this revelation, the Lord declared, as we have discussed, that Moses plainly taught these very things to the children of Israel and was attempting to sanctify and deliver these ordinances (that is, the ordinances of the temple) to them so that "they might behold the face of God."[6] Because they hardened their hearts, however, they could not endure the Lord's presence, and the holy priesthood, with its sanctifying ordinances that are designed to prepare man for a fulness, was removed from them.[7] The lesser or preparatory priesthood remained, which holds the key to being in the presence of angels,[8] but the priesthood that prepares man for the presence of God's glory[9] was lost from the body of Israel until the coming of the Lord in the flesh.[10]

Notice the line of emphasis throughout this discourse: We must receive the ordinances of the holy priesthood, without which "the power of godliness is not manifest unto men in the flesh,"[11] in order to withstand the full glory of the Lord.[12] With this in mind, let's once again consider the content on either side of the Lord's aside on priesthood, including the "oath and covenant" of the priesthood that follows it. Recall that the discourse is immediately preceded by the Lord's declaration that he will come

in his glory to the temple at the New Jerusalem, and it is immediately followed by the declaration that the sons of Moses will be filled with the glory
of the Lord in that temple. (Recall as well that Moses was trying to prepare his people to receive the Lord in his glory.) The context on each side
of the discourse on priesthood makes the need for the discourse clear: No
one will be able to abide the presence of the Lord when he comes in his
glory save those (as "the sons of Moses") who have received the sanctifying ordinances of the holy priesthood. Those ordinances make it possible
for us in the flesh to commune with—and survive—the glory of God.
They are the key to knowing God in his fulness—that is, the "key of the
knowledge of God."[13]

"OBTAINING" THE PRIESTHOOD; "RECEIVING" THE PRIESTHOOD

This background helps to clarify a second interesting feature in the
text of the oath and covenant. Verse 33 reads as follows: "For whoso is
faithful unto the obtaining these two priesthoods . . . and the magnifying
their calling, are sanctified by the Spirit unto the renewing of their bodies." This verse is clearly speaking of those who hold the priesthood—those
who have been faithful unto the "obtaining" of the Aaronic and
Melchizedek Priesthoods. If they magnify their calling, this verse says, they
will be sanctified and enabled to abide the glory of God. Since we learned
in earlier verses that preparation for the Lord's glory requires that we receive the ordinances of the holy priesthood—that is, the ordinances of the
temple—"magnifying their calling" in this context must include the receiving of the sanctifying ordinances of the temple.

Which brings us to verses 35 through 37: "*And also* all they who *receive* this priesthood receive me, saith the Lord; For he that receiveth my
servants receiveth me; And he that receiveth me receiveth my Father; And
he that receiveth my Father receiveth my Father's kingdom; therefore all
that my Father hath shall be given unto him" (emphasis added). "And
this," the Lord declares, "is according to the oath and covenant which belongeth to the priesthood."[14]

Notice the interesting juxtaposition: First the Lord talks about those who are faithful unto the *"obtaining"* of these priesthoods.[15] These are they who, he says, "become the sons of Moses and of Aaron"[16]—that is, the *holders* of the priesthood. If those who "obtain" the priesthood are the holders of the priesthood, then who is the Lord referring to in verse 35 when he adds, "And also all they who *receive* this priesthood receive me"? One possible reading of this verse is that the Lord is simply using the word *receive* as a synonym for *obtain,* and that this verse and those that follow are simply referring to blessings obtainable by those who have "obtained" the priesthood—that is, the sons of Moses and of Aaron. This is frequently how these verses are interpreted. However, I believe that the text suggests an alternative and better reading.

First of all, if the Lord had wanted simply to continue to reference those who *hold* the priesthood, he could easily have continued to use the word *obtain* instead of introducing the new word *receive.* But he didn't do this. And, in fact, from this point on, he uses the word *receive* exclusively. That is, the body of what is known as the oath and covenant of the priesthood applies to those who "receive" the priesthood. If those who "receive" the priesthood constitute a different or larger group than those who "obtain" the priesthood, then the oath and covenant of the priesthood applies as much to some non-priesthood holders as it does to those who hold the priesthood. The prefatory "and also" in verse 35 (*"And also* all they who receive this priesthood receive me") adds to the implication that the Lord is now beginning to speak about another group, not limited to the members of the first he had just referenced.

The most clarifying feature of all, however, is provided by the context we have already discussed. Back in verse 23 we learned that Moses was trying to prepare "the children of Israel" (notice—not just the priesthood holders, but the children of Israel generally) so they could "behold the face of God"[17]—beholding his face in this context meaning, according to verse 24, beholding the *fulness* of his glory. Prior to that (in verses 19 through 22), we learned that one can survive such an encounter only if he or she has first *received* the sanctifying ordinances of the holy priesthood. Notice: the text does not say that only those who *hold* the holy Melchizedek Priesthood can see the face of God and live. Rather, it reveals that all those who *receive* the ordinances of that priesthood (and, by implication, keep the covenants associated with them) may see the face of God and live. Women, for example, although they do not hold the Melchizedek Priesthood, have as great a right to receive the sanctifying ordinances of that priesthood as any man does. In addition, no one who holds the priesthood can administer those sanctifying ordinances to himself. It is as necessary for a priesthood holder to "receive" the ordinances of the holy priesthood as it is for one who does not hold the priesthood. Whether male or female, priesthood holder or not, none can abide the presence of the fulness of the glory of the Father and qualify to receive all that he has unless they first *receive* the ordinances of the holy priesthood that make such communion and blessings possible.

It follows that no one, by simply obtaining the holy priesthood, can qualify for the blessings of the oath and covenant that pertain to it. Those blessings apply to those who *receive* the priesthood of the temple—those ordinances that endow us with the requisite "powers of godliness" to abide the Lord's presence at his coming. This, on the revelation's own terms, must include women as well as men.

In this light, the central verses that comprise the oath and covenant of the priesthood (D&C 84:33–40) make clear and beautiful sense:

> For whoso is faithful unto the obtaining these two priesthoods of which I have spoken, and the magnifying their calling, are sanctified by the Spirit unto the renewing of their bodies. They become the sons of Moses and of Aaron and the seed of Abraham, and the church and kingdom, and the elect of God.[18]

> And also all they who receive this priesthood receive me, saith the Lord; For he that receiveth my servants receiveth me; And he that receiveth me receiveth my Father; And he that receiveth my Father receiveth my Father's kingdom; therefore all that my Father hath shall be given unto him. And this is according to the oath and covenant which belongeth to the priesthood.[19]

> Therefore, all those who *receive* the priesthood, receive this oath and covenant of my Father, which he cannot break, neither can it be moved.[20]

Since all mankind must receive the priesthood ordinances of the temple in order to abide the fulness of the Lord's glory, it follows that the central mission of the priesthood is, as it was for Moses, to prepare mankind by getting them to the temple where they can receive the priesthood ordinances and covenants that will sanctify and prepare them for his glory and presence. The Father and the Son can choose to show themselves at less than their full glory. However, if we are to know them as they really are, we need to see and abide with them in the fulness of their glory. It is therefore the Melchizedek Priesthood, which administers the sanctifying ordinances and covenants of the temple that are set apart for that purpose, that holds the "key of the knowledge of God."[21] The lesser or Aaronic Priesthood holds the key to being in the presence of angels,[22] but it is the Melchizedek Priesthood that holds the key to being in the presence of God.[23]

This knowledge of God is vital to all mankind, as all must be prepared to receive the glory of God. It is therefore no coincidence that the balance of D&C 84 is devoted to missionary work—first to the worthiness of those priesthood holders who would take the gospel to the world[24] and then to instructions regarding how to take the gospel to the world.[25] In this context, the entire purpose of missionary work is to help prepare the world for the coming of God.

Jesus was born into the world at a level of glory that mankind in the flesh could endure—telestial glory. His mortal flesh, Paul taught, was a veil[26] that shielded us from a brightness of glory that mankind could not then endure. When he comes again a second time, he will appear at a terrestrial level of glory, meaning that all those who have not lived at least a terrestrial law will not be able to survive his coming, but shall burn as "stubble."[27] His Second Coming will then usher in a thousand-year period of preparation known as the Millennium, a period that will be necessary to prepare all mankind for the coming of celestial glory—the coming of the glory of the Father. And what will be the focus of our efforts during the Millennium? The performing of temple ordinances for all who have ever lived. For it is only through those ordinances that mankind is prepared to survive the fulness of the glory of Father. This is according to the oath and covenant pertaining to the priesthood. "No one can reject this covenant," the Lord tells us elsewhere, "and be permitted to enter into my glory."[28] For this covenant "was instituted for the fulness of my glory."[29]

"I," the Lord proclaims in his conclusion to the revelation, "have put forth my hand to exert the powers of heaven; ye cannot see it now, yet a little while and ye shall see it, and know that I am, and that I will come and reign with my people."[30] In preparation for that day, he in effect announces through this revelation: "Receive the ordinances of the holy priesthood in the temple. For without the ordinances and their associated covenants, no one can see the face of God—that is, a *fulness* of the glory of the Father—and live." "I am able to make you holy,"[31] he reassures us. His oath or promise to us is that if we receive those ordinances and keep the covenants associated with them, he will sanctify us and make us holy so that we can dwell with him.

APPENDIX C

THE SCRIPTURAL ACCOUNTS OF CREATION

GENESIS

Background to creation story:
- None

MOSES

Background to creation story (chapter 1):
- Moses talks with God face-to-face (1:2, 31)
- God refers to Moses as "my son" (1:4, 6, 7, 40)
- Moses is told that he is "in the similitude of [the] Only Begotten" (1:6)
- Moses is told that God created this earth and "worlds without number" by the "word of my power . . . which is mine Only Begotten," or Christ (1:32–33)
- Moses is told that the purpose of these worlds is: "to bring to pass the immortality and eternal life of man" (1:39)
- The Lord calls this purpose "my work and my glory" (1:39)
- Moses is given a vision "concerning this earth" and is directed to record the things that the Lord should speak concerning it (1:40)

ABRAHAM

Background to creation story (chapter 3):
- Abraham talks with God face-to-face (3:11)
- God refers to Abraham as "my son" (3:12)
- Abraham could see no end to "those things which [the Lord's] hands had made" (3:12)
- Vision of the stars and planets (3:1–17)
  - If two stars/planets exist, one whose reckoning of time is longer than another, there shall be another star/planet whose reckoning of time is longer still (3:7–8)
  - There were many great ones—stars—which were near unto the throne of God (3:2)
  - These are "the governing ones" (3:3)
  - One among them—the "greatest" (3:16)—is "nearest unto the throne of God," or as God says: "nearest unto me" (3:2–3, 16)
  - This great one is called "Kolob" *because* it is nearest unto God (3:3)
  - The great one is "set . . . to govern" the earth and other planets of the same order (3:3, 9)
  - "Kolob is after the reckoning of the Lord's time" (3:9), which is one day to each of our 1,000 years (3:4)
- Vision of spirits (3:19–23)
  - If two spirits exist, one being more intelligent than the other, there shall be another more intelligent than they (3:19)
  - There were many noble and great ones (3:22) who dwelt in the midst of God (3:21)
  - These will be made "rulers" (3:23)
  - "And there stood one among them that was like unto God" (3:24)
  - God rules "in the heavens above, and in the earth beneath, in all wisdom and prudence, over all the intelligences [Abraham's] eyes have seen from the beginning" (3:21)
  - God sent the one who was like unto God to make an earth and "prove them herewith, to see if they will do all things whatsoever the Lord their God shall command them" (3:24–25)

GENESIS (CHAPTER 1)

DAY ONE

[1]In the beginning God created the heaven and the earth. [2]And the earth was without form, and void; and darkness was upon the face of the deep. And the Spirit of God moved upon the face of the waters.

[3]And God said, Let there be light: and there was light. [4]And God saw the light, that it was good: and God divided the light from the darkness. [5]And God called the light Day, and the darkness he called Night. And the evening and the morning were the first day.

DAY TWO

[6]And God said, Let there be a firmament in the midst of the waters, and let it divide the waters from the waters. [7]And God made the firmament, and divided the waters which were under the firmament from the waters which were above the firmament: and it was so. [8]And God called the firmament Heaven. And the evening and the morning were the second day.

MOSES (CHAPTER 2)

DAY ONE

[1] . . . I am the Beginning and the End, the Almighty God; by mine Only Begotten I created these things; yea, in the beginning I created the heaven, and the earth upon which thou standest. [2]And the earth was without form, and void; and I caused darkness to come up upon the face of the deep; and my Spirit moved upon the face of the water; for I am God.

[3]And I, God, said: Let there be light; and there was light. [4]And I, God, saw the light; and that light was good. And I, God, divided the light from the darkness. [5]And I, God, called the light Day; and the darkness, I called Night; and this I did by the word of my power, and it was done as I spake; and the evening and the morning were the first day.

DAY TWO

[6]And again, I, God, said: Let there be a firmament in the midst of the water, and it was so, even as I spake; and I said: Let it divide the waters from the waters; and it was done; [7]And I, God, made the firmament and divided the waters, yea, the great waters under the firmament from the waters which were above the firmament, and it was so even as I spake. [8]And I, God, called the firmament Heaven; and the evening and the morning were the second day.

ABRAHAM (CHAPTER 4)

DAY ONE

[1]And then the Lord said: Let us go down. And they went down at the beginning, and they; that is the Gods, organized and formed the heavens and the earth. [2]And the earth, after it was formed, was empty and desolate, because they had not formed anything but the earth; and darkness reigned upon the face of the deep, and the Spirit of the Gods was brooding upon the face of the waters.

[3]And they (the Gods) said: Let there be light; and there was light. [4]And they (the Gods) comprehended the light, for it was bright; and they divided the light, or caused it to be divided, from the darkness. [5]And the Gods called the light Day, and the darkness they called Night. And it came to pass that from the evening until morning they called night; and from the morning until the evening they called day; and this was the first, or the beginning, of that which they called day and night.

DAY TWO

[6]And the Gods also said: Let there be an expanse in the midst of the waters, and it shall divide the waters from the waters. [7]And the Gods ordered the expanse, so that it divided the waters from the waters which were under the expanse from the waters which were above the expanse; and it was so, even as they ordered. [8]And the Gods called the expanse, Heaven. And it came to pass that it was from evening until morning that they called night; and it came to pass that it was from morning until evening that they called day; and this was the second time that they called night and day.

GENESIS (CHAPTER 1)

DAY THREE

9And God said, Let the waters under the heaven be gathered together unto one place, and let the dry land appear: and it was so.

10And God called the dry land Earth; and the gathering together of the waters called he Seas: and God saw that it was good.

11And God said, Let the earth bring forth grass, the herb yielding seed, and the fruit tree yielding fruit after his kind, whose seed is in itself, upon the earth: and it was so. 12And the earth brought forth grass, and herb yielding seed after his kind, and the tree yielding fruit, whose seed was in itself, after his kind: and God saw that it was good.

13And the evening and the morning were the third day.

DAY FOUR

14And God said, Let there be lights in the firmament of the heaven to divide the day from the night; and let them be for signs, and for seasons, and for days, and years: 15And let them be for lights in the firmament of the heaven to give light upon the earth: and it was so.

MOSES (CHAPTER 2)

DAY THREE

9And I, God, said: Let the waters under the heaven be gathered together unto one place, and it was so; and I, God, said: Let there be dry land; and it was so. 10And I, God, called the dry land Earth; and the gathering together of the waters, called I the Sea; and I, God, saw that all things which I had made were good.

11And I, God, said: Let the earth bring forth grass, the herb yielding seed, the fruit tree yielding fruit, after his kind, and the tree yielding fruit, whose seed should be in itself upon the earth, and it was so even as I spake. 12And the earth brought forth grass, every herb yielding seed after his kind, and the tree yielding fruit, whose seed should be in itself, after his kind; and I, God, saw that all things which I had made were good;

13And the evening and the morning were the third day.

DAY FOUR

14And I, God, said: Let there be lights in the firmament of the heaven, to divide the day from the night, and let them be for signs, and for seasons, and for days, and years; 15And let them be for lights in the firmament of the heaven to give light upon the earth: and it was so.

ABRAHAM (CHAPTER 4)

DAY THREE

9And the Gods ordered, saying: Let the waters under the heaven be gathered together unto one place, and let the earth come up dry; and it was so as they ordered; 10And the Gods pronounced the dry land, Earth; and the gathering together of the waters, pronounced they, Great Waters; and the Gods saw that they were obeyed.

11And the Gods said: Let us prepare the earth to bring forth grass; the herb yielding seed; the fruit tree yielding fruit, after his kind, whose seed in itself yieldeth its own likeness upon the earth; and it was so, even as they ordered. 12And the Gods organized the earth to bring forth grass from its own seed, and the herb to bring forth herb from its own seed, yielding seed after his kind; and the earth to bring forth the tree from its own seed, yielding fruit, whose seed could only bring forth the same in itself, after his kind; and the Gods saw that they were obeyed.

13And it came to pass that they numbered the days; from the evening until the morning they called night; and it came to pass, from the morning until the evening they called day; and it was the third time.

DAY FOUR

14And the Gods organized the lights in the expanse of the heaven, and caused them to divide the day from the night; and organized them to be for signs and for seasons, and for days and for years; 15And organized them to be for lights in the expanse of the heaven to give light upon the earth; and it was so.

GENESIS (CHAPTER 1)

DAY FOUR (continued)

[16]And God made two great lights; the greater light to rule the day, and the lesser light to rule the night: he made the stars also. [17]And God set them in the firmament of the heaven to give light upon the earth, [18]And to rule over the day and over the night, and to divide the light from the darkness: and God saw that it was good.

[19]And the evening and the morning were the fourth day.

DAY FIVE

[20]And God said, Let the waters bring forth abundantly the moving creature that hath life, and fowl that may fly above the earth in the open firmament of heaven. [21]And God created great whales, and every living creature that moveth, which the waters brought forth abundantly, after their kind, and every winged fowl after his kind: and God saw that it was good. [22]And God blessed them, saying, Be fruitful, and multiply, and fill the waters in the seas, and let fowl multiply in the earth.

[23]And the evening and the morning were the fifth day.

MOSES (CHAPTER 2)

DAY FOUR (continued)

[16]And I, God, made two great lights; the greater light to rule the day, and the lesser light to rule the night, and the greater light was the sun, and the lesser light was the moon; and the stars also were made even according to my word. [17]And I, God, set them in the firmament of the heaven to give light upon the earth, [18]And the sun to rule over the day, and the moon to rule over the night, and to divide the light from the darkness; and I, God, saw that all things which I had made were good;

[19]And the evening and the morning were the fourth day.

DAY FIVE

[20]And I, God, said: Let the waters bring forth abundantly the moving creature that hath life, and fowl which may fly above the earth in the open firmament of heaven. [21]And I, God, created great whales, and every living creature that moveth, which the waters brought forth abundantly, after their kind, and every winged fowl after his kind; and I, God, saw that all things which I had created were good. [22]And I, God, blessed them, saying; Be fruitful, and multiply, and fill the waters in the sea; and let fowl multiply in the earth;

[23]And the evening and the morning were the fifth day.

ABRAHAM (CHAPTER 4)

DAY FOUR (continued)

[16]And the Gods organized the two great lights, the greater light to rule the day, and the lesser light to rule the night; with the lesser light they set the stars also; [17]And the Gods set them in the expanse of the heavens, to give light upon the earth, and to rule over the day and over the night, and to cause to divide the light from the darkness. [18]And the Gods watched those things which they had ordered until they obeyed.

[19]And it came to pass that it was from evening until morning that it was night; and it came to pass that it was from morning until evening that it was day; and it was the fourth time.

DAY FIVE

[20]And the Gods said: Let us prepare the waters to bring forth abundantly the moving creatures that have life; and the fowl, that they may fly above the earth in the open expanse of heaven. [21]And the Gods prepared the waters that they might bring forth great whales, and every living creature that moveth, which the waters were to bring forth abundantly after their kind; and every winged fowl after their kind. And the Gods saw that they would be obeyed, and that their plan was good. [22]And the Gods said: We will bless them, and cause them to be fruitful and multiply, and fill the waters in the seas or great waters; and cause the fowl to multiply in the earth.

[23]And it came to pass that it was from evening until morning that they called night; and it came to pass that it was from morning until evening that they called day; and it was the fifth time.

GENESIS (CHAPTER 1)

DAY SIX

24And God said, Let the earth bring forth the living creature after his kind, cattle, and creeping thing, and beast of the earth after his kind: and it was so. 25And God made the beast of the earth after his kind, and cattle after their kind, and every thing that creepeth upon the earth after his kind: and God saw that it was good.

26And God said, Let us make man in our image, after our likeness: and let them have dominion over the fish of the sea, and over the fowl of the air, and over the cattle, and over all the earth, and over every creeping thing that creepeth upon the earth.

27So God created man in his own image, in the image of God created he him; male and female created he them. 28And God blessed them, and God said unto them, Be fruitful, and multiply, and replenish the earth, and subdue it: and have dominion over the fish of the sea, and over the fowl of the air, and over every living thing that moveth upon the earth.

29And God said, Behold, I have given you every herb bearing seed, which is upon the face of all the earth, and every tree, in the which is the fruit of a tree yielding seed; to you it shall be for meat. 30And to every beast of the earth, and to every fowl of the air, and to every thing that creepeth upon the earth, wherein there is life, I have given every green herb for meat: and it was so.

31And God saw every thing that he had made, and, behold, it was very good. And the evening and the morning were the sixth day.

MOSES (CHAPTER 2)

DAY SIX

24And I, God, said: Let the earth bring forth the living creature after his kind, cattle, and creeping things, and beasts of the earth after their kind: and it was so; 25And I, God, made the beasts of the earth after their kind, and cattle after their kind, and everything which creepeth upon the earth after his kind; and I, God, saw that all these things were good.

26And I, God, said unto mine Only Begotten, which was with me from the beginning: Let us make man in our image, after our likeness; and it was so. And I, God, said: Let them have dominion over the fishes of the sea, and over the fowl of the air, and over the cattle, and over all the earth, and over every creeping thing that creepeth upon the earth.

27And I, God, created man in mine own image, in the image of mine Only Begotten created I him; male and female created I them. 28And I, God, blessed them, and said unto them: Be fruitful, and multiply, and replenish the earth, and subdue it, and have dominion over the fish of the sea, and over the fowl of the air, and over every living thing that moveth upon the earth.

29And I, God, said unto man: Behold, I have given you every herb bearing seed, which is upon the face of all the earth, and every tree in the which shall be the fruit of a tree yielding seed; to you it shall be for meat. 30And to every beast of the earth, and to every fowl of the air, and to every-thing that creepeth upon the earth, wherein I grant life, there shall be given every clean herb for meat; and it was so, even as I spake.

31And I, God, saw everything that I had made, and, behold, all things which I had made were very good; and the evening and the morning were the sixth day.

ABRAHAM (CHAPTER 4)

DAY SIX

24And the Gods prepared the earth to bring forth the living creature after his kind, cattle and creep-ing things, and beasts of the earth after their kind; and it was so, as they had said. 25And the Gods organized the earth to bring forth the beasts after their kind, and cattle after their kind, and every thing that creepeth upon the earth after its kind; and the Gods saw they would obey.

26And the Gods took counsel among themselves and said: Let us go down and form man in our image, after our likeness; and we will give them dominion over the fish of the sea, and over the fowl of the air, and over the cattle, and over all the earth, and over every creeping thing that creepeth upon the earth.

27So the Gods went down to organize man in their own image, in the image of the Gods to form they him, male and female to form they them.

28And the Gods said: We will bless them. And the Gods said: We will cause them to be fruitful and multiply, and replenish the earth, and subdue it, and to have dominion over the fish of the sea, and over the fowl of the air, and over every living thing that moveth upon the earth.

29And the Gods said: Behold, we will give them every herb bearing seed that shall come upon the face of all the earth, and every tree which shall have fruit upon it; yea, the fruit of the tree yielding seed to them we will give it; it shall be for their meat.

30And to every beast of the earth, and to every fowl of the air, and to every thing that creepeth upon the earth, behold, we will give them life, and also we will give to them every green herb for meat, and all these things shall be thus organized.

31And the Gods said: We will do everything that we have said, and organize them; and behold, they shall be very obedient. And it came to pass that it was from evening until morning they called night; and it came to pass that it was from morning until evening that they called day; and they numbered the sixth time.

GENESIS (CHAPTER 2)

DAY SEVEN

¹Thus the heavens and the earth were finished, and all the host of them. ²And on the seventh day God ended his work which he had made; and he rested on the seventh day from all his work which he had made. ³And God blessed the seventh day, and sanctified it: because that in it he had rested from all his work which God created and made.

⁴These are the generations of the heavens and of the earth when they were created, in the day that the Lord God made the earth and the heavens, ⁵And every plant of the field before it was in the earth, and every herb of the field before it grew: for the Lord God had not caused it to rain upon the earth, and there was not a man to till the ground.

⁶But there went up a mist from the earth, and watered the whole face of the ground. ⁷And the Lord God formed man of the dust of the ground, and breathed into his nostrils the breath of life; and man became a living soul.

MOSES (CHAPTER 3)

DAY SEVEN

¹Thus the heaven and the earth were finished, and all the host of them. ²And on the seventh day I, God, ended my work, and all things which I had made; and I rested on the seventh day from all my work, and all things which I had made were finished, and I, God, saw that they were good; ³And I, God, blessed the seventh day, and sanctified it; because that in it I had rested from all my work which I, God, had created and made.

⁴And now, behold, I say unto you, that these are the generations of the heaven and of the earth, when they were created, in the day that I, the Lord God, made the heaven and the earth, ⁵And every plant of the field before it was in the earth, and every herb of the field before it grew. For I, the Lord God, created all things, of which I have spoken, spiritually, before they were naturally upon the face of the earth. For I, the Lord God, had not caused it to rain upon the face of the earth. And I, the Lord God, had created all the children of men; and not yet a man to till the ground; for in heaven created I them; and there was not yet flesh upon the earth, neither in the water, neither in the air;

⁶But I, the Lord God, spake, and there went up a mist from the earth, and watered the whole face of the ground. ⁷And I, the Lord God, formed man from the dust of the ground, and breathed into his nostrils the breath of life; and man became a living soul, the first man also; nevertheless, all things were before created; but spiritually were they created and made according to my word.

ABRAHAM (CHAPTER 5)

DAY SEVEN

¹And thus we will finish the heavens and the earth, and all the hosts of them. ²And the Gods said among themselves: On the seventh time we will end our work, which we have counseled; and we will rest on the seventh time from all our work which we have counseled. ³And the Gods concluded upon the seventh time, because that on the seventh time they would rest from all their works which they (the Gods) counseled among themselves to form; and sanctified it. And thus were their decisions at the time that they counseled among themselves to form the heavens and the earth.

⁴And the Gods came down and formed these the generations of the heavens and of the earth, when they were formed in the day that the Gods formed the earth and the heavens, ⁵According to all that which they had said concerning every plant of the field before it was in the earth, and every herb of the field before it grew; for the Gods had not caused it to rain upon the earth when they counseled to do them, and had not formed a man to till the ground.

⁶But there went up a mist from the earth, and watered the whole face of the ground. ⁷And the Gods formed man from the dust of the ground, and took his spirit (that is, the man's spirit), and put it into him; and breathed into his nostrils the breath of life, and man became a living soul.

GENESIS (CHAPTER 2)

[8]And the Lord God planted a garden eastward in Eden; and there he put the man whom he had formed. [9]And out of the ground made the Lord God to grow every tree that is pleasant to the sight, and good for food; the tree of life also in the midst of the garden, and the tree of knowledge of good and evil.

[10]And a river went out of Eden to water the garden; and from thence it was parted, and became into four heads. [11]The name of the first is Pison: that it is which compasseth the whole land of Havilah, where there is gold; [12]And the gold of that land is good: there is bdellium and the onyx stone. [13]And the name of the second river is Gihon: the same is it that compasseth the whole land of Ethiopia. [14]And the name of the third river is Hiddekel: that it is which goeth toward the east of Assyria. And the fourth river is Euphrates.

[15]And the Lord God took the man, and put him into the garden of Eden to dress it and to keep it. [16]And the Lord God commanded the man, saying, Of every tree of the garden thou mayest freely eat: [17]But of the tree of the knowledge of good and evil, thou shalt not eat of it: for in the day that thou eatest thereof thou shalt surely die. [18]And the Lord God said, It is not good that the man should be alone; I will make him an help meet for him.

MOSES (CHAPTER 3)

DAY SEVEN (continued)

[8]And I, the Lord God, planted a garden eastward in Eden, and there I put the man whom I had formed. [9]And out of the ground made I, the Lord God, to grow every tree, naturally, that is pleasant to the sight of man; and man could behold it. And it became also a living soul. For it was spiritual in the day that I created it; for it remaineth in the sphere in which I, God, created it, yea, even all things which I prepared for the use of man; and man saw that it was good for food. And I, the Lord God, planted the tree of life also in the midst of the garden, and also the tree of knowledge of good and evil.

[10]And I, the Lord God, caused a river to go out of Eden to water the garden; and from thence it was parted, and became into four heads. [11]And I, the Lord God, called the name of the first Pison, and it compasseth the whole land of Havilah, where I, the Lord God, created much gold; [12]And the gold of that land was good, and there was bdellium and the onyx stone. [13]And the name of the second river was called Gihon; the same that compasseth the whole land of Ethiopia. [14]And the name of the third river was Hiddekel; that which goeth toward the east of Assyria. And the fourth river was the Euphrates.

[15]And I, the Lord God, took the man, and put him into the Garden of Eden, to dress it, and to keep it. [16]And I, the Lord God, commanded the man, saying; Of every tree of the garden thou mayest freely eat, [17]But of the tree of the knowledge of good and evil, thou shalt not eat of it, nevertheless, thou mayest choose for thyself, for it is given unto thee; but, remember that I forbid it, for in the day thou eatest thereof thou shalt surely die.

[18]And I, the Lord God, said unto mine Only Begotten, that it was not good that the man should be alone; wherefore, I will make an help meet for him.

ABRAHAM (CHAPTER 5)

DAY SEVEN (continued)

[8]And the Gods planted a garden, eastward in Eden, and there they put the man, whose spirit they had put into the body which they had formed. [9]And out of the ground made the Gods to grow every tree that is pleasant to the sight and good for food; the tree of life, also, in the midst of the garden, and the tree of knowledge of good and evil.

[10]There was a river running out of Eden, to water the garden, and from thence it was parted and became into four heads.

[11]And the Gods took the man and put him in the Garden of Eden, to dress it and to keep it. [12]And the Gods commanded the man, saying: Of every tree of the garden thou mayest freely eat, [13]But of the tree of the knowledge of good and evil, thou shalt not eat of it; for in the time that thou eatest thereof, thou shalt surely die. Now I, Abraham, saw that it was after the Lord's time, which was after the time of Kolob; for as yet the Gods had not appointed unto Adam his reckoning.

[14]And the Gods said: Let us make an help meet for the man, for it is not good that the man should be alone, therefore we will form an help meet for him.

[15]And the Gods caused a deep sleep to fall upon Adam; and he slept, and they took one of his ribs, and closed up the flesh in the stead thereof; [16]And of the rib which the Gods had taken from man, formed they a woman, and brought her unto the man. [17]And Adam said: This was bone of my bones, and flesh of my flesh; now she shall be called Woman, because she was taken out of man; [18]Therefore shall a man leave his father and his mother, and shall cleave unto his wife, and they shall be one flesh.

GENESIS (CHAPTER 2)

DAY SEVEN (continued)

¹⁹And out of the ground the Lord God formed every beast of the field, and every fowl of the air; and brought them unto Adam to see what he would call them: and whatsoever Adam called every living creature, that was the name thereof. ²⁰And Adam gave names to all cattle, and to the fowl of the air, and to every beast of the field; but for Adam there was not found an help meet for him.

²¹And the Lord God caused a deep sleep to fall upon Adam, and he slept: and he took one of his ribs, and closed up the flesh instead thereof; ²²And the rib, which the Lord God had taken from man, made he a woman, and brought her unto the man. ²³And Adam said, This is now bone of my bones, and flesh of my flesh: she shall be called Woman, because she was taken out of Man. ²⁴Therefore shall a man leave his father and his mother, and shall cleave unto his wife: and they shall be one flesh.

²⁵And they were both naked, the man and his wife, and were not ashamed.

MOSES (CHAPTER 3)

DAY SEVEN (continued)

¹⁹And out of the ground I, the Lord God, formed every beast of the field, and every fowl of the air; and commanded that they should come unto Adam, to see what he would call them; and they were also living souls; for I, God, breathed into them the breath of life, and commanded that whatsoever Adam called every living creature, that should be the name thereof. ²⁰And Adam gave names to all cattle, and to the fowl of the air, and to every beast of the field; but as for Adam, there was not found an help meet for him.

²¹And I, the Lord God, caused a deep sleep to fall upon Adam; and he slept, and I took one of his ribs and closed up the flesh in the stead thereof; ²²And the rib which I, the Lord God, had taken from man, made I a woman, and brought her unto the man. ²³And Adam said: This I know now is bone of my bones, and flesh of my flesh; she shall be called Woman, because she was taken out of man. ²⁴Therefore shall a man leave his father and his mother, and shall cleave unto his wife; and they shall be one flesh.

²⁵And they were both naked, the man and his wife, and were not ashamed.

ABRAHAM (CHAPTER 5)

DAY SEVEN (continued)

¹⁹And they were both naked, the man and his wife, and were not ashamed.

²⁰And out of the ground the Gods formed every beast of the field, and every fowl of the air, and brought them unto Adam to see what he would call them; and whatsoever Adam called every living creature, that should be the name thereof.

²¹And Adam gave names to all cattle, to the fowl of the air, to every beast of the field; and for Adam, there was found an help meet for him.

NOTES

INTRODUCTION: THE STORY BENEATH THE SCRIPTURAL STORY

1. See Luke 24:19.
2. See Luke 24:21.
3. Luke 24:23.
4. See Luke 24:14–15, 18–21.
5. Luke 24:17.
6. Luke 24:25–27, emphasis added.
7. Luke 24:36.
8. Luke 24:37.
9. Luke 24:38.
10. Luke 24:41.
11. Luke 24:44–46, emphasis added.
12. See Luke 24:52–53.
13. 2 Corinthians 3:14.
14. 2 Nephi 11:4, emphasis added.
15. Moses 5:7.
16. Moses 6:63, emphasis added.
17. See Moses 8:19–21, 23.
18. See Moses 8:25.
19. See Moses 8:27; Genesis 6:9.
20. See Moses 8:21.
21. See Genesis 6:22; 7:5.
22. See Moses 8:18.
23. See Genesis 6:18.
24. See Genesis 6:18.
25. See Genesis 7:1, 7.
26. Alma 34:14.
27. See Appendix A for a list of key Christ similitudes in the Old Testament. These similitudes are strung together to tell the story of Jesus' life in chapter 22. Chapter 22 also tells the story of the restoration of the gospel that is revealed from beneath the surface of the Old Testament.
28. See chapter 10.
29. See chapter 2.
30. See chapter 8.
31. See chapter 14.
32. 2 Nephi 11:4.
33. Luke 24:45.
34. Luke 24:27.
35. Luke 24:45.
36. See Luke 24:41, 52–53.

CHAPTER 1: THE PARALLEL CREATION

1. See, for example, Hyrum Andrus, *Doctrinal Commentary on the Pearl of Great Price* (Deseret Book, 1967), 137–82.
2. Abraham 3:22.
3. See Abraham 3:16.
4. See Abraham 3:5–8.
5. See Abraham 3:2.
6. Abraham 3:3.
7. See Abraham 3:2–3, 9, 16.
8. Abraham 3:3, 9.
9. See Abraham 3:19.
10. See Abraham 3:21–22.
11. Abraham 3:23.
12. Abraham 3:24.

13. Abraham 3:21, 24–25.
14. See Abraham Facsimile no. 2, explanation to fig. 1.
15. See Abraham Facsimile no. 2, explanation to fig. 2.
16. See Abraham 3:28; Isaiah 14:12–15.
17. Revelation 12:9.
18. See D&C 6:13; 14:7.
19. Abraham 3:24.
20. Abraham 3:25.
21. Abraham 3:26.
22. Abraham 3:26.
23. See D&C 76:50–70, 92–95.
24. See Abraham 4:2. See also Genesis 1:2; Moses 2:2.
25. See Genesis 1:2; Moses 2:2; Abraham 4:2.
26. See Genesis 1:3–5; Moses 2:3–5; Abraham 4:3–5.
27. See Genesis 1:6–8; Moses 2:6–8; Abraham 4:6–8.
28. See Genesis 1:11–12; Moses 2:11–12; Abraham 4:11–12.
29. See Genesis 1:14–18; Moses 2:14–18; Abraham 4:14–18.
30. Genesis 1:17–18. See also Moses 2:17–18; Abraham 4:17–18.
31. See Genesis 1:20–25; Moses 2:20–25; Abraham 4:20–25.
32. See Genesis 1:26–27; Moses 2:26–27; Abraham 4:26–27.
33. See Genesis 1; Genesis 2:18, 21–25; Moses 3:18, 21–25; Abraham 5:14–19.
34. See Moses 4:14.
35. See D&C 2:3; 49:16–17; 88:18–20; Moses 1:38–39.
36. Moses 2:1; see also Moses 1:32.
37. See, for example, John 8:12.
38. See Genesis 1:2–5; Moses 2:2–5; Abraham 4:2–5.
39. Isaiah 42:5.
40. See Genesis 1:6–8; Moses 2:6–8; Abraham 4:6–8.
41. Jeremiah 2:13.
42. John 15:1.
43. See Genesis 1:9–13; Moses 2:9–13; Abraham 4:9–13.
44. See D&C 88:6–13.
45. See Genesis 1:14–18; Moses 2:14–18; Abraham 4:14–18.
46. See Genesis 1:20–23; Moses 2:20–23; Abraham 4:20–23.
47. See, for example, John 10:11, 14.
48. See, for example, John 1:29.
49. See, for example, Matthew 9:6.
50. See Genesis 1:24–31; Moses 2:24–31; Abraham 4:24–31.
51. Mosiah 3:19, emphasis added.
52. Mosiah 5:8–9.
53. See D&C 14:9.
54. Moses 2:5.
55. Moses 2:7.
56. Abraham 4:7.
57. Abraham 4:12, emphasis added.
58. Abraham 4:18, emphasis added.
59. Abraham 4:21, emphasis added.
60. Abraham 4:31, emphasis added.
61. Abraham 3:25.
62. D&C 88:35.
63. Matthew 26:39.
64. See Articles of Faith 1:10.
65. See Malachi 3:2; 4:1; Isaiah 51:3; 2 Nephi 8:1–3.
66. D&C 88:18–19.
67. D&C 88:20.

CHAPTER 2: THE FALL AND REDEMPTION OF AGENCY

1. See Abraham 3:25–26.
2. Moses 4:1, emphasis added.
3. Moses 4:3.
4. See D&C 29:36–38.
5. Moses 4:4.
6. Moses 3:16–17.
7. See D&C 93:30; 2 Nephi 2:11–13.
8. D&C 93:31, 39.
9. D&C 29:40.
10. Moses 4:4.
11. Mosiah 16:3–5.
12. John 8:34.
13. Moses 4:15–17.
14. Moses 4:18–19.
15. D&C 93:29.
16. See D&C 93:29, 38.

17. 2 Nephi 2:29.
18. 1 Corinthians 13:12.
19. 1 Nephi 13:27.
20. Alma 12:6.
21. See Moses 4:14.
22. Galatians 6:3.
23. 1 Nephi 15:3.
24. D&C 64:22.
25. See Alma 5:10–14.
26. Moses 4:6.
27. 2 Nephi 2:24.
28. 2 Nephi 2:16.
29. D&C 29:39.
30. 2 Nephi 2:11.
31. Ezekiel 36:26.
32. 2 Nephi 2:26, emphasis added.
33. 2 Nephi 9:8–9.
34. Mosiah 16:4.
35. Moses 5:9, emphasis added.
36. See 2 Nephi 2:29.
37. Mosiah 14:6; see also James E. Faust, "The Atonement: Our Greatest Hope," *Ensign,* November 2001, 18–20.
38. Hebrews 4:15.
39. Joseph Fielding Smith, *Doctrines of Salvation* (Bookcraft, 1954–56), 1:129; see also *Teachings of Ezra Taft Benson* (Bookcraft, 1988), 14–15.
40. 2 Corinthians 5:21.
41. Luke 22:44.
42. Jack Welch, "Toward Becoming a Gospel-Scholar," *This People,* Summer 1998, 52.
43. James E. Faust, "Atonement: Our Greatest Hope," 19, quoting John Taylor, *The Mediation and Atonement* (Deseret News, 1882), 150.
44. James E. Talmage, *Jesus the Christ* (Deseret Book, 1979), 613.
45. Hebrews 4:15.
46. Moses 7:26.
47. Moses 4:21.
48. Moses 5:9.
49. Moses 5:13.
50. Mosiah 16:5.
51. 2 Nephi 1:13.
52. 2 Nephi 2:26–27, emphasis added.
53. 2 Nephi 2:28–29, emphasis added.
54. 2 Nephi 2:25, emphasis added.

CHAPTER 3: GOD AND MAN AFTER THE FALL

1. Moses 3:17.
2. D&C 88:22, emphasis added.
3. Moses 6:57, emphasis added.
4. *Teachings of the Prophet Joseph Smith,* sel. Joseph Fielding Smith (Deseret Book, 1976), 367.
5. JST, Exodus 33:20, emphasis added.
6. JST, Exodus 34:1.
7. Alma 42:14.
8. Romans 3:23.
9. When Jesus was born into this mortal realm, his premortal glory was cloaked, as it were, by the veil of his flesh (see Hebrews 10:20) to the level of a telestial glory so that all mankind could be with him in the flesh.
10. See, for example, John 14:9; Bruce R. McConkie, *Doctrinal New Testament Commentary,* 3 vols. (Bookcraft: 1973), 1:730–31.
11. See, for example, D&C 93:3–5, John 5:19; 14:10.
12. John 14:9.
13. McConkie, *Doctrinal New Testament Commentary,* 1:731.
14. Moses 1:1.
15. Joseph Fielding Smith, *Doctrines of Salvation,* 1:27.
16. See Moses 1:9.
17. See Moses 1:10.
18. See Moses 1:12–22.
19. See Moses 2 and 3.
20. See Moses 3–5.
21. See Moses 6–8.
22. The book of Moses is a collection of revelations received by the Prophet Joseph Smith as he pondered upon the Bible, in accordance with a commandment he received from the Lord to commence upon an inpired translation of the Bible. The revelations compiled in the book of Moses give

additional details to the events and stories recorded in Genesis chapters 1–6.

23. Moses 1:12.

24. See also Abraham 3:12.

25. See Moses 1:8, 23, 42.

26. Ether 3:14.

27. Mosiah 5:7.

28. Alma 22:15.

29. Alma 5:7.

30. Alma 5:14.

31. Bruce R. McConkie, *The Promised Messiah* (Deseret Book, 1978), 352.

32. McConkie, *Promised Messiah,* 351–52, emphasis added.

33. "The Father and The Son: A Doctrinal Exposition by The First Presidency and The Twelve," in James E. Talmage, *Articles of Faith* (Deseret Book, 1984), 424.

34. See Articles of Faith 1:4.

35. See Articles of Faith 1:4.

36. Alma 5:26–27.

37. Mosiah 4:12.

38. Mosiah 15:11, 22.

39. Mosiah 5:8–9.

40. Moses 1:4, emphasis added.

41. Moses 1:4–5.

42. McConkie, *Doctrinal New Testament Commentary,* 3:184.

43. See Moses 1:11.

44. Ether 3:13.

45. See Hebrews 10:20.

46. See D&C 88:22–24.

47. See Malachi 3:2; 4:1.

48. Moses 5:5.

49. Moses 5:7–8.

50. Moses 6:52, numbering added.

51. Moses 6:64–68, emphasis added.

52. Moses 6:62.

53. 2 Nephi 32:5.

54. Moses 1:6.

55. D&C 93:3.

56. John 17:21.

57. D&C 35:2, emphasis added.

58. John 8:41.

59. Moses 1:26.

CHAPTER 4: EXPLORING THE ABRAHAMIC COVENANT

1. See Abraham 1:5–15.

2. Abraham 1:2.

3. Abraham 1:4.

4. JS–H 1:38–39, emphasis added. See also Malachi 4:5–6.

5. For a discussion of Elijah and his mission, see chapter 16 of this book.

6. D&C 110:11–16, emphasis added.

7. See Moses 7:69.

8. Genesis 17:7.

9. D&C 132:6.

10. See D&C 132:4–7.

11. Abraham 1:3.

12. *History of the Church,* 7 vols. (Deseret Book, 1948), 4:207.

13. See D&C 84:19–23. For a discussion of these verses, see Appendix B.

14. Moses 5:59.

15. Facsimile no. 2, fig. 3, in the book of Abraham.

16. See Moses 5:59; D&C 107:42–52; 138:41.

17. D&C 138:41.

18. For more on that possibility, see Alma E. Gygi, "I Have a Question: Is It Possible That Shem and Melchizedek Are the Same Person?" *Ensign,* November 1973, 15–16.

19. See JST, Genesis 14:27, 32–36; Hebrews 7:8. See also chapter 21 of this book, which discusses dispensations.

20. See D&C 84:14; Abraham 1:2.

21. Abraham 1:2.

22. The most detailed account in Genesis of the Lord's covenant with Abraham is contained in the narrative after Abraham turned ninety-nine years old in Genesis 17. However, a portion of the covenant was communicated to Abraham two chapters earlier in Genesis, and another portion was reiterated five chapters later, after Abraham was saved from having to sacrifice Isaac. The Abraham account

does not mention Abraham's age at the time he received the covenant.

23. Abraham 3:12.
24. Genesis 17:7.
25. See Genesis 17:5.
26. Genesis 17:8. See also Genesis 15:7, 18; Abraham 2:6.
27. Abraham 1:4.
28. See Genesis 17:2–6; 22:17.
29. Abraham 2:9.
30. Abraham 2:11. See also Genesis 22:18.
31. Abraham 2:6, 8–11.
32. Abraham 2:9.
33. Abraham 2:10, emphasis added.
34. See Genesis 22:17.
35. Abraham 2:11.
36. Galatians 3:16, 20, 26–29. Verse 20 is quoted from the JST.
37. Abraham 2:11.
38. Galatians 3:29.
39. JST, Genesis 14:28–29.
40. See D&C 110:12–16.
41. See Malachi 4:5–6.
42. D&C 132:30–31, emphasis added.
43. See D&C 110:12–16. For more on Elijah and his mission, see chapter 16 of this book.
44. Moses 5:59.
45. D&C 132:4. For a discussion of how the Melchizedek Priesthood ordinances of the temple are set apart to prepare us to enter into the presence of the glory of God, see Appendix B.
46. D&C 132:7.
47. D&C 132:31.
48. Abraham 1:4.
49. See D&C 132:12–15, 18.
50. Abraham 2:11.
51. D&C 107:3.
52. Malachi 4:6. For a further discussion of this prophecy in Malachi, see chapter 16 of this book.

CHAPTER 5: ANOTHER LOOK AT ABRAHAM AND ISAAC

1. Genesis 22:7.
2. See Genesis 22:2.

3. Genesis 22:8.
4. Genesis 22:8.
5. Genesis 17:18.
6. See Genesis 17:20.
7. See Genesis 21:14.
8. Genesis 21:14.
9. See Genesis 16:1–2.
10. See Genesis 16:11, 15.
11. See Genesis 17:1–21.
12. See Genesis 17:15–16.
13. See Genesis 17:17.
14. Genesis 17:18.
15. See Genesis 17:20.
16. See Genesis 17:19, 21
17. Genesis 21:8–10.
18. Genesis 21:11.
19. See Genesis 21:9 (where Ishmael mocks the one who is in similitude of Christ).
20. See Genesis 21:10, 12.
21. See Genesis 17:20–21; 21:10; 22:2.
22. See Genesis 21:14.
23. See Genesis 21:15–16.
24. See Genesis 16:12.
25. See Genesis 21:17.
26. See Genesis 21:19.
27. Genesis 21:11, emphasis added.
28. Genesis 21:14.
29. See Genesis 21:16–19.
30. See Genesis 21:15.
31. See Ether 12:27—God gives men weaknesses so that humility may result, so that his grace may be sufficient for them.
32. Genesis 22:10–12, emphasis added.
33. Abraham 1:15.
34. Abraham 1:16.
35. Genesis 22:12, emphasis added.
36. Genesis 22:13.
37. Matthew 27:42.
38. Genesis 22:7–8.
39. Luke 15:17–20, 32.

CHAPTER 6: CHRIST AND THE PATRIARCHAL ORDER

1. See Genesis 27:1–35.
2. See chapter 7 for a full discussion of

this and other matters concerning Jacob's children.

3. See Abraham 1:2–4.
4. See Abraham 1:26–27.
5. See chapter 5.
6. See Genesis 25:29–34.
7. See Genesis 27:1–35.
8. Genesis 27:36.
9. D&C 93:21.
10. Colossians 1:15.
11. Matthew 1:25.
12. See, for example, D&C 77:11.
13. D&C 93:22.
14. Genesis 11:26 appears to suggest that Abraham was the firstborn in his family, as it states that "Terah lived seventy years, and begat [Abraham], Nahor, and Haran." Does the fact that Abraham's name was listed first mean that he was the firstborn? Evidence suggests not. In Acts 7:4, we learn that Abraham moved to the land of Canaan from the land called Haran "when his father [Terah] was dead." However, if Terah died at the age of 205 (Genesis 11:32), and Abraham departed Haran when he was either 62 (Abraham 2:14) or 75 (Genesis 12:4), then Terah would have been 130 to 143 years of age, not 70, when Abraham was born. This means that one of Abraham's brothers was born at least 50 years before Abraham—most likely the son named Haran, the father of Lot, the nephew who accompanied Abraham to Canaan. Given the 50 years difference, it is very possible that the other son, Nahor, also was older than Abraham, and that Abraham was the youngest of the three.
15. 1 Chronicles 5:1.
16. See Genesis 35:22.
17. See 1 Chronicles 5:1.
18. Genesis 25:23.
19. See Genesis 25:27–28; 27:1–35.
20. Genesis 48:19.
21. See Genesis 48:16–20.

22. Isaiah 53:2–4.
23. 1 Corinthians 15:45.
24. D&C 93:22.
25. See Galatians 4:7.
26. See Luke 15:11–32.
27. See Genesis 35:9–10.
28. See Genesis 49:8–10.
29. See Genesis 49:22–24.
30. See Genesis 48:13–19.

CHAPTER 7: TEMPORAL AND SPIRITUAL SALVATION THROUGH JOSEPH

1. Genesis 37:3.
2. Genesis 37:4.
3. Genesis 37:18.
4. Genesis 37:19.
5. See Genesis 37:5–11.
6. Genesis 37:20, emphasis added.
7. Genesis 37:6–7.
8. Genesis 37:8.
9. Genesis 37:9.
10. Genesis 37:10.
11. Genesis 37:11, emphasis added.
12. Genesis 39:1.
13. See Genesis 50:26.
14. Genesis 39:3.
15. Genesis 39:5.
16. See Genesis 39:7–12.
17. See Genesis 39:13–20.
18. See Genesis 41:25–31.
19. See Genesis 41:33–36.
20. See Genesis 41:40–43.
21. See Genesis 41:46–49.
22. Genesis 41:54.
23. Genesis 41:54.
24. Genesis 41:57.
25. See Genesis 42:2.
26. Genesis 42:2.
27. Genesis 42:5–6.
28. Genesis 42:8.
29. Genesis 42:6.
30. Genesis 42:9.
31. JST, Genesis 48:8–10, emphasis added.
32. JST, Genesis 48:10–11, emphasis added.

33. JST, Genesis 50:25, emphasis added.
34. See 1 Nephi 5:14–16.
35. Ether 13:7.
36. Deuteronomy 33:13–15, emphasis added.
37. See Joshua 13:6–19:48.
38. See Joshua 13:7–8; 16:1–17; 18.
39. 1 Nephi 2:20.
40. Ether 13:5–8, emphasis added.
41. 3 Nephi 15:13–14.
42. 3 Nephi 15:19.
43. JST, Genesis 50:31.
44. Ezekiel 37:16–17.
45. See JST, Genesis 50:31.
46. 3 Nephi 21:1, 7.
47. 2 Nephi 30:3–7.
48. See JST, Genesis 50:30, 33.
49. See Jeremiah 31:9; JST, Genesis 48:5; Genesis 48:17–20; Brigham Young, in *Journal of Discourses,* 26 vols. (Latter-day Saints' Book Depot, 1854–1886), 2:268–69.
50. See Joseph Fielding Smith, *Doctrines of Salvation,* 2:250–51; 3:250–51.
51. D&C 133:30–33, emphasis added.
52. JST, Genesis 48:10.
53. See Genesis 37:3; Matthew 3:17.
54. See Genesis 37:6–11; Mark 14:61–62; John 8:12, 58.
55. See Genesis 37:8, 11; Luke 23:1–2; John 1:11.
56. See Genesis 37:12–17; Matthew 4:19.
57. See Genesis 37:13–17; Ezekiel 34:11–12.
58. See Genesis 37:18–20; Matthew 27:1.
59. See Genesis 37:25–28; Matthew 27:3.
60. Seventeen-year-old Joseph for twenty pieces of silver (Genesis 37:25–28; Leviticus 27:5); thirty-three-year-old Jesus for thirty pieces of silver (Matthew 27:3; Exodus 21:32).
61. See Genesis 39:7–12; Matthew 4:10.
62. See Genesis 41:46; Luke 3:23.
63. See Genesis 42:1–6, 25; John 6:48–57.
64. See Genesis 42:25; 44:1; 2 Nephi 9:50.
65. See Genesis 34; 42:18–44; Alma 5:33–34.
66. Genesis 45:1–8, 14–15, emphasis added.
67. Genesis 42:21.

CHAPTER 8: THE EXODUS: DELIVERANCE THROUGH THE DELIVERER

1. Exodus 1:8.
2. Exodus 1:7.
3. See Exodus 1:14.
4. In Exodus 6:16–20, we learn that Moses was the son of Amram, who was the son of Kohath, who was the son of Levi, son of Jacob/Israel. Kohath was part of the original group (although likely a young boy at the time), including his father, Levi, who came down to live in Egypt during the famine. (See Genesis 46:8–11.) With only Amram between Kohath and Moses in the family lineage, the length of time that could reasonably have passed from the entry of Israel into Egypt to Moses' birth is unlikely to have exceeded 140 years (that would mean that both Kohath and Amram would have been about seventy when their sons in question were born). Adding another eighty years to that number for the age of Moses at the time of the Exodus, the Exodus 6 passages suggest a sojourn of no more than 220 years from Israel's entry into Egypt to its exodus.
5. See Exodus 1:11.
6. See Exodus 32:1–8.
7. Isaiah attached the name "Egypt" to a country he saw in vision—a country in the midst of which he saw "an altar to the Lord" (that is, a temple) and at the border of which he saw a distinctive monument or "pillar." (Isaiah 19:19.) What nation on earth has a

monument more distinctive at its borders than the Statue of Liberty, for example, or a temple more prominently displayed in its heartland than the Salt Lake Temple (or perhaps a later temple in the New Jerusalem)?

8. See Exodus 3:1.
9. Exodus 3:1.
10. JST, Exodus 3:2, emphasis added.
11. Exodus 3:5.
12. See, for example, Joseph Fielding Smith, *Doctrines of Salvation,* 3:131–32.
13. See Neal A. Maxwell, *Not My Will, But Thine* (Bookcraft, 1988), 46.
14. Joseph Fielding Smith, *Doctrines of Salvation,* 2:131.
15. *Discourses of Brigham Young,* sel. John A. Widtsoe (Deseret Book, 1954), 416, emphasis added.
16. Exodus 3:9–10.
17. See Exodus 2:14.
18. Exodus 3:11.
19. Exodus 3:12.
20. Exodus 3:12.
21. Exodus 3:13.
22. Exodus 3:14.
23. Exodus 3:15.
24. Exodus 4:1.
25. See Exodus 4:2–4.
26. Exodus 4:6.
27. NIV, Exodus 4:6.
28. Exodus 4:6.
29. See Exodus 4:7.
30. Exodus 4:5.
31. Exodus 4:9.
32. See, for example, Moses 5:7.
33. See Moses 1:32–33; 2:1.
34. Moses 5:8.
35. Moses 5:9.
36. Moses 6:52.
37. See, for example, Moses 5:6–8; 6:59–60.
38. See Moses 6:63.
39. See Moses 1:4, 6, 7, 40.
40. See Moses 6:65–68, 5:59; see also chapter 3 of this book.
41. See Moses 1:1–2.
42. See Moses 1:26; Exodus 3:12; D&C 84:23–24.
43. Moses 1:26.
44. See Exodus 2:15.
45. See Exodus 4:29–31.
46. See, for example, Exodus 5:20–21; 14:11–12; 32:1–8.
47. See Exodus 5:6–21.
48. See Exodus 7:14–24.
49. See Exodus 8:1–15.
50. See Exodus 8:16–19.
51. See Exodus 8:20–32.
52. See Exodus 9:1–7.
53. See Exodus 9:8–12.
54. See Exodus 9:18–35.
55. See Exodus 10:4–6, 12–20.
56. See Exodus 10:21–23.
57. See Exodus 11:4–10; 12:12–13.
58. See Exodus 7:22, 24; 8:7–8.
59. Exodus 8:19.
60. See, for example, Exodus 8:12–13, 30–31; 9:33; 10:18–19.
61. Exodus 12:12.
62. Exodus 9:14.
63. Exodus 15:26, emphasis added.
64. See, for example, Exodus 11:3.
65. Exodus 9:17.
66. See, for example, Exodus 8:22–23; 9:4, 26; 10:23.
67. Exodus 11:1, 4–5.
68. See Exodus 12:1–2.
69. See Exodus 12:3, 5.
70. See Exodus 12:6.
71. See Exodus 12:46.
72. See Exodus 12:6.
73. See Exodus 12:7, 22.
74. See Exodus 12:8.
75. See Exodus 12:15, 19.
76. See Exodus 12:8, 15, 18–20.
77. See Exodus 12:8.
78. See Exodus 12:11.
79. See Exodus 12:14, 26–27.
80. See Exodus 12:24, 28, 50.
81. See Exodus 12:3.
82. 2 Nephi 9:10.
83. 3 Nephi 11:14, emphasis added.
84. See Exodus 12:13.

85. See, for example, Matthew 16:6; LDS Bible Dictionary, 723.
86. See, for example, Matthew 13:33.
87. Moses 1:6.
88. See JST, Genesis 50:24, 29; Matthew 2:1–6.
89. See Exodus 1:15–16, 22; Matthew 2:16.
90. See Exodus 2:1–5; Matthew 2:13–15.
91. See Exodus 24:18; 34:28; Matthew 4.
92. See Moses 1:20–21; Matthew 4:10.
93. See Moses 1:25; Exodus 14:21–29; Luke 8:24–25.
94. See Exodus 3:11; 4:10–18; Matthew 26:39.
95. Prefigured in Moses 1:6, 26.
96. See JST, Galatians 3:19–20.

CHAPTER 9: THE TEMPLE AS THE WAY OF ESCAPE AND RETURN

1. Exodus 19:4–6.
2. Exodus 19:7.
3. Exodus 19:8.
4. See Exodus 19:8.
5. See Exodus 19:10–15, 21–25.
6. See Exodus 20–23.
7. Exodus 24:3.
8. Exodus 24:3.
9. See Exodus 24:4–8.
10. See Exodus 24:12.
11. See Exodus 24:18.
12. Exodus 25:1, 8–9, 22.
13. D&C 84:23, emphasis added. See also Appendix B.
14. See Exodus 13:21–22.
15. See, for example, Exodus 16:11–35; 17:3–7.
16. See, for example, Revelation 5:8.
17. See, for example, Exodus 32:9–14; Numbers 14:11–23.
18. See Numbers 13:1–20.
19. Numbers 13:27.
20. Numbers 13:31.
21. Numbers 14:8.
22. Numbers 14:2.
23. See Numbers 14:22–23, 38.
24. See Exodus 32:1–6.

25. See Exodus 30:10; Leviticus 16; Hebrews 9:6–7.
26. See D&C 84:19–25.
27. Exodus 19:6.
28. See Exodus 25:22.
29. See D&C 84:25.
30. Numbers 16:48.
31. See D&C 84:19–25.
32. John 14:6.
33. Matthew 3:15.
34. Hebrews 10:19–20.
35. See Exodus 26:31–33.
36. See Exodus 25:31–37.
37. See 1 Kings 6:32; 7:49.
38. See Genesis 3:16–24; Moses 4:22–31.
39. See Genesis 3:21; Moses 4:27.
40. See Genesis 3:24; Moses 4:31.
41. See Moses 5:5–6.
42. See Moses 6:64–66.
43. See Exodus 27:1–8.
44. See Exodus 30:17–21.
45. See Moses 5:13.

CHAPTER 10: UNDERSTANDING THE LAW OF MOSES

1. See Exodus 32:1–6.
2. Exodus 32:8.
3. See Exodus 24:3–8.
4. D&C 84:24.
5. JST, Exodus 33:20, emphasis added.
6. See D&C 84:20–23.
7. See D&C 84:24–25.
8. Alma 42:5.
9. JST, Exodus 34:1, emphasis added.
10. See D&C 84:19–25.
11. D&C 84:25.
12. See, for example, Hebrews 9:1, 6–7.
13. See Exodus 25:22; 29:43–46.
14. Hebrews 9:8, emphasis added.
15. Alma 42:4.
16. D&C 84:26.
17. D&C 84:27.
18. See, for example, Alma 13.
19. See D&C 84:19, 24–27; 107:18–20. See also Appendix B herein.
20. Mosiah 13:29–30, emphasis added.

21. See Romans 3:19–20; James 2:10; 2 Nephi 2:5; Alma 42:18.

22. For any violation of the law, a sin offering had to be made in order to satisfy the demands of justice under the law (see the first seven chapters of Leviticus). This involved the sacrifice of an unblemished animal or fowl, as determined under the law by such factors as the type of sin, the wealth of the sinner, and so on. Only parts of the animal were burned, and the rest was eaten. The priests offered up the sacrifice for the sinner, and through the animal's death the sinner was reconciled with the law (see, for example, Leviticus 4:20). Once a year, on the Day of Atonement, a special sin offering was made on behalf of all of Israel. On that day, the High Priest would enter the Holy of Holies and there at the mercy seat on the ark of the covenant offer the blood of the lamb as a sacrifice for his own sin and the sins of all of Israel (see Hebrews 9:1, 6–7).

23. See Hebrews 9:8; 10:4.

24. Alma 34:14.

25. Numbers 21:6.

26. See Numbers 21:7.

27. See Numbers 21:8–9.

28. Alma 33:19.

29. John 3:14–15.

30. Mosiah 13:30.

31. See, for example, Genesis 3:1.

32. 3 Nephi 12:19, emphasis added.

33. Romans 3:20.

34. Romans 3:19.

35. 3 Nephi 12:21.

36. 3 Nephi 12:22.

37. 3 Nephi 12:27–29.

38. 3 Nephi 12:5.

39. 3 Nephi 12:7.

40. 3 Nephi 12:8.

41. D&C 121:45.

42. Matthew 23:23.

43. Ether 12:27.

44. Moroni 10:32.

CHAPTER 11: DISCOVERING DEUTERONOMY

1. See Moses 5:7–12.

2. See Moses 1:40.

3. Moses 6:7.

4. Moses 5:59.

5. See Genesis 28:10–22.

6. Moses 1:26.

7. See Exodus 32:11–14; Numbers 14:11–20.

8. Deuteronomy 33:1.

9. Deuteronomy 34:5.

10. Moses 1:6.

11. See Deuteronomy 34; Alma 45:19.

12. Deuteronomy 31:16.

13. Deuteronomy 31:19–22.

14. NIV, Deuteronomy 32:1–2, emphasis added.

15. Exodus 16:13–15.

16. See John 6:58.

17. D&C 121:45.

18. Deuteronomy 33:13, emphasis added.

19. NIV, Deuteronomy 33:13.

20. Genesis 28:12.

21. See Genesis 28:13–15.

22. See Marion G. Romney, "Temples— the Gates to Heaven," *Ensign,* March 1971, 16.

23. Genesis 28:18.

24. Genesis 28:22.

25. Genesis 28:16.

26. Exodus 17:6.

27. 1 Corinthians 10:1, 4.

28. Deuteronomy 9:9–11.

29. See 3 Nephi 15:9; Alma 34:14–15.

30. See, for example: Helaman 5:12; Matthew 7:24–27; Moses 7:53; D&C 6:34; Psalm 71:1–3; 3 Nephi 11:39–40; Jacob 4:15; D&C 11:24.

31. 1 Corinthians 3:11.

32. Helaman 5:12.

33. NIV, Deuteronomy 32:5.

34. John 8:41.

35. NIV, Deuteronomy 32:4.

36. NIV, Deuteronomy 32:5.

37. See Moses 1:6.

38. NIV, Deuteronomy 32:6.
39. NIV, Deuteronomy 32:11.
40. NIV, Deuteronomy 32:15.
41. Deuteronomy 8:11–18.
42. See NIV, Deuteronomy 32:15–18.
43. See, for example, Deuteronomy 28:15–68.
44. NIV, Deuteronomy 32:20.
45. NIV, Deuteronomy 32:26.
46. NIV, Deuteronomy 32:20.
47. Deuteronomy 4:27–28.
48. See NIV, Deuteronomy 32:26–27.
49. NIV, Deuteronomy 32:37–38.
50. NIV, Deuteronomy 32:39.
51. NIV, Deuteronomy 32:36, emphasis added.
52. Deuteronomy 4:29–31.
53. NIV, Deuteronomy 32:43.
54. Deuteronomy 30:1–3.
55. See D&C 84:19–25. See also chapters 9 and 10 and Appendix B herein.
56. NIV, Deuteronomy 33:13.
57. D&C 121:45.
58. See Deuteronomy 32:1–2.
59. Deuteronomy 33:16–17.
60. Deuteronomy 31:21.

CHAPTER 12: EARLY YEARS IN THE PROMISED LAND: THE PATTERN OF FALL AND REDEMPTION

1. See chapter 8 herein.
2. See Numbers 14. Moses was taken from Israel for another reason before they were allowed to pass into the promised land (see D&C 84:24–25).
3. Deuteronomy 20:16–18.
4. Deuteronomy 7:2–3.
5. Exodus 4:22–23.
6. Deuteronomy 7:4–6.
7. D&C 133:7.
8. See Malachi 3:2; 4:1.
9. See Alma 7:14; 11:37.
10. Joshua 11:15.
11. See Joshua 6.
12. See Joshua 6:21.
13. See Joshua 2; 6:17, 22–25.
14. See Joshua 8.
15. See Joshua 10.
16. Joshua 11:16–17.
17. Joshua 11:23.
18. Joshua 13:1.
19. Joshua 13:1.
20. See Joshua 14–21.
21. Joshua 23:5, 12–13.
22. Judges 1:19.
23. Judges 1:21.
24. Judges 1:27.
25. Judges 1:29.
26. Judges 1:30.
27. Judges 1:31–32.
28. Judges 1:33.
29. Judges 1:34.
30. Judges 3:7.
31. Judges 3:12.
32. Judges 4:1.
33. Judges 6:1.
34. Judges 10:6.
35. Judges 13:1.
36. Judges 3:8.
37. Judges 3:12–14.
38. Judges 4:2–3.
39. Judges 6:1.
40. Judges 10:7–9.
41. Judges 13:1.
42. See Judges 3:9, 15; 4:3; 6:6; 10:11.
43. See Judges 3:9–10,15; 4:4–5,14; 6:12–16; 10:15–18; 11:1, 5–11.
44. See Judges 3:10, 28–30; 4:23; 8:28; 11:32–33.
45. See Judges 3:11, 30; 5:31; 8:28.
46. See Judges 4:17, 21–22.
47. Judges 6:15.
48. Judges 11:1.
49. See Judges 11:2–3.
50. Judges 11:1.
51. Judges 11:5–11.
52. Judges 13:2–5.
53. See, for example, Judges 14:19; 15:3–5, 14–15; 16:28–30.
54. Judges 14:4.

CHAPTER 13: SAMUEL AND THE
MESSIANIC KINGDOM

1. 1 Samuel 1:10.
2. See 1 Samuel 1:17–20.
3. Compare 1 Samuel 2:1–10 with Luke 1:46–55.
4. See 1 Samuel 1:28.
5. Luke 1:33.
6. 1 Samuel 1:24; 2:11.
7. Luke 2:42–43; 46.
8. NIV, 1 Samuel 2:26.
9. Luke 2:52.
10. See 1 Samuel 12:12, 17; 13:13; Matthew 23:27.
11. See, for example, 1 Samuel 3:21–4:1.
12. Luke 4:37.
13. 1 Samuel 3:20.
14. 1 Samuel 4:3.
15. See Joshua 6.
16. 1 Samuel 4:3.
17. 1 Samuel 4:5.
18. See 1 Samuel 4:6–8.
19. 1 Samuel 4:10.
20. 1 Samuel 4:11.
21. 1 Samuel 4:17.
22. 1 Samuel 4:13–18.
23. 1 Samuel 4:13.
24. 1 Samuel 5:1.
25. 1 Samuel 5:2.
26. 1 Samuel 5:3.
27. 1 Samuel 5:3.
28. 1 Samuel 5:4.
29. 1 Samuel 5:6.
30. 1 Samuel 5:10. See also 1 Samuel 5:7, 9.
31. 1 Samuel 5:11.
32. 1 Samuel 6:3.
33. See Leviticus 4–6.
34. See 1 Samuel 6:1.
35. 1 Samuel 6:8.
36. 1 Samuel 6:12.
37. 1 Samuel 6:12.
38. 1 Samuel 6:13.
39. 1 Samuel 6:19.
40. See Exodus 19:21.
41. 1 Samuel 6:19.
42. 1 Samuel 7:1.
43. 1 Samuel 7:2.
44. 1 Samuel 7:3.
45. 1 Samuel 7:4.
46. 1 Samuel 7:5.
47. 1 Samuel 7:6.
48. 1 Samuel 7:7.
49. 1 Samuel 7:8.
50. 1 Samuel 7:9.
51. 1 Samuel 7:10.
52. 1 Samuel 8:5, 20.
53. Neal A. Maxwell, *Things As They Really Are* (Deseret Book, 1978), 54.
54. 3 Nephi 21:6.
55. See Daniel 2:34–45.
56. 1 Nephi 15:13.
57. 1 Nephi 13:42.
58. 2 Nephi 30:2.
59. See Zechariah 12:10–11.
60. See Zechariah 13:1–2.
61. See Zechariah 13:9.
62. Zechariah 14:3–5.
63. Zechariah 14:9.
64. 1 Samuel 8:20.
65. Genesis 14:18.
66. Judges 8:22.
67. Judges 8:23, emphasis added.
68. Judges 21:25, emphasis added.
69. 1 Samuel 8:4–5, emphasis added.
70. See 1 Samuel 8:6.
71. See 1 Samuel 8:11–18.
72. 1 Samuel 8:19–20.
73. 1 Samuel 8:7–8.
74. 1 Samuel 8:22.
75. See 1 Samuel 12:15–13:1.
76. See NIV, 1 Samuel 7:1–3.
77. See 1 Samuel 7:3.
78. See 1 Samuel 7:5–9.
79. See 1 Samuel 7:10.
80. See 1 Samuel 12:16–18.
81. 1 Samuel 12:16–19.
82. 1 Samuel 12:14, 23.
83. 1 Samuel 12:13, emphasis added.
84. See 1 Samuel 12:14–15, 25.
85. 1 Samuel 10:25.

Chapter 14: David, Saul, Jonathan, and the Allegory of Salvation

1. 1 Samuel 15:17.
2. See Acts 13:21.
3. 1 Samuel 11:13.
4. See 1 Samuel 10:26–27; 11:12–13.
5. 1 Samuel 9:21.
6. See 1 Samuel 13:5–12.
7. See 1 Samuel 15:3–9.
8. 1 Samuel 15:26, 28.
9. 1 Samuel 16:13.
10. See 1 Samuel 10:27; 11:12–13.
11. See 1 Samuel 17:40–54.
12. 1 Samuel 17:58.
13. 1 Samuel 18:1, 3–4, emphasis added.
14. 1 Samuel 23:17–18.
15. 1 Samuel 19:2.
16. 1 Samuel 15:28.
17. Matthew 22:39.
18. 1 Samuel 18:6–9, emphasis added.
19. 1 Samuel 18:12.
20. 1 Samuel 20:4.
21. See 1 Samuel 23:16.
22. See 1 Samuel 18:11; 19:10.
23. See, for example, 1 Samuel 18:25; 19:1, 11; 20:31; 23:8, 14.
24. See 1 Samuel 22:11–19.
25. See, for example, 1 Samuel 23:18.
26. See 1 Samuel 19:12.
27. See 1 Samuel 27:1.
28. See 1 Samuel 22:1–2.
29. 1 Samuel 24:2–4.
30. See 1 Samuel 24:4–7.
31. 1 Samuel 24:8.
32. 1 Samuel 24:8.
33. 1 Samuel 24:9–11.
34. See 1 Samuel 26:2–12.
35. 1 Samuel 26:16–20.
36. 2 Samuel 1:11–12, 17, 23, 27, emphasis added.
37. 1 Samuel 25:36.
38. See, for example, 1 Samuel 25:25.
39. See 1 Samuel 25:15–16.
40. See 1 Samuel 25:4–8.
41. 1 Samuel 25:10–11.

42. See, for example, 1 Samuel 20:32–33; 25:17.
43. 1 Samuel 26:21, emphasis added.
44. 1 Samuel 25:13.
45. 1 Samuel 25:21.
46. For a complete examination of the story of Abigail, and its allegorical application, see James L. Ferrell, *The Peacegiver* (Deseret Book, 2004).
47. 1 Samuel 25:18.
48. 1 Samuel 25:20, 23–25, 28, 31, emphasis added.
49. 1 Samuel 25:30.
50. 1 Samuel 25:24.
51. 1 Samuel 25:28.
52. See 1 Samuel 25:25.
53. See, for example, 3 Nephi 12:21–30; Moroni 10:22.
54. D&C 64:9.
55. D&C 1:10.
56. James 2:13.
57. Matthew 6:14–15; 3 Nephi 13:14–15. See also Matthew 5:7; 6:12; 18:32–35; Mark 11:25–26; Ephesians 4:32; D&C 82:1; 88:40.
58. Luke 6:37.
59. Matthew 18:35.
60. Matthew 18:34.
61. 1 Samuel 25:32–33, 35.
62. See Matthew 25:40, 45.
63. Matthew 7:2.
64. 1 Samuel 24:16–20.
65. 1 Samuel 26:21.
66. 1 Samuel 25:24.

Chapter 15: The Houses of the Kings and the House of the Lord

1. See 2 Samuel 2:4.
2. See 2 Samuel 2:8–10.
3. See 2 Samuel 3:1.
4. See 2 Samuel 5:1–5.
5. See 1 Samuel 7:1; 2 Samuel 6:1–17.
6. 2 Samuel 6:17.
7. 1 Chronicles 17:4–6.
8. 1 Chronicles 17:10–14.
9. 1 Kings 9:4–7.

10. See D&C 84:38 and chapter 4 herein.
11. 1 Corinthians 3:9.
12. See Hebrews 3:6.
13. See chapter 4 herein.
14. See Revelation 21:22.
15. 1 Kings 11:4.
16. 1 Kings 11:11.
17. See 1 Kings 11:26–28.
18. 1 Kings 11:31.
19. 1 Kings 11:38.
20. See 1 Kings 12.
21. See James E. Talmage, *Articles of Faith*, 294; 3 Nephi 15:15; the Apocryphal book of 2 Esdras 13:41–46.
22. See 1 Kings 12:26–27.
23. 1 Kings 12:28–29.
24. 1 Kings 12:29–30.
25. 2 Chronicles 14:2–4.
26. 2 Chronicles 15:18.
27. 2 Chronicles 17:9.
28. 2 Chronicles 20:4–12.
29. See 2 Chronicles 24:4.
30. 2 Chronicles 24:18.
31. See 2 Chronicles 29:3–20.
32. See 2 Kings 21:3–8; 23:4.

CHAPTER 16: ELIJAH AND THE FOUR GREAT SEPARATIONS

1. 1 Kings 16:30.
2. 1 Kings 16:33.
3. 1 Kings 15:26.
4. See 1 Kings 18:22–40.
5. See JS–H 1:36.
6. Malachi 3:1–3.
7. Malachi 3:2.
8. Malachi 3:3–7.
9. Malachi 3:3, emphasis added.
10. Malachi 3:6.
11. Malachi 3:7.
12. Malachi 3:7. See also Appendix B. (In speaking of the "offering in righteousness" spoken of in the scriptures, the Prophet Joseph Smith referred to the presentation, in the holy temple, of "a book containing

the records of our dead, which shall be worthy of all acceptation." See D&C 128:24.)
13. For a full discussion of the priesthood pertaining to the temple, and its importance in preparing man to receive the Lord in his glory, see Appendix B.
14. See chapter 4 herein.
15. Malachi 3:7.
16. Malachi 4:1–6 (as revised in JS–H 1:37–39).
17. Malachi 4:1.
18. Malachi 4:4.
19. Malachi 4:5, as revised in JS–H 1:38.
20. Malachi 4:5, as revised in JS–H 1:39. See also chapter 4 herein for a discussion of the Abrahamic covenant—the blessings of the fathers, and "the right whereunto I should be ordained [in the priesthood] to administer the same" (Abraham 1:2).
21. See the discussion in chapter 4 herein.
22. JS–H 1:38.
23. Malachi 3:7.
24. Malachi 3:7.
25. Malachi 3:4.
26. D&C 131:2–4.
27. D&C 84:19.
28. D&C 107:19.
29. See Appendix B.

CHAPTER 17: THE LORD'S QUESTION TO JONAH

1. For an extended, practical examination of the story of Jonah, and its allegorical application, see James L. Ferrell, *The Peacegiver*.
2. See, for example, Deuteronomy 32:23–26.
3. See Hosea 7:11; 8:9; 10:6; 11:11.
4. Jonah 1:2.
5. Jonah 1:3.
6. Jonah 1:3.
7. See Jonah 1:7.
8. See Jonah 1:8–12.
9. See Jonah 1:13–14.

10. See Jonah 1:17.
11. See Jonah 2:1–10.
12. Jonah 2:10.
13. Jonah 3:1–2.
14. Jonah 3:3.
15. JST, Jonah 3:10.
16. Jonah 4:1.
17. See Jonah 4:2.
18. Jonah 4:2.
19. Jonah 4:11.
20. For a detailed discussion of the chiastic form, see John W. Welch, "What Does Chiasmus in the Book of Mormon Prove?" chapter 11 in Noel B. Reynolds, *Book of Mormon Authorship Revisited* (BYU Religious Studies Center, 1982; reprinted by F.A.R.M.S., 1996).
21. Jonah 2:8.
22. See Jonah 1:5.
23. See Jonah 1:4.
24. See Jonah 1:6.
25. Jonah 1:13, emphasis added.
26. Matthew 18:32–33, emphasis added.
27. Matthew 18:34–35.
28. Matthew 18:35, emphasis added.
29. See Alma 42:29–30.
30. See Jonah 1:1.
31. See Jonah 1:3.
32. See Jonah 1:4.
33. See Jonah 1:5.
34. See Jonah 1:6.
35. See Jonah 1:9.
36. Jonah 1:15.
37. See Jonah 1:17.
38. Jonah 2:2.
39. Jonah 2:4.
40. 2 Chronicles 36:23.
41. Luke 11:28–30, 32, emphasis added.
42. See Jonah 2:7–9.
43. Matthew 12:39–40, emphasis added.
44. Jonah 2:2.
45. Jonah 2:6.
46. Jonah 2:3.
47. Jonah 2:5.
48. Jonah 2:3.
49. Jonah 2:5.
50. Jonah 2:4.
51. Matthew 27:46.
52. Jonah 2:4.
53. Luke 23:46.
54. See Jonah 2:9.

CHAPTER 18: THE HOUSE OF ISRAEL AS A TYPE AND SHADOW

1. 2 Nephi 6:4, emphasis added.
2. 3 Nephi 23:3, emphasis added.
3. Isaiah 46:10.
4. Isaiah 49:5–6, emphasis added.
5. Luke 2:29–33, emphasis added.
6. Matthew 12:17–21.
7. Isaiah 52:14.
8. Bruce R. McConkie, *The Mortal Messiah,* 4 vols. (Deseret Book, 1979–81), 4:354.
9. 3 Nephi 20:46, emphasis added.
10. 3 Nephi 21:9.
11. See 3 Nephi 21:11.
12. See 3 Nephi 21:26–28.
13. McConkie, *Mortal Messiah,* 4:354.
14. See chapter 8 herein for a discussion of how the United States can be considered modern "Egypt."
15. Ezekiel 37:11.
16. Ezekiel 37:12, 14.
17. See Ezekiel 37:15–22.
18. See Ezekiel 37:17, 20.
19. Ezekiel 37:21.
20. See JST, Genesis 50:31; 2 Nephi 3:12; 29:12–14; D&C 27:5.
21. Isaiah 19:20.

CHAPTER 19: THE DISPENSATIONS OF THE LORD'S PEOPLE

1. See chapter 17 herein.
2. Moses 6:63.
3. See Matthew 19:30; 20:16; 1 Nephi 13:42; D&C 29:30.
4. See 1 Nephi 13:42.
5. See D&C 29:30, in context.
6. Revelation 1:11.
7. Moses 5:57.
8. 2 Thessalonians 2:3.
9. Moses 5:13.
10. Enoch and his city had been taken up into heaven earlier, so that with

Noah's family on the ark, only the wicked were destroyed in the flood. However, the wicked included everyone else who then walked the earth.

11. See Matthew 10:1–2; 16:13–19; 17:1–12; 18:18.
12. Ephesians 1:10.
13. Acts 3:19–21.
14. See Ephesians 1:10.
15. See D&C 128:17–21.
16. See Alma 13.
17. See Appendix B herein.
18. See Moses 7:38–39.
19. See 1 Peter 3:19; D&C 138.
20. See 1 Corinthians 15:29.
21. *Millennial Star,* 16:220.
22. D&C 128:18.

CHAPTER 20: JOB, DAVID, AND THE SUFFERING OF THE LORD

1. See Job 1:6–11.
2. Job 1:10–11.
3. Job 1:12.
4. See Job 1:13–19.
5. Job 1:20–21.
6. Job 1:22.
7. Job 2:5.
8. See Job 2:6.
9. Job 2:7.
10. Job 2:12.
11. Job 2:12.
12. Job 2:13.
13. Alma 7:11–12, emphasis added.
14. 2 Nephi 9:21–22, emphasis added.
15. D&C 19:18.
16. See Alma 7:11.
17. John 9:2.
18. Isaiah 52:14; 53:2–4, emphasis added.
19. Luke 4:23, emphasis added.
20. Alma 7:12.
21. D&C 121:1.
22. See D&C 121:7–46.
23. D&C 121:10.
24. D&C 122:8.
25. 2 Nephi 9:21.
26. 2 Nephi 9:7.

27. For a full discussion of this, see chapter 2 herein.
28. See Isaiah 52:14.
29. Matthew 26:28. See also chapter 2 herein.
30. See D&C 19:18.
31. See 2 Samuel 11.
32. Psalm 69:1.
33. D&C 19:18.
34. Psalm 69:20.
35. Matthew 26:37–40.
36. Psalm 22:1.
37. Psalm 69:3.
38. Psalm 22:15.
39. John 19:28.

CHAPTER 21: THE WISDOM OF THE SCRIPTURES

1. Proverbs 1:2.
2. Proverbs 1:3.
3. Proverbs 1:4–5.
4. Proverbs 1:6.
5. Proverbs 4:7.
6. Moroni 7:46.
7. See 1 Kings 11:1–11.
8. 1 Kings 3:12.
9. Ecclesiastes 1:16–18.
10. Ecclesiastes 2:12–17.
11. Proverbs 8:11.
12. Proverbs 1:33.
13. Proverbs 3:16.
14. Proverbs 3:18.
15. Proverbs 4:9.
16. Proverbs 8:18.
17. Proverbs 8:35.
18. Proverbs 9:11.
19. Ecclesiastes 2:26.
20. Proverbs 1:20–21.
21. Proverbs 3:13.
22. Proverbs 3:16.
23. Proverbs 3:17.
24. Proverbs 3:18.
25. Proverbs 3:19.
26. Proverbs 1:23.
27. Proverbs 1:24–26.
28. Proverbs 1:28–31.
29. Proverbs 4:8.

30. Proverbs 4:9.
31. Proverbs 8:1.
32. Proverbs 8:7–8.
33. Proverbs 8:14.
34. Proverbs 8:17.
35. Proverbs 8:17.
36. Proverbs 8:23–26.
37. Proverbs 8:27–31.
38. Proverbs 8:32.
39. Proverbs 8:32.
40. Proverbs 8:35.
41. Proverbs 9:5.
42. Proverbs 9:11.
43. 1 Corinthians 1:20–24, emphasis added.
44. Ecclesiastes 2:17.
45. 1 Corinthians 1:26–31, emphasis added.
46. Proverbs 8:3, emphasis added.
47. Proverbs 3:18, emphasis added.
48. Proverbs 4:9, emphasis added.
49. Proverbs 3:17, emphasis added.
50. Proverbs 9:13. The NIV translation of this verse identifies her as "the woman Folly."
51. See, for example, Proverbs 2:16–19; 5:1–23; 6:23–29; 7:1–27; 9:13–18.
52. See Proverbs 7:3–4.
53. See Proverbs 7:10.
54. Proverbs 7:12.
55. See Proverbs 7:11.
56. See Proverbs 7:11.
57. See Proverbs 7:13, 18.
58. See Proverbs 7:16–17.
59. See Proverbs 7:19–20.
60. See Proverbs 7:25.
61. Proverbs 7:21–22.
62. Proverbs 7:22.
63. Proverbs 7:25, emphasis added.
64. Proverbs 7:27.
65. See 1 Kings 11:3.
66. See 1 Kings 11:2.
67. 1 Kings 11:4.
68. Proverbs 7:22.
69. Proverbs 5:22.
70. Proverbs 5:7–8.
71. Proverbs 6:25.
72. Proverbs 2:18.
73. Proverbs 4:8–10.
74. Proverbs 8:35–36.
75. Ecclesiastes 12:8.
76. Ecclesiastes 12:13.
77. Proverbs 1:7.
78. Proverbs 3:5–7.
79. 1 Corinthians 1:30.
80. 1 Corinthians 1:30.

CHAPTER 22: THE OLD TESTAMENT'S UNIFIED TESTIMONY

1. See 1 Nephi 13:28.
2. Luke 24:27.
3. Luke 24:38.
4. 2 Nephi 11:4.
5. Isaiah 46:10.
6. See Ezekiel 37:17–19.
7. Luke 24:52.

APPENDIX B: THE LATTER-DAY RESTORATION OF THE LOST TEMPLE ORDINANCES

1. *History of the Church,* 1:286–87.
2. See D&C 84:6–16.
3. See D&C 84:19.
4. See D&C 84:20–21 (along with verses 6–17).
5. See D&C 84:22. The passage can seem ambiguous as to whether it is saying that one must have received the ordinances of the holy priesthood or have the power of godliness in order to see the face of God and live. However, since it says that the power of godliness is not manifest unto man without the ordinances, it reduces to the same point: One must have received the ordinances of the holy priesthood in order to survive the glory of the Father. However, this seems not to square with Joseph Smith's experience in the First Vision, for he saw the face of God and survived without having received the ordinances of the temple. However, the statement "see the face of God . . . and live" has to do with seeing the

fulness of the glory of God (D&C 84:22), not some lesser portion. The Father (and the Son, for that matter) can choose to show themselves at less than their full glory. However, if we are to really know them as they are, we need to see them as they really are, in the fulness of their glory. This is why the Melchizedek Priesthood holds "the key to the knowledge of God," for we can know him only by being with him, and it is through the ordinances and accompanying covenants of the holy priesthood that we are sanctified to be able to dwell in the fulness of his glory.

6. D&C 84:23.
7. See D&C 84:24–25.
8. See D&C 13.
9. See D&C 107:18–20.
10. See D&C 84:26–28.
11. D&C 84:21.
12. See D&C 84:23–25.
13. D&C 84:19. See also D&C 107:18–19.
14. D&C 84:39.
15. D&C 84:33.
16. D&C 84:34.
17. D&C 84:23.
18. D&C 84:33–34. These verses are about those who hold the priesthood and who, having themselves received the sanctifying ordinances of that priesthood, now administer those ordinances to others.
19. D&C 84:35–39. The oath and covenant that pertains to the priesthood applies to all who receive the ordinances of the Melchizedek Priesthood.
20. D&C 84:40, emphasis added.
21. D&C 84:19.
22. See D&C 13.
23. See D&C 107:18–20.
24. See D&C 84:43–62.
25. See D&C 84:62–120.
26. See Hebrews 10:20.
27. Malachi 4:1.
28. D&C 132:4.
29. D&C 132:6.
30. D&C 84:119.
31. D&C 60:7.

INDEX